Proceedings of
the Sixth International Conference on

Quantum Communication, Measurement and Computing

Edited by

Jeffrey H. Shapiro
Massachusetts Institute of Technology
Cambridge, Massachusetts, USA

Osamu Hirota
Tamagawa University
Machida, Tokyo, JAPAN

RP **Rinton Press**

Library of Congress Control Number: 2003091544

12 Castleton Road
Princeton, New Jersey 08540
USA
rinton@rintonpress.com
http://www.rintonpress.com

Published by Rinton Press, Inc.

Printed in the United States of America

ISBN 1-58949-030-4

The Sixth International Conference on
Quantum Communication, Measurement and Computing

Massachusetts Institute of Technology
Cambridge, Massachusetts 02139, USA
July 22-26, 2002

Organizing Committee

Jeffrey H. Shapiro (Chair)	MIT, USA
G. Mauro D'Ariano	Univ. of Pavia, Italy
Gerald Gilbert	MITRE Corporation, USA
Peter Knight	Imperial College, UK
Prem Kumar	Northwestern Univ., USA
Gerard Milburn	Univ. of Queensland, Australia
Masanao Ozawa	Tohoku Univ., Japan

Advisory and Award Committee

Osamu Hirota (Chair)	Tamagawa Univ., Japan
Stephen Barnett	Univ. of Strathclyde, UK
V. P. Belavkin	Univ. of Nottingham, UK
Paul A. Benioff	Argonne National Lab., USA
Charles Bennett	IBM, USA
Carlton M. Caves	Univ. of New Mexico, USA
David DiVincenzo	IBM, USA
Christopher Fuchs	Lucent Technologies, USA
Daniel Gottesman	Perimeter Inst., Canada
Philippe Grangier	Inst. d'Optique, France
Alexander S. Holevo	Steklov Mathematical Inst., Russia
Pawel Horodecki	Univ. of Gdansk, Poland
Richard Hughes	Los Alamos National Lab., USA
Richard Jozsa	Bristol Univ., UK
Hoi-Kwong Lo	MagiQ Technologies, USA
Andrew Steane	Oxford Univ., UK
Paolo Tombesi	Univ. di Camerino, Italy
David Wineland	NIST, USA
William Wootters	Williams College, USA
Horace P. Yuen	Northwestern Univ., USA

2002 International Quantum Communications Award

The International Award on Quantum Communications was established by the Research Institute of Tamagawa University to acknowledge an individual or a group of individuals for pioneering contributions to the development of quantum communications.

The First International Award on Quantum Communications was presented, in 1996, to Dr. Charles Bennett, Professor Carl Helstrom, Professor Alexander Holevo, and Professor Horace Yuen at the Third International Conference on Quantum Communication and Measurement, held at Mt. Fuji-Hakone Land, Japan.

The Second International Award on Quantum Communications was presented, in 1998, to Professor Jeffrey Kimble and Dr. Peter Shor at the Fourth International Conference on Quantum Communication and Measurement, held at Northwestern University, USA.

The Third International Award on Quantum Communications was presented, in 2000, to Dr. Paul Benioff, Dr. David Wineland, and Dr. Chris Monroe at the Fifth International Conference on Quantum Communication, Measurement and Computing held in Capri, Italy.

The Fourth International Award on Quantum Communications was presented at the Sixth International Conference on Quantum Communication, Measurement and Computing (QCMC'02) to:

Professor **David Deutsch** of Oxford University, UK
for fundamental contributions to quantum computing that include pioneering work on the quantum Turing machine

Professor **Serge Haroche** of École Normale Supérieure, France
for fundamental contributions to quantum state generation that include pioneering work on quantum superposition

Professor **Benjamin Schumacher** of Kenyon College, USA
for fundamental contributions to quantum information theory that include pioneering work on quantum data compression

The awards were presented at the QCMC'02 banquet. Professors Deutsch, Haroche, and Schumacher each received a certificate from Tamagawa University and a check in the amount of USD 4,500.

Preface

This volume contains contributions based on the papers presented at the Sixth International Conference on Quantum Communication, Measurement and Computing (QCMC'02), which was held from July 22-26, 2002 on the campus of the Massachusetts Institute of Technology (MIT). The conference drew together 318 researchers from 28 countries and covered topics in quantum information theory, theoretical and experimental aspects of quantum computing, quantum communication systems, quantum cryptography, new quantum effects and their experimental realizations, generation detection and applications of nonclassical light, quantum noise, quantum measurement theory, and quantum control. MIT President Charles Vest opened QCMC'02 with welcoming remarks. The conference program featured plenary talks by Professors David Deutsch, Serge Haroche, and Benjamin Schumacher, who are the winners of the Fourth International Award on Quantum Communications. Professor Deutsch was unable to attend QCMC'02, but nevertheless was able to give his lecture via a two-way videoconference between Oxford, UK and Cambridge, USA. The 45 invited talks, from the world's leading researchers in quantum communication, measurement and computing, formed the core of the conference program and provided the many graduate students and postdoctoral researchers who attended with excellent coverage of these fields. There were also 26 contributed talks and 78 poster presentations, and the entire program was accommodated in the five-day conference without resorting to parallel sessions. Many lively discussions transpired during the continental breakfasts, the coffee breaks, the lunches, and the poster sessions, as well as at the conference's three social events: the opening reception on July 21 at the MIT Faculty Club, the evening visit (with dinner buffet) to the John F. Kennedy Library and Museum on July 23, and the conference banquet and award presentation at the Cambridge Marriott Hotel on July 25.

QCMC'02 would not have been possible without the generous support of its sponsors: Tamagawa University, the Army Research Office, the National Security Agency, the Advanced Research and Development Activity, the Research Laboratory of Electronics at MIT, the Cambridge-MIT Institute, the MITRE Corporation, MagiQ Technologies, Inc., and the Communications Research Laboratory.

Moreover, the conference would not have run as smoothly as it did without the hard work of many people at MIT. Ms. Cathi Levine, Ms. Marie Seamon, and the rest of the staff at MIT Conference Services were superb in handling all of the logistical details for QCMC'02. Mr. William Smith of the Research Laboratory of Electronics (RLE) provided essential help with the fundraising and financial arrangements for the conference. Mr. David Foss of RLE saw to it that the participants had readily-available access to the Internet. Ms. Krista Van Guilder of RLE designed the QCMC'02 logo, the conference web site, poster and program, as well as the cover for these proceedings. Mr. Greg Hren took the photographs that appear on the conference web site and in these proceedings. Ms. Josephina Lee of RLE ensured that the flood of submissions which came in response to the QCMC'02 call for papers were promptly logged and acknowledged.

Jeffrey H. Shapiro
Osamu Hirota

Organizing Committee for the Sixth International Conference on Quantum Communication, Measurement and Computing (QCMC'02)

Standing, left to right : Masanao Ozawa, Peter Knight, Osamu Hirota (Chair, Advisory and Award Committee), Jeffrey Shapiro (Principal Organizer), Mauro D'Ariano
Seated, left to right : Gerald Gilbert, Prem Kumar
Not pictured: Gerard Milburn

Participants of the Sixth International Conference on Quantum Communication, Measurement and Computing (QCMC'02)

CONTENTS

Part II — Entangled Photons

Part III — Quantum Information and Coding

Part IV — Quantum Imaging and Quantum Processing with Linear Optics

Part V — Spin-Based Quantum Computation

Part VI — Quantum Dynamics, Geometry, and Simulation

Part VII — Quantum Control and Measurement

Part VIII — Quantum Cryptography and Bit Commitment

Part IX — Quantum Computation and Decoherence

Part X — Quantum Communication and Coding

Part XI — Sources of Nonclassical Light

Part I

Entanglement

THE CHARACTERIZATION OF GAUSSIAN OPERATIONS AND DISTILLATION OF GAUSSIAN STATES

GÉZA GIEDKE AND J. IGNACIO CIRAC

Max-Planck-Institut für Quantenoptik,
Hans-Kopfermann-Strasse 1, D-85748 Garching, Germany

We characterize the class of all physical operations that map Gaussian states to Gaussian states. We show that this class coincides with that of all operations which can be performed on Gaussian states using active and passive linear optics and homodyne measurements. For bipartite systems we characterize the actions which can be implemented by local operations and classical communication, as well as those requiring ppt-preserving maps. Using this we show that Gaussian states cannot be distilled by local Gaussian operations and classical communication.

1 Introduction

Many applications of quantum information require the ability to prepare general states and to perform arbitrary transformations with them. However, there are physical systems where the set of transformations that can be implemented is very restricted. For example, in quantum optical systems linear transformations involving beam splitters, phase plates, polarizers, and homodyne measurements are readily implemented but more general ones can only be performed with a low efficiency. Moreover, with these tools and a squeezer one can generate only a small class of states, the so–called Gaussian states. Nevertheless, many quantum information protocols have been found within the realm of linear optics: entanglement generation,[1] teleportation,[2] key distribution,[3] quantum error correction,[4] cloning,[5] some of which have already been implemented.[6] For the moment it is not known how (or whether) important operations such as entanglement distillation or a (useful) depolarization of continuous variable states can be implemented with linear optics. This raises the question which transformations can be realized by the concatenation of such operations, i.e. the tools currently available in the lab. This question was partially answered in Ref. 7, where a subclass of operations that transform Gaussian states into Gaussian states has been mathematically characterized, namely those which are *trace-preserving*. The relation of these maps to some of the experimentally feasible operations has been discussed in Ref. 8 The operations considered in Refs. 7 and 8 do not include measurements. However, one of the main strengths of linear optics is the efficient measurement of the field quadratures by homodyne detection. Furthermore, measurements and classical communication are an essential ingredient in certain basic quantum information protocols such as quantum teleportation[9] or entanglement distillation.[10] Thus it is important to find a mathematical characterization of *all* the physical actions that can be applied to Gaussian states including not trace-preserving operations.

Here we give a full solution to this problem by providing a simple description of all Gaussian operations. As an important application we discuss the question of distillation of Gaussian states by local Gaussian operations and classical communication. It was recently shown[11] that the entanglement of a symmetric two-mode Gaussian state of two parties cannot be increased with the help of another copy of that state and a homodyne measurement. Here we give a proof that distillation is not possible for an arbitrary number of modes per site, general Gaussian states and general Gaussian operations.

2 Gaussian States and Operations

As usual[21] we describe Gaussian states by the *displacement* d and the *correlation matrix* (CM) γ. The density matrix of an n-mode Gaussian state is

$$\rho = \pi^{-n} \int_{\mathrm{R}^{2n}} dx e^{-x^T \gamma x/4 - id^T x} W(x), \tag{1}$$

where $W(x) = \exp\left[-ix^T R\right], x \in \mathrm{R}^{2n}$ is the displacement operator on $\mathcal{H}$ and $R = (X_1, P_1, \ldots, X_n, P_n)$ are the quadrature operators. γ is a $2n \times 2n$ real symmetric matrix and $d \in \mathrm{R}^{2n}$; each pair (γ, d) describes a Gaussian state as long as $\gamma \geq iJ_n$, where $J_n = \bigoplus_{k=1}^{n} J_1, \quad J_1 = \begin{pmatrix} 0 & -1 \\ 1 & 0 \end{pmatrix}$. Physical actions are mathematically described by completely positive (cp) maps acting on the corresponding density operators. The best way to characterize them is the isomorphism[13] between cp maps (physical actions) and positive operators (unnormalized states).

Operations. Given a cp map $\mathcal{E}$ acting on bounded operators $\mathcal{B}(\mathcal{H})$, we define the positive operator $E \in \mathcal{B}(\mathcal{H}) \otimes \mathcal{B}(\mathcal{H})$ as follows

$$E_{12} = (\mathcal{E} \otimes 1)(|\Phi\rangle_{12}\langle\Phi|). \tag{2}$$

From this definition it is easy to see that

$$\mathcal{E}(\rho) \propto \mathrm{tr}_2[E_{12}^{T_2} \rho_2] = \mathrm{tr}_{23}(E_{12}\rho_3 \left|\Phi\right\rangle_{23} \left\langle\Phi\right|) \tag{3}$$

These equations have a direct physical meaning. Equation (2) tells us that given $\mathcal{E}$, we can always obtain the state E by preparing a maximally entangled state and acting with the map on the second subsystem, and, conversely, (3) says that given the state $E \in \mathcal{B}(\mathcal{H}) \otimes \mathcal{B}(\mathcal{H})$ and a state $\rho \in \mathcal{B}(\mathcal{H})$, we can effectively apply $\mathcal{E}$ to ρ by projecting the systems 2 and 3 into $|\Phi\rangle$ (e.g., by a "Bell measurement") obtaining $\mathcal{E}(\rho)$ (probabilistically).

Now we define a *Gaussian completely positive map* (gcp map) $\mathcal{G}$ by the properties that both $\mathcal{G}$ and $1 \otimes \mathcal{G}$ map Gaussian states to Gaussian states. With the help of the isomorphism it is straight forward to characterize them:[21,20] a Gaussian map $\mathcal{G}$ on n modes is isomorphic to a (unnormalized) Gaussian state G of $2n$ modes

$$G = \int_{\mathrm{R}^{4n}} dx e^{-\frac{1}{4}x^T \Gamma x + iD^T x - C} W(x), \tag{4}$$

with Γ, D, C real and $\Gamma \geq iJ$. Since all Gaussian states can be generated from the vacuum state by unitary Gaussian operations and discarding subsystems[14] and the Bell measurement can be realized by homodyne detection this shows that all Gaussian operations are feasible with these means.

Now we determine the action of the map $\mathcal{G}$ on a Gaussian state in terms of the CMs. Apart from normalization, we have $\mathcal{G} : \rho_{\gamma,d} \mapsto \rho_{\gamma',d'}$, and we find:

$$\gamma' = \tilde{\Gamma}_1 - \tilde{\Gamma}_{12} \frac{1}{\tilde{\Gamma}_2 + \gamma} \tilde{\Gamma}_{12}^T, \quad d' = D_1 + \tilde{\Gamma}_{12} \frac{1}{\tilde{\Gamma}_2 + \gamma} (D_2 + d), \tag{5}$$

where we have denoted

$$\Gamma = \begin{pmatrix} \Gamma_1 & \Gamma_{12} \\ \Gamma_{12}^T & \Gamma_2 \end{pmatrix}, D = \begin{pmatrix} D_1 \\ D_2 \end{pmatrix}, \tag{6}$$

and $\tilde{\Gamma} = (1 \oplus \Lambda)\Gamma(1 \oplus \Lambda)$, where $\Lambda = \mathrm{diag}(1, -1, 1, -1, \dots, -1)$. Thus, we have that all gcp maps on $\mathcal{B}(\mathcal{H})$ are characterized by a correlation matrix $\Gamma \geq iJ_{2n}$ and a displacement vector D. In order to derive Eqs. (5), we just use Eq. (3), replacing E_{12} by G and ρ_2 by a Gaussian state $\rho_{\gamma,d}$ as in Eq. (1) and obtain $\rho_{\gamma',d'} \propto \mathrm{tr}_2(G^{T_2} \rho_{\gamma,d})$.

Examples. It is instructive to see how familiar Gaussian operations are encoded in (Γ, D). Obviously, the identity operation corresponds to the maximally entangled state Φ, i.e., to $(\Gamma = \lim_r \gamma(r), D = 0)$, where $\gamma(r) = \begin{pmatrix} A_r & C_r \\ C_r & A_r \end{pmatrix}$. Here $A_r = \cosh r 1$ and $C_r = \sinh r \Lambda$ are $2n \times 2n$ square matrices. The CM $\gamma(r)$ describes n identical two–mode squeezed vacuum states and in the limit the (improper) maximally entangled state $|\Phi\rangle = \sum_k |k\rangle\,|k\rangle$. Performing a displacement operation on Φ leaves the CM unchanged, but produces a displacement, hence we have $[\Gamma = \gamma(r \to \infty), D = (D_1, 0)]$. A Gaussian unitary transformation corresponds to a *symplectic* transformation $\gamma \mapsto S^T \gamma S$ of the CM;[14] thus the Gaussian operation corresponding to S has the CM

$$\Gamma = \lim_{r \to \infty} \begin{pmatrix} \cosh r S^T S & \sinh r S^T \Lambda \\ \sinh r \Lambda S & A_r \end{pmatrix}.$$

Finally, we consider Gaussian measurements. The typical measurement is homodyne detection, which realizes the von Neumann measurement of the operator X. More generally, any projection into a pure Gaussian state is a Gaussian operation; and each such projection can be embedded in a positive-operator-valued measure (POVM) of the form $M_\gamma = \{|\gamma, d\rangle\,\langle\gamma, d| : d \in \mathrm{R}^{2n}\}$ corresponding to a generalized Gaussian measurement. The CM which corresponds to the measurement of an m-mode POVM M_{γ_p} on a $n + m$-mode system (and tracing over the measured modes) is given by

$$\Gamma = \begin{pmatrix} A_r & C_r & 0 \\ C_r & A_r & 0 \\ 0 & 0 & \gamma_p^{-1} \end{pmatrix} \tag{7}$$

and a displacement $D = (0, 0, d)^T$. Note that the first row corresponds to system "1", while the second and third row refer to system "2". This represents a straightforward generalization of the situation considered in Section 2 to maps which decrease the number of modes present. Evaluating Eq. (3) for a $n+m$ mode Gaussian state with CM $\gamma = \begin{pmatrix} A & C \\ C^T & B \end{pmatrix}$, we obtain

$$\gamma' = A - C\frac{1}{B+\gamma_p}C^T, \qquad d' = \frac{1}{2}C\frac{1}{B+\gamma_p}d, \tag{8}$$

which corresponds to the change in CM derived in Ref. 11 for projections into pure Gaussian states. Homodyne detection represents the limiting case in which the CM γ_p becomes infinitely squeezed. In this limit, the inverse in Eqs. (8) is to be understood as the pseudo-inverse.

The operations above are all isomorphic to *pure* Gaussian states and represent the *noise-free Gaussian operations.* Noise added to the CM describing the operation directly translates into noise added to the output, i.e., we have that $\Gamma' = \Gamma + P \geq \Gamma$ implies that $G_{\Gamma'}(\gamma) \geq G_\Gamma(\gamma) \forall \gamma \geq iJ$, as shown in Ref. 21.

Deterministic Operations Note that it was shown in Refs. 19 and 21 that the transformation Eqs. 5, which is in general not trace-preserving can be turned into a deterministic, trace-preserving operation mapping $\rho_{\gamma,d}$ to $\rho_{\gamma',\tilde{\Gamma}_{12}(\tilde{\Gamma}_2+\gamma)^{-1}d}$ by conditionally displacing the output state. (To do this, γ and Γ must be known.) This is true even if γ is a multi-party state, since displacements can be done locally. It is a curious feature of Gaussian operations that even measurements change the CM deterministically.

3 Bipartite systems and Entanglement Distillation

In this section we consider Gaussian maps $\mathcal{G}$ on bipartite systems. To determine whether a Gaussian operation $\mathcal{G}$ can be implemented with *local operations* on the subsystems A and B (LOCC) or whether interaction between the system is necessary, we can use the the ideas of Ref. 15, which extend the isomorphism[13] to bipartite systems. This allows to read off the answer from the state G isomorphic to $\mathcal{G}$: If G is separable, then it can be generated by LOCC, and thus $\mathcal{G}$ can be implemented (probabilistically) by LOCC. Note that following the discussion above this can be done *deterministically* for Gaussian operations, provided the CM of the state on which we act is known. If G is entangled, two cases can be distinguished: if G has positive partial transpose (ppt), the corresponding map can be implemented with a so-called ppt-preserving channel, otherwise full-fledged quantum interaction between A and B is needed.

The separability criterion for Gaussian states[16] allows us to decide for every given map, whether it is separable, ppt preserving or neither. Moreover, the characterization of separable CMs given in Ref. 17, namely that γ is separable iff $\exists\gamma_A, \gamma_B \geq iJ$ such that $\gamma \geq \gamma_A \oplus \gamma_B$ implies that — except for added correlated noise — all Gaussian LOCC operations are of product form.[21,19]

Distillation. Entanglement distillation[10] is a process in which two distant parties A and B transform a large number of copies of a bipartite mixed entangled state ρ_{AB} (jointly written as $\rho_{AB}^{\otimes n}$) into a state $\psi_{AB}^{(n)}$, which, as n goes to infinity approaches a pure maximally entangled state. To this end, A and B are allowed to perform arbitrary LOCC on $\rho_{AB}^{\otimes n}$. We consider a partially entangled Gaussian state with CM γ_{AB} and want to check if a separable Gaussian map can distill the entanglement. To this end we define a function $V(\gamma)$ to quantify the entanglement of a general bipartite CM. Let $V(\gamma_{AB})$ be the largest value $p \leq 1$ such that $\gamma_{AB} \geq p(\gamma_A \oplus \gamma_B)$, for some CMs γ_A and γ_B. Note that for a maximally entangled Gaussian state $V = 0$ [for this and further properties of $V(\gamma)$ see Ref. 21], and therefore a Gaussian distillation protocol should decrease $V(\gamma_{AB})$. In general we start with an arbitrary number copies of the state with CM γ_{AB}, i.e. a state with the CM $\bigoplus_{k=1}^{n} \gamma_{AB}$. As shown in Ref. 21, V does not change when adding more copies of the same state. The question then is, whether there is a local Gaussian operation $\mathcal{G}$ that produces from these states an output state γ'_{AB} with $V(\gamma'_{AB}) < V(\gamma_{AB})$ or even allows to reach $V \to 0$ in the limit of infinitely many copies.

In the following we show that with local Gaussian operations it is impossible to decrease V at all. Our proof makes no assumptions on the size or type of the entangled state considered or the local Gaussian operations performed. In particular, it covers any number of copies of a $n \times n$-mode input state.

We consider a separable Gaussian completely positive map acting on two systems A and B. As discussed above, the action of such a map on the correlation matrix γ_{AB} is completely characterized by another correlation matrix Γ acting on an extended space of systems A, A$'$, B and B$'$. The fact that the map is separable implies that $\Gamma = \Gamma_{AA'} \oplus \Gamma_{BB'} + P$, where P is a positive matrix. According to Sec.2 this means that Γ can be implemented by first performing the (completely uncorrelated) operation corresponding to $\Gamma_{AA'} \oplus \Gamma_{BB'}$ and then performing random displacements of the resulting state according to a probability distribution depending on P and the CM γ_{AB} of the input state. Since these displacements do not increase the entanglement, we can concentrate on the effect of the product transformation $\Gamma_{AA'} \oplus \Gamma_{BB'}$.

It follows quickly[21] that V cannot be increased at all by product operations. Thus the maximally entangled state cannot be approached (not even in the limit of infinitely many copies of γ_{AB}). Thus entanglement distillation of Gaussian states with Gaussian means is impossible. More generally, $V(\gamma_{AB})$

restricts all state transformations that can be achieved by Gaussian LOCC.

4 Conclusions

We have characterized all the physical actions that can be performed using linear optics, squeezers, and homodyne measurements. We have also characterized those that can be implemented with LOCC and those that can be implemented using ppt-preserving maps. We have shown that Gaussian states cannot be distilled by local Gaussian operations and classical communication.

Acknowledgments

We acknowledge valuable discussions with J. Eisert and J. Fiurášek. We acknowledge support by the European Union under the project EQUIP (contract IST-1999-11053).

References

1. M. Reid *et al.*, Phys. Rev. A **34**, 1260 (1986).
2. L. Vaidman, Phys. Rev. A **49**, 1473 (1994); S. Braunstein *et al.*, Phys. Rev. Lett. **80**, 869 (1998).
3. T. Ralph, Phys. Rev. A **61**, 010303R; M. Hillery, *ibid.* **61**, 022309; M. Reid, *ibid.* **62**, 062308; S. Pereira *et al.*, *ibid.* **62**, 042311 (2000); D. Gottesman *et al.*, *ibid.* **63**, 22309 (2001);
4. S. Braunstein, Phys. Rev. Lett. **80**, 4084 (1998).
5. N. Cerf *et al.*, Phys. Rev. Lett. **85**, 1754 (2000).
6. A. Furusawa *et al.*, Science **282**, 706 (1998); C. Silberhorn *et al.*, Phys. Rev. Lett. **86**, 4267 (2001).
7. B. Demoen *et al.*, Lett. Math. Phys. **2**, 161 (1977).
8. J. Eisert *et al.*, Phys. Rev. Lett. **89**, 097901 (2002).
9. C. Bennett *et al.*, Phys. Rev. Lett. **70**, 1895 (1993).
10. C. Bennett *et al.*, Phys. Rev. Lett. **76**, 722 (1996).
11. J. Eisert *et al.*, Phys. Rev. Lett. **89**, 137903 (2002).
12. A. Perelomov, *Generalized Coherent States*, Springer Verlag (1986).
13. A. Jamiołkowski, Rep. Math. Phys. **3**, 275 (1972).
14. R. Simon *et al.*, Phys. Rev. A **49**, 1567 (1994).
15. I. Cirac *et al.*, Phys. Rev. Lett. **86**, 544 (2001).
16. G. Giedke *et al.*, Phys. Rev. Lett. **87**, 167904 (2001).
17. R. Werner *et al.*, Phys. Rev. Lett. **86**, 3658 (2001).
18. G. Vidal *et al.*, Phys. Rev. A **65**, 032314 (2002).
19. J. Fiurášek, Phys. Rev. Lett. **89**, 137904 (2002).
20. J. Fiurášek, Phys. Rev. A **66**, 012304 (2002).
21. G. Giedke *et al.*, Phys. Rev. A **66**, 032316 (2002).

ON DIRECT DETECTION OF ENTANGLEMENT PROPERTIES OF UNKNOWN STATES

PAWEL HORODECKI

Faculty of Applied Physics and Mathematics, Technical University of Gdańsk, Gdańsk, Poland
E-mail: pawel@mif.pg.gda.pl

ARTUR K. EKERT, CAROLINA MOURA ALVES, DANIEL K. L. OI

Department of Applied Physics and Mathematics, University of Cambridge, Cambridge, CB3 OWA, United Kingdom

L. C. KWEK

Department of Natural Sciences, National Institute of Education, Nanyang Technological University, 1 Nanyang Walk, Singapore 637616

The recent development of methods for detecting entanglement of unknown quantum state is described. In particular, the fundamental limitations due to the linearity of quantum mechanics are discussed. Then both qualitative and quantitative methods of entanglement detection are shortly presented.

1 Introduction

Quantum information processing requires quantum resources. One of them is quantum entanglement. It is the key ingredient of quantum teleportation, quantum dense coding, some schemes of quantum cryptography and quantum computing (see Refs. 1,2). In general, a mixed state ϱ_{AB} is entangled (is not entangled) if it cannot (can) be written in the form $\varrho_{AB} \sum_i p_i|\phi_i\rangle\langle\phi_i| \otimes |\psi_i\rangle\langle\psi_i|$. We shall consider systems $m \otimes n$ that are defined on the Hilbert space $\mathcal{C}^d \otimes \mathcal{C}^{d'}$ that corresponds to the system of two spins $s = (d-1)/2$, $s' = (d-1)/2$.

Consider some physical device that is supposed to produce a quantum resource — entanglement of given systems. Then it is important to know whether the device works properly i.e., whether it produces the resource we need. We assume no *a priori* knowledge about the device. The only information is that it is memoryless and stationary. This means that it produces copies of bipartite quantum systems in the same state:

$$\boxed{\text{SOURCE}} \rightarrow \varrho_{AB} \otimes \varrho_{AB} \otimes \ldots \otimes \varrho_{AB}, \tag{1}$$

and that we can perform global measurements. We are supposed to test the output with respect to the following questions: (i) whether the state ϱ_{AB} is entangled or not; and (ii) how much entanglement there is in the system. However, we would like to answer the above in a more optimal way than just reconstructing the state. This it what distinguishes the present approach from typical methods, in which knowledge about the entanglement of the bipartite density matrix was *a priori* given. So far the approach been applied to pure quantum states.[3,4]

For general mixed states, the problem was that the only directly measurable entanglement test (the entanglement witnesses method, see Ref. 2) was not very strong when there is no prior knowledge about the state. On the other hand, the most powerful positive-maps method[5,6] (see Appendix), provided on basis of positive maps theory, were purely mathematical tests that involved unphysical transformations (positive but not completely-positive maps) and required full prior knowledge about the density matrix ϱ_{AB}. Quite surprisingly the unphysical maps can be in a sense implemented in the laboratory *via* their *structural physical approximations.* This leads to the method of entanglement detection that we shall briefly review in this paper.

2 Structural physical approximations and separability tests

Quantum mechanics is a linear theory and some fundamental restrictions follow from linearity. It is known that if the source (1) produces a single copy of the state, then the well-known no-cloning theorem does not allow us to make another copy. There are some further restrictions. Suppose that the source produces two copies. Then, for instance, the *transformation* $\varrho\otimes\varrho \to \varrho^2/\mathrm{Tr}(\varrho^2)$ is physically impossible.[8] If, however, we are more modest and want only to perform the *measurement* $\varrho \otimes \varrho \to \mathrm{Tr}(\varrho^2)$, than it can be achieved (see Sec. 3). Looking for powerful entanglement detection methods one faces another problem, namely the *unphysical* character of the positive-maps separability criteria (see Appendix). For instance, the PPT test[6] involves the map that corresponds to partial time reversal[7] that obviously cannot be physically implemented.

Structural physical approximations — In Ref. 8 (see, in this context, Ref. 9) there is the following general formula for structural physical approximation (SPA) $\overline{\Theta}$ of any unphysical linear Hermitian map $\Theta : \mathcal{M}_d \to \mathcal{M}_{d'}$[a] that acts on any state ϱ,

$$\overline{\Theta}(\varrho) = \left[\frac{\lambda\lambda'}{\lambda d d' + \alpha}\right]\frac{I}{d'} + \left[\frac{1}{\lambda d d' + \alpha}\right]\Theta(\varrho), \tag{2}$$

where $\lambda = \max[0, -a]$ and a is the minimal eigenvalue of the $d' \otimes d'$ operator $[\mathrm{I}\otimes\Theta](|\Psi_+\rangle\langle\Psi_+|)$ with $|\Psi_+\rangle = \frac{1}{\sqrt{d}}\sum_{i=1}^{d'}|i\rangle|i\rangle$. We also define $\alpha = \max_\varrho \Theta(\varrho)$. Note that the structure of the output of approximate map $\overline{\Theta}$ is identical to that of original map Θ up to rescaling by the factor $1/(\lambda\lambda' + \alpha)$ and the trivial "noise" due to the rescaled maximally-mixed state I/d' that is added.

Application to entanglement/separability tests — The above idea was applied [10] to maps of the kind $\Theta = I\otimes\Lambda$, where Λ is some chosen positive but not completely-positive map. The corresponding map $\overline{\mathrm{I}\otimes\Lambda}$ can be implemented

---

[a]Here $\mathcal{M}_d$ stands for complex $d \times d$ matrices.

physically with probability $p = Tr([\overline{\mathrm{I} \otimes \Lambda}](\varrho)$ for given ϱ. This corresponds to the transformation:

$$\varrho \underset{prob.p}{\longrightarrow} \varrho' \equiv \frac{\overline{\mathrm{I} \otimes \Lambda}(\varrho)}{\mathrm{Tr}(\overline{\mathrm{I} \otimes \Lambda}(\varrho))} = p^{-1}\left[q\frac{I}{d'} + (1-q)[\mathrm{I} \otimes \Lambda](\varrho)/a\right], \tag{3}$$

with parameters satisfying $0 \leq q \leq 1$ and $0 \leq a$ satisfying $\mathrm{Tr}\{[I \otimes \Lambda](\varrho)\} \leq a$ (for details of parameters q, a see Ref. 10). Note that $p = 1$ for trace-preserving Λ. Now, because of the form (3) the mathematical positive maps separability test (see Appendix) can be easily seen to be equivalent to the following[10] *physical separability condition: for any separable state ϱ the new state ϱ' has all eigenvalues not less than $q/d'p$.* Thus we have reduced the problem of physical detection of entanglement to the detection of the spectrum of some new state ϱ' that is produced from the initial state ϱ in some physical process (i.e., the implementation of the map $\overline{\mathrm{I} \otimes \Lambda}$). There is a method[11] of spectrum detection without state reconstruction if the collective measurements are allowed. We shall present a novel method of spectrum estimation that utilizes quantum interferometry and can be implemented as a quantum computational network.[12]

3 Estimation of spectrum and entanglement detection

Let us introduce the unitary shift operator defined as

$$V_{(n)}|\phi_1\rangle \otimes |\phi_2\rangle ... \otimes |\phi_n\rangle = |\phi_n\rangle \otimes |\phi_1\rangle ... \otimes |\phi_{n-1}\rangle. \tag{4}$$

We define the *controlled shift* operation U_{V_n}. This is a unitary transformation of the system composed of a single control qubit and n systems of d-level structure. It acts on the Hilbert space $\mathcal{H} = \mathcal{C}^2 \otimes (\mathcal{C}^d)^{\otimes n}$ and is defined by

$$U_{C-V_{(n)}} = |0\rangle\langle 0| \otimes I + |1\rangle\langle 1| \otimes V_n \tag{5}$$

It can be built with $n-1$ controlled "swaps" being just $U_{V_{(n)}}$ with $n = 2$. Let us now recall the form of Hadamard gate H and phase gate U_ϕ:

$$H = \frac{1}{\sqrt{2}}\begin{bmatrix} 1 & 1 \\ 1 & -1 \end{bmatrix}, \quad U_\phi = \frac{1}{\sqrt{2}}\begin{bmatrix} e^{i\phi} & 0 \\ 0 & 1 \end{bmatrix}. \tag{6}$$

The interferometric network[12] corresponds to the unitary operation

$$U_n = [H \otimes I^{\otimes n}] \circ [U_{C-V_{(n)}}] \circ [U_\phi H \otimes I^{\otimes n}]. \tag{7}$$

If we put $\varrho_n \equiv |0\rangle\langle 0| \otimes \varrho^{\otimes n}$ as the input to the above network then for $\phi = 0$ measurement of Pauli matrix σ_z on the control qubit gives[12]

$$\langle \sigma_z \rangle = \mathrm{Tr}(V_n \varrho^{\otimes n}) = \mathrm{Tr}(\varrho^n), \tag{8}$$

because the shift operation satisfies $\mathrm{Tr}(V_{(n)} A_1 \otimes ... \otimes A_n) = \mathrm{Tr}(A_1 A_2 ... A_n)$ for any matrices $\{A_i\}$. Then, in order to evaluate the spectrum of the density matrix of the d-level system it is enough to run the above protocol for

$n = 2, 3, ..., n$. The final measurements on the control qubit will give $\mathrm{Tr}(\varrho^2)$, $\mathrm{Tr}(\varrho^3)$, ... ,$\mathrm{Tr}(\varrho^d)$. These numbers are enough to reconstruct the spectrum of ϱ. Note that this requires only estimation of $d-1$ parameters instead of d^2-1 needed in tomographic methods. The alternative procedure would be to measure the Hermitian part of V_n.[8]

Detecting entanglement — To check the physical separability condition given in Sec. 2, we combine the SPA method with spectrum detection. Given any bipartite $d \otimes d$ state ϱ, we first apply the physical transformation $\varrho \rightarrow \varrho' = [\mathrm{I} \otimes \Lambda](\varrho)$ then detect just the spectrum of ϱ'. Comparison to quantum state estimation shows that the present protocol requires slightly fewer copies $[(d^4 + d^2 + 2)/2]$ of the initial states in one round and many fewer estimated parameters ($d^2 - 1$ instead of $d^4 - 1$). The method can be generalized to other $n \otimes m$ systems and to the multipartite case. For the PPT test,[6] the method involves the map[10]

$$[\widetilde{\mathrm{I} \otimes T}](\varrho) = \frac{d}{d^3+1} I \otimes I + \frac{1}{d^3+1}[\mathrm{I} \otimes T](\varrho), \tag{9}$$

which for two qubits can be easily realized physically with the help of random Pauli transformations. Because for two qubits the PPT test is necessary and sufficient for separability, the present method leads to a *sharp two-qubit entanglement test* that requires estimation of only three parameters. Note that in the above $\varrho^{\otimes n}$ plays the role of *data of quantum structure.* The process can be viewed as a new kind of quantum computing that solves binary problem ("entangled/not entangled") with initial quantum data structure. The presented scheme of direct check of the PPT test can be immediately used[13] to detect the computable entanglement measure.[14] Indeed, the present version of the PPT test allows us to infer the original of $[I \otimes T](\varrho)$, which is enough to compute the measure of Ref. 14.

Quantum capacity test — There exists a natural procedure for producing the bipartite two-qubit state ϱ_{Λ_1} from a one-qubit channel Λ_1 by sending half of a maximally-entangled pair down the channel. It can be shown[12] that the present test of the PPT criterion gives a sharp test for zero two-way capacity $Q_{\leftrightarrow}$ of the channel.

Direct measurement of entanglement of formation — Quite recently it has been shown[13] that, somewhat surprisingly, for two qubits the entanglement of formation E_f [15] can be detected directly despite its nonlinearity. We shall only sketch here the idea of the result. For two qubits $E_f(\varrho) = h[(1+\sqrt{1-C(\varrho)^2})/2]$, where Shannon binary information is $h(x) \equiv -x\log_2(x) - (1-x)\log_2(1-x)$ and an important state function called the concurrence[16] is defined as

$$C(\varrho) = \max[\sqrt{\lambda_1} - \sqrt{\lambda_2} - \sqrt{\lambda_3} - \sqrt{\lambda_4}, 0]. \tag{10}$$

Here, the positive and decreasing numbers $\{\lambda_i\}_{i=1}^4$ are the eigenvalues of (the non-Hermitian) matrix $\varrho\tilde{\varrho}$, with $\tilde{\varrho} = \sigma_y \otimes \sigma_y \varrho^* \sigma_y \otimes \sigma_y$ and Pauli matrices σ_y.

The following scheme (see Ref. 13 for details) allows us to determine the $\{\lambda_i\}$ and, consequently, the concurrence:

$$\varrho\otimes\varrho \xrightarrow{\Lambda_1} \varrho_1 \Longrightarrow \langle M_1\rangle = \sum_i \lambda_i, \quad \varrho\otimes\varrho\otimes\varrho\otimes\varrho \xrightarrow{\Lambda_2} \varrho_2 \Longrightarrow \langle M_2\rangle = \sum_i (\lambda_i)^2$$

$$\varrho\otimes\varrho\otimes\varrho\otimes\varrho\otimes\varrho\otimes\varrho \xrightarrow{\Lambda_3} \varrho_3 \Longrightarrow \langle M_3\rangle = \sum_i (\lambda_i)^3$$

$$\varrho\otimes\varrho\otimes\varrho\otimes\varrho\otimes\varrho\otimes\varrho\otimes\varrho\otimes\varrho \xrightarrow{\Lambda_4} \varrho_4 \Longrightarrow \langle M_4\rangle = \sum_i (\lambda_i)^4 \qquad (11)$$

where the $\{\Lambda_k\}$ are some SPA maps similar to $\overline{I\otimes T}$, and the $\{\langle M_k\rangle\}$ are mean values of some observables $\{M_k\}$ measured on systems in states $\varrho_k \equiv \Lambda_k(\varrho^{\otimes k})$. In comparison with state reconstruction, this protocol needs 33% of copies more in one round (20 instead of 15) but requires estimation of *almost four times fewer* parameters (4 instead of 15).

4 Discussion

We have presented methods for qualitative and quantitative detection of quantum entanglement without prior knowledge about the quantum state. These methods utilize structural physical approximations (SPA) of unphysical maps and a quantum interferometric network involving the quantum-controlled unitary shift operation. They allow us to estimate the nonlinear function $\mathrm{Tr}(\varrho^n)$, and to detect entanglement with many fewer parameters to estimate than are required for quantum state reconstruction. The described process can be viewed as a special kind of quantum computing, namely that of quantum data structure. In particular, entanglement detection corresponds to a kind of binary decision problem that involves the question:"Is there entanglement in the system?". The quantum network can be also used in a test for zero capacity in a quantum channel, for entropy estimation, and for efficient detection of the mean values of observables.[12] It can be also generalized to the distant laboratories paradigm, but that demonstration shall be presented elsewhere. An interesting open problem is to improve the present approach and provide an optimal protocol for entanglement detection and estimation. For this purpose, the notion of optimality should be precisely defined. Another problem is[13] to extend the approach to detect the minimal information needed to perform an entanglement distillation protocol or , perhaps, distillable entanglement and quantum capacities themselves. This, however, would require general analytical formulas, whose lack is a longstanding open problem.

Appendix

Here we shall briefly review the positive-maps separability criterion.[5] This method corresponds to testing separability *via* positive linear maps, $\Lambda : \mathcal{M}_n \rightarrow$

$\mathcal{M}_m$. The map is *positive* if it maps any state into an operator with nonegative spectrum. The map is *completely positive* iff $[\mathrm{I}_k \otimes \Lambda]$ is positive for the identity map $\mathrm{I}_k : \mathcal{M}_k \rightarrow \mathcal{M}_k$ for any k. It has been shown[5] that any bipartite $n \otimes m$ state ϱ is separable if and only if the matrix

$$[\mathrm{I} \otimes \Lambda](\varrho) \equiv \begin{bmatrix} \Lambda(\tilde{\varrho}_{1,1}) & \Lambda(\tilde{\varrho}_{1,2}) & ... & \Lambda(\tilde{\varrho}_{1,m}) \\ ... & ... & ... & ... \\ \Lambda(\tilde{\varrho}_{m,1}) & ... & ... & \Lambda(\tilde{\varrho}_{m,m}) \end{bmatrix} \tag{12}$$

has nonegative spectrum for any positive map Λ. Here $n \times n$ submatrices are defined as $[\tilde{\varrho}_{i,j}]_{\mu,\nu} = \langle i, \mu | \varrho | j, \nu \rangle$. The criterion above is nontrivial *only* for those maps that are positive but *not* completely positive, i.e., are *not* physical. In fact one can make some further restrictions but they are not needed here.

Acknowledgments

The work is supported by EU grant EQUIP, contract No. IST-1999-11053.

References

1. D. Bouwmeester, A. K. Ekert, and A. Zeilinger Eds., *The physics of quantum information: quantum cryptography, quantum teleportation, quantum computation.* (Springer, New York, 2000).
2. G. Alber, T. Beth, M. Horodecki, P. Horodecki, R. Horodecki, M. Röttler, H. Weinfurter, R. F. Werner, and A. Zeilinger; *Quantum information: an introduction to basic theoretical concepts and experiments.*, volume 173 of *Springer Tracts in Modern Physics*, (Springer, Berlin, 2001).
3. J. M. G. Sancho and S. F. Huelga, Phys. Rev. A **61**, 032314 (2000).
4. A. Acin, R. Tarrach, and G. Vidal, Phys. Rev. A, **61**, 062307 (2000).
5. M. Horodecki, P. Horodecki, and R. Horodecki, Phys. Lett. A, **223**, 1 (1996).
6. A. Peres, Phys. Rev. Lett. **77**, 1413 (1996).
7. A. Sanpera, R. Tarrach, and G. Vidal, Phys. Rev. A, **58**, 826 (1998).
8. P. Horodecki, quant-ph/0111036.
9. V. Buzek, M. Hillery, and R. F. Werner, Phys. Rev. A **60**, 2626 (1999).
10. P. Horodecki and A. Ekert, Phys. Rev. Lett. **89**, 127902 (2002).
11. M. Keyl, R. F. Werner, Phys. Rev. A **64**, 052311 (2001).
12. A. K. Ekert, C. M. Alves, D. L. Oi, M. Horodecki, P. Horodecki, and L. C. Kwek, Phys. Rev. Lett., **88**, 047905 (2002).
13. P. Horodecki, quant-ph/0111082.
14. R. F. Werner and G. Vidal, Phys. Rev. A **61**, 042303 (2000).
15. C. H. Bennett, D. P. DiVincenzo, J. Smolin and W. K. Wootters, Phys. Rev. A **54**, 3814 (1997).
16. W. K. Wootters, Quant. Inf. Comp. **1**, 27 (2001).

GENERIC ENTANGLEMENT GENERATION AND A DUALITY IN ENTANGLEMENT FOR IDENTICAL OBJECTS

SOUGATO BOSE

Institute for Quantum Information, California Institute of Technology, Pasadena, CA 91125, USA
Department of Physics and Astronomy, University College London, Gower St., London WC1E 6BT, UK
E-mail: sougato.bose@qubit.org

DIPANKAR HOME

Physics Department, Bose Institute, Calcutta 700009, India

A general scheme for deterministically entangling any degree of freedom of two uncorrelated identical particles from independent sources is presented. The method works through a combination of two particle interferometry, non-absorbtive which way detection and feedback. We discuss the wide range of applicability of our scheme. We also present a curious duality in entanglement for identical quantum objects. Compared to quantum statistics, this dualism is a more general property of identical quantum objects.

1 Introduction

Suppose we are given the task of entangling *any* variable of two independent identical particles of *any* type. The particles in question may not interact with each other or with any other quantum system which can mediate entanglement. This rules out most *known* mechanisms for entanglement generation[1,2,3] which involve either a direct interaction between the systems involved (such as photon-photon interaction during down conversion[1]) or indirect transfer of entanglement due to their interaction with other quantum systems. In this paper, we will present a very general method of entangling two identical particles from independent sources which does not fall into any of the above categories. In fact, it exploits *quantum indistinguishability* as the important entangling mechanism, rather than explicit interactions.

We first describe the basic idea. Two identical particles in orthogonal states of the degree of freedom to be entangled (for example, opposite orientations in the case of spin) are mixed at a beam splitter. Then the subensemble of cases when the two particles exit the beam splitter through separate outputs is selected. If the degree of freedom to be entangled is kept unmeasured, then because of indistinguishability, the output channels automatically become the new identity labels of the particles. The relevant degree of freedom of the two particles is then found to be entangled. The procedure can be repeated if the particles do not exit the beam splitter through separate channels. In this way, as we shall describe in greater detail in the next section, the particles can be entangled with nearly unit efficiency.

As a second part of our paper, we show a curious dualism in entanglement stemming from the impossibility of distinguishing identical quantum objects through their superselected innate properties (such as mass, charge etc.). This dualism is independent of quantum statistics (i.e. it holds for bosons, fermions and anyons)

2 A detailed description of the entangling procedure

Our setup is depicted in Fig.1. It consists of a beam splitter with input channels A and B, output channels C and D and which-channel detectors P_C in C and P_D in D. These detectors are assumed to be *nonabsorbing* and are able to *determine the path without disturbing the spin.* Now consider two identical particles in different spin states (say $|\uparrow\rangle$ and $|\downarrow\rangle$) incident simultaneously on the beam splitter from arms A and B as shown in Fig.1. This state, in second quantized notation, is described as $a^{\dagger}_{A\uparrow}a^{\dagger}_{B\downarrow}|0\rangle$ where $|0\rangle$ is the vacuum state and $a^{\dagger}_{A\uparrow}$ and $a^{\dagger}_{B\downarrow}$ are creation operators for $\uparrow$ spin in path A and $\downarrow$ spin in path B respectively. We will label the state concisely as $|A\uparrow;B\downarrow\rangle$. For fermions, $|A\uparrow;B\downarrow\rangle = -|B\downarrow;A\uparrow\rangle$ and for bosons $|A\uparrow;B\downarrow\rangle = |B\downarrow;A\uparrow\rangle$. The transformation done by the beam splitter is[4]

$$
\begin{aligned}
|A\uparrow;B\downarrow\rangle \rightarrow \frac{1}{\sqrt{2}}\{\frac{1}{\sqrt{2}}(|D\uparrow;C\downarrow\rangle \pm |D\downarrow;C\uparrow\rangle)\}& \\
+\frac{i}{2}(|C\uparrow;C\downarrow\rangle + |D\uparrow;D\downarrow\rangle),& \qquad (1)
\end{aligned}
$$

where the $+$ sign stands for fermions and the $-$ sign stands for bosons. After the detectors click, the combined state of the particles and the detectors is

$$
\begin{aligned}
&\frac{1}{\sqrt{2}}\{\frac{1}{\sqrt{2}}(|D\uparrow;C\downarrow\rangle \pm |D\downarrow;C\uparrow\rangle)\}|P_C^*\rangle|P_D^*\rangle \\
&\oplus\frac{i}{2}(|C\uparrow;C\downarrow\rangle|P_C^*\rangle|P_D\rangle \oplus |D\uparrow;D\downarrow\rangle|P_C\rangle|P_D^*\rangle), \qquad (2)
\end{aligned}
$$

where $\{|P_C\rangle,|P_D\rangle\}$ and $\{|P_C^*\rangle,|P_D^*\rangle\}$ are the unexcited and excited (corresponding to detection of one or more particles) detector states respectively. In the above $\oplus$ has been used to indicate the lack of *coherence* between orthogonal detector states. When the detectors are found in the state $|P_C^*\rangle|P_D^*\rangle$, the state of the particles is projected onto $\frac{1}{\sqrt{2}}(|D\uparrow;C\downarrow\rangle \pm |D\downarrow;C\uparrow\rangle)$. The spin part of this state can be rewritten in the first quantized notation (using the paths as particle labels) as $|\psi^{\pm}\rangle_{CD} = \frac{1}{\sqrt{2}}(|\uparrow\rangle_D|\downarrow\rangle_C \pm |\downarrow\rangle_D|\uparrow\rangle_C)$ (spin entangled state). It is legitimate to use the paths as particle labels because the particles are *identical.*

While the above method is successful only 50 percent of the time, we can make this process arbitrarily efficient via feedback. In the setup of Fig.1), when P_C and P_D do not click in coincidence, it is fed back again into the

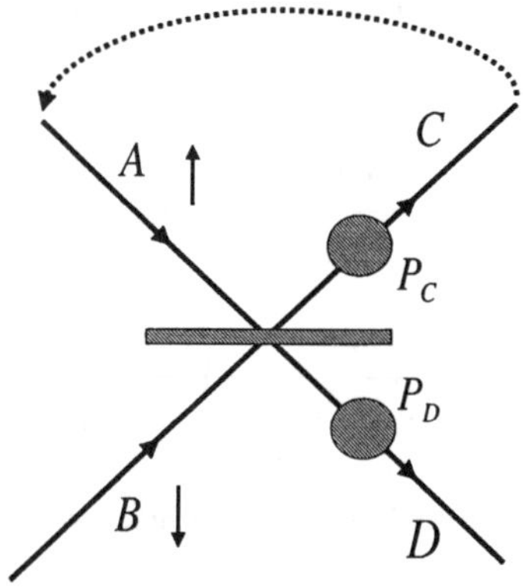

Figure 1. The setup for generating entangled states using quantum indistinguishability. The feedback loop is shown in the figure as a dotted line. If the particles bunch in the same output channel, they are fed back into the beam splitter. This is recursively continued till the particles antibunch, in which case they are entangled.

beam splitter. The incident state is $|A \uparrow; A \downarrow\rangle$ or $|B \uparrow; B \downarrow\rangle$ during such a feedback. On passing through the beam splitter, if there is anti-coincidence in the detectors P_C and P_D, the state generated is $\frac{1}{\sqrt{2}}(|\uparrow\rangle_D|\downarrow\rangle_C \mp |\downarrow\rangle_D|\uparrow\rangle_C)$. For coincidence, the feedback procedure is again repeated. The procedure is repeated until the pair anti-bunches. Here, the probability of failure decreases exponentially (2^{-N}) with the number N of feedback rounds, while the required resources (a single beam splitter and a pair of detectors) remain unchanged. Thus by increasing the number N of feedback rounds, the efficiency of our entanglement generation procedure can be increased arbitrarily. In fact one can continue the process *until* the particles anti-bunch and get entangled, which means the process can be regarded as *deterministic.*[5]

3 Physical Implementations

Though we have illustrated the method in the last section with spin as the variable being entangled, our entangling method is very general and applicable to any degree of freedom of any species of particles.[5] All one needs for our procedure are particles for which beam splitters exist (and it exists for example, for electrons, neutrons, atoms and macromolecules[6]) and which have at least two commuting degrees of freedom. One of these degrees of freedom, usually the one which remains coherent for a longer time (such as the spin degree of freedom), is chosen to be the variable to be entangled. The other degree of freedom is used for the non-absorptive which-way detection. Physical implementations of our scheme with various types of particles is described

Particle type	Entangled Variable	Detection Variable
Electrons	Spin	Charge
Neutrons	Momentum	Spin
Ions	Internal Levels	Charge
Neutral Atoms	Momenta	Internal Levels
Macro-molecules	Vibrations	Spin/Charge/Internal Levels

Table 1. Implementations of our generic entangling scheme with various kinds of particles.

in the table 1.

Duality in entanglement for identical quantum objects

When two particles are identical (i.e. not distinguishable through innate attributes such as mass, charge etc.), one needs *at least two dynamical variables* to meaningfully describe an entangled state of the particles. In a suitable quantum state such as $\frac{1}{\sqrt{2}}(|D\uparrow; C\downarrow\rangle \pm |D\downarrow; C\uparrow\rangle)$, when one of the variables (the positions as denoted by C and D in our case) denotes the identity of the particle, the other variable (the spin in our case) appears *entangled.* However, the above state can *equally well* be rewritten in first quantized notation as $|D_\uparrow C_\downarrow\rangle + |C_\uparrow D_\downarrow\rangle$ (for both bosons and fermions), where the spins have been used to label the particles and their paths are entangled. One simply has to separate the particles spatially corresponding to their spin states (using a polarization beam splitter or a Stern-Gerlach) in a direction orthogonal to the $C - D$ direction. Non-local correlations can between the spatial variables of the two particles can then be tested by mixing paths C and D in each location of definite spin.

References

1. P. G. Kwiat *et. al.*, *Phys. Rev. Lett.* **75**, 4337 (1995).
2. A. Furusawa *et. al.*, *Science* **282**, 706 (1998).
3. E. Hagley *et. al.*, *Phys. Rev. Lett.* **79**, 1 (1997); C. A. Sackett *et. al.*, *Nature* **404**, 256 (2000).
4. R. Loudon, *Phys. Rev. A***58**, 4904 (1998).
5. S. Bose and D. Home, *Phys. Rev. Lett.* **88**, 050401 (2002).
6. M. Arndt *et. al.*, *Nature* **401**, 680 (1999).

HOW MUCH STATE ASSIGNMENTS CAN DIFFER

TODD A. BRUN

Institute for Advanced Study, Einstein Drive, Princeton, NJ 08540
Phone: 609-734-8335, FAX: 609-951-4489, email: tbrun@ias.edu

The state that an observer attributes to a quantum system depends on the information available to that observer. If two or more observers have different information about a single system, they will in general assign different states. Is there any restriction on what states can be assigned, given reasonable assumptions about how the observers use their information? We derive necessary and sufficient conditions for a group of general density matrices to characterize what different people may know about one and the same physical system. These conditions are summarized by a single criterion, which we term *compatibility*.

1 Observers with differing information

Suppose there is a physical system $\mathcal{S}$ with an associated Hilbert space $\mathcal{H}_\mathcal{S}$ of (finite) dimension D, and two observers Alice and Bob each acquire information about $\mathcal{S}$ by some means. Based on this information, they describe $\mathcal{S}$ by two *states*: ρ_A and ρ_B, respectively. If the information that Alice and Bob acquire is not the same, then in general $\rho_A \neq \rho_B$.

The question we address in this paper is this: is there any restriction on the possible assignments ρ_A and ρ_B that can be made? We argue that there is; and we term two states ρ_A and ρ_B which could represent two descriptions of the same physical system *compatible*[1].

For the purposes of this paper, we assume that all of the information acquired by Alice and Bob is both *accurate* and *reliable*. By *accurate* we mean the usual: that any measurements were performed and recorded correctly, and that no one deliberately lied to either of them. By *reliable* we mean something rather more subtle: that the information acquired by Alice and Bob has not been rendered incorrect by disturbances to $\mathcal{S}$ unknown to them.

Classically this is a rather straightforward assumption, but quantum mechanically it is not, largely due to the disturbing effects of measurement. If Bob, for instance, were to measure $\mathcal{S}$, that measurement would disturb the system, potentially introducing errors into Alice's state assignment. By assuming that the information of both observers is *reliable*, we are explicitly ruling out such disturbances. What this means technically will become clear below.

2 Compatibility

Intuitively, what should we expect from a criterion for compatibility? First, if ρ_A and ρ_B are both *pure states*, then they should only be compatible if they are identical:

$$\rho_A = \rho_B = |\psi\rangle\langle\psi| \tag{1}$$

for some $|\psi\rangle$. This seems natural, because pure states represent states of *maximal knowledge* (or minimal ignorance).

Rudolph Peierls[2] suggested two criteria for compatibility in the general case:

$$\begin{aligned} \text{PI}: \ & [\rho_A, \rho_B] = 0 \,, \\ \text{PII}: \ & \rho_A \rho_B \neq 0 \,. \end{aligned}$$

These criteria together rule out differing pure state assignments. Criterion PII seems very natural: it is just the statement that ρ_A and ρ_B are not orthogonal, and hence not contradictory. PI is somewhat less obvious. It seems to be reasoned by analogy with compatible observables, in which $[\hat{A}, \hat{B}] = 0$ implies that the observables $\hat{A}$ and $\hat{B}$ can be measured simultaneously.

Unfortunately, in the current case it is much too restrictive. Consider the following example:

$$\begin{aligned} \rho_A &= |\psi\rangle\langle\psi| \\ \rho_B &= p|\psi\rangle\langle\psi| + (1-p)|\phi\rangle\langle\phi| \,, \end{aligned} \tag{2}$$

where $\langle\psi|\phi\rangle \neq 0$. This pair of assignments fails to satisfy PI; but it could easily arise from two observers with different information. For instance, Bob may believe that $\mathcal{S}$ could have been prepared in either state $|\psi\rangle$ or $|\phi\rangle$, while Alice has additional information which rules out the latter.

Let's consider instead one of the following two (equivalent) criteria: ρ_A and ρ_B are compatible if and only if there exist decompositions of ρ_A and ρ_B

$$\begin{aligned} \rho_A &= p_0|\chi\rangle\langle\chi| + \sum_{i>0} p_i|\psi_i\rangle\langle\psi_i| \,, \\ \rho_B &= q_0|\chi\rangle\langle\chi| + \sum_{j>0} q_j|\phi_j\rangle\langle\phi_j| \,, \end{aligned} \tag{3}$$

which share a state $|\chi\rangle$ in common, such that $p_0, q_0 > 0$; or equivalently, if and only if the intersection of their supports is nontrivial,

$$S[\rho_A] \bigcap S[\rho_B] \neq 0 \,, \tag{4}$$

where $S[\rho]$ is the space spanned by the eigenvectors of ρ with nonzero eigenvalues. Note that this definition of compatibility extends straightforwardly to any number of observers, Alice, Bob, Cara, etc. This criterion implies PII, and also implies that pure state assignments must be identical. We show below that this criterion is both necessary and sufficient.

3 Necessity

Assuming Alice and Bob are rational, if they pool their information they should agree on a joint state description ρ_J. Furthermore, since it was assumed that their information was reliable, any measurement outcome to which either of them initially assigned zero probability must *still* have zero probability in the new state ρ_J.

This means that the *null space* of the new state $N[\rho_J]$ must *include* the null spaces of the two states ρ_A and ρ_B:

$$
\begin{aligned}
N[\rho_A] &\subseteq N[\rho_J] \,, \\
N[\rho_B] &\subseteq N[\rho_J] \,,
\end{aligned}
\tag{5}
$$

(where $N[\rho]$ is the space spanned by the eigenvectors of ρ with vanishing eigenvalues). This implies that $N[\rho_J]$ contains the span of $N[\rho_A]$ and $N[\rho_B]$, which implies in turn that

$$
S[\rho_J] \subseteq S[\rho_A] \bigcap S[\rho_B] \,. \tag{6}
$$

In order for such a joint state assignment to exist, therefore, the intersection of the supports of ρ_A and ρ_B must be nontrivial.

4 Sufficiency

Obviously, if one is just given two state assignments $\rho_{A,B}$ it is impossible to know if they are intended to apply to the same system or not. So by sufficiency what we mean is that if the assignments satisfy the compatibility criterion, then they *could* be different descriptions of the same system based on different information.

We prove this by construction. Suppose ρ_A and ρ_B have decompositions (3). These state assignments could have arisen in the following way. Suppose that there are two ancillary systems $\mathcal{A}$ and $\mathcal{B}$ in addition to S, and that both Alice and Bob know that the initial state was

$$
\begin{aligned}
|\Psi\rangle = \frac{1}{N}\Bigg(& |0\rangle_{\mathcal{A}}|0\rangle_{\mathcal{B}}|\chi\rangle_S + \sum_{i>0}\sqrt{\frac{p_i}{p_0}}|0\rangle_{\mathcal{A}}|i\rangle_{\mathcal{B}}|\psi_i\rangle_S \\
& + \sum_{j>0}\sqrt{\frac{q_j}{q_0}}|j\rangle_{\mathcal{A}}|0\rangle_{\mathcal{B}}|\phi_j\rangle_S \Bigg) \,,
\end{aligned}
\tag{7}
$$

where N is a normalization factor, $|0\rangle_{\mathcal{A}}$ and $|j\rangle_{\mathcal{A}}$ are all mutually orthogonal, and similarly for $|0\rangle_{\mathcal{B}}$ and $|i\rangle_{\mathcal{B}}$. Alice then measures subsystem $\mathcal{A}$ and Bob measures $\mathcal{B}$, both getting result 0, but they do not share their results. It is clear that in this case Alice and Bob will make the state assignments ρ_A and ρ_B given in (3). If they were to pool their information, they would both arrive at the joint state assignment $|\chi\rangle$. So any state assignments which satisfy the compatibility criterion *could* arise from observers with different information about the same physical system $\mathcal{S}$.

5 Further questions

Both the problem and the solution are easy to state, but lead one into subtle and interesting questions about how state assignments are made. For example:

1. What restrictions are there on how Alice and Bob acquire their information, if we want it to be *accurate* and *reliable*? How does the case where they perform measurements differ from the case where they get information from a knowledgeable third party?

2. If Alice and Bob pool their information, how do they form a joint state assignment?[3] Rather than giving an all or nothing criterion, is it possible to quantify a *degree* of compatibility between two state assignments?[4]

3. Are there other reasonable notions of compatibility? And if so, do they lead to well-defined compatibility criteria?[5]

All of these questions have been examined to some extent, but much remains open. This just shows how far there is to go in completely understanding state assignment in quantum mechanics.

Acknowledgments

First and foremost, I would like to acknowledge my collaborators Jerry Finkelstein and David Mermin; all technical results of this paper were developed jointly with them. I thank Robin Blume-Kohout, Carl Caves, Jennifer Dodd, Chris Fuchs, David Poulin and Rüdiger Schack for stimulating conversations and feedback, and the organizers of QCMC 2002. This research was supported in part by the Martin A. and Helen Chooljian Membership in Natural Sciences, and by DOE Grant No. DE-FG02-90ER40542.

References

1. Todd A. Brun, J. Finkelstein and N. David Mermin, Phys. Rev. A 65, 032315 (2002).
2. R.E. Peierls, Physics World, 19-21 (January 1991).
3. Kurt Jacobs, quant-ph/0201096.
4. One such measure was suggested by David Poulin and Robin Blume-Kohout in quant-ph/0205033. Another measure, suggested by Alexei Kitaev (private communication), is the maximum trace of a positive operator $\hat{R}$ such that $\rho_A - \hat{R}$ and $\rho_B - \hat{R}$ are both positive.
5. Carlton M. Caves, Christopher A. Fuchs and Rüdiger Schack, quant-ph/0206110.

PHASE SPACE BELL INEQUALITIES, THREE MARGINAL THEOREM AND QUANTUM ENTANGLEMENT MEASURES

G. AUBERSON,[†] G. MAHOUX,[‡] S.M. ROY[◇] AND V. SINGH[◇]

[†]*LPM, Université Montepellier II, F-34095 Montepellier, Cedex 05, France,*
E-Mail: auberson@lpm.univ-monpt2.fr

[‡]*S.Ph.T., Centre d'Études Nucléaires de Saclay, F-91191 Gif-sur-Yvette Cedex, France*
E-mail: mahoux@spht.saclay.cea.fr

[◇]*Tata Institute of Fundamental Research, Mumbai 400 005, India*
E-mail: (SMR) shasanka@theory.tifr.res.in; (VS) vsingh@theory.tifr.res.in

We derive continuous-variable (position, momentum) Bell inequalities as tests of the existence of positive phase-space densities consistent with quantum probability densities. Violation of these inequalities by quantum states also serve as quantitative tests of the quantum entanglement of these states.

1 The Three-Marginal Theorem

Consider a quantum system with a two-dimensional configuration space, and complete commuting sets (CCS) of observables, $\{Q_1, Q_2\}, \{Q_1, P_2\}, \{P_1, Q_2\}$ and $\{P_1, P_2\}$, where $\vec{Q}$ and $\vec{P}$ denote, respectively, the position and momentum operators. The quantum density operator specifies the probability densities for observing particular eigenvalues for any particular CCS, for example, $\langle q_1, q_2|\rho|q_1, q_2\rangle$, but does not specify joint probabilities for different CCS of observables. We pose the following "four-marginal problem". For every quantum state ρ, does there exist a positive-definite phase-space probability density distribution, $D(\vec{q}, \vec{p})$, whose marginals reproduce the quantum probability densities for all four choices of the CCS, i.e.,

$$\int d\vec{p}\, D(\vec{q}, \vec{p}) = \langle \vec{q}\,|\rho|\vec{q}\,\rangle \tag{1}$$

$$\int d\vec{q}\, D(\vec{q}, \vec{p}) = \langle \vec{p}\,|\rho|\vec{p}\,\rangle \tag{2}$$

$$\int dp_1\, dq_2\, D(\vec{q}, \vec{p}) = \langle q_1, p_2\,|\rho|q_1, p_2\,\rangle \tag{3}$$

$$\int dq_1\, dp_2\, D(\vec{q}, \vec{p}) = \langle p_1, q_2\,|\rho|p_1, q_2\,\rangle. \tag{4}$$

For simplicity, we suppress the dependence of $D(\vec{q}, \vec{p})$ on ρ. The Wigner distribution function[1] satisfies the marginal conditions, but does not satisfy the condition of positivity. We prove a no-go theorem, "the Three-Marginal Theorem": there are quantum density operators ρ for which a positive-definite phase-space probability density $D(\vec{q}, \vec{p})$ satisfying the four-marginal conditions does not exist. We thus confirm a longstanding conjecture,[2] and vastly improve on a previous result[3] that forbids reproducing quantum probabilities of an infinite sequence of CCS as marginals of one $D(\vec{q},\vec{p})$. The four-marginal theorem does not refer to Einstein locality. It constitutes a novel Gleason-Kochen-Specker type theorem for infinite-dimensional vector spaces.

2 Four-Marginal Postulate and Quantum Entanglement

We shall show that when Q_i, P_i $(i = 1, 2)$ refer to subsystems 1 and 2, the marginal postulates (1)–(4) with positive $D(\vec{q},\vec{p})$, are necessarily valid for all separable (i.e., non-entangled) quantum states,

$$\rho = \sum_r \lambda_r \rho_{1r} \otimes \rho_{2r} \tag{5}$$

$$\lambda_r \geq 0 \tag{6}$$

$$\sum_r \lambda_r = 1 \tag{7}$$

$$\rho_{ir} = \sum_\alpha \mu_{ir\alpha} |\psi_{ir\alpha}\rangle\langle\psi_{ir\alpha}| \tag{8}$$

$$\mu_{ir\alpha} \geq 0 \tag{9}$$

$$\sum_\alpha \mu_{ir\alpha} = 1. \tag{10}$$

For proof, notice that the positive-definite phase-space density

$$D(\vec{q},\vec{p}) = \sum_r \lambda_r \left(\sum_\alpha \mu_{1r\alpha} |\psi_{1r\alpha}(x_1)|^2 |\tilde{\psi}_{1r\alpha}(p_1)|^2 \right) \times \left(\sum_\beta \mu_{2r\beta} |\psi_{2r\beta}(x_2)|^2 |\tilde{\psi}_{2r\beta}(p_2)|^2 \right), \tag{11}$$

where tildes indicate Fourier transforms, satisfies the four-marginal postulate. A straightforward computation of the integrals in (1)–(4) establishes this result. The relation of the three -marginal theorem with quantum entanglement is quantified by the phase-space Bell inequalities. Any separable state must obey these inequalities. On the other hand, the three-marginal theorem follows from the existence of states which violate the inequalities.

3 Phase-Space Bell Inequalities and Proof of the Three-Marginal Theorem

Let the experimentally measurable probability densities for the four commuting pairs of variables be denoted by $R(q_1, q_2)$, $S(q_1, p_2)$, $T(p_1, q_2)$ and $U(p_1, p_2)$. Suppose that these densities are marginals of one normalized non-negative phase-space density $D(\vec{q},\vec{p})$. Let $F_1(q_1)$, $F_2(q_2)$, $G_1(p_1)$, $G_2(p_2)$ be arbitrary nonvanishing functions. It is

$$\begin{aligned}&\operatorname{sgn}[F_1(q_1)]\{\operatorname{sgn}[F_2(q_2)] + \operatorname{sgn}[G_2(p_2)]\}\\&+ \operatorname{sgn}[G_1(p_1)]\{\operatorname{sgn}[F_2(q_2)] - \operatorname{sgn}[G_2(p_2)]\} = \pm 2.\end{aligned} \tag{12}$$

Multiplying by $D(\vec{q},\vec{p})$ and integrating over phase space, we readily prove the phase-space Bell inequalities,

$$\begin{aligned}-2 \le &\int dq_1 \operatorname{sgn}[F_1(q_1)]\\&\times \left[\int dq_2 \operatorname{sgn}[F_2(q_2)] R(q_1,q_2) + \int dp_2 \operatorname{sgn}[G_2(p_2)] S(q_1,p_2)\right]\\&+ \int dp_1 \operatorname{sgn}[G_1(p_1)]\\&\times \left[\int dq_2 \operatorname{sgn}[F_2(q_2)] T(p_1,q_2) - \int dp_2 \operatorname{sgn}[G_2(p_2)] U(p_1,p_2)\right] \le 2,\end{aligned} \tag{13}$$

These inequalities can be tested experimentally. Further, we can test if quantum mechanics obeys the four-marginal postulate by replacing R, S, T, U by their quantum expressions. We obtain

$$|\mathrm{Tr}(\rho A)| \le 2, \tag{14}$$

where A is the operator obtained by replacing R, S, T, U in the above integrals by $|q_1q_2\rangle\langle q_1q_2|$, $|q_1p_2\rangle\langle q_1p_2|$, $|p_1q_2\rangle\langle p_1q_2|, |p_1p_2\rangle\langle p_1p_2|$ respectively. We have found states[6] $\rho_\pm$ for which $\mathrm{Tr}(\rho_\pm A)$ can approach $\pm 2\sqrt{2}$ as closely as we wish, violating the Bell inequality. This proves the four-marginal theorem. Further, all separable states obey the four-marginal postulate and the above Bell inequalities; hence the violation of $|\mathrm{Tr}(\rho A)| \le 2$ is a measure of the entanglement of ρ. This measure for infinite-dimensional vector spaces supplements considerable previous work[4] for finite-dimensional vector spaces.

Quantum mechanics does permit a positive definite $D(\vec{q},\vec{p})$ which obeys any three of the four marginal conditions. We have constructed the most general such $D(\vec{q},\vec{p})$ extending previous work on two[5] and three marginals.[2] Details of this construction and the three marginal theorem will be published elsewhere.[6]

Acknowledgments

Work supported by the Indo-French Centre for the Promotion of Advanced Research, Project 1501-2.

References

1. E. Wigner, Phys. Rev. **40**, 749 (1932).
2. S. M. Roy and V. Singh, Phys. Letters A **255**, 201 (1999).

3. A. Martin and S. M. Roy, Phys. Letters B **350**, 66 (1995).
4. A. Peres, Phys. Rev. Lett. **77**, 1413 (1996); M. Horodecki et al., Phys. Lett. A **223**, 1 (1996) and Phys. Rev. Lett. **80**, 5239 (1998); R. F. Werner and M. M. Wolf, Phys. Rev. A **61**, 062102 (2000) and **64**, 032112 (2001); N. D. Mermin, Phys. Rev. Lett. **65**, 1838 (1990); S. M. Roy and V. Singh, Phys. Rev. Lett. **67**, 2761 (1991).
5. L. Cohen, J. Math. Phys. **25**, 2402 (1984).
6. G. Auberson, G. Mahoux, S. M. Roy and V. Singh, Phys. Lett. A **300**, 327 (2002), quant-ph/0205185.

ENTANGLEMENT CONCENTRATION VIA DETERMINISTIC TRANSFORMATION

FUMIAKI MORIKOSHI
NTT Basic Research Laboratories, NTT Corporation
3-1 Morinosato-Wakamiya, Atsugi-shi, Kanagawa, 243-0198, Japan
E-mail: fumiaki@will.brl.ntt.co.jp

MASATO KOASHI
CREST Research Team for Interacting Carrier Electronics
School of Advanced Sciences, The Graduate University for Advanced Studies (SOKENDAI)
Hayama, Kanagawa, 240-0193, Japan
E-mail: koashi@soken.ac.jp

We discuss deterministic extraction of Bell pairs from given entangled pure states shared between distant parties. It is shown that pairwise manipulations suffice for optimal deterministic concentration of two-qubit pairs. Deriving the maximum efficiency of the operation, we give an entanglement measure valid in deterministic transformations.

1 Introduction

Quantifying entanglement has attracted great attention recently in that it is expected to give us further insights into not only the weirdness of quantum nonlocality but also its potential as a resource in quantum information processing. One way of quantifying entanglement is to estimate the number of Bell pairs,

$$|\Phi^+\rangle = \frac{1}{\sqrt{2}}(|00\rangle + |11\rangle), \tag{1}$$

extractable from a given entangled state by local operations aided by classical communication (LOCC). That problem for bipartite pure states has already been solved in the case of asymptotically successful transformations.[1] Extraction of maximally-entangled pairs from partially-entangled pairs by LOCC is generally called entanglement concentration, and its limitations and efficiency in probabilistic transformations of finite number of pairs have also been studied.[2,3,4,5,6]

In this paper, we consider another situation in which Bell pairs are extracted from a given entangled state by LOCC with certainty.[7] This reveals a useful feature of deterministic concentration of two-qubit pairs that we need only pairwise manipulations of given pairs instead of manipulating all of them collectively. Moreover, an entanglement measure for deterministic transformations will be derived, which can be generalized to higher dimensions.

2 Tournament-like concentration of two-qubit pairs

Suppose Alice and Bob share n (possibly different) partially-entangled pairs $|\psi_1\rangle \otimes \cdots \otimes |\psi_n\rangle$, where

$$|\psi_i\rangle = \sqrt{a_i}\,|00\rangle + \sqrt{1-a_i}\,|11\rangle \quad \text{with} \quad \frac{1}{2} < a_i < 1, \qquad (i = 1, \ldots, n), \quad (2)$$

and wish to extract as many Bell pairs as possible from these entangled pairs by LOCC with certainty.

Assuming that Alice and Bob obtain k Bell pairs and $(n-k)$ disentangled pairs, i.e.,

$$|\psi_1\rangle \otimes \cdots \otimes |\psi_n\rangle \rightarrow \otimes^k |\Phi^+\rangle \otimes^{n-k} |00\rangle, \quad (3)$$

and applying Nielsen's theorem,[8] one can prove that this concentration is accomplished if

$$a_1 \cdots a_n \leq \frac{1}{2^k}. \quad (4)$$

Inequality (4) gives the maximum number of Bell pairs extractable from the partially-entangled pairs given by Eq. (2),

$$k_{max} = \lfloor -\log_2(a_1 \cdots a_n) \rfloor = \left\lfloor \sum_{i=1}^{n} -\log_2 a_i \right\rfloor, \quad (5)$$

where $\lfloor x \rfloor$ represents the largest integer equal to or less than x.

This implies that the contribution from a partially-entangled state $|\psi_i\rangle = \sqrt{a_i}\,|00\rangle + \sqrt{1-a_i}\,|11\rangle$ can be described as

$$D(\psi_i) \equiv -\log_2 a_i \qquad \left(\frac{1}{2} \leq a_i \leq 1\right). \quad (6)$$

Note that $D(\Phi^+) = 1$ and $D(|00\rangle) = 0$, and $D(\psi)$ does not diverge in $\frac{1}{2} \leq a_i \leq 1$.

On the other hand, it was proved that we can always conserve a sum of $D(\psi_i)$ in deterministic concentration of two pairs by keeping the residual entanglement that is not enough for a Bell pair in a partially-entangled pair.[7,9] We can thus achieve optimal deterministic concentration just by a series of pairwise manipulations without losing any amount of Bell pairs that is supposed to be distilled.

Let us look at the concentration procedure concretely. First Alice and Bob choose two arbitrary entangled pairs. Then they perform a two-pair concentration on them. If they obtain a Bell pair, it is put aside, and the residual entangled pair will be reused in a later pairwise concentration. If the selected two pairs are insufficient for a Bell pair, they gather the entanglement contained in the two pairs into a partially-entangled pair, which will be reused in a later pairwise concentration. They repeat these operations until they achieve the maximum number of Bell pairs. In each pairwise concentration, at least one of the pairs becomes a Bell pair or a disentangled pair, which does not proceed to the next concentration. Thus, we perform a pairwise concentration at most $n-1$ times in a process similar to elimination in a tournament, which requires no collective manipulation of more than two pairs.

3 Entanglement measure for the deterministic concentration

Deterministic entanglement concentration stated above leads to an entanglement measure valid in deterministic transformations. First, we present the conditions for entanglement measures $M(\psi)$ in deterministic transformations of pure states: (i) $M(\psi)=0$ iff $|\psi\rangle$ is separable. (ii) $M(\psi)$ remains unchanged under local unitary transformations. (iii) $M(\psi)$ cannot be increased by deterministic LOCC. These conditions are modified versions of those for entanglement measures proposed by Vedral et al.[10,11] The restriction of deterministic transformations makes the third condition weaker than the counterpart in the original versions,[10,11] which requires the non-increasing property of the *expected* value of the measure when the final states are not unique.

The quantity $D(\psi_i)$ defined by Eq. (6) satisfies the above conditions, thus is considered as an entanglement measure for deterministic transformations. Note that if we allow probabilistic transformations, the expected value of our measure can be increased in some cases. The most fascinating property of the measure $D(\psi)$ is additivity. The additivity shows that the tournament-like concentration procedure does not depend on the way of pairing entangled pairs, because we can always attain the optimality as long as the sum $\sum_i D(\psi_i)$ is conserved.

We can extend the measure to general pure entangled states. Suppose Alice and Bob share a partially-entangled state whose Schmidt number is m,

$$|\psi\rangle=\sum_{j=1}^{m}\sqrt{p_j}\,|j,j\rangle \quad \text{with} \quad \sum_{j=1}^{m}p_j=1, \qquad (m\geq 2), \tag{7}$$

Then, the measure for the state becomes

$$D(\psi)\equiv-\log_2\left(\max_i p_i\right) \qquad \left(0<\max_i p_i\leq 1\right), \tag{8}$$

and also gives the maximum number of Bell pairs extractable from Eq. (7),

$$k_{max}=\left\lfloor-\log_2(\max_i p_i)\right\rfloor. \tag{9}$$

On the other hand, another well-known entanglement measure, entropy of entanglement,[1]

$$E(\psi)\equiv-\sum_{i=1}^{d}p_i\log_2 p_i, \tag{10}$$

represents the amount of entanglement per one copy $|\psi_i\rangle$ in the concentration of an infinite number of identical copies of $|\psi_i\rangle$. The strong restriction of deterministic transformations makes our concentration scheme less efficient than the asymptotically successful concentration, which attains $E(\psi)$ in the asymptotic limit. The reason why there exists a gap between the two measures $D(\psi)$ and $E(\psi)$, and the way of filling it are discussed in Ref. 12 by introducing the notion of error exponents.

4 Conclusion

We have presented a deterministic entanglement concentration scheme for a finite number of partially-entangled pairs. The tournament-like property was revealed in the case of two-qubit pairs. An entanglement measure for the deterministic situation was also presented. Further implications of the quantity in another context of quantum information theory remain to be explored.

Acknowledgments

We are grateful to N. Imoto for valuable discussions. This work was supported by a Grant-in-Aid for Encouragement of Young Scientists (Grant No. 12740243) and a Grant-in-Aid for Scientific Research (B) (Grant No. 12440111) by the Japan Society of the Promotion of Science.

References

1. C. H. Bennett, H. J. Bernstein, S. Popescu, and B. Schumacher, Phys. Rev. A **53**, 2046 (1996).
2. H.-K. Lo and S. Popescu, Phys. Rev. A **63**, 022301 (2001).
3. G. Vidal, Phys. Rev. Lett. **83**, 1046 (1999).
4. S. Bose, V. Vedral, and P. L. Knight, Phys. Rev. A **60**, 194 (1999).
5. D. Jonathan and M. B. Plenio, Phys. Rev. Lett. **83**, 83, 1455 (1999).
6. L. Hardy, Phys. Rev. A **60**, 1912 (1999).
7. F. Morikoshi and M. Koashi, Phys. Rev. A **64**, 022316 (2001).
8. M. A. Nielsen, Phys. Rev. Lett. **83**, 436 (1999).
9. F. Morikoshi, Phys. Rev. Lett. **84**, 3189 (2000).
10. V. Vedral, M. B. Plenio, M. A. Rippin, and P. L. Knight, Phys. Rev. Lett. **78**, 2275 (1997).
11. V. Vedral and M. B. Plenio, Phys. Rev. A **57**, 1619 (1998).
12. M. Hayashi, M. Koashi, K. Matsumoto, F. Morikoshi, and A. Winter, quant-ph/0206097 (2002).

CHARACTERIZING SEPARABLE PURE STATES OF MULTI-QUBIT SYSTEMS

PHILIPPE JORRAND
Leibniz Laboratory 46 av Félix-Viallet 38031 Grenoble Cedex (France)
E-mail: Philippe.Jorrand@imag.fr

MEHDI MHALLA
Leibniz Laboratory 46 av Félix-Viallet 38031 Grenoble Cedex (France)
E-mail: Mehdi.Mhalla@imag.fr

This paper addresses two questions: what conditions should the amplitudes in the pure state $|\psi_N\rangle$ of a system of n qubits ($N = 2^n$) satisfy for this state to be separable (i) into a tensor product of n qubit states $|\psi_N\rangle = |\psi_2\rangle_0 \otimes |\psi_2\rangle_1 \otimes \cdots \otimes |\psi_2\rangle_n$, and (ii), into a tensor product of 2 subsystems states $|\psi_P\rangle \otimes \left|\psi_Q\right\rangle$ with $P = 2^p$ and $Q = 2^q$ such that $p + q = n$? For both questions, necessary and sufficient conditions are proved.

1 Introduction

Two notions of separability are considered: full separability (no entanglement) and $p - q$ separability (test of bipartition).

The state $|\psi_N\rangle$ of a quantum system composed of n qubits is fully separable iff it can be factorized into a tensor product of n qubit states, $|\psi_N\rangle = |\psi_2\rangle_0 \otimes |\psi_2\rangle_1 \otimes \cdots \otimes |\psi_2\rangle_n$, where each $|\psi_2\rangle$ is a qubit state.

Given integers p and q such that $p + q = n$, $|\psi_N\rangle$ is $p - q$ separable iff it can be factorized into a tensor product $|\psi_P\rangle \otimes |\psi_Q\rangle$ of a subsystem state $|\psi_P\rangle$ with a subsystem state $|\psi_Q\rangle$, where $P = 2^p$ and $Q = 2^q$ (i.e., the two subsystems are composed of p and q qubits respectively): $|\psi_N\rangle = |\psi_P\rangle \otimes |\psi_Q\rangle$.

2 Conditions for Full Separability

2.1 Pair-product invariance

$|\psi_N\rangle = \sum_{i=0}^{N-1} \alpha_i |i\rangle$ is pair-product invariant iff: $\forall k \in [1, n], \forall i \in [0, K-1]$, $\alpha_i \alpha_{K-i-1}$ is constant where, for any integer k, K denotes 2^k . The pair-product invariance of the state $|\psi_8\rangle$ of a register of 3 qubits, for example, is visualized in Fig. 1, where the products of pairs of amplitudes linked by arrows with the same shade of gray correspond to the same value of k (i.e., $k = 2$ or $k = 3$) and all have the same value if $|\psi_8\rangle$ is indeed pair-product invariant.

If $|\psi_N\rangle$ is pair-product invariant, many other equalities among products of pairs of amplitudes are satisfied. The definition of pair-product invariance generates one of the minimal sets of such equalities, from which all other equalities can be derived.

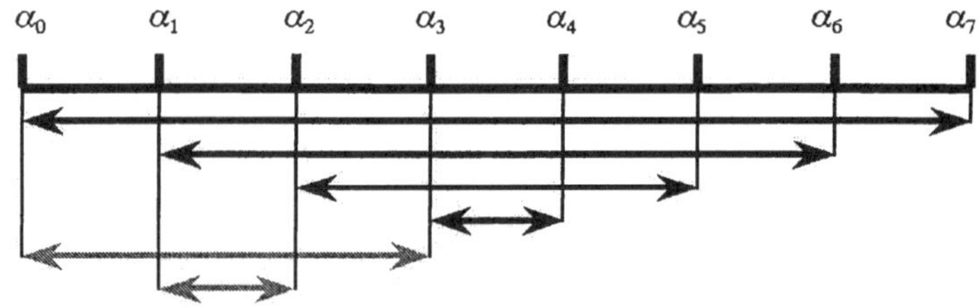

Figure 1. Pair-product invariance of $|\psi_8\rangle$

2.2 Well-formed states

When $|\psi_N\rangle$ has no amplitude equal to zero, $|\psi_N\rangle$ is fully separable iff $|\psi_N\rangle$ is pair-product invariant (for details, see Ref. 4). However, in general, some amplitudes of $|\psi_N\rangle$ are equal to zero. Zeros among the amplitudes of a fully separable $|\psi_N\rangle$ can only originate in zeros among the amplitudes of the $|\psi_2\rangle$ operands in the tensor product which produces $|\psi_N\rangle$. Therefore, zeros follow very specific patterns for their distribution among the N amplitudes of $|\psi_N\rangle$ whenever $|\psi_N\rangle$ is fully separable. As an auxiliary tool for defining these patterns, the set B_N of well-formed bit strings of length N, is defined recursively as follows, where 0^N is a string of N zeros:

$$\begin{aligned} B_2 &= \{01, 10, 11\} \\ B_{2N} &= \{0^N x, x0^N, xx | x \in B_N\} \end{aligned} \tag{1}$$

An amplitude abstraction function f will also be useful, which maps any state $|\psi_N\rangle$ into a bit string of length N:

$$|\psi_N\rangle = \sum_{i=0}^{N-1} \alpha_i\, |i\rangle \Longrightarrow f(|\psi_N\rangle) = x_0 x_1 \ldots x_{N-1}, \tag{2}$$

where $x_i = 0$ iff $\alpha_i = 0, x_i = 1$ otherwise. Then, $|\psi_N\rangle$ is a well-formed state if the zeros among its amplitudes are distributed according to a pattern corresponding to a well-formed bit string of length N:

$$f(|\psi_N\rangle) \in B_N. \tag{3}$$

2.3 Full separability

When a well-formed state $|\psi_N\rangle$ has a number of zero amplitudes, these are placed correctly for this state to be a candidate for full separability. But this is not enough for $|\psi_N\rangle$ to be fully separable; there must also be conditions satisfied by the non-zero amplitudes of $|\psi_N\rangle$, and by them only. For this, all zero amplitudes will first be eliminated from $|\psi_N\rangle$ by a zero deletion function *nozero* yielding a state $nozero(|\psi_N\rangle) = |\psi_K\rangle$ with K, a power of 2, non-zero amplitudes.[4]

Theorem 1 *$|\psi_N\rangle$ is fully separable if and only if $|\psi_N\rangle$ is well-formed and $nozero(|\psi_N\rangle)$ is pair product invariant.*

The proof is by induction on n, the number of qubits, and the complexity of the test is 2^n products and $2 * 2^n$comparisons (see Ref. 4).

3 Conditions for $p - q$ separability

A state $|\psi_N\rangle$ of a register of n qubits is $p-q$ separable iff it can be factorized into a tensor product: $|\psi_N\rangle = |\psi_P\rangle \otimes |\psi_Q\rangle$ with $N = 2^n$, $P = 2^p$, $Q = 2^q$ and $p + q = n$. Let $|\psi_P\rangle$ and $|\psi_Q\rangle$ have the following amplitudes:

$$|\psi_P\rangle = \begin{pmatrix} \beta_0 \\ \vdots \\ \beta_{P-1} \end{pmatrix} \text{ and } |\psi_Q\rangle = \begin{pmatrix} \gamma_0 \\ \vdots \\ \gamma_{Q-1} \end{pmatrix}. \quad (4)$$

Then, the $p - q$ separability of $|\psi_N\rangle$ sets its amplitudes as follows:

$$|\psi_N\rangle = \begin{pmatrix} \alpha_0 \\ \vdots \\ \alpha_{kQ+r} \\ \vdots \\ \alpha_{N-1} \end{pmatrix} = \begin{pmatrix} \beta_0 \\ \vdots \\ \beta_k \\ \vdots \\ \beta_{P-1} \end{pmatrix} \otimes \begin{pmatrix} \gamma_0 \\ \vdots \\ \gamma_r \\ \vdots \\ \gamma_{Q-1} \end{pmatrix} = \begin{pmatrix} \beta_0\gamma 0 \\ \vdots \\ \beta_0\gamma_{Q-1} \\ \vdots \\ \beta_k\gamma_r \\ \vdots \\ \beta_{P-1}\gamma_0 \\ \vdots \\ \beta_{P-1}\gamma_{Q-1} \end{pmatrix}. \quad (5)$$

In other words, $|\psi_N\rangle$ is $p - q$ separable iff $\forall k \in [0, P - 1]$ and $\forall r \in [0, Q - 1]$, $\alpha_{kQ+r} = \beta_k\gamma_r$. This defines a structure for the N amplitudes in $|\psi_N\rangle$. There are P groups of Q amplitudes each: $\alpha_{kQ+r} = \beta_k\gamma_r$ is amplitude number r ($r \in [0, Q - 1]$) in group number k ($k \in [0, P - 1]$). This means that, if $\beta_k = 0$, all amplitudes in group number k are equal to zero, and that the distributions of zeros within all groups obtained with $\beta_k \neq 0$ are the same and are identical to the distribution of zeros within $|\psi_Q\rangle$. These are the main remarks leading to a characterization of $p - q$ separable states, with the following theorem:

Theorem 2 *Let $|\psi_N\rangle$, with $N = PQ$, be a state such that $i_0 = k_0Q + r_0$ is the least index with $\alpha_{i_0} \neq 0$. Then, $|\psi_N\rangle$ is $p - q$ separable if and only if:*

$$\forall k \in [k_0 + 1, P - 1], \forall r \in [r_0 + 1, Q - 1], \alpha_{k_0Q+r_0}\alpha_{kQ+r} = \alpha_{k_0Q+r}\alpha_{kQ+r_0}. \quad (6)$$

This shows that given a pure state $|\psi_N\rangle$ and an integer p we can test the $p-q$ separability in at most 2^n comparisons and $2 * 2^n$ products.[4]

It can be noted that this characterization of $p-q$ separability does not make a special case of states with no zero amplitude before considering the general case. But $p-q$ separability could have been treated in a way similar to full separability, by first introducing a definition for a new pair-product invariance and a new notion of well-formed states reflecting the distribution of zeros in $p-q$ separable states.

4 Conclusion

Although entanglement is at the heart of quantum information processing and communication, the mathematical structure of entanglement is far from being understood. A lot has been learned about entangled pure and mixed states of bi-partitc systems, but Ref. 1 clearly tells that very little is known beyond three-qubit systems. This paper is a contribution to studying separability criteria for n-partite systems, while staying on the safe ground of pure states only, like other recent attempts to understanding entanglement beyond two- or three-partite systems.[2,3] Among the questions directly opened by the approach presented here are (i) the search for values of p and q, with a minimum number of adequate permutations of qubits, to decide whether or not $|\psi_N\rangle$ is $p-q$ separable, and (ii) the relation of pair-product invariance (for both full separability and $p-q$ separability) with measures of entanglement, like concurrence (see for example Ref. 2).

References

1. D. Bruss, quant-ph/0110078.
2. S. Albeverio, and S.-H. Fei, quant-ph/0109073.
3. S. Bravyi, quant-ph/0205021.
4. P. Jorrand, and M. Mhalla, quant-ph/0209125.

QUANTUM ENTANGLEMENT AND PARTICLE STATISTICS

YASSER OMAR, NIKOLA PAUNKOVIĆ, AND SOUGATO BOSE
Centre for Quantum Computation, University of Oxford, United Kingdom
E-mail: yasser.omar@qubit.org

VLATKO VEDRAL
Optics Section, The Blackett Laboratory, Imperial College, United Kingdom

In this work we explore the relationship between quantum entanglement and particle statistics. We present here two protocols showing that particle indistinguishability can enforce a transfer of entanglement from internal to spatial degrees of freedom without any interaction between them and also that useful quantum information processing can be accomplished by particle statistics alone, in our case in an entanglement concentration scheme.

1 Spin-Space Entanglement Transfer

We want to explore the effects of particle statistics on entangled identical particles. For this we must bring them to a fully indistinguishable situation. In our work,[1] we use two pairs of identical particles (fermions or bosons) maximally entangled in their internal degrees of freedom: e.g., spin $\frac{1}{2}$ of electrons and polarization of photons. We make the particles indistinguishable by sending them to beam splitters according to the setup described below (see Fig. 1).

1.1 The Calculations

In order to calculate what happens in the above setup, we write our initial state in the second quantization formalism:

$$\frac{1}{\sqrt{2}}(a^{\dagger}_{A1\uparrow}a^{\dagger}_{A2\downarrow} + a^{\dagger}_{A1\downarrow}a^{\dagger}_{A2\uparrow})\frac{1}{\sqrt{2}}(a^{\dagger}_{B1\uparrow}a^{\dagger}_{B2\downarrow} + a^{\dagger}_{B1\downarrow}a^{\dagger}_{B2\uparrow})|0\rangle, \tag{1}$$

taking into account the commutation ($[a^{\dagger}_i, a^{\dagger}_j]_- = 0$) and anti-commutation ($[a^{\dagger}_i, a^{\dagger}_j]_+ = 0$) relations for bosons and fermions respectively.

The operation of the beam splitter is described by any unitary transformation in SU(2).

1.2 Output State for Fermions with a 50/50 *Beam Splitter*

For clarity, let us consider for the rest of the paper the particular case of 50/50 beam splitters ($\alpha = 1/\sqrt{2}, \beta = -i/\sqrt{2}$). In the case of fermions, the output state is then given by the following diagram (see Fig. 2).

Since the beam splitter transformations are unitary operations, the output states must preserve the two e-bits present in the initial states. In this picture

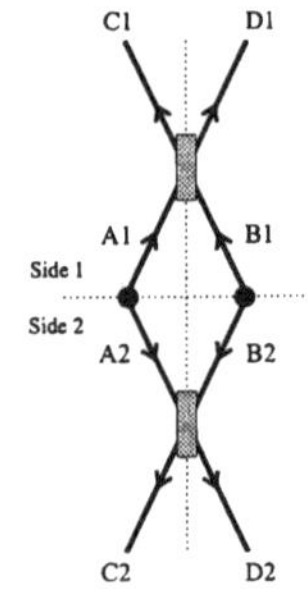

Figure 1. Setup for making particles indistinguishable. Each black circle represents a source of a pair of particles maximally entangled in the internal degrees of freedom. The rectangles represent beam splitters.

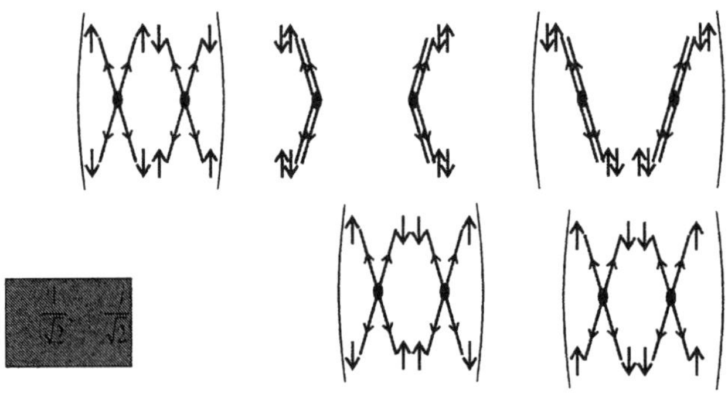

Figure 2. Output state representations for the case of 50/50 beam splitters. The internal degrees of freedom are represented by the arrows.

we can clearly see that the first two terms have 1 unit of entanglement in spin, whereas in the remaining terms the other e-bit is now shared by both the spin and the path degrees of freedom. We thus have a transfer of entanglement from spin to space. It is possible to transfer entanglement from the internal to the spatial degrees of freedom through local actions using only the effects of particle statistics, without any interaction between the spin and the path. It is even possible to extract space-only entanglement by doing local measurements of the spin (or polarization, in the case of bosons).

1.3 Extracting Space-only and Spin-only Entanglement

To extract space-only entanglement, we measure the total spin $\mathbf{S}$ on both sides (1 and 2) along the x axis and then select the $S_x = 0$ results. This way we obtain, both for fermions and bosons, 1 e-bit of entanglement in space. If on the other hand we measure the spatial components of the total wave function and select the anti-bunching results, we will obtain a state with $\log_2 3$ e-bits in spin for fermions, whereas for bosons there will be no entanglement at all in spin. If instead we select bunching, we will obtain exactly the opposite. Under the same situation, fermions and bosons show a difference in their information processing behavior.

2 Entanglement Concentration

We want to show that it is possible to do useful quantum information processing using only the effects of particle statistics.[2] For this, we propose an entanglement concentration protocol based solely on the statistical properties of indistinguishable particles. Again, our scheme requires only 50/50 beam splitters, plus path measurements and one-way communication at the end.

2.1 State to Concentrate

We start with an n-particle state entangled between Alice and Bob with at most 1-ebit of entanglement. As before, we consider identical particles (fermions or bosons) entangled in their internal degrees of freedom: either spin 1/2 for electrons or polarization for photons (see Fig. 3).

Our state is then:

$$|\phi\rangle^n \equiv \alpha|\underbrace{\uparrow\uparrow\cdots\uparrow}_{n}\rangle_A|\downarrow\downarrow\cdots\downarrow\rangle_B + \beta|\downarrow\downarrow\cdots\downarrow\rangle_A|\uparrow\uparrow\cdots\uparrow\rangle_B, \tag{2}$$

with $|\alpha|^2 + |\beta|^2 = 1$ and $|\uparrow\uparrow\cdots\uparrow\rangle_A = \hat{a}^+_{A1\uparrow}\hat{a}^+_{A2\uparrow}\cdots\hat{a}^+_{An\uparrow}|0\rangle$.

2.2 The Protocol

We use two pairs of the type described above, labelled L and R, thus starting with the state $|\varphi\rangle^n \equiv |\phi\rangle^n_L \otimes |\phi\rangle^n_R$.

We perform our protocol, for example, on Bob's side. Our protocol consists of bringing each of Bob's particles into a 50/50 beam splitter and then making a specific measurement on the output particles, as described in the Fig. 3.

Before particles from the left fall into the beam splitter, we apply to each of them a spin flip. This flipping is applied in order to align some spins (or polarizations) in appropriate terms so that we can exploit the statistical effects of the beam splitters later on.

After the particles pass through the beam splitter, Bob performs a path measurement on the first pair using detectors $L1$ and $R1$. Say the particles are fermions: if they bunch, we discard them, and so on. For bosons, we do exactly the opposite. In the limiting case in which we apply this procedure infinitely many times (to an infinitely large state), we obtain the same

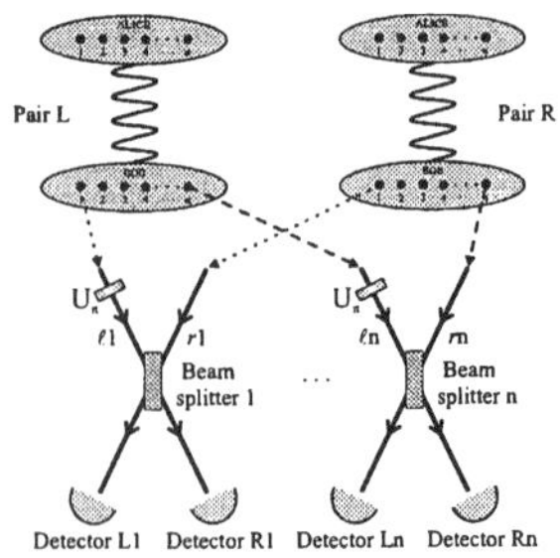

Figure 3. This figure represents the setup for our entanglement concentration protocol using quantum statistics. Initially, Alice and Bob share two pairs of entangled systems, L and R. Each entangled pair is composed of two n-particle states. One of the parties, say Bob, can then convert these pairs into a more entangled pair by performing a set of local operations using only standard 50/50 beam splitters, path measurements and one-way classical communication with Alice.

maximally-entangled state, both for fermions and for bosons, with probability $E^{\infty}(|\phi\rangle^n) = p = |\alpha\beta|^2$, that gives us the efficiency of our entanglement concentration protocol.

3 Future Directions

Future work will comprise investigating more extensive quantum information processing procedures based on the effects of particle statistics, such as entanglement purification, quantum state discrimination, generalization of these procedures using multi-ports beam splitters and the role of indistinguishability in the generation of entanglement. Our approach can also be extended to other types of statistics. Recent experiments suggest that it would be possible to test our results in the near future.

Acknowledgments

Y.O. acknowledges support from Fundação para a Ciência e a Tecnologia from Portugal. N.P. thanks Elsag S.p.A. for financial support. V.V. acknowledges support from Hewlett-Packard company, EPSRC and the European Union project EQUIP.

References

1. Y. Omar, N. Paunković, S. Bose and V. Vedral, *Phys. Rev.* A **65**, 062305 (2002), and references therein.
2. N. Paunković, Y. Omar, S. Bose and V. Vedral, *Phys. Rev. Lett.* **88**, 187903 (2002), and references therein.

TWO-QUBIT MIXED STATES AND THE ENTANGLEMENT-ENTROPY FRONTIER

TZU-CHIEH WEI[1], KAE NEMOTO[2], PAUL M. GOLDBART[1], PAUL G. KWIAT[1], WILLIAM J. MUNRO[3] AND FRANK VERSTRAETE[4]

[1]*Department of Physics, University of Illinois at Urbana-Champaign, 1110 West Green Street, Urbana, Illinois 61801-3080, USA*

[2]*Informatics, Bangor University, Bangor LL57 1UT, UK*

[3]*Hewlett-Packard Laboratories, Filton Road, Stoke Gifford, Bristol, BS34 SQ2, UK*

[4]*Department of Mathematical Physics and Astronomy, Ghent University, Belgium*

Maximally-entangled mixed states are states that, for a given mixedness (entropy), achieve the greatest possible entanglement. For two-qubit systems and for various combinations of entanglement and mixedness measures, we determine the form of the corresponding maximally-entangled mixed states analytically. We show that their forms can vary with the combination of entanglement and mixedness measures chosen. Moreover, for certain combinations, the forms of the maximally-entangled mixed states can change discontinuously at a specific value of the entropy.

1 Introduction

Over the past decade, the entanglement of quantum states has been recognized as a central resource in various aspects of quantum information processing.[1] Given the central status of entanglement, the task of quantifying the degree to which a state is entangled is important, and several measures have been proposed to quantify it.[2] It is worth remarking that even for the smallest Hilbert space capable of exhibiting entanglement, i.e., the two-qubit system, there are aspects of entanglement that remain to be explored.

Among mixed quantum mechanical states, special status should be accorded to those that, for a given value of the entropy (or mixedness), have the largest possible degree of entanglement.[3] The reason is that such states can be regarded as mixed-state generalizations of Bell states, the latter being known to be the maximally-entangled two-qubit *pure* states. Hence, this kind of *mixed* states could be expected to provide useful resources for quantum information processing.

In order to construct maximally-entangled mixed states (MEMS), one needs to define and quantify the notions of both entanglement and mixedness. Yet, different entanglement measures can lead to different orderings of entangled states.[4] There can also be ordering problems for mixedness. These two ordering problems imply that what states constitute MEMS may depend on the measures of both entanglement and mixedness.

The primary objective of this paper is to determine the *frontiers*, i.e., the boundaries of the regions occupied by physically-allowed states in these planes, and to identify the structure of these MEMS under various measures.

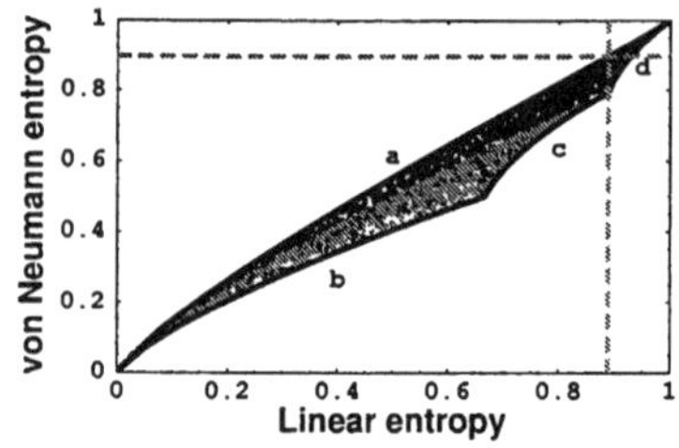

Figure 1. Comparison of two entropies. Dots represent randomly generated states; the segments a, b, c, and d constitute the boundary of physically-allowed states. The figure shows that, e.g., there exist mixed states ρ_1 and ρ_2 for which $S_V(\rho_1) > S_V(\rho_2)$ whereas $S_L(\rho_1) < S_L(\rho_2)$. Dashed lines indicate thresholds of entropies beyond which no states can be entangled.

2 Entanglement and mixedness

In this section we briefly review measures of entanglement and mixedness that we consider.

The entanglement of formation for a mixed state ρ is defined as the minimal average number of maximally-entangled pure states consumed in order to realize the ensemble described by ρ, i.e.,

$$E_F(\rho) \equiv \min_{\{p_i,\psi_i\}} \sum_i p_i\, E(|\psi_i\rangle), \quad \text{with} \quad E(|\psi_i\rangle) \equiv -\mathrm{Tr}\,\rho_B \log(\rho_B), \tag{1}$$

where $\rho_B \equiv \mathrm{Tr}_A|\psi_i\rangle\langle\psi_i|$ and the minimization is taken over $\{p_i\}$ and $\{|\psi_i\rangle\}$ such that $\rho = \sum_i p_i|\psi_i\rangle\langle\psi_i|$. We remark that E_F is, in general, difficult to calculate for mixed states. Fortunately, for the two-qubit case Wootters[5] has derived a closed form for E_F.

Negativity measures the extent to which a state violates the positive partial transpose (PPT) criterion[6] of separability. It equals twice the absolute value of the sum of the negative eigenvalues of the partially-transposed matrix ρ_B^T. In two-qubit systems it can be shown that the partial transpose of a density matrix can have at most one negative eigenvalue[8] and, hence, $N(\rho) = 2\max(0, -\lambda_4)$, where λ_4 is the lowest eigenvalue of ρ^{T_B}. Even though $N = 0$ is not, in general, a sufficient condition for separability (except for two-qubit and qubit-qutrit systems), it is readily computable. We remark that E_F and N can give different orderings for different pairs of states.[4]

The two mixedness measures we consider are linear entropy S_L and von Neumann entropy S_V, defined in two-qubit systems via

$$S_L(\rho) \equiv \frac{4}{3}(1 - \mathrm{Tr}\rho^2), \quad S_V(\rho) \equiv -\mathrm{Tr}(\rho \log_4 \rho); \tag{2}$$

they are properly normalized in the range $[0, 1]$. We illustrate the ordering problem of these two mixedness measures in Fig. 1.

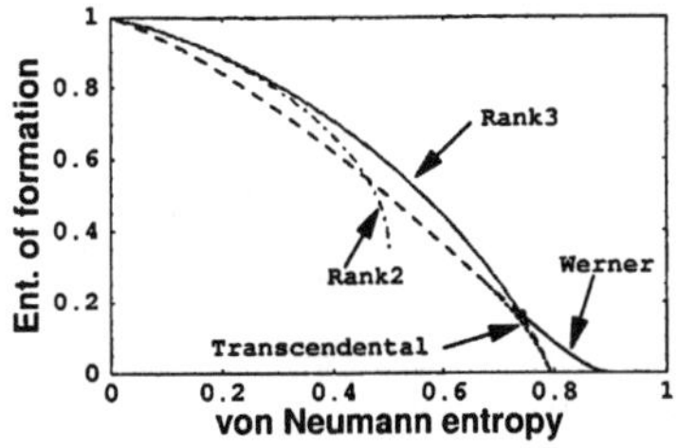

Figure 2. Entanglement frontier: E_F vs. S_V. The physically-allowed region is below the solid curve, i.e., the frontier. The frontier consists of two branches: that given by ρ_i (indicated by "Rank 3") and that given by ρ_{ii} (Werner states). Two additional curves indicated by "Rank 2" and "Transcendental" (not shown) are from those states that also satisfy the stationarity conditions but are not globally maximal.

3 Entanglement-versus-mixedness frontiers

In this section, we describe how to derive and present the forms of MEMS under various measures. Employing the results of Verstraete et al.,[7] it can be shown that the states with maximal E_F or N can be parametrized in the following way[8] (up to local unitary transformations):

$$\rho = \begin{bmatrix} x+\frac{r}{2} & 0 & 0 & \frac{r}{2} \\ 0 & a & 0 & 0 \\ 0 & 0 & b & 0 \\ \frac{r}{2} & 0 & 0 & x+\frac{r}{2} \end{bmatrix}, \quad \text{with } x, a, b, r \geq 0 \text{ and } \mathrm{Tr}(\rho) = 1. \tag{3}$$

Straightforward calculations show that

$$E_F = h\big([1+\sqrt{1-C^2}]/2\big), \quad \text{with } C \equiv \max\{r - 2\sqrt{ab}, 0\}, \tag{4a}$$

$$N = \max\{\sqrt{(a-b)^2 + r^2} - (a+b), 0\}, \tag{4b}$$

where $h(x) \equiv -x\log_2(x) - (1-x)\log_2(1-x)$.

By maximizing entanglement[a] at fixed entropy, we can then derive the forms of MEMS (frontier states) under the four combinations of entanglement and mixedness. We list the results as follows.

I. E_F vs. S_L frontier states. The form of MEMS in this case was derived by Munro et al.[3] and shown to consist of two branches. At the point where the two branches meet, the forms of states on the two sides coincide.

II. N vs. S_L frontier states. There are two inequivalent families of MEMS which give the same frontier:

$$\rho^{(1)}_{\mathrm{MEMS}:N,S_L}(r) = \rho_{\mathrm{Werner}}(r), \quad \rho^{(2)}_{\mathrm{MEMS}:N,S_L}(r) = \begin{bmatrix} \frac{1+\sqrt{3r^2+1}}{6} & 0 & 0 & \frac{r}{2} \\ 0 & \frac{4-2\sqrt{3r^2+1}}{6} & 0 & 0 \\ 0 & 0 & 0 & 0 \\ \frac{r}{2} & 0 & 0 & \frac{1+\sqrt{3r^2+1}}{6} \end{bmatrix}, \tag{5}$$

[a] For the case of E_F, it is equivalent and convenient to maximize C instead.

where the Werner state $\rho_{\rm Werner}(r)$ is defined to be $r|\phi^+\rangle\langle\phi^+| + \frac{1-r}{4}I$.

III. E_F vs. S_V frontier states. The frontier states also consist of two branches:

$$\rho_{\rm MEMS;E_F,S_V} = \begin{cases} \rho_{\rm ii}(C), & \text{for } 0 \le C \le C^*; \\ \rho_{\rm i}(C), & \text{for } C^* \le C \le 1; \end{cases} \quad \text{with } C^* \approx 0.741, \tag{6a}$$

$$\rho_{\rm i}(C) = \begin{bmatrix} \frac{4-\sqrt{4-3C^2}}{6} & 0 & 0 & \frac{C}{2} \\ 0 & \frac{\sqrt{4-3C^2}-1}{3} & 0 & 0 \\ 0 & 0 & 0 & 0 \\ \frac{C}{2} & 0 & 0 & \frac{4-\sqrt{4-3C^2}}{6} \end{bmatrix}, \quad \rho_{\rm ii}(C) = \begin{bmatrix} \frac{2+C}{6} & 0 & 0 & \frac{1+2C}{6} \\ 0 & \frac{1-C}{6} & 0 & 0 \\ 0 & 0 & \frac{1-C}{6} & 0 \\ \frac{1+2C}{6} & 0 & 0 & \frac{2+C}{6} \end{bmatrix}. \tag{6b}$$

Note that at $C = C^*$ the density matrix on each branch can never be the same. Thus as one moves across $C = C^*$ along the frontier, the state changes discontinuously. Moreover, $\rho_{\rm ii}$ is a Werner state: $\rho_{\rm ii}(C) = \rho_{\rm Werner}(r)\big|_{r=(2C+1)/3}$.

IV. N vs. S_V frontier states. In this case the frontier states are Werner states.

We illustrate the entanglement vs. mixedness plane for the case of E_F vs. S_V in Fig. 2.

4 Concluding remarks

We have determined families of maximally entangled mixed states (MEMS) and boundaries of the physically-allowed region in the entanglement-mixedness plane (frontier) under various entanglement and mixedness measures. The frontier states under E_F vs. S_V behave *discontinuously* at a specific point on the frontier. What precise resources the various MEMS furnish remains an open question.

This work was supported in part by NSF, DOE, QUIPROCONE, and EQUIP.

References

1. See, e.g., M. Nielsen and I. Chuang, *Quantum Computation and Quantum Information* (Cambridge University Press, Cambridge, 2000).
2. For a review, see M. Horodecki, Quan. Info. and Comp. **1**, 3 (2001).
3. W. J. Munro et al., Phys. Rev. A **64**, 030302 (2001).
4. J. Eisert and M. B. Plenio, J. Mod. Opt. **46**, 145 (1999); F. Verstraete et al., J. Phys. A **34**, 10327 (2001); S. Virmani and M. B. Plenio, Phys. Lett. A **268**, 31 (2000).
5. W. K. Wootters, Phys. Rev. Lett. **80**, 2245 (1998).
6. A. Peres, Phys. Rev. Lett. **77**, 1413 (1996); M. Horodecki et al., Phys. Lett. A **223**, 1 (1996).
7. F. Verstraete et al., Phys. Rev. A **64**, 012316 (2001).
8. T. C. Wei et al., quant-ph/0208138.

LOCC PROTOCOLS FOR ENTANGLEMENT TRANSFORMATIONS

G. MAURO D'ARIANO[A,B] AND MASSIMILIANO F. SACCHI[A]

(A) Dipartimento di Fisica 'A. Volta', Università di Pavia and Unità INFM via A. Bassi 6, I-27100 Pavia, Italy

(B) Department of Electrical and Computer Engineering Northwestern University, Evanston, IL 60208, USA

We construct the protocols to achieve probabilistic and deterministic entanglement transformations for bipartite pure states by means of local operations and classical communication. A new condition on pure contraction transformations is provided.

The transformation of entangled states by means of local operations and classical communication (LOCC) is a key issue in quantum information processing. In fact, increasing entanglement by means of LOCC with some probability is crucial in practice, since losses and decoherence have detrimental effects in the establishment of entanglement at distance.

In this paper we give a short and simple proof of Lo-Popescu theorem.[1] Then, we provide a new necessary condition for pure-contraction transformations. Finally, we construct explicitly the LOCC protocols to achieve deterministic and probabilistic transformations for bipartite pure states.

We first introduce the main notation. Given a linear operator O we denote by $O^\dagger$, O^*, O^τ, and $O^\ddagger$ the hermitian conjugate, the complex conjugate, the transpose, and the Moore-Penrose inverse of O, respectively. Recall that $O^\ddagger$ is the unique matrix that satisfies $OO^\ddagger O = O$, $O^\ddagger O O^\ddagger = O^\ddagger$, $OO^\ddagger$ and $O^\ddagger O$ hermitian. Notice also that $OO^\ddagger \equiv P_O$ is the orthogonal projector over $\mathrm{Rng}(O)$, whereas $O^\ddagger O \equiv P_{O^\dagger}$ is the orthogonal projector over $\mathrm{Rng}(O^\dagger) \equiv \mathrm{Supp}(O)$. We write the singular value decomposition (SVD) of O as $O = X_O \Sigma_O Y_O$, where Σ_O denotes the diagonal matrix whose entries are the singular values $\sigma_i(O)$ of O taken in decreasing order, and X_O, Y_O are unitary. We write

$$|A\rangle\rangle \equiv \sum_{i,j} a_{ij} |i\rangle_1 \otimes |j\rangle_2, \qquad (1)$$

for the bipartite pure states on the Hilbert space $\mathcal{H}_1 \otimes \mathcal{H}_2$, where $\{|i\rangle_1\}$ and $\{|j\rangle_2\}$ are two orthonormal bases for $\mathcal{H}_1$ and $\mathcal{H}_2$. One can easily check the relation $A \otimes B|C\rangle\rangle = |ACB^\tau\rangle\rangle$. Finally, we use the notation $A \prec B$ for Hermitian operators A and B to denote the majorization relation[2] $\mathrm{eigv}(A) \prec \mathrm{eigv}(B)$, and in the same fashion we will write $A \prec^w B$ and $A \prec_w B$ for super- and sub-majorization.[2]

We give now a simple proof of Lo-Popescu theorem.[1]

Theorem 1. All LOCC on a pure bipartite entangled state $|\Psi\rangle\rangle$ can be reduced to a contraction by Alice and a unitary transformation by Bob. This is due to the equivalence of any Bob contraction M with the Alice contraction N assisted by Bob's unitary transformation U as follows

$$I \otimes M|\Psi\rangle\rangle = N \otimes U|\Psi\rangle\rangle \,, \tag{2}$$

where

$$N = K_{M\Psi^\tau} M K_\Psi \,, \qquad U = K^\dagger_{M\Psi^\tau} K^\dagger_\Psi \,, \tag{3}$$

and K_O is the unitary operator achieving the transposition of the operator O, namely $O^\tau = K_O O K^*_O$.

Proof. To prove that every LOCC can be reduced to an Alice contraction and a Bob unitary transformation it is sufficient to prove Eq. (2), since: *a)* all possible elementary LOCC in a sequence will be reduced to an Alice contraction and a Bob unitary; *b)* the product of two contractions is a contraction; *c)* unitary transformations are particular cases of contraction.

Given the SVD of any linear operator O one has

$$O^\tau = Y^\tau_O \Sigma_O X^\tau_O = (Y^\tau_O X^\dagger_O) O (Y_O{}^\tau X^\dagger_O)^* \equiv K_O O K^*_O \,, \tag{4}$$

with $K_O = Y^\tau_O X^\dagger_O$. Hence

$$\Psi M^\tau = (M\Psi^\tau)^\tau = K_{M\Psi^\tau}(M\Psi^\tau)K^*_{M\Psi^\tau} = K_{M\Psi^\tau} M K_\Psi \Psi K^*_\Psi K^*_{M\Psi^\tau} \,. \tag{5}$$

Then one gets Eq. (2) with N and U given as in Eq. (3).

The main theorem on entanglement transformations is the following.

Theorem 2. The state transformation $|A\rangle\rangle \to |B\rangle\rangle$ is possible by LOCC iff

$$AA^\dagger \prec^w pBB^\dagger \,, \tag{6}$$

where $p \leq 1$ is the probability of achieving the transformation. A necessary condition to be satisfied is $\mathrm{rnk}(A) \geq \mathrm{rnk}(B)$. In particular, the transformation is deterministic ($p = 1$) iff $AA^\dagger \prec BB^\dagger$.

Theorem 2 unifies the results of Nielsen[3] and Vidal.[4]

In the following we provide a new necessary condition for the case of pure-contraction transformation, namely we prove:

Theorem 3. If there is a *pure* LOCC that achieves the state transformation $|A\rangle\rangle \to |B\rangle\rangle$ with probability p, we must have

$$pBB^\dagger \prec_w AA^\dagger. \tag{7}$$

Proof. According to theorem 1, the pure LOCC transformation $|A\rangle\rangle \to |B\rangle\rangle$ occurring with probability p is given by

$$M \otimes U|A\rangle\rangle = \sqrt{p}|B\rangle\rangle \,, \tag{8}$$

and we need to have $MAU^\tau = \sqrt{p}B$. Using the SVD of A and B one has $\tilde{M}\Sigma_A\tilde{U} = \sqrt{p}\Sigma_B$, with $\tilde{M} = X^\dagger_B M X_A$ and $\tilde{U} = Y_A U^\tau Y^\dagger_B$. Then $\tilde{M}\Sigma^2_A\tilde{M}^\dagger = p\Sigma^2_B$, namely

$$\sum_k S_{kl}\sigma^2_k(A) = p\sigma^2_l(B) \,, \tag{9}$$

where $S_{kl} \doteq |\langle l|\tilde{M}|k\rangle|^2$ is a sub-stochastic matrix, since

$$\begin{aligned}\sum_k S_{kl} &= \langle l|\tilde{M}\tilde{M}^\dagger|l\rangle \le ||M^\dagger||^2 \le 1\,, \\ \sum_l S_{kl} &= \langle k|\tilde{M}^\dagger\tilde{M}|k\rangle \le ||M||^2 \le 1\,. \end{aligned} \tag{10}$$

This proves that Eq. (7) is a necessary condition for transformation (8).

To construct the explicit protocols that realize entanglement transformations we will use the following lemma:

Lemma 1. $x \prec^w y \iff$ for some v $\;x \prec v$ and $v \ge y$,
along with Uhlmann theorem:

Theorem 4. For Hermitian operators C and D one has $C \prec D$ if and only if there is a probability distribution p_λ and unitaries W_λ such that

$$C = \sum_\lambda p_\lambda W_\lambda D W_\lambda^\dagger\,. \tag{11}$$

For Lemma 1 a probabilistic transformation can always be performed through two steps: a deterministic transformation $|A\rangle\!\rangle \to |Q\rangle\!\rangle$, followed by a pure-contraction $|Q\rangle\!\rangle \to |B\rangle\!\rangle$ that occurs with probability p.

For the deterministic transformation $|A\rangle\!\rangle \to |Q\rangle\!\rangle$, one needs to find the contractions M_λ and the unitaries U_λ versus the operators W_λ of Eq. (11), where $C = AA^\dagger$ and $D = QQ^\dagger$, such that

$$M_\lambda \otimes U_\lambda |A\rangle\!\rangle = \sqrt{q_\lambda}|Q\rangle\!\rangle\,. \tag{12}$$

The general solution of Eq. (12) is given by

$$M_\lambda = \sqrt{q_\lambda} Q U_\lambda^* A^\ddagger + N_\lambda(1 - AA^\ddagger)\,. \tag{13}$$

To guarantee that M_λ is a contraction we can always take

$$U_\lambda^* = Y_Q^\dagger X_Q^\dagger W_\lambda X_A Y_A\,, \qquad N_\lambda = 0\,. \tag{14}$$

In fact from Eqs. (13) and (14) and using Eq. (11) one has

$$\begin{aligned}\sum_\lambda M_\lambda^\dagger M_\lambda &= \sum_\lambda q_\lambda (A^\ddagger)^\dagger Y_A^\dagger X_A^\dagger W_\lambda^\dagger X_Q Y_Q Q^\dagger Q Y_Q^\dagger X_Q^\dagger W_\lambda X_A Y_A A^\ddagger \\ &= \sum_\lambda q_\lambda (A^\ddagger)^\dagger Y_A^\dagger X_A^\dagger W_\lambda^\dagger Q Q^\dagger W_\lambda X_A Y_A A^\ddagger \\ &= (A^\ddagger)^\dagger Y_A^\dagger X_A^\dagger A A^\dagger X_A Y_A A^\ddagger \\ &= (A^\ddagger)^\dagger A^\dagger A A^\ddagger = (AA^\ddagger)^\dagger AA^\ddagger = AA^\ddagger = P_A\,. \end{aligned} \tag{15}$$

The completeness of the measurement can be guaranteed by the further contraction $M_0 = V(I - AA^\ddagger)$, where V is an arbitrary unitary operator.

Hence, given explicitly Eq. (11) one can perform the contractions M_λ and the unitaries U_λ to achieve the entanglement transformation. The problem of looking for a POVM with minimum number of outcomes (thus minimizing the amount of classical information sent to Bob's side) is reduced to finding the transformation (11) with minimum number of unitaries. One can resort to a constructive algorithm to find a bistochastic matrix D which relates the vectors $\vec{\sigma}_A^2$ and $\vec{\sigma}_Q^2$ of the singular values of A and Q, namely $\vec{\sigma}_A^2 = D\vec{\sigma}_Q^2$. Then Birkhoff theorem allows one to write D as a convex combination of permutation matrices $D = \sum_\lambda q_\lambda \Pi_\lambda$. In terms of Σ_A and Σ_Q one has

$$\Sigma_A^2 = \sum_\lambda q_\lambda \Pi_\lambda^\dagger \Sigma_Q^2 \Pi_\lambda \tag{16}$$

where $\Pi_\lambda = \sum_l |l\rangle\langle\Pi_\lambda(l)|$. In this way one obtains Eq. (11), with $W_\lambda = X_Q \Pi_\lambda X_A^\dagger$. Using Eqs. (13) and (14) for M_λ and U_λ one recovers the result of Ref. 5. Notice that Caratheodory's theorem always allows one to reduce the number of permutations in Eq. (16) to $(d-1)^2+1$, for d-dimensional Alice's Hilbert space.

The second part of the protocol, namely the contraction which provides the state $|B\rangle\rangle$ from $|Q\rangle\rangle$, is present only for probabilistic transformations. It is a pure contraction given by

$$N \otimes V|Q\rangle\rangle = |NQV^\tau\rangle\rangle = \sqrt{p}|B\rangle\rangle \ , \tag{17}$$

where $N = \sqrt{p}X_B\Sigma_B\Sigma_Q^\ddagger X_Q^\dagger$ and $V^\tau = Y_Q^\dagger Y_B$. In fact

$$NQV^\tau = \sqrt{p}X_B\Sigma_B\Sigma_Q^\ddagger\Sigma_Q Y_B = \sqrt{p}X_B\Sigma_B Y_B = \sqrt{p}B \ , \tag{18}$$

where we used the fact that $\Sigma_B\Sigma_Q^\ddagger\Sigma_Q = \Sigma_B$, since for lemma 1 one has $\Sigma_Q^2 \geq p\Sigma_B^2$.

Acknowledgments

This work has been jointly founded by the EC under the program ATESIT (Contract No. IST-2000-29681) and by the USA Army Research Office under MURI Grant No. DAAD19-00-1-0177.

References

1. H.-K. Lo and S. Popescu, Phys. Rev. A **63**, 022301 (2001).
2. R. Bhatia, *Matrix Analysis* (Springer Graduate Texts in Mathematics vol. 169).
3. M. A. Nielsen, Phys. Rev. Lett. **83**, 436 (1999).
4. G. Vidal, Phys. Rev. Lett. **83**, 1046 (1999).
5. J. G. Jensen and R. Schack, quant-ph/0006049.

MANIPULATING QUANTUM ENTANGLEMENT AND GENERATING NONCLASSICAL STATES WITH ATOMS AND PHOTONS IN A CAVITY

SERGE HAROCHE

Département de Physique de l'ENS
24 rue Lhomond 75231, Paris cedex 05, France
and
Collège de France, 11 Place Marcelin Berthelot, 75005, Paris, France

We present recent experiments on quantum information and nonclassical state manipulation performed with circular Rydberg atoms and microwave photons in a cavity.

1 Introduction

Cavity QED is the field of quantum optics which deals with the interaction of isolated atoms with high Q resonators. It has proved to be an ideal testing ground for quantum information physics. We have performed over the last six years a series of demonstration experiments using a versatile Rydberg atom-superconducting cavity set up. In some experiments, the atoms can be considered to be qubit carriers coupled via their interaction with a cavity field containing a small, well controlled number of photons. In this way, quantum nondemolition of single photons has been demonstrated,[1] quantum gates have been operated,[2] and the entanglement of up to three independent quantum systems realized and tested.[3]

In another set of experiments, a coherent field is fed into the cavity by an external classical source and is manipulated by the atoms crossing the cavity. The strength of the field can be progressively increased by feeding higher and higher mean photon numbers into the system. When the field is very weak, it has a marked quantum behavior. As the photon number is progressively increased, it behaves more and more classically. In this way, we can study some aspects of the boundary between the "microscopic" and the "macroscopic" worlds and demonstrate complementarity[4] and decoherence phenomena.[5]

A criterion for deciding whether a state of a microscopic system is classical or quantum is given by analyzing the features of its Wigner function. If this quasi-probability distribution exhibits negative parts, the system cannot be described in classical terms and is essentially quantum. This is the case of Fock states and Schrödinger cat like states of the field. Decoherence manifests itself by the very fast washing out of these negative features, whose study provides a powerful way to study the quantum-classical boundary.

In this short contribution, I briefly describe our set up and analyze three recent experiments belonging to the three categories mentioned above: an experiment in which we have demonstrated a new kind of entanglement procedure between atoms; a demonstration of complementarity at the quantum-classical boundary, and a measurement of a negatively valued Wigner function of the cavity field. More details about our experimental procedures can be found in a recent review paper.[6]

2 Experimental set up

Our set up[6] comprises an open geometry cavity made of two spherical superconducting mirrors facing each other, in a Fabry-Perot configuration. It stores microwave photons for up to 1 msec and lets them interact with Rydberg atoms crossing the cavity one by one, or two by two, at mid-distance between the mirrors. The atoms, effusing from an oven and velocity selected by optical pumping, are prepared in a circular Rydberg state by a pulsed process. The set up is cooled to about 1 K to minimize thermal radiation noise. The atoms are detected after they have crossed the cavity by field ionization. A microwave source can be used to feed a coherent field into the cavity. Some experiments are performed by directly detecting the atomic final energy state and gaining in this way information about the atom-cavity field energy exchange process. In other experiments, atomic state superpositions are used. Atoms are sent across the cavity in a superposition of energy levels and the states are mixed again after the cavity interaction. This is performed with the help of two auxiliary classical microwave field pulses sandwiching the cavity mode. The successive application of these pulses constitutes a Ramsey interferometer. Interference fringes are obtained, in the probability for finding the atom in a given final state, when the frequency of the Ramsey pulses is tuned across a transition between two Rydberg levels. By studying how the phase and amplitude of these fringes is affected by the presence of photons in the cavity, one gains information about the atom-photon interaction process.

3 Atom-atom entanglement by cavity assisted collision

This apparatus can be used to entangle two atoms in a deterministic way. The process can be either a resonant exchange of photons between two atoms that successively cross the cavity, or a nonresonant energy exchange via a virtual photon process involving two atoms simultaneously crossing the cavity. In the first case, the process exploits twice the basic interaction process of an atom with the cavity field (quantum Rabi oscillation). A first atom emits, with 50% probability a photon in the cavity and a second atom catches this photon with 100% probability. The final result is an entanglement between the two atoms.[7]

The atom-atom entanglement process via real cavity photon exchange has a fidelity intrinsically limited by cavity losses and thermal photon background. These limitations can, at least in principle, be avoided by entangling directly the two atoms, without having to rely on the production of an intermediate photon state in the cavity. To achieve this, we make the two atoms interact simultaneously with the cavity.[8] The atoms A_1 and A_2 are prepared, one after the other, in the circular states e and g and have different velocities. Atom A_1 overtakes A_2 at cavity center. Both atoms are later detected by the state-selective field ionization. The closest cavity mode is slightly detuned from the $e \rightarrow g$ transition. Because energy is not conserved, no real photon emission can occur in this case. Atom A_1 can however virtually emit a photon immediately reabsorbed by A_2. This leads, as in the resonant case, to atom-atom entanglement. The system ends up in a superposition of the combined $|e, g\rangle$ and $|g, e\rangle$ states. The quantum mechanical amplitudes of this superposition are periodic functions of $1/\delta$, where δ is the atom-cavity detuning. By repeating the experiment many times, we have reconstructed the joint probabilities $P(e_1, g_2)$ and $P(g_1, e_2)$ for finding finally the atom pair in states e, g and g, e and observed the oscillation of these probabilities versus $1/\delta$.[8] We have in particular realized a situation of maximum entanglement by adjusting δ to the value corresponding to $P(e_1, g_2) = P(g_1, e_2) = 0.5$. We have proposed to use such a process to demonstrate a simple version of Grover's search algorithm.[9]

4 Exploring the quantum classical boundary in a complementarity experiment

The notion of entanglement is deeply related to the concept of complementarity. In an atomic interference experiment, an atom behaves as a "wave" giving rise to interference "fringes" unless it gets entangled with a "which-path" detector able to disclose the path followed by the particle through the apparatus. If the "which-path" detection is effective, the atom behaves like a "particle" and no interference occurs. Which one of the two complementary aspects of the system (wave or particle) is revealed in the experiment depends thus upon the degree of its entanglement with the "which-path" element. This element can be of various kinds, either a part of the system's "environment", or an intrinsic part of the apparatus itself. As an example of this latter situation, if a beam splitter in a double path interferometer is "light" enough to be entangled with the atom when it crosses it, the apparatus cannot behave as a genuine interferometer and the fringes vanish. Discussing complementarity with Einstein, Bohr had analyzed a situation wherein particles are crossing a Young interferometer in which one slit is carried by a very light assembly, free to move independently of the other.[10] In an ordinary Young apparatus with fixed slits, interference fringes reveal the wave nature of the particle. In the Bohr design, the momentum kick imparted to the moving slit by the deflected particle provides which-path information, suppressing the fringes and revealing the corpuscular aspect. As emphasized by Bohr, a quantum description of the slit is essential to understand the experimental conditions determining fringe visibility. There can be a continuous transition from the quantum slit case (very small mass) to the classical one (infinite mass). In between, we expect fringes with a limited contrast, which measures the degree of entanglement between the particle and the interferometer. We have used our cavity QED apparatus to perform a complementarity test very closely related in its principle to this double slit Gedanken experiment.

Following previously published proposals,[11,12] we use, instead of a Young device, a double pulse oscillatory field Ramsey interferometer operating with Rydberg atoms.[4] The field pulses, resonant on a transition between the two atomic energy levels e and g, act as atomic energy beam splitters transforming these states into superpositions, and can give rise to interference effects in the probability for finding the atom in a given final state. The first resonant field pulse is a small coherent field injected through a waveguide inside the long lived cavity mode. Depending upon the average photon number N in this field, it can be considered to be either a microscopic (low N values) or a macroscopic (high N) "beam splitter". The second pulse is produced downstream in the second Ramsey zone. This latter pulse, produced by photons which are fed into a low Q field mode can always be considered to be classical. The first and second pulses are thus respectively equivalent to the moving and fixed slits in the Bohr's design. If the average photon number N in the first pulse is high, Ramsey fringes with maximum contrast are observed. When N is low, the one-photon change produced by the atomic transition from level e to g leads to atom-field entanglement, in the same way as the recoil motion of the moving slit in Bohr's design leads to slit–particle entanglement. The contrast of the resulting Ramsey fringe pattern is then reduced. At the limit where the field in this first pulse is down to the vacuum, the first quantum Ramsey pulse results in maximum atom-"beam-splitter" entanglement and the fringes vanish altogether. We have observed in this way a continuous variation of the fringe contrast, directly related to the amount of entanglement between the atom and the quantum field "beam-splitter".

5 Negative Wigner function measurements

The statistical properties of a single mode field are described by its Wigner function W, which is a quasi-probability distribution in phase space. The existence of negative W-values in some regions of phase space is generally regarded as sign of nonclassical behavior. We have measured the full W function for a single photon field stored in a cavity and observed that it is negative around phase space origin.[13] Measuring the Wigner function can be done in various ways. The tomography method amounts to measuring the fluctuations in quadratures of the field corresponding to various phases and reconstructing W by using the Radon inversion procedure.[14] The negative W function of a single photon in a running field mode has been recently obtained in this way.[15] Other methods are based on the measurement of the photon number distribution in the field.[16] One such method, proposed by Lutterbach and Davidovich[17] and already outlined in Ref. 18 is especially well suited for our cavity QED apparatus. In order to obtain the Wigner function of a field state at a given point in phase space, whose coordinates correspond to a complex amplitude α, one has first to translate this field state by adding to it a coherent field of amplitude $-\alpha$, then measure the average value of the photon number parity operator P in the translated field. This operator is equal to $\exp(-i\pi a^\dagger a)$, where a and $a^\dagger$ are the field photon annihilation and creation operators. The parity operator P appears as an atomic light-shift operator, producing a π-rad phase shift of the coherence between two atomic levels when there is one photon in the mode. The atomic coherence and the average value of the parity operator P can be directly measured by Ramsey interferometry.

Hence the method to measure the Wigner function of a single photon in the cavity with a single atom used to produce and probe the field is as follows. First, a photon is emitted in the cavity by the atom undergoing a transition between Rydberg states e and g. Then, while the atom is still inside it, the cavity is detuned from the Rydberg atom transition by an amount such that the field produces a phase shift of exactly π-rad per photon on the e-g atomic coherence. This coherence in prepared by a first classical Ramsey pulse applied to the atom, immediately after the end of the single photon preparation stage. The cavity field is at the same time translated by injecting a coherent field $-\alpha$ into the cavity. The evolution of the atomic coherence in the translated field is probed at a later time by a second Ramsey pulse and the resulting fringes are obtained by finally detecting the atoms in levels e and g. The phase of these fringes is swept by applying to the atom a short pulse of electric field between the two Ramsey pulses. From the Ramsey fringe signal obtained by averaging a large number of single atom events, one infers directly the expectation value of P in the cavity field translated by $-\alpha$. By repeating the experiment for various α values, we obtain the W function for the single photon field. This function has a typical volcano shape with a negative valley at phase space origin. This experiment is the first one in which the Wigner function of a cavity stored photon is probed. Note however that similar Wigner function studies exhibiting negative W values have been performed on the vibrational states of a single ion in a trap.[19] We plan to extend soon our W function studies to higher photon number Fock states and to Schrödinger cat states of the field, which also have negative parts.

6 Conclusion and perspectives

The cavity QED experiments described above constitute text book illustrations of quantum physics and demonstrate interesting possibilities to use entanglement and state superpositions in order to achieve simple quantum information tasks. They also yield insights into the quantum-classical boundary and decoherence phenomena. Our set up suffers however many limitations, discussed in Ref. 6, which will have to be overcome before pushing the experiments further, with more atoms and more photons. Several improvements are underway, which include using better cavities, with longer damping times, better atomic sources and more efficient detectors. One of our projects involves the study of quasi-classical fields, made of many photons, delocalized in two separate cavities.[20] Such a system would combine, so to speak, the weirdness of Schrödinger cats with the strangeness of nonlocality.

Acknowledgements

This research is carried out with support from the Centre National de la Recherche Scientifique (CNRS), the European Community and the Japan Science and Technology Corporation (JST), in the Program ICORP "Quantum Entanglement".

References

1. G. Nogues *et al.*, Nature **400**, 239 (1999).
2. A. Rauschenbeutel *et al.*, Phys.Rev.Lett. **83**, 5166 (1999).
3. A. Rauschenbeutel *et al.*, Science, **288**, 2024 (2000).
4. P. Bertet *et al.*, Nature **411**, 166 (2001).
5. M. Brune *et al.*, Phys. Rev. Lett. **77**, 4887 (1996).
6. J. M. Raimond, M. Brune and S. Haroche, Rev. Mod. Phys. **73**, 565 (2001).
7. E. Hagley *et al.*, Phys. Rev. Lett. **79**, 1 (1997).
8. S. Osnaghi *et al.*, Phys. Rev. Lett. **87**, 037902 (2001).
9. F. Yamagushi *et al.*, Phys. Rev. A, **66**, 010302-1 (2002).
10. N. Bohr, in *Quantum Theory and Measurement*, (eds. J. A. Wheeler and W. H. Zurek) p. 9, Princeton University Press, (1983).
11. B. G. Englert, H. Walther and M. O. Scully, Appl. Phys. B **54**, 366 (1992).
12. S. B. Zheng, Opt. Comm. **173**, 265 (2000).
13. P. Bertet *et al.*, Phys. Rev. Lett. to be published (2002)
14. K. Vogel and H. Risken, Phys. Rev. A **40**, 2847 (1989).
15. A. I. Lvovsky *et al.*, Phys. Rev. Lett. **87**, 050402 (2001).
16. K. Banaszek and K. Wodkiewicz, Phys. Rev. Lett. **76**, 4344 (1996).
17. L. G. Lutterbach and L. Davidovich, Phys. Rev. Lett. **78**, 2547 (1997).
18. B. G. Englert, N. Sterpi and H. Walther, Opt. Comm. **100**, 526 (1993).
19. D. Leibfried *et al.*, Phys. Rev. Lett. **77**, 4281 (1996).
20. L. Davidovich *et al.*, Phys. Rev. Lett. **71**, 2360 (1993).

OVERLAP AND ENTANGLEMENT WITNESS MEASUREMENTS

RADIM FILIP
Department of Optics, Palacký University,
17. listopadu 50, 772 00 Olomouc, Czech Republic,
e-mail address: filip@optics.upol.cz

MARTIN HENDRYCH
Joint Laboratory of Optics, Palacký University and the Physical Institute of the Czech Academy of Sciences, 17. listopadu 50, 772 00 Olomouc, Czech Republic

MILOSLAV DUŠEK AND JAROMÍR FIURÁŠEK
Department of Optics, Palacký University,
17. listopadu 50, 772 00 Olomouc, Czech Republic

A generic device for direct measurement of overlap, fidelity, purity and Hilbert-Schmidt distance of two density matrices is proposed. Simultaneously, the same apparatus is able to measure an entanglement witness. The experimental demonstration of the overlap measurement for polarization states of the photons is presented.

Any quantum state is characterized by its density matrix operator, which contains all achievable information about the system. Some important properties of a quantum state can be found in a simple way from the overlap $\mathrm{Tr}(\rho^A\rho^B)$ between two density matrices ρ^A and ρ^B, such as the fidelity $\langle\Psi|\rho|\Psi\rangle$ of density matrix ρ with a pure state $|\Psi\rangle$, the purity $\mathrm{Tr}(\rho^2)$ of the state ρ, or the Hilbert-Schmidt distance between two density matrices $d(\rho^A,\rho^B) = \sqrt{\mathrm{Tr}[(\rho^A-\rho^B)^2]/2}$. In this contribution, we propose a new direct method for measuring these parameters without a complete state reconstruction.[1] In addition, we suggest that the same measurement device can be used to measure an entanglement witness. We also briefly present the experimental results of a linear optical implementation of the overlap measurement for the polarization states of photons.[2]

To begin, we describe the components of the generic measurement setup. We assume two systems 0 and 1, treated as the measured objects, for example the modes of electromagnetic field. As a quantum meter, we will utilize an auxiliary qubit A, with basis states $|\uparrow\rangle$ and $|\downarrow\rangle$. The device is composed of two interferometric setups: one working with the main systems 0 and 1 and the other manipulating the auxiliary qubit A. To construct these interferometers, we need the following unitary operations: for the auxiliary qubit, unitary transformations U_H (Hadamard gate) $|\uparrow\rangle \to (|\uparrow\rangle + |\downarrow\rangle)/\sqrt{2}$, $|\downarrow\rangle \to (|\downarrow\rangle - |\uparrow\rangle)/\sqrt{2}$ and phase shift transformation $U_{PS}\,|\uparrow\rangle \to \exp(i\psi)|\uparrow\rangle$, $|\downarrow\rangle \to |\downarrow\rangle$, and for the main systems 0 and 1, a linear coupling represented

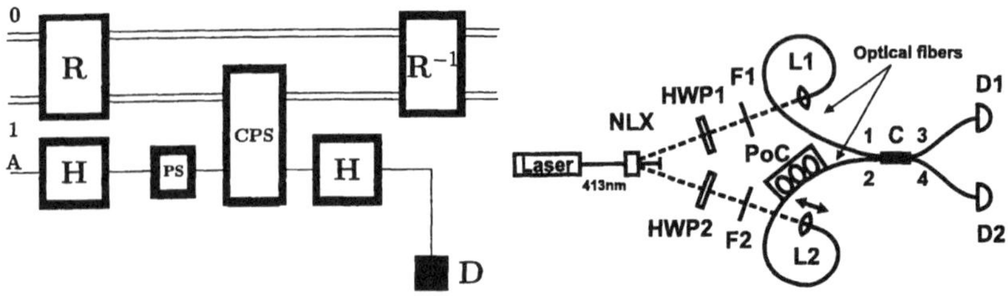

Figure 1. Left: generic measuring device, H – Hadamard gate, CPS – controlled phase shift, PS – phase shift, R – coupling gate, D – detector. Right: experimental setup, LASER – Kr^{+}-ion laser, NLX – nonlinear crystal $LiIO_3$ (type-I), HWP – half-wave plates, F – long-wave pass filters (cut-off at 670 nm), L – lenses, PoC – polarization controller, C – fiber coupler, D – avalanche photodiode.

by unitary operation $U_R = \exp\left[\frac{\pi}{4}(a_0^\dagger a_1 - a_1^\dagger a_0)\right]$, where a_0 and a_1 are annihilation operators of the field modes. These operations U_H, U_R and U_{PS} can be performed by linear systems and their experimental implementations obviously do not represent a principal problem. A key point in the proposed setup is the realization of an efficient controlled phase shift (CPS) operation $U_{CPS} = \exp\left(i\pi a_0^\dagger a_0 |\uparrow\rangle\langle\uparrow|\right)$, which couples the main system 0 and auxiliary qubit system A. This CPS operation is described by the following interaction Hamiltonian $H_I = \hbar\kappa a_0^\dagger a_0 |\uparrow\rangle\langle\uparrow|$, where κ is a real coupling constant and the effective interaction time is set to be equal to π/κ. This kind of interaction can be mediated by an appropriate nonlinear coupling between systems 0 and A, such as found in cavity-QED and trapped-ion experiments. If the state of the auxiliary system is $|\uparrow\rangle$, the above described operation realizes a phase shift about π in system 0, whereas for state $|\downarrow\rangle$, no phase shift is induced. We compound the CPS gate with the coupling U_R operations to the following sequence of transformations $U_X = U_R^\dagger U_{CPS} U_R$ on systems 0 and 1 induced by the auxiliary qubit state. Depending on this qubit state, U_X effectively flips the states of systems 0 and 1 on the output of main systems:

$$U_X|\psi_n\rangle_0|\phi_m\rangle_1|\uparrow\rangle = |\phi_m\rangle_0|\psi_n\rangle_1|\uparrow\rangle, \quad U_X|\psi_n\rangle_0|\phi_m\rangle_1|\downarrow\rangle = |\psi_n\rangle_0|\phi_m\rangle_1|\downarrow\rangle, \tag{1}$$

where $|\psi_n\rangle$ and $|\phi_n\rangle$ are basis states, however, without any change of the basis states $|\uparrow\rangle$ and $|\downarrow\rangle$. If we are able to perform all the above mentioned operations, then the generic measurement can be realized in the way depicted in Fig. 1. The measuring device consists of the main interferometer with the operations U_R, U_R^{-1} on systems 0,1 coupled by a CPS-gate to an auxiliary interferometer with the operations U_H, U_{PS} on the qubit system A. Finally, the detection procedure D of the states $|\uparrow\rangle$ and $|\downarrow\rangle$ on the auxiliary qubit is performed and the corresponding probabilities $p_\uparrow$ and $p_\downarrow$ are determined.

First, we will discuss the overlap $O = \mathrm{Tr}(\rho^A\rho^B)$ measurement for the states ρ^A and ρ^B at the inputs 0 and 1. In the first stage, we calibrate the auxiliary interferometer without the CPS gate by adjusting the phase ψ in such a way that $p_\downarrow = 1$. After this procedure, we use the total apparatus with the CPS gate and measure a decrease of the probability $p_\downarrow$. From this probability, we are able to determine the overlap from the relation $O = 2p_\downarrow - 1$. It is important that only a single parameter has to be estimated to measure the overlap O, irrespective of the complexity of the states ρ^A and ρ^B of the measured systems. Second, we consider a general state ρ of the total system 0 and 1, to demonstrate the entanglement witness measurement with the same measurement setup. After performing the same measurement with the CPS gate included, the same variable $\Delta = 2p_\downarrow - 1$ can be rewritten as an expectation value of the partially-transposed density matrix $\Delta = \langle\Lambda|\rho^{T_1}|\Lambda\rangle$, where the partial transposition is defined by $\rho^{T_1}_{mn,m'n'} = \langle m|_0\langle n|_1\rho^{T_1}|n'\rangle_1|m'\rangle_0 = \rho_{mn',m'n}$, and $|\Lambda\rangle$ is an unnormalized maximally entangled state $|\Lambda\rangle = \sum_j |\phi_j\rangle_0|\phi_j\rangle_1$. According to Peres-Horodecki separability criterion, if Δ is negative we can be sure that the total state is entangled. For positive Δ, however, we are not able to decide whether ρ is entangled or not. Both the overlap and entanglement-witness measurements can be described by a POVM operator Π, viz., $\Delta = \mathrm{Tr}(\rho\Pi)$ with $\Pi = \Pi_+ - \Pi_-$, where the POVM elements Π_+ (Π_-) represent projection onto the symmetric (antisymmetric) subspace of the total space of systems 0 and 1.

Now let us turn our attention to the polarization states of two photons. The states corresponding to the horizontal and vertical linear polarizations will be denoted $|H\rangle$ and $|V\rangle$, respectively. In such a case the projector onto the antisymmetric subspace has the following form $\Pi^- = |\Psi^-\rangle\langle\Psi^-|$, where $|\Psi^-\rangle = \frac{1}{\sqrt{2}}\Big(|H\rangle|V\rangle - |V\rangle|H\rangle\Big)$ is nothing else but a singlet state. What happens if a singlet impinges on a balanced beam splitter? It is an elementary exercise to show that a beam splitter preserves it. Such a state results in a simultaneous detection at both detectors placed in the output modes of the beam splitter. The singlet is the only one of the four Bell states (completing the basis in the Hilbert space of two qubits) that produces such a coincidence detection. The other Bell states make only one of the detectors fire. This fact makes the measurement on two qubits consisting of projectors Π^+ and Π^- experimentally feasible.

The experimental setup forming a Hong-Ou-Mandel interferometer is shown in Fig. 1. In our experiment, visibilities of a Hong-Ou-Mandel dip exceeding 98% were reached. Different time delays were generated by moving the coupling lens L2 and the tip of the fiber towards the nonlinear crystal. Moving the coupling stage 200 μm away from the center of the dip also served to measure the coincidence rate C_{200} on the shoulder for normalization purposes (it represents half of the impinging pair rate). The overlap is calculated from measured data as follows: $\mathrm{Tr}(\rho_A\rho_B) = 1 - 2\mathrm{Tr}(\Pi^-\rho_A \otimes \rho_B) = 1 - \frac{C_0}{C_{200}}$, where C_0 is the coincidence rate when the arms of the interferometer are

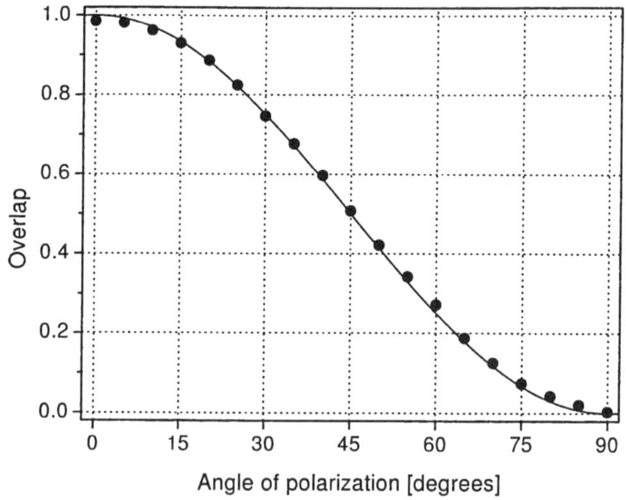

Figure 2. Overlap of two pure states. The first photon is in the state with vertical linear polarization ($\theta = 0$). The other photon is also linearly polarized but its polarization is rotated by angle $\theta > 0$.

balanced. As a simple demonstration, we measured the overlap of two pure states. Photon pairs obtained from downconversion were linearly polarized in the vertical direction. The polarization of photons in Arm 1 was kept fixed and the polarization angle θ of photons in Arm 2 was varied by rotating the half-wave plate HWP2. Thus we measured the overlap between the states $|V\rangle$ and $\cos(\theta)|V\rangle + \sin(\theta)|H\rangle$. The experimental results shown in Fig. 2 are in very good agreement with the theoretically expected dependence $\cos^2(\theta)$ that is also plotted in Fig. 2. Each data point in Fig. 2 has been derived from 50 to 200 one-second measurement periods. On average, 3300 coincidences per second were measured on the shoulder away from the dip. Statistical errors are smaller than the symbols used for the points in the graphs. Other errors stem from the non-unit visibility and optical-path fluctuations. The accuracy of polarization-angle settings was better than $\pm 0.3°$.

Acknowledgments

This research was supported by the Ministry of Education of the Czech Republic, projects LN00A015, VS96028 and RN19982003012.

References

1. R. Filip, Phys. Rev. A **65**, 062320 (2002).
2. M. Hendrych, M. Dušek, R. Filip and J. Fiurášek, quant-ph/0208091.

GEOMETRY OF SOME QUANTUM-MECHANICAL STATE SPACES

JOHAN BRÄNNLUND
Stockholm University
SCFAB, Department of Physics
SE-106 91 Stockholm
Sweden
E-mail: jbr@physto.se

1 Introduction

The state space of quantum mechanics is complex projective space $\mathbb{CP}^N$. For low-dimensional systems, this space can be concretely visualized and properties such as entanglement studied in geometrical terms. For a spin-1/2 particle, the space is simply the Poincaré sphere.

It turns out that it is possible to use coordinates that neatly split the space in two — part of a sphere and a torus.

2 What is $\mathbb{CP}^N$?

Physical quantities like $|\langle\varphi|\psi\rangle|^2$ are unchanged when $|\varphi\rangle \to e^{i\alpha}|\varphi\rangle$ so the Hilbert space description contains some gauge freedom — remove this!

Write $|\psi\rangle = \sum_i Z^i|e_i\rangle$ with Z^i being complex numbers, i.e., $Z^i = (n_0 e^{i\nu_0}, ..., n_N e^{i\nu_N})$.

Normalization $\Rightarrow \sum_i n_i^2 = 1$. Also, use phase freedom to set $\nu_0 = 0$. This is a coordinate system for $\mathbb{CP}^N$. As expected, $\mathbb{CP}^1$ is the Poincaré sphere. The higher-dimensional projective spaces are *not* spheres — there is one spherical part consisting of the $\{n_i\}$ and one torus part coming from the $\{\nu_i\}$.

$\mathbb{CP}^N$ gets a natural metric from the Hilbert space, the so-called *Fubini-Study* metric. For $N = 1$, this is the metric on the sphere, as it should be. In these coordinates, the metric becomes

$$\mathrm{d}s^2 = \sum_i \mathrm{d}n_i^2 + (n\text{-dependent } \mathrm{d}\nu_i \mathrm{d}\nu_j \text{ terms}).$$

3 Visualizing $\mathbb{CP}^2$

This space has coordinates (n_0, n_1, n_2) and (ν_1, ν_2) with the constraint $n_0^2 + n_1^2 + n_2^2 = 1$ so the space is four-dimensional. The sphere can be stereographically projected onto the positive quadrant of the $x-y$ plane (see Fig. 1).

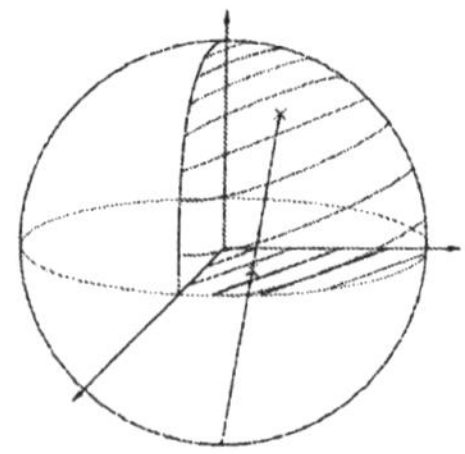

Figure 1. Stereographic projection from the south pole.

This means that $\mathbb{C}P^2$ is a quadrant of a plane with a torus sitting over each point; see Fig. 2.

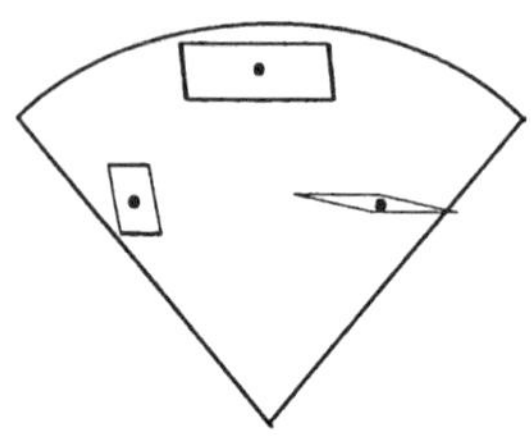

Figure 2. Octant part of $\mathbb{C}P^2$ with some tori shown.

4 Two coupled qubits

For studying entanglement, the simplest nontrivial example is two coupled qubits. This means that the state space is $\mathbb{C}P^3$. Its coordinates are

$$(n_0, n_1 e^{i\nu_1}, n_2 e^{i\nu_2}, n_3 e^{i\nu_3}) \leftrightarrow$$
$$|\psi\rangle = n_0|++\rangle + n_1 e^{i\nu_1}|+-\rangle + n_2 e^{i\nu_2}|-+\rangle + n_3 e^{i\nu_3}|--\rangle.$$

4.1 Separable states

$|\psi\rangle$ is separable if the coefficient matrix C_{ij} in $|\psi\rangle = \sum_{i,j} C_{ij}|ij\rangle$ has rank one. This leads to

$$\begin{cases} n_0 n_3 = n_1 n_2 \\ \nu_3 = \nu_1 + \nu_2 \end{cases}$$

By analogy with $\mathbb{C}P^2$, the n-coordinates can still be stereographically projected, this time into a ball. Doing this, we get the separable surface shown in Fig. 3.

In the torus, the picture is as shown in Fig. 4

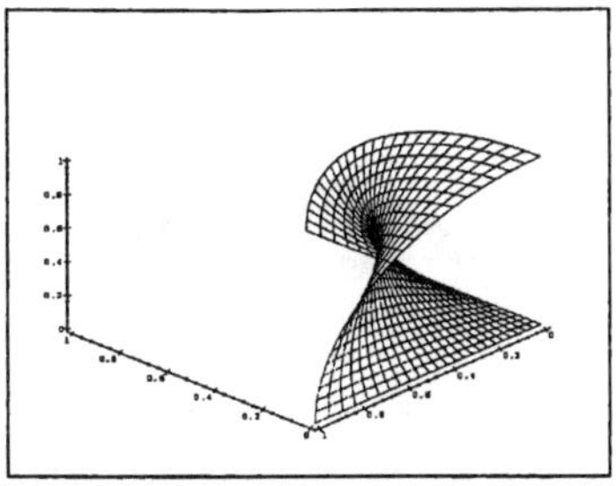

Figure 3. The separable surface in the octant.

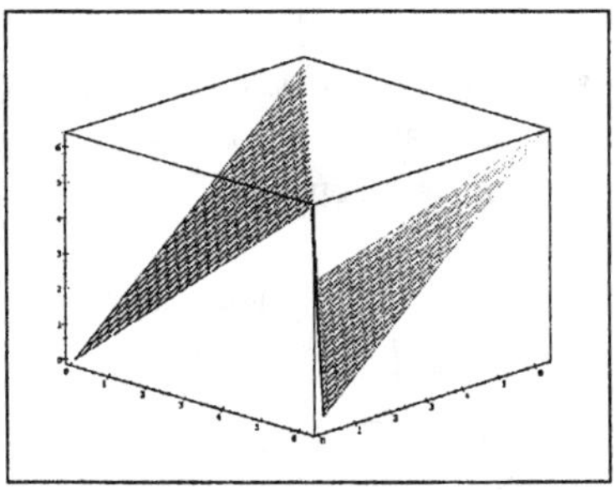

Figure 4. The separable surface in the torus.

4.2 Maximally entangled states

The condition on C_{ij} for $|\psi\rangle$ to be maximally entangled is that $C_{ij} \in \mathrm{SU}(2)$. In terms of the n's and ν's, this means that

$$\begin{cases} n_0 = n_3 \\ n_1 = n_2 \\ \nu_3 = \nu_1 + \nu_2 + \pi \end{cases}$$

which is a line in the octant and a plane in the torus; see Fig. 5.

4.3 Intermediate entanglement

For states between the two extremes of separability and maximal entanglement, things are not quite as nice as before. The line in the octant thickens and one obtains an n-dependent plane in the torus, giving a five-dimensional total space. Also, the topology of the maximally entangled states becomes more complicated; it is $\mathrm{U}(2)\times\mathrm{U}(2)\ /\ \mathrm{U}(1)^3$.

One application of the geometric framework is that there is a natural

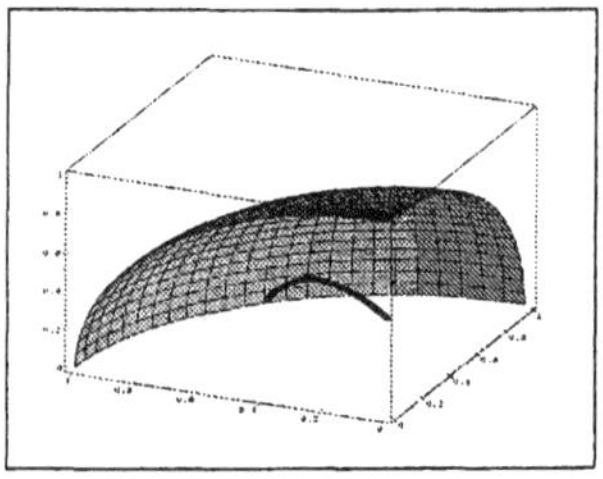

Figure 5. The maximally entangled line in the octant.

measure of entanglement: the minimal distance κ to the separable surface. The result is $\kappa = \max[\sin^2(\sigma), \cos^2(\sigma)]$ where σ is the Schmidt angle. This angle also provides a *stratification* of the full state space $\mathbb{C}P^3$, with maximally entangled and separable states at the two endpoints and states with intermediate entanglement in between; see Fig. 6.

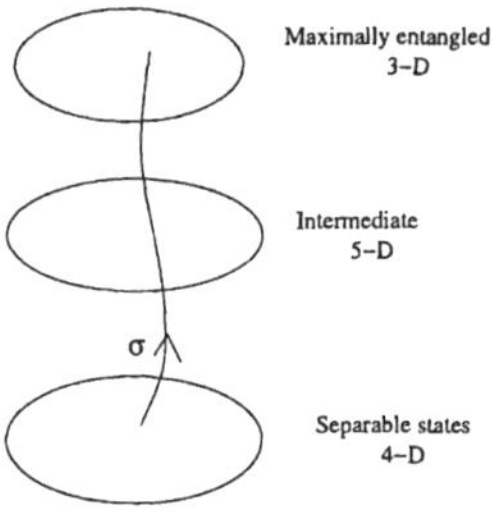

Figure 6. Schematic picture of the stratification of $\mathbb{C}P^3$.

One can compute the volume of these spaces of intermediate entanglement:

$$V = \pi^3 \cos^2(2\sigma)\sin(2\sigma).$$

Dividing this expression by $\pi^3/6$, which is the total volume of $\mathbb{C}P^3$, one obtains a probability density for the Schmidt angle which is maximal for $\tan 2(\sigma) = 1/\sqrt{2} \Rightarrow \sigma \approx 17.6°$ (open question: what is special about this value of σ?).

Further reading

For more details, see Bengtsson, Brännlund and Życzkowski, quant-ph/0108064 (accepted by Int. J. Mod. Phys. A).

ENTANGLEMENT CREATION IN A TWO-ELECTRON SYSTEM

ANDREA BERTONI
INFM - National Research Center S3,
via Campi 213/A, 41100 Modena, Italy - E-mail: bertoni.andrea@unimo.it
and
Advancer Research Center for Electronic Systems, Università di Bologna, Italy

SUSANNA REGGIANI
Advancer Research Center for Electronic Systems, Università di Bologna, Italy

We present a simulative study of the dynamics of entanglement creation between the continuous position variables of two electrons injected in a quantum wire system. The analysis is performed for pure states and the entanglement is computed as the von Neumann entropy of the reduced density matrix of the system. The evolution of the electron wave function is obtained by numerically solving the two-particle time-dependent Schrödinger equation.

1 Introduction

The key requirement of a two-qubit quantum logic gate is the creation of entanglement. Thus, within any physical system proposed for quantum computing hardware, the dynamical evolution that creates highly nonclassical entangled states needs to be accurately investigated.

Recently the authors advanced a proposal for a qubit realized in the frame of a solid-state system based on coupled quantum wires.[1] The two-qubit gate proposed for the universal set is a conditional phase shifter, realized by means of a Coulomb coupler in which two electrons running along two adjacent wires get close enough to give rise to an effective Coulomb interaction. This geometry not only creates the phase factor that entangles the qubit states represented by the electron coordinates orthogonal to the wires, but also creates entanglement between the continuous position variables of the two electrons along the wires. In the present work we analyze the formation of this two-particle entanglement by performing a direct solution of the two-particle time-dependent Schrödinger equation for a number of different geometries and computing the von Neumann entropy of the reduced density matrix at each time step of the physical evolution.

2 Physical system and simulative model

The physical system consists of two Si/SiO_2 quantum wires and the two electrons, at the initial time, are represented by two minimum-uncertainty wave packets with a kinetic energy of 50 meV and a broadening in position of 20 nm.

The coherent transport of the two electrons running along the wires has been simulated in a single parabolic band approximation by solving the time-dependent Schrödinger equation for the two-particle wave function $\Psi(x_1, x_2)$:

$$i\hbar \frac{\partial}{\partial t}\psi(x_1, x_2, t) = -\frac{\hbar^2}{2m}\left(\frac{\partial^2}{\partial x_1^2} + \frac{\partial^2}{\partial x_2^2}\right)\psi(x_1, x_2, t) + V(x_1, x_2)\psi(x_1, x_2, t).$$

To this purpose, the wires have been modeled as 1D devices, as if they have no width in the quantized direction. With this approach, the geometry of the system is incorporated in the two-particle potential

$$V(x_1, x_2) = \frac{e^2}{\varepsilon D(x_1, x_2)}, \text{ with } D(x_1, x_2) = \sqrt{(x_1 - x_2)^2 + (Y_1(x_1) - Y_2(x_2))^2},$$

where e is the electron charge, ε is the silicon dielectric constant, D is the distance between point x_1 in the first wire and point x_2 in the second wire. The functions $Y_1(x_1)$ and $Y_2(x_2)$ contain the geometry of the two wires: $Y_n(x)$ represents the y coordinate of a point that has x coordinate along wire n.

At each time step, the entanglement

$$S(\rho) = -\mathrm{Tr}_1\{\mathrm{Tr}_2(\rho)\log_2[\mathrm{Tr}_2(\rho)]\},$$

is computed, where ρ is the density matrix of the two-particle system.[2] Because the evolution of the wave function is performed in the real (x_1, x_2) space, once the density matrix has been traced over the x_2 coordinate it is diagonalized in order to compute its logarithm. This task, repeated at each time step, represents the main computational effort of the algorithm implemented. The time evolution is obtained by means of a Crank-Nicholson finite difference scheme.

3 Numerical results and conclusions

In Figs. 1–4 we present the value of the two-particle entanglement S as a function of time for four different cases. Each figure also contains the schematic of the wires' geometry with the initial condition for the wave function. In Figs. 1 and 2 a 3D plot of $\psi(x_1, x_2)$ together with the potential $V(x_1, x_2)$ is also shown. It is worth noting that the origin of the x coordinate of each wire corresponds to its left end . The detailed descriptions of the different cases are reported in the captions of the figures.

Acknowledgments

Work partially supported by MURST (National Project on Quantum Computation) and by the US Office of Naval Research (Contract N00014-98-1-0777).

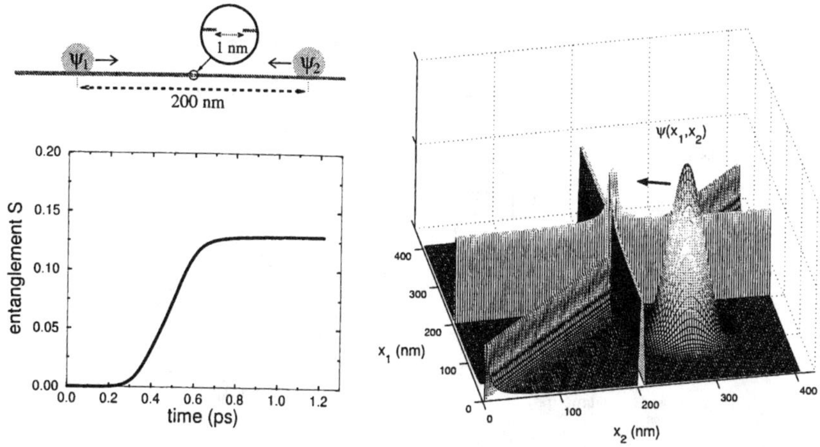

Figure 1. Two electrons propagate in opposite directions along a wire that has a small gap in the middle. Between time $t = 0.3$ ps and $t = 0.6$ ps the electrons bounce back due to both the mutual Coulomb repulsion (with maximum on the diagonal $x_1 = x_2$ of the 3D graph) and the high potential barrier of the gap (the "cross" at $x_1 = 200$ and $x_2 = 200$). The entanglement increases monotonically during the process.

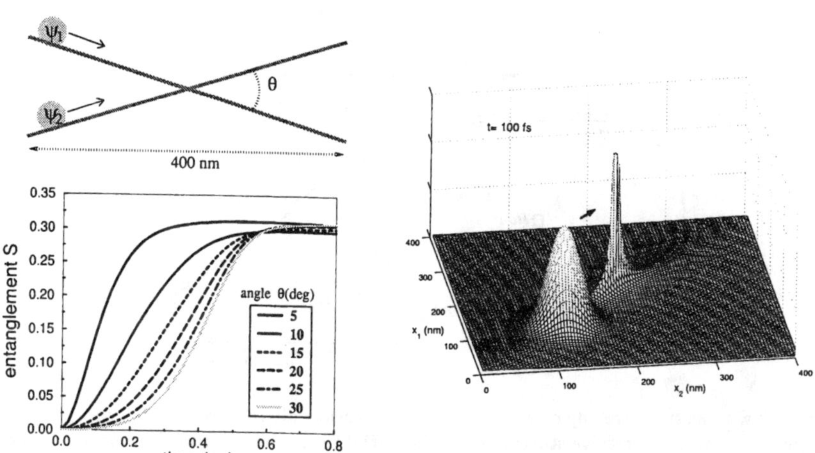

Figure 2. Two electrons propagate along two crossing wires. Together they reach the crossing point, where the two-particle potential $V(x_1 = 200, x_2 = 200)$ is infinite, then they continue along the original wires with a negligible reflected component. This result is different from a classical case and from a solution obtained using a single-particle Hartree approximation: in these two cases the electrons bounce back. The simulation is repeated for different values of the angle between the wires. The entanglement increases monotonically and reaches a value that is independent of the angle θ.

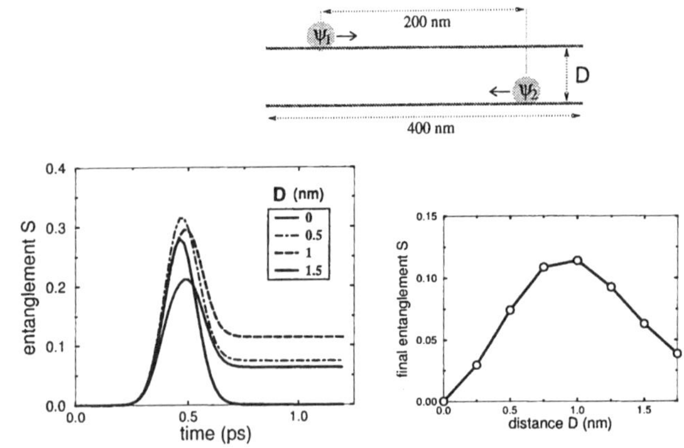

Figure 3. Two electrons are injected in opposite directions along two parallel wires. The entanglement increases while they are approaching each other, then decreases as their transmitted and reflected components separate. The graph on the right shows the final value of the entanglement. The maximum value corresponds to a wire distance D of about 1 nm. The case with D = 0 corresponds to the system of Fig. 1 without the central gap: now the mutual Coulomb repulsion is only responsible for the bouncing back of the electrons. Note that for D = 0 the final state is not entangled.

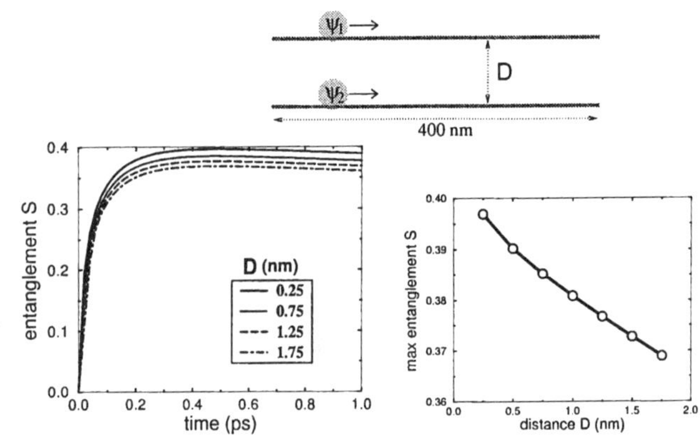

Figure 4. Two electron are injected in the same direction along two parallel wires. The Coulomb interaction is effective starting from the initial time: the value of the entanglement increases immediately and reaches an almost-steady value that is plotted in the right graph for different values of D.

References

1. A. Bertoni et al., J. Mod. Opt. **49**, 1219 (2002). A similar proposal was presented by R. Ionicioiu et al. in Int. J. Mod. Phys. B **15**, 125 (2001).
2. C. H. Bennett et al., Phys. Rev. A **53**, 2046 (1996).

SEMIDEFINITE PROGRAMMING, ENTANGLEMENT WITNESSES AND BOUND ENTANGLED STATES

ANDREW C. DOHERTY

Institute for Quantum Information, California Institute of Technology, Pasadena, California 91125

PABLO A. PARRILO

Institut für Automatik, ETH Zürich, CH-8092, Switzerland

FEDERICO M. SPEDALIERI

Institute for Quantum Information, California Institute of Technology, Pasadena, California 91125

We briefly review a recently proposed set of criteria for separability that may be checked using semidefinite programs. These optimizations allow the construction of explicit entanglement witnesses. We introduce a semidefinite program that achieves the reverse process of constructing bound entangled states from appropriate entanglement witnesses.

The problem of distinguishing between mixed separable states, which can be prepared by local operations and classical communication,[1] and entangled states which cannot has been an active area of recent research in quantum information theory.[2,3,4] A class of convex optimizations know as *semidefinite programs* have proven useful in addressing this problem[5] and seem to have broad application in quantum information theory.[6,7,8] Here we review our earlier results and further illustrate some of the useful properties of semidefinite programs through a simpler example that tests decomposability of entanglement witnesses.

A bipartite mixed state ρ is separable[1] if it can be written as a convex combination of pure product states

$$\rho = \sum p_i |\psi_i\rangle\langle\psi_i| \otimes |\phi_i\rangle\langle\phi_i|, \tag{1}$$

where $|\psi_i\rangle$ and $|\phi_i\rangle$ are state-vectors on the spaces $\mathcal{H}_A$ and $\mathcal{H}_B$ of subsystems A and B respectively, and $p_i > 0, \sum_i p_i = 1$. Several operational criteria that identify entangled states are known. In particular the partial transpose criterion[9,10] is a readily checkable necessary condition for separability. If ρ has matrix elements $\rho_{ik,jl} = \langle i| \otimes \langle k|\rho|j\rangle \otimes |l\rangle$ then the partial transpose ρ^{T_A} is defined by $\rho^{T_A}_{ik,jl} = \rho_{jk,il}$. The partial transpose of a separable state (1) is given by $\sum p_i |\psi_i^*\rangle\langle\psi_i^*| \otimes |\phi_i\rangle\langle\phi_i|$. Thus, if a state is separable it must have a positive partial transpose (PPT). Any state for which ρ^{T_A} is not positive semidefinite is necessarily entangled, although there are PPT entangled states.[11]

In Ref. 5 we introduced a hierarchy of necessary conditions for separability that are also based on readily checkable properties of separable states.

These criteria generalize the positive partial transpose criterion but are strictly stronger. Consider the state $\tilde{\rho}$ defined on $\mathcal{H}_A \otimes \mathcal{H}_B \otimes \mathcal{H}_A$ given by

$$\tilde{\rho} = \sum p_i |\psi_i\rangle\langle\psi_i| \otimes |\phi_i\rangle\langle\phi_i| \otimes |\psi_i\rangle\langle\psi_i|. \tag{2}$$

Firstly $\tilde{\rho}$ is an extension of ρ (that is the partial trace over the third party C is equal to ρ, $\mathrm{Tr}_C[\tilde{\rho}] = \rho$ and $\tilde{\rho}$ is positive). Secondly the state is symmetric under interchanging the two copies of $\mathcal{H}_A$. If we define the swap operator P such that $P|i\rangle \otimes |k\rangle \otimes |j\rangle = |j\rangle \otimes |k\rangle \otimes |i\rangle$, we have $P^2 = I$, and $\pi = (I+P)/2$ is a projector onto the symmetric subspace. Clearly $\pi\tilde{\rho}\pi = \tilde{\rho}$. Finally the extension $\tilde{\rho}$ is a tripartite separable state. This means that it will have positive partial transposes with respect to any of the parties, and in particular we have $\tilde{\rho}^{T_A} \geq 0$ and $\tilde{\rho}^{T_B} \geq 0$. This gives us a separability criterion. *If the state ρ on $\mathcal{H}_A \otimes \mathcal{H}_B$ is separable then there is an extension $\tilde{\rho}$ on $\mathcal{H}_A \otimes \mathcal{H}_B \otimes \mathcal{H}_A$ such that $\pi\tilde{\rho}\pi = \tilde{\rho}$, $\tilde{\rho}^{T_1} \geq 0$ and $\tilde{\rho}^{T_2} \geq 0$.* We may generalize this to an arbitrary number of copies of both $\mathcal{H}_A$ and $\mathcal{H}_B$.

The problem of searching for the extension $\tilde{\rho}$ can be solved efficiently, since it is an example of a *semidefinite program* (SDP).[12] A SDP corresponds to the optimization of a linear function, subject to a linear matrix inequality (LMI). A typical SDP will be

$$\begin{aligned} \text{minimize} \quad & c^T\mathbf{x} \\ \text{subject to} \quad & F(\mathbf{x}) \geq 0, \end{aligned} \tag{3}$$

where c is a given vector of length m, $\mathbf{x} = (x_1, \ldots, x_m)$, and $F(\mathbf{x}) = F_0 + \sum_i x_i F_i$, for some fixed n-by-n Hermitian matrices F_j. The inequality in the second line of (3) means that the matrix $F(\mathbf{x})$ is positive semidefinite. The vector $\mathbf{x}$ is the variable over which the minimization is performed. Each of our new separability criteria may be stated as a semidefinite program.[5]

For every entangled state ρ there is an observable—termed an entanglement witness (EW)—that distinguishes it from all the separable states. An EW W for the entangled state ρ satisfies

$$\mathrm{Tr}[W\rho_{sep}] \geq 0 \quad \text{and} \quad \mathrm{Tr}[W\rho] < 0, \tag{4}$$

where ρ_{sep} is any separable state. The SDP associated with checking any given one of our criteria allows us to construct explicit EWs when state is found not to satisfy it.[5] This is possible because the convexity of SDPs leads to a duality structure analogous to the duality between states and observables and guarantees the existence of "witnesses" to the infeasibility of the SDP that can readily be used to construct EWs. Here we will illustrate this duality by reference to the simpler problem of testing whether an EW is decomposable. The dual SDP to the one written above is

$$\begin{aligned} \text{maximize} \quad & -\mathrm{Tr}(F_0 X) \\ \text{subject to} \quad & X \geq 0 \\ & \mathrm{Tr}(F_i X) = c_i \end{aligned} \tag{5}$$

where the variables of the optimization form an m-by-m matrix X. If the feasibility constraints may be satisfied for some $X > 0$ and $\mathbf{x}$ such that $F(\mathbf{x}) > 0$ the problems are termed strictly feasible and the optimum values of the primal and dual forms are equal and there is a feasible pair $(\mathbf{x}_{\text{opt}}, X_{\text{opt}})$ achieving the optimum.[12] In this case it can be shown that $\text{Tr}[F(\mathbf{x}_{\text{opt}})X_{\text{opt}}] = 0$ and thus $F(\mathbf{x}_{\text{opt}})X_{\text{opt}} = 0$ so the Hermitian matrices $F(\mathbf{x}_{\text{opt}})$ and X_{opt} have orthogonal ranges. This is known as the *complementary slackness* condition.

A sufficient but not necessary condition for Z to be an entanglement witness is for it not to be positive but rather decomposable as $Z = P + Q^{T_A}$, where $P \geq 0, Q \geq 0$. If we know only the matrix elements of Z it may not be clear how to determine whether such a decomposition exists. Consider the following semidefinite program in the dual form

$$\begin{array}{ll} \text{maximize} & -\text{Tr}(P + Q^{T_A})/d_A d_B \\ \text{subject to} & P \geq 0, \quad Q \geq 0 \\ & H(P + Q^{T_A}) = H(Z). \end{array} \tag{6}$$

where $H(Y) = Y - [\text{Tr}(Y)]I/d_A d_B$ is the traceless part of Y (a matrix on $\mathcal{H}_A \otimes \mathcal{H}_B$). The matrix variable X in this case is block diagonal with blocks P and Q ($X = P \oplus Q$). The final equality constraint may be enforced by a finite number ($d_A^2 d_B^2 - 1$) of trace constraints that define F_i and c_i, F_0 is proportional to the identity. By adding a sufficiently large multiple of the identity to any matrix satisfying the trace constraints it is possible to construct an $X > 0$ also satisfying the constraints, hence the optimization is strictly feasible. If the optimum $\eta \geq -\text{Tr}(Z)/d_A d_B$ then for $\epsilon \equiv \text{Tr}(Z)/d_A d_B + \eta \geq 0$ we have $Z = (P_{\text{opt}} + \epsilon I) + Q_{\text{opt}}^{T_A}$ and so Z is decomposable.

We have stated the semidefinite program in its dual form. The primal form is worth considering because when Z is nondecomposable it constructs bound entangled states detected by Z. Using the formulae above the primal form may be shown to be

$$\begin{array}{ll} \text{minimize} & \text{Tr}(Z\rho) - \text{Tr}(Z)/d_A d_B \\ \text{subject to} & \rho \geq 0, \quad \rho^{T_A} \geq 0 \\ & \text{Tr}(\rho) = 1. \end{array} \tag{7}$$

The completely mixed state is strictly positive and feasible so the optima of these two programs are equal and there are $\rho_{\text{opt}}, P_{\text{opt}}, Q_{\text{opt}}$ achieving the optimum. By complementary slackness the range of P_{opt} is orthogonal to the range of ρ_{opt} and the range of Q_{opt} is orthogonal to the range of $\rho_{\text{opt}}^{T_A}$.

Suppose now that the optimum $\eta < -\text{Tr}(Z)/d_A d_B$. So $\text{Tr}(Z\rho_{\text{opt}}) < 0$ and since Z is an EW ρ_{opt} is bound entangled ($\rho_{\text{opt}}^{T_A} \geq 0$ by construction). Since it is a PPT entangled state $\rho_{\text{opt}} = (1-p)\rho_{\text{sep}} + p\delta$ where ρ_{sep} is separable, δ is a so-called edge PPT entangled state and $p > 0$ is the minimum value for which such a decomposition is possible.[13] An edge PPT entangled state δ has the property that for any pure product state $|x, y\rangle$ and $\epsilon > 0$, $\delta -$

$\epsilon|x,y\rangle\langle x,y|$ is either not positive or not PPT. Because $\mathrm{Tr}(Z\rho_{\mathrm{sep}}) \geq 0$, if $p < 1$ then $\mathrm{Tr}(Z\rho_{\mathrm{opt}}) > \mathrm{Tr}(Z\delta)$ but this contradicts the optimality of ρ_{opt} which must therefore be an edge PPT entangled state. For any $P \geq 0$, $Q \geq 0$ we have $\mathrm{Tr}\,(P + Q^{T_A})\rho_{\mathrm{opt}} \geq 0$, so Z cannot be decomposable. Defining $\epsilon = -\mathrm{Tr}(Z\rho_{\mathrm{opt}}) > 0$, we have $Z = P_{\mathrm{opt}} + Q_{\mathrm{opt}}^{T_A} - \epsilon I$, and from the original dual form of the optimization ϵ is the smallest value for which such an expression holds with $P \geq 0$, $Q \geq 0$. The range properties of $P_{\mathrm{opt}}, Q_{\mathrm{opt}}$ and ρ_{opt} mean that this is the canonical form for Z introduced by Lewenstein *et al.*[13]

We have constructed a semidefinite program that has two important properties. Firstly the semidefinite program provides an easy test for decomposability of entanglement witnesses, such as those that arise from Bell inequalities for example.[14,8] Secondly it provides an algorithm for computing bound entangled states from nondecomposable entanglement witnesses or positive maps, examples of which occur in the mathematical physics literature. This is a further example of the usefulness of semidefinite programming in quantum information theory.

Acknowledgments

ACD gratefully acknowledges conversations with Barbara Terhal. This work was supported in part by the National Science Foundation under grant EIA-0086083, the Caltech MURI Center for Quantum Networks administered by the Army Research Office under Grant DAAD19-00-1-0374 and the Caltech MURI Center for Uncertainty Management for Complex Systems.

References

1. R. F. Werner, Phys. Rev. A **40**, 4277 (1989).
2. M. Horodecki, P. Horodecki, and R. Horodecki, quant-ph/0109124.
3. M. Lewenstein *et al.*, J. Mod. Opt. **47**, 2841 (2000).
4. B. M. Terhal, quant-ph/0101032.
5. A. C. Doherty, P. A. Parrilo and F. M. Spedalieri, Phys. Rev. Lett. **88**, 187904 (2002).
6. E. Rains, quant-ph/0008047.
7. K. Audenaert and B. De Moor, quant-ph/0109155.
8. B. M. Terhal, A. C. Doherty and D. Schwab, quant-ph/0210053.
9. A. Peres, Phys. Rev. Lett. **77**, 1413 (1996).
10. M. Horodecki, P. Horodecki, and R. Horodecki, Phys. Lett. A **223**, 1 (1996).
11. P. Horodecki, Phys. Lett. A **232**, 233 (1997).
12. L. Vandenberghe and S. Boyd, SIAM Review **38**, 49 (1996).
13. M. Lewenstein, B. Kraus, P. Horodecki and J. I. Cirac, Phys. Rev. A **63**, 044304 (2001).
14. B. M. Terhal, Phys. Lett. A **271**, 319 (2000).

ON THE WAY TO AN EXPERIMENTAL REALIZATION OF ENTANGLEMENT PURIFICATION

S. GASPARONI, J.-W. PAN, G. WEIHS, AND A. ZEILINGER

Institute for experimental physics, University of Vienna, Boltzmanngasse 5, Vienna

Entanglement is an essential feature in quantum mechanics and has been used since the seminal paper by Einstein, Podolsky, and Rosen.[1] In quantum information processing entangled pairs are often used in different ways; in these schemes the entanglement of the pairs has to be maximal. Different entanglement purification schemes have been developed to improve nonmaximally entangled pairs. Here we concentrate on the realization of such an experiment.

1 Entanglement and its Purification

Entanglement is not only, as remarked by Schrödinger, the essence of quantum mechanics but it is also fundamental for quantum information processing. It is used to transmit the quantum part of the information in quantum teleportation,[2] as well as in quantum dense coding, and it is also at the basics of quantum cryptography.[3] Moreover, its applications are widespread in the developing field of quantum computation and in its new branch based on linear optics.[4] Different ways may be used to generate entanglement; generally some decay process is used wherein a quantity has to be preserved. For example two electrons originating from an atom of unitary angular momentum are correlated in spin. Similarly, photons entangled in polarization are generated by degenerate spontaneous parametric downconversion (SPDC) when one photon spontaneously decays in two photons, both at half the frequency of the incoming photon. The nonideality of these processes results in the nonmaximality of the entanglement of the resulting pairs. It is therefore necessary to think about schemes to purify the entanglement. Here we will discuss two such schemes and their feasibility. Before introducing purification schemes we need a measure of entanglement quality. The one generally used is the overlap of the state in question with a maximally-entangled state, for example with the Bell state $|\Phi^+\rangle$:

$$F = \langle\Phi^+|\rho_{in}|\Phi^+\rangle \tag{1}$$

which is called the fidelity of the state relative to $|\Phi^+\rangle$. An entangled mixed state can be written in terms of its fidelity as

$$\rho_{in} = F(|00\rangle + |11\rangle)(\langle 00| + \langle 11|) + (1-F)(|01\rangle + |10\rangle)(\langle 01| + \langle 10|). \tag{2}$$

For maximally-entangled states the fidelity is obviously 1.

The first purification scheme was proposed by Bennett et.al [5] Their scheme, depicted in Fig. 1, performs a purification of one nonmaximally entangled pair out of two. The first pair is usually called the control pair and

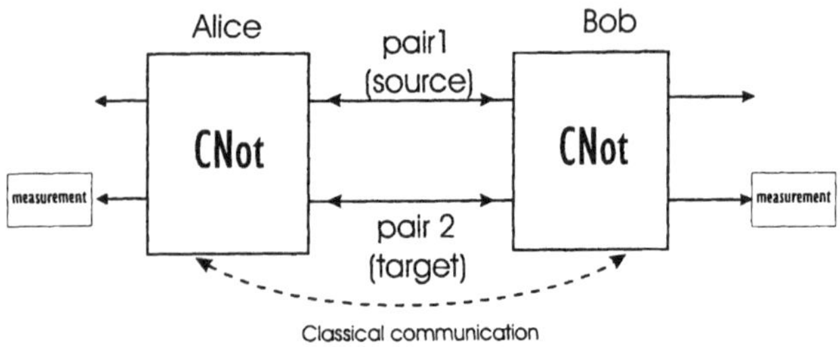

Figure 1. The entanglement purification scheme proposed by Bennett et al. The two qubits are made to interact, from both sides, on a CNOT gate. After this logical operation a z-measurement is performed and the only those cases that are accepted are those in which the target bits at Alice's side and Bob's side are the same.

the second is the target. Let us consider the case in which our pairs are in the state mentioned above, with $F \leq 1$, that is mostly in the $|\Phi^+\rangle$ state. [The initial fidelity has to be greater than 1/2 for the scheme to work.] Each of the two independent qubits is made interact through a controlled-not (CNOT) gate. After the interaction the control pair has been purified when the z-measurement of the two target bits gives the same result. In those cases the fidelity will be increased to the value

$$F' = \frac{F^2 + 1/9(1-F)^2}{F^2 + \frac{2}{3}F(1-F) + \frac{3}{9}(1-F)^2} > F. \tag{3}$$

It is useful to note that such a scheme preserves the input state $|\Phi^+\rangle$. The feasibility of such a scheme is limited by the inefficiency of the CNOT gates that are currently available. Pan et al. thus introduced an alternative scheme that overcomes this technical drawback[6] by using photon polarization state as qubits and replacing the CNOT with high-quality polarizing beam splitters, as shown in Fig. 2. A measurement is performed in the 45° basis on the target pair and, similarly to the previous scheme, the only retained cases are those for which the measurements coincide. This coincidence, which detects the purification events, happens in 1/2 of the cases of the Bennett et al. scheme.

A polarizing beam splitter (PBS) transmits vertically polarized light and reflects horizontally polarized light. Thus, a four-fold detection at the output of the two PBSs selects those cases in which the two incoming photons have the same polarization. If we examine a generally mixed state of the kind ρ, the four-fold detection eliminates the cross-term contribution, which why the fidelity will be increased in the end. A comparison between the two schemes shows that the CNOT and the PBS work in similar ways. In particular, it is clear that two cases are selected in the Bennett et al. scheme: when Alice's side and Bob's side each have two incoming photons of the same polarization; and when Alice's side and Bob's side each have two incoming photons of

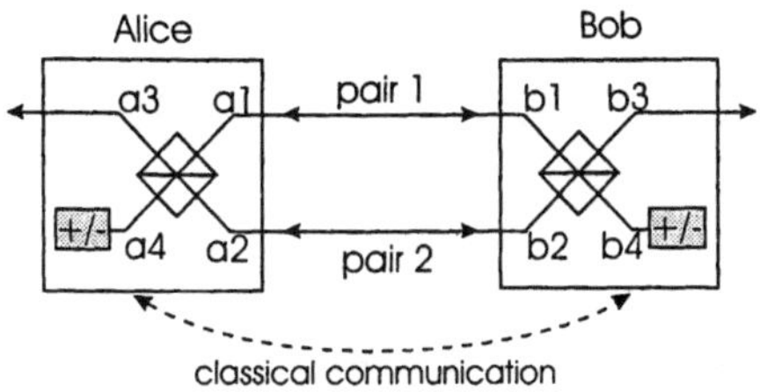

Figure 2. The Pan et al. scheme for entanglement purification. Photons interfere on the PBSs. A measurement is performed on the target photons in the 45° basis, eliminating the cross terms and thus increasing the entanglement of the state.

orthogonal polarizations. The Pan et al. scheme, however, does not include the latter case, thus it success probability is half that of the Bennett et al. scheme.

The experimental setup is shown in Fig. 3. The methods used are similar to other experiments of teleportation[7] or GHZ production:[8] a 798 nm mode-locked laser is used to pump an upconversion process and the upconverted light is used to generate two independent pairs via downconversion. Photons 2 and 4 (1 and 3) interfere at the PBS, where they have to overlap spatially and temporally. The main difficulty in setting up the experiment is the overlap of 2 pairs of photons on PBS1 and PBS2. The setup needs a far greater stability than experiments requiring only overlap of one side. As soon as the two-fold overlap is obtained, there is an interference fringe at the outcomes 1 and 2 because the probability amplitude that a pair is produced on one direction adds to the probability amplitude that one pair is produced in the other direction. The high instability of the fringe shows the stringent stability requirement for proceeding to the last purification steps; see Fig. 4.

Acknowledgments

This work was supported by the Austrian Science Foundation (FWF) and the TMR and the QuComm programs of the European Commission.

References

1. A. Einstein, B. Podolsky, and N. Rosen, Phys. Rev. **47**, 777–780 1935
2. C. H. Bennett, et al., Phys. Rev. Lett. **83**, 3081–3084 1993.
3. T. Jennewein, et al., Phys. Rev. Lett. **84**, 4729–4732 2000.
4. E. Knill, R. Laflamme, and G. J. Milburn, Nature **409**, 46–52 2001.
5. C. H. Bennett, et al., Phys. Rev. Lett. **76**, 722–725 1996.
6. J.-W. Pan, et al., Nature **410**, 1067–1070 2001.
7. D. Bouwmeester, et al., Nature **390**, 575-579 1997.
8. J.-W. Pan, et al., Phys. Rev. Lett. **86**, 4435–4438 2001.

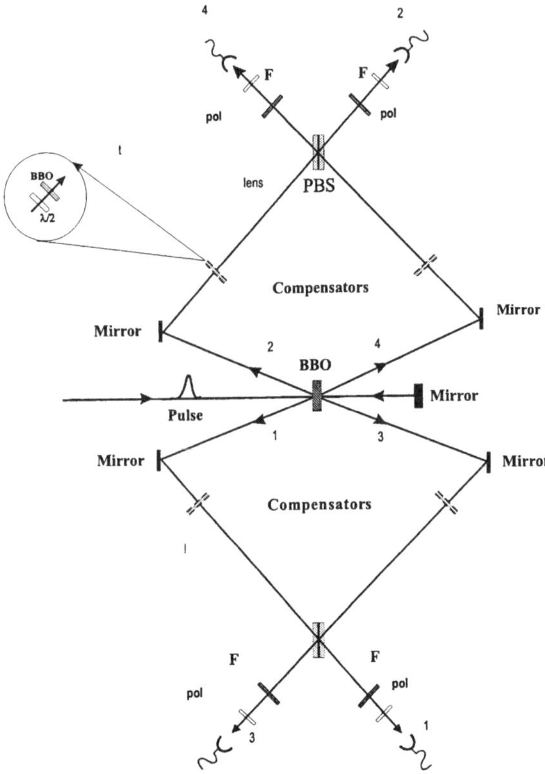

Figure 3. Experimental setup for Pan et al. purification. Two independent EPR pairs are produced via SPDC. Photons on the paths 2(1) and 4(3) must arrive simultaneously and spatially mode-matched. A four-fold coincidence guarantees the purification.

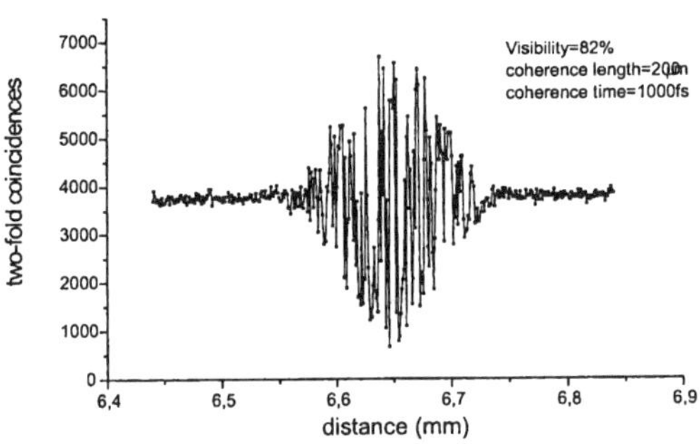

Figure 4. The experimental result proves that there is indeed an overlap of well-matched photons which are well matched. The high instability of the system is seen here, underscoring the premium on phase stability.

DETERMINISTIC REMOTE OPERATIONS: A STATE-OPERATOR APPROACH

BERRY GROISMAN, BENNI REZNIK
School of Physics and Astronomy, Tel Aviv University, Tel Aviv 69978, Israel
E-mail: groisman@post.tau.ac.il

YAKIR AHARONOV
School of Physics and Astronomy, Tel Aviv University, Tel Aviv 69978, Israel
and
Department of Physics, University of South Carolina, Columbia, SC 29208

We present a systematic method for constructing deterministic remote operations on single and multiple systems. The resources needed for an operation on one two-level system are one ebit and a bidirectional communication of two cbits. Our results follow from the properties of a hybrid state-operator object ("stator"), which describes quantum correlations between states and operations.

1 Introduction

The question about types of nonlocal operations which can be generated using a given resource of entangled states and classical communication was recently analyzed.[1,2,3,4,5]

The purpose of this article is to present a systematic approach for constructing a class of deterministic remote unitary transformations, and remote interactions between several distributed systems. We assume that the parties share entangled states and are allowed to perform any local operations and (bidirectional) classical communication.

Our approach relies on the properties of a new hybrid object which we introduce in Sec. 2. This object describes quantum correlations between states of one party, say Alice, and operations acting on an arbitrary state of Bob. It turns out that certain remote operations can be translated to certain properties of this hybrid state-operator object, which we will refer to as a "stator". The possible remote operations are hence associated with properties of the stator alone and are independent of the nature of the state(s) upon which we intend to act remotely. By identifying the appropriate stator we are able to apply a remote operation on an arbitrary state(s).

2 Remote Unitary operations on two-level system

Suppose that Bob has a spin-half particle in the unknown state $|\Psi_B\rangle$ on which Alice and Bob wish to act with a unitary transformation described by a rotation $U_B = \exp[i\alpha\sigma_{n_B}]$ with $\sigma_{n_B}^2 = I_B$ and α an arbitrary real number. We will now show that this transformation can be performed, provided that the axis of rotation $\hat{n}_B$ is known to Bob, and the parameter α of rotation is know to Alice. To this end, they start by using a shared ebit

$$\frac{1}{\sqrt{2}}\Big(|0_a 0_b\rangle + |1_a 1_b\rangle\Big) \otimes |\Psi_B\rangle. \tag{1}$$

Here we denote by the small letters, a and b, the shared ancillary entangled systems of Alice and Bob respectively. Bob starts by performing a CNOT interaction (with respect to σ_{n_B}) between the qubit (b) and his state $|\Psi_B\rangle$, described by the unitary transformation

$$U_{bB} = |0_b\rangle\langle 0_b| \otimes I_B + |1_b\rangle\langle 1_b| \otimes \sigma_{n_B}. \tag{2}$$

This yields the state

$$\frac{1}{\sqrt{2}}\Big(|0_a 0_b\rangle \otimes I_B + |1_a 1_b\rangle \otimes \sigma_{n_B}\Big)|\Psi_B\rangle. \tag{3}$$

Next Bob performs a measurement of σ_x of the entangled qubit to project out a certain value. The resulting state is now

$$\frac{1}{2}(|0_b\rangle \pm |1_b\rangle) \otimes \Big(|0_a\rangle \otimes I_B \pm |1_a\rangle \otimes \sigma_{n_B}\Big)|\Psi_B\rangle. \tag{4}$$

Bob informs Alice of the result of his measurement by sending Alice one classical bit of information. When $\sigma_x = -1$ Alice performs a trivial π-rotation around the $\hat{z}$ axis and flips the $-$ sign to a $+$ sign. The resulting state of the system is now given by

$$\frac{1}{\sqrt{2}}\Big(|0_a\rangle \otimes I_B + |1_a\rangle \otimes \sigma_{n_B}\Big)|\Psi_B\rangle. \tag{5}$$

(Particle b is now disentangled from the particles a and B and we will not give it any further consideration.)

Now Alice performs on her qubit a unitary transformation

$$U_a = e^{i\alpha\sigma_{x_a}}. \tag{6}$$

This yields

$$\frac{1}{\sqrt{2}}\Big(|0_a\rangle \otimes e^{i\alpha\sigma_{n_B}} + |1_a\rangle \otimes \sigma_{n_B} e^{i\alpha\sigma_{n_B}}\Big)|\Psi_B\rangle, \tag{7}$$

i.e., the state of Alice's particle a is correlated with two different transformations on Bob's particle B. By measuring the particle a in z-basis Alice will obtain $e^{i\alpha\sigma_{n_B}}$ acted on B if $\sigma_{z_a} = +1$ or $\sigma_{n_B} e^{i\alpha\sigma_{n_B}}$ acted on B if $\sigma_{z_a} = -1$. In the last case she needs to inform Bob that he must perform a trivial π-rotation, $U_\pi = e^{i\frac{\pi}{2}\sigma_{n_B}}$, which corrects for the extra σ_{n_B} above. This completes the process.

The resources that Alice and Bob require for remote rotation are hence one ebit of shared entanglement and two cbits. For both cbits we have that $p(1) = p(0) = 1/2$, i.e., they are unbiased. Therefore, the exchanged classical communication contains no information on the state of Bob or the angle of rotation.

3 The Stator

We can interpret Eq. (5) as an object $\mathcal{S} = |0_A\rangle \otimes I_B + |1_A\rangle \otimes \sigma_{n_B}$ which acts on Bob's particle B. We call this object a state-operator ("stator"), because it describes quantum correlations between states on Alice's side and operators acting on Bob's system.
This (2-level) stator $\mathcal{S}$ satisfies the *eigenoperator equation:*

$$\sigma_{x_A}\mathcal{S} = \sigma_{n_B}\mathcal{S}. \tag{8}$$

As straightforward consequence $e^{i\alpha\sigma_{x_A}}\mathcal{S} = e^{i\alpha\sigma_{n_B}}\mathcal{S}$. This relation already indicates why stators can be useful for generating remote operations. We note that a unitary operation of Alice gives rise to a similar unitary operation acting on Bob's side.

The purpose of introducing this object is twofold: First, stators simplify considerably the construction of remote unitary operations and interactions via entanglement by providing us with a systematic general approach that can be easily generalized to an arbitrary number of n-level systems. Second, we found that these objects assist us to develop an intuition regarding remote operations that may turn out helpful in other problems.

4 Operations on multiple systems

Consider next the case in which Bob's side has N distinguishable 2-level (spin-half) separate systems in some arbitrary state $|\Psi_{B_{1\ldots N}}\rangle$. The N systems may be distributed to N different remote spatially-separated locations denoted by B_i. To examine the operations possible by our method we further assume that we distribute between Alice and the B_i's a set of N maximally-entangled pairs. As before each B_i has the choice of fixing the local axis of rotation which fixes N generators $\sigma_{n_{B_i}}$, $i = 1, \ldots, N$.

We can repeat the preparation of a stator $\mathcal{S}_i$ for each spin separately. The total stator is then

$$\mathcal{S}_{tot} = \otimes_{i=1}^{N}\Big(|0_{a_i}\rangle \otimes I_{B_i} + |1_{a_i}\rangle \otimes \sigma_{n_{B_i}}\Big). \tag{9}$$

The above stator satisfies an eigenoperator equations $\sigma_{x_i}\mathcal{S}_{tot} = \sigma_{B_i}\mathcal{S}_{tot}$. However, because the different N generators commute, we also have that any *product* of separate eigenoperators is also an eigenoperator. The total number of eigenoperators is then

$$\sum_{m=1}^{N} C_N^m = 2^N - 1. \tag{10}$$

It then follows that Alice has the freedom to select the $2^N - 1$ angles that generate rotations and interactions between the spins.

For example, for two remote spins systems Alice can use two ebits and four cbits to generate the interaction $U_{B_1,B_2} = e^{i\alpha\sigma_{B_1}\sigma_{B_2}}$. Here the local axes of rotation, $\bar{n}_i$ ($\sigma_{B_i} = \bar{n}_i \cdot \bar{\sigma}_{B_i}$), are determined locally by two local observers $B_{1,2}$, and the coupling strength α is controlled by Alice.

The most general remote operation for the case $N = 3$ becomes

$$U_B = \exp\left[i \sum_{m=1}^{3} \alpha_m \sigma_{B_m} + i\frac{1}{2} \sum_{m \neq n} \beta_{mn} \sigma_{B_m} \sigma_{B_n} + i\gamma \sigma_{B_1} \sigma_{B_2} \sigma_{B_3}\right]. \tag{11}$$

5 Conclusion

We presented a systematic method for constructing deterministic remote operations on single and multiple 2-level systems. This method may be generalized to systems of arbitrary dimensions.[6] Our approach requires bidirectional classical communication of unbiased bits between the parties and leaves the control over the generators that act on each system in the hands of the local observers. In this way the control over the full structure of the unitary operation is split between several remote observers. It is also worth mentioning that when the local information is kept secret, the operations cannot be achieved using teleportation-like schemes.

To facilitate the construction of remote operations we have introduced a new object — the stator — that describes correlations between states of one system and operations acting on an arbitrary state of another remote system.

Acknowledgments

The research was supported in part by grant 62/01-1 of the Israel Science Foundation, established by the Israel Academy of Sciences and Humanities and by the Israel MOD Research and Technology Unit.

References

1. D. Collins, N. Linden and S. Popescu, *Phys. Rev.* A **64**, 032302 (2001).
2. J. Eisert, K. Jacobs, P. Papadopoulos, M. B. Plenio, *Phys. Rev.* A **62**, 052317 (2000).
3. J. I. Cirac, W. Dür, B. Kraus and M. Lewenstein, *Phys. Rev. Lett.* **86**, 544 (2001); W. Dür, and J. I. Cirac, *Phys. Rev.* A **64**, 012317 (2001).
4. S. F. Huelga, J. A. Vaccaro, A. Chefles and M. B. Plenio, *Phys. Rev.* A **63**, 042303 (2001); S. Huelga, M.B. Plenio and J. V. Vaccaro, quant-ph/0107110.
5. C.-P. Yang and J. Jea-Banacloche, quant-ph/0107100.
6. B. Reznik, Y. Aharonov, and B. Groisman, *Phys. Rev.* A **65**, 032312 (2002).

QUANTUM OPTOMECHANICAL TELEPORTATION

STEFANO MANCINI, DAVID VITALI AND PAOLO TOMBESI *

INFM, Dipartimento di Fisica, Università di Camerino, 62032 Camerino, Italy

We study the possibility of using optomechanical coupling to teleport a quantum state onto a *macroscopic* mechanical oscillator.

1 Introduction

Quantum state teleportation is undoubtedly one of the most fascinating developments of quantum information processing.[1] Teleportation of an unknown quantum state is its immaterial transport through a classical channel employing one of the most puzzling resources of quantum mechanics: entanglement.[2] A variety of possible experimental schemes have been proposed and a few of them partially realized in the discrete-variable case involving the polarization state of single photons.[3] Successful achievement has also been obtained in the continuous-variable case of an optical field.[4] However, the tantalizing problem of extending quantum teleportation to the macroscopic scale remains open.

Recently, in the perspective of demonstrating and manipulating the quantum properties of bigger and bigger objects,[5] it has been shown[6] how it is possible to entangle two massive macroscopic oscillators, like movable mirrors, by using radiation pressure effects. The creation of such an entanglement at the macroscopic level suggests an avenue for achieving teleportation of a continuous-variable state of a radiation field onto the vibrational state of a mirror.

We consider the usual situation in which an unknown quantum state of a radiation field is prepared by a verifier (Victor) and sent to an analyzing station (Alice). Then we shall provide a protocol that enables Alice to teleport the continuous-variable quantum state of the radiation onto a collective vibrational degree of freedom of a macroscopic, perfectly reflecting, mirror placed at a remote station (Bob).

2 The model

We first consider the well known[7] model of an optical cavity with a totally-reflecting end mirror of mass M, which can move undergoing harmonic oscillations at frequency Ω. A single, laser driven, radiation mode inside the cavity, described by the ladder operators $\hat{a}$, $\hat{a}^\dagger$, optomechanically couples to the moving mirror. The Hamiltonian of such a system is[7]

$$\hat{H} = \hbar\Delta\hat{a}^\dagger\hat{a} - \hbar\Omega\hat{b}^\dagger\hat{b} - \hbar G\left(\alpha\hat{a}^\dagger + \alpha^*\hat{a}\right)\left(\hat{b} + \hat{b}^\dagger\right) , \tag{1}$$

*PRESENTING AUTHOR

where Δ is the detuning between the resonant cavity mode frequency and the frequency of the driving field, whose amplitude is α. Furthermore, $\hat{b}$, $\hat{b}^\dagger$ describe the oscillatory mode of the moving mirror, and G is the optomechanical coupling constant. By choosing $\Delta = -\Omega$ and making the rotating wave approximation (RWA) we end up with an effective Hamiltonian

$$\hat{H}_{eff} = -\hbar G \left(\alpha \hat{a}^\dagger \hat{b}^\dagger + \alpha^* \hat{a} \hat{b} \right) . \tag{2}$$

The Hamiltonian (2) exactly corresponds to that of a parametric amplifier[8] and leads to perfect EPR correlations between the two modes,[2] i.e., between the intracavity radiation field and the mirror's motion. Thus, it would be a suitable Hamiltonian to prepare the two-party state shared by Alice and Bob in the standard continuous-variable teleportation protocol.[9]. Nevertheless, as is usual in teleportation, the two subsystems should be far apart from each other. Thus, if Bob handles the moving mirror, the radiation field should reach (the distant) Alice's site. On one hand, the field leaving the cavity could reach Alice, but in such a case the optomechanical interaction is on during Alice's local operations as well. This has not to be the case for standard teleportation. On the other hand, one could suddenly open the cavity letting the radiation field completely reach Alice, but this is not practical.

We, instead, consider an optomechanical model without the cavity which could be more easily implemented. In particular we consider an intense laser beam impinging on the surface of the mirror, whose radiation pressure realizes an optomechanical coupling.[10] In the limit of small mirror displacements, and in the interaction picture with respect to the free Hamiltonian of the electromagnetic field and the mirror displacement field $\hat{x}(\mathbf{r}, t)$ (we only consider the motion of the mirror along the spatial direction x, orthogonal to its reflecting surface, being $\mathbf{r}$ the coordinate on the mirror surface), one has the following Hamiltonian[11]

$$\hat{H} = - \int d^2\mathbf{r} \, \hat{P}(\mathbf{r}, t) \hat{x}(\mathbf{r}, t) , \tag{3}$$

where $\hat{P}(\mathbf{r}, t)$ is the radiation pressure force.[10] The entire continuum of electromagnetic modes with positive longitudinal wave vector q, transverse wave vector $\mathbf{k}$, and frequency $\omega = \sqrt{c^2(k^2 + q^2)}$ (c being light speed in vacuum) contributes to the radiation pressure force. The mirror displacement $\hat{x}(\mathbf{r}, t)$ is generally given by a superposition of many Gaussian acoustic modes.[11] However, a single-mode description can be adopted whenever detection is limited to a frequency bandwidth that includes only a single mechanical resonance. The simplest choice is the fundamental Gaussian mode with a small waist w, a very large mechanical quality factor Q, a small effective mass M and frequency Ω[11]

$$\hat{x}(\mathbf{r}, t) = \sqrt{\frac{\hbar}{2M\Omega}} \left[\hat{b} e^{-i\Omega t} + \hat{b}^\dagger e^{i\Omega t} \right] \exp(-r^2/w^2) . \tag{4}$$

The interaction Hamiltonian (3) assumes a simple form if we average it over the time interval corresponding to the inverse of the spectral resolution of the optical detection apparatus at Alice's station, $\Delta\nu_{det} \ll \Omega$. This permits us to neglect all terms oscillating faster than Ω (RWA). We also consider an intense driving laser polarized parallel to the mirror surface, with power $\wp$, bandwidth $\Delta\nu_{mode}$ centered around the carrier frequency ω_0, impinging on the mirror with an angle of incidence ϕ_0. If it is sufficiently intense, it can be treated as classical, and it is reflected undisturbed by the mirror. At the same time, it strongly couples the acoustic mode with the two back-scattered sideband modes at frequencies $\omega_1 = \omega_0 - \Omega$ (with annihilation operator $\hat{a}_1$) and $\omega_2 = \omega_0 + \Omega$ (with annihilation operator $\hat{a}_2$). Thus, we end up with the three-mode, effective interaction Hamiltonian[12]

$$\hat{H}_{eff} = -i\hbar\chi(\hat{a}_1\hat{b} - \hat{a}_1^\dagger\hat{b}^\dagger) - i\hbar\theta(\hat{a}_2\hat{b}^\dagger - \hat{a}_2^\dagger\hat{b}), \tag{5}$$

where $\chi = \cos(\phi_0)\sqrt{\wp\Delta\nu_{det}^2\omega_1/2M\Delta\nu_{mode}c^2\Omega}$ and $\theta = \chi\sqrt{\omega_2/\omega_1}$. The physical process described by this interaction Hamiltonian is very similar to a stimulated Brillouin scattering.[8]

3 Teleportation protocol

Eq. (5) contains two interaction terms: the first one, between modes $\hat{a}_1$ and $\hat{b}$, is a parametric-type interaction analogous to Eq.(2),[8] and it is able to generate the EPR-like entangled state which has been used in the continuous-variable teleportation experiment of Ref. 4. The second interaction term, between modes $\hat{a}_2$ and $\hat{b}$, is a beam-splitter-type interaction,[8] which may disturb the entanglement between modes $\hat{a}_1$ and $\hat{b}$ generated by the first term. Therefore, we have to modify the standard teleportation protocol for continuous variables,[9] in order to minimize the disturbing effects of the beam-splitter-type term in Eq. (5).

First of all, the driving mode is filtered out after reflection on the mirror allowing only the modes $\hat{a}_1$ and $\hat{a}_2$ to reach Alice's station (or it could be used by Alice for her measurement purposes). Then Alice performs a heterodyne measurement[8] on the mode $\hat{a}_2$, projecting it onto a coherent state of complex amplitude α. Alice and Bob are left with an entangled state for the optical mode a_1 and the vibrational mode b, conditioned on this measurement result. Realistic initial conditions are given by the vacuum state for the sideband modes, and a thermal state at temperature T, with mean vibrational number $\overline{n} = [\coth(\hbar\Omega/2k_BT) - 1]/2$ for the mechanical mode. In this case, the conditioned entangled state is Gaussian, and characterized by the correlation matrix (independent of α, affecting only first-order moments) $\Gamma_{i,j} = \langle\hat{\mathbf{v}}_i\hat{\mathbf{v}}_j + \hat{\mathbf{v}}_j\hat{\mathbf{v}}_i\rangle/2$ with $\hat{\mathbf{v}} = (\hat{X}_{a_1}, \hat{P}_{a_1}, \hat{X}_b, \hat{P}_b)$ and $\hat{X}_{a_1} = (\hat{a}_1 + \hat{a}_1^\dagger)/\sqrt{2}$, $\hat{P}_{a_1} = -i(\hat{a}_1 - \hat{a}_1^\dagger)/\sqrt{2}$, $\hat{X}_b = (\hat{b} + \hat{b}^\dagger)/\sqrt{2}$, $\hat{P}_b = -i(\hat{b} - \hat{b}^\dagger)/\sqrt{2}$. The coefficients $\Gamma_{i,j}$, depend on the interaction time t,[12] which is determined by the time duration of the driving laser pulse.

Once Alice has performed the heterodyne measurement on $\hat{a}_2$, the standard protocol[9] for continuous-variable quantum teleportation holds. The quantum channel between Alice and Bob is established via the two-mode entangled state described by the correlation matrix Γ. Alice mixes the radiation mode provided by Victor, whose unknown state she wants to teleport, with her part of entangled state (the mode a_1), on a balanced beam splitter. She then carries out homodyne detection at each output port, thereby measuring two commuting quadratures $\hat{X}_+ = \hat{X}_{in} + \hat{X}_{a_1}$ and $\hat{P}_- = \hat{P}_{in} - \hat{P}_{a_1}$. The final step at the sending station is to transmit two classical pieces of information, resulting from the combination of the heterodyne and homodyne measurements she performed, to the receiving terminal. Thus, Bob's local operation (displacement) depends on all Alice's measurements (X_+, P_-, α). To actuate the phase-space displacement, Bob can use again the radiation pressure force. In fact, if the mirror is illuminated by a bichromatic intense laser field with frequencies ϖ_0 and $\varpi_0 + \Omega$, employing again Eq. (3) and the RWA, one is left with an effective interaction Hamiltonian $H_{act} \propto \hat{b}e^{-i\varphi} + \hat{b}^\dagger e^{i\varphi}$, where φ is the relative phase between the two frequency components. Any phase space displacement of the mirror vibrational mode can be realized by using $\hat{H}_{act}$.

When Victor provides an input Gaussian state characterized by a 2×2 symmetric covariance matrix Γ^{in}, the output state at Bob site is again Gaussian, with a covariance matrix Γ^{out}. The input-output relation for these matrices is given by[12]

$$\Gamma_{11}^{\text{out}} = \Gamma_{11}^{\text{in}} + (\Gamma_{11} + 2\Gamma_{13} + \Gamma_{33}) \,, \tag{6}$$

$$\Gamma_{12}^{\text{out}} = \Gamma_{12}^{\text{in}} + (\Gamma_{14} - \Gamma_{12} + \Gamma_{34} - \Gamma_{23}) \,, \tag{7}$$

$$\Gamma_{22}^{\text{out}} = \Gamma_{22}^{\text{in}} + (\Gamma_{22} - 2\Gamma_{24} + \Gamma_{44}) \,. \tag{8}$$

The fidelity F of the described teleportation protocol, defined as the overlap between the input and the output state, can be written as

$$F = (1 + \Gamma_{11} + 2\Gamma_{13} + \Gamma_{33})^{-1} \,, \tag{9}$$

where we have specialized to the case of an input coherent state. In such a case, the upper bound for the fidelity achievable with only classical means is $F = 1/2$.[13] Figure 1 shows the fidelity as a function of the (scaled) interaction time t for different values of the initial mean number $\overline{n}$ of thermal phonons of the mirror acoustic mode. The remarkable result shown is that the maximum value, $F_{max} \simeq 0.85$, is well above the classical bound $F = 0.5$ and it is, surprisingly, independent of the initial temperature of the acoustic mode. However, the time interval within which the classical communication between Alice and Bob has to be done, and the phase space displacement has to be made by Bob, becomes shorter and shorter with increasing temperature. The vibrational state projected by Alice's Bell measurement, indeed, heats up in a time of the order of $(\gamma_m \overline{n})^{-1}$, where γ_m is the mechanical damping constant. The effects of mechanical damping can be instead neglected during the back-scattering process stimulated by the intense laser

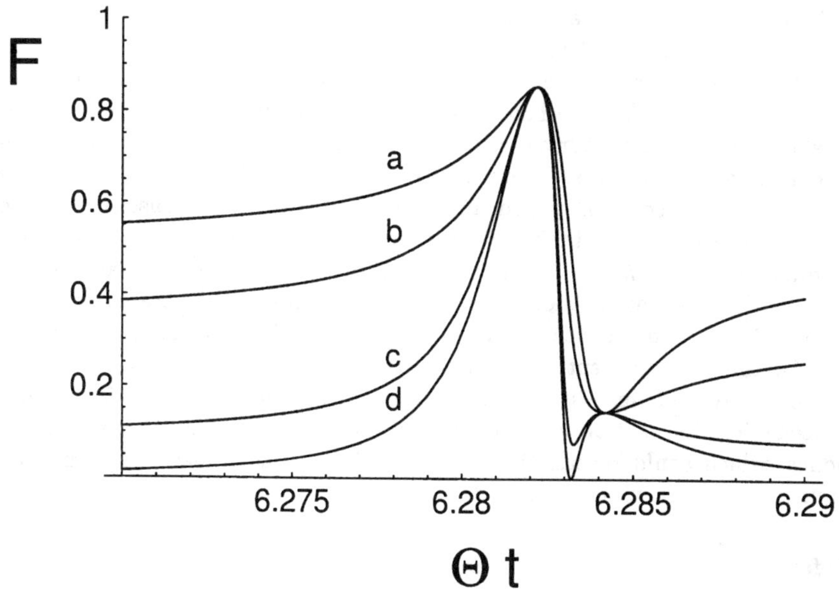

Figure 1. Fidelity F versus the scaled time Θt. Curves a, b, c, d are for $\bar{n} = 0$, 1, 10, 10^3, respectively. The fidelity is periodic in the interaction time, and we show only one of all possible time windows where F reaches its maximum.

beam. In fact, mechanical damping rates of about $\gamma_m \simeq 1\,\text{Hz}$ are available, and therefore negligible with respect to the typical values of the coupling constants $\chi \simeq \theta \simeq 5 \times 10^5\,\text{Hz}$, and $\Theta = \sqrt{\theta^2 - \chi^2} \simeq 10^3\,\text{Hz}$, determining the Hamiltonian dynamics. Such values are obtained with the following choice of parameters: $\wp = 10\,\text{W}$, $\omega_0 \sim 2 \times 10^{15}\,\text{Hz}$, $\Omega \sim 5 \times 10^8\,\text{Hz}$, $\Delta\nu_{det} \sim 10^7\,\text{Hz}$, $\Delta\nu_{mode} \sim t^{-1} \sim 10^3\,\text{Hz}$, and $M \sim 10^{-10}\,\text{Kg}$, which are those used in Fig. 1. These parameters are slightly different from those of already performed optomechanical experiments.[14] However, using a thinner silica crystal and considering higher frequency modes, the parameters we choose could be obtained (see also Ref. 15). These choices show the difficulties one meets in trying to extend genuine quantum effects such as teleportation into the macroscopic domain.

4 Conclusions

We have proposed a simple scheme to teleport an unknown quantum state of the radiation field onto a macroscopic, collective vibrational degree of freedom of a massive mirror. The basic resource of entanglement is attained by means of the optomechanical coupling provided by the radiation pressure.

This scheme could be easily extended in principle to realize a transfer of quantum information between two massive objects.

It is worth remarking that the present teleportation scheme also provides a very powerful *cooling* mechanism for the acoustic mode. As matter of fact, its effective number of thermal excitations soon after the two homodyne measurements at Alice station becomes $\overline{n}_{eff} = 1 + \Gamma_{11} + 2\Gamma_{13} + \Gamma_{33}$. It reduces to $\overline{n} + 1$ in absence of entanglement, where 1 represents the noise introduced by the protocol. Instead, the optomechanical interaction for a proper time permits to achieve $\overline{n}_{eff} = 0.17$, i.e., an 80% reduction of thermal noise at once, at the moment of Alice's measurement, thanks to the entanglement.

Finally, for what concerns the experimental verification of teleportation, that is, the measurement of the final state of the acoustic mode, one can consider a second, intense "reading" laser pulse, and exploit again the optomechanical interaction given by Eq. (5), where now a_1 and a_2 are meter modes, which could reveal, through heterodyne measurements, information about the acoustic mode's state.[16]

References

1. C. H. Bennett, *et al.*, Phys. Rev. Lett. **70**, 1895 (1993).
2. A. Einstein, *et al.*, Phys Rev. **47**, 777 (1935).
3. D. Bouwmeester, *et al.*, Nature (London) **390**, 575 (1997); D. Boschi, *et al.*, Phys. Rev. Lett. **80**, 1121 (1998); T. Jennewein, *et al.*, Phys. Rev. Lett. **88**, 017903 (2002).
4. A. Furusawa, *et al.*, Science **282**, 706 (1998).
5. B. Julsgaard, *et al.*, Nature (London) **413**, 400 (2001).
6. S. Mancini, *et al.*, Phys. Rev. Lett. **88**, 120401 (2002).
7. S. Mancini and P. Tombesi, Phys. Rev. A **49**, 4055 (1994).
8. L. Mandel and E. Wolf, *Optical Coherence and Quantum Optics*, (Cambridge Univ. Press, Cambridge, 1995).
9. L. Vaidman, Phys. Rev. A **49**, 1473 (1994); S. L. Braunstein and H. J. Kimble, Phys. Rev. Lett. **80**, 869 (1998).
10. P. Samphire, *et al.*, Phys. Rev. A **51**, 2726 (1995).
11. M. Pinard, *et al.*, Eur. Phys. J. D **7**, 107 (1999).
12. S. Mancini, *et al.*, quant-ph/0207094.
13. S. L. Braunstein, *et al.*, Phys. Rev. A **64**, 022321 (2001).
14. I. Tittonen, *et al.*, Phys. Rev. A **59**, 1038 (1999); P. F. Cohadon, *et al.*, Phys. Rev. Lett. **83**, 3174 (1999).
15. A. N. Cleland and M. L. Roukes, Nature (London) **392**, 160 (1998).
16. T. Briant, *et al.*, quant-ph/0207049.

A UNIFIED AXIOMATIC APPROACH TO INFORMATION CONTENT OF PHYSICAL STATES

VLATKO VEDRAL
Optics Section, The Blackett Laboratory, Imperial College, London SW7 2BZ, England

ELHAM KASHEFI
Department of Computing, Imperial College, London SW7 2BZ, England

We revisit the axiomatic approach to thermodynamics originally introduced by Giles. We show that his formal theory is general enough to capture both quantum and classical notions of the information content of physical states. In particular, we show that local manipulations of entanglement in quantum information theory and adiabatic transformations of states in thermodynamics have the same underlying mathematical structure. We discuss other possible applications of the Giles' mathematical structure to statistical mechanics and classical information theory of Shannon.

1 Introduction

In this paper we present a general mathematical formalism that we believe can describe key information processing aspects based on different physical theories. This formulation was originally introduced by Giles for the purpose of giving a rigorous mathematical framework for classical thermodynamics.[1] In particular, he wanted to formalize the statement of the second law of thermodynamics and derive a unique quantity, called entropy, which orders thermodynamical states according to their mutual accessibility. His mathematical formalism can be presented in a way that is completely divorced from any underlying physical basis, and this is what potentially allows us to apply it to scenarios other than thermodynamics. In this paper we will first review Giles' original application to thermodynamics, and then show that the same formalism can be interpreted to capture entanglement manipulations in quantum information processing.[2] This allows us to prove in a novel way the uniqueness of the measure of entanglement for pure bipartite states. Because classical information processing can be seen as a special case of quantum information processing, this formalism should also allow us to derive the classical (Shannon) entropy[3] within the same framework, but from the dynamical perspective. This highlights the close relationship between information processing and statistical mechanics in general, as we discuss at the end of the paper, along with other open problems suggested by our work.

2 The Formal Theory

An ideal physical theory should consist of two independent parts: a mathematical theory and a set of rules for interpreting the various mathematical objects involved in the theory. By formalizing a physical theory in such a way as to divorce it from the physical interpretation, it is possible to derive a mathematical structure that may be useful in a completely different physical setting to the original one. We give a brief summary of Giles' mathematical theory[1] and then describe how one can capture thermodynamics and entanglement manipulations with the axioms introduced in this section. The "physical" motivation behind the axioms will then become clearer.

We study a non-empty set $\mathcal{S}$, whose elements are called *states*, in which two operations, $+$ and $\rightarrow$, are defined. The goal is to derive a unique ordering over the states with some particular conditions. In what follows states are denoted by : $a, b, c, \ldots$. In the following axioms we will omit the phrase "for all ...".

Axioms 1-5

(1) *The operation + is associative and commutative.*

(2) $a \rightarrow a$.

(3) $a \rightarrow b \;\&\; b \rightarrow c \Longrightarrow a \rightarrow c$.

(4) $a \rightarrow b \Longleftrightarrow a + c \rightarrow b + c$.

(5) $a \rightarrow b \;\&\; a \rightarrow c \Longrightarrow b \rightarrow c$ *or* $c \rightarrow b$.

A **process** is an ordered pair of states (a, b). The set of all processes is denoted by $\mathcal{P}$ and processes are denoted by $\alpha, \beta, \ldots$. We can extend definitions of $+$ and $\rightarrow$ to $\mathcal{P}$ as follows:

$$(a, b) + (c, d) = (a + c, b + d) \quad (1)$$
$$(a, b) \rightarrow (c, d) \Longleftrightarrow a + d \rightarrow b + c\,. \quad (2)$$

For simplicity, we also define a relation $\subset$ over $\mathcal{S}$. Given states a and b we write $a \subset b$ (and say that a is **contained** in b), if there exists a positive integer n and a state c such that

$$na + c \rightarrow nb \text{ or } nb \rightarrow na + c\ . \quad (3)$$

Informally, the above definition means that a state a is smaller than b if a requires the help of another state c to be converted to or derived from b. Now we can introduce an important class of states, internal states, which serve as a yardstick for ordering the states. A state e is an **internal state** if, given any state x, there exists a positive integer n such that $x \subset ne$. The other important classes of states are the sets of equilibrium and anti-equilibrium states. A state a is an **equilibrium state** if there exists no state b such that

$a \to b$ and $b \not\to a$. A state x is an **anti-equilibrium state** if there exists no state a such that $a \to x$ and $x \not\to a$.

Axioms 6-8

(6) *There exists an internal state.*

(7) *Given a process α, if there exists a state c such that for any positive real number ϵ there exists positive integers m, n and states x, y such that $m/n < \epsilon$, $x \subset mc$, $y \subset mc$, and $(x, y) + n\alpha \to 0$ then $\alpha \to 0$.*

(8) *If a is any state then there exists an anti-equilibrium state x such that $x \to a$. if x and y anti-equilibrium states then so $x + y$.*

We define a real-valued function for ordering the states as follows. An **entropy function**, S, satisfies the following properties:

$$\begin{aligned} &(i)\;\; S(a+b) = S(a) + S(b)\,, \\ &(ii)\;\; a \to b \;\&\; b \to a \Longleftrightarrow S(a) = S(b)\,, \\ &(iii)\;\; a \to b \;\&\; b \not\to a \Longleftrightarrow S(a) < S(b) \\ &(iv)\;\; S(x) = 0 \text{ for every anti-equilibrium state } x\,. \end{aligned} \tag{4}$$

To present the uniqueness theorem for entropy functions we need to define **non-equilibrium component of content function**, a real-valued function Q such that:

$$\begin{aligned} &(i)\;\; Q \text{ is a component of content function}\,, \\ &(ii)\;\; Q(x) = 0 \text{ for every anti-equilibrium state } x\,. \end{aligned} \tag{5}$$

Theorem: *Let S_1 be an entropy function. If Q is a non-equilibrium component of content and λ a positive real number then $\lambda S_1 + Q$ is an entropy function; moreover, any quasi entropy function S may be written in this form.*

This theorem, proved by Giles, states that the measure of order is unique up to an affine transformation. With this we complete the formal part of the theory and turn our attention to several applications. Note that the main point of the formalism is to give conditions under which we can *uniquely* order states of a certain set.

2.1 Thermodynamics

Here we briefly discuss how the formal model introduced in Sec. 2 describes the structure of thermodynamics. Consider S to be the set of all thermodynamical states (e.g., a state of a simple gas is defined once its temperature T and volume V are known, therefore we can say that $a = (T_a, V_a)$). The operation $+$ represents the physical operation of considering two systems together (but independently). Therefore it must naturally be associative and commutative. The operation $\to$ represents an adiabatic process which is meant to convert different physical states into each other. Like any other physical process, it should naturally be reflective and transitive as in axioms 2 and 3. Axiom 4, in the forward direction, is obvious: if state a can be converted into b then the presence of another state c should not alter this fact, i.e., we can convert a and c into b and c by converting a into b while doing nothing to c. In the backward direction, it says that if a process is possible with the aid of another state, then we, in fact, do not need this other state for the process. Thermodynamics deals with macroscopic systems with a large number of degrees of freedom (subsystems). It is in the "asymptotic" limit that this axiom becomes more natural. Finally, axiom 5 is the key property that allows us to compare different states and processes. It says that any two states that are accessible from a third state must be accessible to each other in at least one direction. Not being able to do so would lead to states that would be incomparable, as there would be no physical way of connecting them. Thus a unique way of ordering states would be impossible. Axiom 6 is necessary if we are to compare contents of different states in a unique way. Axiom 7 is the most complex axiom in the theory, although it is strongly motivated by the logic of thermodynamical reasoning. Loosely speaking, it states that if we can transform a into b with an arbitrarily small environmental influence, then this influence can be ignored. This, in some sense, introduces continuity into thermodynamical properties. Axiom 8 is self evident in thermodynamics. A reader interested in a more detailed physical interpretation of the axioms is advised to consult Giles' book.[1]

2.2 Entanglement

In order to describe entanglement manipulations[4,5] within Giles' formal theory, consider $\mathcal{S}$ to be the set of all quantum bipartite pure states and the operation $+$ to be the tensor product $\otimes$. The arrow will be defined in terms of transformations that convert bipartite states by only using local operations on the subsystems separately aided with classical communication between the subsystems (LOCC).[4,5] First, we give the definition of $\subset$ in the quantum setting and then give the precise definition of arrow in the spirit of axiom 7.
Definition. We say that a pure state a is contained in a pure state b, designated as $a \subset b$, iff there exists an integer n and a state c such that either of the following two cases is valid

$$\begin{aligned} &\text{i)} \quad (\forall\epsilon)(\exists\Phi \in \mathbf{LOCC}) : ||\Phi(a^{\otimes n} \otimes c) - b^{\otimes n}|| < \epsilon \qquad (6)\\ &\text{ii)} \quad (\forall\epsilon)(\exists\Phi \in \mathbf{LOCC}) : ||\Phi(b^{\otimes n}) - a^{\otimes n} \otimes c|| < \epsilon \ . \end{aligned}$$

Thus we say that a quantum state a is contained within a state b if, with the help of some other state c, a can be transformed by LOCC into b. Now we define what we mean by a transformation of one quantum state into another.
Definition. We say that a pure state a can be converted into a pure state b,

designated as $a \to b$, iff

$$(\forall\epsilon)(\exists c)(\forall\delta)(\exists n, m \in N,\ \ \Phi \in \mathbf{LOCC} \text{ and } x, y \in \mathcal{S}) \quad (7)$$
$$\text{such that } m/n < \delta\ ,\ x \subset mc\ ,\ y \subset mc \text{ and}$$
$$||\Phi(a^{\otimes n} \otimes x) - b^{\otimes n} \otimes y|| < \epsilon\ .$$

It is important to note that the direction of arrow will reverse in the case of entanglement manipulations. Product states act as equilibrium states in the sense that LOCCs cannot create entanglement out of them and the space of product (disentangled) states is invariant under LOCCs. Likewise, maximally entangled states act as anti-equilibrium states, in the sense that LOCCs naturally tend to destroy entanglement and therefore move "away" from this set. Now, a real-valued function E defined for every state is a **entanglement measure** if

- $E(a \otimes b) = E(a) + E(b)$.
- If $a \to b$ & $b \to a$, then $E(a) = E(b)$.
- If $a \to b$ & $b \to a$, then $E(a) > E(b)$.
- $E(a) = 1$ if a is a maximally entangled state.

Giles' proof of uniqueness of an ordering function is constructive and can be found in Ref. 1. In the case of entanglement manipulations this leads to the following definition for a measure of entanglement:

$$E(a) = \inf\{m/n : y \subset e^{\otimes m} y \to a^{\otimes n} \otimes x\}\,, \quad (8)$$

where e is any maximally entangled state. For a more detailed exposition the reader is encouraged to consult Ref. 2.

2.3 Elementary Classical Information

As a very simple realization of Giles' theory we comment on how to capture the most elementary notion of classical information, namely that the information carried by an event happening with probability p is $\log p$. For this, the states are real numbers $0 < r \leq 1$, $+$ represents multiplication of real numbers, and the arrow is the relation "less then or equal". It is very simple to check that all the axioms are satisfied. Following Giles' construction, we can derive a unique measure for this case, which is then proportional to $\log(p)$. An open question now is to find dynamical processes that naturally lead to this realization and derive the more general Shannon entropy $-\sum_i p_i \log(p_i)$.

3 Discussion and Conclusions

We have shown that the Giles' formal theory not only describes the mathematical foundation of thermodynamics but can also describe entanglement manipulations. This approach to uniqueness of measure of entanglement for pure bipartite states differs from the existing method, in which one looks for a minimal number of conditions for a measure to satisfy such that one could single out a unique one.[6,7]

A natural question to ask is whether the same model can be applied to classical information theory and derive the classical entropy from the dynamical perspective, rather than the usual axioms of Shannon.[3] This could be done by defining the states to be probability distributions (much like in statistical mechanics, where these would correspond to occupation probabilities for the different energy levels). In addition, the arrow would be defined by a stochastic map taking one probability distribution into another one. This is in the same spirit as Penrose's formulation of statistical mechanics.[8] However, in order to derive a unique measure, the notion of arrow needs to be generalized to satisfy all the axioms. We believe this can be done in an asymptotic way by converting multiple copies of the same probability distribution with the aid of another (arbitrary) catalyzer probability distribution. This conjecture remains to be proven. This would not only show that there are deep mathematical connections between thermodynamics, statistical mechanics and information theory, both classical and quantum, but also that they all in fact arise from the same mathematical framework presented here.

Acknowledgments

This work is funded by EPSRC, the European grant EQUIP (contract IST-1999-11053) and Elsag Spa.

References

1. R. Giles, "Mathematical Foundations of Thermodynamics", *International Series of Monographs on Pure and Applied Mathematics*, eds: I. N. Sneddon, M. Stark and S. Ulma, (Pergamon Press, 1964); for a similar approach see the more recent paper by E. H. Lieb and J. Yngvason, *Geom. Funct. Anal.* 334 Part 1 Sp. Iss. SI (2000).
2. V. Vedral and E. Kashefi, *Phys. Rev. Lett.* **89**, 037903 (2002).
3. C. E. Shannon and W. Weaver, *The Mathematical Theory of Communication* (University of Illinois Press, Urbana, IL 1949).
4. V. Vedral, *Rev. Mod. Phys.* **74**, 197 (2002).
5. M. Horodecki, *Quant. Inf. Comp.* **1** 3 (2001).
6. O. Rudolph, *J. Math. Phys.* **42**, 2507 (2001).
7. M. J. Donald, M. Horodecki and O. Rudolph, quant-ph/0105017.
8. O. Penrose, *Foundations of Statistical Mechanics*, (Pergamon Press, 1970).

Part II
Entangled Photons

APPLICATION, GENERATION, AND TEST OF SYMMETRIC ENTANGLED COHERENT STATES

OSAMU HIROTA
Research Institute of Tamagawa University, Tokyo, Japan, and CREST, JST:Japan Science and Technology.
E-mail: hirota@lab.tamagawa.ac.jp

STEVEN. J. VAN ENK
Bell Laboratories, Lucent Technologies, Murray Hill, NJ.USA
E-mail: vanenk@research.bell-labs.com

HIDEO MABUCHI
Norman Bridge Laboratory of Physics, California Institute of Technology, Pasadena CA. USA
E-mail: hmabuchi@caltech.edu

A scheme for generating symmetric, entangled, propagating coherent states with maximum entanglement is proposed, and a method for testing the generated state is discussed.

1 Introduction

Entangled states based on orthogonal states have received much attention in the study of entanglement problems. Our concern, however, is to manipulate an entangled state, based on non-orthogonal states, which might be used as a qubit in quantum optical communication and computing. Discussion of a class of entangled coherent states, which is representative of non-orthogonal states, was first given by Sanders.[1] A fundamental and natural question to ask in this regard is the following. What is the maximum entanglement for an entangled state that is based on non-orthogonal states? To answer this question, a set of entangled states of the coherent states of two bosonic modes—the so-called quasi-Bell states—was defined. It was shown[2,3] that some of these states have one ebit of entanglement, independent of the coherent-state amplitude. The quasi-Bell states have an interesting and potentially useful property in quantum information processing, as shown below and in Refs. 4,5. It is natural, therefore, to seek a generation method for these remarkable states. In this report, we present such a generation method, (using cavity QED initiated by the second author), and we discuss problems in non-locality testing of such states.

2 Entanglement-assisted communication

Let us show one interesting application example of the quasi-Bell states,

$$\begin{aligned}
|\Psi_1\rangle_{AB} &= h_1(|\alpha\rangle_A|-\alpha\rangle_B + |-\alpha\rangle_A|\alpha\rangle_B) \\
|\Psi_2\rangle_{AB} &= h_2(|\alpha\rangle_A|-\alpha\rangle_B - |-\alpha\rangle_A|\alpha\rangle_B) \\
|\Psi_3\rangle_{AB} &= h_3(|\alpha\rangle_A|\alpha\rangle_B + |-\alpha\rangle_A|-\alpha\rangle_B) \\
|\Psi_4\rangle_{AB} &= h_4(|\alpha\rangle_A|\alpha\rangle_B - |-\alpha\rangle_A|-\alpha\rangle_B),
\end{aligned} \tag{1}$$

where the $\{h_i\}$ are normalization constants. The classical communication capacity of two coherent-state signals, $\{|\alpha\rangle, |-\alpha\rangle\}$, is given by

$$C_H = -\frac{1}{2}(1+\kappa)\log(1+\kappa)/2 - \frac{1}{2}(1-\kappa)\log(1-\kappa)/2, \tag{2}$$

where $\kappa = \langle\alpha|-\alpha\rangle$. If Alice and Bob share $|\Psi_2\rangle_{AB}$, then Alice can place the total system in any of the four quasi-Bell states by modulating her qubit with the appropriate unitary operator. The capacity of this system exceeds C_H, even when both systems are constrained to use the same energy. This entanglement-assisted capacity increase is an interesting property of quantum information theory.

3 Generation of propagating entangled coherent states

Producing a quasi-Bell state in propagating modes is essential for sharing entanglement between remote locations, such as in the preceding quantum communication example. For a propagating mode, the state $|\alpha\rangle$ should be understood as a continuous-mode coherent state. In a simple one-dimensional picture, one can define creation and annihilation operators $b^\dagger(\omega)$ and $b(\omega)$ for each mode frequency ω. An eigenstate of the annihilation operator

$$b(\omega)|\{\tilde{\alpha}(\omega)\}\rangle = \tilde{\alpha}(\omega)|\{\tilde{\alpha}(\omega)\}\rangle \tag{3}$$

can always be written as a single-mode coherent state by introducing the new mode operator

$$c_1 = \int d\omega\, \phi_1(\omega)^* b(\omega), \tag{4}$$

with $\phi_1(\omega) = \tilde{\alpha}(\omega)/\sqrt{\int d\omega\, |\tilde{\alpha}(\omega)|^2}$. The state $|\{\tilde{\alpha}(\omega)\}\rangle$ is an eigenstate of c_1 with eigenvalue $\alpha = \sqrt{\int d\omega\, |\tilde{\alpha}(\omega)|^2}$. With c_1 properly defined, this is what we will mean by a coherent state $|\alpha\rangle$ in all that follows. Equivalently, we may work in the time domain by introducing inverse Fourier transforms,

$$b(t) = \frac{1}{\sqrt{2\pi}}\int d\omega\, b(\omega)\exp(-i\omega t), \tag{5}$$

$$\phi_1(t) = \frac{1}{\sqrt{2\pi}} \int d\omega\, \phi_1(\omega) \exp(-i\omega t), \tag{6}$$

$$c_1 = \int dt\, \phi_1(t)^* b(t). \tag{7}$$

This way one can define independent modes by introducing a complete orthonormal set of functions $\{\phi_i(t)\}$ satisfying

$$\int dt\, \phi_i(t)\phi_j^*(t) = \delta_{ij} \tag{8}$$

$$\sum_i \phi_i^*(t)\phi_i(t') = \delta(t - t'). \tag{9}$$

Let us consider here the ideal version of a scheme to produce a propagating entangled coherent state. The idea is inspired by Gheri and Ritsch.[6] Consider an optical Fabry-Perot cavity with two identical mirrors characterized by a decay rate r. The cavity mode is described by a single-mode annihilation operator $c(t)$. If that mode is weakly coupled to a single two-level atom, and the cavity is driven by two input fields $b_{in}^{(1)}(\omega)$ and $b_{in}^{(2)}(\omega)$, a standard calculation shows that the Fourier-transformed annihilation operator of the cavity mode, $c(\omega)$, is

$$c(\omega) = \frac{\sqrt{r}(b_{in}^{(1)}(\omega) + b_{in}^{(2)}(\omega))}{i(\omega - \omega_c) - r + g^2/(i(\omega - \omega_A) - \tau/2)}, \tag{10}$$

where ω_c is the resonance frequency of the cavity, ω_A is the resonance frequency of the atom, g is the coupling between atom and cavity mode, and τ is the spontaneous decay rate of the atom. The output fields emanating from the cavity are, according to standard input-output theory, determined by

$$b_{out}^{(k)}(\omega_c) = b_{in}^{(k)}(\omega_c) + \sqrt{r}c(\omega), \tag{11}$$

for $k = 1, 2$. For an atom far off resonance with the cavity, or to be more precise, when $|\omega_c - \omega_A| \gg g^2/r$, all light at $\omega = \omega_c$ will be transmitted:

$$b_{out}^{(1)}(\omega_c) = -b_{in}^{(1)}(\omega_c), \quad b_{out}^{(2)}(\omega_c) = -b_{in}^{(2)}(\omega_c). \tag{12}$$

On the other hand, if the atomic resonance frequency is chosen such that $\omega_A = \omega_c + \tau/2$, and we are in the strong coupling regime where $g^2 \gg r\tau$ prevails, then the cavity resonance is shifted by so much that all light at $\omega = \omega_c$ will be reflected:

$$b_{out}^{(1)}(\omega_c) = b_{in}^{(1)}(\omega_c), \quad b_{out}^{(2)}(\omega_c) = b_{in}^{(2)}(\omega_c). \tag{13}$$

Now we consider an atom in an equal superposition $(|g_1\rangle + |g_2\rangle)/\sqrt{2}$ of two nondegenerate ground states, where there is a resonant coupling from $|g_1\rangle$ at the cavity frequency, but $|g_2\rangle$ is off resonance. Given two coherent input fields, $|\alpha\rangle_k$ for $k = 1, 2$, at frequency $\omega = \omega_c$, the atom-cavity system will then enact the transformation

$$(|g_1\rangle + |g_2\rangle)|\alpha\rangle_1|\alpha\rangle_2 \to |g_1\rangle|-\alpha\rangle_1|-\alpha\rangle_2 + |g_2\rangle|\alpha\rangle_1|\alpha\rangle_2. \qquad (14)$$

If one subsequently performs a measurement on the atom in the $|\pm\rangle = (|g_1\rangle \pm |g_2\rangle)/\sqrt{2}$ basis, an entangled coherent state $|\Psi_4\rangle_{AB}$ will have been generated if the the outcome is $|-\rangle$. The probability to get that measurement outcome is $P_- = \frac{1}{2}[1-\exp(-4|\alpha|^2)]$, which tends to zero for $\alpha \to 0$. With a probability $P_+ = 1 - P_-$ one produces the state $|\Psi_3\rangle_{AB}$.

4 Non-locality test

We need a physical scheme to check whether or not the output from the preceding atom-cavity system is really the desired entangled coherent state. In general, a non-locality test is used for such a check. First we need two mode-parity operators. The ideal system uses projectors that are based on even and odd coherent states: $\Pi_1 = |\text{even}\rangle\langle\text{even}|$, $\Pi_2 = |\text{odd}\rangle\langle\text{odd}|$. This corresponds to a photon counter that discriminates between even and odd numbers of photons. Alternatively, we can use the Kennedy measurement process from optical communications: $\Pi_1 = I - |-\alpha\rangle\langle-\alpha|$, $\Pi_2 = |-\alpha\rangle\langle-\alpha|$. This corresponds to an energy detector which does not require even/odd photon-number discrimination.

Let us define the following Bell observable, based on the above POVM:

$$\Pi = \Pi_{A1} \otimes \Pi_{B1} - \Pi_{A1} \otimes \Pi_{B2} - \Pi_{A2} \otimes \Pi_{B1} + \Pi_{A2} \otimes \Pi_{B2}. \qquad (15)$$

Here, we have to make the measurement process rotate, but, unfortunately, it does not work. So instead we employ unitary operators, which correspond to rotation, for each field mode, $U_A(\theta_A)$, and $U_B(\theta_B)$. As a result, quantum correlations are given as follows:

$$E(\theta_{Ai}, \theta_{Bj}) = \mathrm{Tr}[U_B^\dagger(\theta_{Bj})U_A^\dagger(\theta_{Ai})\rho_{AB}U_A(\theta_{Ai})U_B(\theta_{Bj})\Pi] \qquad (16)$$

where $i, j = 1$ or 2. The Clauser-Horne-Shimony-Holt form of Bell's inequality is then as follows,

$$S = |E(\theta_{A1}, \theta_{B1}) + E(\theta_{A1}, \theta_{B2}) + E(\theta_{A2}, \theta_{B1}) - E(\theta_{A2}, \theta_{B2})| \le 2. \qquad (17)$$

In order to demonstrate the above inequality, it is essential to realize the unitary rotation operator for even and odd coherent states, or also coherent states. That is, if we use Kennedy's scheme, we need *a rotation for coherent states.* Although rotation for orthogonal states is easily defined, there is a certain restriction for non-orthogonal states. We apply here a channel operator method to discuss a possibility for constructing such a rotation. Let $\{|\psi_{in}(i)\rangle\}, \{|\psi_{out}(i)\rangle\}$ be input and output states for the quantum gate. As a quantum channel, the quantum gate is described by a channel operator,

$$\mathcal{L}\begin{pmatrix} |\psi_{in}(1)\rangle \\ |\psi_{in}(2)\rangle \end{pmatrix} = \begin{pmatrix} |\psi_{out}(1)\rangle \\ |\psi_{out}(2)\rangle \end{pmatrix}. \qquad (18)$$

A quantum channel satisfying $\mathcal{L}\mathcal{L}^\dagger = \mathcal{I}$ is said to be unitary. When the input states are orthogonal states, the general unitary channel can be described by

$$\mathcal{L}_u = \begin{pmatrix} \hat{u}_{11} & \hat{u}_{12} \\ \hat{u}_{21} & \hat{u}_{22} \end{pmatrix} = \begin{pmatrix} \cos(\theta) & -i\sin(\theta)e^{i\phi} \\ -i\sin(\theta)e^{-i\phi} & \cos(\theta) \end{pmatrix}. \tag{19}$$

However, for non-orthogonal input states, the preceding description of a unitary channel has the restriction $\phi = \pm\pi/2$. Thus, in principle, we can construct a rotation for coherent states via the quantum channel

$$\mathcal{L}\begin{pmatrix} |\alpha\rangle \\ |-\alpha\rangle \end{pmatrix} = \begin{pmatrix} \cos(\theta)|\alpha\rangle + i\sin(\theta)|-\alpha\rangle \\ i\sin(\theta)|\alpha\rangle + \cos(\theta)|-\alpha\rangle \end{pmatrix}. \tag{20}$$

Now, we have to find the channel operator from a physical unitary operator or vice versa: $\mathcal{L} \longleftrightarrow U$. We have only one such example, which is known as Yurke-Stoler transform U_{YS}.[7] The Yurke-Stoler state is given by

$$U_{YS}|\alpha\rangle = \exp(-|\alpha|^2)\sum_n \frac{\alpha^n}{\sqrt{n}}\exp(-i\phi_n)|n\rangle, \tag{21}$$

where $\phi_n = \pi/4 - \pi n^2/2$, so that the above equation reduces to

$$U_{YS}|\alpha\rangle = |\Psi_{YS}\rangle = \frac{1}{\sqrt{2}}(|\alpha\rangle - i|-\alpha\rangle). \tag{22}$$

Thus, we have

$$\mathcal{L}_u = \begin{pmatrix} \frac{1}{\sqrt{2}} & \frac{-i}{\sqrt{2}} \\ \frac{-i}{\sqrt{2}} & \frac{1}{\sqrt{2}} \end{pmatrix}. \tag{23}$$

As a result, the rotation angle is fixed in this case, hence we need another idea for realizing an arbitrary angle of rotation which produces tunnelling phenomena.

Let us assume that our measurement scheme is constructed from even and odd coherent states, namely $|\text{even}\rangle = (|\alpha\rangle + |-\alpha\rangle)/\sqrt{2(1+\kappa)}$ and $|\text{odd}\rangle = (|\alpha\rangle - |-\alpha\rangle)/\sqrt{2(1-\kappa)}$. In this case,[8] the displacement operator may be regarded as the rotation operator for even and odd coherent states.

$$|\Psi\rangle = D(i\epsilon)\frac{1}{\sqrt{N}}(|\alpha\rangle + |-\alpha\rangle) = \frac{1}{\sqrt{N}}(e^{i\epsilon\alpha}|\alpha + i\epsilon\rangle + e^{-i\epsilon\alpha}|-\alpha + i\epsilon\rangle) \tag{24}$$

where $N = 2(1+\kappa)$. When $\epsilon \to 0$, $\alpha \to \infty$, and $\epsilon\alpha = \gamma$, it may seem that we can get

$$|\Psi(\gamma)\rangle = \cos(\gamma)|\text{even}\rangle + i\sin(\gamma)|\text{odd}\rangle. \tag{25}$$

However this argument is not valid. Let H_2 be the two-dimensional Hilbert space spanned by the orthogonal basis $\{|\text{even}\rangle, |\text{odd}\rangle\}$, and the domain of displacement operator. The range of the displacement operator is outside of H_2, i.e.,

$$D(i\epsilon)|\alpha\rangle = e^{i\epsilon\alpha}|\alpha + i\epsilon\rangle \notin H_2 \quad \text{and} \quad D(i\epsilon)|-\alpha\rangle = e^{-i\epsilon\alpha}|\alpha + i\epsilon\rangle \notin H_2. \tag{26}$$

So the displacement operator is not a unitary operator on H_2. In fact, the fidelity is,[9]

$$F = \lim_{\substack{\epsilon\to 0\\ \alpha\to\infty}} |\langle\Psi(\gamma)|\Psi\rangle|^2 = \cos^2(\gamma). \tag{27}$$

If we operate N-times as an W-H gate, then the fidelity becomes $F_N = \cos^{2N}(\gamma)$; we cannot interpret such an operation as rotation on H_2.

On the other hand, when one uses the projectors $|\text{even}\rangle\langle\text{even}|$ and $|\text{odd}\rangle\langle\text{odd}|$ as the non-locality test's measurement process, the measurement probabilities become,

$$|\langle\Psi|\text{even}\rangle|^2 = \frac{\exp(-\epsilon^2)}{(1+\kappa)^2}|\cos(\gamma)+\kappa|^2 \cong \cos^2(\gamma) \tag{28}$$

$$|\langle\Psi|\text{odd}\rangle|^2 = \frac{\exp(-\epsilon^2)}{(1+\kappa)^2}\sin^2(\gamma) \cong \sin^2(\gamma), \tag{29}$$

where the approximations are valid for $\epsilon \to 0$ and $\alpha \gg 1$. This represents a possible measurement for the non-locality experiment, but it requires photon counters that can discriminate between even and odd photon numbers and it involves undesirable high-power operation.

In summary, both schemes face difficulties impeding their experimental demonstration.

5 Conclusion

The maximally-entangled coherent state cannot be generated from a unitary process, a situation unlike that for the Yurke-Stoler state. We have proposed another scheme to generate a propagating maximally-entangled coherent state. In addition, we inspected difficulties that will be encountered applying a non-locality test to confirm the generation of these states.

References

1. B. C. Sanders, Phys. Rev. A **45**, 6811, (1992).
2. O. Hirota, and M. Sasaki, in *Quantum Communication, Computing, and Measurement 3*, (Kluwer/Plenum, New York, 2001).
3. S. van Enk and O. Hirota, Phys. Rev. A **64**, 022313, (2001).
4. X. Wang, Phys. Rev. A **64**, 022302, (2001).
5. H. Jeong, M. S. Kim, and J. Lee, Phys. Rev. A **64**, 052308, (2001).
6. K. M. Gheri, and H. Ritsch, Phys. Rev. A **56**, 3187, (1997).
7. B. Yurke. and D. Stoler, Phys. Rev.Lett. **57**, 13, (1986).
8. D. Wilson, H. Jeong, and M. S. Kim, J. Mod. Opt. **49**, 851, (2002).
9. S. Tatsuta and T. S. Usuda, *Proceedings of ISITA-2000*, (2000)

ULTRAFAST GENERATION OF TWO-PHOTON ENTANGLED STATES USING TWO NONLINEAR CRYSTALS

GIOVANNI DI GIUSEPPE,*[2] METE ATATÜRE,†[1] MATTHEW D. SHAW,[2] YING-TSANG LIU,[1] ALEXANDER V. SERGIENKO,[1,2] BAHAA E. A. SALEH,[2] AND MALVIN C. TEICH[1,2]

Quantum Imaging Laboratory,
[1]*Department of Physics and* [2]*Department of Electrical and Computer Engineering, Boston University, 8 Saint Mary's Street, Boston, MA 02215*
webpage: http://www.bu.edu/qil/

Quantum interference experiments with two-photon states generated by spontaneous parametric downconversion of an ultra-short pump pulse impinging on two nonlinear optical crystals are investigated. In particular, we analyze the influence of the frequency and wave-vector distributions on the visibility of the fourth-order polarization interference pattern and its connection with the polarization entanglement.

Photon pairs generated in spontaneous parametric downconversion (SPDC) have recently been employed in a number of interesting applications, such as quantum cryptography, teleportation, computation, metrology, and imaging. As such, considerable attention has been devoted to the design of improved sources of downconverted light. A number of different experimental configurations have been used to generate various types of quantum states, including those entangled in frequency, wave-vector, and polarization. We have recently demonstrated the utility of a model which considers entanglement in frequency and wave vector concurrently,[1] and extended this model to generation media with inhomogeneous distributions of nonlinearity.[2] In this work we present an extension of the latter model to the case of ultrafast pump pulses, and discuss the effect on fourth-order quantum interference patterns.

Let us consider the two-photon state generated in SPDC with an arbitrary pump-pulse profile and an arbitrary longitudinal distribution of nonlinearity. The general form of a two-photon state at the output of the generation medium is

$$|\Psi\rangle = \int d\mathbf{k}_o\, d\mathbf{k}_e\; \Phi(\mathbf{k}_o,\mathbf{k}_e)\; \hat{a}_o^\dagger(\mathbf{k}_o)\hat{a}_e^\dagger(\mathbf{k}_e)|0\rangle, \tag{1}$$

where $\mathbf{k}_{o,e}$ are three-dimensional wave vectors for the signal (ordinarily polarized) and idler (extraordinarily polarized) fields, respectively.

Within the limits of first-order time-dependent perturbation theory, the state function is found[1] to be $\Phi(\mathbf{k}_o,\mathbf{k}_e) = \mathcal{E}_p(\mathbf{k}_o+\mathbf{k}_e)\,\tilde{\chi}[\Delta(\mathbf{k}_o,\mathbf{k}_e)]$, where

*EMAIL: GDG@BU.EDU. ALSO AT: ISTITUTO ELETTROTECNICO NAZIONALE *G. FERRARIS*, STRADA DELLE CACCE 91, I-10153 TORINO, ITALY.
†ALSO AT: 4. PHYSIKALISCHES INSTITUT UNIVERSITÄT STUTTGART PFAFFENWALDRING 57 70550 STUTTGART, GERMANY

$\mathcal{E}_p(\mathbf{k})$ is the complex-amplitude profile of the pump field, $\tilde{\chi}[\Delta(\mathbf{k}_o, \mathbf{k}_e)] = \int dz\, \chi(z) \exp[i\Delta(\mathbf{k}_o, \mathbf{k}_e)]$ is the Fourier transform of the second-order nonlinearity distribution $\chi(z)$ along the longitudinal axis, and $\Delta(\mathbf{k}_o, \mathbf{k}_e) = \mathbf{k}_p - \mathbf{k}_o - \mathbf{k}_e$ is the wave vector mismatch function inside the generation medium. Note that the state function $\Phi(\mathbf{k}_o, \mathbf{k}_e)$ cannot be written as the product of two functions $\Phi_o(\mathbf{k}_o)\Phi_e(\mathbf{k}_e)$, and thus the state is said to be entangled in three-dimensional wave vector, or concurrently entangled in frequency and transverse wave vector.

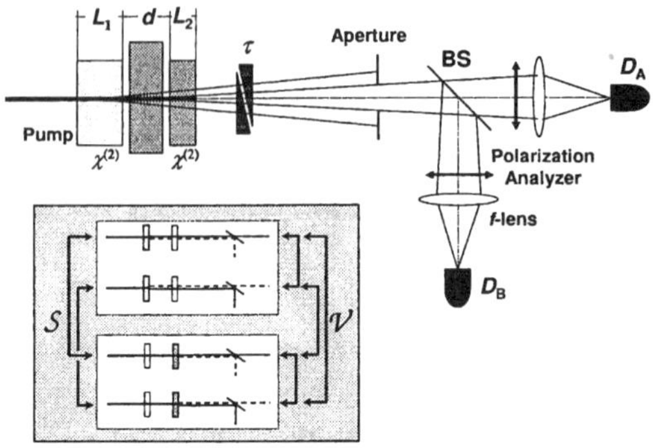

Figure 1. Schematic of a typical experimental arrangement. Collinear type-II SPDC is generated in two bulk crystals separated by a birefringent linear medium. The interferometer consists of a relative time delay τ introduced between signal and idler photons, a non-polarizing beam splitter, and two polarization analyzers. The inset at lower left illustrates the four relevant probability amplitudes for photon pairs from the first and second crystal to be transmitted and reflected from the beam splitter, and how these amplitudes enter into the expressions $\mathcal{S}$ and $\mathcal{V}$ of Eqs. (4) and (5).

We now consider the propagation of the downconverted light generated using the crystal configuration described above through an arbitrary linear optical system to a pair of single-photon detectors, as illustrated in Fig. 1. The probability amplitude for detecting the photon pair at the space-time coordinates $x_A = (\mathbf{x}_A, t_A)$ and $x_B = (\mathbf{x}_B, t_B)$ is given by

$$\mathcal{A}(x_A, x_B) = \int d\mathbf{k}_o\, d\mathbf{k}_e\ \Phi(\mathbf{k}_o, \mathbf{k}_e)\ \Big[\mathcal{H}_A(\mathbf{k}_o)\ \mathcal{H}_B(\mathbf{k}_e)\ e^{-i(\omega_o t_A + \omega_e t_B)} + $$
$$+ \mathcal{H}_A(\mathbf{k}_e)\ \mathcal{H}_B(\mathbf{k}_o)\ e^{-i(\omega_e t_A + \omega_o t_B)}\Big], \quad (2)$$

where the transfer function $\mathcal{H}_{A,B}(\mathbf{k})$ describes the propagation of a mode $\mathbf{k}$ through the optical system from the output plane of the generation medium to detection planes $\mathbf{x}_A$ and $\mathbf{x}_B$, respectively.

Consider SPDC from two crystals of equal thickness L, dispersion coefficients $D = 1/u_o - 1/u_e$ and $\Lambda = 1/u_p - (1/u_o + 1/u_e)/2$ (here $u_{p,o,e}$ are the group velocities for the pump, signal, and idler fields inside each crystal), separated by a birefringent linear medium of thickness d. Let the birefringence of the medium impose a relative temporal delay τ_d between the signal and idler photons generated in the first crystal. When pairs from such a source are allowed to propagate through the interferometer of Fig. 1, the coincidence rate for slow bulk detectors (which integrate over space and time) can be written within the paraxial and quasi-monochromatic field approximations as

$$\mathcal{R}_c(\tau) = \mathcal{R}_\infty \left\{1 + \mathcal{S}(\tau) + v_{pol}\, \mathcal{V}(\tau)\right\}, \tag{3}$$

where τ is the relative optical-path delay between photons, the constant factor $\mathcal{R}_\infty$ is the "shoulder rate", and the polarization analyzer projection factor $v_{\rm pol} = 2\mu_{\rm Ao,Be}\, \mu_{\rm Bo,Ae}/[\mu^2_{\rm Ao,Be} + \mu^2_{\rm Bo,Ae}]$ with $\mu_{ij,lm}$ $(i,l = \text{A, B and } j,m = \text{e, o})$ is the projection of the (i,l)-th photon polarization onto the (j,m)-th analyzer polarization. The interference functions $\mathcal{S}$ and $\mathcal{V}$ are given by

$$\mathcal{S} = 2\epsilon \frac{\rho}{1+\rho^2} \int d\xi\; \Pi_{0,1}(\xi)\; \Pi_{0,1}\left[\xi - \left(1 + \frac{\tau_d}{DL}\right)\right] \cdot \\ \cdot\, \mathcal{G}^{(0)}\left(\xi; \frac{\tau}{DL}\right) \mathcal{C}_p\left[\frac{\Lambda L}{2}\left(1 + \frac{\tau_d}{DL}\right)\right] \cos(\Delta' d) \tag{4}$$

and

$$\mathcal{V}(\tau) = \frac{1}{1+\rho^2} \int d\xi\; \Pi_{0,1}(\xi)\; \Pi_{0,1}\left(2\frac{\tau}{DL} - \xi\right) \cdot \\ \cdot\, \mathcal{G}^{(1)}\left(\xi; \frac{\tau}{DL}\right) \mathcal{C}_p\left[\Lambda L\left(\xi - \frac{\tau}{DL}\right)\right] + \\ + \frac{\rho^2}{1+\rho^2} \int d\xi\; \Pi_{0,1}(\xi)\; \Pi_{0,1}\left[2\frac{\tau}{DL} - 2\left(1 + \frac{\tau_d}{DL}\right) - \xi\right] \cdot \\ \cdot\, \mathcal{G}^{(2)}\left(\xi; \frac{\tau}{DL}\right) \mathcal{C}_p\left[\Lambda L\left(\xi - \frac{\tau}{DL} + \left(1 + \frac{\tau_d}{DL}\right)\right)\right] + \\ + 2\epsilon \frac{\rho}{1+\rho^2} \int d\xi\; \Pi_{0,1}(\xi)\; \Pi_{0,1}\left[2\frac{\tau}{DL} - \left(1 + \frac{\tau_d}{DL}\right) - \xi\right] \cdot \\ \cdot\, \mathcal{G}^{(12)}\left(\xi; \frac{\tau}{DL}\right) \mathcal{C}_p\left[\Lambda L\left(\xi - \frac{\tau}{DL} + \frac{1}{2}\left(1 + \frac{\tau_d}{DL}\right)\right)\right] \cos(\Delta' d), \tag{5}$$

where ρ is the acceptance angle of the interferometer, Δ' is the wave vector mismatch in the inter-crystal medium, $\mathcal{C}_p(t)$ is the temporal autocorrelation of the pump field and the spatiotemporal interference functions $\mathcal{G}^{(j)}(\xi; \frac{\tau}{DL})$ are defined in a previous work.[2]

This equation predicts two deviations from the familiar single-mode theory of interferometry with SPDC. The presence of transverse wave vectors leads to spatial distinguishability between signal and idler photons at the detector plane, and an attendant loss of interference visibility. Similarly, pumping with ultrafast pulses leads to spectral distinguishability between photons, which also leads to reduced visibility.

Figure 2 shows, for a quasi-monochromatic cw pump field, a plot of the visibility function $\mathcal{V}$ where the delay is fixed at the point of maximum interference DL, as a function of the system aperture size r (determining the acceptance angle ρ) and the distance d between crystals where the linear medium separating the crystals is taken to be air. In the limit of very thin crystals, small apertures, and small separation distances, the photons are spatially indistinguishable and Eq. (3) reduces to the conventional single-mode theory.

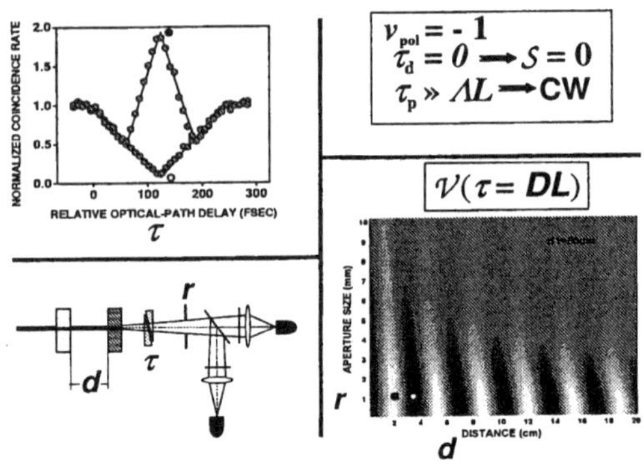

Figure 2. Quantum interference patterns obtained with a cw pump field and two 0.5-mm-long BBO crystals with parallel optical axes separated by an air gap. The lower right inset shows the visibility function $\mathcal{V}(\tau = DL)$ as a function of crystal separation d and aperture diameter r. Note the periodicity in d and decay in r. The upper left inset is a reproduction of experimental data from a previous work, with a fixed acceptance angle $\rho = 3.3$ mrad.

We have reported a model of quantum interference patterns from degenerate collinear type-II SPDC with an arbitrary longitudinal distribution of nonlinearity and an arbitrary pump profile. The model treats a state concurrently entangled in frequency and transverse wave vector. In the case of two crystals separated by an air gap, the structure of the observed quantum interference pattern is seen to depend on the optical path length between the two crystals, the acceptance angle of the optical system, and the bandwidth of the pump.

References

1. M. Atatüre, G. Di Giuseppe, M. D. Shaw, A. V. Sergienko, B. E. A. Saleh, and M. C. Teich Phys. Rev. A **65**, 023808 (2002); *ibid.* **66**, 023822 (2002).
2. G. Di Giuseppe, M. Atatüre, M. D. Shaw, A. V. Sergienko, B. E. A. Saleh, and M. C. Teich Phys. Rev. A **66**, 013801 (2002).

POLARIZATION-ENTANGLED PHOTON PAIRS OBVIATE NEED FOR CALIBRATION IN MATERIAL CHARACTERIZATION

KIMANI C. TOUSSAINT, JR., MATTHEW T. CORBO,
AYMAN F. ABOURADDY, ALEXANDER V. SERGIENKO,
BAHAA E. A. SALEH, AND MALVIN C. TEICH

Quantum Imaging Laboratory, Departments of Electrical & Computer Engineering and Physics, Boston University, 8 *Saint Mary's Street, Boston, MA* 02215 – 2421, *USA*

E-mail: kimani@bu.edu

Quantum entanglement is a peculiar aspect of quantum mechanics that has baffled physicists and philosophers alike. Until recently, it has exclusively been used in many experiments to study the foundations of quantum mechanics. We show how entanglement can be harnessed to obtain ellipsometric data from materials without the need for calibration.

1 Introduction

Ellipsometry[1] is a well-established metrological technique used, particularly in the semiconductor industry, to determine the thickness and optical constants of thin films. The high accuracy required in measuring these parameters necessitates absolute calibration of both the source and the detector. As this is not attainable in practical settings, all ellipsometric techniques employ a reference sample for calibration.

In this paper, we show how quantum ellipsometry alleviates the aforementioned problem by using a two-photon polarization-entangled state generated by type-II spontaneous parametric downconversion (SPDC).[2,3] This is done in a simple setting with a minimal number of optical components.[4,5]

The quantum ellipsometer is illustrated in Fig. 1. A 406-nm cw Kr^+ laser (pump) beam illuminates a nonlinear optical crystal (NLC), beta-barium borate. Quantum mechanics predicts that some of the pump photons disintegrate into pairs, known as signal and idler, which conserve energy (frequency-matching) and momentum (phase-matching).[3,6] For our purposes, we choose the SPDC to be in a configuration known as 'type-II non-collinear'. 'Type-II' refers to the fact that the signal and idler photons have orthogonal polarizations; the term 'non-collinear' indicates that the signal and the idler photons are emitted in two different directions. The idler beam reflects off the sample of interest before it encounters a linear polarizer (A_1) followed by single-photon photodetector (D_1). The signal beam encounters a linear polarization analyzer (A_2), followed by a single-photon photodetector (D_2). The detectors, two avalanche photodiodes operating in the Geiger mode, are part of a circuit that records the coincidence rate of photon pairs. The sample is characterized by the parameters ψ and Δ: ψ is the ratio of the magnitudes

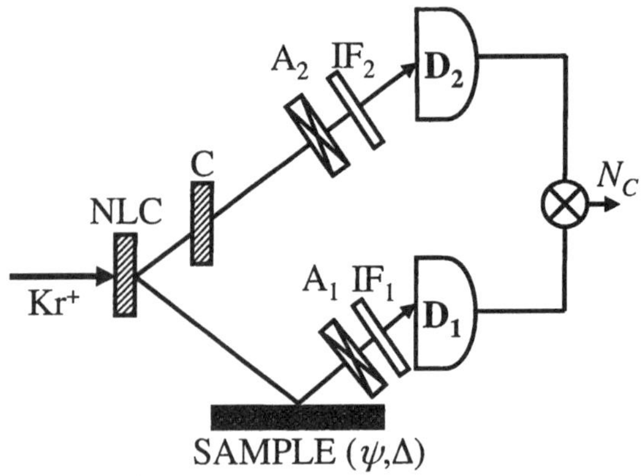

Figure 1. Polarization-entangled twin-photon ellipsometer. NLC stands for nonlinear crystal; C is a birefringent compensator; A_1 and A_2 are linear polarization analyzers; IF_1 and $IF2_2$ are interference filters; D_1 and D_2 are single-photon detectors; and N_c is the coincidence rate. The sample is characterized by the ellipsometric parameters ψ and Δ defined in the text.

of the sample reflection coefficients, R_H and R_V for the p- and s-polarized waves, respectively; Δ is the phase shift between them.

In order to select the degenerate twin photons centered at 812 nm, interference filters (IF_1 and IF_2) with 10-nm bandwidths were placed in front of each detector. Because of the birefringence of the NLC used to generate SPDC, the signal and idler photons emerge from the NLC with a relative time delay that one compensates for by placing an appropriate birefringent material (labelled C in Fig. 1) of suitable thickness in the signal and/or idler path.[2]

The non-classical source and the optical arrangement shown in Fig. 1 exhibit two features that circumvent the two problems noted above, i.e., calibration of the source and of the detector. The first characteristic of quantum ellipsometry is that the source is a twin-photon source; i.e., we are guaranteed on detection of a photon in one of the arms of the setup that its twin is in the other. The second characteristic is the polarization entanglement of the source. Polarization entanglement acts as an interferometer, encompassing both arms of our apparatus, thereby alleviating the need for calibrating the second detector in our coincidence scheme.[4,5]

It can be shown that the measured coincidence rate, N_c, is given by[4,5]

$$N_c = C[\tan(\psi)\cos^2(\theta_1)\sin^2(\theta_2) + \sin^2(\theta_1)\cos^2(\theta_2) \\ +2\sqrt{\tan(\psi)}\cos(\Delta)\cos(\theta_1)\cos(\theta_2)\sin(\theta_1)\sin(\theta_2)], \quad (1)$$

where the constant of proportionality C depends on the efficiencies of the

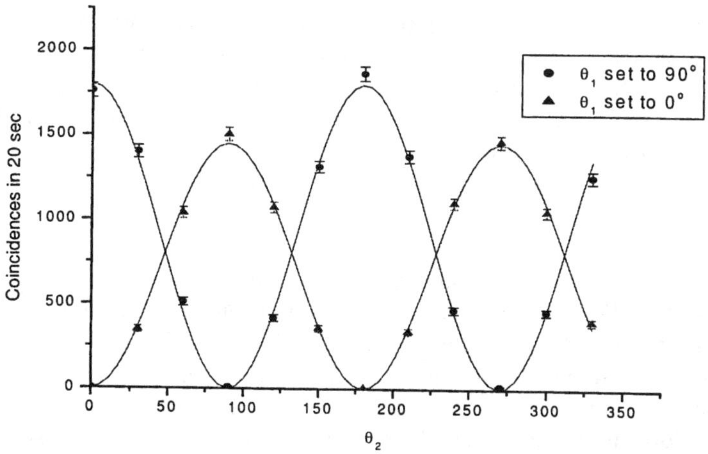

Figure 2. Interference patterns obtained from an experiment on a silicon sample.

detectors and the duration of accumulation of coincidences.[5]

2 Experimental Results

Preliminary experiments have shown that polarization-entangled photon pairs can be used to obtain values of ψ that are comparable to those obtained from traditional ellipsometers.

Using the experimental setup described earlier, a silicon (Si) sample was tested at an angle of incidence of 30°. First, the angle of the analyzer A_1, denoted θ_1, was set to 90° while θ_2 was scanned. Referring to Eq. (1), which, for θ_1=90°, reduces to

$$N_c = C\cos^2(\theta_2), \tag{2}$$

reveals that the amplitude of this curve provides the value for C. Second, θ_1 was set to 0° while θ_2 was again scanned. In this case, Eq. (1) reduces to

$$N_c = C[\tan(\psi)\sin^2(\theta_2)], \tag{3}$$

so that the amplitude of this function is equal to $C\tan(\psi)$. The resulting interference patterns are shown in Fig. 2. One can therefore determine ψ simply by dividing the two functions. Using this approach, ψ was determined to be $40.2 \pm .1°$ for our Si sample. The expected value for ψ at this angle of incidence is 40.4° in accordance with calculations carried out using the appropriate Sellmeier dispersion formula.[7,8]

Unfortunately, the interference patterns obtained using a technique similar to the one described above did not provide a reasonable value for Δ.

The main reason for this comes from the fact that the equations used to obtain ψ assumed that the quantum state of the light emitted by the NLC is a maximally-entangled pure state. In order to obtain Δ, Eq. (1) must include the dependence of the ellipsometric parameters on the actual state of the light that is available in practice.

3 Conclusion

We have shown that, by employing entangled-photon pairs that are generated by type-II SPDC in a non-collinear configuration, one can obtain absolute ellipsometric data from a reflective sample. The underlying physics that permits such ellipsometric measurements resides in the fact that fourth-order (coincidence) quantum interference of the photon pairs, in conjunction with polarization entanglement, emulates an idealized classical ellipsometric setup that utilizes a source and a detector that are both calibrated absolutely.

This work was supported by the Gates Foundation, the National Science Foundation, and by the Center for Subsurface Sensing and Imaging Systems (CenSSIS), an NSF engineering research center. A. V. Sergienko's e-mail address is alexserg@bu.edu.

References

1. R. M. A. Azzam and N. M. Bashara, *Ellipsometry and Polarized Light* (North-Holland, Amsterdam, 1977).
2. P. G. Kwiat, K. Mattle, H. Weinfurter, A. Zeilinger, A. V. Sergienko, and Y. Shih, Phys. Rev. Lett. **75**, 4337 (1995).
3. D. N. Klyshko, *Photons and Nonlinear Optics* (Gordon and Breach, New York, 1988).
4. A. F. Abouraddy, K. C. Toussaint, Jr., A. V. Sergienko, B. E. A. Saleh, and M. C. Teich, Opt. Lett. **26**, 1717 (2001).
5. A. F. Abouraddy, K. C. Toussaint, Jr., A. V. Sergienko, B. E. A. Saleh, and M. C. Teich, J. Opt. Soc. Am. B **19**, 656 (2002). Note that in Eqs. (13)–(15), $\tan^2(\psi)$ should be replaced by $\tan(\psi)$, and $\tan(\psi)$ should be replaced by $\sqrt{\tan(\psi)}$.
6. B. E. A. Saleh and M. C. Teich, *Fundamentals of Photonics* (Wiley, New York, 1991).
7. E. D. Palik, *Handbook of Optical Constants of Solids* (Academic Press, New York, 1985).
8. E. D. Palik, *Handbook of Optical Constants of Solids III* (Academic Press, New York, 1995).

TWO-FREQUENCY-MODE ENTANGLEMENT GENERATION INSIDE AN OPTICAL PULSE BY A NONLINEAR FIBER AND SPECTRAL PULSE SHAPING

MASAHIRO TAKEOKA AND MASAHIDE SASAKI
Communications Research Laboratory,
4-2-1 Nukui-kitamachi, Koganei-city, Tokyo 184-8795, Japan
E-mail: takeoka@crl.go.jp

We propose a novel fiber-based scheme for generating quadrature entanglement between a desired pair of frequency bands. The scheme is based on a nonlinear fiber, a spectral pulse shaper, and an adaptive feedback loop. We numerically evaluated the proposed system and it is predicted that at least −5 dB of the quadrature entanglement is created by preparing an appropriate initial phase spectrum.

1 Introduction

The optical Kerr effect for ultrashort pulses in fiber has been extensively studied for generation of nonclassical optical pulses such as photon-number squeezing or quadrature squeezing.[1] Recently, not only squeezing but also generation of entangled photon pairs has become attractive. Although schemes for entangled-pair generation have almost all been based on parametric down-conversion in $\chi^{(2)}$ materials,[2,3] novel ideas based on the Kerr nonlinearity in fiber have been suggested in several recent papers.[4,5,6] Fiber-based systems for entanglement generation have several advantages compared to $\chi^{(2)}$ systems, e.g., simple apparatus and integrability into present-day fiber-optic communication systems.

It is known that the Kerr nonlinearity causes multimode quantum correlations between intrapulse spectral modes of an optical pulse. Spälter et al.[7] worked on experimental characterization of the multimode entanglement between spectral modes inside a soliton pulse and was able to observe photon-number correlations. It was also recently shown that not only the physical parameters of a fiber, but also the initial pulse envelope strongly affects the generation of quantum correlations.[8] In this paper, we investigate the possibility of quadrature-entanglement generation between two selected frequency bands inside the pulse (the inset of Fig. 1) via a novel adaptive coherent-control system based on an ultrashort pulse laser, a Fourier pulse shaper, and a nonlinear fiber.

2 Proposed system

A schematic of our proposal is shown in Fig. 1. An ultrashort pulse is directed into a programmable pulse shaper in which the pulse envelope is spectrally manipulated.[9] Then the shaped pulse is sent to a fiber to generate

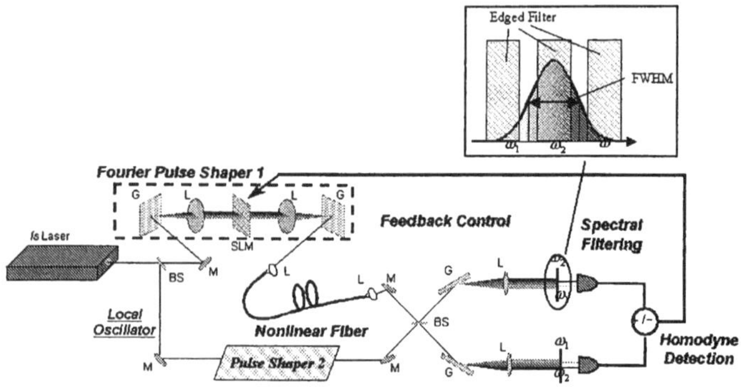

Figure 1. Schematic of the adaptive coherent-control system for generation of entanglement inside an optical pulse.

entanglement due to the Kerr nonlinearity and anomalous dispersion. With the Gaussian-state approximation, the condition for the amplitude and phase quadratures to be entangled is as follows:

$$\langle(\Delta\hat{X}_1 \pm \Delta\hat{X}_2)^2\rangle,\ \langle(\Delta\hat{Y}_1 \mp \Delta\hat{Y}_2)^2\rangle < \frac{1}{4} < \langle(\Delta\hat{X}_1 \mp \Delta\hat{X}_2)^2\rangle,\ \langle(\Delta\hat{Y}_1 \pm \Delta\hat{Y}_2)^2\rangle, \tag{1}$$

where $\Delta\hat{X}_{1,2}$ and $\Delta\hat{Y}_{1,2}$ are the linearized fluctuation operators for the quadratures $\hat{X}_{1,2} = (\hat{a}^\dagger_{1,2} + \hat{a}_{1,2})/\sqrt{2}$ and $\hat{Y}_{1,2} = i(\hat{a}^\dagger_{1,2} - \hat{a}_{1,2})/\sqrt{2}$, respectively. The suffixes 1 and 2 represent the selected two frequency modes of the pulse (the inset of Fig. 1), and $\hat{a}_{1,2}$ and $\hat{a}^\dagger_{1,2}$ are the annihilation and creation operators, respectively, for these two modes. The variances in (1) can be detected by spectrally-resolved homodyne detection with a 50/50 beam splitter and an appropriately-shaped local oscillator (LO) pulse as illustrated in Fig. 1. The two entangled frequency modes are extracted by the spectral filter before the photodetection. The observed entanglement is fed back to the mask of the pulse shaper to optimize the mask pattern. Simulated annealing (SA) is utilized as the optimization algorithm.

Propagation of the pulse in a nonlinear fiber and the spectrally-filtered homodyne detection can be analyzed by the back-propagation method,[10] which calculates the variances of quantum fluctuations within the linearization approximation. We consider the normalized optical field and neglect linear losses and the stimulated Raman scattering. The output field $\hat{a}_{\rm out}(t)$ from the edged spectral filter is given by the input-output relation

$$\hat{a}_{\rm out}(t) = (1-\Gamma(t))^{1/2}\,\hat{a}_{\rm in}(t) + \Gamma(t)^{1/2}\hat{c}(t), \tag{2}$$

where $\hat{a}_{\rm in}(t)$ and $\hat{c}(t)$ are the optical field before filtering and the vacuum field, respectively, and $\Gamma(t)$ is obtained from the bandpass-filter function $\tilde{\Gamma}(\omega)$.

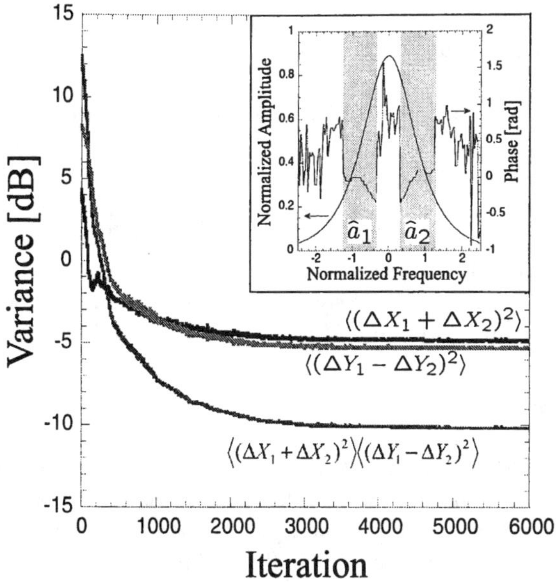

Figure 2. Optimization of the entanglement between two frequency modes inside the pulse by the simulated annealing method. The fiber propagation distance is 3 soliton periods.

The photon-number fluctuation detected by the spectrally-filtered homodyne detector is

$$\Delta\hat{n} = \frac{1}{2}\int [(1-\Gamma(t))\bar{a}_{\mathrm{LO}}(t)\Delta\hat{a}_0(L,t) + \mathrm{H.c.}]\,dt, \tag{3}$$

where $\Delta\hat{a}_0(L,t)$ is the quantum fluctuation of the fiber -propagated field to be measured, L is the fiber length, and $\bar{a}_{\mathrm{LO}}(t)$ is the classical envelope of the LO pulse. The variances of the quadratures in Eq. (1) can be observed by measuring $\langle\Delta\hat{n}^2\rangle$.

3 Numerical evaluation

In our simulation, the initial pulse was assumed to be in a coherent state with a classical envelope of sech(t). The phase mask of the pulse shaper supports the entire pulse spectrum with 128 pixels and 64 gray levels and is set to be zero modulation for all pixels at the beginning of the calculation. The SA algorithm is programmed to minimize the product of the squeezed variance $\langle(\Delta\hat{X}_1+\Delta\hat{X}_2)^2\rangle\langle(\Delta\hat{Y}_1-\Delta\hat{Y}_2)^2\rangle$. Figure 2 shows the result of iterated calculations for 4.7 normalized dispersion lengths of the fiber length L. It shows that the variances $\langle(\Delta\hat{X}_1 + \Delta\hat{X}_2)^2\rangle$ and $\langle(\Delta\hat{Y}_1 - \Delta\hat{Y}_2)^2\rangle$, which are 4.16 dB and 8.21 dB above the shot noise limit (SNL) initially, are clearly squeezed to −4.86 dB and −5.33 dB, respectively. The inset of Fig. 2 is the optimized initial spectrum that is directed into the fiber. The two gray-shaded sidebands are the frequencies of $\hat{a}_1$ and $\hat{a}_2$. By using the phase mask which generates the phase spectrum in the inset of Fig. 2 from the sech pulse, the squashed variances $\langle(\Delta\hat{X}_1 - \Delta\hat{X}_2)^2\rangle$ and $\langle(\Delta\hat{Y}_1 + \Delta\hat{Y}_2)^2\rangle$ are calculated to be 6.76 dB and 11.52 dB above the SNL, respectively. These variances do not reach the minimum uncertainty relation for $\langle(\Delta\hat{X}_1 + \Delta\hat{X}_2)^2\rangle$ and $\langle(\Delta\hat{Y}_1 - \Delta\hat{Y}_2)^2\rangle$. Since the fiber's nonlinearity is not the simple $\chi^{(2)}$ nonlinearity, the interactions inside a pulse do not directly correspond to the simple two-mode squeezing operator. Further theoretical consideration will be necessary to develop a clearer understanding of the interaction mechanism.[11]

4 Conclusion

We have proposed an alternative scheme for generation of frequency-band entanglement inside an ultrashort optical pulse. Once the optimal phase mask is obtained in our system, the frequency entangled pulse is easily generated by pulse shaping and fiber propagation. It provides a greatly simplified system for entanglement generation when compared to other schemes that utilize several cavities or an interferometer with severe requirements for mode or phase locking.

To share the generated entanglement, the pulse should be spectrally decomposed and extracted. The extracted two wavepackets are localized in finite bandwidths and temporal regions. Thus, to measure them or use them for applications such as quantum teleportation, proper preparation of the local oscillator pulse — to match the envelope of the entangled wavepacket — must be carefully considered.

References

1. A. Sizmann and G. Leuchs, Progress in Optics **39**, 373 (1999).
2. P. G. Kwiat, E. Waks, A. G. White, I. Appelbaum, and P. H. Eberhard, *Phys. Rev.* A **60**, R773 (1999).
3. Z. Y. Ou, S. F. Pereira, and H. J. Kimble, *Appl. Phys.* B **55**, 265 (1992).
4. L. J. Wang, C. K. Hong, and S. R. Friberg, *J. Opt.* B **3**, 346 (2001).
5. J. E. Sharping, M. Fiorentino, and P. Kumar, *Opt. Lett.* **26**, 367 (2001).
6. Ch. Silberhorn, P. K. Lam, O. Weiß, F. König, N. Korolkova, and G. Leuchs, *Phys. Rev. Lett.* **86**, 4267 (2001).
7. S. Spälter, N. Korolkova, F. König, A. Sizmann, and G. Leuchs, *Phys. Rev. Lett.* **81**, 786 (1998).
8. M. Takeoka, D. Fujishima, and F. Kannari, *Opt. Lett.* **26**, 1592 (2001).
9. A. M. Weiner, *Prog. Quant. Electr.* **19**, 161 (1995).
10. Y. Lai and S.-S. Yu, *Phys. Rev.* A **51**, 817 (1995).
11. D. Fujishima, F. Kannari, M. Takeoka, and M. Sasaki (submitted).

A FREQUENCY-NONDEGENERATE ENTANGLEMENT SOURCE USING PERIODICALLY-POLED LITHIUM NIOBATE

ELLIOTT J. MASON, MARIUS A. ALBOTA, FRIEDRICH KÖNIG, AND FRANCO N. C. WONG

Massachusetts Institute of Technology, Research Laboratory of Electronics, Cambridge, MA 02139-4307, USA
Email: franco@ncw2.mit.edu

We demonstrate efficient generation of highly nondegenerate photon pairs with a type-I phase-matched, periodically-poled lithium niobate parametric downconverter. The signal photons at 800 nm and the idler photons at 1600 nm were generated in a collinear-propagation configuration with an inferred pair generation rate of 1.4×10^7/s/mW of pump power. Detection of a signal photon triggered a thermoelectrically cooled, 20%-efficient InGaAs avalanche photodiode for the detection of the 1600-nm conjugate idler photon. Using single-mode fibers as spatial mode filters, the signal-conditioned idler-detection probability was $\sim$3.1%.

1 Pair generation

Most applications in discrete-variable quantum information physics make use of entangled photon pairs as an important resource. High brightness of entangled photon-pair sources is essential for future development of this field. For example, a recently proposed singlet-based quantum communication system requires an efficient source of entangled photons at 795 nm for local trapped-Rb quantum memories and at 1.55 μm for fiber-optic entanglement distribution.[1,2] The required photon-pair characteristics for this proposal exemplify those for systems involving resonant coupling to atomic systems as well as efficient fiber-optic delivery. The pairs should be highly nondegenerate, with one photon at 795 nm and the other at 1550 nm. For efficient coupling to a narrowband atomic transition the photons must have bandwidths of only a few tens of MHz. Furthermore, it is important that they are in a well-defined spatial mode for coupling to an atomic cavity (at 795 nm) or to a single mode fiber delivery system (at 1550 nm). The requirements can be met using an optical parametric amplifier (OPA) with a quasi-phase matched nonlinear crystal. By engineering the phase matching, the wavelengths of signal and idler can be freely chosen. A cavity can be utilized to enhance the resonant modes that have narrow bandwidths and well-defined spatial modes. Using a properly designed type-I phase matched downconverter, the outputs propagate collinearly without walkoff. Note that a nonlinear waveguide is not a good choice for a narrowband cavity configuration, because of its high propagation loss. Polarization-entangled photon pairs can be generated using two independent but coherently pumped OPA sources.[3]

In this paper we present experimental results from a single-pass parametric downconverter[4] as a precursor to the narrowband OPA source. The experimental configuration is shown in Fig. 1. We used a 2-cm-long crystal

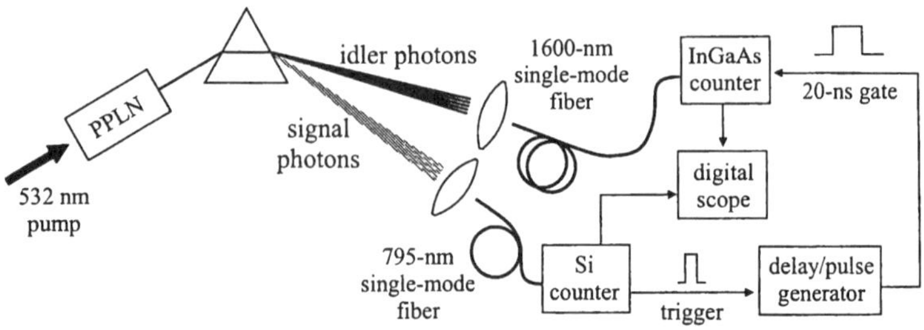

Figure 1. Experimental configuration for pair coincidence measurements. The signal photon is detected by the silicon (Si) photon counter, whose electrical output pulse is used to trigger the gate for the InGaAs detector.

of periodically-poled lithium niobate (PPLN) pumped by a cw frequency-doubled Nd:YVO_4 laser at 532 nm. Phase matching in PPLN was achieved by poling a third-order grating in the crystal with a grating period of 21.6 μm. The confocal parameter of the pump inside the crystal was chosen to be 20 cm, about ten times the crystal length. We obtained tunable outputs centered at 800 nm and 1580 nm by varying the temperature of the crystal between 140°C and 185°C. We characterized the PPLN downconverter by difference-frequency generation (DFG) of tunable ~800 nm light with a strong pump at 532 nm and a 1580-nm tunable probe laser. We measured a temperature tuning coefficient of ~1.3 nm/°C for the 1580-nm tunable source. At a fixed temperature, the DFG showed a bandwidth in the probe wavelength of 1.26 nm (~150 GHz), in good agreement with the expected value for a 2-cm-long PPLN crystal.

In the spontaneous downconversion mode, we inferred a pair-generation rate of 1.4×10^7/s/mW of pump power at 532 nm from our measurements, based on the 54% quantum efficiency of our Si detector and the 85% propagation efficiency of our experimental setup. Typical pump powers were 1–2 mW. When the signal was coupled into a single-mode fiber, the singles rate decreased to 30,000 counts/s/mW, because the spontaneous emission was distributed over many modes and only a single mode was selected by the fiber. Since the photons are produced in pairs, the rate of detected coincidences should be, in principle, equal to the inferred single-mode singles rate. However, the quantum efficiencies of the InGaAs detector (~20%), the idler propagation efficiency (85%), the fiber coupling efficiency (~50%) and the efficiency of collecting the same spontaneous mode in the signal and idler fibers (η_{mode}) reduce the observed coincidence rate. Therefore, we observed a single-mode coincidence rate of only 930 pairs/s/mW with a 3.1% conditional probability for the idler photon detection. A counting histogram is shown in Fig. 2, showing that the coincident idler photons were well localized in time and that dark counts were negligible. By comparing the observed coincidence rate with the

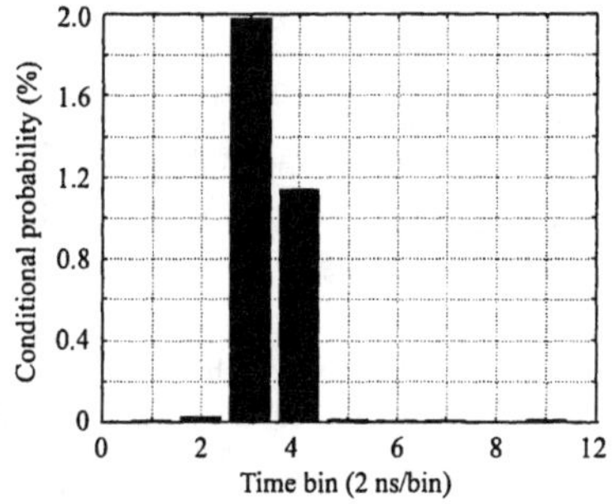

Figure 2. Histogram of signal-conditioned idler detection probability. The width of the distribution is due to the rise time of the detector electronics.

rate predicted from the singles rate, we infer the signal-idler mode-matching efficiency η_{mode} to be 36%. Had the signal and idler fibers collected the same mode ($\eta_{mode} = 1$), the observed conditional probability would have been ~8%.

In order to obtain polarization entanglement, we plan to pump the PPLN crystal from both sides with counter-propagating pump beams. The photon pairs are then extracted and the two signal photons as well as the two idler photons are combined using a polarizing beam splitter to yield the required polarization entanglement at two highly-nondegenerate wavelengths.

2 Detectors

The detection of the 800-nm photon is easily achieved with a commercial silicon photon counting module (PerkinElmer SPCM-AQR-14). For the detection of single photons at 1600 nm we built a compact all-solid-state InGaAs avalanche photodiode detector.[4,5] We used a fiber pigtailed avalanche photodiode [JDS Uniphase (EPM239BA)] that was cooled with a four-stage thermoelectric cooler to −50°C. For single-photon detection the diode was biased just below its breakdown voltage and a gating pulse provided an overbias of 2–4 V at appropriate times. The 20-ns gate pulses had a rise/fall time of 3–4 ns. The avalanche output pulses were then amplified by 40 dB with resultant pulse amplitudes of 1–2 V and rise times of less than 2 ns. We found good operating conditions at a temperature of −50° C, where dark counts were sufficiently low and afterpulsing due to trapped charge carriers was negligible at a gating frequency of 100 kHz. Figure 3 shows typical quantum efficiencies and dark-count probabilities as functions of the overbias voltage. The quantum efficiency reaches 20% at an overbias voltage of 3.5 V, at which point the dark count probability is ~0.1% within the 20-ns gate.

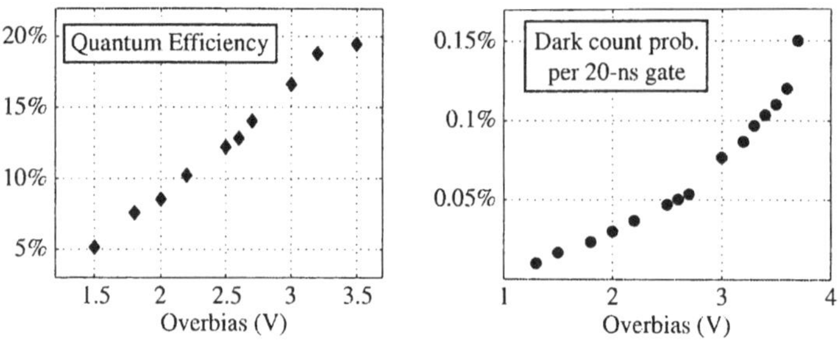

Figure 3. Plots of (left) quantum efficiency and (right) dark count probability of the InGaAs avalanche photodiode with a 20-ns gate at $-50°C$ versus overbias voltage.

3 Conclusion

In conclusion, we have demonstrated efficient parametric downconversion in PPLN with highly-nondegenerate output pairs. The inferred pair-production rate was 1.4×10^7 pairs/s/mW of pump power. We also achieved coincidence detection using a thermoelectrically-cooled InGaAs avalanche photodiode.[4] Future works include the generation of polarization entangled pairs as well as the implementation of a cavity configuration to increase the flux within a certain spectral and spatial mode.

Acknowledgment

This work was supported by the DoD Multidisciplinary University Research Initiative (MURI) program administered by the Army Research Office under Grant DAAD-19-00-1-0177, and by the National Reconnaissance Office.

References

1. J. H. Shapiro, *New J. Phys.* **4**, 47 (2002).
2. S. Lloyd, M. S. Shahriar, J. H. Shapiro, and P. R. Hemmer, *Phys. Rev. Lett.* **87**, 167903 (2001).
3. J. H. Shapiro and N. C. Wong, *J. Opt. B: Quantum Semiclass. Opt.* **2**, L1 (2000).
4. E. J. Mason, M. A. Albota, F. Koenig, and F. N. C. Wong, *Opt. Lett.*, in press (2002).
5. M. A. Albota, "Single-photon detection of 1.55 μm entangled light and frequency upconversion in periodically poled lithium niobate for quantum communication," S. M. Thesis, Massachusetts Institute of Technology (2002).

QUANTUM COMMUNICATIONS WITH TIME-BIN ENTANGLED PHOTONS: LONG-DISTANCE QUANTUM TELEPORTATION AND QUANTUM REPEATERS

N. GISIN, I. MARCIKIC, H. DE RIEDMATTEN, W. TITTEL,* H. ZBINDEN

Group of Applied Physics, University of Geneva, CH-1211, Geneva 4, Switzerland

**also with QUANTOP, University of Aarhus, Denmark*

E-mail: nicolas.gisin@physics.unige.ch

Using 2 km of standard telecom optical fibers, we teleport qubits carried by photons of 1.3 μm wavelength to qubits in another laboratory carried by a photons of 1.5 μm wavelength. The photons to be teleported and the necessary entangled photon pairs are created in two different nonlinear crystals. The measured mean fidelity is of 81.2%. We discuss how this could be used as quantum repeaters without quantum memories.

1 Introduction

Long-distance quantum communication in optical fibers should exploit the standard and widely installed telecom fibers. This standard imposes the wavelength (either around 1300 nm, or around 1550 nm). It does also strongly suggest that polarization encoding is not the optimal choice. Indeed, polarization effects in telecom fibers fluctuate on a time scale from ms to tens of minutes for aerial and underground cables, respectively. These unavoidable fluctuations require active feedback and/or compensation schemes. An alternative consists of encoding the qubits in time-bins. Time-bin qubits have already been used for quantum cryptography,[1] for the production of non-maximally entangled qubits,[2] and to encode quantum states in higher-dimensional Hilbert spaces.[3] In this contribution we present the results of an experimental demonstration of long-distance quantum teleportation, using time-bin qubits. In section 3 we present a potential application of quantum teleportation as "quantum repeaters without quantum memory".

Figure 1 presents a general preparation and measurement scheme for time-bin qubits.[4] In principle, any state can be deterministically prepared and ideal measurements in any basis performed. In practice, however, the switches are replaced by passive couplers, hence inducing a 50% loss. Also, in our experiment we replaced the variable coupler either by a passive coupler (corresponding to a coupling ratio of 50%), or by fibers of appropriate lengths (corresponding to 0% and 100% coupling ratios).[a]

[a]The replacement of the switches is necessary because real and fast switches have losses even larger than 50%. However, real variable couplers could be used.

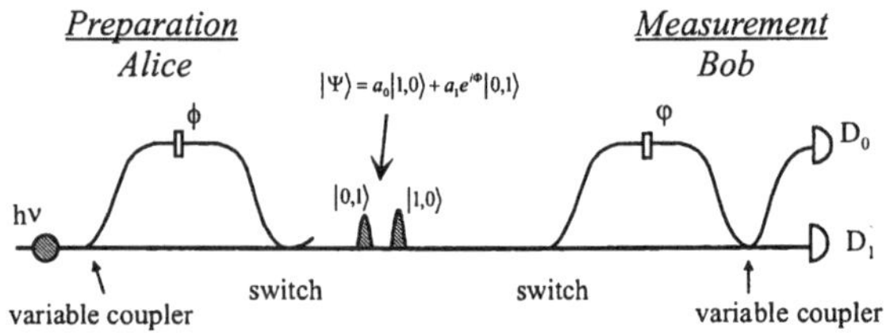

Figure 1. Preparation and measurement of time-bin qubits

2 Quantum teleportation

Our experiment is schematically presented in Fig. 2. For a general introduction to quantum teleportation and previous experiments, we refer to.[5,6,7,8,9] A mode-locked Ti:Sapphire laser produces 150 fs pulses at $\lambda = 710\,\text{nm}$. The

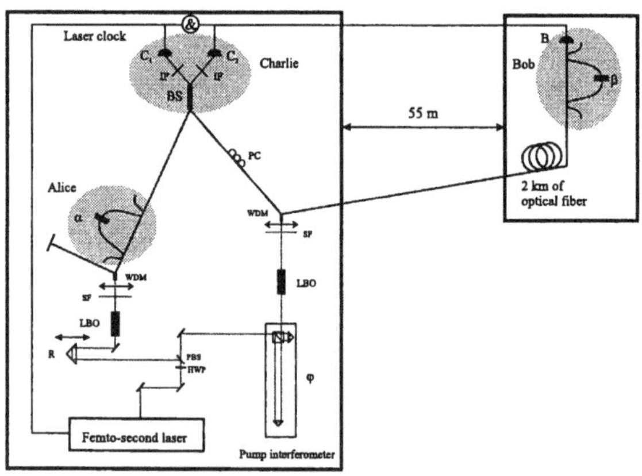

Figure 2. Experimental setup

laser beam is split into two parts. The transmitted beam is used to create entangled time-bin qubits (EPR source) by passing the beam first through an unbalanced bulk Michelson interferometer with optical path-length difference $\Delta\tau = 1.2$ ns and then through a type I nonlinear crystal (LBO) where entangled non-degenerate collinear time-bin qubits at telecom wavelengths (1310 and 1550 nm) are created. The pump light is removed with a silicon filter (SF) and the twin photons are collimated into an optical fiber and separated by a wavelength-division-multiplexer (WDM). The 1310 nm photon is then sent to Charlie and its twin 1550 nm photon to Bob. The entangled state is described by $|1,0\rangle_{\text{Charlie}} \otimes |1,0\rangle_{\text{Bob}} + |0,1\rangle_{\text{Charlie}} \otimes |0,1\rangle_{\text{Bob}}$, where $|1,0\rangle$ and $|0,1\rangle$ represents the first and second time bins, respectively.

The reflected beam is used to create the qubits to be teleported. Similar to the creation of the entangled pairs, the beam is focussed into a LBO crystal creating pairs of photons at 1310 nm and 1550 nm wavelengths. After blocking the pump light and coupling the photon pairs into an optical fiber, the 1550 nm photon is removed using a WDM. Alice passes the 1310 nm photon through a qubit preparation device, thereby creating a state $|\psi_{\text{Alice}}\rangle = a_0|1,0\rangle + a_1 e^{i\alpha}|0,1\rangle$, where $a_0 = 0, 1$ or $1/\sqrt{2}$ and $a_0^2 + a_1^2 = 1$. Alice's qubit is finally sent to Charlie.

Charlie performs the joint Bell-state measurement between the qubit sent by Alice and his part of the pair, with the 50/50 fiber coupler BS. We select only the projection onto the singlet entangled state $|\psi^{(-)}\rangle = |1,0\rangle_{\text{Alice}} \otimes |0,1\rangle_{\text{Charlie}} - |0,1\rangle_{\text{Alice}} \otimes |1,0\rangle_{\text{Charlie}}$. This takes place when the two photons trigger the detectors labelled C1 and C2 in Fig. 2 at times that differ precisely by the time difference $\Delta\tau$ between two time bins. Detectors C1 and C2 are a LN2-cooled passively-quenched Ge avalanche photodiode (APD) and a Peltier-cooled InGaAs APD, respectively.[10] Bob is situated in another lab, 55 m away from Charlie. To simulate a longer distance we added 2 km of optical fiber before the teleported photon reaches Bob's analyzer.

The quality of the teleportation is usually reported in terms of fidelity $\bar{F}$, i.e., the probability that Bob's qubit successfully passes an analyzer testing that it is indeed in the state ψ_{Alice} prepared by Alice, averaged over all possible ψ_{Alice}. The linearity of quantum mechanics implies:

$$\bar{F} = \int \langle\psi_{\text{Alice}}|\rho_{\text{Bob}}|\psi_{\text{Alice}}\rangle d\psi_{\text{Alice}} = \frac{2}{3}F_{\text{equator}} + \frac{1}{3}F_{\text{pole}} \tag{1}$$

where F_{equator} and F_{pole} are the fidelities averaged only over the states corresponding to the equator and the poles of the Poincaré sphere, respectively. In

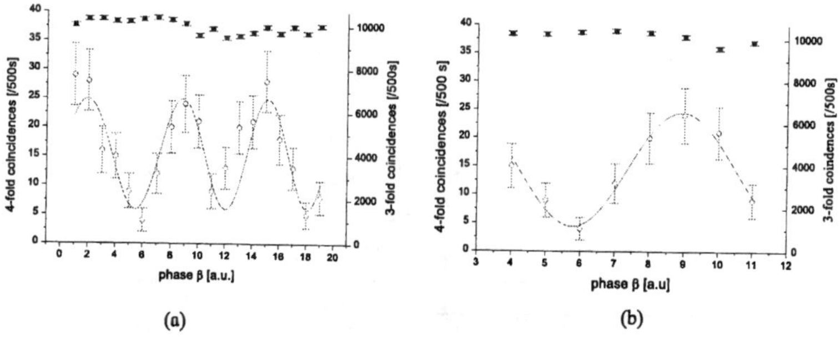

Figure 3. Teleportation of equatorial states. Open circles are 4-fold coincidences (3 photons + laser clock), i.e., detection of Bob's photon conditioned on a successful Bell measurement. Black squares are 3-fold coincidences (Photons C1 + B + laser clock); they should remain constant, since they contains no information about the Bell measurement

our experiment we measured F_{pole} directly, by preparing and measuring each of the two corresponding states: $F_{\text{pole}} = (82.5 \pm 3)\%$. In order to measure

F_{equator}, we prepared various states, using a 50/50 coupler with various phases α, and for each scanned the analyzing interferometer's phase β. From the raw visibility V_{raw} one obtains the fidelity $F = (1 + V_{\text{raw}})/2$. Typically, we obtain $F_{\text{equator}} = (80.5 \pm 2.5)\%$ (Fig. 3a), with best results achieving values up to $(85 \pm 2.5)\%$ (Fig. 3b). Accordingly, the measured fidelity, averaged over all possible states ψ_{Alice} equals $\bar{F} = (81.2 \pm 2.5)\%$.

3 Quantum repeaters without quantum memory

Generally, quantum channels are lossy, hence the probability that a single photon sent by Alice reaches Bob decreases with distance. Because of the no-cloning theorem, there is no way to merely amplify the signal. With noise-free detectors, the attenuation would only affect the bit rate, and protocols like quantum cryptography would provide secure keys for arbitrary distances. However, realistic detectors have a finite probability of dark counts (around 10^{-4} per ns for InGaAs APDs[10]). This noise is independent of the distance, hence there is a limiting distance after which the signal becomes smaller than the noise. In a series of papers, H. Briegel and co-workers[11] have shown that the appropriate use of entanglement purification and of quantum memories allows one, in principle, to realize quantum repeaters which would extend the range of quantum cryptography to unlimited distances, with only a polynomial increase of repeater stations. This is a promising line of research for experimental physics, but it is only fair to say that it will remain a research topic for the years to come. However, without quantum memories and using

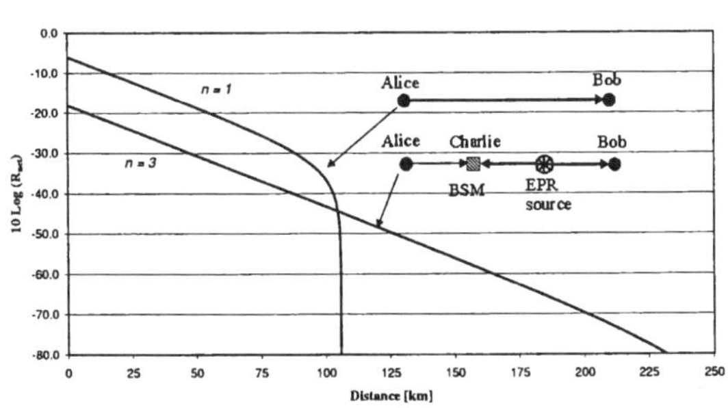

Figure 4. Net count rate as a function of the distance when Alice is directly connected to Bob (n=1) and in the case of teleportation (n=3).

only near-future technologies (like the ones presented in this contribution), there are ways to extends the distances over which secret quantum keys can be distributed, although not to unlimited distances.[12,13,14] Assume that Alice and Bob are connected by a quantum communication channel with transmission coefficient t. Let η denote the photon-counting detector's efficiency and D the dark count probability per transmission (i.e., per qubit). Furthermore, let C and Q be the rates of correctly and incorrectly detected photons: to a good approximation,[b] we have $C = t\eta$, $Q = (1 - t\eta)D$. Accordingly, the total rate of transmission R_{raw} and the QBER (Quantum Bit error Rate) are:

$$R_{\text{raw}} = C + Q \qquad\qquad \text{QBER} = \frac{Q}{C+Q}. \tag{2}$$

The net rate R_{net}, after error correction and privacy amplification, is proportional to the raw rate R_{raw} with a coefficient that depends on the QBER.[12] This coefficient is the difference between the Alice-Bob I_{AB} and the Alice-Eve I_{AE} Shannon mutual informations (or the Bob-Eve one, if smaller). The exact relation between I_{AE} and the QBER depends on the exact eavesdropping model. Our results are essentially independent of the details, though numerical values may differ slightly. For the optimal individual attack, $I_{AB} - I_{AE}$ is almost a linear function of the QBER, hence we use the approximation:

$$R_{\text{net}} \approx R_{\text{raw}} \cdot \left(1 - \frac{\text{QBER}}{15\%}\right) = C - \frac{85}{15}Q. \tag{3}$$

With realistic numbers, $\eta = 0.25$, $D = 10^{-4}$, and an attenuation coefficient $\alpha = 0.25\,\text{dB/km}$ (i.e., $t = 10^{-\alpha L/10}$, L = fiber length), this sets an absolute limit for quantum key distribution around 105 km (even with perfect single-photon sources), see Fig. 4. Consider now the case in which the channel is divided into 3 sections, each of length $L/3$, i.e., with transmission coefficient $t^{1/3}$ (Fig. 4), exactly as in a quantum teleportation experiment. In such a configuration, Bob correctly detects the qubit whenever all 3 photons make it to their detectors, all 3 detectors click and the Bell measurement is successful, i.e., $C^{(3)} = \frac{1}{2}(t^{1/3}\eta)^3 = \frac{1}{2}t\eta^3$. The rate of incorrect detections contains three parts:[c] (i) all 3 photons are lost and there are 3 dark counts, (ii) 2 photons are lost, 1 detected and there are 2 dark counts, (iii) 1 photon is lost, 2 detected and there is one dark count. Accordingly:

$$\begin{aligned} Q^{(3)} &= (1 - t^{1/3}\eta)^3 \cdot D^3 + 3t^{1/3}\eta(1 - t^{1/3}\eta)^2 \cdot D^2 + 3(t^{1/3}\eta)^2(1 - t^{1/3}\eta) \cdot D \\ &= \left(t^{1/3}\eta + (1 - t^{1/3}\eta)D\right)^3 - t\eta^3. \end{aligned} \tag{4}$$

The corresponding net rate, with the same parameters, is also displayed in Fig. 4. Clearly, the division of the channel into 3 trunks and the use of

[b] We checked that a complete analysis doesn't qualitatively change the results

[c] We assumed that the detector noise completely dominates the error rate. This is a reasonable assumption when Alice is directly connected to Bob (i.e., when $n = 1$), see Ref. 15. But, clearly, when the systems gets more complex, optical alignment is less optimal. How this optical contribution to the error rate scales with n depends on the detailed implementation. From our experiment we believe that the "optical error rate" can be maintained quite low.

teleportation significantly increases the maximal distance over which quantum key distribution is possible. The generalization to divisions into n trunks is straightforward. For given parameters the limiting distance increases with n, up to a maximum, and then decreases again.

4 Concluding remarks

Objects are constituted by energy and structure (or matter and form according to Aristotle). In quantum teleportation one teleports neither energy nor matter. However, the ultimate structure of objects is indeed teleported from and place to another, without the object ever being anywhere in between! Admittedly, teleportation of systems much more complex than a simple qubit is still elusive. But the teleportation of qubits could already be useful for quantum cryptography, although much effort will be needed to improve this first long-distance realization, especially the stability of the experimental scheme.

Financial support by the Swiss OFES and NSF within the framework of the European IST project Qucomm and the Swiss National Center for Quantum Photonics is acknowledged. W.T. acknowledges funding by the ESF Programme Quantum Information Theory and Quantum Computation (QIT).

References

1. W. Tittel, J. Brendel, H. Zbinden and N. Gisin, Phys. Rev. Lett. **84**, 4737 (2000).
2. R. Thew, S. Tanzilli, W. Tittel, H. Zbinden, N. Gisin, quant-ph/0203067.
3. H. de Riedmatten, I. Marcikic, H. Zbinden and N. Gisin, to appear in QIC, quant-ph/0204165; and these proceedings.
4. W. Tittel and G. Weihs, Quantum Information & Computation **1**, 32 (2001).
5. C. H. Bennett, G. Brassard, C. Crépeau, R. Jozsa, A. Peres, and W. K. Wootters, Phys. Rev. Lett. **70**, 1895 (1993).
6. D. Bouwmeester, J. W. Pan, K. Mattle, M. Eibl, H. Weinfurter, and A. Zeilinger, Nature **390**, 575 (1997).
7. D. Boschi, S. Branca, F. De Martini, L. Hardy, and S. Popescu, Phys. Rev. Lett. **80**, 1121 (1998).
8. Y.-H. Kim, S. P. Kulik, and Y. Shih, Phys. Rev. Lett. **86**, 1370 (2001).
9. A. Furusawa, J. L. Sorensen, S. L. Braunstein, C. A. Fuchs, H. J. Kimble, and E. S. Polzik, Science **282**, 706 (1998).
10. D. Stucki, G. Ribordy, A. Stefanov, and H. Zbinden, J. of Mod. Optics **48**, 1967 (2001); available from http://www.idQuantique.com.
11. H. Briegel, W. Dur, J. I. Cirac, and P. Zoller, Phys. Rev. Lett. **81**, 5932 (1998).
12. N. Gisin, G. Ribordy, W. Tittel, and H. Zbinden, Rev. Mod. Phys. **74**, 145 (2002).
13. E. Waks, A. Zeevi, and Y. Yamamoto, Phys. Rev. A **65**, 052310 (2002).
14. B. C. Jacobs, T. B. Pittman, J. D. Franson, quant-ph/0204097.
15. D. Stucki, N. Gisin, O. Guinnard, G. Ribordy, H. Zbinden, New J. of Phys. 4, 41.1-41.8 (2002).

TAMING ENTANGLEMENT

PAUL KWIAT, JOE ALTEPETER, DAVID BRANNING, EVAN JEFFREY, NICHOLAS PETERS, AND TZU-CHIEH WEH

Department of Physics, University of Illinois, 1110 W. Green St., Urbana, IL 61801-3080, USA

E-mail: kwiat@uiuc.edu

Using a spontaneous parametric downconversion source of photon pairs, we are working towards the creation of arbitrary 2-qubit quantum states with high fidelity. Currently, all physically allowable combinations of polarization entanglement and mixture can be produced, including maximally-entangled mixed states. The states are experimentally measured and refined via computer-automated quantum-state tomography, and this system has also been used to perform single-qubit and ancilla-assisted quantum process tomography.

Central to the long-term future of quantum information processing is the capability of performing extremely accurate and reproducible gate operations. The restrictions for fault-tolerant quantum computation are extremely demanding: the tolerable error-per-gate operation should be less than 10^{-4} to 10^{-6}. Implementing such precise gate operations and preparing the requisite input states is therefore one of the key milestones for quantum information processing. Using optical realizations of qubits, e.g., polarization states of photons, we have the potential to meet these demanding tolerances. Therefore, although large-scale quantum computers will perhaps never be constructed solely using optical qubits, these systems nevertheless form a unique and convenient test bed with which to experimentally investigate the issues surrounding state creation, manipulation, and characterization, and also ways of dealing with decoherence.

Our primary tool for these investigations is a source of correlated photons produced via the process of spontaneous parametric downconversion: with small probability, a pump photon of appropriate polarization may split into two longer-wavelength daughter photons, subject to energy and momentum conservation (Fig. 1). By triggering on one of these photons, the other is prepared in a single-photon Fock state.[1] We can apply local unitary transformations to the polarizations of these photons using a birefringent half-wave

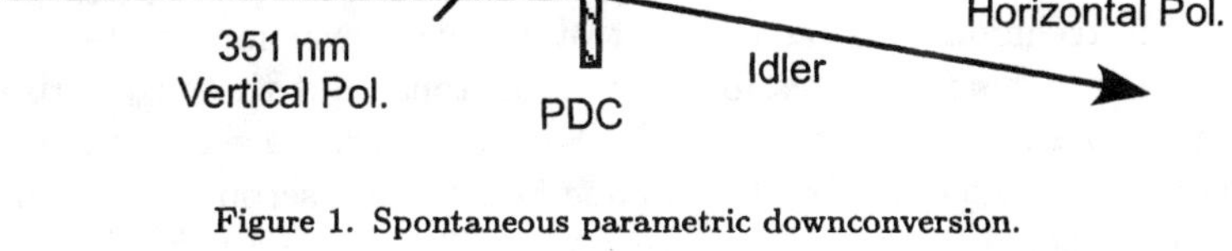

Figure 1. Spontaneous parametric downconversion.

(a)

(b)

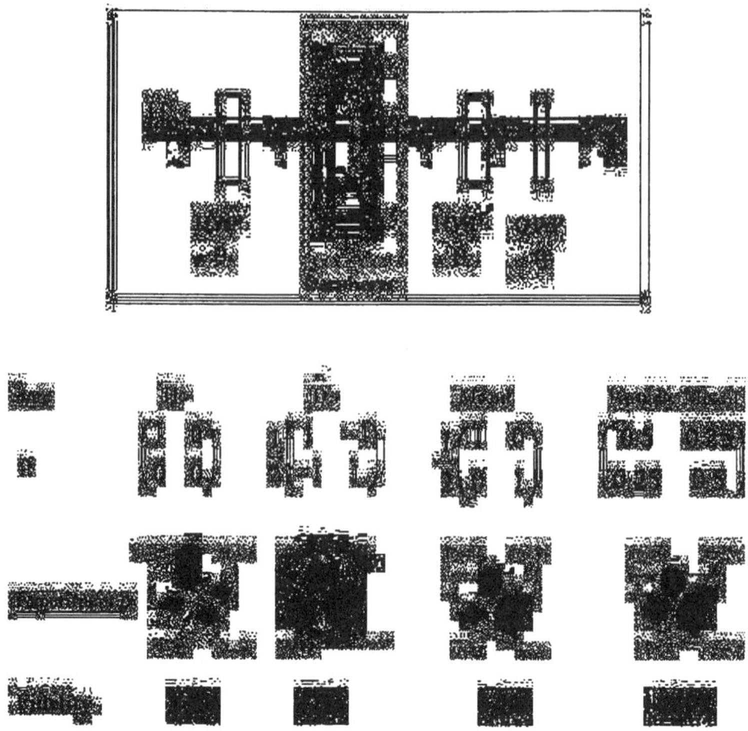

Figure 2. (a) Experimental arrangement for single-photon state creation. The single-photon input to the system comes from one member of a parametric downconversion pair, with the other photon used as a herald. The operation of the decoherer — to separate orthogonal polarizations by much more than the coherence length — is indicated here using a polarizing beam splitter to create a birefringent delay line. (b) A variety of single-qubit states have been generated and reconstructed using quantum state tomography.

plate (HWP) and quarter-wave plate (QWP). We can also introduce decoherence (either independently or collectively) by passing the photons through birefringent delay lines.

Using these techniques for the single photon case, the initial pure horizontal state $|H\rangle$ may be precisely converted into an arbitrary pure or mixed state (Fig. 2). We estimate that we can create and reliably distinguish (with fidelities of 0.998 or better) over 100,000 single-qubit states. Applying these single-qubit techniques to each output of a downconversion crystal, we can create arbitrary *product* states for the two photons. But these comprise only a very small part of the total two-qubit Hilbert space. To access the rest, we must create entangled states; this is done by adding a second downconverter with an orthogonal optic axis as shown in Fig. 3a. A given pair of signal and

(a)

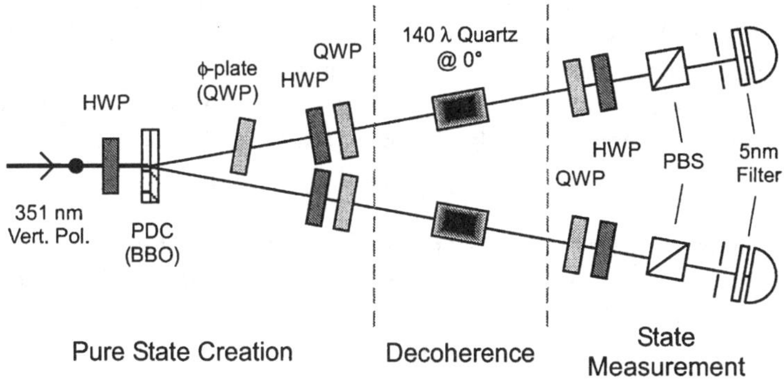

(b)

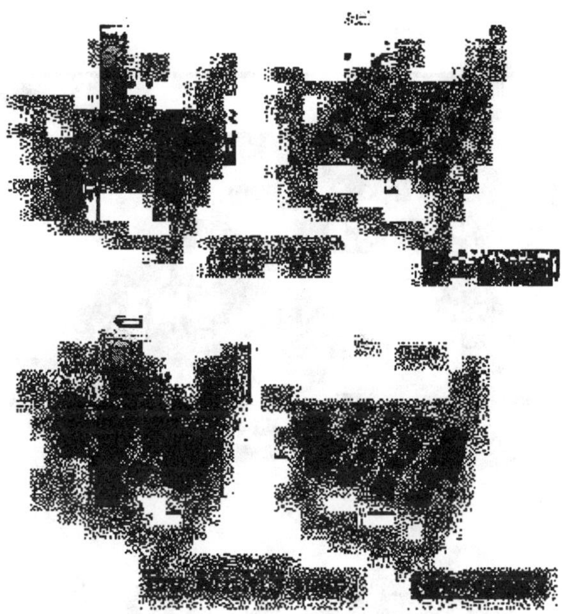

Figure 3. (a) Experimental arrangement for two-photon state creation. (b) A variety of two-qubit states have been generated and reconstructed using quantum state tomography. Also shown are the fidelity of the reconstructed density matrices with the target input states, indicating a high degree of control.

idler photons could have been born in the first crystal, with vertical polarizations, or in the second with horizontal polarizations. These two possibilities cannot be distinguished by any measurements other than polarization, so the quantum state for these photons is a superposition of $|V\rangle|V\rangle$ and $|H\rangle|H\rangle$.

Because each crystal responds to only one pump polarization, the relative weights of the two downconversion processes can be controlled by adjusting the input pump polarization.[2] A birefringent phase plate is also added to one of the outputs to control the relative phase of the two contributions, so that we can create nonmaximally entangled states of the form:

$$|\psi\rangle \propto |H\rangle|H\rangle + \epsilon e^{i\phi}|V\rangle|V\rangle.$$

Combined with the single-photon local unitary transformations, any pure 2-qubit state can be produced. In this way, we have prepared a variety of states (Figs. 3b, 4b).

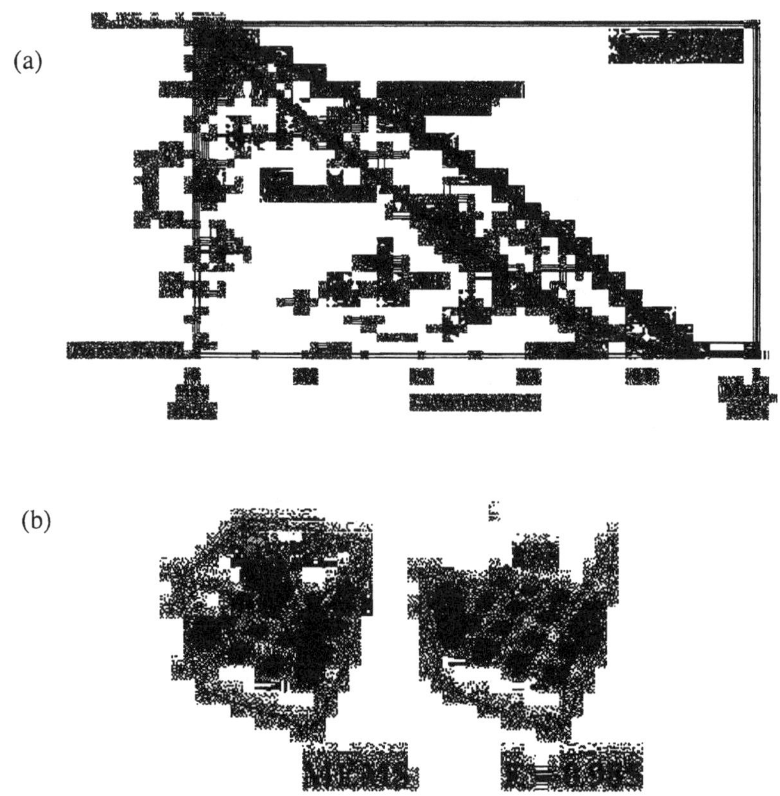

Figure 4. (a) The Tangle-Entropy plane. (b) Tomographic reconstruction of the density matrix for a MEMS (Maximally Entangled Mixed State). F is the fidelity of the measured state with the target.

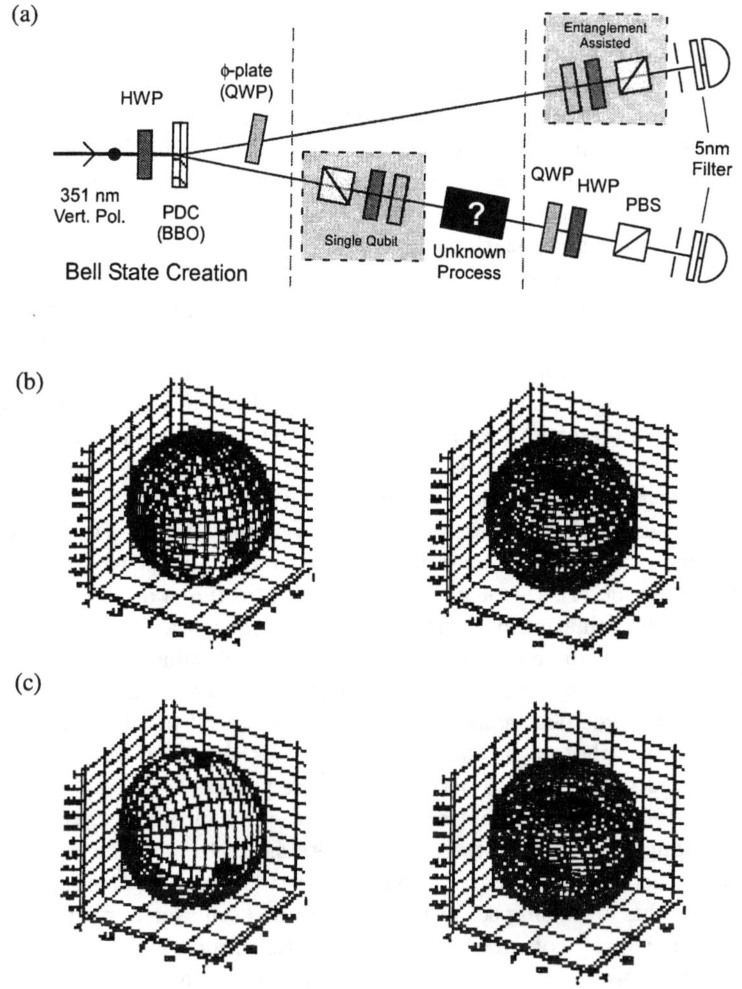

Figure 5. (a) Experimental arrangement for single-qubit and entanglement-assisted quantum process tomography. (b) Tomographic reconstructions for a unitary process (left) and decoherence (right), illustrated as transformations on the Poincaré sphere. The gray mesh spheres represent all possible initial single-qubit states. The dots show the initial states $|H\rangle$, $|V\rangle$, $|45°\rangle$, $|-45°\rangle$, $|L\rangle$, and $|R\rangle$ after the transformations. (c) Entanglement-assisted tomographic reconstructions for the same processes.

The density matrices are tomographically determined by measuring the polarization correlations in 16 bases, and performing a maximum-likelihood analysis to find the legitimate density matrix most consistent with the experimental results.[3] In order to improve the speed and accuracy of our tomographic measurements, we have implemented a fully automated system. In addition to reducing the total time for a measurement, and significantly decreasing the uncertainty in the measurement settings, this automated system will also enable the implementation of an adaptive tomography routine — by making an initial fast estimate of the state, one could spend most of the data collection time making an optimized set of measurements. With this sort of optimal quantum tomography, we hope to reach the ultimate limit in quantum state characterization.

Our automated system has enabled the creation of a large number of states with widely varying degrees of purity and entanglement. A convenient way to display these states is the "Tangle-entropy" plane, shown in Fig. 4. Because it is impossible to have a state that is both completely mixed and completely entangled, there is an implied boundary between states that are physically possible and those that are not: this boundary is formed by the "maximally-entangled mixed states" (MEMS), which possess the largest degree of entanglement possible for their entropies.[4]

Finally, using the modification of our system shown in Fig. 5a, we can realize several methods of quantum process tomography,[5] whose goal is to completely characterize some unknown process affecting a qubit. This process may be any combination of unitary transformations, state-dependent losses, and decoherence. One method is to send a variety of input states through the process, and tomographically determine the output states. Another technique, known as "entanglement-assisted" or "ancilla-assisted" process tomography,[6] exploits the two-photon correlations available at the source, and requires only a single, fixed input state to perform an entire process tomography.

In the future, we will continue to expand our abilities to create an ever-widening range of quantum states and processes, and to push the level of precision with which they are created and characterized with adaptive tomography. Ultimately, this promising set of tools should be useful for implementing and testing various protocols in quantum information processing.

This work was supported in part by the DCI Postdoctoral Research Fellowship Program and by ARDA, and in part under NSF Grant #EIA-0121568.

References

1. C. K. Hong and L. Mandel, *Phys. Rev. Lett.* **56**, 58 (1986).
2. P. G. Kwiat et al., *Phys. Rev. A* **60**, R773 (1999).
3. D. F. V. James et al., *Phys. Rev. A* **64**, 052312 (2001); A. G. White et al., *Phys. Rev. Lett.* **83**, 3103 (1999).
4. T. C. Wei et al., in preparation; W. J. Munro et al., *Phys. Rev. A* **64**, 030302(R) (2001).
5. I. L. Chuang and M. A. Nielsen, *J. Mod. Opt.* **44**, 2455 (1997); J. F. Poyatos et al., *Phys. Rev. Lett.* **78**, 390 (1997).
6. J. B. Altepeter et al., in preparation.

MULTI-PHOTON QUANTUM CRYPTOGRAPHY AND QUANTUM CLONING

GABRIEL DURKIN, CHRISTOPH SIMON, ANTIA LAMAS-LINARES, JOHN HOWELL, DIRK BOUWMEESTER

Centre for Quantum Computation, University of Oxford OX1 3PU, United Kingdom

Department of Physics, Center for Spintronics and Quantum Computation, University of California, Santa Barbara, California 93106

Entangled photons play an important part in quantum optics when exploring the nature of nonlocal quantum correlations. They represent a powerful resource for quantum information experiments, including teleportation and cryptography. In the regime of spontaneous parametric downconversion entangled pair production is still quite inefficient. However, this group has used *stimulated* parametric downconversion to produce photon states entangled both in polarization and photon number. By this technique, the group has significantly increased the probability amplitudes of entangled pairs and entangled states of higher photon number, which make possible new kinds of efficient cryptography protocols and stronger violation of 'locality' through Bell-type measurements. We show in addition, that this entangled photon source can perform effective *universal* quantum cloning of single photons.

1 Stimulated Parametric Downconversion

Type II parametric downconversion (PDC) involves a photon from a pump light source splitting into two photons of lower frequencies within a nonlinear crystal. Part of the work undertaken by this group has been to encourage multi-photon output from downconversion, by a stimulated process.[1] The experimental conditions implemented in our laboratory are such that the phenomenological interaction Hamiltonian for degenerate PDC can be expressed as:

$$\hat{H} = \kappa(\hat{a}_h^\dagger \hat{b}_v^\dagger - \hat{a}_v^\dagger \hat{b}_h^\dagger) + h.c., \tag{1}$$

where $\hat{a}$ and $\hat{b}$ are annihilation operators for the distinct spatial modes or directions of downconverted light, and the subscripts h and v refer to horizontal and vertical polarizations. This Hamiltonian produces a quantum state entangled both in photon number and polarization. There are 4 possible output modes, a_h, a_v, b_h, b_v. The Hamiltonian is responsible for the distribution of entanglement amongst the 4 modes, and its symmetries are inherited by the states. The symmetry in this case is an invariance under any $SU_2 \otimes SU_2$-type transformation of the operators, for example any rotation of polarization within the plane. Consequently, the state has the structure of maximally entangled singlet[a] states $|\psi_{2n}^-\rangle$ in a superposition of increasing photon number.

[a]bipartite singlet states also have $SU_2 \otimes SU_2$ invariance

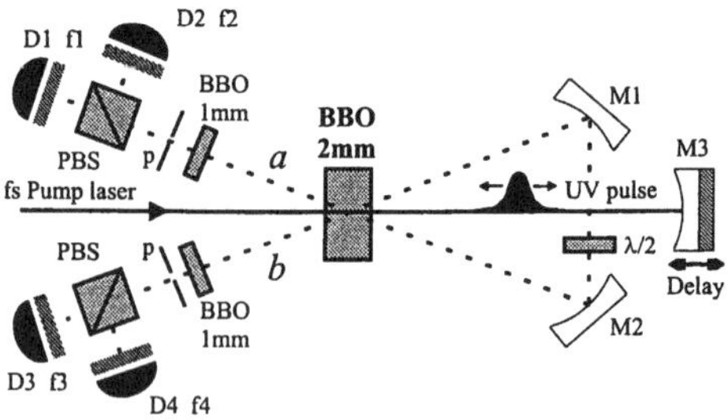

Figure 1. The 'bow-tie' scheme used to engineer high-τ coupling via stimulated downconversion. A frequency-doubled mode-locked Ti:Sa laser (80 MHz repetition rate, $\lambda = 390$ nm) pumps a 2-mm-long β-barium-borate (BBO) crystal. The pump is reflected onto itself by mirror M3, mounted on a computer controlled translation stage. Mirrors M1 and M2 form the feedback loop of the downconversion beams, including a polarization rotation element ($\lambda/2$) for the entangled photons. Photons are detected in avalanche photodiodes D1–D4, once they have traversed the polarizing beam splitters.

The state may be written as:

$$|\mathrm{PDC}\rangle = \frac{1}{\cosh^2(\tau)} \sum_{n=0}^{\infty} \sqrt{n+1}\ \tanh^n(\tau)\ |\psi_{2n}^-\rangle. \tag{2}$$

Here. $\tau = \kappa t/\hbar$ is the effective interaction time. From this point we will employ the short-hand notation $|\alpha, \beta; \gamma, \delta\rangle$ for $|\alpha\rangle_{a_h}|\beta\rangle_{a_v}|\gamma\rangle_{b_h}|\delta\rangle_{b_v}$, where the greek letters denote photon occupancy in each mode. Each singlet has the form

$$|\psi_{2n}^-\rangle = \frac{1}{\sqrt{n+1}} \sum_{p=0}^{n} (-1)^p |(n-p), p\,; p, (n-p)\rangle. \tag{3}$$

The sub-states $|\psi_{2n}^-\rangle$ are maximally entangled singlet states in a joint Hilbert space of $(n+1) \times (n+1)$ dimensions. The two-photon state $|\psi_2^-\rangle = \frac{1}{\sqrt{2}}(|1,0;0,1\rangle - |0,1;1,0\rangle)$, is the familiar Bell singlet analogous to a pair of spin-half particles in an overall spin-zero state. The 4-photon singlet $|\psi_4^-\rangle = \frac{1}{\sqrt{3}}(|2,0;0,2\rangle - |1,1;1,1\rangle + |2,0;0,2\rangle)$ is equivalent to two spin-one particles aligned to a zero joint spin. By photon counting, a particular maximally entangled singlet state can be verified, a method known as post-selection. As to which of the singlet states is post-selected, this is completely probabilistic, and determined by the amplitudes $\sqrt{n+1}\cosh^{-2}(\tau)\ \tanh^n(\tau)$ in (2). The results will exhibit correlations corresponding to the singlet state. The multi-photon (containing four or more photons) singlet states will not be of practical use if their occurrence rate is substantially lower than the lowest order, $|\psi_2^-\rangle$ Bell singlet, as is the case in the *spontaneous* parametric downconversion (SPDC) process. In order that higher photon number singlet states have comparable probability, the interaction parameter τ needs to be sufficiently large. The increased coupling τ could be achieved by lengthening the crystal, but using a larger crystal introduces problems. For this experiment, instead of trying to increase the crystal length, we have reflected the pump laser and downconversion modes back through the same crystal in a bow-tie formation, as shown in Fig. 1. By seeding the crystal in this way, many downconversion pairs are stimulated. Since the beam paths are identical, true indistinguishability is preserved, allowing the highest quality of entanglement to be created, cf. Ref. 1.

2 Using the Stimulated Process in Cryptography

There is a perfect encryption technique, known as the Vernam Cypher,[2] that relies on two communicating parties, Alice and Bob, sharing a random bit string known only to them. This string, the 'key', is equal in length to the message to be communicated secretly. Adding these two bit strings together and publically transmitting the result (known as the cryptogram) Alice can be sure that only someone in possession of the key can decode the message. *Quantum Key Distribution* (QKD) provides a way to generate the key perfectly randomly, between Alice and Bob and in such a way that they would be aware of any eavesdropper. Undetected eavesdropping is prevented by Alice and Bob making measurements in two conjugate bases.

A simple protocol employing the multi-photon states for QKD now follows. From a common source, entangled multi-photon pulses are sent to Alice and Bob via modes a and b respectively. They independently and randomly choose a polarization basis each time a measurement is made, choosing between horizontal/vertical linear, $+45°/-45°$ linear polarizations. On examination of the 4-mode Fock states of (3), it is clear that when their random basis choices coincide, if Alice measures $n-p$ photons in a specific polarization mode (e.g., $+45°$) and p along the orthogonal mode (e.g., $-45°$), then Bob will measure p and $n-p$ along the corresponding polarizations. The correlations are independent of the measurement basis, because of the $SU_2 \otimes SU_2$ invariance of the state (2).

If a third party becomes involved and entangles her probe system with that of Alice and Bob it reduces the quality of the entanglement they share in $|\psi_{2n}\rangle$. Errors are introduced to the correlations, and on comparison of a fraction of their data, Alice and Bob become aware of the eavesdropper, 'Eve'. The multi-photon signals improve matters, as every uniquely identifiable 4-mode number state can represent a letter in their cryptographic alphabet. By increasing the probabilities of high-n singlets, the legitimate users Alice and Bob have a greater vocabulary at their disposal. More precisely, in the absence of losses, the achievable bit rate of their communication (per pulse) will increase significantly with the number of photons, because the number of distinguishable measurements increases. There are $n+1$ such outcomes for each singlet of 2n photons.

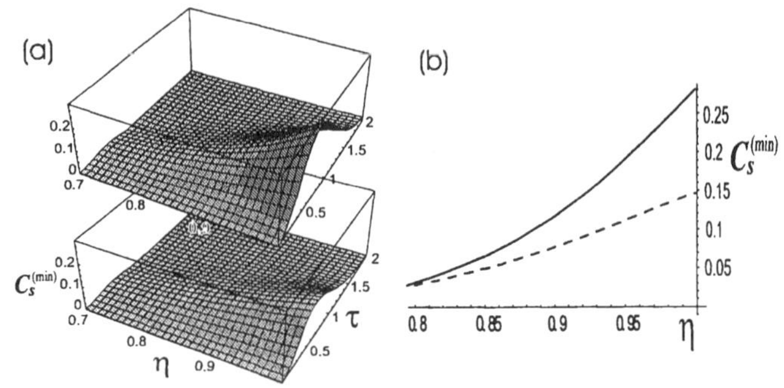

Figure 2. Both graphs show the lower bound on the achievable secure bit rate C_s. In (a) it is plotted as a function of η and τ, where η is the overall transmission, encompassing limited detection efficiency and propagation losses, and τ is the effective interaction time of the source. The upper plot (a) refers to the protocol using both 2-photon and 4-photon results, and the lower plot is for the standard protocol using 2-photon results only. One sees that using 4-photon detections, in addition to 2-photon detections, leads to a significant increase in secure bit rates in the region of low losses. This is shown in (b), where we have plotted the lower bound on C_s for both protocols, at their optimal τ values: $\tau = 0.78$ and $\tau = 0.70$ for the new and old protocols, respectively. The bound on C_s decreases for higher τ values, as can be seen clearly in (a), because the probabilities for 2-photon and 4-photon results are reduced as higher photon numbers become more and more likely. Making use of these higher photon numbers would further increase the bit rates.

We have examined the effect of natural photon losses, modelled by the action of beam splitters in each of the four photon modes. Such losses will introduce errors in the Alice/Bob correlations, because the state after losses no longer exhibits the perfect correlations of the singlets. In QKD one has to assume that all errors are due to Eve's intervention. The maximum value of the secure channel capacity, in the presence of losses, will depend on the type of eavesdropping attack employed, and Eve's ability to maximize her information. In principle all eavesdropping strategies must be considered, a difficult task since the system considered here is very complex.[4] We considered a specific QKD protocol, in which Alice and Bob utilize the detection results when they detect two photons each, in addition to the results when only one photon is detected on each side. We compared this case to the standard protocol, which exclusively uses the 2-photon results.[5] The eavesdropper was allowed to replace the transmission lines with ideal lossless ones, and, in addition, was given control of the source. Knowing that Alice and Bob expect some errors on the lossy lines, she tailors her interference to reproduced the error profiles they expect. She sometimes sends singlet states unmodified, but other times she simply send a particular 4-mode number state, of which she has full knowledge.

Under these conditions, we determined the secrecy capacity for this simple protocol. The results are shown in Fig. 2. It is seen that for low losses the secure bit rate is almost doubled. This improvement would be enhanced if, in addition to 2-photon and 4-photon signals, higher photon number singlets were employed. For a fuller description of our analysis see Ref. 6.

3 Experimental Quantum Cloning

Let us progress to another application employing the entangled photon pairs created in a downconversion process: quantum cloning of a single photon.

The perfect copying of an unknown quantum state is impossible, a direct consequence of the linearity of quantum mechanics.[7] However, it is possible to approximately clone such a state, and a device which copies all possible unknown states to the same degree of accuracy is known as a *universal quantum cloning machine.* We utilized stimulated emission in parametric downconversion to demonstrate a universal cloning for individual quantum systems that is close to optimal. In our experiment the downconversion scheme differs slightly from that used for cryptography. An input photon, siphoned from the pump beam, is injected along the downconversion mode a and passes through the nonlinear crystal having first been prepared in an arbitrary polarization state. If we take as an example an input photon polarized in the horizontal direction, this photon will have associated with it a creation operator $\hat{a}_h^\dagger$. As a consequence of the Hamiltonian (1) the unitary evolution of the system is, to first order:

$$-i\kappa t(a_h^\dagger b_v^\dagger - a_v^\dagger b_h^\dagger)a_h^\dagger|0\rangle \Rightarrow \frac{1}{\sqrt{3}}(\sqrt{2}|2,0;0,1\rangle - |1,1;1,0\rangle). \tag{4}$$

Here we see that the photon distribution $|2,0;0,1\rangle$, with the 2 output photons in the same mode as the injected photon, is twice as likely to occur in a measurement as the alternative (where the output photons are in mutually orthogonal polarizations). It can be interpreted that the two photons in mode a are the *clones* of the input photon. It is impossible to determine which of the two output photons both in mode $\hat{a}_h^\dagger$ was the input photon, and which was the downconverted photon. Therefore the two exiting photons are *both* approximate copies of the input. To determine the fidelity of the clones we take the average cloning success over both exiting photons. Looking again at (4), with probability 2/3 the clones are in the same mode as the input, i.e., the cloning is perfect. With probability 1/3 the two output clones are in different modes. In this case, on average the cloning is 50% perfect. Adding up these probabilities: $F = \frac{2}{3} \times 1 + \frac{1}{3} \times \frac{1}{2} = \frac{5}{6}$.

This was shown to be the optimal fidelity for the universal cloning of a single photon.[8] Note that in this example the input photon was chosen to be of horizontal polarization, but because of the Hamiltonian symmetry, the same results hold for input photons of any polarization. Therefore, this experiment represents a demonstration of truly *universal* cloning, in line with the proposal of Ref. 9. More details of our experiment can be found in Ref. 10.

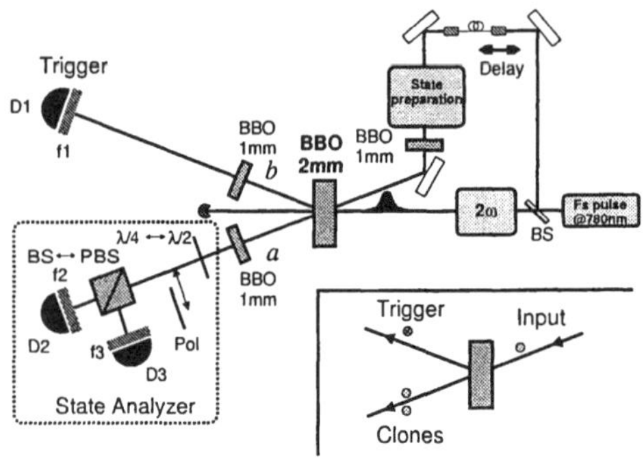

Figure 3. Setup for cloning by stimulated emission. A tiny part of each Ti:Sa pump pulse is split off at the beam splitter and then attenuated below the single-photon level, thus probabilistically preparing the input photon. Its polarization state can be adjusted at will. The major part of every pulse from the laser is frequency doubled and used to pump the nonlinear crystal (2-mm-long βBO), where photon pairs entangled in polarization are created in the modes a and b. A delay line containing a single-mode optical fiber facilitates superimposing the input photon and the a photon produced in the crystal. For perfect overlap, the two photons in mode a after the crystal are indistinguishable and both are optimal clones of the input photon. Note that both clones are in the same mode.

References

1. A. Lamas-Linares, J. C. Howell, and D. Bouwmeester, *Nature* **412**, 887 (2001).
2. C. E. Shannon, *Bell Syst. Tech. J* **50**, 656 (1949).
3. A. Peres, *Quantum Theory: Concepts and Methods* **ch 9**, p.282 Kluwer Acad. (1998).
4. A. Ekert, B. Hutner, G. Massimo Palma, and A. Peres, *Phys. Rev. A* **50**, 2 (1994).
5. T. Jennewein, C. Simon, G. Weihs, H. Weinfurter, and A. Zeilinger, Phys. Rev. Lett **84**, 4729 (2000).
6. G. Durkin, C. Simon, and D. Bouwmeester, *Phys. Rev. Lett.* **88**, 18 (2002).
7. W. K. Wootters, W. H. Zurek, *Nature* **299**, 802 (1982); D. Dieks, *Phys. Lett. A* **92**, 271 (1982).
8. D. Bruß, A. Ekert, and C. Macchiavello, *Phys. Rev. Lett.* **81**, 2598 (1998).
9. C. Simon, G. Weihs, and A. Zeilinger, *Phys. Rev. Lett.* **84**, 2993 (2000).
10. A. Lamas-Linares, C. Simon, J. C. Howell, and D. Bouwmeester, *Science* **296**, 712 (2002).

OBSERVATION OF PHOTONS EMITTED DURING INHIBITED SPONTANEOUS EMISSION

DAVID BRANNING AND PAUL KWIAT
Department of Physics, University of Illinois, 1110 W. Green St., Urbana, IL 61801-3080, USA
E-mail: branning@uiuc.edu

ALAN MIGDALL
Optical Technology Division, NIST, Gaithersburg, MD, 20899-8441, USA

We present the results of an experiment to observe inhibited spontaneous emission of a parametric downconverter by an optical cavity that is switched off in a time that is short compared with the round trip time of the light. The question is, can photons be detected immediately, or only after some retardation time? Our results are consistent with the cavity QED prediction that photons can be counted immediately.

When an excited atom is placed near a mirror, it is allowed to radiate only into the set of electromagnetic modes that satisfy the boundary conditions imposed by the mirror. If none of these modes are compatible with the emission modes of the atom, it will not radiate. This phenomenon, known as inhibited spontaneous emission, has been observed for atoms, for trapped electrons, and for parametric downconverters (PDC's), in which incident pump photons spontaneously decay into pairs of lower-energy signal and idler photons.[1]

In 1995, Fearn *et al.*[2] proposed an interesting thought experiment: suppose an excited atom is placed in an inhibiting cavity, and after some time, one mirror of the cavity is instantaneously replaced by a photon-counting detector. Will the photodetector count a photon immediately (because the counter-propagating field amplitudes have been in the cavity all along), or will there be some round-trip delay due to the necessity of the atom first seeing the changed mode structure of the cavity, and then radiating a photon into this new mode structure?

The experiment is currently impractical to carry out for atoms, but because very long cavities can be used to inhibit a PDC, it is possible to perform the variation shown in Fig. 1(a) using an electro-optic switch (Pockels cell).[3] A pump laser beam is directed into a PDC, where pairs of signal and idler photons may be created (Process 1). The pump, signal, and idler beams are reflected back into the PDC, where there is another chance for downconversion to occur (Process 2). Because there is no way to distinguish which downconversion process gives rise to the detected photons at A [see Fig. 1(b)], interference is possible; the relative phases are adjusted via a dispersive "tilt glass," to produce fringes at detector A (see Fig. 2).

The "sudden mirror replacement" experiment is conducted with the tilt

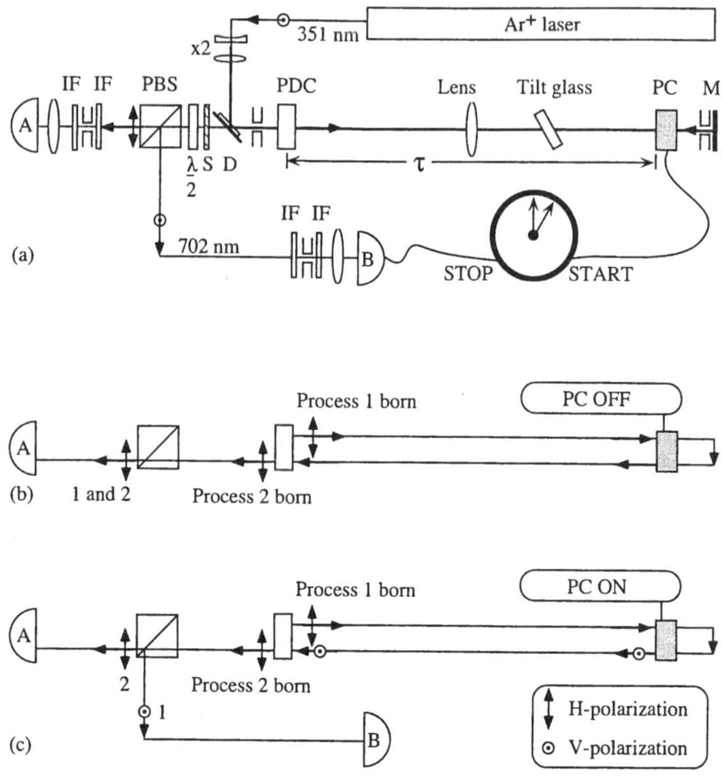

Figure 1. (a) Experimental arrangement. The PDC is a 6.25-mm KDP crystal, and the PC is 44.7 mm of KD*P. The Schott glass (S), dichroic mirror (D), and interference filters (IF) allow only the downconversion to impinge on the avalanche photodiode detectors A and B. (b) With the PC off, Process 1 and Process 2 photons go to the same detector. (c) With the PC on, Process 1 photons are rotated from H to V, and deflected to detector B.

glass fixed at the fringe minimum, where the emission is (partially) frustrated (Fig. 2). The Pockels cell (PC) is activated and quickly (within 7.5 ns) rotates the signal and idler polarizations by 90 degrees. The Process 1 light in the cavity now travels through the PDC without interfering, and is directed by the polarizer (PBS) to detector B [Fig. 1(c)].

The question is, how soon after the cavity is switched off will photons be registered at B? The two plausible scenarios in the thought experiment lead to two different answers: if photons (or photon amplitudes) were present in the cavity all along, then the delay should be τ (the propagation time from the PC to the PDC) plus a propagation time from the PDC to the detector. On the other hand, if the PDC had to wait to emit light until the mode structure was changed, this would incur an extra round-trip delay of 2τ (from

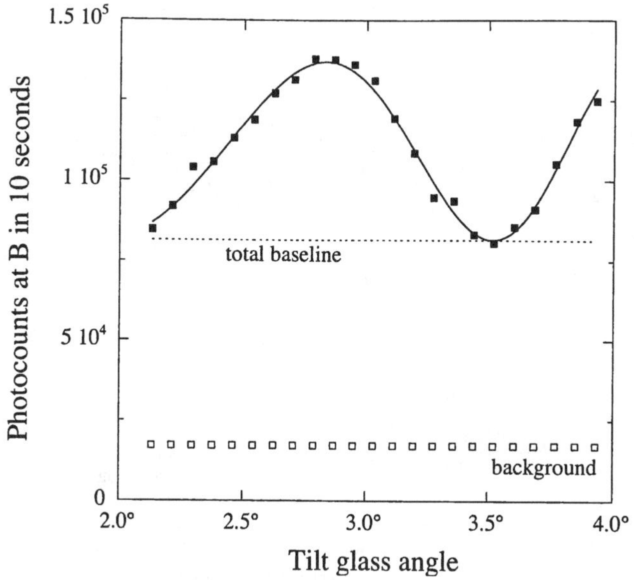

Figure 2. Single-channel interference fringe obtained by scanning the tilt glass incidence angle within the cavity. The background-corrected fringe visibility is (30 ± 1)%. The difference between the minimum and the background is the non-interfering total baseline rate.

the PC to the PDC and back). These two possibilities can be experimentally distinguished so long as the switching time is less than 2τ. In our experiment, the PC has a rise time of 7.5 ns and it is (1856 ± 5) mm away from the center of the PDC, so $2\tau = (12.37 \pm 0.03)$ ns.

The experimental results are shown in Fig. 3. The dots record the number of photon counts at various time delays, starting from just before the activation of the PC. For comparison, the photon arrivals from a HeNe laser in the same apparatus are shown as a thin line. The HeNe light is not suppressed or enhanced by the cavity, and must arrive at the early time. The downconversion arrivals are consistent with this early arrival, and inconsistent with an additional delay of 2τ by 29 standard deviations.

An important caveat is that because the fringe in Fig. 2 does not have perfect visibility, we observe a non-interfering rate of downconversion that is always taking place from both Process 1 and Process 2 (the "total baseline rate"). It is then hardly surprising that some photons arrive at detector B at the same time as the HeNe photons. The only photons that can be unambiguously identified as having come from an inhibited spontaneous emitter are those which remain after this baseline is subtracted. The mean counting rate

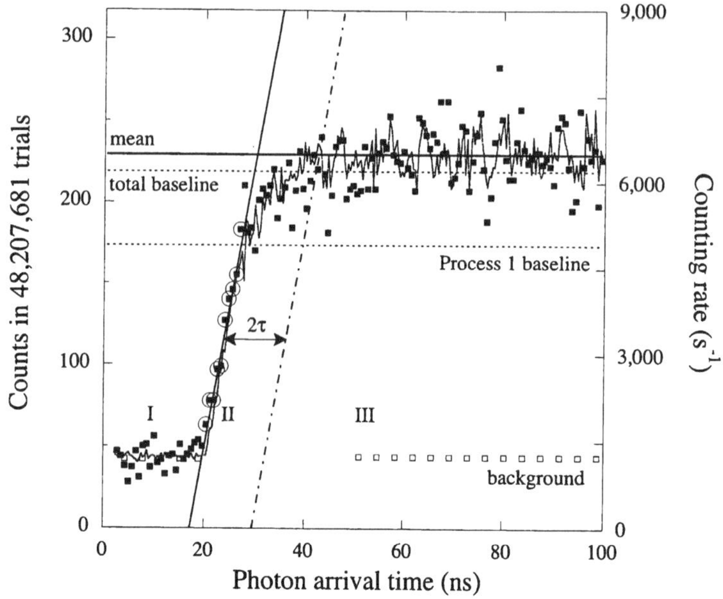

Figure 3. Arrival-time data for downconverted photons in the cavity (dots) and for a HeNe beam (solid line.) In region I, the Pockels cell has not been activated and no photons arrive at B. In region II, the Pockels cell voltage is rising. In region III, the photon counting rate at B reaches a steady-state value that is 2.2 standard deviations above the total baseline rate (see Fig. 2); this rate is also 28 standard deviations above the baseline rate of photons from only Process 1.

above background in region III of Fig. 3 is (5252 ± 74) s^{-1}. This exceeds the baseline rate (after correction for background, drifts, and PC efficiency[4]) by (290 ± 130) s^{-1}, or 2.2 standard deviations. Alternatively, we note that detector B can only register Process 1 photons (see Fig. 1), which are suppressed by 30% at the fringe minimum in Fig. 2 (along with the Process 2 photons). The mean counting rate in region III of Fig. 3 exceeds this suppressed "Process 1 baseline rate" by (1576 ± 57) s^{-1}, or 28 standard deviations.

References

1. T. J. Herzog, J. G. Rarity, H. Weinfurter, and A. Zeilinger, *Phys. Rev. Lett.* **72**, 629 (1994).
2. H. Fearn, R. J. Cook, and P. W. Milonni, *Phys. Rev. Lett.* **74**, 1327 (1995).
3. H. Weinfurter *et al.*, Ann. New York Acad. Sci. **755**, 61 (1995).
4. D. Branning, P. G. Kwiat, and A. L. Migdall, in preparation.

COUNTERPROPAGATING ENTANGLED PHOTONS IN A WAVEGUIDE WITH PERIODIC NONLINEARITY

MARK C. BOOTH, METE ATATÜRE, GIOVANNI DI GIUSEPPE, ALEXANDER V. SERGIENKO, BAHAA E. A. SALEH AND MALVIN C. TEICH

Quantum Imaging Laboratory, Boston University,
8 Saint Mary's Street, Boston, Massachusetts 02215, USA

The conditions required for spontaneous parametric downconversion in a waveguide with periodic nonlinearity in the presence of an unguided pump field are established. We find that counterpropagating beams exhibit narrow bandwidth permitting the generation of quantum states that possess discrete-frequency entanglement. Such states may be useful for experiments in quantum optics and technologies that benefit from frequency entanglement.

1 Introduction

Entangled photons, which may be generated through the process of spontaneous parametric downconversion (SPDC) in a crystal with $\chi^{(2)}$ nonlinearity, have long been in the spotlight for quantum-optics experiments.[1,2] SPDC suffers from low conversion efficiency, on the order of 10^{-9} entangled-photon pairs per mode per pump photon, which ultimately limits their use for many practical applications. Quasi-phase matching in crystals with periodic nonlinearity, however, offers the promise of increased photon-pair production.[3] Furthermore, with the integration of a waveguide structure, it is possible to control the spatial characteristics of the downconverted photons while still maintaining a substantial increase in conversion efficiency.[4] It turns out that the waveguide structure imparts yet another critically important feature: the possibility of generating counterpropagating signal and idler photons. We compare the crystal tuning characteristics and spectral properties of counterpropagating beams to those for copropagating beams under typical experimental conditions.

2 Conditions for counterpropagating SPDC

We consider the specific example of a PPLN waveguide, with a $\chi^{(2)}$ nonlinearity that is modulated as a square wave in the z-direction. Because in a series expansion of this nonlinearity, the dominant Fourier components are of order $m = \pm 1$, the PPLN waveguide tuning characteristics result primarily from the $m = \pm 1$ curves, as shown in Fig. 1.

If we consider an example in which the pump-beam angle is 80°, there are signal-idler wavelength combinations of approximately 880 nm/1350 nm ($m = -1$, dashed curve, open circles) and 930 nm/1240 nm ($m = +1$, solid

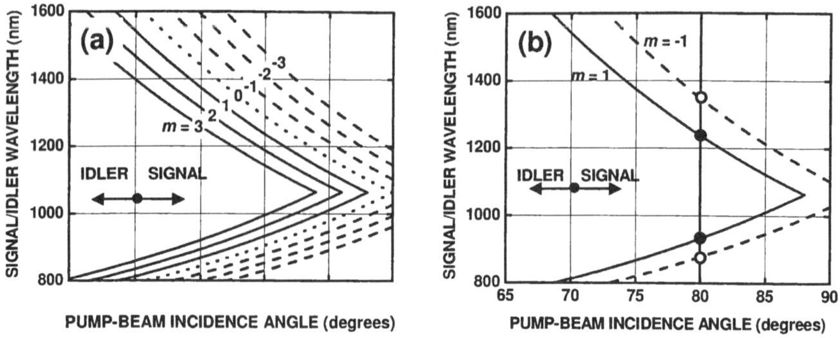

Figure 1. Tuning curves for perfect QPM with various values m: (a) Signal and idler wavelengths versus pump-beam incidence angle θ for grating vector orders $m = 0, \pm1, \pm2$, and ±3 with a poling period $\Lambda = 6.8\ \mu$m. (b) Subset of tuning curves in (a) for $m = \pm1$ with the poling period $\Lambda = 6.8\ \mu$m. The signal photon propagates in the positive z-direction and the idler photon counterpropagates in the negative z-direction as shown by the inset. The pump wavelength is $\lambda_p = 532$ nm in both (a) and (b). Circles in (b) indicate the two signal-idler combinations possible for a pump-beam incidence angle of 80°: 880 nm/1350 nm ($m = -1$, dashed curve, open circles) and 930 nm/1240 nm ($m = +1$, solid curve, solid circles).

curve, solid circles). This quantum state can be represented by

$$|\Psi^{(2)}\rangle \sim c_1|880, 1350\rangle + c_2|930, 1240\rangle, \qquad (1)$$

where the constants c_1 and c_2 are determined mainly by the pump properties. By simply selecting the pump-beam incidence angle to be 74.6°, for example, the two-photon quantum state given above can be readily tuned to new signal-idler wavelength combinations of 810 nm/1550 nm and 860 nm/1380 nm.

3 Spectral properties of counterpropagating SPDC

We also consider effects on the spatio-temporal distribution of downconverted light imparted by the finite crystal length and the modal structure of the waveguide. In a comparison of the tuning curves and spectral properties of counterpropagating beams to those for copropagating beams under typical experimental conditions, we find that the counterpropagating beams retain a narrow bandwidth across many signal-idler wavelength combinations, unlike the results shown in Fig. 2(a) for copropagating beams. This finding supports the claim that a superposition of two counterpropagating nondegenerate photons pairs occurs naturally within the PPLN waveguide structure.

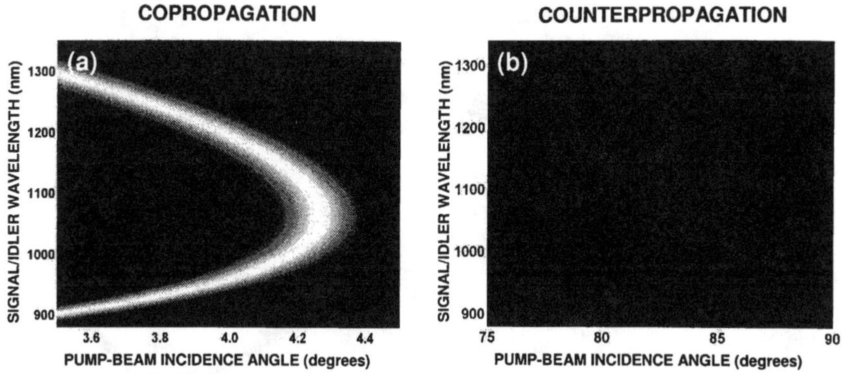

Figure 2. (a) Calculated signal and idler spectra versus pump-beam incidence angle for copropagating beams in a 1-mm PPLN waveguide with a poling period $\Lambda = 7.4$ μm and positive grating vector K_m ($m = 1$). The pump wavelength is $\lambda_p = 532$ nm. (b) Calculated signal and idler spectra versus pump-beam incidence angle for counterpropagating beams in a 1-mm PPLN waveguide with a poling period $\Lambda = 6.8$ μm and $m = \pm 1$. The pump wavelength is $\lambda_p = 532$ nm. Although this plot includes all the information pertaining to the spectra of the downconverted light, it is visually indistinguishable from the plot presented in Fig. 1(b).

4 Application to quantum communication

Copropagating entangled photons generated by SPDC have previously been observed in periodically poled silica fibers (PPSFs) by directly coupling of the pump beam.[5] If the pump beam is coupled to the core medium in a scheme analogous to that of a cladding-pumped fiber laser, it would be possible to generate counterpropagating signal and idler photons directly in the poled fiber. Due to the inherent narrow bandwidth of the counterpropagating beams, a dispersion-free quantum communication apparatus could be realized as illustrated in Fig. 3.

5 Conclusions

It is possible to control the superposition of two or more counterpropagating nondegenerate photon pairs by tuning the pump-beam incidence angle, by appropriately changing the pump field profile using, e.g., a superposition of pump angles, and by engineering the periodicity of the nonlinearity. Such a quantum state cannot be generated in bulk nonlinear media, nor in media with periodic structures, but they are generated naturally in media with both periodic nonlinearity and a waveguiding structure. Although we primarily discussed theoretical results for a PPLN waveguide, the results are general and will also apply, for example, to a periodically-poled cladding-pumped fiber with $\chi^{(2)}$ nonlinearity.

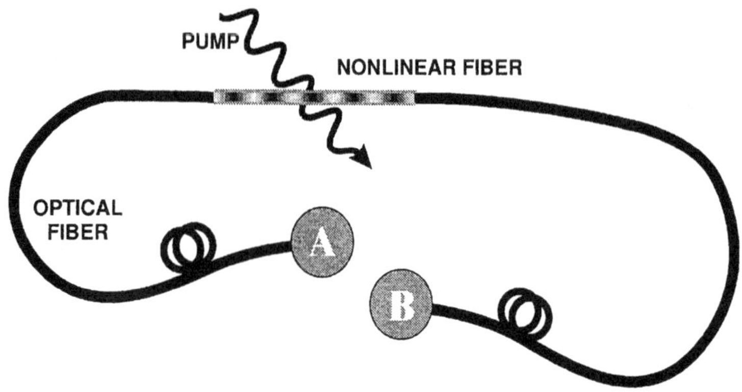

Figure 3. Application to quantum communication. The pump beam (which is guided in the fiber cladding) couples to the core medium as it propagates. Since the core medium has a modulated nonlinearity (illustrated as striations), counterpropagating entangled photons can be generated directly within the communication fiber to provide dispersion-free quantum communication between Alice (A) and Bob (B).

Acknowledgements

This work was supported by the National Science Foundation; the Center for Subsurface Sensing and Imaging Systems (CenSSIS), an NSF Engineering Research Center; the Defense Advanced Research Projects Agency (DARPA); and the David and Lucile Packard Foundation.

References

1. J. Peřina, Z. Hradil, and B. Jurčo, *Quantum Optics and Fundamentals of Physics* (Kluwer, Boston, 1994), Chaps. 7 and 8.
2. L. Mandel and E. Wolf, *Optical Coherence and Quantum Optics* (Cambridge, Cambridge, 1995), Chap. 22.
3. S. Tanzilli, H. De Riedmatten, W. Tittel, H. Zbinden, P. Baldi, M. De Micheli, D. B. Ostrowsky, and N. Gisin, *Electron. Lett.* **37**, 26-28 (2001).
4. K. Banaszek, A. B. U'Ren, and I. A. Walmsley, *Opt. Lett.* **26**, 1367-1369 (2001).
5. G. Bonfrate, V. Pruneri, P. G. Kazansky, P. Tapster, and J. G. Rarity, *App. Phys. Lett.* **16**, 2356-2358 (1999).

CONTINUOUS-VARIABLE POLARIZATION ENTANGLEMENT

N. KOROLKOVA, J. HEERSINK, CH. SILBERHORN, G. LEUCHS

Zentrum für Moderne Optik, Universität Erlangen, Staudtstr. 7/B2, 91058 Erlangen, Germany

T. C. RALPH

Department of Physics, University of Queensland, St Lucia, QLD 4072, Australia

R. LOUDON

Department of Electronic Systems Engineering, Essex University, Colchester CO4 3SQ, UK

Quantum information with continuous variables conventionally exploits quantum variables with canonic commutation relations, like position and momentum, or quadrature field components. In contrast, this contribution is devoted to quantum continuous polarization variables. The relevant observables are quantum Stokes operators which obey the SU(2) algebra with a commutator which is not a c-number but an operator. In this paper, we review the concept of polarization squeezing and the new concept of continuous-variable polarization entanglement using quantum Stokes parameters. We discuss the prospects and specific features of such nonclassical polarization states for quantum communication.

1 Quantum Stokes operators

The Hermitian Stokes operators are defined as quantum versions of their classical counterparts:[1,2]

$$\begin{aligned} \hat{S}_0 &= \hat{a}_x^\dagger \hat{a}_x + \hat{a}_y^\dagger \hat{a}_y, & \hat{S}_1 &= \hat{a}_x^\dagger \hat{a}_x - \hat{a}_y^\dagger \hat{a}_y, \\ \hat{S}_2 &= \hat{a}_x^\dagger \hat{a}_y + \hat{a}_y^\dagger \hat{a}_x, & \hat{S}_3 &= i\left(\hat{a}_y^\dagger \hat{a}_x - \hat{a}_x^\dagger \hat{a}_y\right), \end{aligned} \tag{1}$$

where the x and y subscripts label the creation, destruction and number operators of quantum harmonic oscillators associated with the x and y photon polarization modes. The creation and destruction operators have the usual commutation relations,

$$\left[\hat{a}_j, \hat{a}_k^\dagger\right] = \delta_{jk} \qquad j,k = x,y. \tag{2}$$

The Stokes operator $\hat{S}_0$ commutes with all the others,

$$\left[\hat{S}_0, \hat{S}_i\right] = 0, \qquad i = 1,2,3 \tag{3}$$

but the operators $\hat{S}_1$, $\hat{S}_2$ and $\hat{S}_3$ satisfy the commutation relations of the SU(2) Lie algebra, for example

$$\left[\hat{S}_2, \hat{S}_3\right] = 2i\hat{S}_1. \tag{4}$$

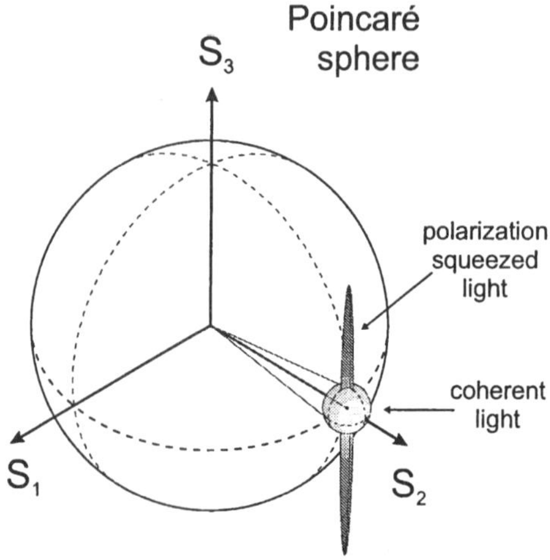

Figure 1. Representations of quantum polarization states of bright coherent and bright amplitude-squeezed light on the Poincaré sphere. The latter shows polarization squeezing in the parameters $\hat{S}_0$, $\hat{S}_1$, and $\hat{S}_2$, with anti-squeezing in $\hat{S}_3$.

The other commutation relations are obtained by a cyclic permutation of indices. Apart from the factor of 2 and the absence of Planck's constant, this is identical to the commutation relation for components of the angular momentum operator. Simultaneous exact measurements of the quantities represented by these Stokes operators are thus impossible in general and their means and variances are restricted by the uncertainty relations

$$V_2V_3 \geq \left|\langle\hat{S}_1\rangle\right|^2, \qquad V_3V_1 \geq \left|\langle\hat{S}_2\rangle\right|^2, \qquad V_1V_2 \geq \left|\langle\hat{S}_3\rangle\right|^2, \tag{5}$$

Here V_j is a convenient shorthand notation for the variance $\langle\hat{S}_j^2\rangle - \langle\hat{S}_j\rangle^2$ of the quantum Stokes parameter $\hat{S}_j$.

For the Stokes operators, one can define nonclassical polarizations states which serve then as requisites for quantum information processing. Light is said to be polarization squeezed[3,4,5,6] if the variance of one or more of the Stokes parameters is smaller than the corresponding value for coherent light[3,4,6] or, alternatively, is below the limit given by an equality sign in the uncertainty relations (5).[5] We define a polarization coherent state as follows: $|\psi_{\mathrm{coh}}\rangle = |\alpha\rangle_x|\alpha\rangle_y$, where $|\alpha\rangle$ is a conventional coherent state. The minimum-uncertainty polarization state corresponds to the level given by an equality sign in the uncertainty relations (5). Note, that the polarization coherent state is not a minimum-uncertainty state for all Stokes operators, as the uncertainty relations (5) cannot in general be all simultaneously fulfilled with an equality sign. Usually, one has to deal with polarized light beams, mostly linear or circular polarized. In this case, the Stokes vector is aligned along one of the directions S_j, so that one of the Stokes operators $\hat{S}_j$; $j = 1, 2, 3$ possesses strong coherent amplitude and the other two have zero mean values. Then only one of the uncertainty relations (5) survives and other two are bound from below by zero, allowing for the simultaneous exact measurements of the corresponding variables. For the remaining single conjugate pair of Stokes operators the coherent polarization state is a minimum uncertainty state.

Different methods to generate polarization-squeezed light have been proposed (see Ref. 4 for a review). Frequency-tunable polarization-squeezed light, produced by combining the squeezed vacuum with an orthogonally-polarized strong coherent beam on a polarizing beam splitter, has been applied to quantum state transfer from a light field to an atomic ensemble, thus generating spin squeezing of the atoms in an excited state.[5] A range of polarization squeezed states generated from an optical parametric oscillator has recently been extensively experimentally characterized.[6]

2 Entanglement

Continuous-variable polarization entanglement[4] refers to a quantum non-separable state of two light beams and implies correlations of the quantum uncertainties between one or more pairs of Stokes operators of two spatially-separated optical beams. It has the nature of two-mode squeezing as well as entanglement of the amplitude and phase and has been recently observed in an experiment.[7] Continuous-variable polarization entanglement can be characterized either using the criterion for continuous variable EPR-like correlations by Reid,[8,4] or in terms of non-separability of a quantum state.[9,4] Following the derivation of the sufficient form of the inseparability criterion of Duan et al., [9] one can easily rewrite it for Stokes operators using the uncertainty relations from above, e.g., $V_3 V_1 \geq |\langle \hat{S}_2 \rangle|^2$. For a non-separable state one obtains the condition:

$$V(\hat{S}_{1D} + \hat{S}_{1C}) + V(\hat{S}_{3D} - \hat{S}_{3C}) < 2\left(|\langle S_{2C} \rangle| + |\langle S_{2D} \rangle|\right), \tag{6}$$

which is a sufficient criterion of non-separability for Stokes variables.[4,7] Assuming symmetry between subsystems C and D, so that $\langle S_{2C} \rangle = \langle S_{2D} \rangle = \langle S_2 \rangle$, for a non-separable state we get:

$$\frac{V(\hat{S}_{1D} + \hat{S}_{1C}) + V(\hat{S}_{3D} - \hat{S}_{3C})}{2|\langle S_2 \rangle|} < 2. \tag{7}$$

For some cases it might be advantageous to use the generalized Heisenberg equation $V_3 V_1 \geq |\langle \hat{S}_2 \rangle|^2 + |\langle \Delta\hat{S}_1 \Delta\hat{S}_3 \rangle|^2$, $\Delta\hat{S}_j = \hat{S}_j - \langle \hat{S}_j \rangle$, to derive Eq. (6). Then the following condition for non-separability is obtained:[7]

$$V(\hat{S}_{1D} + \hat{S}_{1C}) + V(\hat{S}_{3D} - \hat{S}_{3C}) \leq 2\sqrt{|\langle S_{2C} \rangle|^2 + |\langle \Delta\hat{S}_{1C} \Delta\hat{S}_{3C} \rangle|^2} + 2\sqrt{|\langle S_{2D} \rangle|^2 + |\langle \Delta\hat{S}_{1D} \Delta\hat{S}_{3D} \rangle|^2}. \tag{8}$$

The current development of methods for quantum information processing based on quantum continuous variables has stimulated interest in the nonclassical polarization states. The correspondence between the algebras of the Stokes operators and the spin operators enables an efficient transfer of quantum information from a freely-propagating optical carrier to a matter system. For implementation of quantum communication protocols, the use of bright polarization-entangled beams allows one to dispense with the experimentally costly local oscillator techniques and combine intense easy-to-handle sources of EPR-entangled light and efficient direct detection. Experiments on the generation of bright pulsed polarization-squeezed and polarization-entangled states using a fiber Sagnac interferometer[4] are currently in progress.[10] Such non-classical polarization states are then well suited for quantum key distribution[4,11] and quantum teleportation with intense light fields.

Acknowledgments

The work was supported by the Deutsche Forschungsgemeinschaft and by the EU grant under QIPC, project IST-1999-13071 (QUICOV).

References

1. G. G. Stokes, Trans. Camb. Phil. Soc. **9**, 399 (1852).
2. M. Born and E. Wolf, *Principles of Optics*, 7th edn (Cambridge University Press, Cambridge, 1999).
3. A. S. Chirkin, A. A. Orlov, and D. Yu. Paraschuk, *Quantum Electron.* **23**, 870 (1993) (translated from *Kvantovaya Electronika* **20**, 999 (1993)); N. V. Korolkova and A. S. Chirkin, *J. Mod. Opt.* **43**, 869 (1996).
4. N. Korolkova, G. Leuchs, R. Loudon, T. C. Ralph, and Ch. Silberhorn, *Phys. Rev. A* **65**, 052306 (2002).
5. J. Hald, J. L. Sorensen, C. Schori, and E. S. Polzik, *J. Mod. Opt.* **47**, 2599 (2000).
6. W. P. Bowen, R. Schnabel, H.-A. Bachor, and P. K. Lam, *Phys. Rev. Lett.* **88**, 093601 (2002).
7. W. P. Bowen, N. Treps, R. Schnabel, and P. K. Lam, quant-ph/0206017.
8. M. D. Reid and P.D. Drummond, *Phys. Rev. Lett.* **60**, 2731 (1988); M. D. Reid, *Phys. Rev. A* **40**, 913 (1989); M. D. Reid, quant-ph/0112038.
9. L.-M. Duan, G. Giedke, J. I. Cirac, and P. Zoller, *Phys. Rev. Lett.* **84**, 2722 (2000).
10. J. Heersink, T. Gaber, S. Lorenz, O. Glöckl, N. Korolkova, G. Leuchs, manuscript in preparation.
11. S. Lorenz, Ch. Silberhorn, N. Korolkova, R.S. Windeler, and G. Leuchs, *Appl.Phys.B* **73**, 855 (2001).

ENGINEERING PHOTONIC ENTANGLEMENT

ALFRED B. U'REN, MANUEL DE LA CRUZ AND IAN A. WALMSLEY
Clarendon Laboratory, Oxford University, Oxford, OX1 3PU, UK
E-mail: walmsley@physics.ox.ac.uk

REINHARD ERDMANN
Rome Air Force Laboratory, Rome, NY, 13439, USA

We discuss the use of quasi-phase-matched downconversion to engineer the amount and type of space-time entanglement present in two-photon states. We also discuss a quantum positioning scheme based on a source of multiple entangled photons and report the implementation of this scheme for the case of two entangled photons.

1 Introduction

Quantum entanglement may be exploited for improved metrology, such as in clock synchronization[1] and positioning[2]. Such schemes often rely on multi-photon states with tailored spectral entanglement. It is therefore important to develop tools to engineer entanglement in the continuous degree of freedom of multi-photon states. Entanglement relies on the coherent addition of quantum amplitudes resulting from multiple interfering pathways. This interference is degraded and indeed can be destroyed if the pathways are in any way distinguishable in principle. A complete analysis must therefore include all degrees of freedom, both observed and non-observed ones. In this paper we discuss the use of quasi phase matching (QPM) and broadband pumping for engineering entanglement as well as a novel multi-photon quantum interference effect which makes use of a specifically tailored multi-photon entangled state.

2 Spatio-temporal Schmidt decompositions

Parametric downconversion (PDC) has been used as source of correlated pairs of photons in many recent experiments ranging from fundamental tests of quantum mechanics to implementations of quantum information technologies. Photon pairs may exhibit correlations between the signal and idler photons in spectral, spatial and polarization degrees of freedom. A practical way of selecting those photon pairs that are maximally entangled is through post-selection via either spatial or spectral filtering. Such an approach can lead to improved interference visibility at the expense of a prohibitive reduction in count rates. It is therefore desirable to develop methods of engineering the photon states at the source. A useful tool for analyzing the entanglement present in the continuous degree of freedom of two-photon states is to make a Schmidt decomposition[3] of the spatio-temporal-polarization state amplitude $S(k_s, \omega_s, \mu_s, k_i, \omega_i, \mu_i)$ into a sum of products of functions: $S(k_s, \omega_s, \mu_s, k_i, \omega_i, \mu_i) = \sum_n \sqrt{\lambda_n} \psi_n(k_s, \omega_s, \mu_s) \phi_n(k_i, \omega_i, \mu_i)$ where $\lambda_{s,i}$, $\theta_{s,i}$ and $\mu_{s,i}$ represent the wavelength, propagation angle and polarization of the signal(s) and idler(i) photons. Figure 1 shows such a numerically-obtained Schmidt decomposition (excluding polarization) of a two-photon PDC state from a KTP QPM grating oriented for non-collinear phase matching centered at 900 nm. The figure shows both the eigenvalue amplitudes λ_n and the five lowest-order $\psi_n(\lambda, \theta)$ and $\phi_n(\lambda, \theta)$ functions. It is found that the resulting entanglement does not necessarily involve the infinitely many degrees of freedom in the frequency-space-polarization continuum with typically only a finite number of Schmidt modes having appreciable eigenvalue magnitudes. The number of such modes is a measure of how much entanglement (including spectral, spatial and polarization degrees of freedom) is present in the photon pairs.[4]

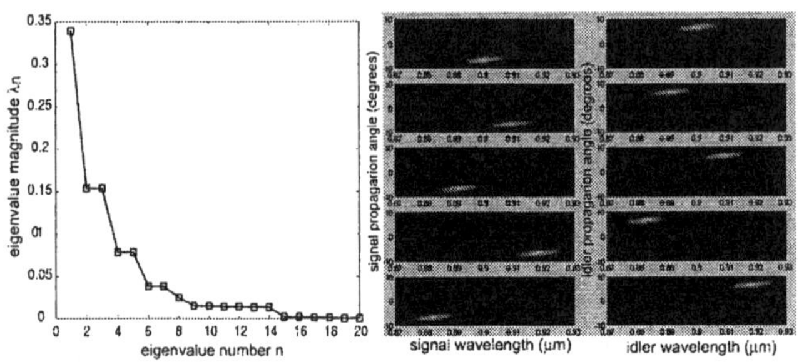

Figure 1. Spatio-temporal Schmidt decomposition

3 Two-photon state engineering using quasi-phase-matching

Nearly all PDC experiments to date have used as source a nonlinear $\chi^{(2)}$ crystal exploiting the principle of birefringent phase-matching. Recently, several groups have studied the generation of PDC using the alternative technique of QPM.[5,6,7,8] It has been shown that QPM leads to the possibility of engineering the temporal properties of the entangled photons.[9] Employing a crystal in a waveguided geometry, on the other hand, leads to the possibility of controlling the spatial characteristics of the downconverted modes.[8]

Producing PDC in nonlinear waveguides dramatically improves the photon collection efficiencies possible in multi-photon coincidence experiments. To illustrate this, Table 1 shows the economy figure of merit $R = R_s/(L \times P)$ for several recent PDC experiments, where R_s is the number of (single) photons detected per second, L the length of the crystal and P the pump power used. As can be seen, waveguide sources have several orders of magnitude higher R values.

GROUP	CRYSTAL	$P[mW]$	$R_s[kHz]$	$R[Hz/(m \cdot W)]$
Kwiat *et al.*[11]	Type I 10 cm KDP	.010	65	6.5×10^7
Weinfurter *et al.*[10]	Type II 2 mm BBO	465	1250	2.7×10^6
Walmsley *et al.* [8]	1 mm KTP waveguide	.022	720	3.3×10^{10}

Table 1. Generating correlated photon pairs efficiently.

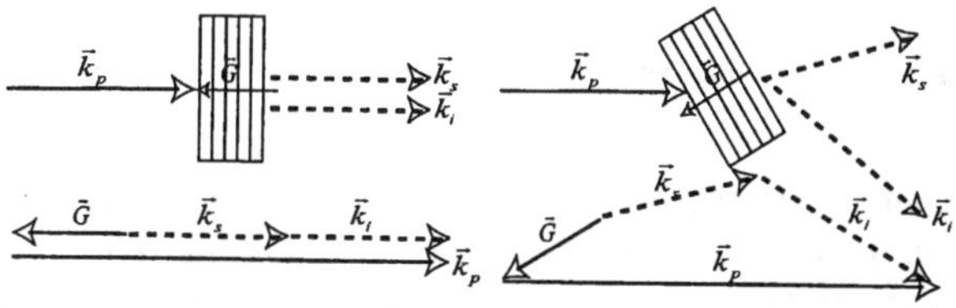

Figure 2. Collinear and non-collinear quasi phase matching

In a typical PDC state (see Fig. 1) the largest eigenvalue Schmidt mode is frequency degenerate. Rotating the QPM structure as shown in Fig. 2 inhibits the degenerate mode. Some examples of collinear and non-collinear QPM phase matching together with their corresponding physical configurations are shown in Fig. 2. On the other hand, by appropriately choosing the beamwaist of the Gaussian pump, it may be shown that it is possible to make the eigenvalue amplitudes decrease quickly enough so that only the first non-degenerate pair is occupied. Thus, PDC generated by a QPM crystal with an appropriately chosen pump can be in the form of a Schmidt Bell state $|\Psi\rangle = |1\rangle_1|1\rangle_2 + |2\rangle_1|2\rangle_2$ where $|i\rangle_j$ represents photon j in Schmidt mode i.

4 Interferometric quantum positioning with slow detectors

Multi-particle spectral entanglement has a number of applications. For example, Giovannetti *et al.*[2] have proposed a positioning scheme making use of a state with a specific kind of frequency entanglement. For this state, the temporal uncertainty in the time of arrival of the photons, and therefore the uncertainty in the inferred position of the emitter with respect to the detectors, diminishes with the number of photons N by a factor $\sqrt{N}$ faster than is possible with an analogous classical system. Unfortunately the scheme requires detectors with a response much faster than the photon wavepacket temporal duration. We propose a quantum interferometric positioning scheme using realistic slow detectors. Consider the following $2N$ photon state:

$$|\Psi^{(2N)}_{\mathrm{AC}}\rangle = \int_{-\infty}^{\infty} d\epsilon f(\epsilon) \prod_{k=1}^{N} a^{\dagger}_{2k-1}(\omega_0 + \epsilon) a^{\dagger}_{2k}(\omega_0 - \epsilon)|\mathrm{vac}\rangle, \qquad (1)$$

where $f(\omega)$ is a function representing the spectral profile of the photon

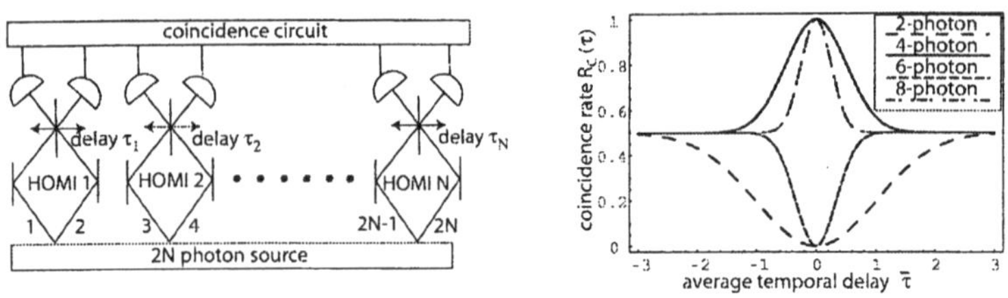

Figure 3. N stacked Hong-Ou-Mandel interferometers and resulting coincidence rate curves.

wavepackets and ω_0 is the central wavepacket frequency. The subscripts of the creation operators represent the (distinguishable) spatial modes in which the photons are emitted. In this scheme $2N$ photons are injected pairwise into N stacked Hong-Ou-Mandel interferometers (HOMI),[12] as depicted in Fig. 3. The $2N$ photons are detected in coincidence upon leaving the output ports of the beam splitters. The resulting coincidence rate is recorded as a function of the temporal delays $\{\tau_1, ..., \tau_N\}$ between the two photons in each HOMI. It can be shown that the coincidence rate function is given as $R_c(\overline{\tau}) \propto 1 + (-1)^N \exp\left[-(\sigma^2 N^2 \overline{\tau}^2)/2\right]$ where $\overline{\tau} = N^{-1}\sum_i \tau_i$ is the average delay, and σ is the spectral profile bandwidth. While for odd N (including the usual two-photon case) the coincidence rate function is a "dip", for even N it becomes a "heap" as depicted in Fig. 3.

The effect described above represents a novel kind of multiple-photon interference which may be used as the basis for a relative quantum positioning scheme. Here we assume that all HOMIs are subjected to the same delay: $\overline{\tau} \to \tau$. The position of an object defining the length of one arm of all $2N$ HOMIs can be determined with a precision dictated by the temporal width of the "dip" or "heap," which improves by a factor of N upon increasing the number of photon pairs (and therefore HOMIs) used.

Suppose that the N HOMIs of Fig. 3 have source and beam splitter in common but are allowed to have vertices defined by the mirrors of each HOMI in distinct locations. Suppose that while all N HOMIs share the left-hand side (LHS) arm, their right-hand side (RHS) arm vertices are used to define the positions of N particles (see Fig. 4). Interference will occur if:

$$\left| \frac{1}{N}\sum_{i=0}^{N} L_i - L_{\text{lhs}} \right| < \frac{2\sqrt{2\ln 2}c}{\sigma N}, \tag{2}$$

where L_{lhs} represents the length of the LHS arm and L_i represents the length of each RHS arm. If interference occurs, the N particles defined by the vertices of the RHS arms lie within a sphere whose radius is inversely proportional to N. The studied interference effect may thus be used to test the degree of localization of the N particles with a precision which scales $\sqrt{N}$ faster than in the case of an analogous ideal classical system.

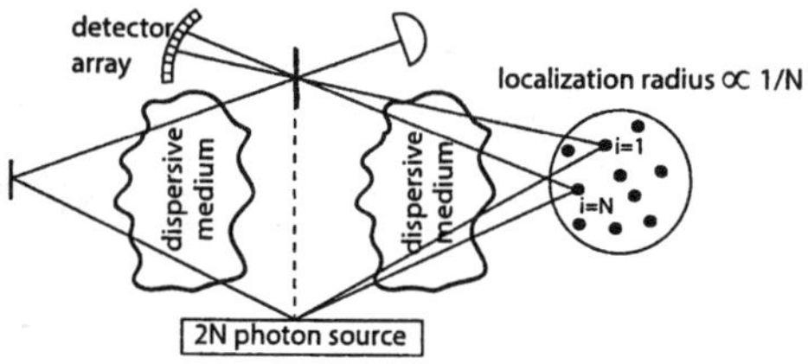

Figure 4. Quantum localizer.

Two-photon positive spectral correlation requires an ultrafast pump.[16] Although no specific methods for generating multi-photon states such as the one in Eq. (1) have been proposed, the added flexibility provided by an ultrafast pump is likely to be necessary. In both the positioning and localization schemes discussed, an ultrafast pulse-pumped source of photons can yield an absolute distance reference obtained through classical timing of pulses.[a]

Temporal pulse broadening, caused by dispersion, reduces the positioning precision in an analogous classical system. A number of quantum states have been shown to be immune to unbalanced to dispersion in various interferometric configurations.[13,14,15] Fourth-order interference in a HOMI pumped by an ultrafast pump is fundamentally different from the continuous-wave (cw) case. Calculations indicate that dispersion in one path can reduce or even eliminate quantum interference.[16,17] Theory also predicts the restoration of interference when identical (balanced) dispersive elements are present in both paths.[14,17,16]

We report experimental results illustrating quantum positioning for the one-pair ($N = 1$) case and show that fourth-order quantum interference, in the configuration discussed above, is free of dispersive effects. A useful feature of the dispersion cancellation effect exhibited by our scheme is that it involves balanced or same-sign dispersion, which is well suited for fiber or atmospheric transmission.

The experimental configuration used (see Fig. 5) is similar to the collinear type II HOMI setup used in prior experiments.[18] Data (see Fig. 5) were taken by monitoring coincidence counts as a function of the translation stage (TS) position. The first plot provides a dispersion-free scan. We also present two unbalanced cases, in which a dispersive element is introduced in one arm. It is seen that increasing the unbalanced dispersive phase term decreases interference visibility and broadens the coincidence rate function. Finally, a scan is included with identical highly dispersive elements. The expected "disper-

[a]Note that the state in Eq. (1) contains positive correlation between alternate photons of the kind required for the Giovannetti *et al.*[2] positioning scheme.

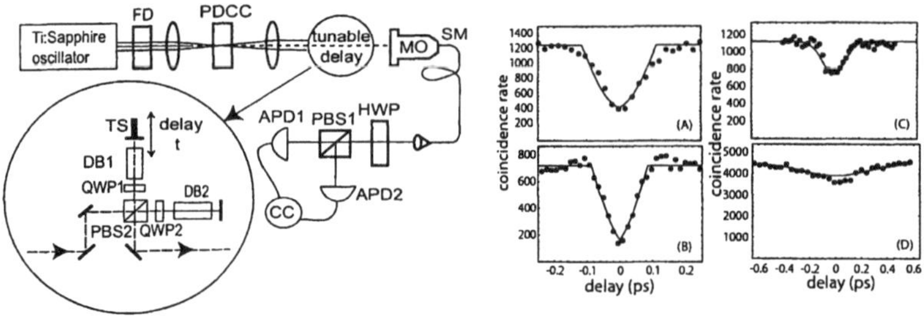

Figure 5. Experimental setup and data. (A) No dispersive glass (B) balanced dispersion (two 10-cm-long S-LAH-60 glass blocks) (C) Unbalanced dispersion (one 6-cm-long BK7 glass block (D) Unbalanced dispersion (one 10-cm-long S-LAH-60 glass block)

sion cancellation" is exhibited in that the high visibility of the dispersion-free profile is recovered, and no temporal broadening observed.

Acknowledgments

We wish to thank K. Banaszek and W. Grice for insightful discussions. This work was partially supported by ARO-administered MURI grant number DAAG-19-99-1-0125.

References

1. V. Giovannetti *et al.*, Phys. Rev. Lett. **87**, 11 (2001).
2. V. Giovannetti, S. Lloyd, and L. Maccone, Nature **412**, 417 (2001).
3. C. K. Law, I. A. Walmsley *et al.*, Phys. Rev. Lett. **84**, 5304 (2000).
4. H. Huang and J. H. Eberly, J. Mod. Opt. **40**, 915 (1993).
5. G. Bonfrate *et al.*, Appl. Phys. Lett. **75**, 2356 (1999).
6. S. Tanzilli *et al.*, Electron. Lett. **37**, 26 (2001).
7. K. Sanaka, *et al.*, Phys. Rev Lett. **86**, 5620 (2001).
8. K. Banaszek, A. U'Ren, and I. Walmsley, Opt. Lett. **26**, 1367 (2002).
9. A. U'Ren, I. Walmsley, Digest of OSA Annual Meeting **ME2**, (2000).
10. C. Kurtsiefer *et al.*, Phys. Rev. A **64**, 023802 (2001).
11. P. G. Kwiat *et al.*, Phys. Rev. A **48**, R867 (1993).
12. C. Hong, Z. Ou, and L. Mandel Phys. Rev. Lett. **59**, 2044 (1987).
13. M. J. Fitch *et al.*, Phys. Rev. A **65**, 054809 (2002).
14. A. Steinberg *et al.*, Phys. Rev. Lett. **68**, 2421 (1992).
15. J. Franson, Phys. Rev. Lett. **45**, 3126 (1992).
16. R. Erdmann, I. Walmsley *et al.*, Phys. Rev. A **62**, 053810 (2000).
17. A. Sergienko *et al.*, Phys. Rev. A **59**, 2359 (1999).
18. W. Grice, R. Erdmann, and I. Walmsley, Phys. Rev. A **57**, R2289 (1998).

ENTANGLED-PHOTON STATE ENGINEERING

A. V. SERGIENKO, G. DI GIUSEPPE, M. ATATÜRE,
B. E. A. SALEH, AND M. C. TEICH
Quantum Imaging Laboratory, Department of Electrical & Computer Engineering and Department of Physics, Boston University, Boston, MA 02215, USA
E-mail: AlexSerg@bu.edu

We have studied experimentally and theoretically the hyper-entanglement of quantum states produced in the nonlinear process of spontaneous parametric downconversion. This simultaneous entanglement in several pairs of quantum variables (frequency, three-dimensional wave vector, and polarization) provides a significant resource for designing complex nonclassical states for quantum information processing and quantum measurement applications.

1 Introduction

In the nonlinear-optical process of spontaneous parametric downconversion (SPDC), in which a laser beam illuminates a nonlinear-optical crystal, pairs of photons are generated in a state that can be entangled[1] concurrently in frequency, momentum, and polarization. A significant number of experimental efforts designed to verify the entangled nature of such states have been carried out on states entangled in a *single* parameter, such as in energy,[2] momentum,[3] or polarization.[4] In general, the quantum state produced by SPDC is not factorizable into independently entangled single-parameter functions. Consequently any attempt to access one parameter is affected by the presence of the others. A common approach to quantum interferometry to date has been to choose a single entangled parameter of interest and eliminate the dependence of the quantum state on all other parameters. For example, when investigating polarization entanglement, spectral and spatial filtering are typically imposed in an attempt to restrict attention to polarization alone.

A more general approach to this problem is to consider and exploit the concurrent entanglement from the outset. In this approach, the observed quantum-interference pattern in one parameter, such as polarization, can be modified at will by controlling the dependence of the state on the other parameters, such as frequency and transverse wave vector. This strong interdependence has its origin in the nonfactorizability of the quantum state into product functions of the separate parameters.

We theoretically and experimentally study how the polarization quantum-interference pattern, presented as a function of relative temporal delay between the photons of an entangled pair, is modified by controlling the optical system through different kinds of spatial apertures. The effect of the spectral profile of the pump field is investigated by using both a continuous-wave and a pulsed laser to generate SPDC. The role of the spatial profile of the pump field is also studied experimentally by restricting the pump-beam diameter at the face of the nonlinear crystal.

Spatial effects in Type-I SPDC have previously been investigated, typically in the context of imaging with spatially resolving detection systems.[5,6] The theoretical formalism presented here for Type-II SPDC is suitable for extension to Type-I in the presence of an arbitrary optical system and detection apparatus. Our study leads to a deeper physical understanding of multi-parameter entangled two-photon states and concomitantly provides a route for engineering these states for specific applications, including quantum information processing.

2 Multi-parameter Entangled-State Generation, Propagation, and Detection

Generation. By virtue of the relatively weak interaction in the nonlinear crystal, we consider the two-photon state generated within the confines of first-order time-dependent perturbation theory:

$$|\Psi^{(2)}\rangle \sim \frac{\mathrm{i}}{\hbar} \int_{t_0}^{t} dt' \; \hat{H}_{\mathrm{int}}(t') \; |0\rangle \, . \tag{1}$$

Here $\hat{H}_{\mathrm{int}}(t')$ is the interaction Hamiltonian, $[t_0, t]$ is the duration of the interaction, and $|0\rangle$ is the initial vacuum state. The interaction Hamiltonian governing this phenomenon is[7]

$$\hat{H}_{\mathrm{int}}(t') \sim \chi^{(2)} \int_V d\mathbf{r} \; \hat{E}_p^{(+)}(\mathbf{r}, t') \, \hat{E}_o^{(-)}(\mathbf{r}, t') \, \hat{E}_e^{(-)}(\mathbf{r}, t') \; + \; \mathrm{H.c.} \, , \tag{2}$$

where $\chi^{(2)}$ is the second-order susceptibility and V is the volume of the nonlinear medium in which the interaction takes place. The operator $\hat{E}_j^{(\pm)}(\mathbf{r}, t')$ represents the positive- (negative-) frequency portion of the jth electric-field operator, with the subscript j representing the pump (p), ordinary (o), and extraordinary (e) waves at position $\mathbf{r}$ and time t', and H.c. stands for Hermitian conjugate. Because of the high intensity of the pump field it can be represented by a classical c-number, rather than as an operator, with an arbitrary spatiotemporal profile given by

$$E_p(\mathbf{r}, t) = \int d\mathbf{k}_p \; \tilde{E}_p(\mathbf{k}_p) e^{\mathrm{i}\mathbf{k}_p \cdot \mathbf{r}} e^{-\mathrm{i}\omega_p(\mathbf{k}_p)t} \, , \tag{3}$$

where $\tilde{E}_p(\mathbf{k}_p)$ is the complex-amplitude profile of the field as a function of the wave vector $\mathbf{k}_p$.

We decompose the three-dimensional wave vector $\mathbf{k}_p$ into a two-dimensional transverse wave vector $\mathbf{q}_p$ and frequency ω_p, so that Eq. (3) takes the form

$$E_p(\mathbf{r},t) = \int d\mathbf{q}_p\, d\omega_p\, \tilde{E}_p(\mathbf{q}_p;\omega_p) e^{i\kappa_p z} e^{i\mathbf{q}_p\cdot\mathbf{x}} e^{-i\omega_p t}, \tag{4}$$

where $\mathbf{x}$ spans the transverse plane perpendicular to the propagation direction z. In a similar way the ordinary and extraordinary fields can be expressed in terms of the quantum-mechanical creation operators $\hat{a}^\dagger(\mathbf{q},\omega)$ for the $(\mathbf{q},\omega)$ modes as

$$\hat{E}_j^{(-)}(\mathbf{r},t) = \int d\mathbf{q}_j\, d\omega_j\; e^{-i\kappa_j z} e^{-i\mathbf{q}_j\cdot\mathbf{x}} e^{i\omega_j t}\, \hat{a}_j^\dagger(\mathbf{q}_j,\omega_j), \tag{5}$$

where the subscript $j = o, e$. The longitudinal component of $\mathbf{k}$, denoted κ, can be written in terms of the $(\mathbf{q},\omega)$ pair as[6,8]

$$\kappa = \sqrt{\left[\frac{n(\omega,\theta)\,\omega}{c}\right]^2 - |\mathbf{q}|^2}, \tag{6}$$

where c is the speed of light in vacuum, θ is the angle between $\mathbf{k}$ and the optical axis of the nonlinear crystal, and $n(\omega,\theta)$ is the index of refraction in the nonlinear medium. Note that the symbol $n(\omega,\theta)$ in Eq. (6) represents the extraordinary refractive index $n_e(\omega,\theta)$ when calculating κ for extraordinary waves, and the ordinary refractive index $n_o(\omega)$ for ordinary waves.

Substituting Eqs. (4) and (5) into Eqs. (1) and (2) yields the quantum state at the output of the nonlinear crystal:

$$|\Psi^{(2)}\rangle \sim \int d\mathbf{q}_o d\mathbf{q}_e\, d\omega_o d\omega_e\; \Phi(\mathbf{q}_o,\mathbf{q}_e;\omega_o,\omega_e)\hat{a}_o^\dagger(\mathbf{q}_o,\omega_o)\hat{a}_e^\dagger(\mathbf{q}_e,\omega_e)|0\rangle, \tag{7}$$

with

$$\Phi(\mathbf{q}_o,\mathbf{q}_e;\omega_o,\omega_e) = \tilde{E}_p(\mathbf{q}_o+\mathbf{q}_e;\omega_o+\omega_e)\, L\,\mathrm{sinc}\left(\frac{L\Delta}{2}\right) e^{-i\frac{L\Delta}{2}}, \tag{8}$$

where L is the thickness of the crystal and $\Delta = \kappa_p - \kappa_o - \kappa_e$ where κ_j ($j = p, o, e$) is related to the indices $(\mathbf{q}_j,\omega_j)$ via relations similar to Eq. (6). The nonseparability of the function $\Phi(\mathbf{q}_o,\mathbf{q}_e;\omega_o,\omega_e)$ in Eqs. (7) and (8), recalling (6), is the hallmark of *concurrent* multi-parameter entanglement.

Propagation. Propagation of the downconverted light between the planes of generation and detection is characterized by the transfer function of the optical system. The biphoton probability amplitude[7] at the space-time coordinates $(\mathbf{x}_A, t_A)$ and $(\mathbf{x}_B, t_B)$ where detection takes place is defined by

$$A(\mathbf{x}_A,\mathbf{x}_B;t_A,t_B) = \langle 0|\hat{E}_A^{(+)}(\mathbf{x}_A,t_A)\hat{E}_B^{(+)}(\mathbf{x}_B,t_B)|\Psi^{(2)}\rangle. \tag{9}$$

The explicit forms of the quantum operators using the transfer function $\mathcal{H}_{ij}$ ($i = A, B$ and $j = e, o$) describing the propagation of a $(\mathbf{q},\omega)$ mode from the nonlinear-crystal output plane to the detection plane can be found in Ref. 6. By choosing optical systems with explicit forms of the functions $\mathcal{H}_{Ae}$, $\mathcal{H}_{Ao}$,

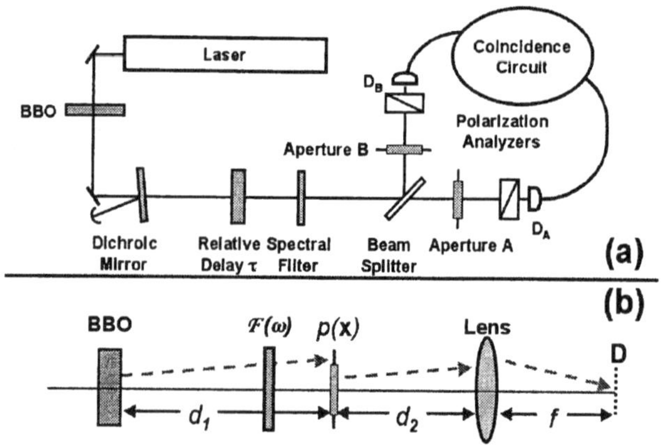

Figure 1. (a) Schematic of the experimental setup for observation of quantum interference using type-II collinear SPDC. (b) Detail of the path from the crystal output plane to the detector input plane. $\mathcal{F}(\omega)$ represents an (optional) filter transmission function, $p(\mathbf{x})$ represents an aperture function, and f is the focal length of the lens.

$\mathcal{H}_{Be}$, and $\mathcal{H}_{Bo}$, the overall biphoton probability amplitude is constructed as desired.

Detection. The formulation of the detection process requires some knowledge of the detection apparatus. Slow detectors, for example, impart temporal integration whereas detectors of finite area impart spatial integration. One extreme case is realized when the temporal response of a *point* detector is spread negligibly with respect to the characteristic time scale of SPDC, namely the inverse of downconversion bandwidth. In this limit the coincidence rate reduces to

$$R = |A(\mathbf{x}_A, \mathbf{x}_B; t_A, t_B)|^2 . \tag{10}$$

On the other hand, quantum-interference experiments typically make use of slow *bucket* detectors. Under these conditions, the coincidence count rate R is readily expressed in terms of the biphoton probability amplitude as

$$R = \int d\mathbf{x}_A d\mathbf{x}_B \, dt_A dt_B \, |A(\mathbf{x}_A, \mathbf{x}_B; t_A, t_B)|^2 . \tag{11}$$

3 Multi-parameter Entangled-State Manipulation

We now apply this formalism[9] to a specific configuration of entangled-photon quantum interferometer illustrated in Fig. 1.

Quantum Interference with Shifted-Ring Apertures. In all existing experimental reports using parametric downconversion the optical elements in the system are placed concentrically about the longitudinal (z) axis.

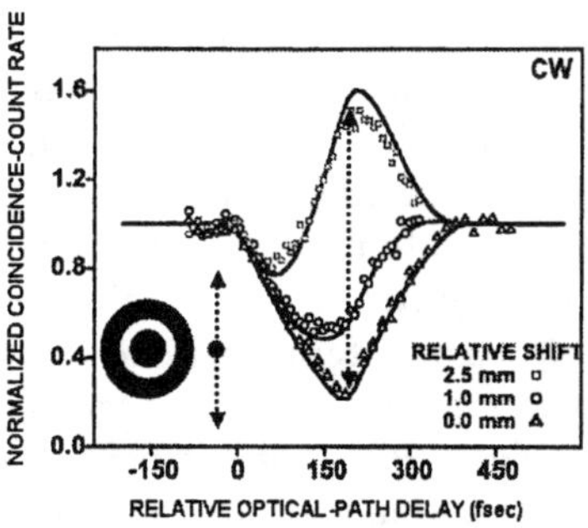

Figure 2. Normalized coincidence-count rate as a function of the relative optical-path delay, for an annular aperture (internal and external diameters of 2 and 4 mm, respectively) in one of the arms of the interferometer in the configuration of Fig. 1. A 7 mm circular aperture is placed in the other arm. The data were obtained using a 351 nm cw pump and no spectral filters. The symbols are experimental results for different relative shifts of the annulus along the direction of the optical axis of the crystal (vertical). The solid curves are the theoretical plots without any fitting parameters.

In this condition, the sole aperture before the beam splitter, as shown in Fig. 1(a), yields the same transfer function as two identical apertures placed in each arm after the beam splitter. We demonstrated experimentally that the observed quantum-interference pattern is also sensitive to a *relative shift* of the apertures in the transverse plane. This extra factor provides yet another degree of control on the quantum-interference pattern for a given aperture form. This new feature provides us with a great deal of flexibility in designing and manipulating polarization entangled quantum states.

Given the experimental setup shown in Fig. 1 with an annular aperture in arm A and a 7 mm circular aperture in arm B, we obtained the quantum-interference patterns shown in Fig. 2. The annular aperture used had an outer diameter of $b = 4$ mm and an inner diameter of $a = 2$ mm. The symbols give the experimental results for various values of the relative shift $|\mathbf{s}_A - \mathbf{s}_B|$, as denoted in the legend. Note that as in the case of the shifted slit, the interference pattern displays a peak rather than the familiar triangular dip usually expected in this type of experiment. Traditionally this effect can be achieved only by polarization analyzer rotation.

4 Conclusion

In summary, we observe that the multi-parameter entangled nature of the two-photon state generated by SPDC allows transverse spatial effects to play a role in polarization-based quantum-interference experiments. The interference patterns generated in these experiments are, as a result, governed in part by the profiles of the apertures in the optical system, which admit wave vectors in specified directions. The observed quantum-interference pattern in one feature, such as polarization (Bell-states), can be modified by controlling the dependence of the state on the other parameters, such as frequency and transverse wave vector. This strong interdependence has its origin in the nonfactorizability of the quantum state into product functions of the separate forms of entanglement. We theoretically and experimentally show how the polarization Bell-state quantum-interference pattern can be modified at will by controlling the optical system through manipulation of its spatial and temporal characteristics. Our study provides a route for engineering hyper-entangled states to be used in quantum-information and quantum-measurement technologies.

References

1. E. Schrödinger, Naturwissenschaften **23,** 807 (1935); **23,** 823 (1935); **23,** 844 (1935) [Translation: J. D. Trimmer, Proc. Am. Phil. Soc. **124,** 323 (1980); reprinted in *Quantum Theory and Measurement*, edited by J. A. Wheeler and W. H. Zurek (Princeton University Press, Princeton, 1983)].
2. C. K. Hong, Z. Y. Ou, and L. Mandel, Phys. Rev. Lett. **59,** 2044 (1987); P. G. Kwiat, A. M. Steinberg, and R. Y. Chiao, Phys. Rev. A **47,** R2472 (1993).
3. J. G. Rarity and P. R. Tapster, Phys. Rev. Lett. **64,** 2495 (1990).
4. Z. Y. Ou and L. Mandel, Phys. Rev. Lett. **61,** 50 (1988); Y. H. Shih and C. O. Alley, Phys. Rev. Lett. **61,** 2921 (1988); Y. H. Shih and A. V. Sergienko, Phys. Lett. A **191,** 201 (1994); P. G. Kwiat, K. Mattle, H. Weinfurter, A. Zeilinger, A. V. Sergienko, and Y. H. Shih, Phys. Rev. Lett. **75,** 4337 (1995).
5. A. Joobeur, B. E. A. Saleh, and M. C. Teich, Phys. Rev. A **50,** 3349 (1994); C. H. Monken, P. H. Souto Ribeiro, and S. Pádua, Phys. Rev. A **57,** 3123 (1998); B. E. A. Saleh, A. Joobeur, and M. C. Teich, Phys. Rev. A **57,** 3991 (1998).
6. B. E. A. Saleh, A. F. Abouraddy, A. V. Sergienko, and M. C. Teich, Phys. Rev. A **62,** 043816 (2000).
7. D. N. Klyshko, *Photons and Nonlinear Optics* (Gordon and Breach Science Publishers, New York, 1988).
8. T. B. Pittman, D. V. Strekalov, D. N. Klyshko, M. H. Rubin, A. V. Sergienko, and Y. H. Shih, Phys. Rev. A **53,** 2804 (1996).
9. M. Atatüre, G. Di Giuseppe, M. D. Shaw, A. V. Sergienko, B. E. A. Saleh, and M. C. Teich, Phys. Rev. A **66,** 023822 (2002).

GENERATING QUANTUM INTERFERENCE AND POLARIZATION ENTANGLEMENT WITH OPTICAL PARAMETRIC AMPLIFIERS

JEFFREY H. SHAPIRO
Research Laboratory of Electronics
Massachusetts Institute of Technology
Cambridge, MA 02139
E-mail: jhs@mit.edu

A traveling-wave treatment of a type-II phase matched optical parametric amplifier (OPA) is reported. It connects the standard Gaussian-state analysis for such a system to the bi-photon wave packet characterization of a parametric downconverter. This treatment reproduces the narrowband (near-resonance) predictions of the lumped-element OPA theory for doubly-resonant operation. Without the near-resonance restriction, a new quantum interference effect emerges: coincidence-counting dips and revivals in a Hong-Ou-Mandel interferometer.

Parametric downconversion sources are intrinsically broadband; THz bandwidths are typical. Our recent proposal for long-distance qubit teleportation,[1] however, requires a high-brightness narrowband source of polarization entanglement, to match the MHz linewidth of its trapped-atom quantum memory.[2] We have shown theoretically[3] that the polarization-combined outputs from a pair of coherently-pumped, doubly-resonant, optical parametric amplifiers (OPAs) will fulfill this need. That analysis employed a lumped-element model for the OPA behavior in the vicinity of the double resonance, and was sufficiently generic to include both type-I and type-II phase matching. In the present paper, we report a traveling-wave treatment of the type-II phase matched, doubly-resonant OPA. When restricted to frequencies close to the double resonance, the new analysis reproduces the lumped-element results. Without this restriction, however, a new quantum interference effect emerges: coincidence-counting dips and revivals in a Hong-Ou-Mandel (HOM) interferometer.[4] Our work is related to that of Lu and Ou,[5] who published a multi-mode lumped-element analysis for the photon statistics of type-I and type-II phase matched OPAs. These authors also presented measurements of the fluorescence spectrum and the photon-counting interarrival statistics for a multi-mode type-I system. They did not, however, discuss polarization entanglement or coincidence-counting dips and revivals.

The configuration we shall consider is shown in Fig. 1(a). A type-II phase matched $\chi^{(2)}$ crystal is embedded in a single-ended, dual-cavity arrangement and subject to single-pass, continuous-wave pumping at frequency ω_P. The polarizing beam splitter in Fig. 1(a) separates the signal and idler beams so that they see identical output couplers but different free-space cavity lengths. For simplicity, we employ a collinear, plane-wave propagation model with no pump depletion, no pump fluctuations, and no excess losses. We also assume perfect phase-matching at degeneracy—the center frequencies of the signal and idler beams are both $\omega_P/2$—with both the signal and idler cavities resonant at this frequency.

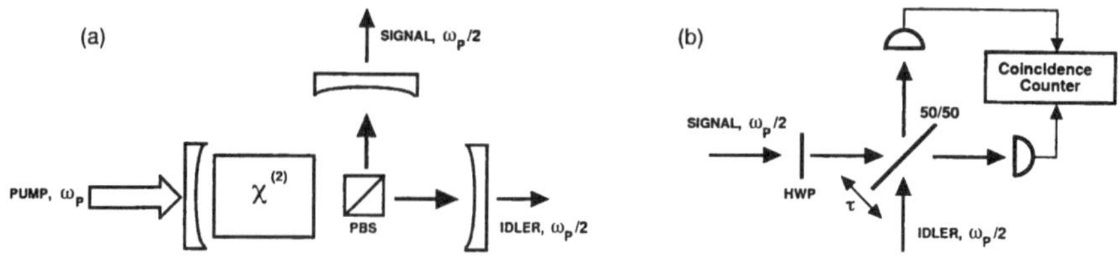

Figure 1. (a): Doubly-resonant, type-II phase matched optical parametric amplifier with continuous-wave pumping. The pump is single pass and enters through a mirror that is totally reflecting for the signal and idler. The polarizing beam splitter (PBS) separates the signal and idler so that they see identical output couplers but different optical cavities. (b): Hong-Ou-Mandel interferometer for measuring quantum interference, via coincidence counting, as the delay, τ, scanned. Because a type-II OPA is assumed, the half-wave plate (HWP) is needed to rotate the signal polarization to match that of the idler.

To analyze the Fig. 1(a) configuration, we start from the coupled-mode equations for the downconversion process without the resonators. With $\hat{E}_S(z,t)$ and $\hat{E}_I(z,t)$ denoting the positive-frequency, photon-units field operators for the relevant polarization components of the signal and idler, respectively, we have that,

$$\frac{\partial \hat{A}_S(z,\omega)}{\partial z} = i\kappa A_P \hat{A}_I^\dagger(z,\omega)e^{i\Delta k z} \text{ and } \frac{\partial \hat{A}_I(z,\omega)}{\partial z} = i\kappa A_P \hat{A}_S^\dagger(z,\omega)e^{i\Delta k z}, \quad (1)$$

for $+z$ propagation within the nonlinear crystal, where $E_P(z,t) = A_P e^{-i(\omega_P t - k_P z)}$ is the classical pump field, and

$$\hat{E}_S(z,t) = \int \frac{d\omega}{2\pi} \hat{A}_S(z,\omega)e^{-i(\omega_P/2+\omega)t + ik_S z}, \quad (2)$$

$$\hat{E}_I(z,t) = \int \frac{d\omega}{2\pi} \hat{A}_I(z,\omega)e^{-i(\omega_P/2-\omega)t + ik_I z}. \quad (3)$$

In Eq. (1), κ is the nonlinear coupling coefficient, and $\Delta k \equiv k_P - k_S - k_I$ gives the phase mismatch at detuning ω in terms of the pump wave number at ω_P, the signal wave number at $\omega_P/2+\omega$, and the idler wave number at $\omega_P/2-\omega$. The parametric interaction entangles the signal mode at frequency $\omega_P/2+\omega$ with the idler mode at frequency $\omega_P/2-\omega$; our sign conventions in Eqs. (2) and (3) makes these entangled modes $\hat{A}_S(z,\omega)$ and $\hat{A}_I(z,\omega)$, respectively. Because the crystal is phase matched at degeneracy, the detuning term $e^{i\Delta k z}$ in Eq. (1) can be replaced with $e^{i\omega\Delta k' z}$, where $\Delta k' \equiv -k_S'(\omega_P/2) + k_I'(\omega_P/2)$

to lowest order in a Taylor-series expansion. For a crystal of length l, with input at $z = 0$ and output at $z = l$, we then find that,

$$\hat{A}_S(l,\omega) = \left[\cosh(pl) - \frac{i\omega\Delta k' l}{2}\frac{\sinh(pl)}{pl}\right] e^{i\omega\Delta k' l/2}\hat{A}_S(0,\omega) + i\kappa A_P l\frac{\sinh(pl)}{pl} e^{i\omega\Delta k' l/2}\hat{A}_I^\dagger(0,\omega), \quad (4)$$

$$\hat{A}_I(l,\omega) = \left[\cosh(pl) - \frac{i\omega\Delta k' l}{2}\frac{\sinh(pl)}{pl}\right] e^{i\omega\Delta k' l/2}\hat{A}_I(0,\omega) + i\kappa A_P l\frac{\sinh(pl)}{pl} e^{i\omega\Delta k' l/2}\hat{A}_S^\dagger(0,\omega), \quad (5)$$

where $p \equiv \sqrt{\kappa^2|A_P|^2 - (\omega\Delta k'/2)^2}$. Equations (4) and (5) comprise a two-mode Bogoliubov transformation, familiar from squeezed-state theory, that is commutator preserving. In the low-gain limit, $\kappa|A_P|l \ll 1$, this transformation converts a pair of vacuum-state input fields, $\hat{E}_S(0,t)$ and $\hat{E}_I(0,t)$, into a a pair of output fields, $\hat{E}_S(l,t)$ and $\hat{E}_I(l,t)$, that contains a bi-photon state, viz., the joint output state of the signal and idler is approximately,

$$|\psi\rangle_{SI} \approx |\mathbf{0}\rangle_S|\mathbf{0}\rangle_I + \int\frac{d\omega}{2\pi}\, i\kappa A_P l e^{-i\omega\Delta k' l/2}\frac{\sin(\omega\Delta k' l/2)}{\omega\Delta k' l/2}|\omega_P/2+\omega\rangle_S|\omega_P/2-\omega\rangle_I, \quad (6)$$

where $|\mathbf{0}\rangle$ denotes the multimode vacuum state, and $|\Omega\rangle$ denotes a single-photon state at frequency Ω. It is now easy to show that this state produces a triangular coincidence-counting dip of width $2|\Delta k' l|$, shown in Fig. 3(a), as delay is scanned in the HOM interferometer shown in Fig. 1(b).

The low-gain approximations to Eqs. (4) and (5) that lead to Eq. (6) are not commutator preserving. Thus, in our treatment of the doubly-resonant OPA, we postpone passage to the low-gain limit until after the effects of the resonant cavities have been calculated. The signal and idler cavities both resonate at $\omega_P/2$; we shall assume that their optical path lengths are the same at this frequency, i.e., $L = n_S(\omega_P/2)l + l_S = n_I(\omega_P/2)l + l_I$ in terms of the signal and idler refractive indices at degeneracy and the lengths of the free-space paths in the signal and idler cavities. Let $\hat{E}_S^{\rm in}(t)$ and $\hat{E}_I^{\rm in}(t)$ denote the input signal and idler field operators—assumed to be in their vacuum states—and $\hat{E}_S^{\rm out}(t)$ and $\hat{E}_I^{\rm out}(t)$ be the resulting output field operators for the signal and idler. Introducing the Fourier relations [cf. Eqs. (2)and (3)],

$$\hat{E}_S(t) = \int\frac{d\omega}{2\pi}\hat{A}_S(\omega)e^{-i(\omega_P/2+\omega)t} \quad \text{and} \quad \hat{E}_I(t) = \int\frac{d\omega}{2\pi}\hat{A}_I(\omega)e^{-i(\omega_P/2-\omega)t}, \quad (7)$$

for these input and output field operators, and passing to the low-gain limit, we find that joint output state of the signal and the idler is approximately,

$$\psi\rangle_{SI} \approx |\mathbf{0}\rangle_S|\mathbf{0}\rangle_I$$

$$+\int\frac{d\omega}{2\pi}\frac{i\kappa A_P l T e^{-i(\omega\Delta k' l/2-\theta)}}{|1-\sqrt{R}e^{i2\omega L/c}|^2}\frac{\sin(\omega\Delta k' l/2)}{\omega\Delta k' l/2}|\omega_P/2+\omega\rangle_S|\omega_P/2-\omega\rangle_I, \quad (8)$$

where θ is a physically unimportant absolute phase, and $R = 1 - T$ is the reflectivity of the output couplers. Comparing the bi-photon terms in Eqs. (6) and (8), we see that the signal and idler cavities have introduced a double-resonance denominator. Our final tasks will be to explore the implications of this denominator in narrowband pair generation, in polarization entanglement generation, and in HOM interferometry.

Our lumped-element analysis of narrowband pair generation from a doubly-resonant OPA[3] predicts that the signal and idler outputs will be in a maximally-entangled state whose normally-ordered (fluorescence) spectrum versus detuning satisfies,

$$\langle \hat{A}_S^{\text{out}\dagger}(\omega)\hat{A}_S^{\text{out}}(\omega')\rangle = \langle \hat{A}_I^{\text{out}\dagger}(\omega)\hat{A}_I^{\text{out}}(\omega')\rangle = 2\pi S^{(n)}(\omega)\delta(\omega-\omega'), \quad (9)$$

with

$$S^{(n)}(\omega) = \left[2G\Gamma^2/(\omega^2+\Gamma^2)\right]^2, \quad (10)$$

where the last equality assumes operation in the low-gain regime, Γ is the common linewidth of the signal and idler cavities, and G^2 is the OPA pump power divided by the threshold power for oscillation. The corresponding fluorescence spectrum obtained from Eq. (8) of our traveling-wave theory is,

$$S^{(n)}(\omega) = \frac{|\kappa A_P l T|^2}{|1-\sqrt{R}e^{i2\omega L/c}|^4}\left(\frac{\sin(\omega\Delta k' l/2)}{\omega\Delta k' l/2}\right)^2 \quad (11)$$

$$\approx \frac{|\kappa A_P l T|^2}{[(2\omega L/c)^2+(1-\sqrt{R})^2]^2}, \quad (12)$$

where the approximation assumes high-Q cavities and $|\omega| \ll \pi c/L \ll 2\pi/|\Delta k' l|$. With the identifications $\Gamma = c(1-\sqrt{R})/2L$ and $G = \kappa|A_P|lT/2(1-\sqrt{R})^2$, we see that the traveling-wave and lumped-element OPA analyses coincide.

To obtain the high-brightness narrowband source of polarization-entangled photon pairs needed for our long-distance teleportation architecture,[1] we combine the signal beams and the idler beams from from a pair of Fig. 1(a) configuration doubly-resonant OPAs on a polarizing beam splitter, as shown in Fig. 2. We have previously used lumped-element analysis[3] to demonstrate that the Fig. 2 arrangement produces the desired singlet-state polarization entanglement when the OPAs are pumped π-rad out of phase. The traveling-wave treatment we have developed in the present paper affords a more complete understanding of the entangled state that is produced by the Fig. 2 setup. In particular, from Eq. (8) we find that the joint output state of the signal and idler in the low-gain regime is,

$$|\psi\rangle_{SI} \approx |\mathbf{0}\rangle_{S_x}|\mathbf{0}\rangle_{I_y}|\mathbf{0}\rangle_{S_y}|\mathbf{0}\rangle_{I_x}$$

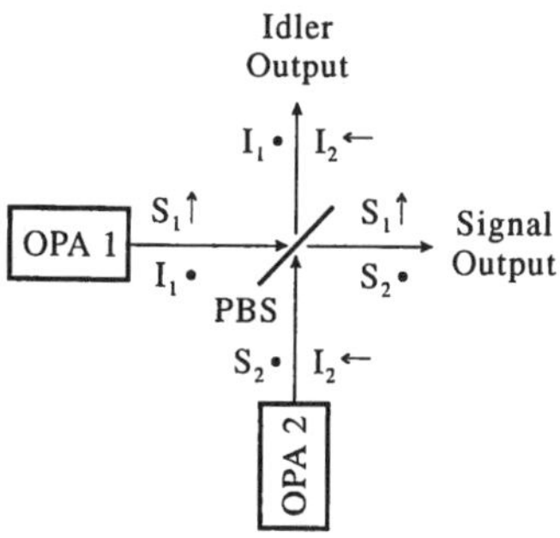

Figure 2. Type-II OPA configuration for generating polarization-entangled photon pairs. Each OPA is a doubly-resonant configuration, as shown in Fig. 1(a). The two OPAs are coherently pumped π-rad out of phase, to produce the singlet state needed for qubit teleportation. For each optical beam, the propagation direction is $\hat{z}$, and $\hat{x}$ and $\hat{y}$ polarizations are denoted by arrows and bullets, respectively. PBS, polarizing beam splitter.

$$+\int \frac{d\omega}{2\pi} S^{(p)}(\omega)(|\omega_P/2+\omega\rangle_{S_x}|\omega_P/2-\omega\rangle_{I_y} - |\omega_P/2+\omega\rangle_{S_y}|\omega_P/2-\omega\rangle_{I_x}), \tag{13}$$

where

$$S^{(p)}(\omega) \equiv \frac{i\kappa A_P l T e^{-i(\omega\Delta k' l/2-\theta)}}{|1-\sqrt{R}e^{i2\omega L/c}|^2}\frac{\sin(\omega\Delta k' l/2)}{\omega\Delta k' l/2}, \tag{14}$$

is the phase-sensitive spectrum. Equation (13) shows the singlet-state behavior that enables qubit teleportation. Moreover, because the Lloyd et al. quantum memory[2] will only respond to the narrowband portion of the biphoton field in the vicinity of the ^{87}Rb line, we can reproduce the teleportation performance analysis of Ref. 1—which employed lumped-element OPA theory—by matching the double resonance at $\omega_P/2$ to the ^{87}Rb line center.

Finally, let us revisit HOM interferometry when the signal and idler inputs come from a doubly-resonant OPA. When the state Eq. (8) is supplied to the interferometer in Fig. 1(b), a series of triangular coincidence-counting dips and revivals occur. The width of each dip is set by the phase-matching bandwidth, i.e., each dip is $2|\Delta k' l|$ wide, just as found for the non-resonated downconverter. The spacing between each coincidence dip is $2L/c$, i.e., a cavity roundtrip. The central (deepest) coincidence dip is as shown in Fig. 3(a) for the non-resonated case. The remaining coincidence dips become progressively shallower as the delay is scanned further from the location of the central dip. The span of the dips-and-revivals region is many cavity lifetimes—for our high-Q, no-excess-loss cavities—as shown by the envelope of their maxima and minima which is plotted in Fig. 3(b). This new quantum interference phenomenon has a simple physical explanation. Signal and idler photon pairs are

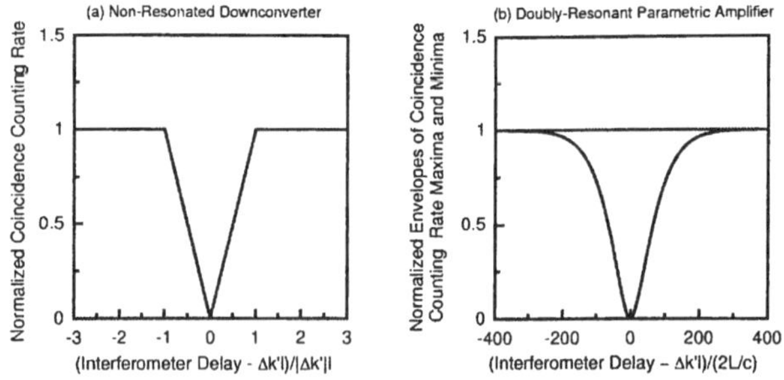

Figure 3. (a): Normalized coincidence-counting rate versus delay for a Hong-Ou-Mandel interferometer whose input is the output state from a (non-resonated) type-II parametric downconverter. The coincidence dip occurs at $\Delta k'l$ and is of width $2|\Delta k'l|$ (b): Envelopes of the coincidence counting rate maxima and minima for a Hong-Ou-Mandel interferometer whose input is the output state from a type-II doubly-resonant optical parametric amplifier with a 5% output coupler ($R = 0.95$). Within these envelopes, triangular coincidence dips occur every $2L/c$ from the central dip at $\Delta k'l$.

created, via parametric downconversion in the $\chi^{(2)}$ crystal, in near simultaneity. Because the crystal is embedded in high-Q cavities that resonate both the signal and idler, each photon in a particular pair will take many cavity lifetimes to leak out through its respective output coupler. A pair from a downconverter (without a resonator) gives rise to a coincidence-counting dip in a HOM interferometer when the delay is adjusted so that indistinguishable photon wave packets present themselves at the two input ports of the interferometer's beam splitter. Because of the optical cavities in the Fig. 1(a) configuration, such interference occurs at a multiplicity of delay settings—separated by multiples of the roundtrip cavity delay—as the component photons of each generated pair leak out of the OPA. In more mathematical terms, the optical cavities have imposed a comb-like structure on the common fluorescence spectrum of the signal and idler beams, and this combs lead to a similar comb-like behavior in the coincidences-versus-delay pattern seen in the HOM interferometer because the latter is in essence a Fourier transform of the former.

References

1. J. H. Shapiro, *New J. Phys.* 4:47 (2002).
2. S. Lloyd, M. S. Shahriar, J. H. Shapiro, and P. R. Hemmer, *Phys. Rev. Lett.* 87:167903 (2001).
3. J. H. Shapiro and N. C. Wong, *J. Opt. B: Quantum and Semiclass. Opt.* 2:L1 (2000).
4. C. K. Hong, Z. Y. Ou, and L. Mandel, *Phys. Rev. Lett.* 59:2044 (1987).
5. Y. J. Lu and Z. Y. Ou, *Phys. Rev. A* 62:033804 (2000).

CREATING HIGH-DIMENSIONAL TIME-BIN ENTANGLEMENT USING MODE-LOCKED LASERS

HUGUES DE RIEDMATTEN, IVAN MARCIKIC, HUGO ZBINDEN AND NICOLAS GISIN

Group of Applied Physics, 1211 Geneva, Switzerland
E-mail: hugues.deriedmatten@physics.unige.ch

We present a new scheme to generate high dimensional entanglement between two photonic systems. The idea is based on parametric downconversion with a sequence of pump pulses generated by a mode-locked laser. We prove experimentally the feasibility of this scheme by performing a Franson-type Bell test using a 2-way interferometer with path-length difference equal to the distance between 2 pump pulses. With this experiment, we can demonstrate entanglement for a two-photon state of at least dimension $d = 11$.

1 Introduction

Entanglement in high-dimensional Hilbert spaces is interesting from a fundamental point of view[1,2,3] as well as from a more applied point of view, in the context of quantum information science.[4,5] Experimentally, only a few experiment have explored entanglement in higher dimensions.[6,7,8,9] In this contribution, we present a new scheme to generate high dimensional time-bin entanglement[10] between two photonic systems. The method is based on parametric downconversion with a sequence of pump pulses with a fixed phase relation.[11] We can thus obtain an entanglement between photons created in a coherent superposition of discrete emission times, given by the successive laser pulses. The coherence between the different pulses can be obtained using a mode-locked laser. We demonstrate the feasibility of this scheme by analyzing the created high-dimensional entangled states with a 2-way interferometer, with path-length difference equal to the distance between two laser pulses.

2 Principle of high-dimensional time-bin entanglement

Suppose that we have sequences of d pump pulses with a fixed phase relation entering a parametric downconverter (PDC). The time difference between two pulses is Δt. If the probability of having more than one pair in d pulses is negligible, the state obtained after the PDC can be written as

$$|\Psi_{PDC}\rangle = \sum_{j=1}^{d} c_j e^{i\phi_j} |j,j\rangle , \tag{1}$$

where $|j,j\rangle$ means that a photon pair is created in pulse or time-bin j, ϕ_j is the phase difference between two pump pulses and $\sum_{j=1}^{d} c_j^2 = 1$. This scheme enables, in principle, the generation of any desired two-photon high-dimensional state by setting the number, the amplitude and the phase of the pump pulses.

The more natural way to analyze states of the form (1) would be to use D-way interferometers. However, building such devices would lead to severe practical difficulties as D increases. Nevertheless, the use of a 2-way interferometer, where the long arm introduces a delay Δt with respect to the short one, permits demonstration of high-dimensional entanglement, as explained below. After the interferometer, a state of the form (1) becomes:[a]

$$|\Psi_{PDC}\rangle \rightarrow |\Psi_{int}\rangle = |1,1\rangle + \sum_{j=2}^{d} |j,j\rangle (1 + e^{2i\delta}) + e^{2i\delta} |d+1, d+1\rangle . \quad (2)$$

The coincidence count rate is given by:

$$R_c \sim 1 + V \cos(2\delta), \quad (3)$$

where V is the visibility of the interference pattern. Equation 2 shows that there are $2d$ different processes that lead to coincidences, among which two are completely distinguishable (the first and the last terms). Hence, if all the terms are taken into account, the maximum visibility is given by:

$$V = \frac{d-1}{d}. \quad (4)$$

Consequently, by measuring a given visibility in this experiment, we can prove that *we have generated entanglement for a two-photon state of at least dimension*[b] $d = \frac{1}{1-V}$. This is a lower bound, because the analyzer is not perfect.

3 Experiment

The experimental setup is shown in Fig. 1. A Ti-Sapphire femtosecond laser (76 MHz, $\lambda_p = 710$ nm, 150 fs) is used to pump a type-I $KNbO_3$ nonlinear crystal, where non-degenerate photon pairs at telecom wavelength (1310/1550 nm) are created by PDC. The created photons are focused into a single-mode optical fiber and directed towards a bulk Michelson interferometer. The physical path-length difference between the two arms corresponds to half the period of the laser, i.e., 6.55 ns $\longleftrightarrow$ 1.95 m. The phase in the long arm can be varied

[a] We consider only the terms involving photons that travel together in the interferometer, because only those terms lead to indistinguishable processes. In practice, this is achieved by selecting a sufficiently small time-coincidence window. The coefficients c_j and ϕ_j are constants, and the state is written without normalization.

[b] In our experiment, however, we don't have trains of exactly d pulses. Actually, as we pump the PDC directly with a pulsed laser, we have an (almost) infinite number of pulses. Here the dimension d is bounded by the probability of creating one photon pair in d pulses and by the stability of the pump laser cavity.

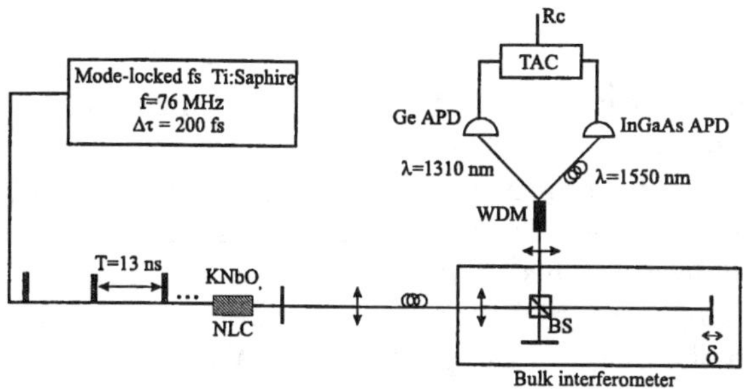

Figure 1. Experimental setup

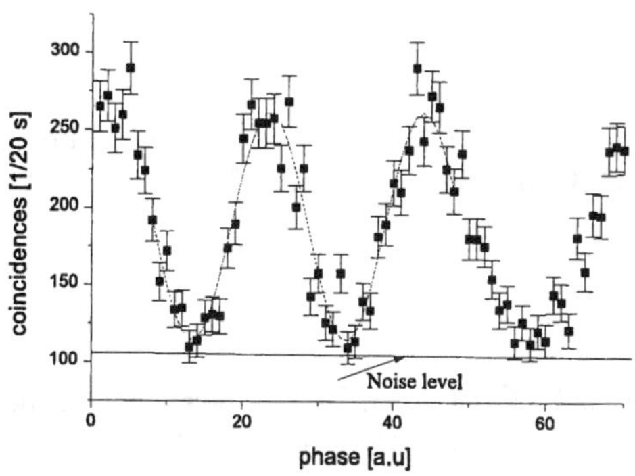

Figure 2. Coincidence count rate as a function of the phase of the interferometer. Black squares are experimental points. The error bars are the statistical errors. The solid line is a sinusoidal fit, from which we can infer a visibility of 91 ± 6%.

with a piezoelectric crystal. The output of the interferometer is focused into a single-mode optical fiber and the photons are separated deterministically by a wavelength division multiplexer (WDM). The 1310 nm and the 1550 nm photons are detected by a LN_2 cooled Ge APD operating in geiger mode and by a Peltier cooled InGaAs APD operating in gated mode, respectively.[12] The signals of the two APDs are finally sent to a time-to-amplitude converter (TAC, Start = Ge, Stop = InGaAs), and the coincidence rate is recorded as a function of the phase shift δ in the interferometer. Figure 2 shows the interference curve. We observe the predicted sinusoidal behavior, and a sinusoidal fit gives a net visibility of 91 ± 6%. The rather high level of noise in the coincidence-count rate is due to the dark counts in the detectors. From this measured visibility, we can infer, using Eq. 4, that *we generated entanglement for a two-photon state of at least dimension* $d = 11$.

4 Conclusion

We presented a new scheme for generating high-dimensional time-bin entanglement between two photons. The method is based on parametric downconversion with a sequence of pump pulses with a fixed phase difference. The necessary coherence between pump pulses can be obtained by using a mode-locked laser. This scheme enables in principle the generation of any desired two-photon high-dimensional state by setting the number, the amplitude and the phase of the pump pulses. We proved experimentally the feasibility of such a scheme by analyzing the high-dimensional entangled state with a 2-way interferometer. The measured visibility of 91 ± 6% allowed us to demonstrate entanglement for a two-photon state of at least dimension $d = 11$.

Acknowledgments

Financial support by the swiss NCCR Quantum Photonics, and by the European project QuComm is acknowledged.

References

1. D. Kaszlikowski, P. Gnacinski, M. Zukowski, W. Miklaszewski, and A. Zeilinger, Phys. Rev. Lett. **85**, 4418 (2000).
2. D. Collins, N. Gisin, N. Linden, S. Massar, and S. Popescu, Phys. Rev. Lett. **88**, 040404 (2002).
3. S. Massar, Phys. Rev. A **65**, 032121 (2002).
4. N. J. Cerf, M.Bourennane, A. Karlsson, N.Gisin, Phys. Rev. Lett. **88**, 127902 (2002).
5. M. Fitzi, N. Gisin, and U. Maurer, Phys. Rev. Lett. **87**, 217901 (2001).
6. A. Lamas-Linares, J. C.Howell and D.Bouwmeester, Nature **412**, 887–890 (2001).
7. J. C. Howell, A. Lamas-Linares, and D. Bouwmeester, Phys. Rev. Lett. **88**, 030401 (2002).
8. H. Weinfurter and M. Zukowski, Phys. Rev. A **64**, 010102 (2001).
9. A. Mair, A. Vaziri, G. Weihs, and A. Zeilinger, Nature **412**, 313–316 (2001).
10. J. Brendel, N. Gisin, W. Tittel, and H. Zbinden, Phys. Rev. Lett. **82**, 2594 (1999),
11. H. de Riedmatten, I. Marcikic, H. Zbinden and N. Gisin, to appear in QIC, quant-ph/0204165,
12. G. Ribordy, J.D. Gautier, H. Zbinden and N. Gisin, 2272-2277 (1998).

MAXIMAL-ENTANGLEMENT GENERATION VIA PULSED PARAMETRIC DOWNCONVERSION

VITTORIO GIOVANNETTI, LORENZO MACCONE, JEFFREY H. SHAPIRO, AND FRANCO N. C. WONG
Massachusetts Institute of Technology,
Research Laboratory of Electronics, 50 Vassar St.
Cambridge, MA 02139, USA

A method to entangle photons in frequency is discussed. It uses short pump pulses and long crystals and allows the generation of maximally-entangled two-photon states that are correlated in frequency and anti-correlated in time of arrival. An experimental setup to test the entanglement of the created states is proposed.

Spontaneous parametric downconversion (SPDC) is the conventional source of entanglement used in most experiments. However, the state generated through SPDC using the customary phase-matching condition is maximally entangled only when a continuous-wave (cw) pump is used.[1,2] In particular one sees that by decreasing the pulse length, the visibility of the interference experiments decreases.[3] Advantages offered by pulsed SPDC have prompted interest in finding ways to retain or to restore the entanglement in this regime.[4]

In this paper a method to achieve maximum entanglement in the pulsed regime is analyzed.[5,6] It does not require any filtering or post-selection, and it utilizes long crystals resulting in high downconversion efficiencies. Although the customary phase-matching condition used in SPDC crystals is appropriate for cw pumping, the phase matching conditions we propose here are designed for pulsed pumps. The biphoton twin-beam state generated by conventional phase matching and cw pumping is given by

$$|\mathrm{TB}\rangle = \int \frac{d\omega}{2\pi}\, \phi(\omega)|\omega_p/2-\omega\rangle_s|\omega_p/2+\omega\rangle_i\ , \tag{1}$$

where $|\omega\rangle$ is the state in which there is one photon at frequency ω and no photons at other frequencies, ω_p is the frequency of the cw pump, $\phi(\omega)$ is the spectral function of the twin-beam state, and s and i refer to the signal and idler modes, respectively. On the other hand, the state that is generated from the method presented here will be shown to be

$$|\mathrm{DB}\rangle = \int \frac{d\omega}{2\pi}\, \phi(\omega)|\omega_p/2+\omega\rangle_s|\omega_p/2+\omega\rangle_i. \tag{2}$$

This state has been previously proposed by Erdmann et al.[5] The state $|\mathrm{TB}\rangle$ is anti-correlated in frequency: the sum of the frequencies of the two downconverted photons is fixed and is equal to the cw pump frequency. In contrast, the state $|\mathrm{DB}\rangle$ is correlated in frequency: the *difference* in the frequencies of the downconverted photons is a fixed quantity. Analogously, whereas the state $|\mathrm{TB}\rangle$ has fixed photon time-of-arrival difference (as shown in the famous "Mandel dip" experiment[7]), the state $|\mathrm{DB}\rangle$ has a fixed photon time-of-arrival *sum*, as can be exhibited with a Mach-Zehnder interferometer. Moreover, whereas the photons of the state $|\mathrm{TB}\rangle$ can be discriminated by a frequency measurement, the photons of $|\mathrm{DB}\rangle$ can be discriminated by a time-of-arrival measurement. In this sense one may claim that the state $|\mathrm{DB}\rangle$ proposed here is the dual of the state $|\mathrm{TB}\rangle$ that is obtained under the customary phase-matching condition used in most entanglement experiments. Among other possible applications, the $|\mathrm{DB}\rangle$ state can be employed in the localization protocols described in Ref. 8 to achieve enhancements and cryptographic advantages in position measurements and clock synchronization.

At the output of a compensated SPDC crystal of length L, pumped with a coherent classical pump with spectrum $|\alpha(\omega)|^2$ (peaked at the average pump frequency ω_p), the biphoton state component is given by

$$|\Psi\rangle = \int \frac{d\omega_s}{2\pi}\frac{d\omega_i}{2\pi}\,\alpha(\omega_s+\omega_i)\Phi_L(\omega_s,\omega_i)\,|\omega_s\rangle_s|\omega_i\rangle_i\,, \tag{3}$$

where a normalization factor has been omitted and the phase-matching function is defined as

$$\Phi_L(\omega_s,\omega_i) = \frac{\sin\left(\Delta k(\omega_s,\omega_i)L/2\right)}{\Delta k(\omega_s,\omega_i)/2}\,, \tag{4}$$

with $\Delta k = k_p(\omega_s+\omega_i) - k_s(\omega_s) - k_i(\omega_i)$, for $k_{p,s,i}$ being the wave vectors of the pump, signal, and idler beams, respectively.

In order to generate the customary twin-beam state $|\mathrm{TB}\rangle$ of Eq. (1), one must use a cw pump, which implies $\alpha(\omega_s+\omega_i) \propto \delta(\omega_p-\omega_s-\omega_i)$ in Eq. (3). The spectral function $\phi(\omega)$ of Eq. (1) can then be obtained from the phase-matching function as $\phi(\omega) \propto \Phi_L(\omega_p/2+\omega,\omega_p/2-\omega)$. This, however, is not the only way one can obtain a maximally frequency-entangled state starting from (3). One of the two frequency integrals may also be eliminated by forcing Φ_L to approach a Dirac delta function, instead of relying on $\alpha\to\delta$ as is done for the $|\mathrm{TB}\rangle$ state. This can be accomplished by taking the limit $L\to\infty$, that transforms the spectral function Φ_L into a Dirac delta $\delta\left(\Delta(\omega_s,\omega_i)/2\right)$. Now we need to impose the additional condition that $\Delta k(\omega_s,\omega_i)=0$ if and only if $\omega_s=\omega_i$. Using the first-order Taylor series approximations for the signal and idler wave vectors around the degeneracy point $\omega_p/2$, the desired Δk condition is obtained if one chooses the crystal wave vectors to satisfy

$$n_p(\omega_p) = \frac{n_s(\omega_p/2)+n_i(\omega_p/2)}{2}, \tag{5}$$

$$k_p'(\omega_p) = \frac{k_s'(\omega_p/2)+k_i'(\omega_p/2)}{2}, \tag{6}$$

where $n_{p,s,i} = c\,k_{p,s,i}/\omega$ and the primes denote first derivatives with respect to ω. Equation (5) is the customary phase-matching condition that is used in the generation of the $|\mathrm{TB}\rangle$ state. On the other hand, Eq. (6) is an "extended phase-matching condition" that ensures that the signal and idler photons are correlated in detuning from $\omega_p/2$ over the entire pump spectrum. Under these conditions and taking the limit $L \to \infty$, the biphoton state $|\Psi\rangle$ of Eq. (3) reduces to the $|\mathrm{DB}\rangle$ state of Eq. (2) with $\phi(\omega) = \alpha(2\omega + \omega_p)$.

1 Experimental characterization

A simple way to characterize the two maximally frequency-entangled states $|\mathrm{TB}\rangle$ and $|\mathrm{DB}\rangle$ is to feed these states into either a Hong-Ou-Mandel interferometer[7] or a Mach-Zehnder interferometer.[9] It can be shown[6] that the output signatures of these interferometers are strongly dependent on the type of frequency correlation between the two downconverted photons. An example of these signatures is given in Fig. 1.

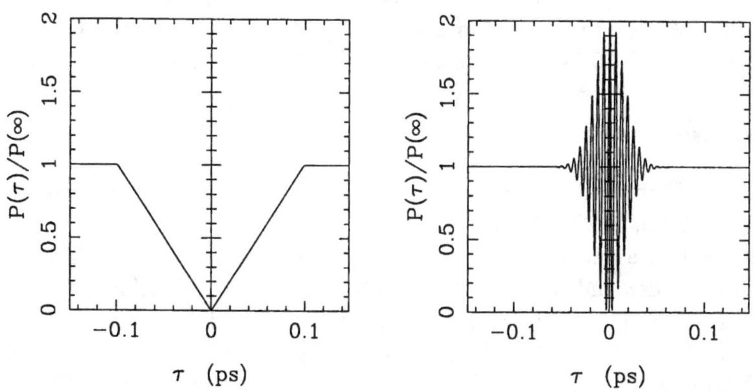

Figure 1. **Left:** Mandel dip in the coincidence rate $P(\tau)$ at the output of a Hong-Ou-Mandel interferometer as a function of the delay τ between the signal and idler beams. The plotted graph refers to a $|\mathrm{TB}\rangle$ input state. The characteristic triangular shape derives from the $\sin(x)/x$ form of the biphoton spectrum in the $|\mathrm{TB}\rangle$ state. Had a $|\mathrm{DB}\rangle$ state been fed into such an interferometer, one would observe a constant $P(\tau)$. **Right:** Peak and fringes in the coincidence rate $P(\tau)$ at the output of the Mach-Zehnder interferometer when the $|\mathrm{DB}\rangle$ state is at the input. The Gaussian envelope derives from the Gaussian spectral profile of the pump beam, and the fringes modulate the envelope at the pump frequency. Had a $|\mathrm{TB}\rangle$ state been fed into the Mach-Zehnder interferometer, one would not see any Gaussian envelope on the fringes. The parameters in the plots are $|k'_p(\omega_p) - k'_s(\omega_p/2)|L = 0.14$ ps (for the left plot) and $\omega_p = 10^{15}$ s^{-1} with a pump bandwidth of 90 THz (for the right plot).

A crystal satisfying both conditions (5) and (6) is difficult to find. However, one can enforce (5) via quasi-phase-matching in a periodically-poled $\chi^{(2)}$ material.[10] In particular, introducing a grating period Λ in the crystal, the zeroth-order term in the $\Delta k(\omega_s, \omega_i)$ expansion (5) is replaced by $n_p(\omega_p) = [n_s(\omega_p/2) + n_i(\omega_p/2)]/2 - 2\pi c/\Lambda\omega_p$. This condition, together with (6), are satisfied, for example, by periodically-poled potassium titanyl phosphate (PPKTP) at a pump wavelength of 790 nm with a grating period of 47.7 μm when propagation is along the crystal's x axis, the pump and idler are y-polarized, and the signal is z-polarized. To what extent is the condition $L \to \infty$ physically realizable? It can be shown,[6] for example, that, for a 167 fs transform-limited pump pulse, a crystal length of the order $0.23\,\text{cm} \ll L \ll 19.7\,\text{cm}$ is sufficient to ensure a high degree of positive-correlated frequency entanglement.

In conclusion, we have shown a potentially realizable method to create photons that are frequency entangled with positive correlation and a procedure to test the generated entanglement to compare it with customary frequency entangled biphotons.

Acknowledgments

This work was supported by the DoD Multidisciplinary University Research Initiative (MURI) program administered by the Army Research Office under Grant DAAG-19-00-1-0177, and by the National Reconnaissance Office.

References

1. M. H. Rubin, D. N. Klyshko, Y. H. Shih, and A. V. Sergienko, Phys. Rev. A **50**, 5122 (1994).
2. W. P. Grice and I. A. Walmsley, Phys. Rev. A **56**, 1627 (1997).
3. T. E. Keller and M. H. Rubin, Phys. Rev. A **56**, 1534 (1997).
4. G. Di Giuseppe, L. Haiberger, F. De Martini, and A. V. Sergienko, Phys. Rev. A **56**, R21 (1997); A. V. Sergienko, *et al.*, *ibid.* **60**, R2622 (1999); D. Branning, W. Grice, R. Erdmann, and I. A. Walmsley, *ibid.* **62**, 013814 (2000); Y.-H. Kim, S. P. Kulik, and Y. Shih, *ibid.* **62**, 011802(R) (2000).
5. R. Erdmann, D. Branning, W. Grice, and I. A. Walmsley, Phys. Rev. A **62**, 053810 (2000).
6. V. Giovannetti, L. Maccone, J. H. Shapiro, and F. N. C. Wong, Phys. Rev. Lett. **88**, 183602 (2002); Phys. Rev. A **66**, 043813 (2002).
7. C. K. Hong, Z. Y. Ou, and L. Mandel, Phys. Rev. Lett. **59**, 2044 (1987).
8. V. Giovannetti, S. Lloyd, and L. Maccone, Nature **412**, 417 (2001); Phys. Rev. A, **65**, 022309 (2002).
9. T. S. Larchuk *et al.*, Phys. Rev. Lett. **70**, 1603 (1993).
10. M. M. Fejer, G. A. Magel, D. H. Jundt, and R. L. Byer, IEEE J. Quantum Electron. **28**, 2631 (1992).

Part III
Quantum Information and Coding

QUANTUM INFORMATION SCIENCE AND COMPLEX QUANTUM SYSTEMS

MICHAEL A. NIELSEN
Department of Physics
The University of Queensland, Queensland 4072, Australia
E-mail: nielsen@physics.uq.edu.au

What makes quantum information science a *science*? This paper explores the idea that quantum information science may offer a powerful approach to the study of *complex quantum systems*.

1 Introduction

My subject in this paper is using quantum information science as an approach to the study of complex quantum systems. The work I describe has involved many collaborators at the University of Queensland and MIT, but I would especially like to emphasize the contribution of Tobias Osborne.

Let me begin by asking what it is that makes quantum information science a science? Friends outside the field sometimes comment that it seems to be largely engineering, with little science. A standard response from physicists is that in the course of building devices like quantum computers, we'll discover lots of interesting physics. This is undoubtedly true, and is an excellent reason for doing quantum information science. But it seems a little like the argument sometimes used to justify going to the moon, namely, that it resulted in valuable spin-off technologies in fields such as computation and aeronautical engineering. This misses a large part of the point, since going to the moon has an *intrinsic worth*, a point obvious even to a small child.

What is the intrinsic worth of quantum information science? In this paper I argue, that quantum information science is a powerful approach to the study of *complex quantum systems*. Related ideas have been advocated previously by many people. Aharonov,[1] Nielsen [2] and Preskill [3] argued that there may be connections between the quantitative theory of entanglement and many-body quantum systems, and there is a burgeoning literature exploring these connections. More explicitly, the concluding paragraph of DiVincenzo's[4] paper on the physical requirements for quantum computation suggests that quantum information science may offer valuable insights into complex quantum systems. This theme was explored in more detail by Osborne and Nielsen,[5,6,7,8] and the present paper is an outgrowth of this work.

2 Complex quantum systems

What is a complex system? Complexity is an elusive concept: it is difficult to define, but we know it when we see it. In response to this difficulty one might ask whether it is possible to quantify complexity. In the 1980s Bennett proposed a measure of complexity called the *logical depth.*[11] The idea is that a system is complex, or logically deep, if a description of the system can be generated by a few simple rules, but those rules require a long time to run. For example, a human body is complex because it is specified by a relatively small amount of information encoded in DNA, but it takes a great deal of processing to get from DNA to the human body. Another example is a regular pattern on a checkerboard, which is not complex because it can be quickly generated by a simple rule. More subtle is the case of a random pattern on a checkerboard. That is not complex either, because there is no simple rule generating the pattern. Indeed, the simplest rule generating the pattern is simply the program which contains (and prints) a complete listing of the states of all the elements of the checkerboard, and this program runs very quickly.

Let me give an example of something complex, that is, with high logical depth. Suppose we take a point, x, in the plane, for example, $x = (0, 0)$. We bounce the point around the plane by repeatedly applying one of the following four rules at random,[12]

$$x \to \begin{bmatrix} 0 & 0 \\ 0 & 0.16 \end{bmatrix} x \text{ with probability } 0.01 \tag{1}$$

$$x \to \begin{bmatrix} 0.85 & 0.04 \\ -0.04 & 0.85 \end{bmatrix} x + \begin{bmatrix} 0 \\ 1.6 \end{bmatrix} \text{ with probability } 0.85 \tag{2}$$

$$x \to \begin{bmatrix} 0.2 & -0.26 \\ 0.23 & 0.22 \end{bmatrix} x + \begin{bmatrix} 0 \\ 1.6 \end{bmatrix} \text{ with probability } 0.07 \tag{3}$$

$$x \to \begin{bmatrix} -0.15 & 0.28 \\ 0.26 & 0.24 \end{bmatrix} x + \begin{bmatrix} 0 \\ 0.44 \end{bmatrix} \text{ with probability } 0.07. \tag{4}$$

When this procedure is repeated a few thousand times an interesting thing happens: with very high probability a fern shape fills in, as illustrated in Fig. 1. Furthermore, the fern is complex in that there is a simple rule generating the fern, but it takes a long time to run.

Bennett formalized these intuitions by defining the logical depth of a data set to be the running time of a near-optimal computer program generating that data set. There are some technicalities hidden in this definition, like the precise meaning of "near-optimal", that I will gloss over. Nonetheless, I would like to give the intuitive flavor of the definition. By "near-optimal" we mean that the program is nearly the shortest possible. The motivating idea is an analogy between computer programs generating data sets and scientific hypotheses. Scientists tend to prefer simple explanations over more complex, so if we think of computer programs as explanations for data sets, then we would prefer short computer programs — simple "explanations" — over longer programs. With this definition, simple repeated structures and random patterns, like the checkerboards described earlier, have low logical depth. Systems like

Figure 1. The fern is formed by iterating the rule in Eqs. (1)-(4) a few thousand times.

the fern have high logical depth because they have simple explanations that take a long time to run.

There is an interesting quantum twist to logical depth. As we know, factoring integers is a hard problem, hard enough that RSA systems offers lots of money to people able to factor large integers: US $200,000 for a 2048-bit integer, at the time of writing. Let's optimistically imagine that it's ten years from now and somebody wants to prove that they have a functioning quantum computer in their lab, but don't want to reveal the details of how they built it. One good way of proving this would be to publish a paper containing the prime factors of a large group of big integers — perhaps the prime factors of all numbers between 10^{1000} and $10^{1000} + 1000000$.

Is this list of factors a complex system? The answer depends on whether the computer in the definition of logical depth is quantum or classical. If it's quantum then it seems likely that this system is *not* logically deep, and thus not complex, because we can quickly generate the list using a short quantum program, namely, Shor's algorithm.[13] If the computer is classical, and there really is no fast classical factoring algorithm, then the list of factors has high logical depth, since there are simple computer programs capable of generating such a list, but they operate very slowly.

Thus, there are two distinct notions of logical depth, classical logical depth, and quantum logical depth. We can summarize the situation by dividing systems into three distinct types. First, there are systems which have both low classical logical depth and low quantum logical depth; these are "simple". Then there are systems that have high classical logical depth, but low quantum logical depth, like the list of prime factors discussed above; these systems might be called "classically complex". Finally, there are systems with both high classical logical depth and high quantum logical depth; the truly "quantum complex" systems. I don't know of any examples with this property, but consider some systems likely candidates, for example, the output of a quantum cellular automata that's been running a long time. Note that systems with high quantum logical depth but low classical logical depth seem unlikely, because a simple, fast classical computer generating a data set can be simulated by a simple, fast quantum computer.

3 Quantum dynamics as a physical resource

I've talked about quantifying complexity in quantum systems, and the information-theoretic viewpoint has led us to the idea that there are at least two, if not more, qualitatively different types of complex system. I'd like now to talk about what we can learn about specific complex quantum systems from quantum information science.

Over the past few years great effort has been devoted to developing a quantitative theory of quantum entanglement. In my opinion a major area in which this theory will be applied is to obtain insights into the properties of complex quantum systems. However, static quantum entanglement is only a small part of the story: it is also interesting to obtain a better understanding of the quantum *dynamics* of complex systems. To achieve this this, my group has focused on quantifying the *strength* of a quantum dynamical operation for information processing.

The motivation for this idea is the observation that quantum dynamics are a *fungible* physical resource, in the sense that it is possible to interconvert different dynamical operations, just as it is possible to convert one type of entangled state to another. More precisely, suppose a system contains n qudits, and the Hamiltonian for the system contains only two-body terms, and so can be represented by a graph whose vertices represent qudits, and whose edges represent the presence of an interaction between those qudits. Finally, suppose the graph is connected, so different qudits aren't cut off from one another. It turns out that by alternating evolution due to such a Hamiltonian with single-qudit gates, we can, in principle, efficiently simulate any quantum computation.[a]

While theoretically interesting, until recently most of these schemes were not practically useful, requiring extremely frequent local control to do simple operations such as the CNOT. Even an optimistic example[16] required $\approx 10^4$ operations to do a CNOT.

Recently, the situation has changed. J.-L. and R. Brylinski[17] have shown that, given any entangling two-qudit unitary U, and local unitaries, it is always possible to do universal quantum computation. However, their proof used ideas from algebraic geometry and the theory of Lie algebras, and it is not clear to me whether their proof implies an efficient constructive method for doing the CNOT. Bremner *et al.*[9] built on this work by giving a *simple, constructive algorithm* for doing a CNOT, and thus universal quantum computation, using any entangling two-qubit unitary operation, and local unitaries.

[a] See,[16,14,15] and references therein.

The algorithm of Ref. 9 turns out to be *near-optimal*, using nearly the minimal possible number of uses of U to simulate a CNOT, and thus shows that quantum dynamical operations are fungible not only in principle, but may be in practice as well.

Knowing that quantum dynamics are a fungible physical resource, and thus qualitatively equivalent to one another, we can try to quantify the *strength* of a dynamical operation. We will now examine some strength measures, basing our discussion on Ref. 10. Let's start by defining a strength measure for an n-qubit unitary operation, U. (This is just one example among many in Ref. 10.) A metric, D, on unitary operations induces a natural strength measure, $K_D(U) \equiv \min_{A,B,\ldots} D(U, A \otimes B \otimes \ldots)$. That is, the strength is the minimal distance between U and the set of local unitaries.

What good is a strength measure? Let me answer by explaining a connection between strength and computational complexity. Imagine we have a strength measure with the following three properties. The first property, *chaining*, says that the strength of a product of two unitary operations, U and V, is less than the sum of their combined strengths, $K(UV) \leq K(U) + K(V)$. The intuition is that the ability to do U and V separately should be *at least* as powerful as the ability to do UV. This property is not always true for the metric-based strength measures, but is true for a large subclass.[10]

The second property, *stability*, says that if we add an extra qubit to our system and do nothing to it, that should not change the strength, $K(U \otimes I) = K(U)$. The metric-based measures do not always satisfy stability, but they do in some instances. The third property, *locality*, says that a strength measure should be zero for products of local unitary operations, $K(A \otimes B \otimes \ldots) = 0$. This is true for the metric-based measures of strength.

Imagine K is a strength measure satisfying these properties, and we want to perform a unitary, U, using CNOT and single-qubit gates. Imagine the circuit contains M CNOTs. Applying the properties, $K(U)$ can be no more than the sum of the strengths of the CNOTs, so $M \geq K(U)/K(\text{CNOT})$. By stability, the strength of CNOT is constant, so if $K(U)$ scales superpolynomially, then so must the number of gates needed to do U. Thus, developing measures of dynamic strength may enable progress on the notoriously difficult problem of proving lower bounds on computational complexity, and thus to gain insight into the enormously complex space of quantum dynamical processes.

Let me conclude by returning to the big picture. I believe that the major scientific task of quantum information science is to develop tools for the study of complex quantum systems. In quantum mechanics we're like chess players who've learnt the rules of the game, but are still trying to figure out the emergent properties those rules imply. We're doing so by developing overarching theories, like the theory of entanglement and of dynamic strength, which let us understand ever more complex phenomena. I expect that as these theories are developed they will enable us to better understand complex systems, not only in information processing, but also in other areas of many-body physics.

Acknowledgements

The point of view in this paper owes a lot to many enjoyable conversations with Jennifer Dodd and Tobias Osborne. Thanks also to Andrew Childs and Tobias Osborne for feedback on an earlier version of this manuscript.[19]

References

1. D. Aharonov. *Phys. Rev. A*, 62(6):2311, 1999.
2. M. A. Nielsen. *Quantum Information Theory*. PhD thesis, University of New Mexico, 1998. arXiv:quant-ph/0011036.
3. J. Preskill. *J. Mod. Opt.*, 47(2):127–137, 2000. arXiv:quant-ph/9904022.
4. D. P. DiVincenzo. *Fortschritte der physik — progress of physics*, 48(9–11):771–783, 2000. arXiv:quant-ph/0002077.
5. M. A. Nielsen. Seminar at the KITP, UC Santa Barbara (2001). http://online.kitp.ucsb.edu/online/qinfo01/nielsen/.
6. T. J. Osborne. *Entanglement and complex quantum systems*. PhD thesis, submitted at the University of Queensland, 2002.
7. T. J. Osborne and M. A. Nielsen. arXiv:quant-ph/0202162, 2002.
8. T. J. Osborne and M. A. Nielsen. *Quantum Information Processing*, 1(1):45–53, 2001. arXiv:quant-ph/0109024.
9. M. J. Bremner, C. M. Dawson, J. L. Dodd, A. Gilchrist, A. W. Harrow, D. Mortimer, M. A. Nielsen, and T. J. Osborne. arXiv:quant-ph/0207072, 2002.
10. M. A. Nielsen, C. M. Dawson, J. L. Dodd, A. Gilchrist, D. Mortimer, T. J. Osborne, M. J. Bremner, A. W. Harrow, and A. Hines. arXiv:quant-ph/0208077, 2002.
11. C. H. Bennett. In W. H. Zurek, editor, *Complexity, entropy and the physics of information*, pp. 137–148. Addison-Wesley, Redwood City, CA, 1990.
12. M. F. Barnsley. *Fractals everywhere*. Academic Press, 1988.
13. P. W. Shor. *SIAM J. Comp.*, 26(5):1484–1509, 1997.
14. C. H. Bennett, J. I. Cirac, M. S. Leifer, D. W. Leung, N. Linden, S. Popescu, and G. Vidal. arXiv:quant-ph/0107035v1, 2001.
15. P. Wocjan, M. Roetteler, D. Janzing, and Th. Beth. *Quantum Information and Computation*, 2(2):133–150, 2002. arXiv:quant-ph/0109063.
16. J. L. Dodd, M. A. Nielsen, M. J. Bremner, and R. T. Thew. *Phys. Rev. A*, 65(4):040301 (R), 2002. arXiv:quant-ph/0106064.
17. J. L. Brylinski and R. Brylinski. *Universal quantum gates*, chapter II in [18]. 2002. arXiv:quant-ph/0108062.
18. R. K. Brylinski and G. Chen, editors. *Mathematics of Quantum Computation*. Computational Mathematics. Chapman & Hall / CRC Press, 2002.
19. M. A. Nielsen. arXiv:quant-ph/0208078.

QUANTUM LIMITS OF MEASUREMENT AND COMPUTING INDUCED BY CONSERVATION LAWS AND UNCERTAINTY RELATIONS

MASANAO OZAWA

Graduate School of Information Sciences, Tôhoku University, Aoba-ku, Sendai, 980-8579, Japan

Mathematical Sciences Research Institute, 1000 Centennial Drive, #5070, Berkeley, California 94720-5070

A quantitative extension of the Wigner-Araki-Yanase theorem is obtained on the limitation on precise, non-disturbing measurements of observables which do not commute with additive conserved quantities, and applied to obtaining a limitation on the accuracy of quantum computing with computational bases which do not commute with angular momentum.

1 Introduction

Errors in quantum computers can be classified into two classes: the static errors—decoherence in qubits arising from the interaction between computational qubits and the environment—and the dynamical errors—imperfection of logic operations arising from the interaction between computational qubits and controllers of quantum gates. The current theory of fault-tolerant quantum computing concludes that if the imperfection is below a certain threshold, the decoherence can be corrected in an arbitrarily large quantum computer.[1] Thus, the fundamental question as to whether quantum computers are physically realizable or not can be reduced to such questions as whether fundamental physical laws lead to an unavoidable imperfection of quantum logic operations or not. On the other hand, it has been known in measurement theory that conservation laws limit the accuracy of measurements, as stated by the Wigner-Araki-Yanase (WAY) theorem:[2,3,4,5] observables which do not commute with bounded additive conserved quantities have no precise, non-disturbing measurements. During computation, a quantum computer usually needs to "measure" internal qubits to perform the branching program. Such "measurements" are carried out by the so-called controlled-not (CNOT) gates. Thus, it is natural to ask whether the WAY theorem leads to a conflict between the accuracy of quantum logic operations and conservation laws.

In this paper, we give a quantitative expression of the WAY theorem to obtain a lower bound on the error and the disturbance. Then, we apply this bound to the implementations of CNOT gates and obtain the following results. If the computational basis is represented by a component of spin and physical implementations obey angular momentum conservation law, any physically realizable unitary operations on the two computational qubits plus the S-2 ancilla qubits cannot implement the CNOT gate within error probability

$1/(4S^2)$. An analogous relation for the bosonic control field is also obtained to show that the error probability has the lower bound $1/(16\bar{n})$, where $\bar{n}$ is the average photon number of the control field. From the above result, we can conclude that in order to avoid entanglement between the computational qubits and the controlling system, we need to use the computational basis which commutes with all conserved quantities, or to use a very large ancilla or a very strong control field to the extent described by the above limitation. The former conclusion is closely related to the proposal of "encoded universality"[6,7] and the latter is closely related to the recent research on imperfect operations caused by the entanglement between qubits and the controlling laser field.[8,9] The present result will give a unified basis for those researches on quantum computing, providing them with rigorous and general, quantitative methods.

2 Error and Disturbance in Quantum Measurement

Let $\mathbf{M}(\mathbf{x})$ be a measuring apparatus with macroscopic output variable $\mathbf{x}$ to measure, possibly with some error, an observable A of the *object* $\mathbf{S}$, a quantum system represented by a Hilbert space $\mathcal{H}_{\mathbf{S}}$. The measuring interaction turns on at time 0 and turns off at time Δt between the object $\mathbf{S}$ and the measuring apparatus $\mathbf{M}(\mathbf{x})$. We assume that the apparatus has two parts, the *probe* $\mathbf{P}$ represented by a Hilbert space $\mathcal{H}_{\mathbf{P}}$ and the *ancilla* $\mathbf{A}$ represented by a Hilbert space $\mathcal{H}_{\mathbf{A}}$, and that the composite system $\mathbf{S}+\mathbf{P}+\mathbf{A}$ evolves unitarily from time 0 to time Δt. Denote by U the unitary operator on $\mathcal{H}_{\mathbf{S}} \otimes \mathcal{H}_{\mathbf{P}} \otimes \mathcal{H}_{\mathbf{A}}$ representing the time evolution of $\mathbf{S}+\mathbf{P}+\mathbf{A}$ in the time interval $(0, \Delta t)$.

At time 0, the object, the probe, and the ancilla are supposed to be in states ψ, ϕ, and ξ, respectively; all state vectors are assumed to be normalized unless stated otherwise. Thus, the composite system $\mathbf{S}+\mathbf{P}+\mathbf{A}$ is in the state $\psi \otimes \phi \otimes \xi$ at time 0. Just after the measuring interaction turns off, the probe is subjected to a local interaction with the subsequent stages of the apparatus. The last process is assumed to precisely measure an observable M in the probe $\mathbf{P}$ and to output the result of the measurement as the value of the macroscopic outcome variable $\mathbf{x}$. The statistical properties of the apparatus $\mathbf{M}(\mathbf{x})$ are then determined by the given quadruple $(\mathcal{H}_{\mathbf{P}} \otimes \mathcal{H}_{\mathbf{A}}, \phi \otimes \xi, U, M)$, which is called the indirect measurement model of $\mathbf{M}(\mathbf{x})$.[10,11] In the Heisenberg picture with the original state $\psi \otimes \phi \otimes \xi$, we shall write $A(0) = A \otimes I \otimes I$, $M(0) = I \otimes M \otimes I$, $A(\Delta t) = U^{\dagger}(A \otimes I \otimes I)U$, and $M(\Delta t) = U^{\dagger}(I \otimes M \otimes I)U$.

We say that measuring apparatus $\mathbf{M}(\mathbf{x})$ *measures* observable A *precisely*, if $A(0)$ and $M(\Delta t)$ have the same probability distribution on any input state ψ. The *error operator* $E(A)$ of apparatus $\mathbf{M}(\mathbf{x})$ for measuring A is defined by $E(A) = M(\Delta t) - A(0)$. The *(root-mean-square) error* $\epsilon(A)$ of apparatus $\mathbf{M}(\mathbf{x})$ for measuring A on input state ψ is, then, defined by $\epsilon(A) = \langle E(A)^2 \rangle^{1/2}$, where $\langle \cdots \rangle$ stands for $\langle \psi \otimes \phi \otimes \xi | \cdots | \psi \otimes \phi \otimes \xi \rangle$. Then, we have

$$\epsilon(A)^2 = \sigma[E(A)]^2 + \langle E(A) \rangle^2 \geq \sigma[E(A)]^2, \tag{1}$$

where $\sigma(X)$ stands for the standard deviation of an observable X in $\psi\otimes\phi\otimes\xi$, i.e., $\sigma(X)^2 = \langle X^2\rangle - \langle X\rangle^2$. It can be shown that apparatus $\mathbf{M}(\mathbf{x})$ measures observable A precisely if and only if $\epsilon(A) = 0$ for any input state ψ.

The apparatus $\mathbf{M}(\mathbf{x})$ is called *non-disturbing*, if $A(0)$ and $A(\Delta t)$ have the same probability distribution on any input state ψ. The *disturbance operator* $D(A)$ of apparatus $\mathbf{M}(\mathbf{x})$ for observable A is defined by $D(A) = A(\Delta t) - A(0)$. The *(root-mean-square) disturbance* $\eta(A)$ of apparatus $\mathbf{M}(\mathbf{x})$ for observable A on input state ψ is, then, defined by $\eta(A) = \langle D(A)^2\rangle^{1/2}$. Then, we have

$$\eta(A)^2 = \sigma[D(A)]^2 + \langle D(A)\rangle^2 \geq \sigma[D(A)]^2. \tag{2}$$

It can be shown that apparatus $\mathbf{M}(\mathbf{x})$ is non-disturbing if and only if $\eta(A) = 0$ for any input state ψ.

3 Quantitative Generalizations of Wigner-Araki-Yanase Theorem

Assume the additive conservation law (ACL) on quantities L_1 of the object $\mathbf{S}$, L_2 of the probe $\mathbf{P}$, and L_3 of the ancilla $\mathbf{A}$. In the Heisenberg picture, we shall write $L_1(0) = L_1\otimes I\otimes I$, $L_1(\Delta t) = U^\dagger(L_1\otimes I\otimes I)U$, $L_2(0) = I\otimes L_2\otimes I$, $L_2(\Delta t) = U^\dagger(I\otimes L_2\otimes I)U$, and so on. Then, the ACL is formulated as

$$L_1(0) + L_2(0) + L_3(0) = L_1(\Delta t) + L_2(\Delta t) + L_2(\Delta t). \tag{3}$$

From Eq. (3), we have the following commutation relations

$$[A(0), L_1(0)] = [L_1(\Delta t), E(A)] + [L_2(\Delta t), D(A)] + [L_3(\Delta t), D(A)], \tag{4}$$

$$[A(0), L_1(0)] = [L_1(\Delta t), E(A)] + [L_2(\Delta t), D(A)] + [L_3(\Delta t), E(A)]. \tag{5}$$

Taking the modulus of the expectations of the both sides of Eq. (4) and applying the triangle inequality, we have

$$|\langle[A(0), L_1(0)]\rangle| \leq |\langle[L_1(\Delta t), E(A)]\rangle| + |\langle[L_2(\Delta t), D(A)]\rangle| + |\langle[L_3(\Delta t), E(A)]\rangle|. \tag{6}$$

By the Robertson uncertainty relation (i.e., $\sigma(X)\sigma(Y) \geq |\langle[X,Y]\rangle|/2$ for any observables X and Y), we have

$$\frac{1}{2}|\langle\psi|[A, L_1]|\psi\rangle| \leq \epsilon(A)\sigma[L_1(\Delta t)] + \eta(A)\sigma[L_2(\Delta t)] + \eta(A)\sigma[L_3(\Delta t)]. \tag{7}$$

Similarly, from Eq. (5), we obtain

$$\frac{1}{2}|\langle\psi|[A, L_1]|\psi\rangle| \leq \epsilon(A)\sigma[L_1(\Delta t)] + \eta(A)\sigma[L_2(\Delta t)] + \epsilon(A)\sigma[L_3(\Delta t)]. \tag{8}$$

Each of the above inequalities, (7) and (8), implies the WAY theorem as follows. If the conserved quantities are bounded, we have $\sigma[L_1(\Delta t)], \sigma[L_2(\Delta t)], \sigma[L_3(\Delta t)] < \infty$. Thus, if the measurement is precise and non-disturbing, i.e., $\epsilon(A) = \eta(A) = 0$ for any state ψ, then we have $[A, L_1] = 0$. Thus, we conclude that observables which do not commute with bounded additive conserved quantities allow no precise, non-disturbing measurement.

Summing up both of the above inequalities and using the inequality $ax + by \le \max\{a, b\}(x + y)$ for $a, b, x, y \ge 0$, we have

$$|\langle\psi|[A, L_1]|\psi\rangle| \le [\epsilon(A) + \eta(A)](2\max\{\sigma[L_1(\Delta t)], \sigma[L_2(\Delta t)]\} + \sigma[L_3(\Delta t)]). \tag{9}$$

Since $\sigma(X) \le \|X\| = \|U^\dagger X U\|$ for any observable X and any unitary operator U, by the inequality $(x + y)^2 \le 2(x^2 + y^2)$ we have

$$\frac{|\langle\psi|[A, L_1]|\psi\rangle|^2}{2(2\max\{\|L_1\|, \|L_2\|\} + \sigma[L_3(\Delta t)])^2} \le \epsilon(A)^2 + \eta(A)^2. \tag{10}$$

4 Physical Implementations of CNOT Gates

Let U_{CN} be a CNOT gate on a 2-qubit system $\mathbf{C} + \mathbf{T}$. Let X_i, Y_i, and Z_i be the Pauli operators of qubit $\mathbf{C}$ for $i = 1$ or qubit $\mathbf{T}$ for $i = 2$ defined by $X_i = |1\rangle\langle 0| + |0\rangle\langle 1|$, $Y_i = i|1\rangle\langle 0| - i|0\rangle\langle 1|$, and $Z_i = |0\rangle\langle 0| - |1\rangle\langle 1|$ with the computational basis $\{|0\rangle, |1\rangle\}$. On the computational basis, U_{CN} acts as $U_{CN}|a, b\rangle = |a, b \oplus a\rangle$ for $a, b = 0, 1$, where $\oplus$ denotes the addition modulo 2. Thus, in particular, we have $U_{CN}|a, 0\rangle = |a, a\rangle$ for $a = 0, 1$. The above relation shows that the unitary operator U_{CN} serves as an interaction between the "object" $\mathbf{C}$ and the "probe" $\mathbf{T}$ for a precise, non-disturbing measurement of Z_1 with probe observable Z_2 without ancilla system. Thus, by the WAY theorem, if there are additive conserved quantities not commuting with Z_1, the unitary operator U_{CN} cannot be implemented correctly.

Let $\alpha = (U, |\xi\rangle)$ be a physical implementation of U_{CN} defined by a unitary operator U on the system $\mathbf{C}+\mathbf{T}+\mathbf{A}$, where $\mathbf{A}$ is the *ancilla*, and a state vector $|\xi\rangle$ of the ancilla. The implementation $\alpha = (U, |\xi\rangle)$ defines a trace-preserving quantum operation $\mathcal{E}_\alpha$ by

$$\mathcal{E}_\alpha(\rho) = Tr_{\mathbf{A}}[U(\rho \otimes |\xi\rangle\langle\xi|)U^\dagger] \tag{11}$$

for any density operator ρ of the system $\mathbf{C} + \mathbf{T}$, where $Tr_{\mathbf{A}}$ stands for the partial trace over the system $\mathbf{A}$. The *gate fidelity*[1] of α is defined by

$$F(\mathcal{E}_\alpha, U_{CN}) = \min_{|\psi\rangle} F(\psi) \tag{12}$$

where $|\psi\rangle$ varies over all state vectors of $\mathbf{C} + \mathbf{T}$, and $F(\psi)$ is the fidelity of two states $U_{CN}|\psi\rangle$ and $\mathcal{E}_\alpha(|\psi\rangle\langle\psi|)$. Then, $1 - F(\mathcal{E}_\alpha, U_{CN})^2$ is a good measure for the worst error probability of the implementation α over all possible input states.[12]

5 Imperfection from Angular Momentum Conservation Law

Let us consider the computational basis defined by the spin component of the z direction and the angular momentum conservation law for the x direction.

Thus, we assume $L_i = X_i$ for $i = 1, 2$, so that $\|L_1\| = \|L_2\| = 1$, and that L_3 is considered as the x-component of the total angular momentum divided by $\hbar/2$ of the ancilla system $\mathbf{A}$. Then, the unitary operator U should satisfy the conservation law $[U, L_1 + L_2 + L_3] = 0$. Letting $A = Z_1$ and $M = Z_2$ and applying Eq. (10), we have

$$\frac{|\langle\psi|[Z_1, X_1]|\psi\rangle|^2}{2[2+\sigma(L_3')]^2} \le \epsilon(Z_1)^2 + \eta(Z_1)^2, \tag{13}$$

where $L_3' = U^\dagger(I \otimes I \otimes L_3)U$.

It can be shown that $U = U_{CN}$ on $\mathcal{H}_\mathbf{T} \otimes \mathcal{H}_\mathbf{C}$ if and only if $\epsilon(Z_1)^2 + \eta(Z_1)^2 = 0$ holds for $\phi = \langle 0\rangle$ and any ψ, ξ. Thus, $\epsilon(Z_1)^2 + \eta(Z_1)^2$ measures the imperfection of U in implementing U_{CN}. Relation (13) suggests that in order to make U more accurately implement U_{CN} we need to make $[Z_1, X_1]$ smaller or make $\sigma(L_3')$ larger.

In order to relate the measure $\epsilon(Z_1)^2 + \eta(Z_1)^2$ to the gate fidelity and to obtain an upper bound for the gate fidelity, assume $\psi = \frac{1}{\sqrt{2}}(|0\rangle + |1\rangle)$ and $\phi = |0\rangle$. Then, we have

$$\epsilon(Z_1)^2 + \eta(Z_1)^2 \le 8[1 - F(\mathcal{E}_\alpha, U_{CN})^2] \tag{14}$$

for any ξ.[12] Since $[Z_1, L_1] = [Z_1, X_1] = 2iY_1$, we have

$$|\langle [Z_1, X_1]\rangle| = 2. \tag{15}$$

Thus, from Eqs. (13)–(15), we have the following fundamental upper bound of the gate fidelity

$$F(\mathcal{E}_\alpha, U_{CN})^2 \le 1 - \frac{1}{4[2+\sigma(L_3')]^2}. \tag{16}$$

In the following, we shall interpret the above relation in terms of notions of the size of implementations for fermionic and bosonic ancillae separately.

We now assume that the ancilla $\mathbf{A}$ comprises qubits. Then, the size $s(\alpha)$ of the implementation α is defined to be the total number n of the qubits included in $\mathbf{C} + \mathbf{T} + \mathbf{A}$. Then, we have $\Delta L_3' \le \|L_3\| = n - 2$. Thus, we have the following upper bound of the gate fidelity

$$F(\mathcal{E}_\alpha, U_{CN})^2 \le 1 - \frac{1}{4s(\alpha)^2}, \tag{17}$$

with $s(\alpha) = n$. Therefore, it has been proven that if the computational basis is represented by the z-component of spin, any implementation with size n which preserves the x-component of angular momentum cannot implement the CNOT gate within the error probability $1/(4n^2)$. In particular, any implementation on $\mathbf{C} + \mathbf{T}$ cannot simulate U_{CN} within the error probability $1/16$.

In current proposals,[1] the external electromagnetic field prepared by the laser beam is considered to be a feasible candidate for the ancilla $\mathbf{A}$ to be coupled with the computational qubits $\mathbf{C}+\mathbf{T}$ via the dipole interaction. Then, the ancilla state ξ is considered to be a coherent state, for which we have $(\Delta N)^2 = \langle \xi | N | \xi \rangle = \langle N \rangle$, where N is the number operator. We assume that the beam propagates to the x-direction with right-hand circular polarization. Then, we have $L_3 = 2N$, and hence $\Delta L_3' = 2\Delta N' = 2\langle N' \rangle^{1/2} \leq 2(\langle N \rangle + 2)^{1/2}$. Thus, Eq. (17) holds with defining the size of implementation α by $s(\alpha) = 2\langle N \rangle^{1/2}$ appropriately for the strong field, and hence Eq. (17) becomes

$$F(\mathcal{E}_\alpha, U_{CN})^2 \leq 1 - \frac{1}{16\langle N \rangle}. \tag{18}$$

Therefore, the lower bound of the error probability is inversely proportional to the average number of photons. This bound is consistent with the recent calculation on error probability based on a "one-photon type" transition Hamiltonian.[9]

In this paper, we have concentrated on CNOT gates, for discussions on other logic operations we refer to the recent publication.[12]

Acknowledgments

This work was supported by the programme "R&D on Quantum Communication Technology" of the MPHPT, by the CREST project of the JST, and by the Grant-in-Aid for Scientific Research of the JSPS.

References

1. M. A. Nielsen and I. L. Chuang, *Quantum Computation and Quantum Information* (Cambridge University Press, Cambridge, 2000).
2. E. P. Wigner, *Z. Physik* **133**, 101 (1952).
3. H. Araki and M. M. Yanase, *Phys. Rev.* **120**, 622 (1960).
4. M. Ozawa, *Phys. Rev. Lett.* **67**, 1956 (1991).
5. M. Ozawa, *Phys. Rev. Lett.* **88**, 050402 (2002).
6. D. Bacon *et al.*, *Phys. Rev. Lett.* **85**, 1758 (2000).
7. D. P. DiVincenzo *et al*, *Nature* (London) **408**, 339 (2000).
8. S. J. van Enk and H. J. Kimble, e-print quant-ph/010788.
9. J. Gea-Banacloche, *Phys. Rev.* A **65**, 022308 (2002).
10. M. Ozawa, *Phys. Rev.* A **62**, 062101 (2000).
11. M. Ozawa, *Phys. Rev.* A **63**, 032109 (2001).
12. M. Ozawa, *Phys. Rev. Lett.* **89**, 057902 (2002).

EXACT AND APPROXIMATE PERFORMANCE OF CONCATENATED QUANTUM CODES

BENJAMIN RAHN
ANDREW C. DOHERTY
HIDEO MABUCHI
Institute for Quantum Information, California Institute of Technology
E-mail: brahn@caltech.edu

Quantum information theorists, as with physicists in many areas, rely on asymptotic limits and expansions in small parameters. However, realistic quantum technologies will be of large but finite scale, and real parameter values may not be sufficiently small; thus methods valid outside these limits are desirable. Here we demonstrate the use of *balanced truncation*,[1] a technique from robust control theory, for studying highly concatenated quantum codes.

We will first review our previous analytic results,[2] in which we derived the effective channel describing an encoded qubit's evolution and propagated these results to concatenation schemes. The calculations for finite levels of concatenation are simple, but the resulting expressions for the effective channel dynamics are cumbersome and ill-conditioned. We will then describe the balanced truncation technique, and use it to find approximate models for these dynamics. Among other results, we derive a model for a 9^4-qubit system requiring only 23 degrees of freedom for accuracy $\sim 10^{-3}$.

1 Summary of Analytic Results

(A more detailed discussion of this section may be found elsewhere.[2])

We consider the following formulation of quantum error correction, depicted in Fig. 1. A logical single-qubit state ρ_0 is perfectly encoded in an N-qubit register by preparing the register in a state $\rho(0)$. The register then evolves via some error dynamics $\rho(0) \mapsto \rho(t) = \mathcal{N}[\rho(0)]$. At time t, a syndrome measurement is made and a corresponding recovery operation is performed. Assuming the measurement and recovery are noiseless, this process returns the system to the codespace; thus its state can be described by a logical single-qubit state. Let ρ_f be the probability-weighted average of the logical qubit states that result from this decoding procedure. For a given code and error model, we wish to know $\rho_f(t)$.

The logical qubit ρ_0 may be parameterized by the expectation values $\langle I\rangle_0$, $\langle X\rangle_0$, $\langle Y\rangle_0$ and $\langle Z\rangle_0$, with $\{I, X, Y, Z\}$ the usual Pauli matrices. Similarly, we parameterize ρ_f by $\langle I\rangle_f$, $\langle X\rangle_f$, $\langle Y\rangle_f$ and $\langle Z\rangle_f$. To describe the evolution of the encoded logical bit, we compute the *effective channel* $\mathcal{G}$ taking ρ_0 to ρ_f. As $\mathcal{G}$ is linear, we may represent $\mathcal{G}$ as the 4×4 matrix taking $\vec{\rho}_0 = (\langle I\rangle_0, \langle X\rangle_0, \langle Y\rangle_0, \langle Z\rangle_0)^{\mathrm{T}}$ to $\vec{\rho}_f = (\langle I\rangle_f, \langle X\rangle_f, \langle Y\rangle_f, \langle Z\rangle_f)^{\mathrm{T}}$.

Figure 1. The error-correction process and an equivalent effective channel $\mathcal{G}$.

Now suppose that the noise $\mathcal{N}$ is given by independent, identical qubit channels $\mathcal{N}^{(1)}$ acting on each qubit of the register, i.e. $\mathcal{N} = \mathcal{N}^{(1)\otimes N}$. Then a code C acts as a map on channels, taking the physical qubit channel $\mathcal{N}^{(1)}$ to the logical qubit channel $\mathcal{G}$. Let the *coding map* for a code C be given by

$$\Omega^C : \mathcal{N}^{(1)} \mapsto \mathcal{G}. \tag{1}$$

Because $\mathcal{N}^{(1)}$ is a qubit channel, just like $\mathcal{G}$ it may be written as a 4×4 matrix. In previous work[2] we showed that the matrix elements of $\mathcal{G} = \Omega^C(\mathcal{N}^{(1)})$ are polynomial functions of the matrix elements of $\mathcal{N}^{(1)}$.

We now consider certain concatenation schemes when the symmetric depolarizing channel acts on each register qubit. The symmetric depolarizing channel is described by $\mathcal{N}_t^{\rm dep}$ diagonal with entries $(1, e^{-\gamma t}, e^{-\gamma t}, e^{-\gamma t})$. From trace preservation the first diagonal element is always 1, so let $[x, y, z]$ denote $\mathcal{N}^{(1)}$ diagonal with entries $(1, x, y, z)$; then $\mathcal{N}_t^{\rm dep} = [e^{-\gamma t}, e^{-\gamma t}, e^{-\gamma t}]$.

First, suppose more generally that the noise model $\mathcal{N}^{(1)} = [x, y, z]$ acts on each physical qubit, and that we encode a logical qubit via the bit-flip (bf) code, with encoding $|0\rangle \mapsto |000\rangle$, $|1\rangle \mapsto |111\rangle$. It can be shown that the effective channel is also diagonal:

$$\Omega^{\rm bf}([x, y, z]) = \left[x^3,\ \tfrac{3}{2}x^2 y - \tfrac{1}{2}y^3,\ \tfrac{3}{2}z - \tfrac{1}{2}z^3\right]. \tag{2}$$

The action on $[x, y, z]$ of the coding map for the phase-flip (pf) code with encoding $|\pm\rangle \mapsto |\pm\pm\pm\rangle$ has a similar form. The concatenation phase-flip(bit-flip) yields the Shor nine-bit code; thus $\Omega^{\rm Shor}([x, y, z]) = \Omega^{\rm pf}(\Omega^{\rm bf}([x, y, z])) =$

$$\left[\tfrac{3}{2}x^3 - \tfrac{1}{2}x^9,\ \tfrac{3}{2}\left(\tfrac{3}{2}z - \tfrac{1}{2}z^3\right)^2\left(\tfrac{3}{2}x^2 y - \tfrac{1}{2}y^3\right) - \tfrac{1}{2}\left(\tfrac{3}{2}x^2 y - \tfrac{1}{2}y^3\right)^3,\ \left(\tfrac{3}{2}z - \tfrac{1}{2}z^3\right)^3\right].$$

Now consider ℓ concatenations of the Shor code under the symmetric depolarizing channel. Let $[\widetilde{x}_\ell(t), \widetilde{y}_\ell(t), \widetilde{z}_\ell(t)]$ be the effective channel $(\Omega^{\rm Shor})^\ell(\mathcal{N}_t^{\rm dep})$. Fig. 2 shows plots of $\widetilde{z}_\ell(t)$ for $0 \le \ell \le 4$; results for $\widetilde{x}_\ell(t)$ and $\widetilde{y}_\ell(t)$ are similar.

2 Balanced Truncation for Approximate Models

The functions $\widetilde{x}_\ell(t)$, $\widetilde{y}_\ell(t)$, and $\widetilde{z}_\ell(t)$ each have the form $\sum_i b_i e^{-a_i \gamma t}$ with the a_i positive integers, the b_i rational, and $\sum_i b_i = 1$. Explicit calculation of the $\widetilde{\sigma}_\ell$ has multiple disadvantages. First, the number of terms in these series grows approximately as 9^ℓ (see Table 1(a)). Further, the magnitude of the b_i grows rapidly: e.g., $|b_i| > 10^{60}$ for 65 of the 352 terms in $\widetilde{z}_3$.

Given $\mathcal{G}(t) = [\widetilde{x}(t), \widetilde{y}(t), \widetilde{z}(t)]$, for each $\widetilde{\sigma}(t)$ we will seek a square matrix A_σ, column vector B_σ and row vector C_σ such that $\widetilde{\sigma}(t) \approx C_\sigma e^{A_\sigma t} B_\sigma$. For

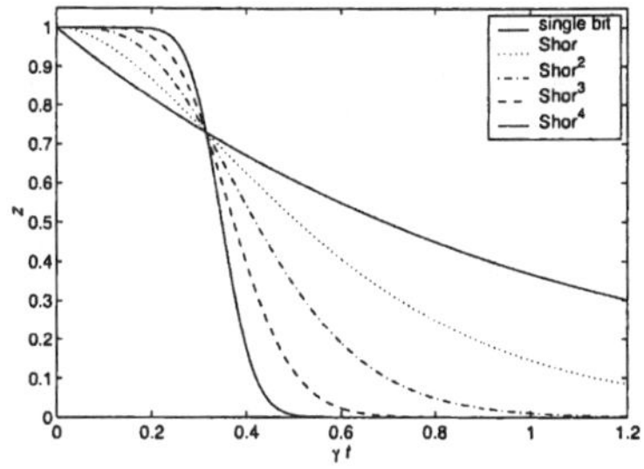

Figure 2. $\widetilde{z}_\ell(t)$ for Shor$^\ell$ concatenation under the depolarizing channel.

ℓ (qubits)	(a) series terms			(b) reduced order		
	$\widetilde{x}_\ell$	$\widetilde{y}_\ell$	$\widetilde{z}_\ell$	$\widetilde{x}_\ell$	$\widetilde{y}_\ell$	$\widetilde{z}_\ell$
0 (1)	1	1	1	1	1	1
1 (9)	2	3	4	2	2	3
2 (81)	13	33	37	4	4	5
3 (729)	118	339	352	5	5	6
4 (6561)	1081	3201	3241	7	7	9

Table 1. (a) Terms in exact series for $\widetilde{\sigma}_\ell(t)$. (b) Order of iteratively reduced realizations.

$n \times n$ A_σ, we say $(A_\sigma, B_\sigma, C_\sigma)$ is an *order n realization* of $\widetilde{\sigma}(t)$. For $\widetilde{\sigma}(t) = \sum_i b_i e^{-a_i\gamma t}$, we can exactly realize $\widetilde{\sigma}(t)$ by choosing A_σ diagonal with entries $-a_i\gamma$, B_σ with entries b_i, and $C_\sigma = (1, 1, \ldots, 1)$. If the a_i are distinct and the b_i non-zero, this realization is *minimal*: there is no lower-order exact realization of $\widetilde{\sigma}(t)$.

To find approximate lower-order realizations we use the technique of *balanced truncation.*[1] Consider a system with input $u(t) \in R$, state $x(t) \in R^n$, dynamics $\dot{x} = Ax + Bu$, and output $y(t) = Cx \in R$; if $u = \delta(t)$, $y = Ce^{At}B$ for $t > 0$. Note that $(A, B, C) \to (TAT^{-1}, TB, CT^{-1})$ leaves $\Psi : u(t) \mapsto y(t)$ unchanged. Balanced truncation numerically constructs a *balancing* transformation T such that in the balanced system, a non-negative real *Hankel Singular Value* (HSV) h_i is associated with each dimension of the state-space R^n. Removing all dimensions with $h_i = 0$ yields a minimal realization; further truncating dimensions with small HSVs introduces a small error in Ψ which, in an appropriate norm, is bounded by the sum of the truncated HSVs.

Consider $\widetilde{z}_2(t)$, with minimal realization of order 37. Balancing the minimal realization, we find that the first five HSVs are $(2.5 \times 10^{-1})/\gamma$, $(3.7\times10^{-2})/\gamma$, $(5.3\times10^{-3})/\gamma$, $(6.0\times10^{-4})/\gamma$, and $(5.4\times10^{-5})/\gamma$. Truncating all but the four most significant dimensions yields an approximation almost indistinguishable from the exact $\widetilde{z}_2(t)$; truncating further mildly degrades the approximation (see the left plot of Fig. 3).

Given A_σ, B_σ and C_σ that yield $f_\sigma(t) = C_\sigma e^{A_\sigma(t)} B_\sigma$ for $\widetilde{\sigma}(t)$, it is easy to construct A', B' and C' that realize any desired polynomial function of the

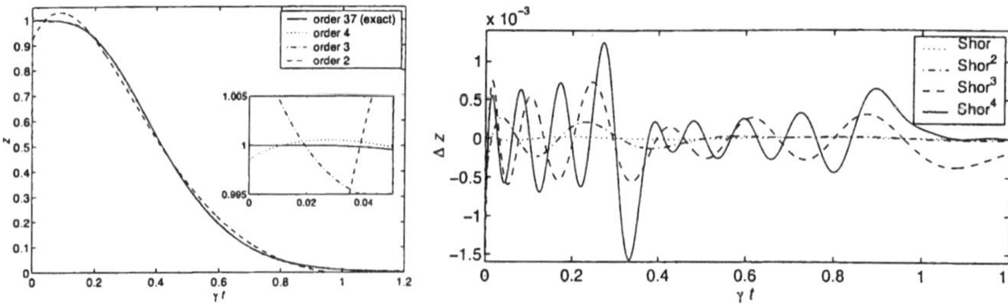

Figure 3. **Left:** Exact $\widetilde{z}_2(t)$, and approximations that result from balanced truncation. The order 4 approximation is only distinguishable from the exact function on the inset. **Right:** Approximation error for $\widetilde{z}_\ell(t)$ generated by iterative reduction with $h_{\min} = (4 \times 10^{-5})/\gamma$.

$f_\sigma(t)$. Thus if the $f_\sigma(t)$ are approximate realizations of the $\widetilde{\sigma}(t)$, we may use this polynomial construction to approximately realize $\Omega^C([\widetilde{x}(t), \widetilde{y}(t), \widetilde{z}(t)])$.

For $\ell > 2$ it is impractical to construct the exact $\widetilde{\sigma}_\ell(t)$ and then apply balanced truncation. Instead, we build approximate realizations for the $\widetilde{\sigma}_\ell(t)$ using a novel iterative approach. Begin with minimal realizations for the $\widetilde{\sigma}_0(t)$ describing $\mathcal{N}_t^{\text{dep}}$. Alternately apply Ω^{bf} and Ω^{pf}; after each concatenation, balance and truncate dimensions with HSVs below some $h_{\min}$. Choosing $h_{\min} = (4 \times 10^{-5})/\gamma$ yields realizations with orders shown in Table 1(b). Comparing to Table 1(a), we see the resulting order reduction is dramatic.

The right plot in Fig. 3 shows the differences between the exact $\widetilde{z}_\ell(t)$ and the results of the iterative reduction method. Results for approximating $\widetilde{x}_\ell(t)$ and $\widetilde{y}_\ell(t)$ are similar. Up to eight 3-qubit concatenations, the worst errors $|\Delta\widetilde{\sigma}_\ell(t)|$ are only $\approx 3 \times 10^{-3}$.

These results suggest balanced truncation is a powerful approximation tool in quantum settings. Future work will further investigate the iterative reduction method, and attempt to find bounds on the approximation errors.

Acknowledgements

This work was partially supported by the Caltech MURI Center for Quantum Networks and the NSF Institute for Quantum Information. B.R. acknowledges the support of an NSF graduate fellowship, and thanks J. Preskill and P. Parrilo for insightful discussions.

References

1. B. Rahn, "A Balanced Truncation Primer," quant-ph/0112066 (2001), and references therein.
2. B. Rahn, A. C. Doherty, and H. Mabuchi, *Phys. Rev. A*, **66**, 032304 (2002).

QUANTUM DECODER FOR SINGLE PHOTON COMMUNICATION

M. SASAKI, M. FUJIWARA, M. TAKEOKA, AND J. MIZUNO
Communications Research Laboratory, Koganei, Tokyo 184-8795, Japan
E-mail: psasaki@crl.go.jp

We present recent experimental progress toward photonic realization of quantum channel coding which deals with reliable transmission of signals at the quantum level. Ambiguity among signals is mainly due to non-orthogonality of quantum states. As a typical model, we consider the ternary symmetric states of a single photon polarization. Optical circuits were implemented for extracting the maximum information from this quantum source by a single-shot measurement, and also for demonstrating the super-additive coding gain by quantum collective decoding.

1 Introduction

Quantum channel coding deals with how reliably one can transmit information over a quantum channel. Given a source of quantum states (letter states), $\{|\psi_x\rangle\}$, one represents messages by block sequences as direct products of the letter states, $\{|\psi_{x_1}\rangle \otimes \cdots \otimes |\psi_{x_n}\rangle\}$. For reliable transmission through a channel with finite errors, one must introduce some redundancy in the codeword representation so as to allow the correction of errors at the receiving side. Messages of k bits are encoded into sequences in length n ($n > k$). It is a matter how to reduce the decoding error while keeping the transmission rate $R = k/n$ as large as possible. The channel capacity C is the maximum rate for error free transmission.[1] Channel capacity theorems were recently extended into the quantum domain, wherein signals are generally conveyed by non-commuting density matrices,[2,3,4] whereas conventional theory deals with the special case of signals conveyed by commuting density matrices. The new capacity theorems indicate that one can attain a higher limit of channel capacity by applying decoding that is assisted by quantum computing (quantum collective decoding). We present recent experimental progress toward photonic realization of quantum channel coding.

2 Optimal single-shot measurement

As a letter source, we consider the ternary-symmetric polarization states of a single photon, $|\psi_0\rangle = |0\rangle$, $|\psi_1\rangle = -\frac{1}{2}|0\rangle - \frac{\sqrt{3}}{2}|1\rangle$, and $|\psi_2\rangle = -\frac{1}{2}|0\rangle + \frac{\sqrt{3}}{2}|1\rangle$, where $|0\rangle$ ($= |H\rangle$) and $|1\rangle$ ($= |V\rangle$) are the horizontally and vertically polarized states. Since they are nonorthogonal states, they cannot be distinguished perfectly. In fact, the minimum average error is $1/3$ when each letter is used with equal a priori probability. The optimal measurement is described by the probability operator-valued measure (POVM) $\{|\mu_x\rangle\langle\mu_x|\}$, with $|\mu_x\rangle =$

$\sqrt{\frac{2}{3}}\,|\psi_x\rangle$.

The measurement minimizing the average error, however, is not the optimal one for channel coding. The optimal measurement for channel coding, $\{\hat{\omega}_y\}$, should maximize the mutual information defined by

$$I(X:Y) = \sum_x P(x) \sum_y P(y|x) \log \left[\frac{P(y|x)}{\sum_{x'} P(x')P(y|x')} \right] \tag{1}$$

where $P(y|x) = \langle\psi_x|\,\hat{\omega}_y\,|\psi_x\rangle$ and $P(x)$ is the *a priori* probability of $|\psi_x\rangle$. The mutual information specifies the maximum transmission rate for which the decoding error P_e can be made arbitrarily small in the limit $n \to \infty$.

In the classical context, a channel model is given as a channel matrix $[P(y|x)]$, and the *a priori* probability $P(x)$ is a variable used to maximize the mutual information. On the other hand, in the quantum context, the measurement strategy may also be optimized for a given and fixed letter state source. For simplicity, we first consider the optimal measurement for the uniform prior distribution, $P(x) = 1/3$ for all x. The optimal measurement is then given by[5] $\hat{\omega}_y = |\omega_y\rangle\langle\omega_y|$, with $|\omega_0\rangle = \sqrt{\frac{2}{3}}\,|1\rangle$, $|\omega_1\rangle = \frac{1}{\sqrt{2}}\,|0\rangle - \frac{1}{\sqrt{6}}\,|1\rangle$, and $|\omega_2\rangle = -\frac{1}{\sqrt{2}}\,|0\rangle - \frac{1}{\sqrt{6}}\,|1\rangle$. The maximum mutual information (accessible information) is $I_1^{\rm Acc} = 0.585$ bits. This can be compared with the maximum mutual information $I_1^{\rm vN} = 0.459$ bits afforded by the standard von Neumann measurement, which is described by a projection of a signal state onto orthogonal bases in the signal Hilbert space.

The optimal measurement can be realized by the polarization interferometer[5] shown in Fig. 1. The performance of this detection circuit has been tested by using heavily-attenuated continuous-wave laser light and single photon counters. Our polarization interferometer exhibits signal-discrimination performance corresponding to 96% of the theoretical maximum $I_1^{\rm Acc}$ at the extrapolated perfect-efficiency point for a single photon counter. Figure 1 (right) shows the experimental mutual information as a function of the relative offset angle between the signal set and the measurement vectors.[6]

Now we consider the classical limit of capacity, which is defined to be the mutual information maximized over both the prior distribution $P(x)$ and the quantum measurement $\{\hat{\pi}_y\}$

$$C_1 = \max_{\{P(x)\}} \max_{\{\hat{\pi}_y\}} I(X:Y). \tag{2}$$

It is this quantity that limits the performance of all modern communications systems. We shall call it here the Shannon limit of the capacity. For the ternary letter states it is known that $C_1 = 0.645$ bits, which is realized by using only two letters with equal probabilities 0.5 and by detecting with the von Neumann measurement .[8,9] Thus the best way of coding based on a separable measurement is to use classical codes for the binary symmetric channel.

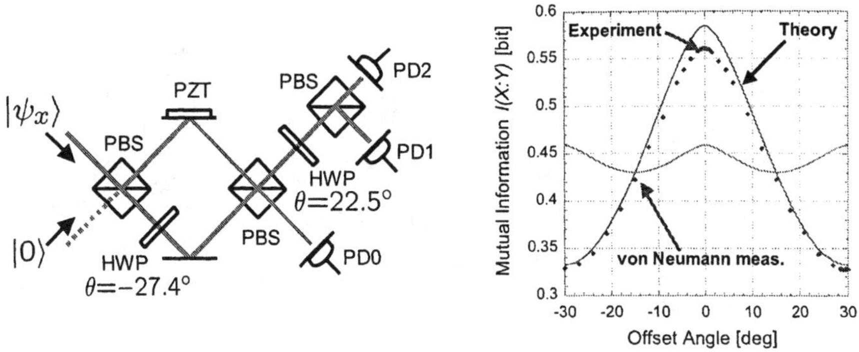

Figure 1. Optical circuit implementation for the accessible information (left), and experimental accessible information (right).

3 Super-additive coding gain

The quantity C_1, however, is not the ultimate capacity allowed by quantum mechanics. To decode the codeword states, one may design a best quantum measurement allowed by quantum mechanics. A well-known example of length-2 coding consists of the set of codewords $\{|\Psi_x\rangle\}$ with $|\Psi_x\rangle = |\psi_x\rangle \otimes |\psi_x\rangle$ ($x = 0, 1, 2$), each of which is used with equal probability, and the two-bit collective decoding based on the square root measurement.[7] The attainable transmission rate in this scheme is $I_2^{\rm SRM}/2 = 0.685$ bits. This suggests that the transmittable information can be increased by more than a factor of two when the transmission resource is doubled. This is indeed an information theoretic quantum coding gain which cannot be seen in classical memoryless channel coding.

Collective decoding essentially includes entanglement control for a received codeword. Unfortunately, however, entangling more than two particles with sufficient precision for attaining super-additive coding gain is something very hard to do at present. So we consider a coding format of polarization and spatial modes of a single photon. Namely, we introduce two spatial modes, Path A and Path B, and make a location qubit $\{|0\rangle_L, |1\rangle_L\}$ in addition to a polarization qubit $\{|0\rangle_P, |1\rangle_P\}$. The state $|0\rangle_L$ means that a photon exists on Path A and no photon on Path B, and vice versa for $|1\rangle_L$. The three length-2 codewords are $|\Psi_x\rangle \equiv |\psi_x\rangle_P \otimes |\psi_x\rangle_L$. This is an example of pulse-position coding, which is often used when the available signal power is severely limited. For this coding format, the super-additive coding gain can be paraphrased as follows: if we double the spatial resources, then we can transmit more than double the information.

The encoder and decoder are depicted in Fig. 2. The circuit consists of half-wave plates and polarizing beam splitters. The decoding performance

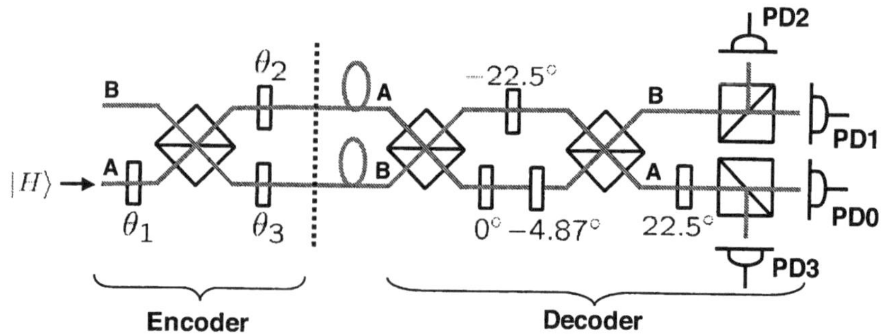

Figure 2. The encoder and decoder for the Peres-Wootters code. A rectangle represents a half-wave plate (HWP) whose fast axis is tipped at the indicated angle from the vertical. A square means a polarizing beam splitter (PBS). The encoder includes 3 HWPs whose angles $(\theta_1, \theta_2, \theta_3)$ are $(45°, 0°, 0°)$, $(-15°, -30°, 15°)$, and $(-15°, 30°, -15°)$, for the codewords, $|\Psi_0\rangle$, $|\Psi_1\rangle$, and $|\Psi_2\rangle$, respectively. The decoder circuit is one possible implementation of the square-root measurement. Detecting a photon at PD0, PD1, or PD2, is assigned to deciding that the codeword sent was $|\Psi_0\rangle$, $|\Psi_1\rangle$, or $|\Psi_2\rangle$, respectively. When the circuit works perfectly, reception of any photon at PD3 is expected.

was tested by measuring single photon counting statistics for constructing the channel matrix in the same way as testing the accessible information. By selecting events at PD0, PD1, and PD2, we can simulate communications of sending and detecting the photons one by one through an almost pure state quantum channel. The mutual information was found to be 0.656 bits per letter. The error bar of ±0.003 bits was mainly due to the thermal drift of the circuit and imperfections of PBSs. This is greater than the theoretical C1. Thus the optical circuit in Fig. 2 exhibits super-additive coding gain.

References

1. C. E. Shannon, Bell System Tech. J. **27**, 379 (Part I) and 623 (Part II) (1948).
2. P. Hausladen, et al., Phys. Rev. A **54**, 1869 (1996).
3. B. Schumacher and M. Westmoreland, Phys. Rev. A **56**, 131 (1997).
4. A.S. Holevo, IEEE Trans. Inf. Theory **IT-44**, 269 (1998).
5. M. Sasaki, et al., Phys. Rev. A **59**, 3325 (1999).
6. J. Mizuno, et al., Phys. Rev. A **65**, 012315 (2002).
7. A. Peres and W. K. Wootters, Phys. Rev. Lett. **66**,1119 (1991)
8. M. Osaki, et al., *Quantum Commun., Comput., and Meas. 2* (Eds. P. Kumar, M. D'Ariano, and O. Hirota, Prenum, NY, 2000) 17.
9. P. W. Shor, quant-ph/0206058.

PREPARING ENCODED STATES IN AN OSCILLATOR

B. C. TRAVAGLIONE
G. J. MILBURN
Centre for Quantum Computer Technology, Department of Physics, University of Queensland, St Lucia, Queensland, Australia

Recently a scheme has been proposed for constructing quantum error-correcting codes that embed a finite-dimensional code space in the infinite-dimensional Hilbert space of a system described by continuous quantum variables. One of the difficult steps in this scheme is the preparation of the encoded states. We show how these states can be generated by coupling a continuous quantum variable to a *single* qubit.

1 Introduction

It appears, in principle, that the laws of quantum mechanics allow certain mathematical problems to be solved more rapidly than can be done using a classical computer.[1] However, in order to accomplish this task, the state of a quantum system must maintain coherence, despite unwanted interactions with the environment. There have been a number of proposed mechanisms for protecting quantum information during a computation.[2,3,4,5,6,7,8] Recently, it has been shown[9] that a d-dimensional quantum system (here we only consider $d = 2$) can be embedded in an infinite-dimensional Hilbert space, such that a universal set of fault-tolerant quantum gates can be implemented using linear optical operations, squeezing, homodyne detection, and photon counting. The qubits are embedded in the continuous system in a manner which protects the quantum information against small shifts in the canonical quantum variables, q (position) and p (momentum). Ideally, the encoded states are an infinite sum of delta functions in both q and p. Of course, such states are non-normalizable, and unphysical. Hence they must be approximated. It has been proposed[9] that these approximate encoded states could be generated by a procedure involving a non-linear interaction Hamiltonian of the form,

$$H' \propto qb^\dagger b, \tag{1}$$

where q is the position operator of one variable, and b ($b^\dagger$) is the annihilation (creation) operator of a second variable. Unfortunately, interactions of the form given in Eq. (1) have proven very difficult to implement. They generally require the radiation pressure of photons to move a macroscopic object (a mirror).[10] Here we show that approximate encoded states can be generated by coupling the continuous variable to a *single* qubit,[11] and performing a sequence of operations similar to a quantum random walk algorithm.[12]

2 Ideal Encoded States

Gottesman et al.[9] discuss how to embed a qubit in a continuous quantum system, so that the extra degrees of freedom within the system can be used to correct errors which arise from unwanted interactions with the environment. Ideally, an encoded zero state, $|\bar{0}\rangle$, will be represented in position space by the wave function

$$\langle q|\bar{0}\rangle = \sum_{s=-\infty}^{\infty} \delta(q - 2\alpha s) = \frac{1}{2\alpha} \sum_{s=-\infty}^{\infty} e^{i\pi sq/\alpha}, \tag{2}$$

and thus in momentum space, it has the wave function

$$\langle p|\bar{0}\rangle = \frac{\sqrt{2\pi}}{2\alpha} \sum_{s=-\infty}^{\infty} \delta(p - \frac{\pi s}{\alpha}) = \frac{1}{\sqrt{2\pi}} \sum_{s=-\infty}^{\infty} e^{-i2sp\alpha}. \tag{3}$$

The wave functions for the encoded zero state are depicted in Fig. 1(a), while Fig. 1(b) depicts the wave functions for the encoded one state. Clearly the zero and one encoded states are orthogonal,

$$\langle \bar{0}|\bar{1}\rangle = 0. \tag{4}$$

For the details of how quantum computation and error recovery is performed with these encoded states we direct the reader to Gottesman et al.[9]

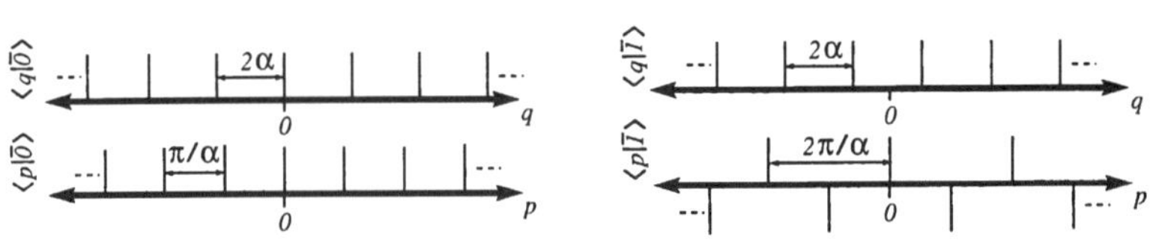

Figure 1. (a) Ideal wave function, in both position and momentum, of the encoded zero state, $|\bar{0}\rangle$. In position space, the wave function is an infinite sum of delta functions, separated by 2α, in momentum space, the wave function is an infinite sum of delta functions separated by π/α. (b) Ideal wave functions of the encoded one state, $|\bar{1}\rangle$.

3 Preparing encoded states using a qubit

Once prepared, it is hoped that the error recovery procedure will be able to maintain the encoded states. However, preparation of the encoded states is not trivial. As has already been stated, we can only prepare approximate encoded states. In this section we show how approximate encoded states can be prepared with the aid of a single ancilla qubit. Our preparation scheme is non-deterministic, in that a valid approximate encoded state will only be prepared with some probability less than one, however, we will know when our preparation procedure has worked.

We shall denote approximate encoded zero and one states with the symbols $|\tilde{0}\rangle$ and $|\tilde{1}\rangle$. As in Gottesman et al., we begin the preparation procedure with the quantum system in the ground state of the oscillator, $|0\rangle$, and apply squeezing in the q quadrature. Using an ancilla qubit, initially in the zero state, $|0\rangle$, the approximate encoded one state, $|\tilde{1}_1\rangle$ is then created by applying the sequence of operators,

$$\hat{H} e^{-i\alpha p_e \sigma_z} \hat{H}. \tag{5}$$

If the qubit is measured in the one state, the encoded variable is discarded and we try again. To create improved approximate encoded states, we iterate the following procedure:
Given $|\tilde{1}_{n-1}\rangle$, and a qubit in the state $|0\rangle$.

- Apply the operators: $$\hat{H} e^{-i2^{n-1}\alpha p_e \sigma_z} \hat{H} \tag{6}$$
- Measure the qubit.
- If the qubit is found in the state $|0\rangle$, then we have created $|\tilde{1}_n\rangle$.
- Else discard and start again.

Fig. 2 depicts the approximate encoded state $|\tilde{1}_3\rangle$, with $\Delta = 0.15$ (initial squeezing) and $\alpha = \sqrt{\pi/2}$. This state will be generated with probability 1/8. The approximate encoded zero state $|\tilde{0}_n\rangle$ is created by displacing the state $|\tilde{1}_n\rangle$ by an amount α in the position variable. Because of the 2^n term in Eq. (6), the average energy of the approximate encoded states will increase exponentially with n, however, it can be shown that the probability of error decreases exponentially with n.

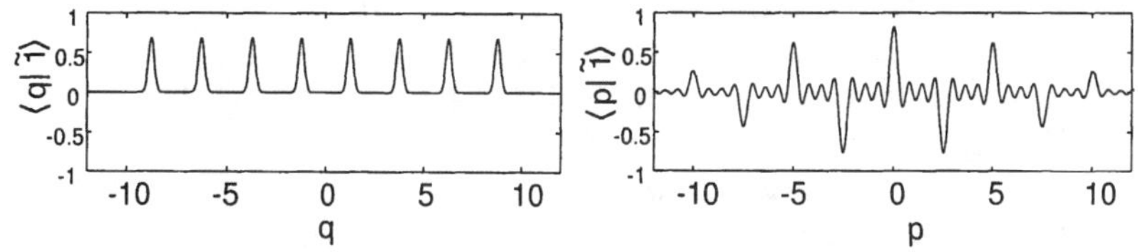

Figure 2. Wave functions, in both position and momentum, of the approximate encoded zero state, $|\tilde{1}_3\rangle$. This approximate encoded state will be generated, with probability 1/8, by first squeezing the continuous variable in momentum quadrature, and then applying the sequence of operations and measurements described in the text.

4 Deterministic error recovery

For robust quantum computation, it is necessary that our encoded states are comb-like in both the position and momentum quadratures, so that small shifts in both position and momentum can be corrected. However, this is not necessary for the ancilla systems used in error recovery. The relative phases between the different 'prongs' in the comb-like state are irrelevant. The reason for this is that we measure the ancilla variable directly after it has interacted with the encoded variable. Thus, after measurement, the relative phase becomes an unimportant global phase.

The invariance of the ancilla variables to relative phases allows us to deterministically prepare ancilla systems for error recovery. The ancilla system states can be prepared using the procedure described in Sec. 3, except that we continue with the preparation procedure for n iterations, irrespective of whether the qubit is measured in the $|0\rangle$ or $|1\rangle$ state.

5 Conclusions

For a quantum computer to become a reality, the daunting task of providing adequate error correction needs to be fulfilled. As the quantum mechanical oscillator is so prevalent in the study of quantum mechanics, it appears to be a natural test bed for quantum computation. Here we have shown how a continuous quantum system can be coupled to a discrete two level quantum system in a manner which allows the continuous quantum system to encode a qubit. This scheme is physically realizable using ion trap quantum computing or cavity QED.

References

1. M. A. Nielsen and I. L. Chuang, *Quantum Computation and Quantum Information* (Cambridge University Press, Cambridge, 2000).
2. P. W. Shor, Physical Review A **52**, 2493 (1995).
3. A. M. Steane, Physical Review Letters **77**, 793 (1996).
4. E. Knill and R. Laflamme, Physical Review A **55**, 900 (1997).
5. H. F. Chau, Physical Review A **55**, 839 (1997).
6. E. M. Rains, *Nonbinary quantum codes* (1997), quant-ph/9703048.
7. D. Gottesman, Physical Review A **54**, 1862 (1996).
8. A. R. Calderbank, E. M. Rains, P. W. Shor, and N. J. A. Sloane, Physical Review Letters **78**, 405 (1997).
9. D. Gottesman, A. Kitaev, and J. Preskill, Physical Review A **64**, 012310 (2001).
10. V. Giovannetti, S. Mancini, and P. Tombesi, *Radiation pressure induced Einstein-Podolsky-Rosen paradox* (2000), quant-ph/0005066.
11. B. C. Travaglione and G. J. Milburn, Physical Review A **66**, 052322 (2002).
12. B. C. Travaglione and G. J. Milburn, Physical Review A **65**, 032310 (2002).

ACCESSIBLE INFORMATION OF 3 SYMMETRIC STATES IN 3-DIMENSIONAL COMPLEX HILBERT SPACE

KOUJI TANAKA   MASAO OSAKI

Research Center for Quantum Communications, Tamagawa University, 6-1-1, tamagawagakuen, Machida-city, Tokyo, 194-8610, JAPAN.

E-mail: osaki@lab.tamagawa.ac.jp

1 Introduction

Accessible information, $I_{\rm ac}$, is one of the most important quantities for evaluating a set of quantum states to be used for classical information transmission.[1] For the lifted trine states in 3-dimensional real Hilbert space, Shor has derived $I_{\rm ac}$ with 3 or 6 detection operators.[2] This result coincides with Davies' theorem.[3,4] Here we try to derive it for 3 symmetric states in 3-dimensional complex Hilbert space.

2 Signal quantum states and their representation

Three Phase-Shift Keyed (3PSK) coherent-state signals comprise one of the most simple symmetric spanning sets for 3-dimensional complex Hilbert space.[5] Their state vectors are represented as follows:

$$|f_1\rangle = |\alpha\rangle, \quad |f_2\rangle = |\alpha e^{2\pi i/3}\rangle, \quad |f_3\rangle = |\alpha e^{-2\pi i/3}\rangle. \tag{1}$$

The symmetry property is given by the unitary operator $\hat{V}$ through the relation $|f_i\rangle = \hat{V}^{(i-1)}|f_1\rangle$, where $\hat{V} = \exp[2\pi i\hat{n}/3]$ and $\hat{n}(= \hat{a}^\dagger\hat{a})$ is the photon number operator. The Gram matrix of these signal quantum states is

$$\boldsymbol{G} = [\langle f_i|f_j\rangle] = \begin{bmatrix} 1 & \kappa & \kappa^* \\ \kappa^* & 1 & \kappa \\ \kappa & \kappa^* & 1 \end{bmatrix}, \tag{2}$$

where κ is an inner product that depends on the signals' average photon number $n_{\rm s}(= |\alpha|^2)$,

$$\kappa = K_{\rm c} + iK_{\rm s} = \exp\left[-3n_{\rm s}/2\right]\left(\cos\left[\sqrt{3}n_{\rm s}/2\right] + i\sin\left[\sqrt{3}n_{\rm s}/2\right]\right). \tag{3}$$

With the symmetric property of the Gram matrix, we can obtain the following orthonormal basis for the signal Hilbert space $\mathcal{H}_{\rm s}$:

$$\begin{aligned} |e_1\rangle &= \frac{1}{\sqrt{3h_1}}\left(|f_1\rangle + e^{-2\pi i/3}|f_2\rangle + e^{2\pi i/3}|f_3\rangle\right), \\ |e_2\rangle &= \frac{1}{\sqrt{3h_2}}\left(|f_1\rangle + e^{2\pi i/3}|f_2\rangle + e^{-2\pi i/3}|f_3\rangle\right), \\ |e_3\rangle &= \frac{1}{\sqrt{3h_3}}\left(|f_1\rangle + |f_2\rangle + |f_3\rangle\right), \end{aligned} \tag{4}$$

where $\{ h_i : i = 1, 2, 3 \}$ are the eigenvalues of the Gram matrix,

$$h_1 = 1 - K_c + \sqrt{3}K_s, \quad h_2 = 1 - K_c - \sqrt{3}K_s, \quad h_3 = 1 + 2K_c. \tag{5}$$

Then the signal quantum state vectors $|f_i\rangle$ can be represented by ordinary column vectors $\vec{f_i}$ in the basis $\{|e_j\rangle\}$, i.e.,

$$\begin{aligned}
\vec{f_1} &= \frac{1}{\sqrt{3}} \left[\sqrt{h_1}, \sqrt{h_2}, \sqrt{h_3}\right]^T, \\
\vec{f_2} &= \frac{1}{\sqrt{3}} \left[\mathrm{e}^{2\pi \mathrm{i}/3}\sqrt{h_1}, \mathrm{e}^{-2\pi \mathrm{i}/3}\sqrt{h_2}, \sqrt{h_3}\right]^T, \\
\vec{f_3} &= \frac{1}{\sqrt{3}} \left[\mathrm{e}^{-2\pi \mathrm{i}/3}\sqrt{h_1}, \mathrm{e}^{2\pi \mathrm{i}/3}\sqrt{h_2}, \sqrt{h_3}\right]^T,
\end{aligned} \tag{6}$$

where $[\cdot]^T$ denotes vector transpose. The unitary operator $\hat{V}$ then has the diagonal matrix representation $\boldsymbol{V} = \mathrm{diag}\left[\mathrm{e}^{2\pi \mathrm{i}/3}, \mathrm{e}^{-2\pi \mathrm{i}/3}, 1\right]$.

3 Symmetric measurement and conditional probabilities

Along with the scheme shown by Shor,[2] the optimal POVM (Positive Operator Valued Measure) is three-fold symmetric for the case of signals that are equally likely *a priori*. Each element of POVM can be a rank-1 operator, so that it is described by some vector in the signal Hilbert space $\mathcal{H}_s$. A (kth) set of symmetric states $\{ |\omega_j^{(k)}\rangle, j = 1, 2, 3 \}$ has a representation $\{\vec{\omega}_j^{(k)}\}$ in the $\{|e_j\rangle\}$ basis given by,

$$\begin{aligned}
\vec{\omega}_1^{(k)} &= \sqrt{p_k}\left[\mathrm{e}^{\mathrm{i}\theta_k^{(1)}} \cos\phi_k \cos\psi_k, \mathrm{e}^{\mathrm{i}\theta_k^{(2)}} \cos\phi_k \sin\psi_k, \sin\phi_k\right]^T, \\
\vec{\omega}_2^{(k)} &= \sqrt{p_k}\left[\mathrm{e}^{\mathrm{i}\theta_k^{(1)}+2\pi \mathrm{i}/3} \cos\phi_k \cos\psi_k, \mathrm{e}^{\mathrm{i}\theta_k^{(2)}-2\pi \mathrm{i}/3} \cos\phi_k \sin\psi_k, \sin\phi_k\right]^T, \\
\vec{\omega}_3^{(k)} &= \sqrt{p_k}\left[\mathrm{e}^{\mathrm{i}\theta_k^{(1)}-2\pi \mathrm{i}/3} \cos\phi_k \cos\psi_k, \mathrm{e}^{\mathrm{i}\theta_k^{(2)}+2\pi \mathrm{i}/3} \cos\phi_k \sin\psi_k, \sin\phi_k\right]^T.
\end{aligned} \tag{7}$$

The domains for the parameters that appear in this representation are as follows:

$$-\frac{\pi}{3} \le \theta_1^{(k)} \le \frac{\pi}{3}, \quad -\pi \le \theta_2^{(k)} \le \pi, \quad 0 \le \phi_k, \psi_k \le \frac{\pi}{2}. \tag{8}$$

For a set consisting of several sets of symmetric states, $\left\{ |\omega_j^{(k)}\rangle, k = 1, 2, \cdots, \right\}$ to be a resolution of the identity, the parameters must satisfy

$$\sum_k p_k = 1, \quad \sum_k p_k u_k = 2/3, \quad \sum_k p_k v_k = 1/3, \tag{9}$$

where $u_k = \cos^2\phi_k$ and $v_k = \cos^2\phi_k \sin^2\psi_k$.

The conditional probabilities for detecting the quantum state $|f_i\rangle$ as $|\omega_j^{(k)}\rangle$ are given by,

$$\left[P^{(k)}(j|i)\right] = \left[\left|\langle\omega_j^{(k)}|f_i\rangle\right|^2\right] = \left[\left|\vec{\omega}_j^{(k)T}\vec{f}_i\right|^2\right] = \frac{p_k}{3}\begin{bmatrix} A_k & B_k & C_k \\ C_k & A_k & B_k \\ B_k & C_k & A_k \end{bmatrix}. \tag{10}$$

4 Mutual information and its maximization

The mutual information is calculated as follows:

$$\begin{aligned} I &= \sum_k \sum_{i=1}^{3} \xi_i \sum_{j=1}^{3} P^{(k)}(j|i) \log\left[\frac{P^{(k)}(j|i)}{\sum_{\ell=1}^{3}\xi_\ell P^{(k)}(j|\ell)}\right] \\ &= \sum_k p_k \cdot \frac{1}{3}\{(A_k+B_k+C_k)\log[3/(A_k+B_k+C_k)] \\ &\quad + A_k\log A_k + B_k\log B_k + C_k\log C_k\} \\ &\equiv \sum_k p_k \cdot F(u_k, v_k, \theta_k^{(1)}, \theta_k^{(2)}), \end{aligned} \tag{11}$$

where equal *a priori* probabilities have been assumed ($\xi_i = 1/3$). The function $F(u_k, v_k, \theta_k^{(1)}, \theta_k^{(2)})$ represents the contribution of kth symmetric measurement to the mutual information. Since the parameters $\theta^{(1)}, \theta^{(2)}$ are independent of the conditions in Eq. (9), $F(u, v, \theta^{(1)}, \theta^{(2)})$ can be maximized over $\theta^{(1)}, \theta^{(2)}$ without regard to the preceding constraints:

$$F_m(u,v) \equiv \max_{\theta^{(1)}} \max_{\theta^{(2)}} F(u, v, \theta^{(1)}, \theta^{(2)}). \tag{12}$$

This double maximization was carried out numerically (see Fig. 1).

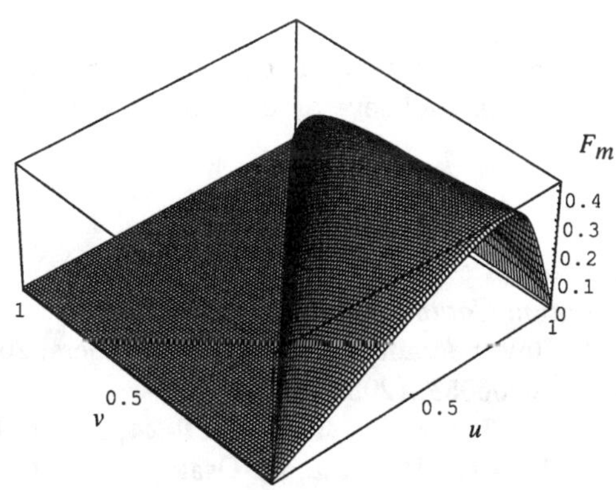

Figure 1. Example of $F_m(u,v)$ for $|\kappa| = 0.80$.

According to the conditions in Eq. (9), I is the convex combination of several $F_m(u_k, v_k)$ with its braycenter at $(u, v) = (2/3, 1/3)$. The maximum value of I, namely, the accessible information I_{ac}, is attained by using at most 3 sets of symmetric measurements because $F_m(u, v)$ is a function with two variables. The maximum value of I obtained using more than 3 sets equals that achieved using only 3 sets. The number of symmetric measurements needed to achieve I_{ac} depends on the shape of $F_m(u, v)$ at $(u, v) = (2/3, 1/3)$. The relations are summarized in Table 1.

Table 1. The shape of $F_m(u, v)$ and the number of symmetric measurements.

shape of $F_m(u, v)$	symmetric measurement
concave	1 set (3 operators)
saddle shape	2 sets (6 operators)
convex	3 sets (9 operators)

The shape of $F_m(u, v)$ is found from its Hessian matrix, whose positive eigenvalues indicate convexity in certain directions. By detailed numerical analysis for $0.01 \leq |\kappa| \leq 0.99$ in steps of 0.01, we have found that saddle shape prevails for $0.70 \leq |\kappa| \leq 0.87$ and for $|\kappa| = 0.98$ and 0.99. The other values of $|\kappa|$ exhibit concavity. There are no $|\kappa|$ values that give convex shape.

5 Conclusion

The number of POVMs needed to achieve the accessible information is 3 or 6 for the case of 3PSK signals in coherent states.

Acknowledgments

We thank P. Shor, A. S. Holevo, C. A. Fuchs, and M. Shoma for their helpful comments, encouragements, and several ideas about this problem.

References

1. A. S. Holevo, Probl. Peredachi Inform. **15**, 3 (1979).
2. P. Shor, in *Quantum Communications and Measurement* (P. Tombesi and O. Hirota eds.) Kluwer Academic/Plenum Publishers, 2001, pp. 107-114. LANL, quant-ph/0206058, (2002).
3. E. B. Davies, IEEE, Trans. Inf. Theory, **IT-24**, 596, (1978).
4. M. Sasaki, S. M. Barnett, R. Jozsa, M. Osaki, and O. Hirota, Phys. Rev. A., **59**, 3325, (1999).
5. M. Osaki, T. S. Usuda, and O. Hirota, Phys. Lett. A, **245**, 189, (1998).

QUANTUM DYNAMICS OF OPEN SYSTEMS FROM THE POINT OF INFORMATION TRANSFER

PETER ŠTELMACHOVIČ[1], MÁRIO ZIMAN[1], VLADIMÍR BUŽEK[1,2]
[1] *Research Center for Quantum Information, SAS, Dúbravská cesta 9, Bratislava, 842 28, Slovakia*
[2] *Department of Mathematical Physics, National University of Ireland, Maynooth, Co. Kildare, Ireland*

One of the most complex phenomena in quantum theory is the dynamics of open systems. In general, one can assume an open system S to be a part of a larger closed system composed of the open system and the environment R. The whole $S+R$ system evolves unitarily, and the question of irreversibility of dynamics of open systems is then a great issue. How do irreversible dynamics of the system S emerge from a unitary evolution of the $S+R$ system? We present an analysis of irreversibility from the point of view of information transfer between the system qudit and reservoir qudits.

1 Introduction

Let us consider the following model: an open system, S, represented by a single qudit (quantum system with d-dimensional Hilbert space) initially prepared in an unknown state $\varrho_S^{(0)}$, and the environment called the reservoir, R, composed of N qudits all prepared in the state ξ, which is arbitrary but the same for all reservoir qudits. We will enumerate the qudits of the reservoir and denote the state of the k-th qudit as ξ_k. From the definition of the reservoir it follows that initially $\xi_k = \xi$ for all k, so the initial state of the reservoir is described by the density matrix $\xi^{\otimes N}$. We will assume that at each time step the system qudit interacts with just a single qudit from the reservoir and let U be a unitary operator representing the interaction between a system qudit and one of the reservoir qudits (see Fig. 1). In what follows we will discuss two different types of evolution: the *deterministic* collision model and the *random* collision model.

2 Deterministic model

We will restrict the evolution in the following way. We will assume that the system qudit can interact with each of the reservoir qudits at most once. Moreover, the reservoir qudits are not allowed to interact with one another. These two additional assumptions lead to a deterministic model of evolution in which the system particle interacts with the reservoir via a sequence of interactions between the system qudit and N reservoir qudits all prepared in the state ξ. The final state of the system is then described by the density

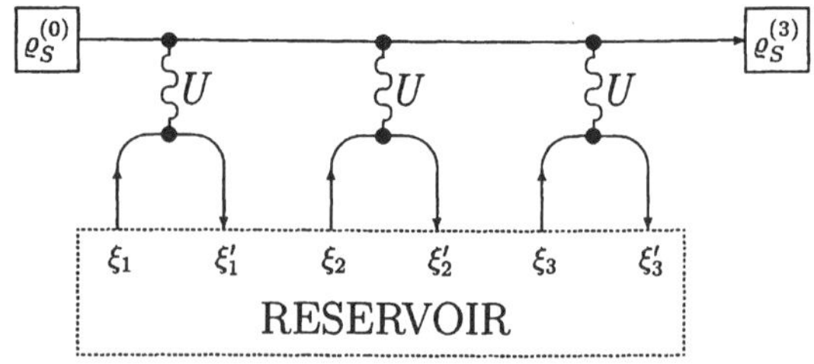

Figure 1. A simple collision-like model of homogenization with just three reservoir qudits involved.

operator

$$\varrho_S^{(N)} = \mathrm{Tr}_R \left[U_N \dots U_1 \left(\varrho_S^{(0)} \otimes \xi^{\otimes N} \right) U_1^\dagger \dots U_N^\dagger \right] , \tag{1}$$

where $U_k := U \otimes (\bigotimes_{j \neq k} \mathbf{1}_j)$ describes the interaction between the k-th qudit of the reservoir and the system qudit. So far we have not specified the unitary transformation U representing the interaction between qudits. Instead, we pose another condition on the evolution of the open system S and the reservoir R. We assume that states of the reservoir qudits change just a little, and that after N interactions the state of the system qudit becomes close to the initial state of the reservoir qudits. Formally,

$$\forall k, 1 \leq k \leq N \dots\dots D(\xi_k', \xi) \leq \delta; \tag{2}$$

$$\forall N \geq N_\delta \dots\dots D(\varrho_S^{(N)}, \xi) \leq \delta\,, \tag{3}$$

where $D(.,.)$ denotes some distance (e.g., a trace norm) between the states under consideration, $\delta > 0$ is a small parameter which is chosen a priori to determine the degree of the homogeneity and $\xi_k' := \mathrm{Tr}_S[U \varrho_S^{(k-1)} \otimes \xi U^\dagger]$ is the state of the k-th reservoir qudit after its interaction with the system qudit. Since all final states are almost identical, we can consider the process to be a quantum homogenization:[1,2] out of N qudits prepared in the same state ξ and a single object prepared in an arbitrary state $\rho_S^{(0)}$ we obtain $N+1$ homogenized objects.

Quantum homogenization that satisfies the conditions given by Eq.(2) and Eq.(3) can be realized by the partial swap operation[1,2]

$$P_{kj}(\eta) = \mathbf{1}_k \otimes \mathbf{1}_j \cos(\eta) + i \sin(\eta) S_{kj}\,, \tag{4}$$

where S_{kj} is the swap operation that acts on the qudits k and j as follows, $S_{kj}|\psi_k\rangle \otimes |\phi\rangle_j = |\phi\rangle_k \otimes |\psi\rangle_j$.

3 Random collision model

The conditions imposed in the case of the deterministic model are a bit restrictive. Therefore now we drop some of them in order to obtain a more realistic model. First of all, we allow the system particle to interact with any of the reservoir particles an arbitrary number of times. Secondly, we allow the reservoir particles to interact with one another. Thus the unitary transformation representing the interaction between two qudits is still described by the partial swap operation (4), but now the sequence of interactions may include all possible pairs of qudits. Such a model is usually called a *random* collision model. The immediate consequence of this is that there is more than one possible sequence for how the system particle can interact with the reservoir. (We are not counting as different those sequences which differ only by permutation of the reservoir particles, because we are free to relabel the reservoir particles.) In other words, the model becomes random and we have to take into account all possible paths or equivalently all possible scenarios of interactions between individual particles.

To illustrate our physical model, let us consider a situation in which a single system qubit is initially prepared in the state $|1\rangle$, while N reservoir qubits are prepared in the state $|0\rangle^{\otimes N}$, where we consider $\{|0\rangle, |1\rangle\}$ to be qubit basis vectors. Due to the sequence of k partial-swap operations (4), the system qubit is changed and is described by the density operator $\varrho^{(k)} = z|1\rangle\langle 1| + (1-z)|0\rangle\langle 0|$, where the parameter z depends on the specific sequence of partial swap interactions. In Fig. 2 we plot the parameter z as a function of the number k of interactions between the system and the reservoir qubits.

4 Reversibility

In both the deterministic as well as the random collision models at the end of the homogenization process all the particles are essentially in the same state (equal to the initial state of the reservoir particles). Since the whole process is unitary, the original information encoded in the state of the system particle cannot be lost — it has simply been transferred into the correlations between the interacting particles.[1,3] So the question is can it be recovered? That is, can we reverse the whole process of the homogenization? It turns out (for more details see Refs. 1,4) that it can be reversed providing the *classical* information about the sequence of interactions is available. If so, then the original *quantum* information, that is the initial state of the system qudit, can be completely recovered from the homogenized system by the specific sequence of inverse partial-swap operations. On the other hand, if the classical information about the order of interactions is not available, then the original quantum information is irreversibly lost in the homogenized system. We conclude that the necessary condition for the recovery of quantum information is the availability of the specific classical information.[4]

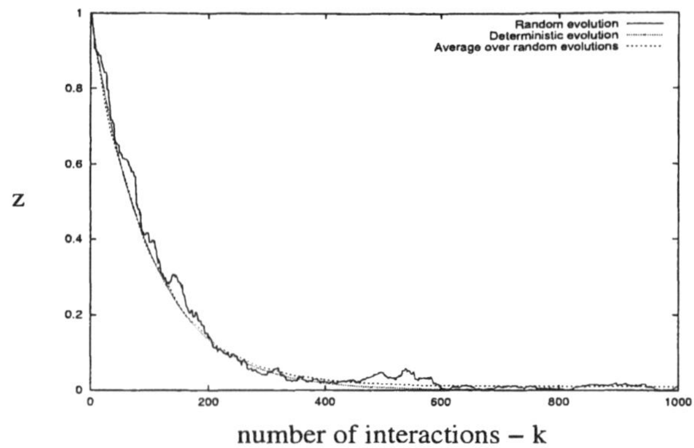

Figure 2. Results of numerical simulations of a quantum homogenization model. We assume a system qubit initially prepared in the state $|1\rangle$, while N reservoir qubits are prepared in the state $|0\rangle^{\otimes N}$. Due to the sequence of k partial-swap operations (4), the system qubit is changed and is described by the density operator $\varrho^{(k)} = z|1\rangle\langle 1| + (1-z)|0\rangle\langle 0|$ We plot the parameter z as a function of number of interactions k between the system and the reservoir qubits for three different cases: the deterministic model (dotted line), a specific trajectory with a random model (solid line), and the outcome of random model averaged over 1000 trajectories (dashed line).

Acknowledgments

This was work supported in part by the European Union projects EQUIP (IST-1999-11053), QUBITS (IST-1999-13021), and by the Slovak Academy of Sciences. We thank Nicolas Gisin, Valerio Scarani, Mark Hillery, and Peter Hakel.

References

1. M. Ziman, P.Štelmachovič, V. Bužek, M.Hillery, V. Scarani, and N. Gisin, Phys. Rev. A **65**, 042105 (2002).
2. D. Nagaj, P. Štelmachovič, V. Bužek, and M. Kim, to appear in Phys. Rev. A.
3. V. Scarani, M. Ziman, P. Štelmachovič, N.Gisin, and V. Bužek, Phys. Rev. Lett. **88**, 097905 (2002).
4. P.Štelmachovič, M. Ziman, and V. Bužek, in preparation.

A SCALABLE QUANTUM ARCHITECTURE USING EFFICIENT NONLOCAL INTERACTIONS

GAVIN K. BRENNEN, DAEGENE SONG, CARL J. WILLIAMS
National Institute of Standards and Technology, 100 Bureau Dr., Gaithersburg, MD 20899-8423, USA
E-mail: gavin.brennen@nist.gov

Many protocols for quantum information processing use a control sequence or circuit of interactions between qubits and control fields wherein arbitrary qubits can be made to interact with one another. The primary problem with many "physically scalable" architectures is that the qubits are restricted to nearest neighbor interactions and quantum wires between distant qubits do not exist. Because of errors, nearest neighbor interactions often present difficulty with scalability. In this paper we describe a generalized quantum architecture that provides efficient nonlocal operations for such a system. We describe a protocol that efficiently performs nonlocal gates between elements of separated static logical qubits using a bus of dynamic qubits that can be used as a refreshable entanglement resource.

For a large scale lattice-model-based quantum computer, one can imagine that interacting distant qubits will become increasingly important with both the complexity of the algorithm and the size of the input data stream. In most lattice models of a quantum computer (*e.g.* neutral atom optical lattice, ^{31}P embedded in Si, quantum dot arrays) the qubits are statically placed, interactions are with nearest neighbors, and quantum wires to connect distant qubits do not readily exist[a]. One solution is to swap states of adjacent qubits in order to connect two distant memory nodes. It is obvious that the operation time scales linearly with distance and moreover the resultant fidelity due to one and two qubit errors associated with swapping falls off exponentially with distance. In principle, swapping could be done in a fault-tolerant manner, but simultaneously preventing correlated errors while providing fault-tolerant operations places severe technical constraints on any physical architecture.

This paper considers a lattice model of quantum computation in which we divide the lattice qubits into static qubits, that contain information, and dynamic qubits, that are used to carry information. We then focus on how a "bus" of dynamic qubits can be used to create the necessary entanglement resource to perform nonlocal gates[5] using entanglement swapping.[1] This approach has the advantage that the "quantum bus" need not meet the same fidelity requirements as fault-tolerant computation, but must only reach the minimal threshold required for entanglement purification.[2]

The efficacy of this protocol depends on the ordering of numerous time scales: including gate times for one- and two-qubit operations, measurement times, and decoherence times. We further divide decoherence into static deco-

[a]It may be possible to swap information from one static qubit to another via a flying qubit by coupling *e.g.* through a cavity, however designing these local couplings is challenging.

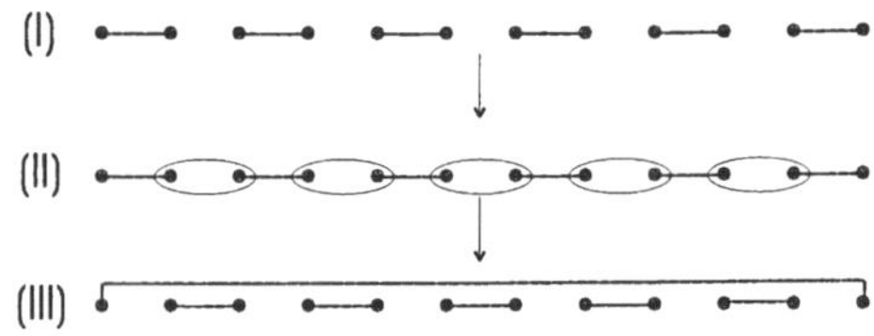

Figure 1. (I) parallel entanglement of adjacent pairs; (II) parallel Bell state measurements across the nodes of the entangled pairs; (III) the result is one long entanglement pair and residual entangled pairs that remain a resource.

herence times for errors that occur when a qubit is *not being manipulated* and dynamic decoherence that results from manipulating the qubits. The architecture we describe below is appropriate to the situation in which the static decoherence time is much longer than the other time scales in the problem, so that the limitation on computation fidelity is due almost completely to dynamical, one- and two-qubit, errors. Our procedure requires Bell-state measurements on the joints between nearest-neighbor entangled pairs, meaning measurement errors must be comparable to dynamical errors. The decoherence times must therefore satisfy $\tau_{meas} \sim \tau_{2bit,1bit} \ll \tau_{static}$.

The procedure for entanglement swapping using nearest neighbor interactions is shown in Fig.1. The process involves three steps: parallel entanglement of adjacent qubits, parallel Bell-state measurement on the joints between pairs, and a single qubit correction gate on one end of the resultant long pair that depends on the measurement record. The order of Bell-state measurements does not affect the single qubit correction gate because the Pauli operators associated with correction for each Bell measurement anticommute (changing the order only introduces a global phase) allowing parallel Bell-state measurements. One consequence of Bell-state measurement is an additional requirement for efficient readout of individual qubits during the computation. We show elsewhere that for measurement fidelities of roughly 0.95, the use of entanglement swapping is exponentially more efficient than swapping.

In Fig.2 we show one possible realization of the overall architecture that would be appropriate for a 5- or 7-qubit quantum error correcting code (QECC).[4] The physical qubits of logical qubit A, denoted A_i, are shown distributed in blocks and connected via entanglement with corresponding partners in logical qubit B. Because these codes are not robust against correlated errors, it is essential that the elements of the logical qubit be distributed with a separation large compared to the correlation length of the reservoir (including control fields). To remain within the code subspace it is necessary to perform nonlocal operations simultaneously on all logical qubits. The inherent parallelism of entanglement swapping lends itself well to performing nonlocal gates between multiple physical qubits that constitute the encoded logical qubits. The details of choosing the size of logic elements and the width

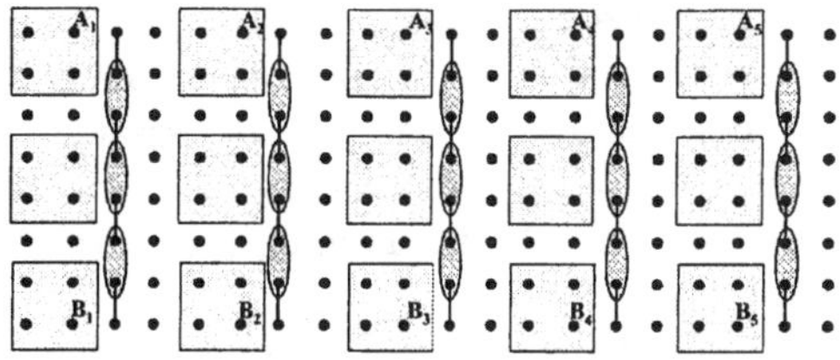

Figure 2. A lattice model of a quantum computer. The qubits in the box correspond to static physical qubits comprising a 5-qubit QECC and the dynamic qubits in the channel are used as a bus to carry information stored in the static qubits. Additional qubits within a box can accommodate concatenated encoding.

of the quantum bus will depend on the specifics of the errors, the dimension of the system, the number of memory nodes, and the size and depth of the coding.

With ideal operations an arbitrarily long entangled pair can be generated with entanglement swapping. However, experimental noise resulting from imperfect control of one- and two-qubit unitary operations and measurement errors, typically produces a mixed state distant pair. Bell-state measurements on a pair of qubits (q_1,q_2) can be realized by single-qubit Hadamards, a CPHASE gate, and finally a measurement in the logical basis of the control bit q_1. We assume that single-bit gates can be performed with high fidelity and introduce a two-qubit unitary error that occurs during the implementation of the CPHASE gate. We term this the controlled phase error (CPE) and describe its action on a state ρ as:

$$S_{CPE} = \int d\phi\, g(\phi)\, U(\phi)\rho U(\phi)^{\dagger}, \tag{1}$$

where $U(\phi) = |00\rangle\langle 00| + |01\rangle\langle 01| + |10\rangle\langle 10| - e^{i\phi}|11\rangle\langle 11|$, is the CPHASE gate with an additional unknown phase sampled from the probability distribution $g(\phi)$. For the case that $g(\phi)$ is symmetric about zero, the map is simply

$$S_{CPE} = p\, U(0)\rho U(0)^{\dagger} + (1-p)\,\rho. \tag{2}$$

This error corresponds to a physical situation in which there is experimental uncertainty in the field strength, timing, or strength of the interaction that imparts an additional unwanted phase during the gate. Measurement error on a binary state can be modelled by associating the experimental outcomes 0 and 1 with two dimensional projectors $P_0 = \eta|0\rangle\langle 0| + (1-\eta)|1\rangle\langle 1|$, and $P_1 = \mathbf{1} - P_0$. This model includes less than perfect detector efficiency η, since there is a probability $(1-\eta)$ that a detector reading of 0 actually corresponds to the qubit being in state $|1\rangle$, and conversely for 1. In many systems the efficiency can be improved at the cost of lengthening measurement time.

The noisy CPE map after entanglement swapping over n pairs produces a mixed state $\rho_{1,l}$ of length $l = 2 + 2n$ in nearest neighbor units that is a convex sum of Bell diagonal and logical basis diagonal states. The single bit correction gate on one end depends on two bits of classical information about the measurement record over the intervening $l - 1$ ordered qubits: $\sigma_M \equiv \sigma_{\oplus m_{even}, \oplus m_{odd}}$ where $\sigma_{0,0} \equiv \mathbf{1}, \sigma_{0,1} \equiv \sigma_x, \sigma_{1,0} \equiv \sigma_z, \sigma_{1,1} \equiv -i\sigma_y$. The fidelity is defined as the overlap of the mixed resource with a maximally-entangled Bell state, $F_l = \langle \phi^+ | \sigma_M^1 \rho_{1,l} \sigma_M^{1\dagger} | \phi^+ \rangle$ given here by:

$$F_l(p, \eta) = 1/4(1 + p^{l-1}(2(2\eta - 1)^{(l-1)/2} + (2\eta - 1)^{l-1}). \quad (3)$$

The fidelity falls off exponentially with distance, as does swapping without measurement, because it requires at least $l/2$ swaps to connect two qubits a distance l apart and each swap requires at least 2 maximally-entangling gates (such as $\sqrt{\text{SWAP}}$) meaning $F_l^{SWAP} < p^l$. The advantage of entanglement swapping is that the entanglement resource is degraded (in a well characterized manner) rather than the relevant quantum information, and the resource itself can be purified without the overhead of fault-tolerant gates at the swap level. In addition, the time to implement parallel entanglement swapping is $T_{entswap} = 4\tau_{1bit} + 2\tau_{2bit} + \tau_{meas}$ *independent of length*, and it can be much faster than the minimal swapping time $T_{swap} = 2l\tau_{2bit}$, provided a high-efficiency measurement does not take too long.

After entanglement swapping to a state with a minimum threshold fidelity, multiple mixed-state pairs within a channel can be purified using standard protocols.[2] The analysis of purification with noisy operations has been done by Dür *et.al*[3] For a system in which the different fidelity times are known, one may find that for sufficiently long separations one may want to break the protocol into two pieces, purify each piece and follow with entanglement swapping as in the quantum repeaters proposal.[3]

In conclusion, we have described a scalable quantum architecture that provides efficient nonlocal operations based on a system restricted to static qubits and nearest neighbor interactions. The prescribed architecture is appropriate to a system whose dominant source of error is noisy unitaries and measurement. A future publication will describe several extensions of this work, including additional error models, specifics on the tradeoff between this protocol and swapping, and how the bus addressability can be relaxed by using multiple species of qubits.

References

1. M. Zukowski, *et al.*, *Phys. Rev. Lett.* **71**, 4287 (1993).
2. C.H. Bennett, *et al.*, *Phys. Rev. Lett.* **76**, 722 (1996).
3. W. Dür, *et al.*, *Phys. Rev.* A **59**, 169 (1999).
4. J. Preskill, *P. Roy. Soc. Lond. A Mat.* **454**, 385 (1998).
5. J. Eisert, *et al.*, *Phys. Rev.* A **62**, 52317 (2000).

OPTICAL INFORMATION

ANDREI N. SOKLAKOV
RÜDIGER SCHACK
Department of Mathematics, Royal Holloway, University of London, Egham, Surrey TW20 0EX, UK

A typical experimental setup of single-atom cavity QED consists of a two-level atom interacting with a single mode of the electromagnetic field inside an optical cavity. The cavity is externally driven and the output is continuously monitored via homodyne measurements. In a recent paper,[1] we have calculated the rate at which the measurements provide information about the quantum state of such a system and investigated the link between this rate and the optical information,[2] i.e., the rate at which the measurements provide information about the position of the atom inside the cavity. Here we further analyze the flow of information about the quantum state of the system. We present a systematic procedure for calculating higher-order terms in the power series expansion for the information gain. To illustrate the procedure, we compute the second-order term in the all-on-resonance case with strong driving.

Consider a system composed of a single two-level atom interacting with a single electromagnetic mode of a high-finesse optical cavity, which is externally driven. This system can be characterized by five real parameters. These are the strength of the atom-cavity coupling g, the cavity field decay rate κ, the driving strength E, and two detunings: the detuning of the atomic resonance ω_a from the driving laser frequency ω_0, $\Delta_a = \omega_a - \omega_0$, and the detuning of the cavity resonance ω_c from the driving laser frequency, $\Delta_c = \omega_c - \omega_0$. In the frame rotating at the driving laser frequency, the system evolution in the absence of measurements is described by the master equation

$$\dot{\varrho} = -i[H, \varrho] + \kappa(2a\varrho a^\dagger - a^\dagger a\varrho - \varrho a^\dagger a)\,, \tag{1}$$

where ϱ is the joint density operator for the atom and the intracavity field, and

$$H = \Delta_c a^\dagger a + \Delta_a \sigma^\dagger \sigma + iE(a^\dagger - a) + ig(a^\dagger \sigma - \sigma^\dagger a)\,. \tag{2}$$

The intra-cavity mode is coupled to the environment via a partially transparent mirror. In the homodyne detection scheme, the output field is added to a reference field at a beam splitter and then analyzed by two photodetectors. This measurement setup is characterized by two extra parameters: the photodetectors' efficiency η, and the complex parameter $\beta = |\beta|e^{i\phi}$, where $|\beta|$ is the reference field's strength, and ϕ is its phase relative to the driving laser.

The evolution of the state, ϱ, of an open quantum system subject to a continuous measurement can often be described by a stochastic master equation of the form[3,4,5]

$$d\varrho = \mathcal{L}(\varrho)dt + \mathcal{M}(\varrho)dW\,, \tag{3}$$

which is to be understood in the sense of the Itô stochastic differential calculus.[6] Any particular measurement record is represented by some realization of the stochastic process $W(t)$. The superoperator $\mathcal{L}$ is linear and defines the "unconditional" evolution, i.e., the evolution in the absence of measurements as given by Eq. (1). By contrast, the superoperator $\mathcal{M}$ is nonlinear and accounts for the effects of the measurement. For homodyne measurements, it is given by[4,5]

$$\mathcal{M}(\varrho) = \sqrt{2\kappa\eta}\left(e^{-i\phi}a\varrho + e^{i\phi}\varrho a^{\dagger} - \mathrm{tr}\left[\varrho(e^{-i\phi}a + e^{i\phi}a^{\dagger})\right]\varrho\right). \quad (4)$$

By definition, the entropy of a system described by a density matrix ϱ is

$$H(\varrho) \equiv -\mathrm{tr}(\varrho \ln \varrho) = \mathrm{tr}[\sum_{n=1}^{\infty} \frac{(-1)^n}{n}(\tilde{\varrho}^{n+1} + \tilde{\varrho}^n)], \quad (5)$$

where $\tilde{\varrho} = \varrho - \mathbb{1}$. The average rate of entropy change in the presence of continuous observations is given by

$$\langle H_1(\varrho)\rangle = \lim_{\Delta t \to 0}\left\langle \frac{H(\varrho+\delta) - H(\varrho)}{\Delta t}\right\rangle, \quad (6)$$

where the average $\langle\cdot\rangle$ is taken over all possible measurement outcomes observed over the time Δt, and

$$\delta = \mathcal{L}(\varrho)\Delta t + \mathcal{M}(\varrho)\Delta W. \quad (7)$$

The quantity (6) determines the rate R_Q at which we acquire information about the quantum state of the system, via the relation $R_Q = -\langle H_1(\varrho)\rangle$.

Let ϱ_0 be the state of the system at time t_0. Using the Fokker-Planck equation[6] that corresponds to the stochastic master equation (3) one can show that during the period of time $t - t_0 = \Delta t$ the average change of system entropy is given by the Taylor-like series

$$\langle \Delta H(\varrho_0)\rangle = \langle H_1(\varrho_0)\rangle\Delta t + \langle H_2(\varrho_0)\rangle\frac{(\Delta t)^2}{2!} + \cdots + \langle H_n(\varrho_0)\rangle\frac{(\Delta t)^n}{n!} + O(\Delta t^{n+1}), \quad (8)$$

where the coefficients obey the recursive relation

$$\left\langle H_{n+1}(\varrho)\right\rangle = \lim_{\Delta t\to 0}\left\langle \frac{\langle H_n(\varrho+\delta)\rangle - \langle H_n(\varrho)\rangle}{\Delta t}\right\rangle. \quad (9)$$

In an earlier paper[1] we have shown that

$$\langle H_1(\varrho)\rangle = \sum_{n=1}^{\infty}\frac{(-1)^n}{n}\mathrm{tr}\Big([(n+1)\tilde{\varrho}^n + n\tilde{\varrho}^{n-1}]\mathcal{L}(\varrho) + \sum_{s=0}^{n-1}(s+1)\tilde{\varrho}^s\mathcal{M}(\varrho)\tilde{\varrho}^{n-1-s}\mathcal{M}(\varrho) + \sum_{s=0}^{n-2}(s+1)\tilde{\varrho}^s\mathcal{M}(\varrho)\tilde{\varrho}^{n-2-s}\mathcal{M}(\varrho)\Big). \quad (10)$$

This formula is valid without any restrictions on the superoperators $\mathcal{L}$ and $\mathcal{M}$, and hence the above recursive formula provides a systematic procedure for calculating higher-order corrections to $\langle \Delta H(\varrho_0) \rangle$. For the next term in the series, we obtain

$$\langle H_2(\varrho) \rangle = \lim_{\Delta t \to 0} \sum_{n=1}^{\infty} \frac{(-1)^n}{n\,\Delta t} \left(\lambda(\tilde{\varrho}, \delta, n) + \mu(\tilde{\varrho}, \delta, n) + \mu(\tilde{\varrho}, \delta, n-1) \right), \qquad (11)$$

where

$$\lambda(\tilde{\varrho}, \delta, n) \equiv \mathrm{tr}\Big\langle \big[(n+1)(\tilde{\varrho}+\delta)^n + n(\tilde{\varrho}+\delta)^{n-1}\big]\mathcal{L}(\varrho+\delta) - \big[(n+1)\tilde{\varrho}^n + n\tilde{\varrho}^{n-1}\big]\mathcal{L}(\varrho) \Big\rangle, \qquad (12)$$

and

$$\mu(\tilde{\varrho}, \delta, n) \equiv \sum_{s=0}^{n-1} (s+1)\,\mathrm{tr}\Big\langle (\tilde{\varrho}+\delta)^s \mathcal{M}(\varrho+\delta)(\tilde{\varrho}+\delta)^{n-1-s}\mathcal{M}(\varrho+\delta) - \tilde{\varrho}^s \mathcal{M}(\varrho)\tilde{\varrho}^{n-1-s}\mathcal{M}(\varrho) \Big\rangle. \qquad (13)$$

We now illustrate the use of this formalism for the all-on-resonance case, $\omega_a = \omega_c = \omega_0$, in the strong driving regime, $E/g \gg 1$, in the steady state. The steady state, defined by $\mathcal{L}(\varrho_{\rm ss}) = 0$, is the natural state into which the system relaxes before the measurements start. In this case we have

$$\mathcal{L}(\varrho) = \big[E(a^\dagger - a) + g(a^\dagger \sigma - \sigma^\dagger a), \varrho\big] + \kappa(2a\varrho a^\dagger - a^\dagger a \varrho - \varrho a^\dagger a), \qquad (14)$$

and the steady state is given by[7]

$$\varrho_{\rm ss} = \frac{1}{2}\left(|\alpha; +\rangle\langle \alpha; +| + |\alpha^*; -\rangle\langle \alpha^*; -| \right). \qquad (15)$$

Here $|\alpha; +\rangle$ and $|\alpha^*; -\rangle$ are two orthogonal quantum states defined by

$$|\alpha; \pm\rangle = \frac{1}{\sqrt{2}} |\alpha\rangle \left(|{\rm g}\rangle \pm i|{\rm e}\rangle \right), \qquad (16)$$

where $|\alpha\rangle$ is the coherent field state with amplitude

$$\alpha = \frac{E}{\kappa}\left[1 - \left(\frac{g}{2E}\right)^2 + i\frac{g}{2E}\sqrt{1 - \left(\frac{g}{2E}\right)^2} \right]. \qquad (17)$$

We now compute $\langle H_2(\varrho_{\rm ss}) \rangle$. Let $\delta_{\rm ss} = \mathcal{L}(\varrho_{\rm ss})\Delta t + \mathcal{M}(\varrho_{\rm ss})\Delta W = \mathcal{M}(\varrho_{\rm ss})\Delta W$. Because for any linear $\mathcal{L}$ we have $\langle \mathcal{L}(\delta_{\rm ss}) \rangle = 0$, and noticing that $[\varrho_{\rm ss}, \delta_{\rm ss}] = 0$, we obtain

$$\lambda(\tilde{\varrho}_{\rm ss}, \delta_{\rm ss}, n) = \mathrm{tr}\Big\langle n\big[(n+1)\tilde{\varrho}_{\rm ss}^{n-1} + (n-1)\tilde{\varrho}_{\rm ss}^{n-2}\big]\delta_{\rm ss}\mathcal{L}(\delta_{\rm ss}) + O(\delta_{\rm ss}^3) \Big\rangle. \qquad (18)$$

Since $\tilde{\varrho}_{ss}$ is proportional to the identity in the two-dimensional space spanned by the vectors (16), this equation has the form

$$\lambda(\tilde{\varrho}_{ss}, \delta_{ss}, n) = \mathrm{tr}\Big\langle \delta_{ss}\mathcal{L}(\delta_{ss})\Big\rangle f(n) + O(\Delta t^2)\,, \tag{19}$$

where f is some function whose precise form is not important here. Using Eq. (14) it is easy to show that for any state of the form (15) we have $\mathrm{tr}\big\langle \delta_{ss}\mathcal{L}(\delta_{ss})\big\rangle = 0$, and so we can neglect $\lambda(\tilde{\varrho}_{ss}, \delta_{ss}, n)$.

Similar calculations for the μ-terms give

$$\begin{aligned}\mu(\tilde{\varrho}_{ss}, \delta_{ss}, n) = {} & \frac{n(n+1)}{2}\mathrm{tr}\Big(\tilde{\varrho}_{ss}^{n-1}\Big\langle \big(\mathcal{M}(\varrho_{ss}+\delta_{ss})\big)^2 - (\mathcal{M}(\varrho_{ss}))^2\Big\rangle \\ & + (n-1)\tilde{\varrho}_{ss}^{n-2}\Big\langle \delta_{ss}\big(\mathcal{M}(\varrho_{ss}+\delta_{ss})\big)^2\Big\rangle\Big) + O(\Delta t^2) \\ & = 16\nu^4\,\frac{n(n+1)}{2^n}(-1)^{n-1}\Delta t + O(\Delta t^2)\,, \end{aligned} \tag{20}$$

where $\nu = \sin\phi\,\sqrt{2\kappa\eta}\,\mathrm{Im}(\alpha)$. The general expression for the second time derivative $\langle H_2(\varrho_{ss})\rangle$ is obtained by substituting this result into Eq. (11) neglecting $\lambda(\tilde{\varrho}_{ss}, \delta_{ss}, n)$ as explained above. We find

$$\langle H_2(\varrho_{ss})\rangle \propto \sum_{n=1}^{\infty}\frac{n^2-3n}{2^n} = 0\,. \tag{21}$$

This shows that the first-order result from Ref. 1 is accurate up to the second order in Δt. It is possible to obtain this particular result in a considerably simpler way by specializing the above calculations at an earlier stage. The calculation was given in this generic form for the purpose of illustration only. A more detailed version of this paper is available as part of a technical report[8].

ANS would like to thank Kevin Birnbaum, Jeff Kimble, and Theresa Lynn for many helpful discussions. Part of this work was carried out at the Institute for Quantum Information at Caltech, the hospitality of which is gratefully acknowledged. This research was partially funded by project Q-ACTA of the IST-FET program of the EU.

References

1. A. N. Soklakov and R. Schack, *Phys. Rev. A*, to be published.
2. C. J. Hood *et al.*, *Science* **287**, 1447 (2000).
3. V. P. Belavkin and P. Staszewski, *Phys. Rev. A* **45**, 1347 (1992).
4. H. M. Wiseman and G. J. Milburn, *Phys. Rev. A* **47**, 642 (1993).
5. H. M. Wiseman and G. J. Milburn, *Phys. Rev. A* **47**, 1652 (1993).
6. C. W. Gardiner, *Handbook of Stochastic Methods* (Springer, Berlin, 1985).
7. P. Alsing and H. J. Carmichael, *Quantum Opt.* **3**, 13 (1991).
8. A. N. Soklakov, technical report RHUL-MA-2002-1 (Department of Mathematics, Royal Holloway, University of London, 2002), http://www.rhul.ac.uk/mathematics/techreports.

Part IV

Quantum Imaging and Quantum Processing with Linear Optics

ROLE OF ENTANGLEMENT IN QUANTUM HOLOGRAPHY

BAHAA E. A. SALEH, AYMAN F. ABOURADDY,
ALEXANDER V. SERGIENKO, AND MALVIN C. TEICH
Quantum Imaging Laboratory, Departments of Electrical & Computer Engineering, Boston University, 8 *Saint Mary's Street, Boston, MA* 02215, *USA*
E-mail: besaleh@bu.edu

Two optical beams in a two-photon state may be used for distributed imaging. Coherent imaging and holography truly require spatial entanglement in the source and cannot be achieved using a classical source with correlations but without entanglement.

1 Introduction

Light in a single-photon pure quantum state may exhibit interference, e.g., in a Young's double-slit configuration, and may in principle be used for coherent imaging and holography. In a multipath holographic configuration, the hologram is the spatial distribution of the probability density function $p(\mathbf{x})$ for detecting the photon at the position $\mathbf{x}$ in the detection plane. Such function is of course measured by use of an ensemble of single-photon experiments. No advantage is gained, however, by use of such quantum state, as opposed to conventional light in the coherent state.

Similarly, light in a two-beam two-photon state exhibits fourth-order (or coincidence) interference that may also be utilized for incoherent imaging[3,4] and coherent imaging and holography.[2,5,6] The hologram is a spatial distribution obtained from the joint probability density function $p(\mathbf{x}_1, \mathbf{x}_2)$ for detecting the photons at positions $\mathbf{x}_1$ and $\mathbf{x}_2$. This paper addresses the role of two-particle spatial entanglement in such imaging systems and whether the same information extracted from an entangled-based system can be retrieved

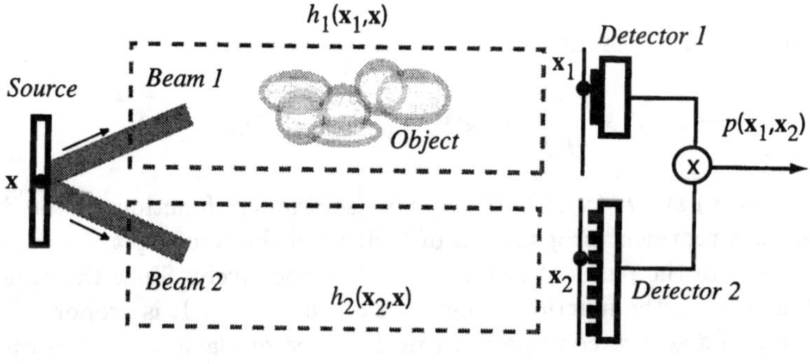

Figure 1. Two-beam distributed imaging system

by classical means.

2 Pure-State Two-Photon Imaging

Consider a two-beam light source in a two-photon arbitrary quantum state. As illustrated in Fig. 1, the object is placed in the path of one of the beams, say beam 1, and two photodetectors are used to record the arrival of the two photons in the two beams. Detector 1 is a single point detector of finite area A placed in beam 1 after the object, and detector 2 is a bank of point detectors (or a single point detector whose position is scanned) used to detect the photon in beam 2 with high spatial resolution. The hologram is a record of the spatial distribution

$$I(\mathbf{x}_2) = \int_A p(\mathbf{x}_1, \mathbf{x}_2) d\mathbf{x}_1, \tag{1}$$

which is the probability density for detecting a photon in beam 1 anywhere within the detector area A, and a photon in beam 2 at position $\mathbf{x}_2$. In this configuration, the beam that interacts with the object is observed with no spatial resolution (since the detector is a single-pixel camera), whereas the other beam is measured with high spatial resolution using the many-pixel detector.

Is coherent imaging possible under these conditions? The answer is obviously dependent on the quantum state of the two-photon light source. However, in the limit in which the state is separable, the readings of the two detectors are independent and therefore the multi-pixel detector in beam 2 provides no information about the object in beam 1. Since beam 1 is measured with no spatial resolution, no imaging is possible.

For an arbitrary pure two-photon quantum state

$$|\Psi\rangle = \iint d\mathbf{x} d\mathbf{x}' \psi(\mathbf{x}, \mathbf{x}') |1_{\mathbf{x}}\rangle |1_{\mathbf{x}'}\rangle, \tag{2}$$

the photon coincidence rate is[7]

$$p(\mathbf{x}_1, \mathbf{x}_2) \propto \left| \iint d\mathbf{x} d\mathbf{x}' h_2(\mathbf{x}_2, \mathbf{x}') \psi(\mathbf{x}, \mathbf{x}') h_1(\mathbf{x}_1, \mathbf{x}) \right|^2, \tag{3}$$

where $h_1(\mathbf{x}_1, \mathbf{x})$ and $h_2(\mathbf{x}_2, \mathbf{x})$ are the impulse response functions of the linear systems that represent propagation of light from the source plane to the detector planes in the paths of beams 1 and 2, respectively. Since the object is placed in beam 1, the function h_1 depends on the object. It is proportional to the optical field generated at point $\mathbf{x}_1$ in the detector plane when the object is illuminated by a point source at position $\mathbf{x}$ in the source plane. The function h_2 is similarly defined and is independent of the object.

Based on Eq. (3), the measurement $p(\mathbf{x}_1, \mathbf{x}_2)$ may be regarded as the coherent image created when a wave emitted by a point source at $\mathbf{x}_1$ travels through a cascade of three linear systems of impulse response functions $h_1(\mathbf{x}, \mathbf{x}_1)$, $\psi(\mathbf{x}', \mathbf{x})$, and $h_2(\mathbf{x}_2, \mathbf{x}')$, respectively. The state function $\psi(\mathbf{x}', \mathbf{x})$ therefore serves as the impulse response function of a coherent system that couples the two beams into one single *coherent* optical system. This description is consistent with Klyshko's advanced wave interpretation.[1] In the maximally-entangled case, $\psi(\mathbf{x}', \mathbf{x}) = \psi_o(\mathbf{x})\delta(\mathbf{x}-\mathbf{x}')$, so that the intermediate system is equivalent to modulation by a complex pupil function $\psi_o(\mathbf{x})$. On the other hand, if the state function is separable, $p(\mathbf{x}_1, \mathbf{x}_2)$ is also separable so that the two beams are decoupled, and the measurement of the photon in beam 2 provides no information about the object in beam 1.

A coherent imaging system may be used for holography if the wave scattered from the object is mixed with a reference wave reaching the detector via a separate path. In the two-beam two-photon setup depicted in Fig. 1, one cannot regard beam 2 as the reference wave. After all, beams 1 and 2 together constitute cascaded serial, and not parallel, parts of a single optical system. To record a hologram of the object, beam 1 must be split into two parallel paths, one scattered from the object and another serving as a reference. For a weakly scattering object, the unscattered wave can serve as this path, as in Gabor holography. Mathematically, this is represented by writing the impulse response function h_1 as a sum $h_1 = h_{1o} + h_{1r}$ of systems representing these two paths. By substitution into Eq. (3) and expanding the square of the sum we obtain the usual four components of conventional holography.[6]

When detector 1 is of finite area A, the apparatus measures the image $I(\mathbf{x}_2)$ given by Eq.(1). In view of Eq.(3), the overall imaging process becomes equivalent to a partially-coherent system since the contributions of points within the area A to the image $I(\mathbf{x}_2)$ are added incoherently. In the limit in which A covers the entire plane, $I(\mathbf{x}_2)$ equals the marginal probability density function for measuring a photon in beam 2 at position $\mathbf{x}_2$ given that a photon has been measured anywhere in beam 1. In this case, if the object is a pure phase object, i.e., does not absorb photons, the imaging system is not capable of extracting any information about the object. Note, however, that for an absorptive object, the two-beam two-photon imaging system is capable of recovering information about the object, even if the single-pixel detector 1 extends over the entire plane. For example, if detector 1 takes the form of an integrating sphere with an opening through which beam 1 enters and scatters from the object therein, the high-resolution measurement on the external beam 2 does yield information about the object, even though the position of the photon scattered from the object is not recorded. This is not applicable to pure phase objects.

3 Mixed-State Maximally-Correlated Two-Photon Imaging

Can similar results be obtained by employing a two-photon source that exhibits classical statistical correlations but not entanglement? That is, can distributed quantum-imaging be achieved without entanglement? To answer this question we take a mixed state that exhibits the strongest possible classical correlations, i.e., one for which the density operator is

$$\hat{\rho} = \int d\mathbf{x}\,\gamma(\mathbf{x})|1_{\mathbf{x}}, 1_{\mathbf{x}}\rangle\langle 1_{\mathbf{x}}, 1_{\mathbf{x}}|. \tag{4}$$

This state represents a superposition of photon-pair emission probabilities from various locations within the source. In this case,[5]

$$p(\mathbf{x}_1, \mathbf{x}_2) = \int d\mathbf{x}|h_2(\mathbf{x}_2, \mathbf{x}')|^2\gamma(\mathbf{x})|h_1(\mathbf{x}_1, \mathbf{x})|^2. \tag{5}$$

This function is generated when the object is illuminated by a point source at $\mathbf{x}_1$ (through system h_1), and the resultant coherent image is detected in the source plane, modulated by the function $\gamma(\mathbf{x})$, and imaged incoherently through the optical system h_2. The overall system is incoherent.

4 Can Distributed Imaging be Implemented Classically?

Can the holographic information extracted by a two-beam two-photon source in an entangled state be extracted by use of a classical source? The answer depends on the conditions placed on the measurement apparatus. In the absence of any restrictions, the function $p(\mathbf{x}_1, \mathbf{x}_2)$ in Eq.(3), may be measured by placing a classical point source at $\mathbf{x}_1$ and detecting the light with the multi-pixel detector in beam 2 after it has traveled backward through the object. This is consistent with the advanced-wave interpretation.[1] Other classical implementations are also possible.[8]

Consider, however, a restricted measurement apparatus. Specifically, assume that the object and the single-pixel photodetector are placed within a closed chamber that has an opening (aperture) through which beam 1 enters and scatters from the object before reaching the detector, as illustrated in Fig. 2. The first restriction is that beam 1 may travel through the aperture into the chamber but it cannot travel out of the aperture in the opposite direction. This condition implies a specific space-time configuration for the measurement apparatus. The second restriction is that the spatial distribution of the optical wave crossing the aperture is prespecified and fixed within the aperture and cannot be changed during the course of the experiment. If either condition were not met, one could mimic the information extracted by an entangled-photon source by use of a classical source.

The function $p(\mathbf{x}_1, \mathbf{x}_2)$ in Eq.(3) may be measured classically in two ways, each of which violates one of the above constraints. (i) One could replace the detector with a source and measure the back-propagated wave using detector

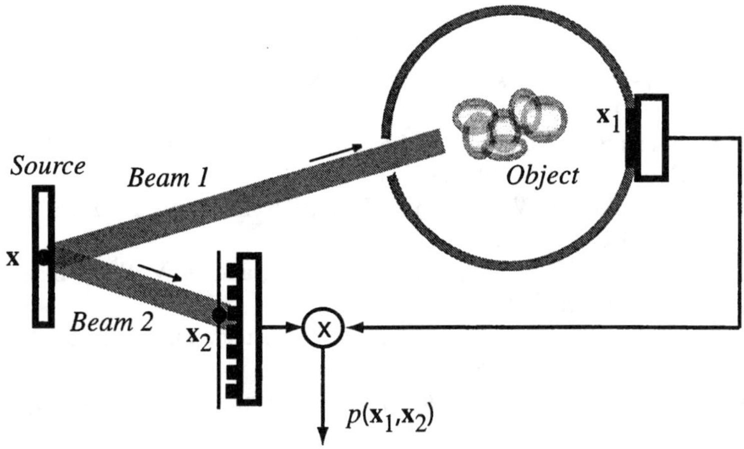

Figure 2. Configuration for coherent imaging with two beams traveling in prescribed directions

2; this of course violates the first constraint. (ii) Alternatively, one may dispense with the system h_2 altogether and employ a bank of classical fields using point sources at $\mathbf{x}_2$ scanned in such a way that full information is recovered from the readings of the single-pixel detector at $\mathbf{x}_1$ inside the chamber. Here, the second constraint is violated since the aperture field is modified.

5 Conclusion

A source of light in the form of two beams in a two-photon quantum state may be used for distributed coherent imaging and holography. One beam probes the object and is measured with a single-pixel detector while the other is measured with high spatial resolution. The photon coincidence rate, measured as a function of position in the second beam, forms a *coherent* image of the object only when the two beams are entangled. Two classically-correlated beams cannot be used for coherent imaging. If the single-pixel detector has an extended area, then the imaging system becomes partially coherent, even in the maximally-entangled case. When the probe distribution is prespecified and the light must travel in a prescribed direction, this distributed imaging system cannot be mimicked by a classical imaging system.

Acknowledgments

This work was supported by the National Science Foundation, by the David & Lucile Packard foundation, and by the Center for Subsurface Sensing and Imaging Systems, an NSF Engineering Research Center.

References

1. D. N. Klyshko, *Zh. Eksp. Teor. Fiz.* **94**, 82 (1988) [*Sov. Phys. JETP* **67**, 1131 (1988)].
2. A. V. Belinskii and D. N. Klyshko, *Zh. Eksp. Teor. Fiz.* **105**, 487 (1994) [*Sov. Phys. JETP* **78**, 259 (1994)].
3. D. V. Strekalov, A. V. Sergienko, D. N. Klyshko, and Y. H. Shih, *Phys. Rev. Lett.* **74**, 3600 (1995).
4. T. B. Pittman, Y. H. Shih, D. V. Strekalov, and A. V. Sergienko, *Phys. Rev. A* **52**, R3429 (1995).
5. A. F. Abouraddy, B. E. A. Saleh, A. V. Sergienko, and M. C. Teich, *Phys. Rev. Lett.* **87**, 123602 (2001).
6. A. F. Abouraddy, B. E. A. Saleh, A. V. Sergienko and M. C. Teich, *Optics Express*, **9**, 498 (2001)
7. A. F. Abouraddy, B. E. A. Saleh, A. V. Sergienko and M. C. Teich, *J. Opt. Soc. Am. B* **19**, 1174 (2002).
8. R. S. Bennink, S. J. Bentley, and R. W. Boyd, *Phys. Rev. A* **89**, 113601 (2002).

QUANTUM IMAGING AND QUANTUM LITHOGRAPHY

YANHUA SHIH
Department of Physics, University of Maryland, Baltimore County, Baltimore, MD 21250, U.S.A.
E-mail: shih@umbc.edu

Quantum imaging has many interesting features that are useful for practical applications. Quantum imaging can be nonlocal and can reach a much higher spatial resolution, even beyond the diffraction limit. Our recent experimental demonstration of quantum lithography has beaten the classical limit by a factor of two.

One of the most surprising consequences of quantum mechanics is the entanglement of two or more spatially distant particles.[1] In a maximally entangled two-particle system, the value of an observable (either space-time or spin observable) for neither single subsystem is determinate. However, if one of the subsystems is measured to be at a certain value for that observable, then the other one is 100% determined, *regardless of the distance between the particles.* In other words, each of the two subsystems may have completely random values for some physical observable, but the correlations (*nonlocal*) of the two subsystems are determined with certainty.[1]

Even though there are still questions in regards to fundamental issues of quantum theory, quantum entanglement has started to play an important role in practical engineering applications such as quantum imaging and quantum lithography.

Quantum imaging has many interesting features that are useful for different applications. For example, quantum imaging can be nonlocal,[2] which is useful for secure two-dimensional information transfer. Quantum imaging can reach a much higher spatial resolution, even beyond the diffraction limit of classical imaging,[3,4] which is useful for lithography and other microsystem fabrication technology.

Quantum lithography is a topic that has recently attracted much attention. Classical optical lithography technology is facing its limit due to the diffraction effect of light. However, this classical limit can be surpassed, surprisingly, by utilizing the quantum nature of entangled N-photon states. In an idealized experimental situation, the spatial resolution of the lithography imaging can be N-times finer than that of the classical limit.[3,4]

We have realized a proof-of-principle quantum lithography experiment recently.[4] The experiment demonstrated the working principle of an N-photon lithography scheme that has the potential to beat the diffraction limit of classical lithography a factor of N.

Figure 1 shows a schematic picture of a microscope used for lithography. A classical light source is used to make a reduced-size image of a complicated pattern, for example a lithography pattern for building up p-n junctions of

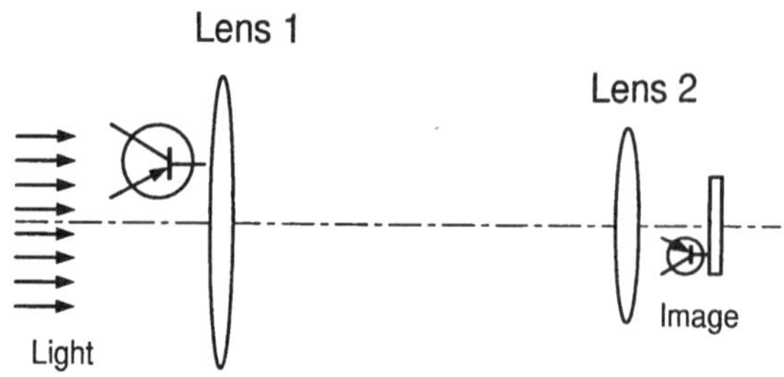

Figure 1. Schematic of a microscope used for optical lithography. Note: the transistor indicates a complicated lithography pattern, which is used to build up p-n junctions of millions of transistors and other components of an integrated circuit.

millions of transistors, on the surface of a silicon chip. The spatial resolution of the reduced image cannot be pushed beyond the diffraction limit. In other words, one cannot reduce the size of the image beyond the diffraction limit. How then can one improve the spatial resolution? Classically, the only choice is to reduce the wavelength of the light. However, when the wavelength is too short, for example in the X-ray region, the optical microscope will stop working. There are no effective lenses that work at such short wavelengths. Quantum theory provides us another choice: keep the optical wavelength, but make use of an N-photon entangled state. One would then be able to achieve a spatial resolution that is equivalent to using classical light with wavelength λ/N .

To demonstrate the quantum lithography idea experimentally, one could compare the spatial resolution of microscope images obtained using classical and entangled multi-photon states. It is not an easy job, especially in the case of $N = 2$. To have a clear demonstration, the experiment has to be done in a clever way. What we did was to measure the interference-diffraction patterns of a single slit and a double slit in the Fourier transform plane (or far-field) of a lens. We know that the first lens of a lithography microscope makes a Fourier transform of the "object" and the second lens transforms it back to a reduced-size image. If one could measure the Fourier transform of the "object" and show that the Fourier transform for the N-photon entangled light of wavelength λ is equivalent to that for classical light of wavelength λ/N, one would see immediately that the spatial resolution of the reduced-size image obtained by the second lens will be N times better. In our recent experiment, we have measured the Fourier transforms of single-slits and double-slits, which are playing the role of the "complicated" pattern for lithography. We found that *under certain experimental conditions*, the two-photon double-slit interference-diffraction pattern has a spatial interference modulation period that is smaller and a diffraction pattern width that is narrower, by factors of two, than those of the classical case. This two-photon entangled state result is thus equivalent to using classical light of wavelength $\lambda/2$. Thus the reduced-size image has the potential to beat the diffraction limit of classical lithography a factor of N, when we use an N-photon entangled state.

The diffraction pattern of a single slit is well-known to be $\text{sinc}^2(\beta)$, where $\beta = (\pi a/\lambda)\sin\theta \simeq (\pi a/\lambda)\theta$, a is the width of the slit, and θ is the diffraction angle. When β reaches π, the superposition of the wavelets results in a minimum intensity. The $\text{sinc}^2(\beta)$ pattern determines the minimum width one can obtain. Usually, this minimum width is called the "diffraction limit."

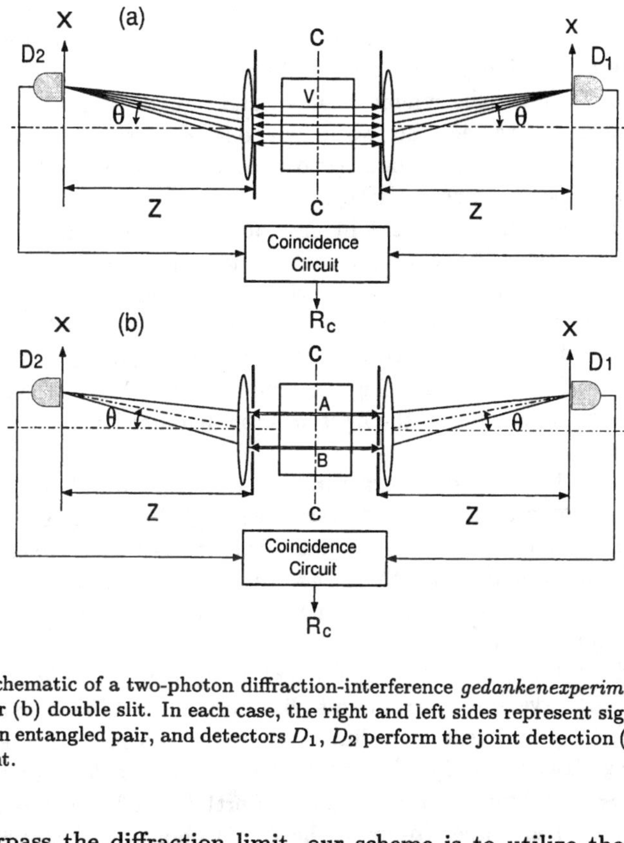

Figure 2. Schematic of a two-photon diffraction-interference *gedankenexperiment* using (a) single slit, or (b) double slit. In each case, the right and left sides represent signal and idler photons of an entangled pair, and detectors D_1, D_2 perform the joint detection (coincidence) measurement.

To surpass the diffraction limit, our scheme is to utilize the entangled nature of an N-particle system. To understand the physics of this scheme, consider the single-slit *gedankenexperiment* from Fig. 2(a). An entangled photon pair of wavelength λ can be generated anywhere in region V. However, photons belonging to the same pair can only propagate (1) *oppositely* (momentum entanglement) and (2) *horizontally* (position entanglement). Single slits are placed symmetrically on the left and right sides of the entangled photon source. A photon-counting detector is placed in the far-field zone (or the Fourier transform plane, if lenses are placed following the slits) on each side, and the coincidences between the "clicks" of both detectors are registered. The two detectors scan symmetrically, i.e., for each coincidence measurement, both detectors have equal x-coordinates. A two-photon joint detection is the result of the superposition of the two-photon amplitudes, which are indicated in the figure by straight horizontal lines. To calculate two-photon diffraction, we need to "superpose" all possible two-photon amplitudes. Unlike the classical case, this superposition is a double integral involving the two slits and the two-photon amplitudes (parallel lines in Fig. 2). By straightforward calculation,[4] the two-photon counterpart of the classical intensity, the joint detection counting rate, is found to be $\text{sinc}^2(2\beta)$, which is a narrower distribution than the classical pattern by a factor of two. This narrower pattern is the same diffraction pattern one would observe classically for wavelength $\lambda/2$. Now if we "fold" the symmetrical left and right sides of the experimental setup together and replace the two independent detectors with a film that is sensitive only to two-photon light (two-photon transition material), then in principle, we have two-photon lithography.

If one replaces the single slit in the above setup with a double-slit, Fig. 2(b), it is also interesting to see that under the half-width diffraction pattern, the double-slit two-photon spatial interference pattern has a higher modulation frequency, as if the wavelength of the light were reduced to one-half its original value. To observe the two-photon interference, one has to "erase" the first-order interference by enforcing the condition $\delta\theta > \lambda/b$ on the experiment, where $\delta\theta$ is the divergence of the light, b is the distance between the two slits, and λ is the wavelength.

The heart of this *gedankenexperiment* is a special two-photon source: the pair has to be generated in such a desired entangled way as described above; i.e., *precise momentum-momentum and position-position entanglement.* We have found and demonstrated that, *under certain conditions*, the two-photon state generated via spontaneous parametric down conversion (SPDC) satisfies the above requirements.

The schematic setup of the experiment is illustrated in Fig. 3. It is basically the "folded" version of the double-slit interference-diffraction experiment shown in Fig. 2(b). The 458 nm line of an Argon ion laser is used to pump a 5-mm-long BBO (β-BaB_2O_4) crystal, which is cut for degenerate collinear type-II phase matching, to produce pairs of orthogonally polarized signal (e-ray of the BBO) and idler (o-ray of the BBO) photons. Each pair emerges from the crystal collinearly, with $\omega_s \simeq \omega_i \simeq \omega_p/2$, where ω_j $(j = s, i, p)$ are the frequencies of the signal, idler, and pump, respectively. The pump is then separated from the signal-idler pair by mirror M, which is coated for reflectivity $R \simeq 1$ for the pump and transmissivity $T \simeq 1$ for the signal-idler. For further pump suppression, a cutoff filter F is used. The signal-idler beam passes through a double-slit, which is placed close to the output side of the crystal, and is reflected by two mirrors, M_1 and M_2, onto a pinhole P followed by a polarization beam splitter PBS. The signal and idler photons are separated by the beam splitter and are detected by the photon counting detectors D_1 and D_2, respectively. The output pulses of each detector are sent to a coincidence counting circuit with a 1.8 ns acceptance time window for signal-idler joint detection. Both detectors are preceded by 10-nm-bandwidth spectral filters centered at the degenerate wavelength, 916 nm. The whole block containing the pinhole, the PBS, the detectors, and the coincidence circuit can be considered as a two-photon detector. Instead of moving two detectors together as indicated in Fig. 2, we rotate the mirror M_1 to "scan" the spatial interference-diffraction pattern relative to the detectors.

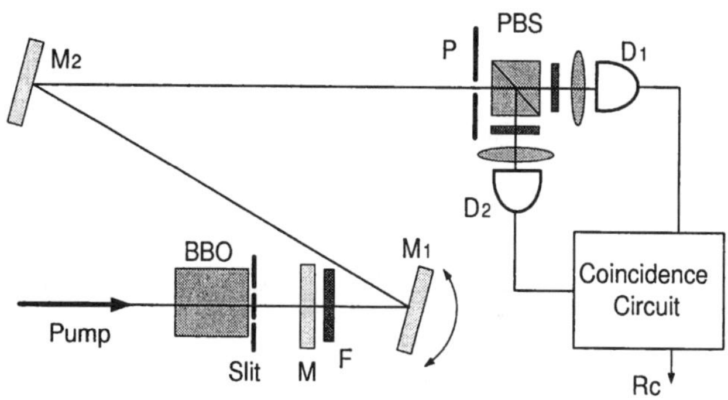

Figure 3. Schematic of the experimental setup. Details are given in the text.

One important point to be emphasized is that the double-slit must be placed *as close as possible* to the output surface of the BBO crystal. Only in this case, can the observed diffraction pattern be narrower than in the classical case by a factor of 2.

Figure 4 reports the experimental results. In our experiment, the width of each slit was $a = 0.13$ mm. The distance between the two slits was $b = 0.4$ mm. The distance between the slits and the pinhole P was 4 m. Figure 4(a) shows the distribution of coincidences versus the rotation angle θ of mirror M_1. The spatial interference period and the first zeros of the envelope were measured to be 0.001 and ± 0.003 radians, respectively.

For comparison, we also measured the first-order interference-diffraction pattern of a classical light source with 916 nm wavelength by the same double-slit in the same experimental setup, see Fig. 4(b). The spatial interference period and the first zeros of the envelope were measured to be 0.002 and ± 0.006 radians, respectively.

In both "classical" and "quantum" cases, we obtain similar standard Young's two-slit interference-diffraction pattern, $\text{sinc}^2[(\pi a/\lambda)\theta]\cos^2[(\pi b/\lambda)\theta]$. However, the wavelength that fits the Fig. 4(b) (classical light) data is 916 nm, but for the curve in Fig. 4(a) (entangled two-photon source) it is 458 nm. Two-photon diffraction has clearly "beaten" the classical limit by factors of 2.

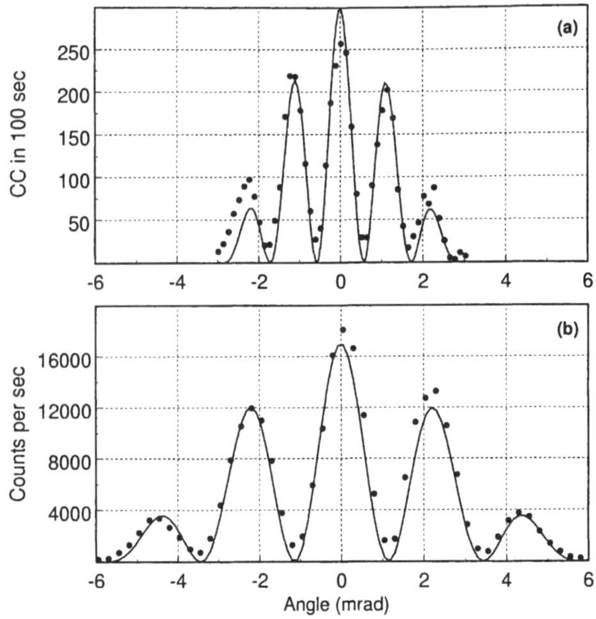

Figure 4. (a): Experimental measurement of the coincidences for the two-photon double-slit interference-diffraction pattern. (b): Measurement of the interference-diffraction pattern for classical light in the same experimental setup. With respect to the classical case, the two-photon pattern has a higher spatial-frequency interference modulation and a narrower diffraction pattern width, by factors of 2.

Acknowledgments

The author thanks M. D'Angelo and M.V. Chekhova for their intelligent and hard experimental work during the demonstration of quantum lithography. This research was supported, in part, by ARDA-NSA, ONR, and NSF.

References

1. A. Einstein, B. Podolsky, and N. Rosen, Phys. Rev. **47**, 777 (1935).
2. T.B. Pittman, Y.H. Shih, D.V. Strekalov, and A.V. Sergienko, Phys. Rev. A **52**, R3429 (1995); D.V. Strekalov, A.V. Sergienko, D.N. Klyshko, and Y.H. Shih, Phys. Rev. Lett., **74**, 3600 (1995).
3. A.N. Boto et al., Phys. Rev. Lett., **85**, 2733 (2000).
4. D'Angelo, M.V. Chekhova, and Y.H. Shih, Phys. Rev. Lett., Vol. 87, 013602 (2001).
5. See, e.g., E. Hecht, *Optics*, Addison-Wesley Publishing, 2nd Edition (1989).

QUANTUM IMAGING AND METROLOGY

HWANG LEE, PIETER KOK, AND JONATHAN P. DOWLING
Exploration Systems Autonomy, Section 367, MS 126-347
Quantum Computing Technologies Group
Jet Propulsion Laboratory, California Institute of Technology
4800 Oak Grove Drive, Pasadena, CA 91109-8099

The manipulation of quantum entanglement has found enormous potential for improving performances of devices such as gyroscopes, clocks, and even computers. Similar improvements have been demonstrated for lithography and microscopy. We present an overview of some aspects of enhancement by quantum entanglement in imaging and metrology.

In state-of-the-art optical-lithographic, semiconductor etching techniques, the Rayleigh diffraction limit puts a lower bound on the feature size that can be printed on a chip. This limit states that the minimal resolvable feature is on the order of $\lambda/4$, where λ is the wavelength of the light used. Classically, if you want to etch features of size 50 nm and smaller, you will be forced to use optical radiation with wavelengths less than 200 nm. Hence, in the optical lithographic community great efforts are put into producing commercial lithographic schemes that utilize wavelengths in the hard UV and X-ray regimes.[1] However, such an approach introduces severe technological and commercial difficulties. For example, mirrors and lenses that are cheap and well understood in the optical regime are much less common and much harder (and more expensive) to make in the UV and X-ray regions of the spectrum, and the problems become worse the shorter you go. Recently, it has been shown, however, that the Rayleigh diffraction limit in optical lithography can be circumvented by the use of path-entangled photon number states.[2]

Fundamentally, optical light beams used for lithography are quantum-mechanical in nature: they are superpositions of photon-number states. This quantum language allows us to taylor non-classical states of light, in which it is possible to program nonlocal correlations between photons. Typically, one photon contains information about the location and the momentum of other photons in the stream.[3] If the proper nonlocal correlations are employed, you can actually manipulate the location at which the light strikes the lithographic substrate, such that features of size $\lambda/4N$ can be etched using N photons of wavelength λ. The use of such an effect was also proposed in sub-natural linewidth spectroscopy.[4]

This remarkable property of quantum-correlated photons has been recognized for some years in the context of quantum optical interferometers. In a typical optical interferometer in which ordinary coherent laser light enters via only one port, the phase sensitivity in the shot-noise limit scales as $\Delta\varphi = 1/\sqrt{\bar{n}}$ where $\bar{n}$ is the mean number of photons.[5] It would seem that any desired sensitivity $\Delta\varphi$ could be attained by simply increasing the laser power. However, when the intensity of the laser ($\bar{n}$) becomes too large, the power fluctuations at the interferometer's mirrors introduce additional noise terms that limit the device's overall sensitivity. Much of the early interest in squeezed light emphasized overcoming this signal-to-noise barrier. In the early 1980s it was demonstrated that squeezing the vacuum in the unused input port of the interferometer causes the phase sensitivity to beat the standard shot-noise limit.[6] The total laser power required for a given amount of phase sensitivity φ is thus greatly reduced.

In 1986, Yurke and collaborators, as well as Yuen, considered the question of phase noise reduction using correlated particles in number states, incident upon both input ports of a Mach-Zehnder interferometer.[7,8,9] They showed that if N quantum particles entered into each input port of the interferometer in nearly equal numbers (and in a highly entangled fashion), then, for large N, it was indeed possible to obtain an asymptotic phase sensitivity of $1/N$, instead of $1/\sqrt{N}$. This is the best you can do using number states in only one input port, and it indicates that the photon counting noise does not originate from the intensity fluctuations of the input beam.[10] Similar observations were made by many authors for optical interferometers[11,12,13,14] as well as Ramsey-type atom interferometers.[15,16,17,18] Wineland and co-workers, in particular, have shown that the optimal frequency measurement can be achieved by using *maximally entangled states.*[16] These maximally entangled states are of a particular interest, since they have a similar form as the ones required for quantum lithography.

Let us take a look at the quantum enhancement due to maximally entangled states, using standard parameter estimation. Consider an ensemble of N two-state systems in the state:

$$|\varphi\rangle = \frac{1}{\sqrt{2}}(|0\rangle + e^{i\varphi}|1\rangle) \tag{1}$$

where $|0\rangle$ and $|1\rangle$ denote the two basis states. The phase information can be obtained by measurement of an observable $\hat{A} = |0\rangle\langle 1| + |1\rangle\langle 0|$. The expectation value of $\hat{A}$ is then given by

$$\langle\varphi|\hat{A}|\varphi\rangle = \cos\varphi\,. \tag{2}$$

When we repeat this experiment N times, we obtain $\langle\varphi_R|\hat{A}_R|\varphi_R\rangle = N\cos\varphi$, where $|\varphi_R\rangle = |\varphi\rangle_1 \ldots |\varphi\rangle_N$, and $\hat{A}_R = \bigoplus_{k=1}^{N} \hat{A}^{(k)}$. Since $\hat{A}_R^2 = \mathbb{1}$, the variance of $\hat{A}_R$, given N samples, is readily computed to be $(\Delta A_R)^2 = N(1-\cos^2\varphi) = N\sin^2\varphi$. According to estimation theory[19], we have

$$\Delta\varphi_{\mathrm{SL}} = \frac{\Delta A_R}{|d\langle\hat{A}_R\rangle/d\varphi|} = \frac{1}{\sqrt{N}}\,. \tag{3}$$

This is the standard variance in the parameter φ after N trials. In other words, the uncertainty in the phase is inversely proportional to the square root of the number of trials. This is called the *shot-noise limit.*

Now consider an entangled state

$$|\varphi_N\rangle \equiv \frac{1}{\sqrt{2}}|N,0\rangle + e^{iN\varphi}|0,N\rangle \,, \tag{4}$$

where $|N,0\rangle$ and $|0,N\rangle$ are collective states of N particles, defined as

$$\begin{aligned} |N,0\rangle &= |0\rangle_1|0\rangle_2 \cdots |0\rangle_N \\ |0,N\rangle &= |1\rangle_1|1\rangle_2 \cdots |1\rangle_N . \end{aligned} \tag{5}$$

The relative phase $e^{iN\varphi}$ is accumulated when each particle in state $|1\rangle$ acquires a phase shift of $e^{i\varphi}$. An important question now is what we need to measure in order to extract the phase information. Recalling the single-particle case of $\hat{A} = |0\rangle\langle 1| + |1\rangle\langle 0|$, we need an observable that does what the operator $|0,N\rangle\langle N,0| + |N,0\rangle\langle 0,N|$ does. For the given state of Eq. (4), we can see that this can be achieved by an observable, $\hat{A}_N = \bigotimes_{k=1}^{N} \hat{A}^{(k)}$. The expectation value of $\hat{A}_N$ is then

$$\langle\varphi_N|\hat{A}_N|\varphi_N\rangle = \cos N\varphi \,. \tag{6}$$

Again, $\hat{A}_N^2 = \mathbb{1}$, and $(\Delta A_N)^2 = 1 - \cos^2 N\varphi = \sin^2 N\varphi$. Using Eq. (3) again, we obtain the so-called Heisenberg limit (HL) of the minimal detectable phase:

$$\Delta\varphi_{\rm HL} = \frac{\Delta A_N}{|d\langle\hat{A}_N\rangle/d\varphi|} = \frac{1}{N} \,. \tag{7}$$

The precision in φ is increased by a factor $\sqrt{N}$ over the standard noise limit. Of course, the preparation of a quantum state such as Eq. (4) is essential to the given protocol.[20]

In quantum lithography, we exploit the $\cos N\varphi$ behavior, exhibited by Eq. (6), to draw closely spaced lines on a suitable substrate.[2] Entanglement-enhanced frequency measurements[16] and gyroscopy[18] exploit the $\sqrt{N}$ increased precision given by Eq. (7). The physical interpretations of A_N and the phase φ will differ in the different protocols. Three distinct physical representations of this construction are of particular interest.

First, in a Mach-Zehnder interferometer [as depicted in Fig. 1(a)] the input light field is divided into two different paths by a beam splitter, and recombined by another beam splitter. The phase difference between the two paths is then measured by balanced detection of the two output modes. Secondly, in Ramsey-type spectroscopy, atoms are put in a superposition of the ground state and an excited state with a $\pi/2$-pulse [see Fig. 1(b)]. After a relative phase shift is accumulated by the atomic states during the free evolution, the second $\pi/2$-pulse is applied and the internal state of the outgoing atom is measured. The third system is given by a qubit that undergoes a Hadamard transform H, then picks up a relative phase and is transformed back with a second Hadamard transformation [Fig. 1(c)]. This representation is more mathematical than the previous two, and it allows us to extract the unifying mathematical principle that underlies the three systems.

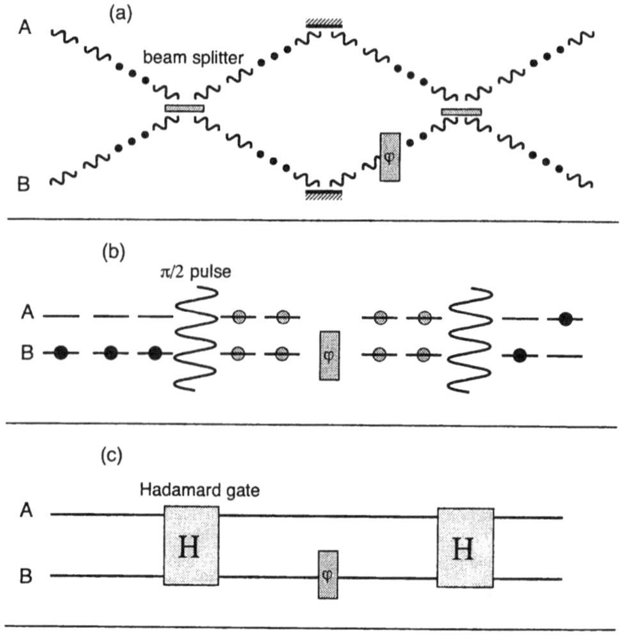

Figure 1. Three distinct representations of phase measurement: (a) a Mach-Zehnder interferometer, (b) Ramsey spectroscopy, and (c) a generic quantum logic gate. The two basis states of a qubit, $|0\rangle$ and $|1\rangle$, may be regarded as the atomic two levels, or the two paths in a Mach-Zehnder interferometer. The state $|\varphi\rangle$ can be regarded as a single photon state just before the second beam splitter in the Mach-Zehnder interferometer, or the single atom state just before the second $\pi/2$-pulse in the Ramsey interferometer.

In all three protocols, the initial state is transformed by a discrete Fourier transform (beam splitter, $\pi/2$-pulse or Hadamard), then picks up a relative phase, and is transformed back again. The Hadamard transform is the standard (two-dimensional) "quantum" finite Fourier transform, such as used in the implementation of Shor's algorithm.[21] The phase shift, which is hard to measure directly, is applied to the transformed basis. The result is a bit flip in the initial basis $\{|0\rangle, |1\rangle\}$, and this is readily measured. We call the formal equivalence between these three systems the *quantum Rosetta stone.*[22] In discussing quantum computer circuits with researchers from the fields of quantum optics or atomic clocks, we find the "quantum Rosetta stone" a useful tool. For example, in a Ramsey-type atom interferometer, noting that $\hat{A} \equiv \sigma_x = H\sigma_z H$, and

$$\hat{A}_N = \bigotimes_{k=1}^{N} \hat{A}^{(k)} = \left(\bigotimes_{k=1}^{N} H^{(k)}\right) \hat{A}'_N \left(\bigotimes_{k=1}^{N} H^{(k)}\right), \tag{8}$$

we need to measure $\hat{A}'_N = \bigotimes_{k=1}^{N} \sigma_z^{(k)}$ after the second beam splitter (see

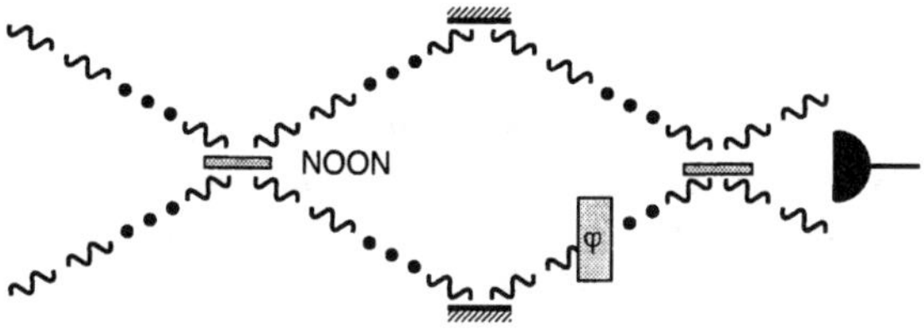

Figure 2. Quantum interferometry. NOON represents the maximally entangled state $|N,0\rangle + |0,N\rangle$ as given in Eq. (5). After the second beam splitter, an obsevable $\hat{A}'_N$ is measured.

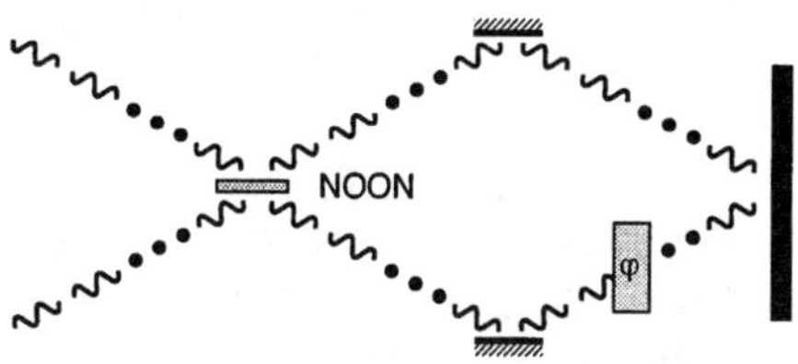

Figure 3. Quantum lithography. NOON represents the maximally path-entangled state. N-photon absorption scheme is analogous to a direct measurement of the observable $\hat{A}_N$.

Fig. 2). On the other hand, a direct optical measurement of $\hat{A}_N$ corresponds to an N-photon absorption scheme in quantum lithography.

Such an enhancement of a factor of $\sqrt{N}$ in quantum metrology is known to be the best possible precision permitted by the uncertainty principle.[23] It is also interesting to see that exploiting quantum correlations yields a $\sqrt{N}$ enhancement in Grover's search algorithm, which has also been shown to be optimal.[24] Is this $\sqrt{N}$ enhancement over the classical protocols universal? It certainly does seem so. But then Shor's algorithm shows its exponential improvement over the best *known* classical algorithm.

We like to end this article with the "Williams-Dowling Inverse-Shor Conjecture".[25] Assume that the best *known* classical factoring algorithm is the best *possible* one. Then, according to Conjecture 1, the quantum Rosetta stone tells us that there must exist an interferometric measurement strategy for phase sensitivity that is exponentially bettter than the shot-noise limit (the best classical strategy). However, we know that this is false. Conjecture 2, therefore, tells us that according to the quantum Rosetta stone, Shor's algorithm is a $\sqrt{N}$ improvement over the *best, but unknown* classical protocol. Thus, there exists a classical algorithm that is exponetially faster than the best known one, though quadratically slower than the quantum algorithm!

Acknowledgments

This work was carried out by the Jet Propulsion Laboratory, California Institute of Technology, under a contract with the National Aeronautics and Space Administration. We wish to thank C. P. Williams, and D. J. Wineland for stimulating discussions. We would like to acknowledge support from the ONR, ARDA, NSA, and DARPA. P.K. and H.L. would also like to acknowledge the National Research Council.

References

1. E. Yablonovich and R.B Vrijen, Opt. Eng. **38**, 334 (1999).
2. A.N. Boto *et al.*, Phys. Rev. Lett. **85**, 2733 (2000).
3. M. D'Angelo, M.V. Chekhova, and Y. Shih, Phys. Rev. Lett. **87**, 013602 (2001).
4. U.W. Rathe and M.O. Scully, Lett. Math. Phys. **87**, 297 (1995).
5. For example, see, M.O. Scully and M.S. Zubairy, *Quantum Optics* (Cambridge University Press, Cambridge, UK, 1997).
6. C.M. Caves, Phys. Rev. D **23**, 1693 (1981).
7. B. Yurke, Phys. Rev. Lett. **56**, 1515 (1986).
8. B. Yurke, S.L. McCall, and J.R. Klauder, Phys. Rev. A **33**, 4033 (1986).
9. H.P. Yuen, Phys. Rev. Lett. **56**, 2176 (1986).
10. M.O. Scully and J.P. Dowling, Phys. Rev. A **48**, 3186 (1993).
11. M.J. Holland and K. Burnett, Phys. Rev. Lett. **71**, 1355 (1993).
12. M. Hillery and L. Mlodinow, Phys. Rev. A **48**, 1548 (1993).
13. C. Brif and A. Mann, Phys. Rev. A **54**, 4505 (1996).
14. T. Kim *et al.*, Phys. Rev. A **57**, 4004 (1998).
15. J. Jacobson, G. Björk, Y. Yamamoto, Appl. Phys. B **60**, 187 (1995).
16. J.J. Bollinger *et al.*, Phys. Rev. A **54**, R4649 (1996).
17. P. Bouyer and M.A. Kasevich, Phys. Rev. A **56**, R1083 (1997).
18. J.P. Dowling, Phys. Rev. A **57**, 4736 (1998).
19. C.W. Helstrom, *Quantum detection and estimation theory*, Mathematics in Science and Engineering **123** (Academic Press, New York, 1976).
20. H. Lee, P. Kok, N.J. Cerf, and J.P. Dowling, Phys. Rev. A **65**, 030101 (2002); P. Kok, H. Lee, and J.P. Dowling, Phys. Rev. A **65**, 052104 (2002); J. Fiurásek, Phys. Rev. A **65**, 053818 (2002); C.C. Gerry, A. Benmoussa, and and R.A. Campos, Phys. Rev. A **66**, 013804 (2002).
21. A. Ekert and R. Jozsa, Rev. Mod. Phys. **68**, 733 (1996).
22. H. Lee, P. Kok, and J.P. Dowling, "A quantum Rosetta stone for interferometry," (in press) J. Mod. Opt., quant-ph/0202133 (2002).
23. Z.Y. Ou, Phys. Rev. Lett. **77**, 2352 (1996).
24. C. Zalka, Phys. Rev. A **60**, 2746 (1999).
25. C.P. Williams, private communication.

EFFICIENT LINEAR OPTICS QUANTUM COMPUTATION

G. J. MILBURN, T.RALPH, A. GILCHRIST, A. WHITE
Centre for Quantum Computer Technology, Univ. of Queensland, St. Lucia, Australia

W.J.MUNRO
Hewlett Packard Laboratories, Bristol, UK

V. KENDON
Imperial College of Science, Technology and Medicine, London, UK

The standard approach for implementing quantum gates seeks appropriate unitary operators from the class of unitary operators that are universal for quantum computation. In reality this requires that we specify the interaction hamiltonian between the physical systems which encode the qubits. In the case of qubits encoded in terms of single photon states this presents a major problem as the required interactions are quartic in the field amplitudes, and thus require high order optical nonlinearity, which is typically small, lossy and slow. While we can anticipate that experimental progress will eventually overcome these problems, at present it is not possible to implement the required gates in a unitary fashion for qubits encoded in single photon states.

However, quantum states do not only change by unitary processes. Non-unitary state change is required when we make a measurement and need to update the description of the state for future analysis or processing. In the KLM proposal[1] non-unitary state change was suggested as a means for implementing quantum gates. The required measurements are discriminating single photon detection, and the qubits are encoded in single photon states. Both the measurement and the qubit state encoding present major technical challenges. However, with these capabilities in hand, the scheme needs only networks of linear optical elements such as beam splitters, polarizers and phase shifters. No additional optical nonlinearity is required.

Nondeterministic gates cannot be cascaded to implement a quantum algorithm. The success probability beyond a few gates would be too small. The key idea in making do with nondeterministic gates is to borrow the idea of Gottesman and Chuang and implement gates by teleportation.[4] In that scheme, implementation of a gate is reduced to preparing the appropriate entangled resource for teleportation. Then it is possible to use nondeterministic gates 'off-line' to prepare the required resource and only complete the teleportation when we know the right resource has been prepared.

Of course, the teleportation process itself is nondeterministic when implemented with linear optics. It is possible to make the process nearly deterministic by using entangled states of n photons in $2n$ modes. At first sight this would seem to add a considerable degree of complexity to the linear optical networks required to prepare the resources. A considerable saving can be made once it is realized that the teleportation of gates always fails in a very special way that corresponds to measurement of the qubit. Thus if we regard the failure of teleportation as failure of the gate, we will always know when an error has occurred and more importantly, what kind of error it is, viz, a measurement of the qubit in the computational basis. Given this knowledge, it is possible to design simple error-correction codes that can correct for the failure of the gate due to failure of teleportation. It is this feature that makes the linear optics quantum computing proposal efficient. Indeed one can show that, at the expense of many photon entangled states for error-correction codes, any error probability less than unity can be corrected in principle. A simple two-qubit code can correct for errors which occur with probability less than 50% and this would probably suffice for simple networks.

While failure of a teleportation gate is an error intrinsic to the protocol and cannot be avoided, photon loss error is also likely to be important in an experimental context. Photons can be lost due to absorption at the linear optical elements (likely to be unimportant) and due to failure of mode matching at optical elements (very likely to be a problem). Two other kinds of error are reducible to photon loss: failure of the single photon source to produce a photon in the right polarization or spatio-temporal mode; and failure of the photon counter to detect a photon. It will be a technological challenge to reduce these errors as much as possible. However error correction codes can be used to mitigate the effect of photon loss. Such codes are also based on teleportation and are described in detail in Ref. 1. A fault tolerance analysis based on such codes indicates that photon loss errors will need to be kept below 1% for scalable computation to be possible. This will require significant advances in photon counting technology. We shall return to this and related issues below.

We choose the traditional encoding of photonic qubits based on a "dual rail" logic, using two modes and one photon: $|0\rangle_L = |1\rangle_1 \otimes |0\rangle_2$ and $|1\rangle_L = |0\rangle_1 \otimes |1\rangle_2$. The modes could be two input modes to a beam splitter distinguished by different wave vector directions, or they could be distinguished by polarization. A single qubit gate is easily implemented by the linear transformation $a_i(\theta) = U(\theta)^\dagger a_i U(\theta)$ with $U_{12}(\theta) = \exp\left[i\theta(a_1^\dagger a_2 + a_1 a_2^\dagger)\right]$. The effect of this unitary in the logical basis is a single qubit rotation, $|0\rangle_L \to \cos\theta_1|0\rangle_L - i\sin\theta_1|1\rangle_L$.

In addition to a single qubit gate, universal quantum computation requires at least a two qubit gate. A simple choice is the conditional sign shift gate, $|x\rangle_L|y\rangle_L \to e^{i\pi x.y}|x\rangle_L|y\rangle_L$. We now describe how a non-unitary implementation of this gate can be done with linear optical transformations, ancilla modes and single photon detection. Under the right circumstances, the conditional states conditioned on observed counts at the ancilla modes will produce the required conditional phase shift.

We seek to implement a conditional nonlinear sign shift (NS) for the state of mode a_1 defined by,

$$|\psi\rangle = \alpha_0|0\rangle_0 + \alpha_1|1\rangle_1 + \alpha_2|2\rangle_1 \to \alpha_0|0\rangle_1 + \alpha_1|1\rangle_1 - \alpha_2|2\rangle_1 \quad (1)$$

We use two ancilla modes, a_2, a_3 which can be regarded as a representing a single qubit in dual rail logic: $|0\rangle_L = |1\rangle_2|0\rangle_3 \ \ |1\rangle_L = |0\rangle_2|1\rangle_3$. In the ***first step***, single qubit rotation is performed on modes 2 and 3, prepared in state $|0\rangle_L$, with the unitary operator $U_{23}(\theta_1)$, namely, $|0\rangle_L \to \cos\theta_1|0\rangle_L - i\sin\theta_1|1\rangle_L$. In the *second step*, mode a_2 of this qubit is coupled to the signal mode,

$$U_{12}(\theta_2)\left[\cos\theta_1|0\rangle_L - i\sin\theta_1|1\rangle_L\right]|\psi\rangle_1 \quad (2)$$

where $|\psi\rangle_1$ is the signal input state. In the *third step* a final qubit rotation through an angle θ_3 is again performed on modes a_2, a_3 with the unitary $U_{23}(\theta_3)$, and a photon counter records a count on each of the qubit modes. The required conditional state is obtained by projecting the output state onto the ancilla states $|1\rangle_2|0\rangle_3$. For the desired NS gate we need to choose the beam splitter parameters to obtain the conditional state in Eq. (1). The projection leads to an unnormalized state, which when normalized gives the probability of this event. The solution, $\theta_1 = \theta_2 = 22.5^o$, $\theta_2 = 114.47^o$, has success probability $\lambda^2 = 1/4$.

Knill et al.[1] showed how this kind of nondeterministic nonlinear sign-shift gate could be used to implement a CNOT gate. The implementation requires two uses of the NS gate and thus the probability of success is 1/16. The scheme however contains two nested, balanced Mach-Zehnder interferometers. This can be considerably simplified at the expense of a small decrease in success probability. A major simplification is achieved by biasing the NS gates. The parameters θ_1 and θ_3 in the NS gates to zero, i.e., the beam splitters are totally reflective. This removes the interferometers from both NS gates, greatly reducing their complexity. All the conditional moments of the original CNOT gate are reproduced, but with the probabilities of the non-zero moments reduced from 1/16 to approximately 1/20. All other properties of the original gate are retained. The details are given in Ralph et al.[5]

As previously discussed, we can use teleportation[4] to enable nondeterministic gates to function in a nearly deterministic way. A basic quantum teleportation protocol for transferring the state $\alpha_0|0\rangle_b + \alpha_1|1\rangle_b$ to one of two modes 3, 4 begins with adjoining the "entangled" state, $|t_2\rangle_{1234} = \frac{1}{\sqrt{3}}\left[|0011\rangle + |1001\rangle + |1100\rangle\right]$ where $|jklm\rangle = |j\rangle_1 \otimes |k\rangle_2 \otimes |l\rangle_3 \otimes |m\rangle_4$. (We omit normalization for convenience.) We then couple the target qubit mode to modes 1, 2 of the ancilla by the three point QFT $\hat{F}_3$ on modes a_0, a_1, a_2. This can be done with linear optics[3] and is defined by the unitary transformation,

$$a_0 \to \frac{1}{\sqrt{3}}(a_0 + a_1 + a_2)$$

$$a_1 \to \frac{1}{\sqrt{3}}(a_0 + e^{-2\pi i/3}a_1 + e^{2\pi i/3}a_2)$$

$$a_2 \rightarrow \frac{1}{\sqrt{3}}(a_0 + e^{2\pi i/3}a_1 + e^{-2\pi i/3}a_2).$$

The total state is thus,

$$|\Psi\rangle = \frac{1}{\sqrt{3}}\left[\alpha_0|000\rangle|1\rangle_3|1\rangle_4 + (\alpha_0|010\rangle|0\rangle_3|1\rangle_4 + \alpha_1|100\rangle|1\rangle_3|1\rangle_4)\right.$$
$$\left. +(\alpha_0|011\rangle|0\rangle_3|0\rangle_4 + \alpha_1|110\rangle|0\rangle_3|1 \rightarrow ngle_4) + \alpha_1|111\rangle|0\rangle_3|0\rangle_4\right].$$

We now consider photon counting on modes a_0, a_1, a_2. As the QFT cannot change the total number of photons, it is clear that a total count of 0 or 3 corresponds to a teleportation failure. In fact, when we count 0 or 3 we have determined that the input qubit was 0 or 1, respectively. Thus $p_{fail} = p_0 + p_1 = 1/3$, and the success probability is therefore $p_{succ} = 1 - 1/3 = 2/3$.

To improve the probability of successful teleportation to $1 - 1/(n+1)$, we use the entangled state $|t_n\rangle_{1\ldots(2n)} = \sum_{j=0}^{n} |1\rangle^j|0\rangle^{n-j}|0\rangle^j|1\rangle^{n-j}$, where $|a\rangle^j$ means $|a\rangle|a\rangle\ldots$, j times. The modes are labelled from 1 to $2n$, left to right. Note that the state exists in the space of n bosonic qubits, where the kth qubit is encoded in modes $n+k$ and k (in this order), and may be prepared by nondeterministic gates. To teleport the state $\alpha_0|0\rangle_b + \alpha_1|1\rangle_b$ using $|t_n\rangle$ we first apply an $n+1$ point Fourier transform $\hat{\mathbf{F}}_{n+1}$ on modes 0 to n. and then measure the number of photons in each of the modes 0 to n. Suppose the total count is k. It is possible to show[1] that if $0 < k < n+1$, then the teleported state appears in mode $n+k$ and only needs to be corrected by applying a phase shift. The modes $2n - l$ are in state 1 for $0 \leq l < (n-k)$ and can be reused in future preparations requiring single bosons. The modes are in state 0 for $n - k < l < n$. If $k = 0$, we learn that the input state is measured and projected to $|0\rangle_b$; if $k = n+1$, it is projected to $|1\rangle_b$. The probability of these two events is $1/(n+1)$, regardless of the input.

There are two problems with the methods shown so far. The first is that for large n, the obvious networks for preparing the required states have very low probabilities of success. It is therefore desirable to avoid using the methods with large n. The second problem is that to get decent success probabilities for coupling gates does require large n, particularly if it is necessary to meet the accuracy requirements of reliable quantum computing.

To achieve exponential improvements in the probability of success for gates and state production with small n, we can use quantum codes and exploit the properties of the failure behavior of teleportation protocols described above. Failure of t_n corresponds to a measurement of the Pauli matrix, Z, with probability $1/(n+1)$.

This can be corrected with a simple code. Consider the simple two-qubit code $|0\rangle_L = |00\rangle + |11\rangle$ and $|1\rangle_L = |01\rangle + |10\rangle$. Suppose the measurement error is on the first qubit;

$$\alpha|0\rangle_L + \beta|1\rangle_L = \alpha(|00\rangle + |11\rangle) + \beta(|01\rangle + |10\rangle) \overset{meas.\ 0}{\longrightarrow} \alpha|00\rangle + \beta|01\rangle. \quad (3)$$

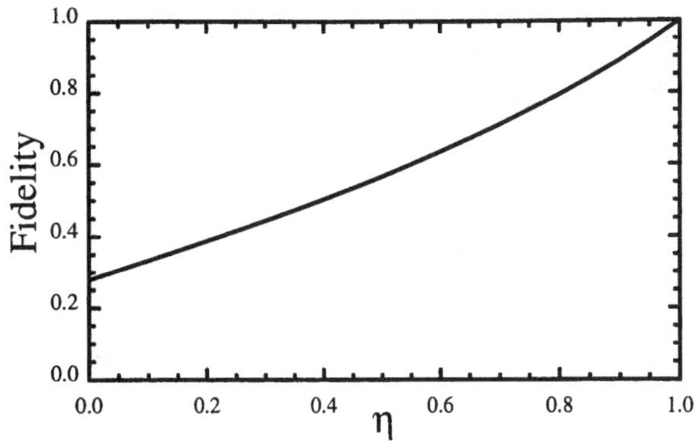

Figure 1. Average fidelity for the NS gate versus the probability that the ancilla photon is lost at input.

We now discard the first qubit and adjoin another ancilla prepared in the zero logical state to give the state $(\alpha|0\rangle + \beta|1\rangle)|0\rangle_a$. A simple two-qubit gate $U = \exp[-i\pi Y X_a/4]$ can then recover, however in the linear optics scheme we must implement such gates by teleportation. It is possible to iterate these and similar error correction methods to efficiently achieve essentially perfect quantum computation. This iteration is known as *concatenation* and underlies the accuracy threshold theorems of fault tolerant quantum computation.[7,8]

We turn now to photon loss, specifically the special case of the NS gate in which the ancilla photon is lost. Correct operation is given in Eq. (1). However if the ancilla is missing, but the detectors still give a (1,0) count, we get the conditional transformation $|\psi\rangle \xrightarrow{\Upsilon} 2^{-1/4}(\alpha_1|0\rangle + 2\alpha_2(1-\sqrt{2})|1\rangle)$.

Let us suppose that the probability for missing the photon in the ancilla is $1-\eta$. The output state is then a mixed state, $\rho_{out} = \mathcal{E}[\psi_{in}]/\mathrm{tr}(\mathcal{E}[\psi_{in}])$, where $\mathcal{E}[\psi_{in}] = \frac{\eta}{4}U_{NS}|\psi_{in}\rangle\langle\psi_{in}|U_{NS}^\dagger + (1-\eta)\Upsilon|\psi_{in}\rangle\langle\psi_{in}|\Upsilon^\dagger$. We can now average the fidelity over all 2-photon input states:

$$\bar{F} = \int d\psi \frac{\mathcal{E}[\psi_{in}]}{\mathrm{tr}(\mathcal{E}[\psi_{in}])}$$

to get an idea of the overall performance due to this kind of error. The results are shown in Fig. 1

Fortunately, photon loss can be detected and corrected with nondeterministic teleportation gates; the details are in.[1] The fault tolerant threshold for this error is 99%. As failure to detect a photon can be subsumed in a photon loss error, this indicates that detectors must operate with efficiencies greater than 99%, a tall order for current technologies.

To conclude, we summarize the physical requirements for linear optics quantum computation: (i) single photon sources, (ii) fast efficient single-photon detectors, (iii) low photon absorption, and (iv) fast electro-optic feed forward. There is currently a great deal of interest in schemes for single photon sources and recently a particularly useful scheme was demonstrated.[9] We expect that reliable and fast single photon sources are not far away. In the mean time, however, the basic elements of linear optics QC can be demonstrated with conditional nondeterministic single photon sources, such as are used in parametric downconversion experiments.[10] The requirement for fast single-photon detectors that can distinguish zero, one and two photons is a difficult one to meet with current technology, but is achievable by a variety of means. The requirement of fast electro-optic feed forward is perhaps the biggest hurdle to overcome for demonstrating a simple quantum circuit, but recent suggestions for photon memories[11] will help mitigate these difficulties.

The difficulty of detecting single photons with high efficiency may be overcome by exploiting the fact that fluorescence shelving measurements of atomic bound states can be extremely efficient and a number of schemes have been suggested.[12,13] Indeed it is even possible to imagine non-unitary gates that exploit this fact directly. Such a scheme was described in Ref. 14; it uses cavity storage of pulses, stimulated Raman interaction and efficient fluorescence atomic state measurements to obtain a conditional NS gate with success probability >98%.

References

1. E. Knill, R. Laflamme and G. J. Milburn, Nature **409**, 46, (2001).
2. G. J. Milburn, Phys. Rev. Lett. **62**, 2124–2127 (1988).
3. M. Reck, A. Zeilinger, H. J. Bernstein, and P. Bertani, Phys. Rev. Lett. **73**, 58–61 (1994).
4. D. Gottesman, and I. L.Chuang, Nature **402**, 390–393 (1999).
5. T. C. Ralph, A. G. White, W. J. Munro and G. J. Milburn, Phys. Rev. A **65**, 012314 (2001).
6. T. H. Cormen, C. E. Leiserson, and R. L. Rivest, *Introduction to Algorithms*, MIT Press, Cambridge, Mass, (1990).
7. E. Knill, R. Laflamme, and W. H. Zurek, Science **279**, 342–345 (1998).
8. J. Preskill, Proc. R. Soc. Lond. A **454**, 385–410 (1998).
9. C. Santori, et al. Nature **419**, 594 (2002).
10. J. D. Franson, M. M. Donegan, M. J. Fitch, B. C. Jacobs, and T. B. Pittman, Phys. Rev. Lett. **89**, 137901 (2002)
11. T. B. Pittman, B. C. Jacobs, and J. D. Franson, Phys. Rev. A **66**, 042303 (2002), T. B. Pittman, J. D. Franson, *Cyclical Quantum Memory for Photonic Qubits*, quant-ph/0207041 (2002).
12. A. Imamoglu, quant-ph/0205196 (2002).
13. D. F. James and P. G. Kwiat, quant-ph/0206049 (2002).
14. A. Gilchrist and G. J. Milburn, *Conditional phase shifts using trapped atoms* quant-ph/0208157 (2002).

UNIVERSAL-NOT GATE AND QUANTUM CLONING

F. DE MARTINI, F. SCIARRINO AND C. SIAS

Instituto Nazionale di Fisica della Materia, Dipartimento di Fisica, Universita' "La Sapienza", Roma, 00185 Italy

An arbitrary quantum state cannot be "cloned" perfectly, i.e., reproduced with "fidelity" $F = 1$ into $M > 1$ states identical to the original, by any conceivable physical device. The main root of this impossibility resides in the linearity of quantum mechanics. A second "quantum impossibility" process, based on the complete positivity character of any quantum operation, forbids the realization of a universal NOT gate, i.e., one that flips exactly *any* input qubit into an orthogonal one. We report an experimental demonstration of the process of cloning an $N = 1$ input qubit into $M = 2$ output qubits by a quantum-injected optical parametric amplifier (OPA). By the same apparatus, realization of a universal NOT gate is also demonstrated. The two processes will be found to be *universal* and *optimal*, i.e., the measured *fidelities* of both processes $F < 1$ will be found to be close to their respective theoretical limits.

Information encoded in a quantum system has to obey the rules of quantum physics, which impose strict bounds on possible manipulations of quantum information. The common origin of these bounds is that all quantum-mechanical transformations have to be represented by completely positive maps, which in turn impose a constraint on the fidelity of the corresponding quantum-mechanical measurements. That is, an unknown state of a qubit cannot be precisely determined (reconstructed) from a measurement performed on a finite ensemble of identically prepared qubits.[1,2,3] In particular, the mean fidelity of the best possible (optimal) state estimation strategy based on measurement of N identically-prepared qubits is $F = (N+1)/(N+2)$. One of the obvious consequences of this estimation bound is that unknown states of quantum systems cannot be cloned (copied) perfectly.[4] Certainly if this would be possible, then one would be able to violate the bound on the fidelity of estimation. Moreover, it would be possible to utilize quantum nonlocality for superluminal signaling.[5] Another transformation which cannot be performed perfectly on an unknown state of a qubit is the spin flip by the universal-NOT gate, i.e., the operation $|\Omega\rangle \Longrightarrow |\Omega^{\perp}\rangle$, where the state $|\Omega^{\perp}\rangle$ is orthogonal to the original $|\Omega\rangle$.[6] Spin flipping is indeed an *anti-unitary*, i.e., a time reversal, transformation.[2] Despite the fact that neither of these maps can be performed perfectly, one still may ask what are their best possible (optimal) approximations, i.e., what is the "optimal" universal cloner and what is the "optimal" universal-NOT (U-NOT) gate. The *universality* condition is required to ensure that all inputs (in unknown states) are transformed with the same *fidelity*. Investigation of these universal optimal transformations, which are also called universal quantum machines, is extremely important since it reveals bounds on optimal manipulations of quantum information. Consequently, in recent years, theoretical investigation of the Universal Optimal Quantum Cloning Machine (UOQCM) and on the U-NOT gate has been very thorough.

The first machine to be investigated theoretically was the *optimal universal quantum cloner* of qubits. The action of this cloner can be described by a simple covariant (ensuring universality) transformation:[7]

$$|\Omega\rangle|\downarrow\rangle_C|\downarrow\rangle_{AC} \Longrightarrow \sqrt{2/3}|\Omega\rangle|\Omega\rangle|\Omega^{\perp}\rangle_{AC} - \sqrt{1/3}|\{\Omega,\Omega^{\perp}\}\rangle|\Omega\rangle_{AC}, \quad (1)$$

where the first (unknown) state vector in the left-hand side of Eq.(1) corresponds to the system to be cloned, the second state vector describes the system on which the information is going to be copied (the "blank" qubit) represented by the "cloning channel" (C), and the third state vector represents the cloner itself. The state $|\Omega^{\perp}\rangle$ is the *antipode* of $|\Omega\rangle$ on the Bloch sphere, and $|\{\Omega,\Omega^{\perp}\}\rangle$ is the completely symmetric state of two qubits. In the present work the cloner is a qubit, associated with the "anti-cloning channel" (AC). Assume that the blank qubit and the cloner are initially in the known state $|\downarrow\rangle$. At the output of the cloner we find two qubits (the original and the copy) in the state $\rho = (2/3)|\Omega\rangle|\Omega\rangle\langle\Omega|\langle\Omega| + (1/3)|\{\Omega,\Omega^{\perp}\}\rangle\langle\{\Omega,\Omega^{\perp}\}|$. The density operator ρ describes the best possible approximation to the perfect cloning process, viz. the state $|\Omega\rangle|\Omega\rangle$. The fidelity of this transformation, $F = 5/6$, does not depend on the input state. After the cloning transformation, the cloner is left in the state $\rho_{AC} = (1/3)|\Omega^{\perp}\rangle\langle\Omega^{\perp}| + (1/3)\mathbf{I}$, where $\mathbf{I}$ is the identity operator. This last density operator represents the best possible approximation to the action of the spin-flip (U-NOT) operation permitted by quantum mechanics; the fidelity of its U-NOT transformation, $F^* = \langle\Omega^{\perp}|\rho_{out}|\Omega^{\perp}\rangle = 2/3$, equals the fidelity of estimation.[6]

In quantum optics it is possible to realize universal quantum machines by associating a cloning machine with a photon amplification process, e.g., involving a nonlinear (NL) medium in an optical parametric amplifier (OPA).[8,9] This can be done by virtue of the isomorphism between logical qubit states and photon polarization states. In an OPA with non-degenerate modes, it is generally supposed that N photons, prepared identically in an arbitrary quantum state $|\Omega\rangle$ of *polarization* ($\overrightarrow{\pi}$) are injected into the amplifier on the input mode k_1. The amplifier then generates on C, the same output "cloning mode", $M > N$ copies of the input qubit $|\Omega\rangle$ and on AC, the output "anti-cloning mode", it produces $M - N$ states $|\Omega^{\perp}\rangle$, thus realizing a quantum NOT gate. Here we will report the experimental demonstration of the process of cloning $N = 1$ input photons into $M = 2$ output photons by a *quantum injected,* nondegenerate OPA operating in a $\overrightarrow{\pi}$*-entangled* configuration[9] (see Fig. 1). The loss of fidelity due to the amplification will agree with the limiting value expected from quantum theory *(optimality property)*, regardless of the input $\overrightarrow{\pi}$-state *(universality property)*.

Because of the U-condition, it is convenient to cast the interaction Hamiltonian in the form:

$$\widehat{H}_{int} = i\hbar\chi\left(\widehat{a}^{\dagger}_{\Psi}\widehat{b}^{\dagger}_{\Psi\perp} - \widehat{a}^{\dagger}_{\Psi\perp}\widehat{b}^{\dagger}_{\Psi}\right) + h.c., \qquad (2)$$

where the field operators $\widehat{a}$ and $\widehat{b}$ act on the C and AC modes, respectively. Assume the input single photon, $N = 1$, in the mode k_1 has polarization Ψ. We will use $\widehat{a}^{\dagger}_{\Psi}|0,0\rangle_{k_1} = |1,0\rangle_{k_1}$ to denote this input state, where $|m,n\rangle_{k_1}$ is the k_1-mode state containing m photons of polarization Ψ and n photons of polarization $\Psi^{\perp}$. Initially, the mode k_2 in unexcited, the OPA inputs start out in the product state $|1,0\rangle_{k_1} \otimes |0,0\rangle_{k_2}$ and evolve according the Hamiltonian from Eq. (2):

$$\begin{aligned} U|1,0\rangle_{k_1} \otimes |0,0\rangle_{k_2} &\simeq |1,0\rangle_{k_1} \otimes |0,0\rangle_{k_2} \\ &+ g\left(\sqrt{2}\,|2,0\rangle_{k_1} \otimes |0,1\rangle_{k_2} - |1,1\rangle_{k_1} \otimes |1,0\rangle_{k_2}\right), \qquad (3) \end{aligned}$$

where g is the gain of the parametric amplifier. This approximation for the state vector describing the two modes at times $t > 0$ is sufficient for all cases in which the coupling value is small, as in our experiment: $g \sim 0.11$. The two addenda in Eq. (3) represent, respectively, the process in which the k_1-mode input photon did not interact in the nonlinear medium, and the process of first-order amplification in the OPA. The state $|2,0\rangle_{k_1}$, corresponding to the state $|\Psi\Psi\rangle$ of mode k_1, describes the cloning of the original photon. The state $|0,1\rangle_{k_2}$, representing a single k_2-mode photon of polarization $\Psi^{\perp}$, is the *flipped* version of the input. To see that stimulated emission is responsible for creation of the flipped qubit, let us compare the state (3) with the output of the OPA when vacuum is injected into the nonlinear crystal. In this case, we obtain to the same order of approximation:

$$\begin{aligned} U|0,0\rangle_{k_1} \otimes |0,0\rangle_{k_2} &\simeq |0,0\rangle_{k_1} \otimes |0,0\rangle_{k_2} \\ &+ g\left(|1,0\rangle_{k_1} \otimes |0,1\rangle_{k_2} - |0,1\rangle_{k_1} \otimes |1,0\rangle_{k_2}\right). \qquad (4) \end{aligned}$$

The cloner (C) state components that contain two photons, i.e., the k_1-mode state vectors $|2,0\rangle_{k_1}$ and $|1,1\rangle_{k_1}$ from Eq. (3), have different amplitudes whose probability ratio (signal-to-noise ratio) is $R = 2$. Likewise, the *qubit flipping* portion of the anti-cloner (AC) state, viz., the k_2-mode state vector $|0,1\rangle_{k_2}$, appears with different amplitudes in Eqs. (3) and (4) and is also realized with signal-to-noise ratio $R = 2$. The preceding signal-to-noise ratios were directly measured in the present experiment. As we shall see, the *fidelities* F of the Universal Cloner and the U-NOT gate, were easily determined from the measured R values.

Universality – Despite the microscopic analysis just given, we note that the *universality* property is indeed a macroscopic feature of the OPA. Thus, it can be tested equally well either by injection of *classical*, e.g., *coherent* fields, or *quantum* states of radiation, e.g., single-photon Fock-states. We have achieved the first by injecting an attenuated *coherent* laser field using

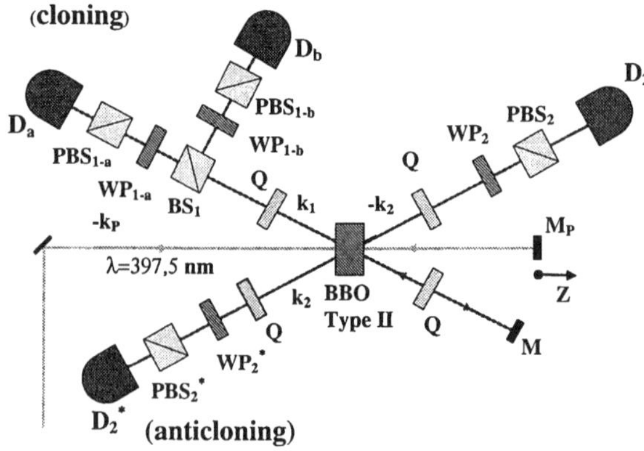

Figure 1. Schematic diagram of the *quantum injected* optical parametric amplifier (OPA) in entangled configuration. The OPA active element was NL crystal BBO cut for type II phase-matching. A single photon pair was emitted by the SPDC process in the BBO crystal towards the *right side* of the figure. One of the particles was detected, after polarization $\vec{\pi}$-filtering by D_2, and provided the *trigger* signal, i.e., the *signature* of the injection event. The twin particle, back reflected by the mirror M, provided the $N = 1$ *quantum injection* into the OPA. Its time superposition with the UV pump in the NL crystal pulse was ensured by micrometric adjustements of the coordinate **Z** of the UV mirror M_p. Fixed quartz plates Q inserted on input and output modes k_1 and k_2 compensated for beam walk-off effects due to the NL crystal's birefringence.

a variation of the setup shown in Fig. 1. The *universality* condition was demonstrated by studying the amplified pulses on the OPA's AC channel. We have verified that the amplification curves were almost identical for different $\vec{\pi}$-state inputs. Each injected coherent pulse was amplified to an average photon number $M \approx 5 \times 10^3$ on the output AC mode. The demonstration of universality is implied by the insensitivity of the *quantum injected* OPA's gain, g, to the $\vec{\pi}$-rotation angles.

Optimality – Figure 1 shows the *self-injected* OPA apparatus that realized the UOQCM process. To perform the cloning experiment, PBS_2^* was removed. Because of the verified universality of OPA amplification, we only considered OPA injection by a single photon in just one $\vec{\pi}$-state, e.g. horizontal polarization $|H\rangle$. The R-measurement was carried out by a 4-coincidence technique, involving all D's of the apparatus, and by suitable changes of the settings of the $\vec{\pi}$-filtering devices on the C channel. The signal-to-noise ratio value obtained from Fig. 2 allowed us to determine the UOQCM *fidelity* according to $F = (2R+1)/(2R+2) = 0.810 \pm 0.008$.[a] The setup in Fig. 1 was also used to perform the U-NOT experiment. The difference

[a]A 1 → 2 cloning experiment with OPA injection provided by an attenuated coherent pulsed laser field has been reported recently in Ref. 10.

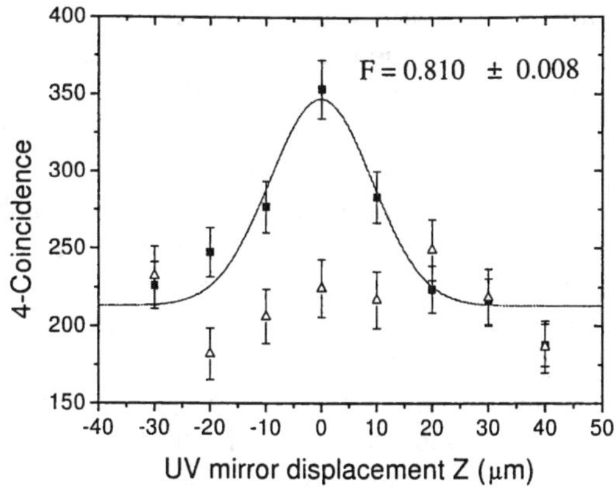

Figure 2. Demonstration of the UOQCM realized by the cloning (C) output channel, k_1.

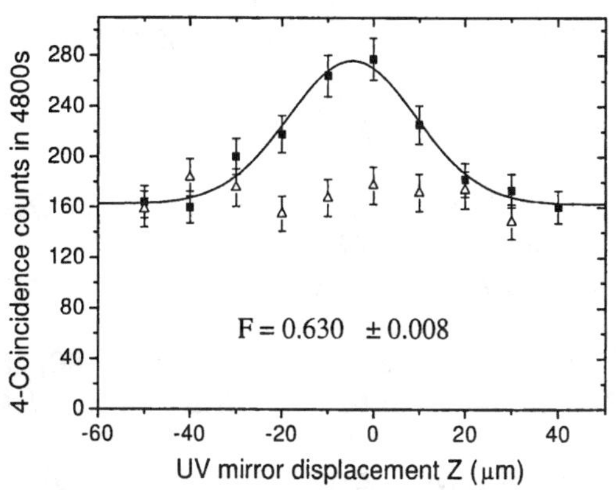

Figure 3. Demonstration of the U-NOT gate realized by the anti-cloning (AC) output channel, k_2.

from the cloning experiment consists of the different measurement devices coupled to the output C and AC channels. Here the C channel, k_1, is simply coupled by a *normal* beam splitter (BS) to detectors D_a and D_b; a coincidence event involving these detectors is the *signature* of a *cloning* event. The AC channel, k_2, is coupled to a $\overrightarrow{\pi}$-analyzer consisting of the set ($PBS_2^* + WP_2^* + D_2^*$). The signal-to-noise ratio, determined by the 4-coincidence data shown in Fig. 3, was $R = 1.69 \pm 0.06$ implying that the U-NOT *fidelity* was $F = R/(R+1) = 0.630 \pm 0.008$.

As a concluding remark, it is well known that an alternative to the U-NOT method for flipping qubits consists of manufacturing the orthogonal qubits based on measurement of the input qubits. The fidelities F of the two alternatives are the same. However, the U-NOT gate does not destroy the input qubit in the irreversible state reduction implied by measurement; it is just redistributed into several qubits at the output. Because this redistribution is governed by a unitary transformation, the process is in principle reversible, something which is definitely not the case for the measurement-based flipping operation. We also want to stress that, to the best of our knowledge the present U-NOT experiment is the first systematic attempt to realize an anti-unitary gate. Obviously, the fidelity of the gate is strictly determined by the structure of quantum mechanics. A remarkable aspect of the present work is that both the quantum cloner and the U-NOT gate are realized by the *same* physical apparatus, by the same unitary transformation, and hence by the same quantum logic network. To the best of our knowledge it is not well understood yet why these two processes are so closely related.

We are indebted with V. Buzek, S. Popescu and C. Simon for very enlightening discussions and suggestions. This work has been supported by the FET European Network on Quantum Information and Communication (Contract IST-2000-29681: ATESIT) and by PAIS-INFM 2002 (QEUPCO).

References

1. A. S. Holevo, *Probabilistic and Statistical Aspects of Quantum Theory* (North-Holland, Amsterdam, 1982).
2. S. Massar and S. Popescu, Phys. Rev. Lett. **74**, 1259 (1995); N. Gisin and S. Popescu, Phys. Rev. Lett. **83**, 432 (1999).
3. R. Derka, V. Buzek and A. Ekert, Phys. Rev. Lett. **80**, 1571 (1998).
4. G. Ghirardi (1981); W.K.Wootters and W.K. Zurek, *Nature* (London) **299**, 802 (1982).
5. N. Herbert, Found. of Phys. **12**, 1171 (1982); L. Mandel, Nature (London), **304**, 188 (1983); N. Gisin, Phys. Lett. A **259** (1999); C. Simon, V. Buzek and N. Gisin, Phys. Rev. Lett. **87**, 170405 (2001).
6. V. Buzek, M. Hillery and R. F. Werner, Phys. Rev. A **60**, R2626 (1999).
7. V. Buzek and M. Hillery, Phys. Rev. A **54**, 1855 (1996); N. Gisin, and S. Massar, Phys. Rev. Lett. **79**, 2153 (1997); D. Bruss, A. Ekert and C. Macchiavello, Phys. Rev. Lett. **81**, 2598 (1998); R. F. Werner, Phys. Rev. A **58**, 1827 (1998).
8. F. De Martini, Phys. Rev. Lett. **81**, 2842 (1998); F. De Martini, V. Mussi and F. Bovino, Opt. Comm. **179**, 581 (2000); F. De Martini, G. Di Giuseppe and S. Padua, Phys. Rev. Lett. **87**, 150401 (2001).
9. C. Simon, G. Weihs and A. Zeilinger, Phys. Rev. Lett. **84**, 2993 (2000).
10. A. Lamas-Linares, C. Simon, J. C. Howell and D. Bouwmeester, Science 1068972 (2002).

PROGRESS IN LINEAR-OPTICS QUANTUM COMPUTING

J. D. FRANSON, M. M. DONEGAN, M. J. FITCH,
B. C. JACOBS, AND T. B. PITTMAN

Johns Hopkins University, Applied Physics Laboratory, Laurel, MD 20723, USA
E-mail: franson@jhuapl.edu

Quantum logic operations can be performed using linear optical elements, ancilla photons, and corrections based on the results of measurements made on the ancilla. We have recently demonstrated several basic quantum logic operations using single photons, a technique for feed-forward control, a new source of single photons on pseudo-demand, and a quantum memory device for single photons.

1 Introduction

Knill, Laflamme, and Milburn (KLM) recently showed[1] that quantum logic operations can be performed using linear optical elements, such as beam splitters and phase shifters. The input qubits, represented by single photons, are combined with additional photons (ancilla) using linear optical elements, after which measurements are made on the ancilla. In the original KLM approach, the output of a logic device is only accepted if the measurements yield specific results (post-selection), whereas the results are always accepted in an alternative approach that we recently suggested.[2] In either case, measurement-dependent corrections are applied to the output and the quantum-mechanical measurement process projects out a final state that corresponds to the desired logical output in the limit of a large number n of ancilla.

We have proposed[3] several quantum logic devices of this kind, including a quantum parity-check, quantum encoder, and a destructive controlled-NOT gate that performs the logical function of a conventional CNOT operation while destroying the control qubit in the process. These basic devices can be combined to implement a full (non-destructive) CNOT gate as described in Ref. 3. Our CNOT implementation makes use of polarization-encoded qubits,[4] which avoids the phase instabilities that can occur when using interferometers.

In the remainder of this paper, we will describe recent experimental demonstrations of a quantum parity-check and a destructive CNOT gate.[5] We have also implemented[6] the feed-forward techniques required to correct the output of the logic gates, along with a new source of single photons on pseudo-demand,[7] and a quantum memory device for single photons.[8] A "high-fidelity" approach[2] to linear-optics quantum computing will also be briefly discussed.

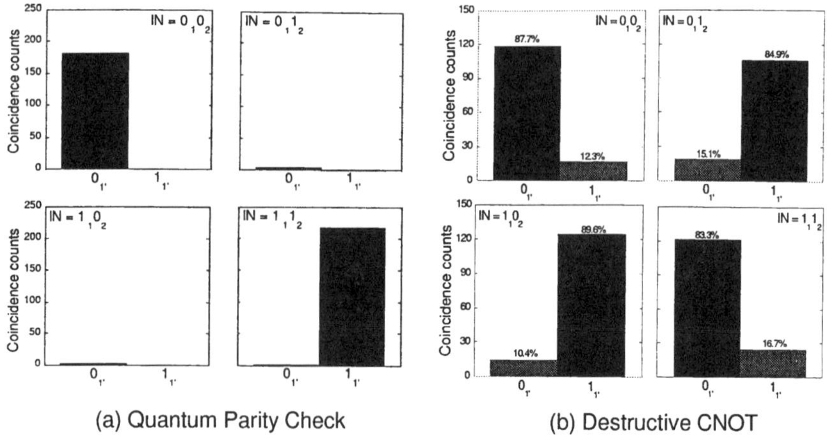

Figure 1. Results from (a) the quantum parity-check experiment, and (b) the destructive CNOT experiment.

2 Experiments

We have performed several proof-of-principle experiments in which a pair of photons was produced using parametric downconversion. The polarizations of the photons could be controlled using wave plates to form superpositions of input states to the logic devices to be tested. The outputs of the logic devices were measured using polarization analyzers and single-photon detectors. All of the current experiments were performed in the coincidence basis, in which the detection of the output photons was required in order to ensure the performance of the correct logic operation.

The results from an experimental demonstration[5] of the quantum parity-check are shown in Figure 1(a). The logical output of the device is shown for all of the possible values of the input qubits. The dark areas represent the correct logical output and the shaded areas represent errors. In this case the errors were on the order of 1%. Similar results were also obtained for superposition states of the input qubits, which shows that the device maintains the coherence of the output qubits.

Figure 1(b) shows the experimental results[5] from a destructive CNOT logic gate. The intended function of this device is to flip or invert the value of the target qubit if and only if the control qubit has the value 1. Once again, the dark areas represent the correct result and the shaded areas, which were on the order of 13% in this experiment, represent errors. Most of this error rate was due to mode mismatch, and we are in the process of repeating the experiment using single-mode fibers in an effort to reduce the error rate.

As mentioned above, real-time corrections must be made to the output

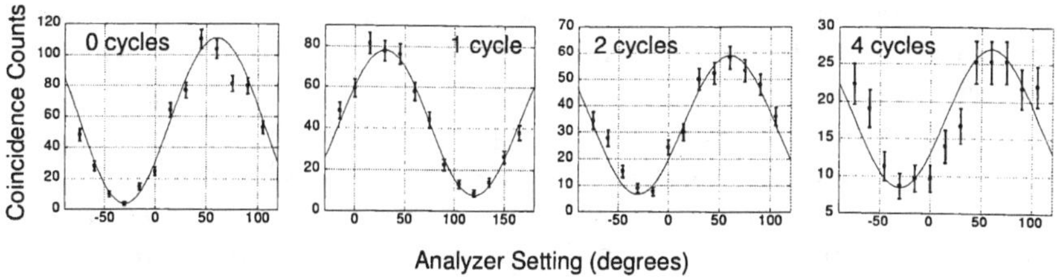

Figure 2. Input and output polarization states in the quantum memory experiment.

of the logic devices when certain results are obtained from the measurements made on the ancilla photons. We have applied these feed-forward corrections to the output of the quantum parity check using a high-speed Pockels cell and a short length of optical fiber to delay the output while the electronics applied the required voltage to the cell.[6] The Pockels cell in this experiment had a rise time of approximately 10 ns, which was sufficient for a real-time correction to the output.

Large numbers of single-photons will be required in a linear-optics approach to quantum computing. We have recently demonstrated[7] a new source of single photons that are available at periodic time intervals that can be synchronized with the cycle time of a quantum computer, which we refer to as a source of single photons on pseudo-demand. In this approach, the detection of one member of a downconverted pair of photons caused the second photon to be switched into an optical storage loop using a high-speed Pockels cell. After it was known that a single photon was present in the loop, it could be switched out of the storage loop when needed. The experimental results showed a loss of approximately 17% per cycle time,[7] which we expect to reduce in the future using low-loss switches.

A storage loop and high-speed switch can also be used to implement a quantum memory device for single photons. Here the switch must not affect the state of polarization of the photonic qubit. We have performed a proof-of-principle demonstration[8] of a memory device[9] of this kind in which a Sagnac interferometer was used as the high-speed switching element. The experimental results of Figure 2 show the polarization of the input qubit and that of the output after four cycles through the device. The performance of the memory device is also being improved using an optical fiber implementation.

3 High-fidelity quantum logic operations

The logic devices originally suggested by KLM[1] give the correct output after post-selection with a failure probability that scales as $1/n$. We have recently proposed[2] an alternative approach in which the output of the logic devices is always accepted (no post-selection), while the entangled state of the ancilla photons is chosen to maximize the fidelity of the output. This results in an intrinsic error rate of $(1/n)^2$, which we expect to have practical advantages in quantum computing applications. In particular, our high-fidelity approach allows a specific error threshold to be met with a smaller number of ancilla photons than in the original KLM approach, assuming that the error correction code must be able to correct for the most general errors. Reducing the number of ancilla photons will reduce the probability of an error in the generation of the ancilla photons, which in turn will make it easier to achieve the error threshold.

4 Summary

We have performed proof-of-principle demonstrations of basic quantum logic operations using single photons, feed-forward control techniques, a new source of single photons on pseudo-demand, and a quantum memory device for single photons. All of these devices have errors on the order of 15% per operation and their performance would have to be greatly improved for any practical applications. Nevertheless, these results represent a first step towards the long-term goal of linear-optics quantum computing.

Acknowledgments

This work was funded by ONR, ARO, NSA, ARDA, and IR&D funds.

References

1. E. Knill, R. Laflamme, and G. J. Milburn, Nature **409**, 46 (2001).
2. J. D. Franson, M. M. Donegan, M. J. Fitch, B. C. Jacobs, and T. B. Pittman, Phys. Rev. Lett. **89**, 137901 (2002).
3. T. B. Pittman, B. C. Jacobs, and J. D. Franson, Phys. Rev. A **64**, 062311 (2001).
4. M. Koashi, T. Yamamoto, and N. Imoto, Phys. Rev. A. **63**, 030301 (2001).
5. T. B. Pittman, B. C. Jacobs, and J. D. Franson, Phys. Rev. Lett. **88**, 257902 (2002).
6. T. B. Pittman, B. C. Jacobs, and J. D. Franson, to appear in Phys. Rev. A (2002); quant-ph/0204142.
7. T. B. Pittman, B. C. Jacobs, and J. D. Franson, to appear in Phys. Rev. A (2002); quant-ph/0205103.
8. T. B. Pittman and J. D. Franson, submitted to Phys. Rev. A (2002); quant-ph/0207041.
9. S. Lloyd, M. S. Shahriar, J. H. Shapiro, and P. R. Hemmer, Phys. Rev. Lett. **87**, 167903 (2001).

QUANTUM COMPUTATION WITH COHERENT STATES

A. GILCHRIST, T.C. RALPH, W.J. MUNRO, AND G.J. MILBURN
Department of Physics and Center for Quantum Computer Technology, University of Queensland, QLD 4072, Brisbane, Australia.
E-mail: alexei@physics.uq.edu.au

We extend a previous proposal for performing deterministic quantum computation using coherent states and linear optics by examining a new version of one of the gates which offers several advantages.

In a previous paper[1] a scheme was put forward to perform deterministic quantum computation using coherent states and linear optics. The scheme was shown to function in the limit of large coherent states, which is very challenging. In this paper we examine a variation on one of the proposed gates that allows much weaker coherent states to be used while still retaining very high fidelity. The basic qubit encoding will be in coherent states and the vacuum, that is the logical qubits are $|0\rangle_L = |0\rangle$ and $|1\rangle_L = |\alpha\rangle$. These qubit states are not orthogonal, but become approximately orthogonal for $|\alpha|$ even moderately large, that is $\langle 0|\alpha\rangle = \exp(-|\alpha|^2/2)$ (for instance with $|\alpha| = 4$, $|\langle 0|\alpha\rangle|^2 \sim 10^{-7}$).

The scheme assumes that we have a source that can produce, as resource states, the superposition states:

$$|c_\pm\rangle = \mathcal{N}_\pm(\alpha)(|0\rangle \pm |\alpha\rangle) \tag{1}$$

where $\mathcal{N}_\pm(\alpha) = (2 \pm 2\exp\{-|\alpha|^2/2\})^{-1/2}$. A powerful feature of the scheme is that we can generate entanglement between two modes using a 50:50 beam-splitter, that is

$$|c_+\rangle|0\rangle \longrightarrow |cc_+\rangle = \mathcal{N}_+(\sqrt{2}\alpha)(|0,0\rangle + |\alpha,\alpha\rangle) \tag{2}$$

which in the logical basis, is the Bell state $(|00\rangle + |11\rangle)/\sqrt{2}$.

The Hadamard H, Phase S_θ, and the controlled-sign CSIGN gates form a universal set for quantum computation.[2] All of these gates can be implemented in an approximate way in this scheme. The S_θ gate can be implemented by a small phase shift δ, which has the effect

$$P_\delta|\alpha\rangle = |e^{i\delta}\alpha\rangle \sim S_\theta|\alpha\rangle \tag{3}$$

and no effect on the $|0\rangle$ state. This gate is a phase gate in the sense that for small δ the overlap with the original state is $\langle\alpha|e^{i\delta}\alpha\rangle \approx e^{-i\delta|\alpha|^2}$ and we can set $\delta = \theta/|\alpha|^2$. Similarly, the CSIGN gate can be implemented with a weak beam-splitter B_δ,

$$B_\delta|\alpha,\alpha\rangle = |e^{i\delta}\alpha, e^{i\delta}\alpha\rangle \sim -|\alpha,\alpha\rangle, \tag{4}$$

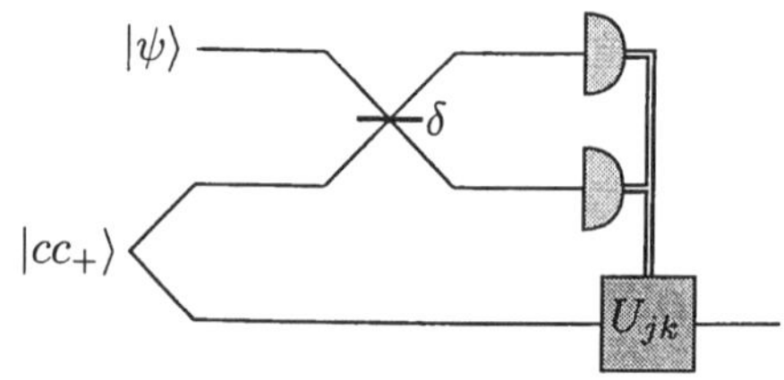

Figure 1. Implementing a 'clean' H gate by use of entanglement.

where we again choose δ so that $\langle \alpha, \alpha | e^{i\delta}\alpha, e^{i\delta}\alpha \rangle \approx e^{2i\delta|\alpha|^2} = -1$. All the other terms are left (approximately) unchanged. A circuit for implementing the Hadamard gate will be discussed below.

There are essentially two approximations in the above transformations. The first is that the states are slightly distorted away from the 0–α subspace. The second is that the transformations are done *inside* the ket, and only in the overlap or due to an appropriate projection are they equivalent to the appropriate phases *outside* the ket. In the remainder of this paper we will analyze a circuit that can address both these problems.

In order to focus on the circuit we'll imagine that we have some apparatus that emulates a destructive 'cat' von Neumann measurement, so that we have at our disposal the projectors, $|c_+\rangle\langle c_+|$ and $|c_-\rangle\langle c_-|$. Note that although the projectors are orthogonal for all α, for small α they are not complete, but in the limit in which $\exp(-|\alpha|^2)$ can be considered negligible $\mathcal{N}_+ = \mathcal{N}_- = 1/\sqrt{2}$ and $|c_+\rangle\langle c_+| + |c_-\rangle\langle c_-| = |0\rangle\langle 0| + |\alpha\rangle\langle\alpha|$, which is the identity in the 0–α subspace and so the projectors form a complete set.

With these measurement projectors, consider implementing the circuit in Fig. 1, which is an extension of the originally proposed H gate with the addition of an entangled state.

The input state into the circuit is

$$|\phi_{\text{in}}\rangle = \mathcal{M}(a|0\rangle + b|\alpha\rangle)\mathcal{N}_+(\sqrt{2}\alpha)(|00\rangle + |\alpha\alpha\rangle), \tag{5}$$

where a and b are the coefficients encoding the qubit with $|a|^2 + |b|^2 = 1$, and $\mathcal{M} = [1 + 2\exp(-|\alpha|^2/2)\text{Re}(ab^*)]^{-1/2}$ is the normalization required to take into account the non-orthogonality of the qubits. After the first two modes are mixed on a beam splitter of reflectivity $\cos^2(\delta)$ the output state is described by

$$\begin{aligned}|\phi_{\text{out}}\rangle = \mathcal{M}\mathcal{N}_+(\sqrt{2}\alpha)(a|0,0,0\rangle + a|is\alpha, c\alpha, \alpha\rangle \\ +b|c\alpha, is\alpha, 0\rangle + b|e^{i\delta}\alpha, e^{i\delta}\alpha, \alpha\rangle),\end{aligned} \tag{6}$$

where $c = \cos(\delta)$ and $s = \sin(\delta)$, and we will choose $\delta = \pi|\alpha|^{-2}/2$.

In order to implement the H gate we need to measure in the 'cat basis' and depending on the outcome of such a measurement we may need to correct

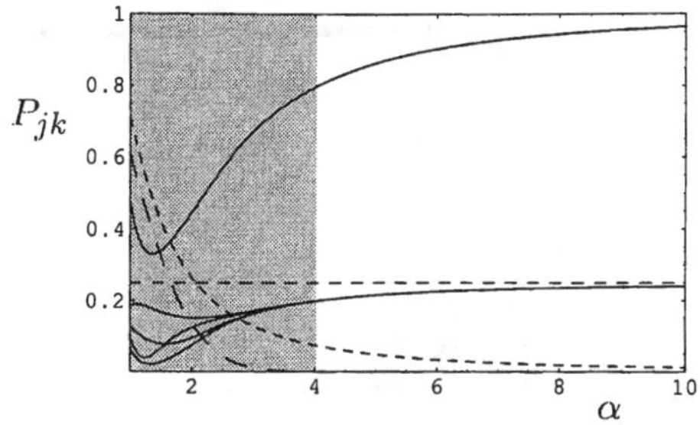

Figure 2. Probability of detecting $c_j c_k$ (lower four solid curves) and total probability (upper solid curve) given an input state $|\alpha\rangle$. The limiting probability is 1/4 for large $|\alpha|$. Also plotted is $\exp(-|\alpha|^2/2)$ (long-dashed curve), which characterizes how quickly the qubit states become orthogonal and the projectors complete; the grayed area is where we'll take these problems to be significant. The dominant error is characterized by $|\langle 0|is\alpha\rangle|$ (fine-dashed curve) which is due to the distortion introduced by the beam splitter.

the resulting output state. If we measure $c_j c_k$ in the first two modes (where $c, j \in \{+, -\}$) then we have to apply the correction unitary U_{jk} where $U_{++} = I$, $U_{+-} = S_\pi$, $U_{-+} = X$ and $U_{--} = XS_\pi$. We can implement the X gate (bit-flip) by first introducing phase shift of π and then displacing the coherent states by α, $X = D(\alpha)P_\pi$. Implementing the sign gate S_π has to be done via a small phase shift as before and will run into the same approximations.

First we will examine the probability of obtaining the various measurement combinations. The probability of detecting $c_j c_k$ in the first two modes is

$$P_{jk} = \mathrm{Tr}\{|c_j c_k\rangle\langle c_j c_k||\phi_{\mathrm{out}}\rangle\langle\phi_{\mathrm{out}}|\}. \tag{7}$$

These probabilities are plotted in Fig. 2. The dominant source of errors is not the non-orthogonality of the qubit states but is due to the beam splitter distorting the states slightly and is characterized by the overlap

$$\langle 0|is\alpha\rangle = e^{-\frac{1}{2}s^2|\alpha|^2} \approx e^{-\frac{\pi}{8}|\alpha|^{-2}}. \tag{8}$$

Note that the total probability approaches one fairly slowly — the missing probability is due to distortion to states outside the 0–α subspace.

The state immediately after measuring $c_j c_k$ will be

$$\rho_{jk} = \frac{1}{P_{jk}}\mathrm{Tr}_{ab}\{|c_j c_k\rangle\langle c_j c_k||\phi_{\mathrm{out}}\rangle\langle\phi_{\mathrm{out}}|\}, \tag{9}$$

so that the final output state with corrections applied can be written as

$$\rho = P_{++}\rho_{++} + P_{-+}X\rho_{-+}X + P_{+-}S_\pi\rho_{+-}S_\pi^\dagger + P_{--}XS_\pi\rho_{--}S_\pi^\dagger X. \tag{10}$$

The first two terms produce a clean state in terms of $|0\rangle$ and $|\alpha\rangle$ and the last two terms distort the state due to the application of the S_π gate. To

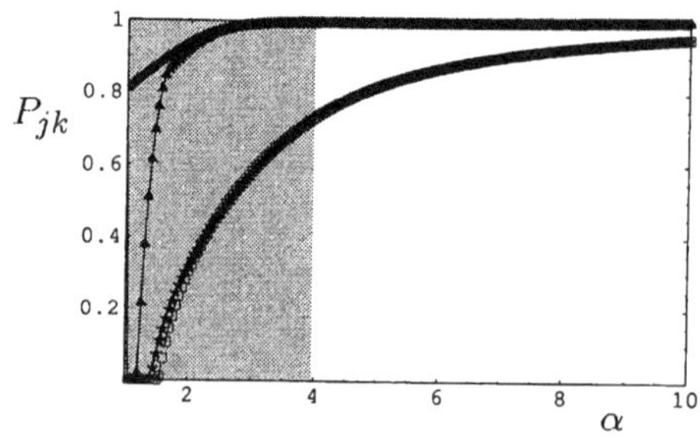

Figure 3. Minimum fidelity of output state ρ_{jk} compared against the action of an ideal Hadamard gate. The top two curves are for ρ_{++} and ρ_{-+} which do not require a sign gate S_π, the bottom two curves are for ρ_{+-} and ρ_{--} which do require a sign gate. The minimum fidelity was computed numerically over all input states with $|a|^2 + |b|^2 = 1$.

characterize the degree of error introduced by the gate we compare this state against the output of an ideal Hadamard gate, which for the purposes of the comparison we'll assume produces the state $|\phi_H\rangle = \mathcal{M}_H[(a+b)|0\rangle + (a-b)|\alpha\rangle]/\sqrt{2}$, where $\mathcal{M}_H = [1 + 2\exp(-|\alpha|^2/2)(|\alpha|^2 - |\beta|^2)]^{-1/2}$. We will use this state on the understanding that the comparison is only meaningful when α is sufficiently large that $\exp(-|\alpha|^2/2)$ can be taken to be zero.

The minimum fidelity, $F_{jk} = \min(\sqrt{\langle\phi_H|\rho_{jk}|\phi_H\rangle})$, for each set of measurement results is shown in Fig. 3. The minimization has been carried out numerically over all qubit input states. It is clear from the figure that for the terms that result in having to apply the S_π gate the errors are much greater. In contrast, when we do not need to make this correction we can exploit the entanglement to project the gate onto a 'clean' 0–α subspace.

This gate can then be used to clean up the approximations in this scheme by chaining together two H gates. This results in both projecting out the desired phases and cleaning up the qubit states with a probability approaching 50%. When we obtain a result that would require the application of S_π we could cycle the output through a pair of H gates again, and in this way with probability approaching one implement a cleaning gate.

AG would like to acknowledge support by the New Zealand Foundation for Research, Science and Technology under grant UQSL0001. This work was supported by the Australian Research Council.

References

1. T. C. Ralph, W. J. Munro, and G. J. Milburn, quant-ph/0110115.
2. M. A. Nielsen and I. L. Chuang, *Quantum Computation and Quantum Information*, (Cambridge Univ. Press, Cambridge, 2000).

GENERATION OF LARGE PHOTON-NUMBER CAT STATES USING LINEAR OPTICS AND QUANTUM MEMORY

N. J. CERF,[1] J. FIURÁŠEK,[2] S. IBLISDIR,[1] AND S. MASSAR[1,3]

[1] *Ecole Polytechnique, CP 165, Université Libre de Bruxelles, B-1050 Bruxelles, Belgium*

[2] *Department of Optics, Palacký University, 17. listopadu 50, 77200 Olomouc, Czech Republic*

[3] *Service de Physique Théorique, CP 225, Université Libre de Bruxelles, B-1050 Bruxelles, Belgium*

A recursive method for producing path-entangled states of light is presented. These states may find applications in quantum lithography and high-precision interferometric measurements. The required resources are single-photon sources, linear optics components, and photodetectors. Adding a quantum memory greatly enhances the yield in comparison with the previously known schemes.

Entangled states play a fundamental role in quantum information processing as they are basic ingredients in various tasks such as quantum teleportation, quantum key distribution, or quantum computing.[1] Entanglement has also been shown to be a useful resource for high-precision frequency measurements and for quantum lithography.[2,3] In this paper, we will focus on the entangled states needed in the latter applications, that is, photon-number path-entangled states or *cat states.* These states are of the form

$$|N_+\rangle_{a,b} = \frac{1}{\sqrt{2N!}}(a^{*N} + b^{*N})|0\rangle, \tag{1}$$

where a^* and b^* denote the bosonic creation operators for two modes of the electromagnetic field, and $|0\rangle$ denotes the vacuum state. Deterministic schemes to produce cat states using $\chi^{(3)}$ nonlinearity have been proposed.[4,5] Unfortunately, the presently available $\chi^{(3)}$ couplings are about 10^{16} times weaker than the required values, which makes these schemes out of the scope of current technology. Recently, however, alternative schemes that only require photon-number state sources, linear optics components (beam splitters and phase shifters), and photodetectors have been proposed for $N = 4$ at first,[6] and then for an arbitrary photon number N.[7,8,9] These schemes are unfortunately *probabilistic*, and the probability $p(N_+)$ of a successful state preparation scales exponentially poorly with N for all of these schemes. Typically, if N is even, $p(N_+)$ scales as c^{-N} with the constant $c = \sqrt{2}\, e$ for the Ref. 7 scheme and $c = e$ in Ref. 8. This is so because these schemes work by adding (or subtracting) the photons one by one (or two by two), each step having a non-unity probability of success. Such a multiplicative process (the yield is a product of success probabilities) naturally scales exponentially.

In this paper, we will demonstrate that using a *tree-like* structure for the linear optics circuit makes it possible to significantly enhance the yield. We will describe a recursive scheme that generates a state of the form of Eq. (1) when N is a power of 2 with an approximate yield of

$$(4\sqrt{\pi})^{-\log_2 N} N^{(1-\log_2 N)/4}. \tag{2}$$

Thus, in contrast with the previous schemes, the scaling is *sub-exponential* in N, which exploits the fact that only $\log_2(N)$ recurrence levels are needed in the tree. As we will see, the price to pay is that a quantum memory (or fast optical switches) is required in addition to the other optical components.

The basic operation in our method is the transformation T_N, which probabilistically transforms two cat states of N photons into one cat state containing $2N$ photons, that is, $T_N : |N_+\rangle_{a,b} \otimes |N_+\rangle_{c,d} \to |2N_+\rangle_{a,b}$ with probability $p(T_N)$. The transformation T_N is realized as follows. First, change the phase of mode d as $d \to e^{i\pi/N} d$. Next, combine the modes a and c at a 50/50 beam splitter and modes b and d at another 50/50 beam splitter. Defining the action of a 50/50 beam splitter on two impinging modes a and b as $a \to (a - ib)/\sqrt{2}$ and $b \to (-ia + b)/\sqrt{2}$, we obtain the 4-mode state

$$\frac{1}{2^{N+1} N!}\left((a^* + ic^*)^N + (b^* + id^*)^N\right)\left((ia^* + c^*)^N - (ib^* + d^*)^N\right)|0\rangle. \tag{3}$$

Finally, measure the number of photons contained in modes c and d. The transformation succeeds if *no* photon is detected in these two modes, in which case we get the (unnormalized) state

$$\frac{1}{2^{N+1} N!}\left((a^*)^{2N} - (b^*)^{2N}\right)|0\rangle. \tag{4}$$

Transforming the phase of mode b as $b \to e^{i\pi/2N} b$ then yields the desired state $|2N_+\rangle_{a,b}$ with a success probability $p(T_N) = \frac{(2N)!}{2^{2N+1}(N!)^2}$. Upon using the Stirling formula, we get

$$p(T_N) \simeq \frac{1}{\sqrt{4\pi N}}\left(1 + O(1/N)\right). \tag{5}$$

Remarkably, $p(T_N)$ does not decrease exponentially with N as if the photons had been added one by one, but only as $1/\sqrt{N}$, so the successive steps of our iterative process keep a reasonably good efficiency as N increases.

Consider first a naive scheme that does not use a quantum memory. Starting from N one-photon states $|1_+\rangle$, which are easily obtainable with a single-photon source and a beam splitter, one probabilistically produces $N/2$ states $|2_+\rangle$, then $N/4$ states $|4_+\rangle$, and so on until one gets the desired state $|N_+\rangle$. What is the overall probability $p(N_+)$ to produce $|N_+\rangle$ with this procedure? Solving the recurrence equation $p(2N_+) = p(N_+)^2 p(T_N)$, we get

$$p(N_+) = \frac{2N!}{(2N)^N} \simeq \sqrt{8\pi N}\,(2e)^{-N}\left(1 + O(1/N)\right). \tag{6}$$

The reason why this success probability decreases exponentially with N is that we require all the $(N-1)$ individual transformations T at all recurrence levels to succeed simultaneously. Since each transformation T has a non-unity probability of success, the probability that they all succeed is exponentially small.

Let us now show that we can strongly improve on this by using a quantum memory. We start with $|1_+\rangle^{\otimes M_1}$ where the number M_1 of states we need to prepare initially will be determined below. Suppose that, after a few steps, we have obtained the state $|n_+\rangle^{\otimes M_n}$, assuming M_n is an even number. We carry out the transformation T_n on each pair of states, which produces on average M_{2n} states $|2n_+\rangle$ where $M_{2n} = \frac{M_n}{2}P(T_n)$. We then discard the states for which the transformation failed and only keep those for which it succeeded (there are, on average, M_{2n} such states). We use these states to construct the state $|4n_+\rangle$, and so on. If we want to produce M_N cat states $|N_+\rangle$ (where N is a power of 2) with a probability of order one, then, solving the above recurrence using Eq. (5), we find that the average number M_1 of states $|1_+\rangle$ that are needed initially is

$$M_1 \simeq (4\sqrt{\pi})^{\log_2 N} N^{(\log_2 N-1)/4}\left(M_N + \mathcal{O}(\sqrt{M_N})\right), \quad (7)$$

which immediately implies Eq. (2). This shows that the resources (i.e., the number of single photons, of operations T_n, of beam splitters, of photodetections, etc.) needed for generating a cat state increase only sub-exponentially with N. This recursive scheme thus requires many fewer operations than the naive scheme, but the dynamics are now conditional on whether the operations T_n succeed or not. Such conditional dynamics require fast optical switches[10] in order to store the photons in a loop, or, alternatively, a quantum memory[11] in which the photon states can be stored. These extra technological resources make our scheme much more demanding than those based only on linear optics, single photon sources, and photodetectors,[6,7,8,9] but $\chi^{(3)}$ couplings are still not required. Note that we may start our recursion from two-photon cat states $|2_+\rangle$ (instead of $|1_+\rangle$), since they can be deterministically generated from two one-photon states using a beam splitter,[12] resulting in an extra factor of 4 in the yield Eq. (2).

Our scheme is sensitive to various imperfections such as the losses in the beam splitters, imperfect mode-matching, etc. Let us focus on one of them, namely the non-unity detector efficiency $\eta < 1$. The probability that the detector does not click when it has absorbed j photons is given by $(1-\eta)^j$. At first sight, it seems that the main source of errors will be due to the events in which no photon is detected in modes c and d when a photon has actually been absorbed in either one of the detectors. By expanding Eq. (3) in a series in c^* and d^*, we find that the probability that there is a single photon in mode c or d is $p(c^*c + d^*d = 1) = \frac{2N}{2^{2N}}$. This probability is thus exponentially smaller than $p(T_N)$, so this event can in fact be neglected in good approximation. Next, if we calculate the probability that two photons are in mode c or d, $p(c^*c+d^*d = 2) = \frac{(2N-2)!}{2^{2N+1}(N-1)!^2} \simeq \frac{P(T_N)}{4}$, we find that, for large N, the probability that one decides that T_N succeeded when it actually failed is approximately given by $(1-\eta)^2/4$. So we conclude that our scheme is robust with respect to detector inefficiencies up to the second order in $(1-\eta)$.

We thank Stefano Pironio and JiangFeng Du for contributing to stimulating discussions and the European Science Foundation for its financial support. S.I. acknowledges support from the FRIA foundation (Belgium). S.M. is Research Associate of the FNRS (Belgium). This work was partly funded by the European Union under the project EQUIP (IST-FET programme).

References

1. M. Nielsen and I. Chuang, *Quantum Computation and Quantum Information* (Cambridge University Press, Cambridge, 2000).
2. J. J. Bollinger, W. M. Itano, D. J. Wineland, and D. J. Heinzen, *Phys. Rev. A* **54**, R4649 (1996).
3. A. N. Boto, P. Kok, D. S. Abrams, S. L. Braunstein, C. P. Williams, and J. P. Dowling, *Phys. Rev. Lett.* **85**, 2733 (2000).
4. G.J. Milburn, *Phys. Rev. Lett.* **62**, 2124 (1989).
5. C. C. Gerry and R. A. Campos, *Phys. Rev. A* **64**, 063814 (2001).
6. H. Lee, P. Kok, N. J. Cerf, and J. P. Dowling, *Phys. Rev. A* **65**, 030101 (2002).
7. P. Kok, H. Lee, and J. P. Dowling, *Phys. Rev. A* **65**, 052104 (2002).
8. J. Fiurášek, *Phys. Rev. A* **65**, 053818 (2002).
9. X. B. Zou, K. Pahlke, and W. Mathis, *Phys. Rev. A* **66**, 014102 (2002).
10. P. G. Kwiat, A. G. White, J. R. Mitchell, O. Nairz, G. Weihs, H. Weinfurter, and A. Zeilinger, *Phys. Rev. Lett.* **83**, 4725 (1999).
11. C. Schori, B. Julsgaard, J. L. Sorensen, and E. S. Polzik, *Phys. Rev. Lett.* **89**, 057903 (2002).
12. C. K. Hong, Z. Y. Ou, and L. Mandel, *Phys. Rev. Lett.* **59**, 2044 (1987).

EFFICIENT LINEAR OPTICAL QUANTUM COMPUTATION

G. J. PRYDE, J. L. O'BRIEN, T. B. BELL, N. K. LANGFORD,
G. J. MILBURN, T. C. RALPH AND A. G. WHITE

*Centre for Quantum Computer Technology, Department of Physics,
The University of Queensland, 4072, AUSTRALIA
e-mail: pryde@physics.uq.edu.au, job@physics.uq.edu.au
web: http://www.quantinfo.org*

We consider realizing the efficient linear optical quantum computing scheme of Knill, Laflamme and Milburn [Nature **409**, 46 (2001)]. A number of the issues in implementing a coincidence-basis version of a CNOT gate are addressed experimentally, including source brightness and mode quality.

1 Introduction

Photons are attractive qubits, being well isolated from the environment, easy to manipulate singly, and easily produced. They are widely used in applications such as quantum cryptography, where only single qubit manipulations are required. However, it is extremely difficult to realize two-qubit interactions between single photons (required for quantum gates such as the CNOT) because of the large nonlinearities requiredċiteAephraim

Knill *et al.* have proposed using *conditional measurements* to obtain large nonlinearities, allowing scalable linear optical quantum computation (LOQC).[2] Conditional measurements imply a non-deterministic interaction, but a teleportation protocol can, in principle, be used to obtain deterministic gates. An efficient CNOT gate has a stringent set of requirements: a heralded single photon source; efficient, number-discriminating photon counters; deterministic Bell measurements to implement the teleportation protocol; quantum memory; and near-ideal non-deterministic CNOT circuitry.

We focus on the last of these via a linear, coincidence basis CNOT (CC-NOT) gate requiring only a two photon input.[3] This gate is a practical non-deterministic CNOT and an ideal test-bed for the issues of experimental realization of efficient LOQC networks. Here we experimentally address a number of issues associated with building the coincidence basis gate.

2 Source issues, interferometry and tomography

The circuit of the CCNOT is shown in the logic diagram of Fig. 1. One of the key requirements for building the CCNOT is an approximation to a single photon source that has both good spatial mode quality and high brightness. This is critical, since CNOT circuits contain both classical and nonclassical interferometers with stringent high visibility requirements to obtain good gate fidelity. Acquisition of photon statistics on practical time scales implies the

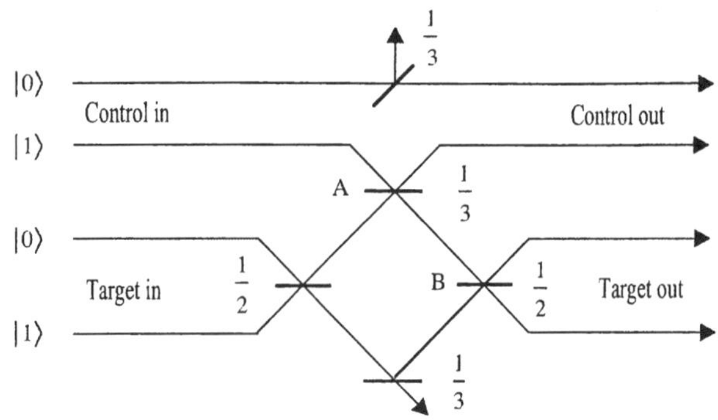

Figure 1. Dual rail logic representation of the coincidence CNOT gate, showing the reflectivities of the beam splitters. Nonclassical interference occurs at beam splitters labelled "A" and "B".

need for a high brightness source because of the various inefficiencies inherent in the circuit construction — the 11% base efficiency of the design,[3] coupled with photon losses from the non-unity efficiency detectors and the optical interfaces in the setup, for example. High brightness sources are also of interest for CNOT designs that require a 4-photon input,[2] since present 4-photon production rates are on the order of 5 events per second,[4] compared with up to 4×10^5 two-photon events per second.[5]

Presently, the most mature approximation to single photon sources is spontaneous parametric downconversion (SPDC), which also has the advantage of automatically producing correlated photon pairs. We have explored a variety of techniques for obtaining the required source brightness and mode quality. These include careful choice of the downconversion phase matching conditions and the use of optical fiber coupling. In the former case, we use a BBO nonlinear crystal cut for type II operation and choose a phase matching condition such that each member of a correlated pair of photons is emitted into a beam-like optical mode.[6] Figure 2 shows a coincidence measurement of the mode shape and intensity, made by scanning an iris across one of the beams and recording the coincidence counts. The near-Gaussian intensity profile of this mode lends itself to the idea that it might be efficiently fiber coupled for further spatial mode filtering and ease of delivery in the experiment. We have investigated the approach of coupling to single mode fiber for a number of other phase matching conditions in type II cut BBO, which have other attractions such as momentum degeneracy of the downconverted photon pair or a simplified experimental geometry. The mode filtering characteristics of single mode fiber have allowed high visibility nonclassical interference to be observed, as discussed below.

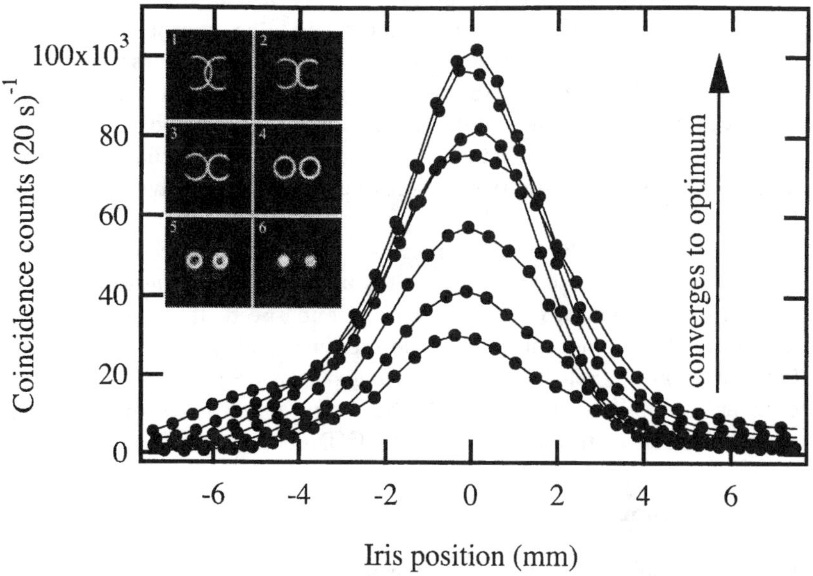

Figure 2. Coincidence measurement of the SPDC mode shape at, and surrounding, the optimal beam-like condition. The inset shows CCD images of the cones collapsing, with the coincidence data corresponding to small variations ($\leq 0.14°$) of the phase matching angle around image 6 (optimal condition).

The core of the CCNOT gate is nonclassical interference which, when coupled with conditional measurement, allows two-qubit operation. In order to obtain high gate fidelity, a high-visibility nonclassical interference is required. We have observed high-visibility nonclassical interference experimentally, both in the spatially degenerate and spatially nondegenerate configurations. Consequently, we have maximum flexibility in the quantum optical circuits that we will be able to construct.

Using a collinear nonclassical interferometer[7] and fiber coupled detectors, we were able to observe a "Hong-Ou-Mandel" dip (HOM)[8] with 90% visibility using 0.36 nm bandwidth (FWHM) filters. Calculations show that the remaining 10% visibility can almost entirely be accounted for by uncompensated longitudinal walkoff. Implementation of walkoff compensation will allow higher bandwidths to be collected and a corresponding increase in photon counting rates achieved.

We have also observed a 80.4%-visible spatially nondegenerate HOM, achieved using fiber coupling to produce high quality spatial modes. The remaining 20% visibility is probably due to mode mismatch, which can be compensated by optimizing the experimental geometry.

Regardless of the exact gate configuration implemented, it is necessary to fully characterize the gate performance. This can be achieved using quantum state tomography of the output qubits[9] enabling quantum process tomography on the gate.[10] Process tomography completely characterizes both the coherent and decohering elements of the gate's transfer function. For the CCNOT described here, the qubits are encoded in photon polarization, so these methods involve preparing identical ensembles of particular quantum states and measuring the Stokes parameters of the photons involved before and after the gate.[10]

Measuring the Stokes parameters on an ensemble requires collecting a large amount of photon statistics, this underscores the necessity of a bright source. Furthermore, for both accuracy and speed, it is highly desirable to automate the tomography, since the measurement process involves repeated (and preferably rapid) accurate setting of the optical axes of a number of quarter and half wave plates. We have developed an automated system to allow complete characterization of the CCNOT or any other gate.

3 Conclusion

We have developed practical source and circuit technology towards implementation of a coincidence-basis CNOT gate using linear optics elements. By varying the phase matching conditions in SPDC and using fiber optics, we have been able to achieve both high brightness and good mode quality. The gate is presently under construction, but the key element of high visibility nonclassical interference has been demonstrated in a number of experimental configurations. The ability to accurately and quickly analyze gate function has been developed.

This work was supported by the Australian Research Council and the US Army Research Office.

References

1. K. J. Resch *et al.*, Phys. Rev. Lett. **87**, 123603 (2001).
2. E. Knill, R. Laflamme and G. J. Milburn, Nature **409**, 46, (2001).
3. T. C. Ralph *et al.*, Phys. Rev. A **65**, 062324 (2002).
4. J. C. Howell *et al.*, Phys. Rev. Lett. **88**, 030401 (2002).
5. C. Kurtsiefer *et al.*, Phys. Rev. A **64**, 023802 (2001).
6. S. Takeuchi, Opt. Lett. **26**, 843 (2001); C. Kurtsiefer *et al.*, J. Mod. Opt. **48**, 1997 (2001).
7. Y. H. Shih *et al.*, Phys. Rev. A **50**, 23 (1994).
8. C. K. Hong *et al.*, Phys. Rev. Lett, **59**, 2044 (1987).
9. A. G. White *et al.*, Phys. Rev. Lett. **83**, 3103 (1999).
10. I. L. Chuang and M. A. Nielsen, J. Mod. Opt. **44**, 2455 (1997).

Part V

Spin-Based Quantum Computation

SPIN SQUEEZING VIA CONTINUOUS QND FEEDBACK

L. K. THOMSEN AND H. M. WISEMAN
Centre for Quantum Dynamics, School of Science, Griffith University, Brisbane, Queensland 4111, Australia.
E-mail: l.thomsen@sct.gu.edu.au, h.wiseman@mailbox.gu.edu.au

S. MANCINI
INFM, Dipartimento di Fisica, Università di Camerino, I-62032 Camerino, Italy.
E-mail: s.mancini@campus.unicam.it

Conditional spin squeezing can be achieved by continuous quantum-nondemolition measurement of an atomic sample. We show that simultaneous feedback of the measurement results can control the quantum state such that the squeezing becomes unconditional. For very strong cavity coupling, the squeezing approaches the Heisenberg limit. Squeezing is also produced at weaker couplings and even in free space, thus presenting a simple experimental test for quantum feedback.

1 Introduction

There have been many recent proposals for creating the quantum correlations between atoms that characterizes spin squeezing, of which, some are schemes based on quantum nondemolition (QND) measurements.[1] These schemes, since they are determined by measurement, represent conditional squeezing of the atomic ensembles. However, it would be preferable to develop unconditional, i.e., deterministically reproducible, squeezing, especially in regard to the field of quantum information. It would be ideal to prepare the same squeezed spin state regardless of the measurement record.

In our scheme we suggest that unconditional spin squeezing can be achieved via continuous feedback of the QND measurement results.[2] The scheme involves monitoring the output of a probe field sensitive to atoms in a particular internal state. This will conditionally squeeze the collective angular momentum of the sample. The results of this measurement are then used to drive the system into the unconditional squeezed state, by continuously shifting the mean collective angular momentum vector to a fixed direction. In this sense it is a continuous (with coherent feedback) version of the alternating measurement and incoherent feedback scheme presented by Mølmer for the production of sub-Poissonian number correlations.[3]

2 QND Feedback Scheme

The feedback scheme is based on a QND measurement of the total population difference between two internal states $|1\rangle$ and $|2\rangle$, i.e., the collective angular momentum operator J_z. In general, the interaction of a single atom with a far-detuned probe laser field is $\hbar\Omega^2(j_z+\frac{1}{2})/4\Delta$, where Ω is the Rabi frequency,

Δ is the detuning. Now the probe could be set up as either a cavity field or a free space field, and as discussed later, the type of interaction leads to different limiting values for the squeezing.

In both cases, the deterministic evolution of the system of N atoms due to this type of interaction is given by the same expression.[4] It is

$$\dot{\rho} = M\mathcal{D}[J_z]\rho, \tag{1}$$

where $\mathcal{D}[r]\rho \equiv r\rho r^\dagger - (r^\dagger r\rho + \rho r^\dagger r)/2$. For the cavity situation $M = 8\chi^2 P/\hbar\omega\kappa^2$ where $\chi = g^2/4\Delta$, g is the one-photon Rabi frequency, and κ is the cavity decay rate, while for free space $M = \theta^2 P/\hbar\omega$ where $\theta = \hbar\omega\gamma^2/8A\Delta I_s$, γ is the atomic linewidth, A is the cross-sectional area, and I_s is the saturation intensity. For both, P and ω are the probe laser power and frequency.

The QND measurement of J_z is effected by the homodyne detection of the output probe field. The conditioned evolution of the system due to this measurement is $d\rho_c(t) = M\mathcal{D}[J_z]\rho_c dt + \sqrt{M}dW(t)\mathcal{H}[J_z]\rho_c$, where $dW(t)$ is an infinitesimal Wiener increment. The corresponding photocurrent is $I_c(t) = 2\sqrt{M}\left\langle J_z\right\rangle_c + \zeta(t)$, where $\zeta(t) = dW(t)/dt$. This evolution causes a decrease in the variance of J_z (i.e., spin squeezing), as well as a stochastic shift of the mean J_z away from its initial value of zero. This shift is equal to

$$d\left\langle J_z\right\rangle_c = 2\sqrt{M}dW(t)(\Delta J_z)_c^2 \approx 2\sqrt{M}I_c(t)dt\left\langle J_z^2\right\rangle_c, \tag{2}$$

where the approximation assumes that $\left\langle J_z\right\rangle_c = 0$, which will be relevant when the feedback is in place. The average or unconditioned evolution, Eq. (1), is simply recovered by taking the ensemble average of all possible conditioned states, i.e., $\rho(t) = \mathrm{E}[\rho_c(t)]$. This leads to a spin state with J_z variance equal to $J/2$. In other words, the unmonitored measurement does not affect J_z and the squeezed character of the individual conditioned states is lost.

To retain the reduced fluctuations of J_z in the average evolution, we feed back the measurement results to continuously drive the system into the $\left\langle J_z\right\rangle_c = 0$ squeezed state. The idea is to cancel the stochastic shift of $\left\langle J_z\right\rangle_c$ due to the measurement. This requires a feedback Hamiltonian of the form

$$H_{\mathrm{fb}}(t) = \lambda(t)I_c(t)J_y/\sqrt{M}, \tag{3}$$

where $\lambda(t)$ is a time-varying feedback strength. Applying quantum feedback theory[5] to find the total stochastic master equation, we can calculate the conditioned shift of the mean J_z due to the feedback. Again using the assumption that $\left\langle J_z\right\rangle_c = 0$ we have

$$d\left\langle J_z\right\rangle_{\mathrm{fb}} \approx -\lambda(t)I_c(t)dt\left\langle J_x\right\rangle_c/\sqrt{M}. \tag{4}$$

Since the idea is to produce $\left\langle J_z\right\rangle_c = 0$ via the feedback, the approximations above and in Eq. (2) apply and we find that the required feedback strength is $\lambda(t) = 2M\left\langle J_z^2\right\rangle_c/\left\langle J_x\right\rangle_c$. Based on this assumption that the feedback works, we can also find an approximate analytical expression for $\lambda(t)$:[4]

$$\lambda(t) \approx Me^{Mt/2}(1 + NMt)^{-1}. \tag{5}$$

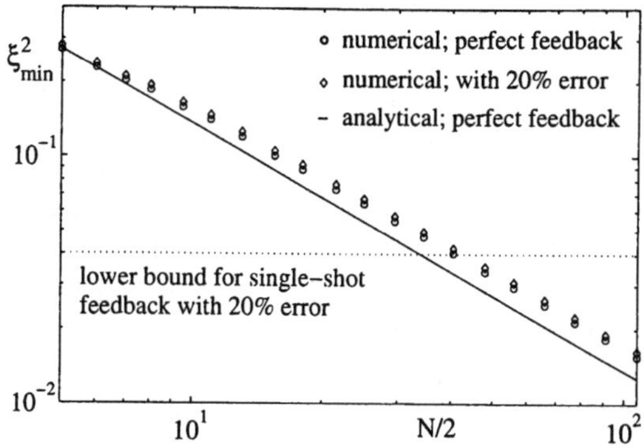

Figure 1. Squeezing parameter minimum. The numerical results with $\lambda(t)$ given by Eq. (5) (circles) and $\lambda(t) \times 120\%$ (diamonds) approach $3.33/N$ and $3.49/N$ respectively. The dotted line is the lower-bound for single-shot feedback with a 20% error, while the solid line is the analytical expression Eq. (8).

The total unconditioned evolution for our continuous QND measurement and feedback scheme is given by the master equation[5]

$$\dot{\rho} = M\mathcal{D}[J_z]\rho - i\lambda(t)[J_y, J_z\rho + \rho J_z] + \lambda(t)^2\mathcal{D}[J_y]\rho/M. \tag{6}$$

The terms in this equation describe, respectively, the measurement back-action, the feedback driving, and the noise introduced by the feedback.

We can now determine, both analytically and numerically, the degree of squeezing produced by this scheme. For our model, the spin squeezing parameter of Sørensen and co-workers[6] becomes

$$\xi_z^2 = N\langle J_z^2\rangle / \langle J_x\rangle^2 \simeq \lambda(t)N/2M\langle J_x\rangle \approx e^{Mt}(1+NMt)^{-1}, \tag{7}$$

which is less than one if J_z is squeezed. This has a minimum at $t_* \approx 1/M$ of

$$\xi^2_{\text{min}} \approx e/N, \quad N \gg 1. \tag{8}$$

Thus, the minimum attainable squeezing parameter asymptotically approaches an inverse dependence on the sample size, i.e., the Heisenberg limit.[7]

Numerical solution of the master equation (6) allows us to obtain exact values for the squeezing parameter and its minimum, which is plotted in Fig. 1 along with Eq. (8). The analytical coefficient ($e \approx 2.72$) represents an error of $\sim 18\%$ compared to the numerical fit ($3.33/N$), however the N^{-1} scaling is confirmed. Figure 1 also shows our scheme, as opposed to a single-shot method, is very robust to any experimental errors in the feedback strength. For the latter approach, a relative error of ϵ in the feedback strength gives an error of $(\Delta J_z^{\text{err}})^2 \sim \epsilon^2 N/4$, which will dominate the total variance for $N \gg 1$. Thus ξ^2_{min} will have a lower bound of ϵ^2, and will never scale as N^{-1}. On the other hand, as shown in Fig. 1, a large (20%) error in $\lambda(t)$ for continuous feedback does not affect the N^{-1} scaling.

3 Atom losses

Experimentally, the limit to squeezing will most likely be dominated by spontaneous atom losses due to absorption of QND probe light. In terms of the measurement strength M, the total number of atoms lost by time t is $\Delta N = \alpha MNt$,[4] where $\alpha = \kappa\gamma/g^2$ for the cavity interaction and $16\pi^2 A/\lambda^2$ (λ is the probe wavelength) for free space. Since, from Eq. (5), the time to reach an arbitrary amount of squeezing is $t \sim 1/NM\xi^2$, we find that $\Delta N \sim \alpha/\xi^2$. Now, the maximum number of atoms that can be lost without destroying a given amount of squeezing scales as $\Delta N_{\max} \sim (N\xi^2)\ln(1/\xi^2)$.[7] So to achieve that level of squeezing we need $\Delta N \sim \Delta N_{\max}$, which gives

$$\xi^2 \sim \sqrt{\alpha/N}. \tag{9}$$

To produce any squeezing we therefore require $\alpha < N$, for $\xi^2 \sim 1/\sqrt{N}$ we need $\alpha \sim 1$, and for the Heisenberg limit we need $\alpha \sim 1/N$.

For the cavity interaction the requirement for Heisenberg limited squeezing becomes $g^2 \sim N\kappa\gamma$, which is the very strong coupling regime. As found by André and Lukin,[7] $\xi^2 \sim 1/\sqrt{N}$ squeezing will be observed for $g^2 \sim \kappa\gamma$, and the generation of any squeezing, i.e., $\xi^2 < 1$, will be observed for $g^2 N > \kappa\gamma$. As might be expected, the free space model will not reach the Heisenberg limit, which requires an unrealistic $A \sim \lambda^2/16\pi^2 N$. The limiting value for free space squeezing is near $1/\sqrt{N}$, since this would be produced if $A \sim \lambda^2/16\pi^2$, and to achieve any squeezing we only require $A < N\lambda^2/16\pi^2$. So for the free space regime we still expect a significant amount of squeezing to be possible.

Acknowledgments

We wish to thank Klaus Mølmer and Eugene Polzik for useful discussions.

References

1. A. Kuzmich, L. Mandel, and N. P. Bigelow, Phys. Rev. Lett. **85**, 1594 (2000); L.-M. Duan, *et al.*, Phys. Rev. Lett. **85**, 5643 (2000); D. A. R. Dalvit, J. Dziarmaga, and R. Onofrio, Phys. Rev. A **65**, 053620 (2002).
2. L. K. Thomsen, S. Mancini, and H. M. Wiseman, Phys. Rev. A **65**, 061801(R) (2002).
3. K. Mølmer, Eur. Phys. J. D **5**, 301 (1999).
4. L. K. Thomsen, S. Mancini, and H. M. Wiseman, quant-ph/0208162.
5. H. M. Wiseman, Phys. Rev. A **49**, 2133 (1994); **49**, 5159(E) (1994); **50**, 4428(E) (1994).
6. A. Sørensen, *et al.*, Nature **409**, 63 (2001).
7. A. André and M. D. Lukin, Phys. Rev. A **65**, 053819 (2002).

PAVING THE ROAD FOR AN ALL-OPTICAL SPIN-BASED QUANTUM COMPUTER

E. PAZY,[1,2] E. BIOLATTI,[2,3] I. D'AMICO,[2] P. ZANARDI,[2] F. ROSSI[2,3]
[1]*Ben-Gurion University of the Negev, Beer-Sheva 84105 Israel*
E-mail: epazy@bgumail.bgu.ac.il
[2]*Institute for Scientific Interchange (ISI), Villa Gualino, Viale Settimio Severo 65, I-10133 Torino, Italy*
[3]*Dipartimento di Fisica, Politecnico di Torino, C.so Duca degli Abruzzi 24, I-10129 Torino, Italy*

T. CALARCO,[4,5] AND P. ZOLLER[4]
[4]*Institute for Theoretical Physics, University of Innsbruck, A-6020 Innsbruck, Austria,*
[5]*ECT, I-38050 Villazzano (TN), Italy*

Interband optical excitations in semiconductor quantum dots can be manipulated by ultrafast laser pulses. As such they are natural candidates for optical-based implementation schemes of quantum computation. The main drawback in such schemes is the unavoidable coupling to the lattice environment i.e., phonons. In this paper we shall present an optically-based implementation scheme which largely overcomes the phonon decoherence problem by using the electronic spin degrees of freedom as qubits and the optically-excited charge degrees of freedom as auxiliary states to implement the required quantum gates and final state measurement.

1 Ideal model

1.1 Quantum register

Semiconductor quantum dot (QD) based implementation schemes for quantum computation hold great promise, due to recent advances in nanostructure fabrication and characterization and to the possibility of integrating them into existing computational devices. In such semiconducting systems the charge carriers are confined in all spatial dimensions, giving rise to a discrete spectrum which manifests itself in a sharp photo luminescence spectrum. For this reason QDs are also refereed to as "artificial atoms". It therefore seems natural to try to incorporate into QD implementation schemes many of the useful techniques employed in the field of quantum optics, in which admirable progress has been made. As we shall show one has to take care in using this naive analogy in considering solid-state QIP schemes, since there are many modifications arising from the nature of the underlaying lattice in semiconducting materials, i.e., electronic band structure, phonons and anisotropy.

Coherent manipulation of excitons in quantum dots has been recently observed experimentally,[1] fulfilling the necessary requirements for quantum information processing (QIP). It has been proposed to use these excitons as qubits,[2] but their coherent oscillations are highly susceptible to decoherence, whereas the spin degree of freedom of an excess conduction electron in a QD enjoys relatively long coherence time. In order to reduce decoherence rates we propose using the spin of an excess electron confined to a QD as the qubit degree of freedom.[a] Our quantum register consists of an array of GaAs-based self-assembled[b] QDs: each QD containing one excess conduction electron whose spin degree of freedom defines the qubit states $|0\rangle, |1\rangle$.

1.2 Pauli-blocking based switching

We aim to implement the needed QIP manipulations — gating and final measurement — by coupling the spin to ultra-fast laser pulses. In order to couple to the spin degree of freedom we employ the Pauli-blocking effect, which has been experimentally verified in QDs.[3] The spin conditional switching of charged excitonic states is obtained in the following way: by shining a σ^+ polarized laser pulse on the QD, due to the Pauli exclusion principle a electron-heavy hole pair is created only if the excess electron — already present in the QD — has a spin projection 1/2. Thus with a π-pulse we obtain an exciton conditional to the spin state (qubit): $\alpha|0\rangle + \beta|1\rangle \to \alpha|0\rangle + \beta|x^-\rangle$, where the charged exciton state $|x^-\rangle$ plays the role of an auxiliary state needed to obtain the desired phase, i.e., it will be annihilated via a second laser pulse once the required gate operation has been completed.

Once we have the ability to selectively, depending on the spin state of the excess electron, excite an auxiliary exciton we can implement quantum gates as well as the final measurement process via the quantum jump method. We start by giving examples how this can be achieved in an ideal case with no lattice-induced effects and discuss the modifications in the next section. A two-qubit phase gate is obtained using the following effective Hamiltonian (for details see Ref. 7)

$$H_{\text{eff}} = \hbar \sum_{\nu=a,b} \left[\frac{\Omega(t)}{2} \left(|1\rangle_\nu \langle x^-| \right) + \text{h.c.} \right] + \Delta E_{ab} |x^-\rangle_a \langle x^-| \otimes |x^-\rangle_b \langle x^-|, \quad (1)$$

where this Hamiltonian describes two neighboring QDs, denoted $\{a, b\}$, coupled to a laser pulse with Rabi frequency $\Omega(t) = 2\mu^{eh} E(t)/\hbar$ and biexcitonic shift,[2] ΔE_{ab}. Corrections to this effective Hamiltonian due to higher energy levels in the QD can be neglected under the constraint Ω, Δ, $\Delta E_{ab}/\hbar$, and the Fourier width of the pulse τ^{-1} to be much smaller than the QD level spacing ($\approx$ 25 meV). Using the the above Hamiltonian and the following pulse sequence: (i) apply a π-pulse to the two QDs, (ii) wait for time $\Delta t \propto \theta/\Delta E_{ab}$

[a] This was first proposed in the seminal paper by Loss and DiVincenzo,[4] but they considered electrical modulated gating and QDs.

[b] Using self-assembled QDs offers us the ability to address each dot individually in an energy selective manner, since there is an inherent fluctuation in the size of the QDs due to the growth technique.

to accumulate the phase θ, and (iii) bring the QDs to their original state by applying a further π-pulse, one obtains the required two-qubit phase gate.

The final state measurement, i.e., measuring the spin state of the excess electron in the QD, is obtained by the quantum jump technique (e.g. Ref. 5): when the original state of the spin in a QD is $|1\rangle$ a fluorescence pattern is obtained. Whereas the state $|0\rangle$ is completely decoupled from the laser field, since it Pauli blocks exciton creation. The fluorescence is governed by[6]

$$\kappa_{rec}\tilde{\rho}^{(0)}_{x^-x^-}(t|t_0) = -\frac{d}{dt}\left[\tilde{\rho}^{(0)}_{11}(t|t_0) + \tilde{\rho}^{(0)}_{x^-x^-}(t|t_0)\right], \tag{2}$$

where $\tilde{\rho}^{(0)}$ is the reduced density matrix for a two-level system, $|1\rangle, |x^-\rangle$ in the sub-space in which no photons have been emitted, since t_0 and $\kappa_{rec} \approx 10^9 sec^{-1}$ is the recombination rate. Equation (2) describes the decay of the trace of $\tilde{\rho}$, i.e., the probability of emitting a photon.

The optical implementation of a single-qubit gate is a bit more elaborate and requires an energetically inverted heavy/light hole structure, as can be obtained in II-VI semiconductors grown under strain. Details regarding the single-qubit implementation can be found in Ref. 7.

2 Lattice based complications

We have shown how the problem of decoherence can be partially overcome by utilizing the spin as our quantum memory, but there is an inherent anisotropy due to the underlying lattice which induces a complicated valance band structure involving heavy and light hole mixing. A realistic QD will exhibit mixing of the heavy and light hole states, which we incorporated in our model by adding a $\varepsilon|0\rangle_\nu\langle x^-|$ term to the effective Hamiltonian, Eq. (1). This term invalidates the assumption of perfect Pauli blocking with σ^+ light and can be viewed as a rotation by an angle $-\varepsilon$ in the $\{|0\rangle, |1\rangle\}$ space. The mixing parameter ε will typically be of the order of the lattice constant, a, to a typical length scale defining the QD in our case $a/L \approx 0.1$ where L is the size of the dot in the growth direction. In Fig. 1 we show numerical results verifying the possibility of using the modified effective Hamiltonian for performing a two-qubit phase gate. The simulation was performed using an adiabatic procedure involving a detuned laser pulse, with a Gaussian shape both for the Rabi frequency $\Omega(t) = \Omega_0 \exp(-t^2/\tau_\Omega^2)$ and for the detuning $\Delta(t) = \Delta_0[1 - \exp(-t^2/\tau_\Delta^2)]$. It should be mentioned that the same adiabatic procedure exploited in this simulation can also be used to reduce unwanted decoherence of excitons during the gating operations,[8] and to perform single-qubit operations.[7] Introducing mixing to the quantum-jump measuring techniques requires one to treat a three-level lambda configuration in which the measurement is done by distinguishing the photon emission obtained when the initial state is $|1\rangle$ from the one obtained when starting in the $|0\rangle$ state.[8] In constructing single-qubit operations one is confronted by complications due

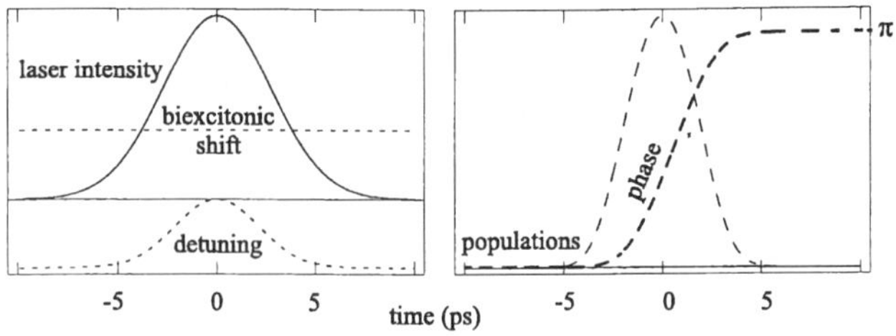

Figure 1. Left panel: pulse shapes and biexcitonic shift. Right panel: biexcitonic population obtained starting from an initial state $|11\rangle$ (dashed line), $|00\rangle$, $|01\rangle$ or $|10\rangle$ (indistinguishable on the plot scale – solid line), and accumulated phase. Parameters: $\Delta E_{ab} = 3\,\text{meV}$, $\Delta_0 = \Delta E_{ab}/\hbar$, $\tau_\Omega = 3.86\,\text{ps}$, $\tau_\Delta = 3\,\text{ps}$, $\delta = 1\,\text{meV}$ and a peak Rabi frequency $\hbar\Omega_0 = 8\,\text{meV}$.

to an inherent anisotropy in semiconducting QDs due to the existence of a preferred direction (the QD symmetry axis), the growth direction. Optical single-qubit operations requires shining light in the in-plane direction, which can be done in a waveguide configuration.[9]

3 Summary

We introduced a proposal for all optical spin-based QIP based on electrons confined to QDs. We emphasized the specific problems arising for the underlying semiconducting lattice and hinted at how they can be overcome, making it possible to successfully bring together ideas from spintronics and optoelectronics and merge them into an ultrfast spin-based QIP implementation scheme.

References

1. T. H. Stievater *et al.*, Phys. Rev. Lett. **87**, 133603 (2001); H. Kamada, *ibid* **87**, 246401 (2001).
2. E. Biolatti *et al.*, Phys. Rev. Lett. **85**, 5647 (2000); E. Biolatti *et al.*, Phys. Rev. B **65**, 075306 (2002).
3. N. H. Bonadeo *et al.*, Phys. Rev. Lett. **81**, 2759 (1998); G. Chen *et al.*, Science **289**, 1906 (2000).
4. D. Loss and D. P. DiVincenzo, Phys. Rev. A **57**, 120 (1998).
5. A. Imamoglu, Fortschr. Phys. **48**, 987 (2000).
6. P. Zoller *et al.*, Phys. Rev. A **35**, 198 (1986).
7. E.Pazy, *et al.*, to appear in J. Supercond.
8. T. Calarco *et al.*, work in progress.
9. J. S. Weiner *et al.*, Appl. Phys. Lett **47**, 664 (1985).

EXPLORING LARGE NUCLEAR SPIN SYSTEMS IN THE SOLID STATE USING NMR

CHANDRASEKHAR RAMANATHAN, HYUNGJOON CHO, PAOLA CAPPELLARO, GREGORY S. BOUTIS, DAVID G. CORY

Department of Nuclear Engineering, Massachusetts Institute of Technology, Cambridge, MA 02139

E-mail: sekhar@mit.edu

In this paper we illustrate the dynamics of a solid-state spin system in two regimes: in the short-time, few-spin limit when evolving under a non-secular Hamiltonian, and in the the long-time, many-spin limit when evolving under the secular dipolar Hamiltonian of the spin system. In the short-time limit we describe the creation of spin states containing multiple quantum coherences using solid-state nuclear magnetic resonance techniques, and show how the properties of these states can be inferred by encoding them in different basis representations. We also explore the sensitivity of these states to noise and decoherence. In the long-time limit we measure the rate of spin diffusion of single and two-spin correlations in a single crystal of calcium fluoride.

1 Introduction

In the approach to designing and implementing a scalable quantum computer, it is essential that we develop the ability to accurately perform desired unitary transformations in a large Hilbert space, as well as understand the sensitivity to decoherence of states in this space. The nuclear spins in a dielectric solid such as calcium fluoride have very long spin-lattice relaxation times, ranging from minutes to days depending on the concentration of paramagnetic impurities present in the crystal. It is therefore possible to investigate the dynamical behavior of these spins under the action of their mutual dipolar couplings and applied radio frequency perturbations, while they are essentially isolated from their environment. Average Hamiltonian theory provides a framework within which we can design experiments in which the internal Hamiltonian of the spins is modulated by radio frequency pulses so that the spins appear to evolve under a suitably designed effective Hamiltonian.[1]

2 Growth of multiple quantum coherences

In a strong magnetic field ($B_0\hat{z}$), an N spin-1/2 system has 2^N stationary states. The magnetic quantum number of theses states is given by $M_z = \sum_i m_{zi} = (n_{|+1/2\rangle} - n_{|-1/2\rangle})/2$, where $m_{zi} = \pm 1/2$ is the eigenvalue of the ith spin in the system. The difference in M_z values between the two levels connected by a transition is referred to as the *coherence number*. However, it is also useful to discuss multiple quantum coherences for states of a system.[2,3] When the state is expressed in the eigenbasis of the system, the presence of

Table 1. Description of the MQ experiment in the z and x bases.

	z basis	x basis
initial state	I_z	$-\frac{i}{2}\left[I_x^+ - I_x^-\right]$
initial coherence number	0	± 1
MQ Hamiltonian	$\sum_{i<j} d_{ij}\left[I_i^+ I_j^+ + I_i^- I_j^-\right]$	$\sum_{i<j} d_{ij}\left[\{2I_{xi}I_{xj} - \frac{1}{2}(I_{xi}^+ I_{xj}^- + I_{xi}^- I_{xj}^+)\} - \frac{1}{2}\{I_{xi}^+ I_{xj}^+ + I_{xi}^- I_{xj}^-\}\right]$
coherence number selection rule	± 2	$0, \pm 2$
coherences	even	odd

a non-zero matrix element $\langle z_i|\rho|z_j\rangle$, indicates the presence of an n-quantum coherence, where $n = M_z(z_j) - M_z(z_i)$. Since $M_z = \sum_i m_{zi}$ is a good quantum number, we use a collective rotation about the axis of quantization, $\sum_i I_z^i$, to characterize it,

$$\langle z_i|\exp(-i\phi\sum_i I_z^i)\rho\exp(+i\phi\sum_i I_z^i)|z_j\rangle = \exp(in\phi)\langle z_i|\rho|z_j\rangle \ . \qquad (1)$$

A generalized coherence number reports on the response of the system to any collective rotation of the spins (about the x axis for example), which is equivalent to expressing the state of the spins in a basis in which the apparent axis of quantization is given by the axis of rotation, and can be obtained from the eigenbasis via a similarity transformation. By encoding the MQ coherences in different, non-commuting bases, we gain access to more information about the state of the spin system.

In our experiments, the homonuclear dipolar Hamiltonian of the spins in a solid is modulated so that the effective Hamiltonian corresponds to a double quantum (DQ) Hamiltonian $\overline{\mathcal{H}} = \sum_{i<j} d_{ij}(I_i^+ I_j^+ + I_i^- I_j^-)$ (when expressed in the z-basis), where d_{ij} is the strength of the dipolar coupling between the spins i and j. We allow the spin system to evolve under this Hamiltonian for varying durations, and then encode the resulting states produced in either the x or z basis. Table 1 shows the initial state, Hamiltonian, and selection rules for this experiment, starting from a thermal equilibrium state in the two bases.. Thus, starting from an initial Zeeman state, we see that under the DQ Hamiltonian only even-order coherences in the z basis and only odd-order coherences in the x basis are produced. Figure 1(a) show the growth of multiple quantum coherences in the two bases. The even and odd selectivity can clearly be seen.

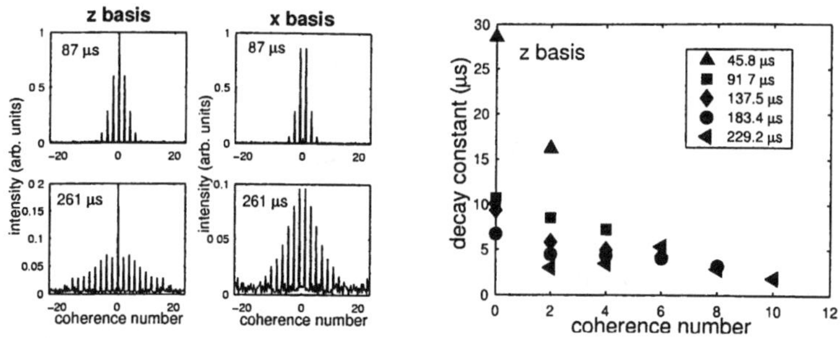

Figure 1. (a) z-basis and x-basis coherences observed after evolution under the DQ Hamiltonian for $87\,\mu s$ and $261\,\mu s$, respectively. The coherences are seen to grow in both bases. (b) Decay of z-basis coherences under the secular dipolar Hamiltonian. The decay rates change depending on the length of time the DQ Hamiltonian is allowed to evolve before the decay is observed.

3 Decay of multiple quantum coherences

We also measured the rate at which the multiple quantum coherences decay under the secular dipolar Hamiltonian. The decay was measured following evolution of the spin system under the DQ Hamiltonian for differing amounts of time ranging from $45.8\,\mu s$ to $229.2\,\mu s$. The secular dipolar Hamiltonian does not mix coherence numbers, so each of the coherence orders should decay independently.

The results are shown in Figure 1(b). It can be seen that although the decay rates initially vary with coherence number at short times, this variation is damped out following long evolution under the DQ Hamiltonian. Coherence number becomes increasingly inadequate to characterize the decay properties of the spin system. The zero-quantum subspace is not a true decoherence free subspace (DFS) in the presence of strong spin-spin coupling.

4 Spin diffusion

Spin diffusion is the spatial transport of spin coherence due to the flip-flop term, $I_+^i I_-^j + I_-^i I_+^j$, in the homonuclear dipolar Hamiltonian. The concept of spin diffusion was introduced by Bloembergen in 1949 to account for the unexpectedly fast relaxation times found in paramagnetic doped crystals.[4]

Figure 2 shows the experimental data obtained for Zeeman and dipolar diffusion, for particular values of the gradient. Dipolar diffusion is seen to be significantly faster than Zeeman diffusion. Table 2 summarizes the experimental results and compares them to theoretical predictions. Although the Zeeman diffusion measurements agree with existing theories, there is a significant discrepancy between the dipolar diffusion measurement and theory.

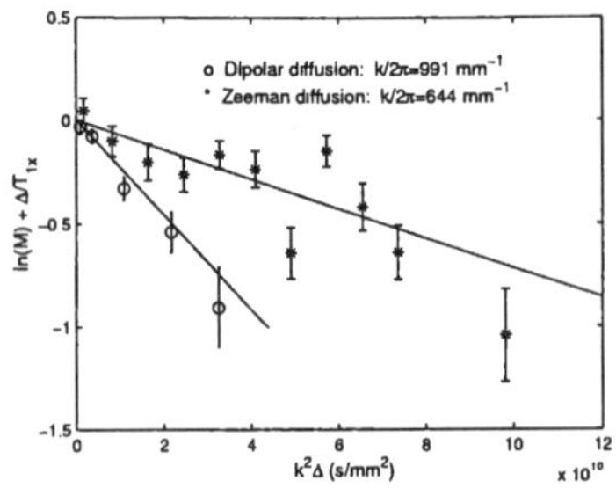

Figure 2. Decay of the measured signal due to diffusion under a magnetic field grating. The data are fit to $M = M_0 \exp(-k_m^2 D\Delta) \exp(-\Delta/T_{1x})$, where Δ is the time during which spin diffusion occurs, and T_{1x} is the relevant spin lattice relaxation time (T_1 for Zeeman order, T_{1D} for dipolar order). Only a single value of k_m is shown to reduce clutter in the figure, but the fit shown was performed with respect to the full data set.

Table 2. Summary of the experimental and theoretical results for spin diffusion

This measurement	[001]	[111]
$D_E^{\|\|}$ [x 10^{-12}cm^2/s]	29 ± 3	33 ± 4
$D_Z^{\|\|}$ [x 10^{-12}cm^2/s]	6.4 ± 0.9	4.4 ± 0.5
Theoretical studies of $D_E^{\|\|}$ and $D_Z^{\|\|}$		
$D_E^{\|\|}$ [5] [x 10^{-12}cm^2/s]	8.53	7.43
$D_E^{\|\|}$ [6] [x 10^{-12}cm^2/s]	13.3	-
$D_Z^{\|\|}$ [5] [x 10^{-12}cm^2/s]	6.98	4.98
$D_Z^{\|\|}$ [6] [x 10^{-12}cm^2/s]	7.43	-
$D_Z^{\|\|}$ [7] [x 10^{-12}cm^2/s]	8.22	6.71

Acknowledgments

We would like to thank Dr. Josesph Emerson and Dr. Timothy Havel for illuminating discussions. This research was funded by DARPA DSO.

References

1. U. Haeberlen and J. S. Waugh, *Phys. Rev.* **175**, 453 (1968).
2. W.S. Warren, D.P. Weitekamp, and A. Pines, *J. Chem. Phys.* **73** 2084 (1980).
3. Y.-S. Yen and A. Pines, *J. Chem. Phys.* **78**, 3579 (1983).
4. N. Bloembergen, *Physica* **15**, 386 (1949).
5. P. Borckmans and W. Walgraef, *Physica* **68**, 157 (1973).
6. C. Tang and J. S. Waugh, *Phys. Rev. B.* **45**, 748 (1992).
7. A. G. Redfield and W. N. Yu, *Phys. Rev.* **169**, 443 (1968), **177**, 1018 (1969).

PSEUDO-DIGITAL QUBITS: A GENERAL APPROACH

MARK FRIESEN, ROBERT JOYNT, AND M. A. ERIKSSON
Physics Department, University of Wisconsin-Madison, Madison, WI 53706, USA
E-mail: friesen@cae.wisc.edu, maeriksson@facstaff.wisc.edu

Pseudo-digital coupling has recently been proposed as a simple but robust technique for reducing gating errors in quantum dot quantum computers. Here, we discuss the technique in the context of simulations on silicon heterostructures. Additionally, we generalize and extend the pseudo-digital concept to other settings. In particular, we consider superconducting charge qubits and suggest a simple circuit for implementing dual, pseudo-digital working points.

Quantum computers are essentially analog devices. As such, errors can easily accumulate, to the point that calculations are ruined. Fortunately, large-scale computations are still feasible, due to the development of quantum error-correcting codes.[1] Nevertheless, error management remains a primary concern in the development of quantum hardware.[2] In addition to environmental influences, errors can also arise due to the imperfect implementation of quantum gates. Such errors are more likely at high clock speeds. As we shall show, hardware-based error suppression becomes the key for treating speed-induced gating errors.

Scalable devices are especially susceptible to gating errors, since large-scale applications typically need to run very fast. In this work we focus on two important scalable systems. First, we review our previous results on semiconductor quantum dot devices. Then we extend our results to superconducting qubits. Semiconductors are particularly strong candidates for scalability, because of compatibility with established microelectronics technologies. In silicon-based devices, the decoherence properties are particularly good.[3,4,5] However operating speeds must be much greater than decoherence times; for electron-spin qubits in Si quantum dots this still necessitates clock rates of order GHz.[6] At this speed, the voltage pulses used to implement gate operations can only be administered with 1% accuracy per gate, even using state-of-the-art electronics.[6] Such error rates are far above the fault-tolerance threshold.[7] To make matters worse, the response of the qubit exchange coupling J to a gate voltage pulse V is exponential in conventional gating schemes [Fig. 1(a)], so that even small errors in V induce large errors in J. We would like to modify this conventional gating architecture to enable a more digital response function for $J(V)$, so that fluctuations in V do not affect J, at least at special working points.

In Ref. 6 we described a hardware-based technique that provides such pseudo-digital working points, allowing two orders of magnitude improvements in gate error rates. In this scheme, $J(V)$ does not actually become flat (digital). Instead, it attains a maximum at a special working point. Fig-

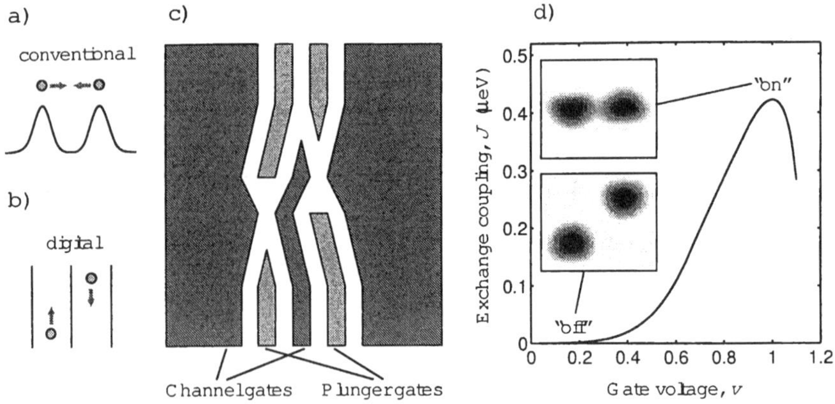

Figure 1. Pseudo-digital coupling in quantum dots. (a) In the conventional gating scheme, a quantum barrier separates the two qubits. Lowering the barrier causes electrons to move towards each other on a line. Electronic exponential tails are responsible for the exponential dependence of $J(V)$. (b) In the pseudo-digital scheme, electrons move past each other in channels. (c) The top-gate structure used in the simulations (top-view). (d) The calculated exchange coupling J as a function of plunger gate voltages V. (See Ref. 6.)

ure 1(c) gives a top-view of the improved, pseudo-digital gating architecture. The gates are to be lithographically patterned over a silicon-germanium heterostructure as described in Ref. 8. In this design, the active layer is a strained silicon quantum well, containing a controlled number of electrons. The top-gates provide lateral electrostatic confinement for forming quantum dots. The structure of Fig. 1(c) defines two coupled quantum dots, each containing a single electron. The dots are bistable, meaning that the electron can sit on either side of the dot, as controlled by the plunger gates. The main idea of the design is that electrons move within their dots in parallel channels, as in Fig. 1(b). When the electrons are at their closest approach, the exchange coupling J attains a maximum, as borne out in simulations [Fig. 1(d)].[6] The maximum of $J(V)$ serves as the "on" working point, while the exponentially small value of $J(V)$ when the qubits are well separated serves as the "off" working point.

The pseudo-digital control we have been discussing is very general, because its implementation requires only the presence of a maximum (or more generally, an extremum) in the qubit coupling J. To illustrate this point, the coupling J between two quantum dot qubits can be expressed as a function of the relative coordinates (x, y) of the two electrons [Fig. 2(a)]. At first glance, the plot suggests no obvious extrema except at the unlikely working point $x = y = 0$, corresponding to the complete overlap of the two electrons. However in the architecture of Fig. 1(c), electrons are made to move in channels, corresponding to a 1D trajectory in (x, y) (Fig. 2(a), solid line). Constraining electron motion in this way allows us to define an arbitrary local maximum,

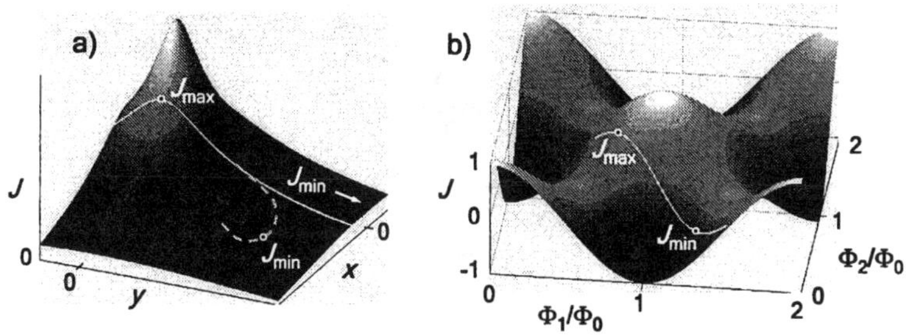

Figure 2. 1D coupling trajectories (white lines) plotted on 2D coupling-parameter space. (a) Quantum dots: x and y reflect the relative positions of the qubits, controlling the exchange coupling J. (b) Superconducting charge qubits: Φ_1 and Φ_2 reflect the magnetic flux through the two qubits, controlling the Josephson coupling.

or "on" state. (We could similarly define a pseudo-digital "off" state, with $J > 0$, using a more complicated gate geometry: Fig. 2(a), dashed line.)

So far, we have discussed pseudo-digital coupling only in the context of interactions that depend on the physical positions of the qubits. Intriguingly, this technique applies equally well to qubit interactions in which position plays no role. We consider a well known design for superconducting charge qubits (Fig. 3),[9] made up of dc-SQUIDs threaded by individually-controlled magnetic fluxes Φ_i and coupled by a common LC oscillator mode. The number of Cooper pairs on each lower island is tuned by separate voltage sources. By varying the flux, the effective Josephson coupling can be tuned on each qubit, enabling single-qubit operations. Two-qubit operations can also be accomplished by turning on the Josephson coupling in two qubits simultaneously. Under appropriate conditions,[9] the qubit coupling strength reduces to $J \propto \cos(\pi\Phi_1/\Phi_0)\cos(\pi\Phi_2/\Phi_0)$, where Φ_0 is the flux quantum. The parameters Φ_1 and Φ_2 control J, providing a natural 2D control basis for two-qubit operations [Fig. 2(b)], analogous to the (x, y) basis used for quantum dots [Fig 2(a)].

To implement a pseudo-digital coupling for the charge qubit, we now need to define a 1D trajectory through (Φ_1, Φ_2). We desire the trajectory to exhibit a local maximum J_{max} as well as a local minimum J_{min}. The ability to define arbitrary working points provides a means to compensate for device-to-device variations that may prevent working at the ideal working points. For the technique to be effective, the qubits cannot stray from their trajectories. Some uncertainty *along* the trajectory can be tolerated however–this is the main concept behind pseudo-digital control. We enforce the single-trajectory requirement using the simple circuit shown in Fig. 3. A single current source I parameterizes the trajectory between the desired working points. The regular shape of $J(\Phi_1, \Phi_2)$ in Fig. 2(b) makes it easy to identify an appropriate trajectory. In fact, a straight line in (Φ_1, Φ_2) works well. The flux

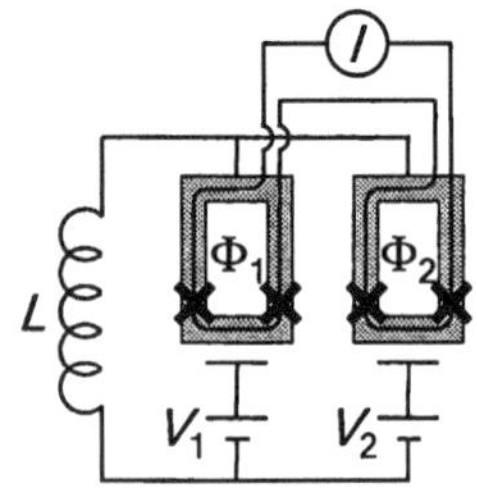

Figure 3. Superconducting charge qubits, coupled through an LC oscillator, and controlled via external fluxes Φ_1 and Φ_2 and gate voltages V_1 and V_2.[9] An additional current source is introduced to control Φ_1 and Φ_2.

through the ith qubit is generated by an external current loop, $\Phi_i = L_i I + \phi_i$, where L_i is the loop inductance and ϕ_i is a constant external-flux bias. The desired linear trajectory $\Phi_1(I) = b\Phi_2(I) + c$ can be achieved by adjusting the circuit parameters such that $L_1 = bL_2$ and $\phi_1 = b\phi_2 + c$. With this circuit, fast switching between the working points can be accomplished, without incurring significant errors. The key is to use a *single* current source to enforce the qubit coupling trajectory.

We have shown how to extend the pseudo-digital coupling scheme to superconducting charge qubits, in addition to quantum dot qubits. However the principle is very general: (1) identify a 2D coupling control space, (2) identify a suitable 1D trajectory for qubits in that control space, (3) use hardware to confine qubits to their trajectories. Indeed, many quantum settings possess the necessary degrees of freedom to implement pseudo-digital control.

References

1. J. Preskill, Proc. R. Soc. London A **454**, 385 (1998).
2. J. Levy, Phys. Rev. A **64**, 052306 (2001).
3. D. Loss and D. P. DiVincenzo, Phys. Rev. A **57**, 120 (1998).
4. B. E. Kane, Nature **393**, 133 (1998).
5. R. Vrijen, *et al.*, Phys. Rev. A **62**, 012306 (2000).
6. M. Friesen, R. Joynt, and M. A. Eriksson, quant-ph/0208105.
7. A. M. Steane, quant-ph/0207119.
8. M. Friesen, *et al.*, cond-mat/0208021.
9. Y. Makhlin, G. Schon, and A. Shnirman, Rev. Mod. Phys. **73**, 357 (2001).

INITIALIZATION AND SCALABILITY OF NMR QUANTUM COMPUTERS

MASAHIRO KITAGAWA
AKIRA KATAOKA
TAKAHIRO NISHIMURA*
Graduate School of Engineering Science, Osaka University
1–3 Machikaneyama-cho, Toyonaka, Osaka 560–8531, Japan
E-mail: kitagawa@ee.es.osaka-u.ac.jp

Bulk-ensemble quantum computation using solution NMR is so far the most successful experimental scheme to demonstrate quantum algorithms. However the lack of entanglement and scalability are often criticized. We present initialization schemes which may restore entanglement, improve the scalability, and achieve real quantum computation without exponential resources other than that of Hilbert space.

1 Introduction

Bulk-ensemble NMR quantum computation was enabled by ingenious initialization schemes which make an effective pure state[1,2,3] out of the thermal equilibrium state near the maximum entropy point. It has been so far most successful in demonstrating quantum algorithms.[4] However, the states used in NMR experiments are separable and therefore contain no entanglement[5,6] and furthermore exponentially huge physical resources such as the numbers of molecules[7] or experiments are used. In this paper, we present initialization schemes which may restore entanglement, improve the scalability, and achieve real quantum computation without exponential resources other than that of Hilbert space.

The simplest answer to this problem would be to cool all the spins down to T=0 K. Then the states of all molecular quantum computers would be initialized to $|0\rangle^{\otimes n}$. However it is not that simple. First of all, T=0 K is never reached. We need a scenario which works not only at 0 K. That is, we still need some scheme to extract the pure state signal out of the mixed states. We will start by lowering the temperature in existing initialization schemes. Secondly, if the material is simply cooled, it is frozen into a solid in which the dipolar interactions make the computational basis including $|0\rangle^{\otimes n}$ non-stationary. We have to decouple dipolar interactions by applying special pulse sequences. Alternatively we may seek the possibility of refrigerating spins without actually refrigerating materials.[8,9]

---

*NOW AT NEC CORPORATION

2 Logical Labeling with Typical Sequences

Exhaustive averaging,[3] which requires 2^n-1 experiments, is out of question from the computational complexity viewpoint, and will never be used for real quantum computation. By real quantum computation, we mean exponential speed-up over classical computation without requiring exponentially huge physical resources other than that of Hilbert space.

Logical labeling[1] also suffers from the exponentially small population of effective pure state at room temperature. However if the origin of the problem is the extremely small polarization at room temperature, it is natural to seek the possibility of improving it by lowering the temperature. We have generalized logical labeling[1] to arbitrary temperature by using typical sequences $\{|0\rangle^{\otimes np}|1\rangle^{\otimes nq}\}$ as the background (np is treated as an integer for simplicity) and the most probable state $|0\rangle^{\otimes n}$ as the signal state.[10]

Under the effective Hamiltonian of homonuclear solution NMR, the thermal equilibrium states can be well-approximated by the density operator $\rho^{\otimes n}$ with $\rho{=}p|0\rangle\langle 0|{+}q|1\rangle\langle 1|$ (*i.i.d.*) where $p{=}(1{+}\delta)/2$, $q{=}1{-}p$, $\delta{=}\tanh(\alpha)$, and $\alpha{=}\hbar\omega/2k_BT$. Unitary logical labeling transforms it into

$$\rho' = P(0)\underbrace{|0\rangle\langle 0|}_{n-m}\otimes[(1-\epsilon)\underbrace{I/2^m}_{m}+\epsilon\underbrace{|0\rangle\langle 0|}_{m}] + \sum_{a\neq 0} P(a)\underbrace{|a\rangle\langle a|}_{n-m}\otimes\underbrace{\rho_a}_{m} .$$

The first term is the conditional effective pure state and its population $P(0) > 1/\sqrt{2\pi n}$ scales very well.

Entanglement is restored if p is large enough. However, the population ϵ of the effective pure state still decreases exponentially with n. This is the limit of using a single signal state, because any state is subject to exponentially small population for increasing n at finite temperature.

Our generalization has revealed that the number of qubits available is given by $m{\approx}nH(p)$, where $H(p){=}{-}p\log p - (1{-}p)\log(1{-}p)$ is the entropy. We lose qubits by lowering the temperature. The counter-intuitive nature of logical labeling is the consequence of using the most typical states as the signal-less background.

3 Typical Sequences as Signal States

The last two considerations naturally lead to the following conclusions: (a) we should use as many signal states as possible; (b) all signal states should give the same result; and (c) the typical states should be used as signal state rather than background.[10]

Each of the typical states $\mathcal{A} = \{|0\rangle^{\otimes np}|1\rangle^{\otimes nq}\}$ has probability of $2^{-nH(p)}$, and the number of the typical states is $|\mathcal{A}| = \binom{n}{np} \approx 2^{nH(p)}/\sqrt{2\pi npq}$. If all the typical states give the same result, the signal strength is in proportion to the population of the signal states $P(x \in \mathcal{A}) = 2^{-nH(p)}|\mathcal{A}| \approx 1/\sqrt{2\pi npq}$, which scales very well.

One way of doing this is by unitary Schumacher compression[11] S which transforms the thermal equilibrium state into

$$\rho' = \sum_{x=0}^{|\mathcal{A}|-1} 2^{-nH(p)} \underbrace{|0\rangle\langle 0|}_{n[1-H(p)]} \otimes \underbrace{|x\rangle\langle x|}_{nH(p)} + \sum_{y\notin\mathcal{A}} P(y) S \underbrace{|y\rangle\langle y|}_{n} S^{\dagger}.$$

The number of qubits available is $m{\approx}n[1-H(p)]$, which is very reasonable because we gain qubits by lowering the temperature and all qubits are available in the limit of $T{=}0$.

The notion of initialization by data compression has been first presented by Schulman and Vazirani in their scalable initialization scheme.[12] However their algorithm relies on Monte Carlo simulation and therefore has not been explicitly given.

The notion itself is very natural from an information theoretical viewpoint, as shown in Fig. 1. Such a compression can be regarded as a one-to-one transformation from 2^{nH} typical states to compressed states.

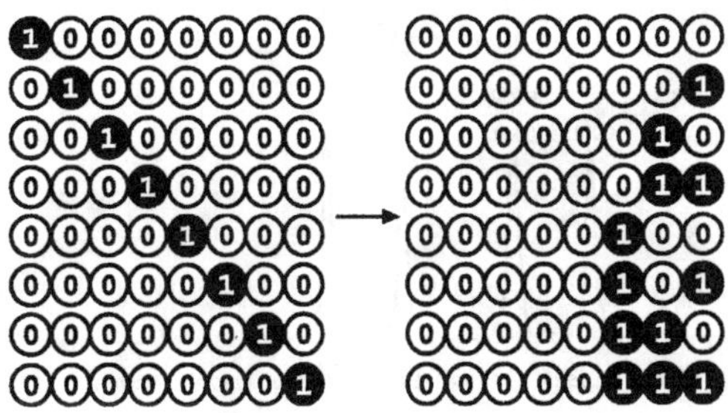

Figure 1. Initialization by compression: the typical states (left) are transformed into the compressed states (right) with common initialized substate.

4 Experimental Demonstration

We have experimentally demonstrated initialization by compression[13] using the molecules shown in Fig. 2. We have prepared the pseudo low temperature state of $n{=}4$ and $p{=}3/4$, the equal mixture of the pseudo typical states, $|0001\rangle$, $|0010\rangle$, $|0100\rangle$ and $|1000\rangle$ as shown in Fig. 3(a) by exhaustive averaging. Application of the simple compression circuit shown in Fig. 4 has transformed it into the equal mixture of $|0000\rangle$, $|0001\rangle$, $|0010\rangle$ and $|0011\rangle$ as shown in Fig. 3(b), in which the leading two qubits are successfully initialized to $|00\rangle$. However, such a compression circuit is not necessarily efficient. In general, the brute-force implementations may take $O(2^{nH})$ rather than poly(n).

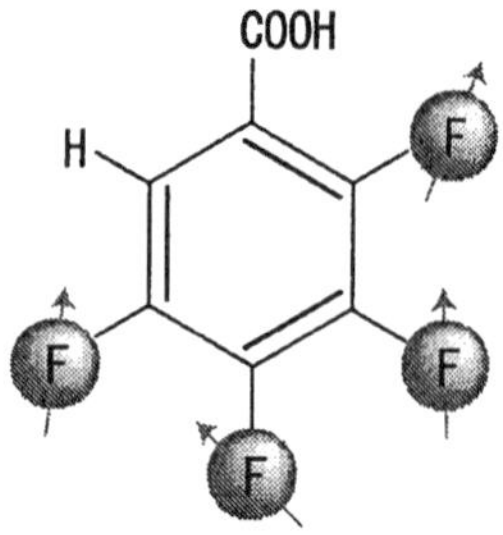

frequency [Hz]	F_1	F_2	F_3
F_0 : −18714.9	18.88	20.88	−8.50
F_1 : −21301.3		−2.62	20.17
F_2 : −13792.2			−13.53
F_3 : −11966.9			

Figure 2. Molecule for 4-qubit experiments

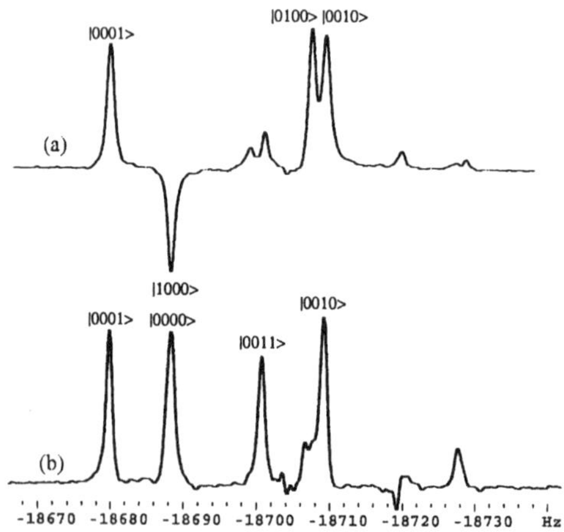

Figure 3. Initialization by compression experiment: (a) pseudo typical state, (b) compressed state

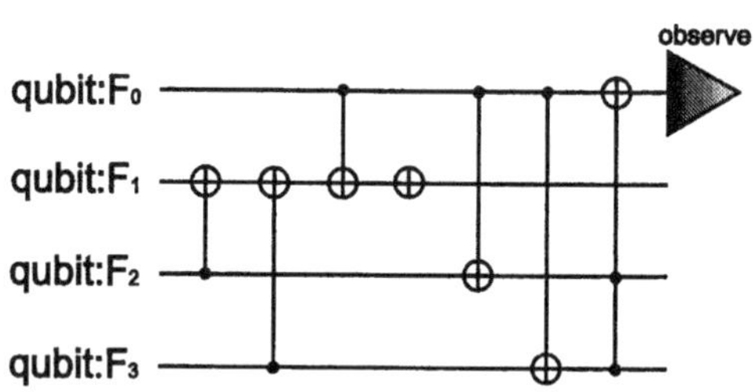

Figure 4. brute-force compression circuit

5 Efficient Initialization Scheme

The data compression circuit for initialization of NMR quantum computers is subject to the special requirements: (a) no clean qubit is initially available; (b) no state reduction by measurement is available; and (c) the total computational complexity must be poly(n). The first requirement makes the application of existing compression algorithms very difficult, because they take availability of clean workspace for granted. For example, the Schumacher compression circuit of Cleve and DiVincenzo[15] requires $2\sqrt{n} + \log(n)$ clean qubits and therefore cannot be used. The second requirement is specific to NMR.

The third requirement rejects brute-force implementations which take $O(2^n)$ steps. However, if it is applied to $\log(n)$ qubits instead of n, it completes in poly(n) steps. Therefore $\log(n)$ clean qubits may be available by pre-compression of $\log(n)/(1-H)$ qubits in $O(n^{cH/(1-H)})$ steps.

By replacing additions and comparisons which require $2\sqrt{n}$ work qubits in the enumerative coding circuit[15] with Draper's in-place additions[14] based on QFT (Quantum Fourier Transformation), we have developed an efficient initialization circuit which requires only $O(n^4)$ steps and $\log(n)$ clean ancilla qubits, as shown in Fig. 5. The clean $\log(n)$ qubits can be supplied in poly(n) steps, as discussed above. The overall scheme can be further improved to operate in $O(n^3)$ steps. However the scheme shown here is efficient enough to prove that the NMR quantum computation can be done in polynomial steps including the initialization phase and is therefore eligible for real quantum computation.

In summary, we have investigated the initialization problem of NMR quantum computers and have developed an efficient initialization scheme that enables real quantum computation using NMR.

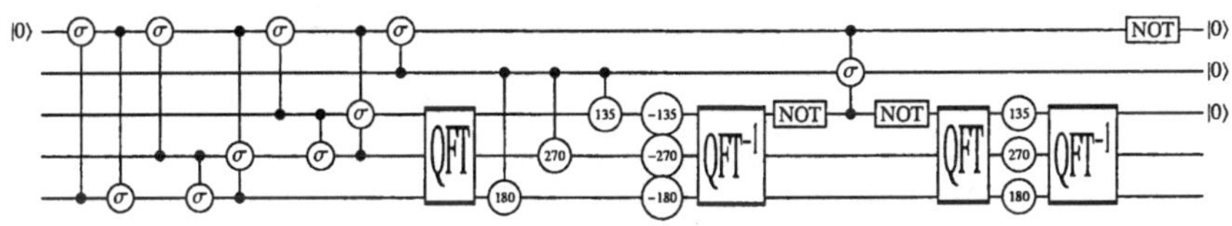

Figure 5. efficient compression circuit

Acknowledgments

This work has been supported by CREST of JST (Japan Science and Technology Corporation). MK would like to acknowledge Prof. A. Fujiwara for enlightening discussions and K. Takeda for useful discussions on dynamic nuclear polarization. The authors would like to thank A. Kagawa for experimental cooperation and K. Nagashima for discussion.

References

1. N. Gershenfeld and I. L. Chuang, *Science* **275**, 350–356 (1997).
2. D. G. Cory, A. F. Fahmy and T. F. Havel, *Proc. Natl. Acad. Sci. USA* **94**, 1634–1639 (1997).
3. E. Knill, I. Chuang and R. Laflamme, *Phys. Rev. A* **57**, 3348–3363 (1998).
4. L. M. K. Vandersypen, M. Steffen, G. Breyta, C. S. Yannoni, M. H. Sherwood, and I. L. Chuang, *Nature* **414**, 883–887 (2001).
5. S. L. Braunstein, C. M. Caves, R. Jozsa, N. Linden, S. Popescu and R. Schack, *Phys. Rev. Lett.* **83**, 1054–1057 (1999).
6. R. Schack and C. M. Caves, *Phys. Rev. A* **60**, 4354–4362 (1999).
7. N. Linden and S. Popescu, *Phys. Rev. Lett.* **87**, 047901 (2001).
8. M. Iinuma, Y. Takahashi, I. Shaké, M. Oda, A. Masaike, T. Yabuzaki and H. M. Shimizu, *Phys. Rev. Lett.* **84**, 171–174 (2000).
9. K. Takeda, T. Takegoshi, and T. Terao, *Chem. Phys. Lett.* **345**, 166–170 (2001).
10. M. Kitagawa, "Initialization, Entanglement and Scalability in Bulk-Ensemble NMR Quantum Computation," *EQIS'01* (2001).
11. B. Schumacher, *Phys. Rev. A* **51**, 2738–2747 (1995).
12. L. J. Schulman and U. Vazirani, In *Proc. 31st STOC*, 322–329 (1999).
13. T. Nishimura, A. Kagawa, A. Kataoka and M. Kitagawa, "Initialization of NMR quantum computer at low temperature using data compression process," *ISQC'02*.
14. T. G. Draper, quant-ph/0008033.
15. R. Cleve and D. P. DiVincenzo, *Phys. Rev. A* **54**, 2636–2650 (1996).

MOLECULAR QUANTUM COMPUTING APPLYING OPTIMAL CONTROL THEORY: THEORETICAL REALIZATION OF QUANTUM GATES AND ALGORITHMS IN THE MODEL SYSTEM ACETYLENE

CARMEN M. TESCH AND REGINA DE VIVIE-RIEDLE
Max-Planck-Institut für Quantenoptik, 85741 Garching, Germany
E-mail: Carmen.Tesch@mpq.mpg.de; rdv@mpq.mpg.de

An overview of a new molecular approach to quantum computing is given. The vibrational modes of molecules are used to encode qubit systems. Specially formed femtosecond laser pulses in the infrared regime act as ultrafast quantum gates. They are calculated using optimal control theory. Global quantum gates and algorithms are reported.

1 Concepts

Quantum computation is a fast growing field in quantum information theory. First basic ideas have been discussed and experimental efforts have been made,[1,2,3,4,5] although it is still unknown which method is the most effective and elegant way leading to the first quantum computing machine.

In this paper we give an overview of our recent work on a new molecular approach to quantum computing in which the vibrational normal modes of molecules in an ensemble are used to encode qubit systems.[6,7] In each mode a certain degree of excitation is referred to as $|0\rangle$, another degree of excitation in the same mode is referred to as $|1\rangle$. The number of utilizable qubits in an N-atomic molecule scales as $3N$.

For the realization of quantum gates within and between the qubits we apply single shaped-femtosecond laser pulses in the infrared (IR) regime. These pulses are calculated using optimal control theory (OCT), which is a very powerful tool in molecular femtosecond physics.[8,9]

For initial state preparation, once again shaped-femtosecond laser pulses can be used. A preparation of the vibrationless ground state, fundamentals, overtones and combination modes is optionally possible. The readout of our quantum register could be achieved by applying standard laser diagnostics (LIF, SEP, REMPI etc.).

The interaction between different qubits is a system inherent property: It is an electromagnetic interaction that is mediated via the molecular bondings. For designing globally applicable laser pulses in just one qubit, this interaction has to be suppressed; in the case of conditional gates, this influence is explicitly used. Both cases can be realized in our OCT functional.

2 Optimal Control Theory

One possible goal in OCT is to find a laser field $\varepsilon(t)$ (= quantum gate), which drives a system from initial states $\psi_{ik}(t = 0) = \phi_{ik}$ to final target states $\psi_{ik}(t = T) = \phi_{fk}$ at a fixed time t=T. The initial and target states correspond to vibrational eigenstates of the molecules (= qubit basis states). Algorithmic schemes allow the formulation of the optimization problem in terms of the following functional:

$$K\left(\psi_{ik}(t), \psi_{fk}(t), \varepsilon(t)\right) = \sum_k |\langle\psi_{ik}(T)|\phi_{fk}\rangle|^2 - \int_0^T \alpha|\varepsilon(t)|^2 dt$$
$$-2\Re\left[\langle\psi_{ik}(T)|\phi_{fk}\rangle \int_0^T \langle\psi_{fk}(t)| \left[\frac{i}{\hbar}\left[H_0 - \mu\varepsilon(t)\right] + \frac{\partial}{\partial t}\right] |\psi_{ik}(t)\rangle dt\right].$$

The first term gives the overlap of the laser-driven wavefunctions $\psi_{ik}(t)$ and the desired target states ϕ_{fk} , which we refer to as population ratio (or fidelity in special cases). The second term represents the laser field $\varepsilon(t)$, which drives the system wavefunctions towards the target states. The laser field intensity is limited by the penalty factor α. The last term mainly ensures that the time dependent Schrödinger equation is fulfilled at all times.

The Hamilton operator H_0, and the dipole moment vector field μ, are calculated *ab initio* using a quantum chemical package (GAUSSIAN98). Therefore all molecular characteristics of the electronic and nuclear movement and their interactions are included in our calculations.

Varying the above functional with respect to its variables leads to a set of $2k + 1$ coupled differential equations. The solution is found iteratively, and results in the optimal quantum gate $\varepsilon(t)$ that operates on each qubit basis state in the correct way.

3 Two Qubit Model System Acetylene

In addition to this principle concept for molecular quantum computation processes, we present our calculations for a two-dimensional model system: acetylene (C_2H_2). Acetylene contains five different normal modes, denoted ($n_1n_2n_3n_4n_5$), two of which are IR-active. A normal-mode analysis has shown that one coordinate is sufficient for a description of the IR-active asymmetric CH-stretching mode (n_3; 3289 cm^{-1}) and the cis-bending mode (n_5; 727 cm^{-1}). Zero quanta in each IR-active mode we refer to as $|0\rangle$, one quantum in each mode we refer to as $|1\rangle$. Our two-qubit basis is defined in the following way: $|00\rangle$:= (00000); $|10\rangle$:= (00100); $|01\rangle$:= (00001); $|11\rangle$:= (00101).

We calculated a two-dimensional *ab initio* potential energy surface. On this surface we solved the corresponding Schrödinger equation in order to get the vibrational eigenfunctions of this system. We calculated 80 eigenfunctions up to an energy of 23150 cm$^-$1, but only four of them were used to define our qubit system.

4 Quantum Gates

Using our optimal control algorithm, we calculated a universal set of quantum gates: the identity, the NOT, the Π and the Hadamard operation in each qubit, and, in addition, the controlled-NOT gates (see Fig. 1).

The achieved ratios are always in the range of 95 to 99%. The preparation of entanglement could also be demonstrated with a fidelity of more than 96%.

The optimal quantum gates were analyzed in the time and frequency domains. The laser field intensity is in the range of 10^{10} to 10^{12} W/cm^2.

The structural complexity of the pulses was investigated by calculating the so-called mask functions. These functions are the direct interface between theory and experiment; they are applied to pulse shapers in order to form pre-specified pulses. Mask functions always follow a pixel scheme (defining transmission and phase), today more than 600 pixels are already commercially available. To form our quantum gates only 60 pixels are needed, which means that our quantum gates are simply structured.

We analyzed the physical mechanism by which our quantum gates work, and found that in most cases higher vibrational excitation (ladder climbing) is intermediately involved. For more details about quantum gates see Refs. 6,10.

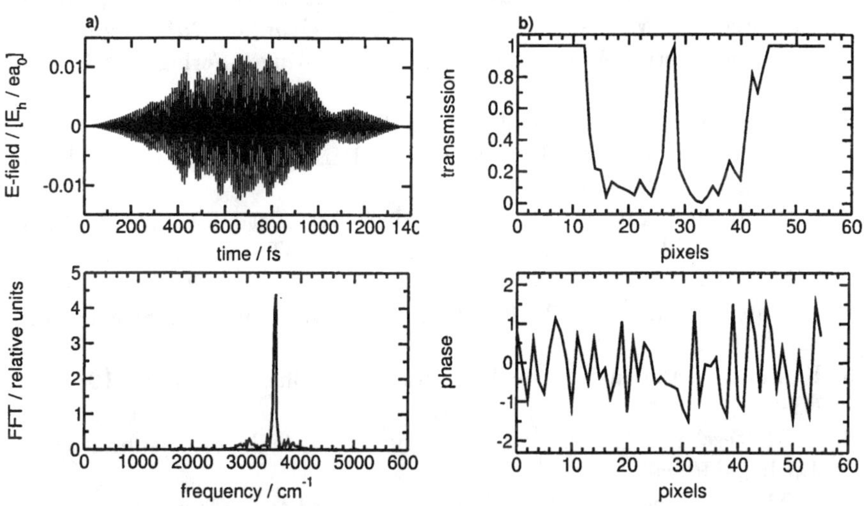

Figure 1. (a) CNOT-gate acting on the first qubit. Its efficiency is more than 97%. (b) Mask function of the CNOT for an experimental realization. The number of pixels indicates a low complexity for the gate.

5 Algorithms

After having calculated global quantum gates, one should be able to run every quantum algorithm. In our case, we have chosen to simulate the Deutsch-Jozsa algorithm, which is often used for proof-of-principle demonstrations in quantum computing. The Deutsch-Jozsa algorithm enables one to determine, in only one step, whether an unknown function U_f is constant or balanced.

To simulate the Deutsch-Jozsa algorithm we translated its single logic steps to our qubit notation and identified the operations with our calculated quantum gates.[11] We applied them successively for all four possible functions U_f, which we have also identified with quantum gates.

The measurement process was simulated using a numerical projection onto our basis states. The correct result (balanced or constant function U_f) is found with a probability of more than 94%. The errors that occurred mainly disappear out of the qubit system, and therefore bear little disturbing influence on the computational space. Having in mind that in an experiment one deals with an ensemble, the detection will give the correct result with certainty.[11]

References

1. M. Brune, F. Schmidt-Kaler, A. Maali, J. Dreyer, E. Hagley, J.M. Raimond, and S. Haroche, Phys. Rev. Lett. **76**, 1800 (1996).
2. J. I. Cirac and P. Zoller, Phys. Rev. Lett. **74**, 4091 (1995).
3. H. C. Nägerl, F. Schmidt-Kaler, J. Eschner, R. Blatt, W. Lange, H. Baldauf and H. Walther, in *The Physics of Quantum Information*, ed. D. Bouwmeester, A. Ekert, A. Zeilinger, (Springer-Verlag, Berlin Heidelberg, 2000).
4. J. A. Jones and M. Mosca, J. Chem. Phys. **109**, 1648 (1998).
5. R. Marx, A. F. Fahmy, J. M. Myers, W. Bermel and S. J. Glaser, Phys. Rev. A **62**, 012310 (2000).
6. C. M. Tesch and R. de Vivie-Riedle, Phys. Rev. Lett. **89**, 157901 (2002).
7. C. M. Tesch, L. Kurtz and R. de Vivie-Riedle, Chem. Phys. Lett. **343**, 633 (2001).
8. H. Rabitz, R. de Vivie-Riedle, M. Motzkus and K. Kompa, Science **288**, 824 (2000).
9. K. Sundermann and R. de Vivie-Riedle, J. Chem. Phys. **110**, 1896 (1999).
10. C. M. Tesch, U. Troppmann, and R. de Vivie-Riedle, to be submitted to J. Chem. Phys.
11. C. M. Tesch and R. de Vivie-Riedle, submitted to J. Chem. Phys.

SUPEROSCILLATIONS AND TUNNELING TIMES

NOAM EREZ

School of Physics and Astronomy, Tel Aviv University, Tel Aviv 69978, Israel
E-mail: noamer@post.tau.ac.il

The tunneling particle is considered as a pre- and post-selected system and its dwell time under the barrier turns out to be the conditional expectation value of the position of a "clock" degree of freedom weakly coupled to it. Such a value, called a "weak value", typically falls outside the eigenvalue spectrum of the operator. The appearance of unusual weak values has been associated with a unique interference structure called "superoscillations". A general property of superoscillations is proved, and the relation of superoscillations to anomalous tunneling times is discussed for a model system.

1 Introduction

It is proposed that superoscillations[a] play an important role in the interferences that give rise to superluminal effects. This is demonstrated for a Schrödinger particle tunneling through the potential:

$$V(x) = \Sigma_{i=0}^{n-1}\alpha_i\delta(x - L_i);\ L_0 = 0. \tag{1}$$

This barrier allows a wave packet to "travel" in zero time (in the low-energy approximation), and with negligible distortion, a distance that is arbitrarily longer than its width.[16] The peak is shown to result from a superoscillatory superposition at the tail. It is to be stressed that causality is not violated. The signal velocity (a measure of the time it takes for an *abrupt* signal to traverse the barrier) is always subluminal. However, the group-delay time (related to the group velocity) and the conditional dwell time both turn out to be zero (in the low-energy limit). This can be explained by a reshaping of the (forward) tail of the packet which travels ahead of the peak.[5–11] The probability of finding the particle on the far side of the barrier is exponentially small (in the width, etc.) and even though a local peak appears, it is no greater than the probability of finding a particle there in the absence of the barrier. For extensive reviews of tunneling times, see Refs. 2–4. We follow the notation of Ref. 4.

2 Superoscillations and Weak Values

It has been shown by Aharonov[17] that when a pre- and post-selected system is subjected to a nondisturbing "weak" measurement, the outcome of the measurement, known as the "weak value", can attain values outside the spectrum

---

[a]Band-limited functions that over a finite interval approximate functions with spectra outside their band

of the eigenvalues of the measured observable.[18] In fact, for any nontrivial (i.e., not proportional to the identity) operator, the initial and final states can be chosen so as to make the weak value with respect to them assume any desired value in the complex plane. From the point of view of the pointer, this means that a superposition of shifts of its position wave function, proportional to the eigenvalues, can amount to a shift corresponding to a value falling outside that spectrum. For the momentum wave function (in the case under consideration, concentrated about 0), this means that multiplying it by a superposition of exponentials with frequencies in some range can be, to arbitrary precision, approximated by multiplication by a single exponential with frequency proportional to the weak value.

This phenomenon was further investigated by Berry[15], who gave it the name superoscillations. He showed, by asymptotic and numerical estimates for a number of such functions, that outside the interval over which the superoscillations take place the function is everywhere exponentially (in the length of that interval) larger. He therefore postulated this exponential penalty for superoscillations in general. These functions were not square integrable, and they approximated over the special interval an equally non-square-integrable pure exponential with some high frequency.

For the original physical problem with square-integrable wave functions however, this cannot be the case. In fact, it is true that any square-integrable function over an interval, I, can be approximated arbitrarily well by a *square-integrable* function with spectrum in any preassigned band.[1] A bandlimited function is analytic, and so cannot *exactly* coincide with a function whose spectrum is not in that band. One may therefore suspect that the closer the approximation, the greater the norm of the approximating function, $||g||$.[b] This can be proven using the theory of Pollak[1] (see discussion).

What about the length of the interval? Let I be our interval, f (the function to be approximated) and g be two square-integrable functions. Suppose also that the spectra of the two functions are disjoint ($\hat{f}\hat{g} = 0$). Define $f_1 = f\chi_I$, $f_2 = f - f_1$, and likewise $g_{1,2}$. Then, from the orthogonality of f and g, it follows that $-(f_2, g_2) = (f_1, g_1)$, and if $f_1 \simeq g_1$, the right-hand side is approximately $||f_1||^2 \simeq ||f_1|| ||g_1||$, and the left is, by the Cauchy-Schwartz inequality, less than or equal to $||f_2|| ||g_2||$. As we increase the length of the interval, $||f_1||$ increases at the expense of $||f_2||$, and $||g_2||$ increases as $||f_2||^{-1}$. More precisely, if $||f_1 - g_1|| < \epsilon$,

$$||g_2|| \geq \frac{||f_1||^2 + ||g_1||^2 - ||f_1 - g_1||^2}{2||f_2||} \geq \frac{||f_1||^2 - \epsilon||f_1|| - \epsilon^2}{||f_2||}. \qquad (2)$$

[b] $||f||^2 = \int |f|^2$

3 The dwell time and superoscillations

The results quoted in the introduction were shown by calculating the transmission coefficient, $t(k)$. The calculation of t can be done in a way suggestive of superoscillations. Let us explain this for the case of 2 delta functions (the $n = 2$ case in (1), i.e., the"Fabry-Perot interferometer").

Suppose a quasimonochromatic wave packet with wave number k arrives at the first delta spike. The transmitted component is the same as the original wave, except for an attenuation and phase which are independent of k. At the second delta spike, the wave splits into a (approximately unattenuated) reflected wave and a transmitted one which, apart from a k-independent multiplicative constant, is the same as the impinging wave. The reflected component is again reflected at the first delta, and arrives at the second delta with an additional phase of $2kL$, but with approximately the same amplitude as the original transmitted wave. In a like manner, one gets additional transmitted waves with additional phases of $2nkL, n = 2, 3, ...$, and amplitudes which decrease very slowly. Thus we get the following formal sum for the resulting amplitude of the wave (up to a multiplicative constant):

$$\sum_n e^{ikx}(e^{ik2L})^n = \frac{e^{ikx}}{1 - e^{2ikL}} = e^{ikx}\frac{e^{-ikL}}{-2i \sin kL}, \tag{3}$$

which is in agreement with a direct calculation.[c] This is an example of superoscillations, because a sum of positive wave vectors results in a negative one (or, equivalently, a sum of positive shifts that results in a negative shift). This is true in the following sense: for $|k| << 1/L$ the denominator of the right-hand side can be considered constant. However, in such a small interval the function does not really oscillate, so it really doesn't have a well-defined frequency. To really speak about superoscillations we need to have a large number of delta functions. This leads to a condition on the wave function.

The same kind of calculation can be done for the wave function of our clock's "pointer". Then this superoscillatory sum would correspond to a series of positive time readings interfering to give zero. This derivation shows that for this system the dwell and group-delay times not only coincide, but are also described by the same mechanism.

4 Discussion

The fact that the set of functions on an interval I, obtained by the restriction to it of all the functions with spectra limited to some arbitrary band, is dense [in $L_2(I)$] was discovered earlier by Pollak and his collaborators.[1] This was

[c]This sum of course diverges, the physical reason being that we neglected the attenuation upon reflection. The correction is easy to make and does not change the results.

done in the context of "band-limited and time-limited" functions in classical communication theory and, although related to Heisenberg's inequality, seems to be unknown in the physics community. Although Landau's theory has been applied to problems of sampling, its implications for the more interesting problem, from a physical point of view, of approximation in L_2 are apparently yet to be studied.

References

1. D. Slepian and H. O. Pollak, Bell. Sys. Tech. J. **40**, 43 (1961) and Bell. Sys. Tech. J. **41**, 1295(1962); H. J. Landau and H. O. Pollak, Bell. Sys. Tech. J. **40**, 65 (1961).
2. E. H. Hauge and J. A. Støvneng, Rev. Mod. Phys. **61**, 917 (1989).
3. R. Landauer and T. Martin, Rev. Mod. Phys. **66**, 217 (1994).
4. R. Y. Chiao and A. M. Steinberg, Progress in Optics **XXXVII**, 345 (1997).
5. R. Y. Chiao, P. G. Kwiat, and A. M. Steinberg, Sci. Am. **269**(2), 52 (1993).
6. A. M. Steinberg, J. Phys. I (France) **4**, 1813 (1994).
7. A. M. Steinberg, La Recherche **281**, 46 (1995).
8. Y. P. Wang and D. L. Zhang, Phys. Rev. A **52**, 2597 (1995).
9. B. Lee and W. Lee., Superlattices and Microstructures **18**, 277 (1995).
10. G. Diener, Phys. Lett. A **223**, 327 (1996).
11. B. Lee, Opt. Soc. Am. Annual Meeting Abstracts, p. 185 (1996).
12. A. M. Steinberg, Phys. Rev. A **52**, 32 (1995).
13. A. M. Steinberg, Phys. Rev. Lett. **74**, 2405 (1995).
14. Y. Aharonov, D. Albert, and L. Vaidman, Phys. Rev. Lett. **60**, 1351 (1988)
15. M. V. Berry, J. Phys. A **27**,L391 (1994); *Quantum Coherence and Reality*, edited by J. A. Anandan and J. Safko (World Scientific, Singapore, 1994).
16. Y. Aharonov, N. Erez, and B. Reznik, Phys. Rev. A, **65**, 052124 (2002)
17. Y. Aharonov, P. G. Bergman, and J. L. Lebowitz Phys. Rev. **134**, B1410 (1964); Y. Aharonov, A. Casher, D. Albert, and L. Vaidman. Phys. Lett. A **124**, 199 (1987); Y. Aharonov and L. Vaidman, J. Phys. A **24**, 2315 (1991); B. Reznik and Y. Aharonov. Phys. Rev A **52**, 2538 (1995).
18. Y. Aharonov, J. Anandan, S. Popescu, and L. Vaidman, Phys. Rev. Lett. **64**, 2965 (1990).

FUNDAMENTAL LIMITATION ON QUBIT OPERATIONS DUE TO THE BLOCH-SIEGERT OSCILLATION

M. S. SHAHRIAR AND PRABHAKAR PRADHAN

Department of Electrical and Computer Engineering, Northwestern University
Evanston, IL 60208 and
Research Laboratory of Electronics, Massachusetts Institute of Technology
Cambridge, MA 02139

We show that if the Rabi frequency is comparable to the Bohr frequency, so that the rotating wave approximation is inappropriate, an extra oscillation is present with the Rabi oscillation. We discuss how the sensitivity of the degree of excitation to the phase of the field may pose severe constraints on precise rotations of quantum bits involving low-frequency transitions. We present a scheme for observing this effect in an atomic beam.

It is well known that the amplitude of an atomic state is necessarily complex valued. The electric or magnetic field generated by an oscillator, on the other hand, is real valued, composed of the sum of two complex components. In describing semiclassically the atom-field interaction involving such a field, one often side-steps this difference by making the so-called rotating wave approximation (RWA), under which only one of the two complex components is kept, and the counterrotating part is ignored. We discuss how the sensitivity of the degree of excitation to the phase of the field poses severe constraints on precise rotations of quantum bits involving low-frequency transitions. We also present a scheme for observing this effect in an atomic beam.

We consider an ideal two-level system in which a ground state $|0\rangle$ is coupled to an excited state $|1\rangle$, and $0 \leftrightarrow 1$ transitions are magnetic dipolar with transition frequency ω, and the magnetic field is of the form $B = B_0 \cos(\omega t + \phi)$. We now summarize briefly the two-level dynamics without the RWA. In the dipole approximation, the Hamiltonian can be written as:

$$\hat{H} = \epsilon(\sigma_0 - \sigma_z)/2 + g(t)\sigma_x, \tag{1}$$

where $g(t) = -g_0\left[\exp(i\omega t + i\phi) + \text{c.c.}\right]/2$, σ_i are Pauli matrices, and $\epsilon = \omega$ corresponds to resonant excitation. The state vector is written as:

$$|\xi(t)\rangle = \begin{pmatrix} C_0(t) \\ C_1(t) \end{pmatrix}. \tag{2}$$

We perform a rotating wave transformation by operating on $|\xi(t)\rangle$ with the unitary operator $\hat{Q}$, where: $\hat{Q} = (\sigma_0 + \sigma_z)/2 + \exp(i\omega t + i\phi)(\sigma_0 - \sigma_z)/2$. The Schrödinger equation then takes the form (setting $\hbar = 1$): $|\dot{\tilde{\xi}}\rangle = -i\tilde{H}(t)|\tilde{\xi}(t)\rangle$, where the effective Hamiltonian is given by

$$\tilde{H} = \alpha(t)\sigma_+ + \alpha^*(t)\sigma_-, \tag{3}$$

with $\alpha(t) = -(g_0/2)[\exp(-i2\omega t - i2\phi) + 1]$, and in the rotating frame the state vector is

$$|\tilde{\xi}(t)\rangle \equiv \hat{Q}|\xi(t)\rangle = \begin{pmatrix} \tilde{C}_0(t) \\ \tilde{C}_1(t) \end{pmatrix}. \tag{4}$$

Now, by making the rotating wave approximation (RWA), corresponding to dropping the fast oscillating term in $\alpha(t)$, one ignores effects (such as the Bloch-Siegert shift) of the order of (g_0/ω), which can easily be observed in experiment if g_0 is large.[1,2] Otherwise, by choosing g_0 to be small enough, one can make the RWA for any value of ω. We explore here both regimes, and we find the general results without the RWA.

From Eqs. (3) and (4), we get two coupled differential equations:

$$\dot{\tilde{C}}_0(t) = i(g_0/2)[1 + \exp(-i2\omega t - i2\phi)]\,\tilde{C}_1(t) \tag{5}$$

$$\dot{\tilde{C}}_1(t) = i(g_0/2)[1 + \exp(+i2\omega t + i2\phi)]\,\tilde{C}_0(t). \tag{6}$$

We choose $|C_0(0)|^2 = 1$ for the initial condition, and proceed to find approximate analytical solutions of Eqs. (5) and (6). Due to the periodic nature of the effective Hamiltonian, the general solution to Eqs. (5) and (6) can be written in the form:

$$|\tilde{\xi}(t)\rangle = \sum_{n=-\infty}^{\infty} \begin{pmatrix} a_n \\ b_n \end{pmatrix} \exp[n(-i2\omega t - i2\phi)]. \tag{7}$$

Inserting Eq. (7) in Eqs. (5) and (6) we get for all n :

$$\dot{a}_n = i2n\omega a_n + ig_0(b_n + b_{n-1})/2, \tag{8}$$

$$\dot{b}_n = i2n\omega b_n + ig_0(a_n + a_{n+1})/2. \tag{9}$$

Here, the coupling between a_0 and b_0 is the conventional one when the RWA is made. The couplings to the nearest neighbors, $a_{\pm1}$ and $b_{\pm1}$, are detuned by an amount 2ω, and so on. To lowest order in (g_0/ω), we can ignore terms with $|n| > 1$, thus yielding a truncated set of six equations for $\dot{a}_0, \dot{b}_0, \dot{a}_{\pm1}, \dot{b}_{\pm1}$. Now consider g_0 to have a time dependence of the form $g_0(t) = g_{0M}[1 - \exp(-t/\tau_{sw})]$, where the switching time constant τ_{sw} is large compared to other characteristic time scales such as $1/\omega$ and $1/g_{0M}$. Then, these equations can be solved by the method of adiabatic elimination, which is valid to first order in $\eta \equiv (g_0/4\omega)$. [Note $\eta(t) = \eta_0[1 - \exp(-t/\tau_{sw})]$, where $\eta_0 \equiv (g_0M/4\omega)$]. To solve the set of equations above, we consider first a_{-1} and b_{-1}. Define $\mu_{\pm} \equiv (a_{-1} \pm b_{-1})$, then one can write $\dot{\mu}_{\pm} = -i(2\omega + g_0/2)\mu_{\pm} \pm ig_0 a_0/2$. Adiabatic following then yields (again, to lowest order in η) $a_{-1} \approx 0$ and $b_{-1} \approx \eta a_0$. Likewise, we can show that $a_1 \approx -\eta b_0$ and $b_1 \approx 0$. The only nonvanishing (to lowest order in η with $|C_0(t=0)|^2 = 1$) terms in the solution of Eqs. (5) and (6) are:

$$C_0(t) = \cos(g_0'(t)t/2) - i\eta e^{-i(2\omega t+2\phi)}\sin(g_0'(t)t/2), \tag{10}$$

$$C_1(t) = ie^{-i(\omega t+\phi)}[\sin(g_0'(t)t/2) - i\eta e^{+i(2\omega t+2\phi)}\cos(g_0'(t)t/2)], \tag{11}$$

where $g_0'(t) = 1/t \int_0^t g_0(t)dt = g_0\left[1 - (t/\tau_{sw})^{-1}\exp(-t/\tau_{sw})\right]$.

To lowest order in η, this solution is normalized at all times. Note that if one applies this excitation to an ensemble of atoms using a $\pi/2$-pulse and then measures the population of state $|1\rangle$ after the excitation terminates (at $t = \tau$, when $g'(\tau)\tau/2 = \pi/2$), the output signal will be

$$|C_1(g_0'(\tau), \phi)|^2 = \frac{1}{2}\left[1 + 2\eta\sin(2\omega\tau + 2\phi)\right], \tag{12}$$

which contains information about both the amplitude and the phase of the driving field B. This clearly indicates that the Rabi transition probability depends on the total phase $\phi_\tau = \omega\tau + \phi$ of the driving field.

A physical realization of this result can be best appreciated by consider-

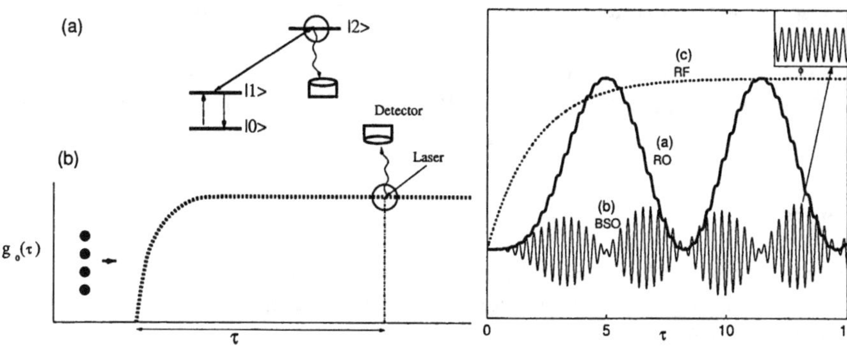

Figure 1. Left: Schematic illustration of an experimental arrangement for measuring the phase dependence of the population of the excited state $|1\rangle$: (a) The microwave field couples the ground state ($|0\rangle$) to the excited state ($|1\rangle$). A third level, $|2\rangle$, which can be coupled to $|1\rangle$ optically, is used to measure the population of $|1\rangle$ via fluorescence detection. (b) The microwave field is turned on adiabatically with a switching time-constant τ_{sw}, and the fluorescence is monitored after a total interaction time of τ. Right: Illustration of the Bloch-Siegert Oscillation (BSO): (a) The population of state $|1\rangle$, as a function of the interaction time τ , showing the BSO superimposed on the conventional Rabi oscillation. (b) The BSO oscillation (amplified scale) by itself, produced by subtracting the Rabi oscillation from the plot in (a). (c) The time-dependence of the Rabi frequency. Inset: BSO as a function of the absolute phase of the field with fixed τ.

ing an experimental arrangement of the type illustrated in the left panel of Fig. 1; a plot of the associated Rabi oscillations is shown in the right panel of Fig. 1. Under the RWA, curve (a) on the right in Fig. 1 represents the conventional Rabi oscillation. However, we notice here some additional oscillation—magnified and shown separately in curve (b) of this panel—that is produced by subtracting the conventional Rabi oscillation, $\sin^2(g(t)/2)$, from curve (a). That is, curve (b) in the right panel of Fig. 1 corresponds to what we call the Bloch-Siegert Oscillation (BSO), given by $\eta\sin(g_0'(\tau)\tau)\sin(2\phi_\tau)$. These analytical results agree very closely with the results obtained via direct numerical integration of Eqs. (5) and (6). Note that the BSO is at twice the frequency of the driving field, and its amplitude vanishes when all the atoms are in a single state. This oscillation will be stronger when the ratio of the resonance frequency to the Rabi frequency is large.[3,4,5] One should keep track of the phase of the excitation field at the location of the qubit[6,7] for low-energy qubit systems[8,9,10] with fast driving fields.

In conclusion, we have shown that when a two-level atomic system is driven by a strong periodic field, the Rabi oscillation is accompanied by another oscillation at twice the transition frequency. This extra oscillation can limit the qubit operations in Rabi flopping without a proper matching of the parameters. However, it has been shown that this phase has potential application in teleportation. By making use of distant entanglement, this mechanism may enable teleportation of the phase of a field that is encoded in the atomic state amplitude, and has potential applications to remote frequency-locking.[11,12,13,14]

We wish to acknowledge support from DARPA grant No. F30602-01-2-0546 under the QuIST program, ARO grant No. DAAD19-001-0177 under the MURI program, and NRO grant No. NRO-000-00-C-0158.

References

1. A. Corney, *Atomic and Laser Spectroscopy* (Oxford University Press, 1977); L. Allen and J. Eberly, *Optical Resonance and Two Level Atoms* (Wiley, 1975).
2. F. Bloch and A. J. F. Siegert, Phys. Rev. **57**, 522 (1940); J. H. Shirley, Phys. Rev. **138**, B979 (1965); S. Stenholm, J. Phys. **64**, 1650 (1973); N .F. Ramsey, *Molecular Beams* (Clarendon Press, 1956).
3. D. Bouwmeester, A. Ekert, and A. Zeilinger, eds., *The Physics of Quantum Information* (Springer, 2000).
4. A. M. Steane, Appl. Phys. **B64**, 623 (1997); A. M. Steane et al., quant-ph/0003097.
5. D. Jonathan, M. B. Plenio, and P. L. Knight, quant-ph/0002092.
6. P. Pradhan and M. S. Shahriar, presented at the Progress In Electromagnetic Research Symposium 2002, Cambridge, MA (July 2002).
7. P. Pradhan and M. S. Shahriar, Bulletin of the American Physical Society, **47** 878 (2002).
8. J. E. Thomas et al., Phys. Rev. Lett. **48**, 867 (1982).
9. M. S. Shahriar and P. R. Hemmer, Phys. Rev. Lett. **65**, 1865 (1990).
10. M. S. Shahriar et al., Phys. Rev. A. **55**, 2272 (1997)
11. R. Jozsa et al., Phys. Rev. Lett. **85**, 2010 (2000).
12. S. Lloyd, M. S. Shahriar, J. H. Shapiro, and P. R. Hemmer, Phys. Rev. Lett. **87**, 167903 (2001).
13. G. S. Levy et al., Acta Astronaut **15**, 481 (1987).
14. M. S. Shahriar, Proceedings of the Conference on Quantum Optics 8, Rochester, NY, July 2001.

Part VI

Quantum Dynamics, Geometry, and Simulation

A QUBIT-STATE READOUT ANALYSIS: QUANTUM TRAJECTORIES VS. MASTER EQUATION APPROACH

HSI-SHENG GOAN

Center for Quantum Computer Technology, University of New South Wales, Sydney, NSW 2052 Australia

We demonstrate the connection between the quantum trajectory approach and the master equation approach of the "partially"-reduced density matrix by studying an initial charge qubit state readout experiment that uses a low-transparency point contact (PC) detector. We analyze an important ensemble quantity for the readout experiment, $P(N,t)$, the probability distribution of finding N electrons that have tunneled through the PC barrier in time t. The simulation results for $P(N,t)$ using 10000 quantum trajectories and the corresponding measurement records are, as expected, in very good agreement with those obtained from Fourier analysis of the "partially"-reduced density matrix. However, the quantum trajectory approach provides more information and more physical insight into the ensemble and time averaged quantity $P(N,t)$.

The problem of a charge qubit measured by a detector (or interacting with an environment) has attracted much attention recently.[1,2,3,4] In this paper, we consider the case of an electron coherently tunneling between two coupled quantum dots (CQD's) subject to a measurement using a low-transparency point contact (PC) or tunnel junction.[1,3,4] The double-dot system forms a single charge qubit, and the measurement corresponds to a continuous time readout of the occupancy of the quantum dot. This problem has been discussed using the traditional (unconditional) master equation approach,[1] by tracing over the environmental (detector) degrees of freedom to obtain the reduced density matrix for the system alone. In that approach, the influence of the PC reservoirs, the decoherence effect for example, on the CQD system can be analyzed. However, no information about the experimentally-observed quantity, namely the electron counts or current through PC, is extracted. An alternative approach, recently developed in Ref. 2 and referred here as the master equation approach of the "partially"-reduced density matrix, is to take a trace over the environmental (detector) microscopic degrees of freedom but keep track of the number of electrons N that have tunneled through the PC barrier during time t. Although this "partially"-reduced density matrix approach provides us with information about the initial qubit state, by measuring the number of accumulated electrons passing through the PC, it is still in an ensemble and time average sense. In other words, the system dynamics are still deterministic in this approach. Hence, it cannot describe the conditional dynamics of the CQD qubit system in a single realization of continuous measurements, which reflects the stochastic nature of electrons tunneling through the PC barrier.

On the other hand, in the quantum trajectory approach [3,4] no average or

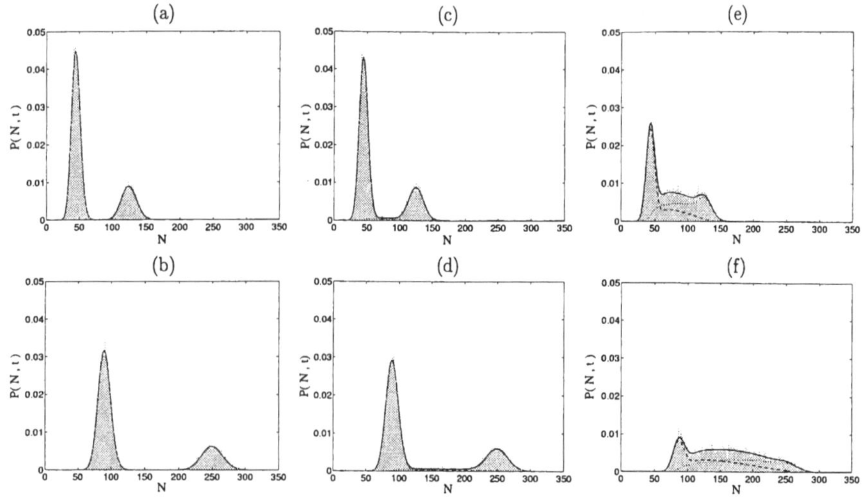

Figure 1. Probability distribution $P(N,t)$ for $\mathcal{E} = 0$ and a fixed value of Γ_d, but with different ratios of $(\Omega/\Gamma_d) = 0$ for (a) and (b), 0.05 for (c) and (d), and 0.2 for (e) and (f). The detection time for (a), (c) and (e) is up to $t = 10/\Gamma_d$, and for (b), (d) and (f) is to $t = 20/\Gamma_d$. The quantities $\rho_{aa}(N,t)$, $\rho_{bb}(N,t)$ and $P(N,t)$ obtained from Fourier analysis are represented in each plot as dashed, dotted, and solid lines, respectively. The shaded region in each plot is the simulation result from 10000 quantum trajectories and their corresponding detection records.

trace over the environmental (detector) states is taken as far as the system evolution is concerned. Instead, repeated continuous-time measurements are made. The stochastic element in the quantum trajectory corresponds exactly to the consequence of the random outcomes of the detection record. Hence we are propagating *in parallel* (self-consistently) the information of a conditioned (stochastic) state evolution [or conditional density matrix evolution $\rho_c(t)$], and a detection record $dN_c(t)$ in a continuous measurement process. In Refs. 3 and 4, the difference and connection between the (conditional) quantum trajectory approach and the (unconditional) master equation approach of the reduced density matrix were emphasized. To our knowledge, however, no direct connection between the quantum trajectory approach and the master equation approach of the "partially"-reduced density matrix has been formally established and reported until recently.[5] In Ref. 5, we have shown that the master equation for the reduced or "partially"-reduced density matrix can be obtained when an average or "partial" average is taken on the conditional, stochastic master equation (quantum trajectory equation) over the possible outcomes of the measurement. This provides a unified picture for these seemingly different approaches in the literature.

Here we demonstrate further the connection between the quantum trajectory approach and the "partially"-reduced density matrix approach, by analyzing an important quantity for the CQD initial qubit state-readout measurement: $P(N,t)$ the probability distribution[2] of finding N electrons that have tunneled through the PC barrier in time t. Each quantum trajectory resembles a single history of the system state in a single run of a continuous-time measurement experiment. We can, therefore, use many possible realizations of quantum trajectories and their corresponding detection records to simulate measurement experiments on a single quantum system. In our case, the quantity $P(N,t)$ can be simulated by building the histogram of the accumulated number of electrons $N_c(t) = \sum dN_c(t)$ up to time t for many realizations of the detection records, and then normalizing the distribution to one. Figure 1 shows that the probability distributions $P(N,t)$, each constructed from 10000 realizations (in shades), are, as expected, in very good agreement with those obtained from Fourier analysis of the partially-reduced density matrix (solid lines). It was shown[4,2] that there is an optimal time window $t_{\rm m} \ll t \ll t_{\rm mix}$ for a confident readout measurement to be performed. In the regime of small (Ω/Γ_d) ratio,[4,2] the measurement (localization) time $t_{\rm m} \sim t_{\rm loc} \approx (1/\Gamma_d)$ is much smaller than the mixing time $t_{\rm mix} \approx (\Gamma_d^2 + \mathcal{E}^2)/(4\,\Omega^2\,\Gamma_d)$. Here Ω and $\mathcal{E}$ are the coherent tunneling frequency and energy mismatch between the CQD's, respectively, and Γ_d (known as the decoherence rate in the reduced density matrix approach) represents the interaction strength between the CQD qubit and the PC detector. For symmetric ($\mathcal{E} = 0$) CQD's, Figs. 1(a)-(d) show that the $P(N,t)$ distribution's peak splits into two with weights closely corresponding to the initial values of the qubit's diagonal density matrix elements, $\rho_{aa}(0) = 0.75$ and $\rho_{bb}(0) = 0.25$, where a, b denote the CQD qubit's charge states. In Figs. 1(e) and (f) the valley between the two-peak structure of $P(N,t)$ is gradually filled up and a single broad plateau develops [i.e., $t_{\rm m}$ ($t_{\rm loc}$) and $t_{\rm mix}$ are on the same time scale]. Thus, no good initial qubit state-readout measurement can be performed in this case.

Note that $t_{\rm m}$ ($t_{\rm loc}$) and $t_{\rm mix}$ are basically statistical ensemble-average quantities. Many different individual realizations of quantum trajectories and their corresponding measurement records can provide physical insight into and aid in the interpretation of the ensemble average properties. For example, we can gain more physical insight into the occurrence of mixing, i.e., the occurrence of the overlap region between the two distributions in $P(N,t)$. The typical quantum trajectories whose accumulated electron detection number falls in the two-peak regions are shown in Fig. 2(a)-(c). Those in the overlap regions are shown in Figs. 2(d)-(f). Note that the accumulated electron detection number of the first half of the time evolution in Fig. 2(d) (i.e., for detection time up to $t = 10/\Gamma_d$), actually falls in the peak region of $\rho_{aa}(N,t)$. Within the readout time t, if the qubit changes its state, then its accumulated electron number very probably falls into the valley region between the peaks of the two distributions. For fixed Γ_d, as Ω increases, the chance for the state-changing transitions to happen in each individual realization of quantum

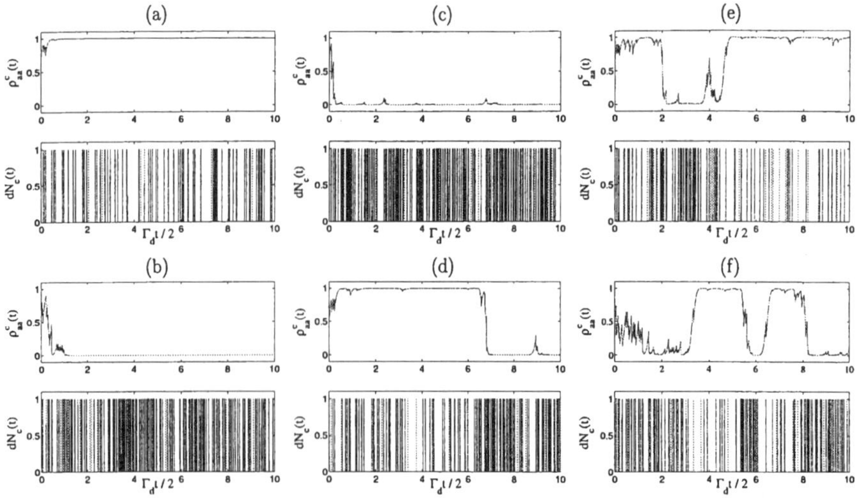

Figure 2. Typical quantum trajectories and corresponding detection records for $P(N,t)$ shown in Fig. 1. The ratios of (Ω/Γ_d) for (a) and (b) is 0, for (c) and (d) is 0.05, and for (e) and (f) is 0.2. Other parameters are the same as in Fig. 1.

trajectories increases. If the ratio (Ω/Γ_d) is increased further, the probability for more state-changing transitions within the same readout time interval also increases [see, e.g., Figs. 2(e) and (f)]. As a result, more weights of the distributions move to fill the valley and the two peaks transform into a broad plateau [see Figs. 1(e) and (f)].

In summary, we have demonstrated that the quantum trajectory approach not only gives the same results as the master equation approach of the "partially" reduced density matrix, but more appealingly provides more information and aids in the interpretation of the ensemble average properties, such as the occurrence of the mixing behavior in $P(N,t)$ discussed here.

References

1. S. A. Gurvitz, Phys. Rev. B **56**, 15215 (1997); quant-ph/9808058.
2. A. Shnirman and G. Schön, Phys. Rev. B **57**, 15400 (1998); Y. Makhlin, G. Schön, and A. Shnirman, Rev. Mod. Phys. **73**, 357 (2001).
3. A. N. Korotkov, Phys. Rev. B **60**, 5737 (1999); Phys. Rev. B **63**, 115403 (2001).
4. H.-S. Goan *et al.*, Phys. Rev. B **63**, 125326 (2001); H.-S. Goan and G. J. Milburn, Phys. Rev. B **64**, 235307 (2001).
5. H.-S. Goan, to appear in the Proceedings of the 26th International Conference on Physics of Semiconductors, Edinburgh, UK (IOP, 2002).

NON-ADIABATIC VACUUM INDUCED BERRY PHASE

SOUGATO BOSE[†], ANGELO CAROLLO[°‡], IVETTE FUENTES-GURIDI[°], MARCELO FRANÇA SANTOS[°] AND VLATKO VEDRAL[°]

[°]*Blackett Laboratory, Imperial College, London SW7 2BZ, UK*

[†]*Clarendon Laboratory, Parks Road Oxford OX1 3PU, UK*

[‡]*INFM, unità di ricerca di Palermo, via Archirafi 36, 90123 Italy*

We investigate quantum effects in geometric phases arising when a two-level system is interacting with a quantized electromagnetic field.

1 Introduction

The concept of geometric phase has attracted a great deal of interest since Berry[1] showed that the state of a quantum system, slowly evolving along a cyclic path, manifests a purely geometric feature, namely the Berry phase. The origin of this phenomenon relies on the geometric nature of state spaces and has been studied in many different systems such as spins, polarized light and atomic physics.[2] Recent works have explored their application in interferometry and quantum computation.[3,4]

Earlier works on the subject suggest how to observe these phases in quantum systems adiabatically driven by external classical devices or sources. The prototypical example is that of a two-level system whose adiabatic evolution is accomplished through the interaction with a slowly varying *classical* electromagnetic field.

In more recent works, it has been shown that new effects can be observed in the geometric phase of a system when the quantized nature of the interacting field is taken into account. In Refs. 5,6, the authors show that a two-level atom interacting with two quantized modes of the electromagnetic field according to the Hamiltonian

$$\begin{aligned} H(\theta,\phi) &= \omega\sigma_{22} + \nu(a^\dagger a + b^\dagger b) + \\ &+ \lambda[(\cos\frac{\theta}{2} a e^{-i\frac{\phi}{2}} + \sin\frac{\theta}{2} b e^{i\frac{\phi}{2}})\sigma_{21} + h.c.]. \end{aligned} \tag{1}$$

presents the following geometric phase

$$\chi^{\pm}_{n,m} = \frac{1}{2}\gamma\left[n - m + \frac{1}{2}(1-\cos\theta_n)\right], \tag{2}$$

if the system is initially prepared in an eigenstate $|\psi^{\pm}_{n,m}\rangle$ of $H(\theta,\phi)$ and then is adiabatically driven through a cyclic path in the θ and ϕ parameters space, where γ is the solid angle subtended by the cyclic loop in the Poincaré's sphere. The phase's dependence on the photon number is not trivial, and can be measured by using an interference procedure between any of the eigenstates $|\psi^{\pm}_{n,m}\rangle$ and the ground state $|g,0,0\rangle$, which is the only state that acquires no geometric phase. The most remarkable case is obtained in the resonant case ($\Delta = 0$) with initial state $|e,0,0\rangle = \frac{1}{\sqrt{2}}(|\psi^+_{0,0}\rangle + |\psi^-_{0,0}\rangle)$. Indeed, even though the field is in its vacuum state the geometric operations performed on the degrees of freedom of the field determine a Berry's phase

$$\chi_{zero} = \frac{\gamma}{4}. \tag{3}$$

In Ref. 7, the authors present an experimental proposal to measure this effect in cavity QED, implemented by rotating the polarization of an external classical field made to interact with both the atoms and the internal quantized cavity modes through the dispersive lambda scheme proposed in Ref. 8.

However, both the theoretical and experimental approaches to the problem present some difficulties that justify the search for new ideas. From the theoretical point of view, the modification of the classical parameters θ, ϕ may lead to the conclusion that the effect observed is not necessarily induced by the quantization of the electromagnetic field. Furthermore, the requirement of adiabatic evolution of the system may be very challenging experimentally, at least for the moment.

In this paper, we present calculations for the non-adiabatic evolution of an entangled state of the atom-field system, that, under certain conditions acquires the same geometric phase, as predicted in Refs. 5,7.

Whenever a system undergoes a cyclic evolution, it acquires, according to the definition of Aharanov and Anandan, a geometric phase that depends only on the path traversed by the system. In the definition of Berry, the geometric phase is obtained as the effect of the cyclic and adiabatic variation of an Hamiltonian. Aharanov and Anandan have extended this idea to a much more general framework. They have demonstrated that the geometric phase is completely independent of the dynamics, providing that the initial and final states of the evolution are the same (up to a phase factor). This means that regardless of the Hamiltonian that generates the evolution, a system that traverses a particular kind of closed path in the projective Hilbert space always acquires the same geometric phase. An extreme example of the non-adiabatic geometric phase is that acquired by a system evolving under a time-independent Hamiltonian. In this scenario, a system prepared in a superposition of eigenstates, after a specific choice of time T, may return to its original state and eventually acquire a geometric phase.

In the setup that we are presenting, the system is initially prepared in an entangled state of the atom and two fields modes. It then evolves under a time-independent Hamiltonian involving only the degrees of freedom of the modes. Consider a two-level system and two harmonic modes with the same frequency ν. Assume that we can prepare the system in the initial state:

$$|\psi_{in}\rangle = e^{-iJ_y\theta}|\phi\rangle, \tag{4}$$

where

$$|\phi\rangle = \cos\alpha/2|e,n,n'\rangle + \sin\alpha/2|g,n+1,n'\rangle \tag{5}$$

and J_y is the y component two-mode displacement operator J defined by

$$J_z = \frac{1}{2}(a^\dagger a - b^\dagger b) \quad J_x = \frac{1}{2}(a^\dagger b + ab^\dagger), \quad J_y = \frac{1}{2i}(a^\dagger b - ab^\dagger). \qquad (6)$$

Assume now that the dynamics of the system are described, in the interaction picture, by the Hamiltonian:

$$H_{int} = \hbar\beta J_z, \qquad (7)$$

where β is a (constant) parameter. Thus, the state evolves according to:

$$|\psi(t)\rangle = \exp -i\beta J_z t|\psi_{in}\rangle, \qquad (8)$$

and after a time $T = 4\pi/\beta$ the state completes a closed loop.

Using the Aharanov and Anandan definition of geometric phase,[6] it is easy to show that, after a cyclic evolution, the state (4) acquires a geometric phase equal to:

$$\chi_{(n,m)} = i\int_0^T \langle\psi(t)|\frac{d}{dt}|\psi(t)\rangle dt = \frac{1}{2}\gamma\left[n - m + \frac{1}{2}(1 - \cos\alpha)\right], \qquad (9)$$

where $\gamma = 4\pi(1 - cos\theta)$ is the solid angle that the parameters θ and ϕ of the Hamiltonian (1) would span if the same evolution (8) had been performed by means of an adiabatic evolution of the Hamiltonian (1). In the special case of $\alpha = \pi/2$ (the maximally entangled state) and $n = m = 0$, we obtain the result:

$$\chi_0 = \gamma/4.$$

As expected, these results are formally equivalent to those already obtained in Ref. 5 for the case of adiabatic evolution. The physical origin of the $\gamma/4$ term is related to the existence of a vacuum state of the field interacting with the two-level system. In Ref. 5 it is the adiabatic evolution of the interaction between atom and modes that gives rise to the geometric phase (9). The existence of the vacuum state allows the system to acquire a geometric phase even when no excitations are initially present in the field. Thus, the $\gamma/4$ term cannot have an interpretation in a classical description of the field, simply because "no excitation" of the field, in such a model, corresponds trivially to "no field".

An analogous explanation can be given in the non-adiabatic case. In order to observe a vacuum effect in the geometric phase, we need to prepare the system in an entangled state of atom and modes. It is the entanglement, in this case, which formally allows the system to acquire the $\gamma/4$ term. This is equivalent to saying that the initial interaction between the atom and a quantized field is the cause of such a peculiar effect.

We have shown that it is possible to obtain the same geometric phase as that generated in the adiabatic case in a setup in which the atom and modes evolve freely, without interaction with any external classical device.

The setup that we have presented clarifies the physical origin of the vacuum-induced geometric phase from a new perspective. This effect appears to be related to the entanglement between the two-level system and the field modes, or, in other words, to the interaction that couples the atom and the vacuum state of the modes.

The setup presented offers also advantages for an experimental observation of the vacuum Berry phase. One of the conditions required in Ref. 5 is that the evolution of the system be adiabatic. The adiabatic-evolution assumption is usually a strong requirement from an experimental perspective, an evolution that needs a long time to be completed needs a system robust against interaction with the environment. We have avoided this requirement in our non-adiabatic approach.

Acknowledgments

This research has been partly supported by the European Union, EPSRC, Hewlett-Packard and EU under Grant Nos. TMR ERB FMR XCT 96-0087 and IST 1999-11053-EQUIP. I. F.-G. would like to thank CNCT (Mexico) Grant no. 115569/135963 for financial support. MFS acknowledges the support of CNPq.

References

1. M. V. Berry, *Proc. Roy. Soc. A* **329**, 45 (1984).
2. A. Shapere and F. Wilczek, eds., *Geometric Phases in Physics.* World Scientific, Singapore, (1989).
3. J. Jones, V. Vedral, A. Ekert, and G. Castagnoli, *Nature* **403**, 869 (1999).
4. G. Falci, R. Fazio, G. M. Palma, J. Siewert, and V. Vedral, *Nature* **407**, 355 (2000).
5. I. Fuentes-Guridi, A. Carollo, S. Bose, and V. Vedral, quant-ph/0202128, to appear in Phys. Rev. Lett.
6. Y. Aharonov and J. Anandan, *Phys. Rev. Lett.* **58**, 1593 (1987).
7. A. Carollo, A. M. França-Santos, and V. Vedral, quant-ph/0204164, submitted to Phys. Rev. Lett.
8. M. F. Santos, E. Solano, and R. L. de Matos Filho, *Phys. Rev. Lett.* **87**, 093601 (2001).

NON-MARKOVIAN STOCHASTIC SCHRÖDINGER EQUATIONS

JAY M. GAMBETTA AND H. M. WISEMAN

School of Science, Griffith University, Nathan, Brisbane 4111, Australia
E-mail: j.gambetta@mailbox.gu.edu.au
E-mail: h.wiseman@mailbox.gu.edu.au

Do stochastic Schrödinger equations (SSEs) have a physical interpretation? In the Markovian limit, the answer is yes, SSEs are evolution equations for the system state conditioned on continuously monitoring the bath.[1] In a previous paper[2] we addressed the non-Markovian case. Although we used quantum measurement theory to define two stochastic unravelings, we concluded that the SSE or quantum trajectory of the state through time is a fiction. In this paper we present a perturbative procedure that allows one to numerically solve diffusive non-Markovian Stochastic Schrödinger equations, for a wide range of memory functions.

1 Introduction

In nature a quantum system is most likely found in an entanglement with at least one other quantum system. An example of this is a two level atom (TLA) immersed in an environment of harmonic oscillators (the electromagnetic field). This type of quantum system, a small system interacting with a larger system (the bath), is called an open quantum system.[1] The system-bath interaction causes the two systems to entangle, resulting in a combined state $|\Psi(t)\rangle$ whose evolution can be theoretically determined by the Schrödinger equation. However, due to the many degrees of freedom of the bath, this is generally impractical and it is best to describe the TLA by the reduced state, $\rho_{\rm red}(t)$. The evolution of $\rho_{\rm red}(t)$ is found by averaging $|\Psi(t)\rangle\langle\Psi(t)|$ over all the possible bath states, and has the general (non-Markovian) form[3]

$$\dot{\rho}_{\rm red}(t) = -i[\hat{H}_{\rm int}(t), \rho_{\rm red}(t)] + \int_0^t \mathcal{K}(t,s)[\hat{\sigma}]\rho_{\rm red}(s)ds, \qquad (1)$$

where $\hat{H}_{\rm int}(t)$ is the system Hamiltonian in the interaction picture, $\mathcal{K}(t,s)[\hat{\sigma}]$ is the 'memory superoperator' representing how the bath affects the TLA, and $\hat{\sigma}$ is the lowering operator for the TLA. The problem with equation (1) is that without some form of approximation, in general, it is unsolvable.

In this paper we use non-Markovian stochastic Schrödinger equations (SSEs), initially developed by Strunz, Diósi, and Gisin[4] and later generalized to include real-valued noise by us[2], to provide a perturbative procedure for solving this equation. Like the enlarged-Hilbert space SSE method,[5] our method by definition will enforce the positive requirement of $\rho_{\rm red}(t)$. Unlike it, however, our numerical solution only involves a Hilbert space equal to that of the TLA.

2 Non-Markovian SSEs

A non-Markovian SSE is a stochastic differential equation for the system state vector $|\psi_z(t)\rangle$ depending on some (non-white) noise $z(t)$. It has the property that when $|\psi_z(t)\rangle\langle\psi_z(t)|$ is averaged over all possible $z(t)$ one obtains ρ_{red}. It should be noted that for a single $\rho_{\text{red}}(t)$, $z(t)$ can take many different functional forms, and we label these different forms a stochastic unraveling.[2]

In Ref. 2 we showed that non-Markovian SSEs can be derived from quantum measurement theory (QMT), with the different unravelings corresponding to different measurements on the bath. The two unravelings we considered were the 'coherent' or 'DSG'[4] unraveling and the 'quadrature' unraveling. As in the Markov limit, we can define at least two SSEs for each unraveling: one for $z(t)$ chosen from an ostensible distribution (a guessed distribution) and the other for its actual distribution. The former gives a SSE linear in the unnormalized state $|\tilde{\psi}_z(t)\rangle$, whereas the latter gives a SSE non-linear in the normalized state $|\psi_z(t)\rangle$. In Ref. 2 we came to the conclusion that the solution of the actual non-Markovian SSE at time t gives the state the system will be in if a measurement of the bath is performed at that time and gives a certain result which depends on the whole history of $z(t)$. For the coherent unraveling the linear non-Markovian SSE has the form

$$\partial_t|\tilde{\psi}_z(t)\rangle = \left[\frac{-i}{\hbar}\hat{H}_{\text{int}}(t) + z^*(t)\hat{\sigma} - \hat{\sigma}^{\dagger}\,{}^{(0)}\hat{F}_z(t)\right]|\tilde{\psi}_z(t)\rangle. \tag{2}$$

Here ${}^{(0)}\hat{F}_z(t)$ is an operator given by

$${}^{(0)}\hat{F}_z(t) = \int_0^t \alpha(t-s)\,{}^{(0)}\hat{f}_z(t,s)ds, \tag{3}$$

where ${}^{(0)}\hat{f}_z(t,s)$ is defined by $\frac{\delta}{\delta z^*(s)}|\tilde{\psi}_z(t)\rangle = {}^{(0)}\hat{f}_z(t,s)|\tilde{\psi}_z(t)\rangle$. In Eq. (2) the noise function $z(t)$ is complex and has the following correlation functions

$$\mathrm{E}[z(t)z^*(s)] = \alpha(t-s), \qquad \mathrm{E}[z(t)z(s)] = 0, \tag{4}$$

where $\alpha(t-s)$ is called the memory function.

The actual non-Markovian SSE for the coherent unravelling is

$$d_t|\psi_z(t)\rangle = \Big[-\frac{i}{\hbar}\hat{H}_{\text{int}}(t) - (\hat{\sigma}^{\dagger} - \langle\hat{\sigma}^{\dagger}\rangle_t)\,{}^{(0)}\hat{F}_z(t) + \Big\langle(\hat{\sigma}^{\dagger} - \langle\hat{\sigma}^{\dagger}\rangle_t)\,{}^{(0)}\hat{F}_z(t)\Big\rangle_t$$
$$+z^*(t)(\hat{\sigma} - \langle\hat{\sigma}\rangle_t)\Big]|\psi_z(t)\rangle, \tag{5}$$

where the noise function has the form $z^*(t) = z_\Lambda^*(t) + \int_0^t \alpha^*(t-s)\langle\hat{\sigma}^{\dagger}\rangle_s ds$, with $z_\Lambda(t)$ having the same correlations as $z(t)$ does in the linear case.

For the quadrature unraveling the linear non-Markovian SSE has the form

$$\partial_t|\tilde{\psi}_z(t)\rangle = \left[-\frac{i}{\hbar}\hat{H}_{\text{int}}(t) + z(t)\hat{\sigma} - \hat{\sigma}_x\,{}^{(0)}\hat{Q}_z(t)\right]|\tilde{\psi}_z(t)\rangle, \tag{6}$$

where the noise function $z(t)$ is real and has the correlation function $\tilde{\mathrm{E}}[z(t)z(s)] = \beta(t-s)$. The functional operator ${}^{(0)}\hat{Q}_z(t)$ in this equation differs from the coherent unraveling by being dependent on real noise.

3 Perturbation Method

To solve the non-Markovian SSE, and hence find $\rho_{\mathrm{red}}(t)$, for the coherent or quadrature unravelings we have to work out the operator functionals ${}^{(0)}\hat{F}_z(t)$ and ${}^{(0)}\hat{Q}_z(t)$, respectively. This has been done exactly only for systems for which an analytical solution for $\rho_{\mathrm{red}}(t)$ may be found by other means[4] or for systems with a small number of bath modes.[2,4] Our general perturbation method is explained in great detail in Ref. 6. In this paper we consider the TLA and memory functions of the form $\alpha(t-s) = \beta(t-s) = \frac{\gamma\kappa}{4}e^{-\kappa|t-s|/2}$.

The perturbation method works by taking the time derivative of Eq. (3) and using the above form for $\alpha(t-s)$; this gives

$$\partial_t {}^{(0)}\hat{F}_z(t) = \frac{\gamma\kappa}{4}\hat{\sigma} - \frac{\kappa}{2}{}^{(0)}\hat{F}_z(t) + \int_0^t \alpha(t-s)\partial_t {}^{(0)}\hat{f}_z(t,s)ds. \tag{7}$$

To find the third term we use $\partial_t \frac{\delta}{\delta z^*(s)}|\tilde{\psi}_z(t)\rangle = \frac{\delta}{\delta z^*(s)}\partial_t|\tilde{\psi}_z(t)\rangle$, this allows us to write

$$\partial_t {}^{(0)}\hat{f}_z(t,s) = -\frac{i}{\hbar}[\hat{H}_{\mathrm{int}}(t), {}^{(0)}\hat{f}_z(t,s)] + z^*(t)[\hat{\sigma}, {}^{(0)}\hat{f}_z(t,s)] - [\hat{\sigma}^\dagger {}^{(0)}\hat{F}_z(t), \\ {}^{(0)}\hat{f}_z(t,s)] - \hat{\sigma}^\dagger \frac{\delta}{\delta z^*(s)}{}^{(0)}\hat{F}_z(t). \tag{8}$$

Thus Eq. (7) becomes

$$\partial_t {}^{(0)}\hat{F}_z(t) = \frac{\gamma\kappa}{4}\hat{\sigma} - \frac{\kappa}{2}{}^{(0)}\hat{F}_z(t) + z^*(t)[\hat{\sigma}, {}^{(0)}\hat{F}_z(t)] - \frac{i}{\hbar}[\hat{H}_{\mathrm{int}}(t), {}^{(0)}\hat{F}_z(t)] \\ -[\hat{\sigma}^\dagger {}^{(0)}\hat{F}_z(t), {}^{(0)}\hat{F}_z(t)] - \hat{\sigma}^\dagger {}^{(1)}\hat{F}_z(t), \tag{9}$$

where ${}^{(1)}\hat{F}_z(t)$ is a first-order functional. It is equal to $\int_0^t \alpha(t-s){}^{(1)}\hat{f}_z(t,s)ds$, where ${}^{(1)}\hat{f}_z(t,s)$ is defined by $\frac{\delta}{\delta z^*(s)}{}^{(0)}\hat{F}_z(t) = {}^{(1)}\hat{f}_z(t,s)$.

If we knew the form of ${}^{(1)}\hat{F}_z(t)$ then Eq. (9) could be solved exactly. If it is not known we can generate $\partial_t {}^{(1)}\hat{F}_z(t)$ in terms of ${}^{(0)}\hat{F}_z(t)$, ${}^{(1)}\hat{F}_z(t)$ and ${}^{(2)}\hat{F}_z(t)$ and so forth up to order n. The perturbation method is basically to truncate the set of differential equations to order n with a guessed value for ${}^{(n)}\hat{F}_z(t)$. In Ref. 6 we discuss what is the best choice for this guess.

4 The driven TLA

To illustrate this perturbation method we use a Hamiltonian (in the interaction picture) of the form

$$\hat{H}_{\mathrm{int}}(t) = \hbar\frac{\Delta}{2}\hat{\sigma}_z + \hbar\frac{\chi}{2}\hat{\sigma}_x, \tag{10}$$

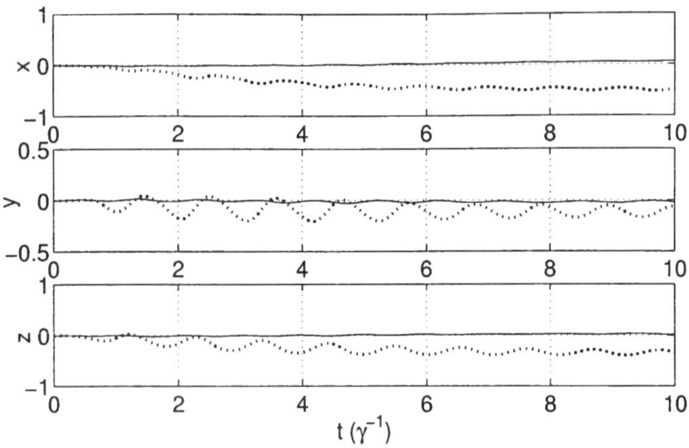

Figure 1. This figure depicts the Bloch vector components for the difference between the reduced state calculated from the enlarged system method[5] and our perturbative method. The dotted lines correspond to the zeroth order and the solid line corresponds to the first order.

where $\Delta = \omega_0 - \Omega$ and χ are the detuning and the driving, respectively. Figure 1 shows graphically that the reduced state calculated from an ensemble of first-order perturbative non-Markovian SSEs (for both unravelings) is closer to the reduced state calculated via the enlarged system method than is the zeroth order. In this figure all calculations were done using the initial system state $|\psi(0)\rangle = |e\rangle$ with system parameters $\gamma = 1$, $\kappa = 1$, $\chi = 5$ and $\Delta = 3$. Time is measured in units γ^{-1}.

References

1. H. J. Carmichael, *An Open Systems Approach to Quantum Optics* (Springer-Verlag, Berlin, 1993).
2. J. M. Gambetta and H. M. Wiseman, Phys. Rev. A **66**, 012108 (2002).
3. S. Nakajima, Prog. Theor. Phys. **20**, 948 (1958); R. Zwanzig, J. Chem. Phys. **33**, 1338 (1960).
4. L. Diósi, N. Gisin and W. T. Strunz, Phys. Rev. A **58**, 1699 (1998); W. T. Strunz, L. Diósi, and N. Gisin, Phys. Rev. Lett. **82**, 1801 (1999); L. Diósi and W. T. Strunz, Phys. Lett. A **235**, 569 (1997).
5. A. Imamoḡlu, Phys. Rev. A **50**, 3650, (1994); P. Stenius and A. A. Imamoḡlu, Quantum Semiclass. Opt. **8**, 283 (1996).
6. J. M. Gambetta and H. M. Wiseman, quant-ph/0208169.

ENCODED UNIVERSALITY FOR GENERALIZED ANISOTROPIC EXCHANGE INTERACTIONS

JIRI VALA AND K. BIRGITTA WHALEY

Department of Chemistry and Pitzer Center for Theoretical Chemistry
University of California, Berkeley, CA 94720, USA
E-mail: jvala@uclink.berkeley.edu

Quantum computation is known to be universal as long as arbitrary single-qubit and entangling two-qubit unitary operations can be applied in a quantum circuit.[1,2] Since these operations are generated by the Hamiltonian, universality is linked fundamentally to the physical structure of the system of qubits. Recently, Whaley and coworkers[3,4,5,6,7] have established a new paradigm of *encoded universality*, within which a lack of universality of non-generic intrinsic physical interactions can be overcome by a suitable encoding of the states representing quantum logic into a two and higher dimensional subspace of the system Hilbert space. The significance of these encoded universality schemes for quantum computation lies in the fact that they require active manipulation only of two-particle exchange interactions, and hence avoid other sources of decoherence like application of additional control fields.

In this work we develop the encoded universality for the generalized anisotropic exchange interaction[8] that results from asymmetry in the exchange tensor and incorporation of additional cross-terms in the Hamiltonian: $\hat{\mathbf{H}}_{ij} = \frac{1}{2}\sum_{\alpha=x,y} J_{ij}^{\alpha}\sigma_i^{\alpha}\sigma_j^{\alpha} + \frac{1}{2}\sum_{\alpha\neq\beta=x,y} J_{ij}^{\alpha\beta}\sigma_i^{\alpha}\sigma_j^{\beta}$. This generalized asymmetric anisotropic Hamiltonian can be seen to split into two distinct parts, symmetric ($\hat{\mathbf{H}}_{ij}^{s}$) and antisymmetric ($\hat{\mathbf{H}}_{ij}^{a}$), that act on orthogonal two-dimensional sectors of the four-dimensional Hilbert space spanned respectively by $\{|01\rangle, |10\rangle\}$ and $\{|00\rangle, |11\rangle\}$:

$$\begin{aligned}\hat{\mathbf{H}}_{ij} &= \frac{1}{2}[J_{ij}^{s}(\sigma_i^x\sigma_j^x + \sigma_i^y\sigma_j^y) + J_{ij}^{a}(\sigma_i^x\sigma_j^x - \sigma_i^y\sigma_j^y)] \\ &+ \frac{1}{2}[K_{ij}^{s}(\sigma_i^x\sigma_j^y - \sigma_i^y\sigma_j^x) + K_{ij}^{a}(\sigma_i^x\sigma_j^y + \sigma_i^y\sigma_j^x)], \qquad (1)\end{aligned}$$

where $J_{ij}^{s} = \frac{1}{2}(J_{ij}^{xx} + J_{ij}^{yy})$, $J_{ij}^{a} = \frac{1}{2}(J_{ij}^{xx} - J_{ij}^{yy})$, $K_{ij}^{s} = \frac{1}{2}(J_{ij}^{xy} + J_{ij}^{yx})$ and $K_{ij}^{a} = \frac{1}{2}(J_{ij}^{xy} - J_{ij}^{yx})$.

The asymmetric anisotropic interaction including these cross-terms is part of a more general model considered by Terhal and DiVincenzo[9] in the framework of fermionic quantum computation.[10,11] The anisotropic exchange is employed in some of the recent proposals for solid-state implementation of quantum computation, e.g., using quantum dots in cavities.[12] The cross terms arise from contributions such as spin-orbit coupling.[13]

Considering first the anisotropic exchange Hamiltonian without cross terms, we construct a universal encoding using the algebraic approach of Kempe et al.[5,6,7] In the case of three-qubit encoding, the operators from the commutant of the Lie algebra generated by the Hamiltonian possess a block diagonal structure, $\hat{\mathbf{X}}_{\mathcal{B}} = \bigoplus_{k=1}^{4} \sigma_k^x$ and $\hat{\mathbf{Z}}_{\mathcal{B}} = \bigoplus_{k=1}^{4} \sigma_k^z$, when expressed in the permuted standard basis set. The complete SU(2) algebra is generated over each 2×2 block. The structure of the commutant representation indicates that the Lie algebra $\mathcal{L}$ generated by the Hamiltonian splits as $M(\mathbb{C}^4) \otimes \mathcal{I}_2$. The Hilbert space of this system splits accordingly into two four-dimensional subspaces, $\mathcal{H}^8 = \mathcal{H}^4 \oplus \mathcal{H}^4$, which are characterized by even and odd bit-string parity. These subspaces are not mixed by the parity-preserving interaction (1).

The four-dimensional subspaces thus define two independent codes that are spanned by the following two sets of code words:

$$(I)\ \{|000\rangle, |110\rangle, |101\rangle, |011\rangle\} \quad \text{and} \quad (II)\ \{|111\rangle, |001\rangle, |010\rangle, |100\rangle\}. \qquad (2)$$

We now apply the Hamiltonian, acting simultaneously and identically on both subspaces $\mathcal{H}^4$, to pairs of physical qubits in the three-qubit code words and analyze the action of these interactions and of their commutators.

We start with the exchange coupling H^{12} between the physical qubits 1-2, for instance. In either code space, this interaction is represented by the matrix $(J^a \sigma_x) \otimes (J^s \sigma_x)$. The lower right block, acts as a σ_{34}^x operation over the code words 3 and 4, e.g., the states $|101\rangle$ and $|011\rangle$ from (I), with coupling strength J^s. The antisymmetric component, which is the top left 2×2 block of this matrix, acts on the other two orthogonal states from the code, namely on $|000\rangle$ and $|110\rangle$ from (I). This also results in an encoded $\bar{\sigma}^x$ operation, but with coupling strength J^a. This is the first element required for an encoded SU(2) operation.

The second element is an encoded $\bar{\sigma}^y$ operation. This operation is generated through the commutator of a pair of Hamiltonian operators. For instance, taking the commutator of interactions between physical qubits 1-3 and qubits 2-3 yields $[H^{13}, H^{23}] = i[(J^a)^2 - (J^s)^2]\sigma_{34}^y$. The operator σ_{34}^y possesses a similar structure as H^{12}, but the lower right 2×2 block acts as encoded $\bar{\sigma}^y$ on the states 3 and 4 of the code (I) for instance, $|101\rangle$ and $|011\rangle$, whereas the upper left block containes only zero elements. That means that part of the interaction which changes the occupation number by two, like the antisymmetric component of the corresponding H^{12}, is eliminated via the commutation relations.

The third and last element required for an encoded SU(2) operation is encoded $\bar{\sigma}^z$. It can be easily verified that this operation is now obtainable from a second-level commutator of the Hamiltonian with the encoded $\bar{\sigma}^y$ operation: e.g., $[H^{12}, \sigma_{34}^y] = i2J^s\sigma_{34}^z$. Analogous sets of operators can be defined starting from the other two exchange Hamiltonians, i.e., H^{13} and H^{23}. In total therefore, we have three distinct ways of defining the logical qubit from each of the subspaces (I) and (II), with arbitrary SU(2) operations possible on any of these six possible sets of qubits.

The inclusion of the cross-product terms transforms the Hamiltonian operators into hermitian matrices of the same structure, whose coupling coefficients $\tilde{J}^a$ and $\tilde{J}^s$ are now complex numbers. The result of the commutation relation is again proportional to the $\bar{\sigma^y}$ operation. For instance, $[\tilde{H}^{13}, \tilde{H}^{23}] = i(|\tilde{J}^a|^2 - |\tilde{J}^s|^2)\sigma^y_{34}$. However now only two of the three possible commutation relations between pairs of complex Hamiltonian matrices of the three-qubit code will generate encoded $\bar{\sigma^y}$. Encoded $\bar{\sigma}^z$ and $\bar{\sigma}^x$ are generated via the higher-level commutators.

Since the encoded $\bar{\sigma}^y$ operations for a given Hamiltonian are generated via the commutation relations with the other two available (and equally strong) interactions among three physical qubits, the most suitable layout structure is an equilateral triangle. To additionally accomodate the two-qubit logical operations, it is convenient to arrange triangles of physical qubits representing logical qubits into a linear chain with alternating triangle orientations.[8] With this layout, it can be shown that an entangling two-qubit gate — namely, an element of the local equivalence class [CNOT][14,15] — is obtained by applying the encoded $\bar{\sigma}^z$ operation onto the triplet of physical qubits that connects two logical qubits.[8]

Implementation of encoded SU(2) operations is achieved using conjugation by unitary operations, as also considered by Kempe et al.[5,16] and Lidar and Wu.[17] The antisymmetric terms in the Hamiltonian complicate the situation, since the conjugating sequence of the unitary evolutions in general mixes different states of the code space. We note however that the simultaneous effect of the symmetric and antisymmetric terms of the Hamiltonian (1) can be eliminated by choosing a suitable duration of the exchange interaction. We illustrate the procedure on an example in which cross terms in the Hamiltonian are absent, i.e., $K^a_{ij} = K^s_{ij} = 0$. Since $[\hat{\mathbf{H}}^s_{ij}, \hat{\mathbf{H}}^a_{ij}] = 0$ for any i and j, the unitary evolution operator generated by the Hamiltonian (1) splits into a product $U(\tau) = \exp(-i\hat{\mathbf{H}}^s_{ij}\tau)\exp(-i\hat{\mathbf{H}}^a_{ij}\tau)$. For a suitably chosen time duration, one of the terms can be made to generate the identity from the interaction Lie group if $J^s_{ij} \neq J^a_{ij}$. Simultaneously, the effect of the other term can be tuned to provide the desired transformation. For instance, the unitary evolution generated by the σ^y_{34} operator, resulting from the commutation relation $[H^{13}, H^{23}]$, can be obtained under some conditions from the following conjugation, $\hat{\mathbf{U}}(\sigma^y_{34}, \phi) = e^{-i\sigma^y_{34}\phi} = e^{iH^{13}\theta/2}e^{iH^{23}\phi'/2}e^{-iH^{13}\theta/2}$, where $\phi' = \phi/J^s$ and θ is the time duration satisfying simultaneously $\theta = 0(\text{mod } \pi)/J^a = \frac{\pi}{2}(\text{mod } \pi)/J^s$. Due to the asymmetry of the exchange coupling terms ($J^s \neq J^a$) and the unitarity of the quantum evolution, this condition can always be fulfilled. Development of a conjugating procedure for the generalized exchange Hamiltonian (1), where $K^a_{ij} \neq 0$ and $K^s_{ij} \neq 0$, is possible within the same framework. In that case, the encoded $\bar{\sigma}^y$ operation is directly available from the cross terms with appropriate choice of conjugation timings.[8]

In the present work we have demonstrated that encoded universality can be achieved for generalizations of the anisotropic exchange interaction that remove the symmetry between exchange components acting in the x and y directions and also incorporate cross-product terms in the Hamiltonian. Rewriting the generalized Hamiltonian in terms of its symmetric and antisymmetric components, we found that it is possible to completely eliminate the effect of the antisymmetric term of the Hamiltonian on quantum evolution, either by judicious use of commutation relations or by imposing a suitable timing of the operations. This allowed encoded single-qubit and two-qubit operations to be formulated in short discrete-gate sequences analogous to those previously derived for the symmetric anisotropic (XY) Hamiltonian.[16]

Acknowledgments

The authors' work was sponsored by the Air Force Laboratory, Air Force Material Command, USAF, under Contract No. F30602-01-2-0524, and by the Defense Advanced Research Projects Agency (DARPA) and the Office of Naval Research under Grant No. FDN 00014-01-1-0826.

References

1. D. P. DiVincenzo, *Phys. Rev. A* **51**, 1015 (1995).
2. A. Barenco et al., *Phys. Rev. A* **52**, 3457 (1995).
3. D. Bacon et al., in *Proc. International Conference on Experimental Implementation of Quantum Computation*, Rinton Press, Australia, p. 257, e-print quant-ph/0102140 (2001).
4. D. P. DiVincenzo et al., *Nature* **408**, 337 (2000).
5. J. Kempe, D. Bacon, D. Lidar, and K. Whaley, *Phys. Rev. A* **63**, 042307 (2001).
6. J. Kempe, Ph.D. thesis, University of California, Berkeley (2001).
7. J. Kempe, D. Bacon, D. P. DiVincenzo, and K. B. Whaley, *Quantum Information and Computation* **1**, 241 (2001).
8. J. Vala and K. B. Whaley, *Phys. Rev. A* **66**, 022304 (2002).
9. B. M. Terhal and D. P. DiVincenzo, *Phys. Rev. A* **65**, 032325 (2001).
10. S. B. Bravyi and A. Y. Kitaev, quant-ph/0003137.
11. L. Valiant, in *Proc. 33rd ACM Symp. Theory of Computing*, ACM (2001).
12. A. Imamoglu et al., *Phys. Rev. Lett.* **83**, 4204 (1999).
13. T. Moriya, *Phys. Rev.* **120**, 91 (1960).
14. Y. Makhlin, quant-ph/0002045.
15. J. Zhang, J. Vala, K. B. Whaley, and S. Sastry, quant-ph/0209120.
16. J. Kempe and K. B. Whaley, *Phys. Rev. A* **65**, 052330 (2002).
17. D. Lidar and L.-A. Wu, *Phys. Rev. Lett.* **88**, 017905 (2001).

GATE-LEVEL SIMULATION OF QUANTUM CIRCUITS

GEORGE F. VIAMONTES, MANOJ RAJAGOPALAN,
IGOR L. MARKOV, AND JOHN P. HAYES
The Univ. of Michigan, Advanced Computer Architecture Lab., Ann Arbor, MI 48109-2122
E-mail: {gviamont,rmanoj,imarkov,jhayes}@eecs.umich.edu

Simulating quantum computation on a classical computer is a difficult problem. The matrices (operators) representing quantum gates, and vectors modeling qubit states grow exponentially with an increase in the number of qubits. However, by using a new data structure called the Quantum Information Decision Diagram (QuIDD) that exploits the structure of quantum operators, many of these matrices and vectors can be represented in a form that grows polynomially. Using QuIDDs, we implemented a general-purpose quantum computing simulator in C++ called QuIDDPro and tested it on Grover's algorithm. We observed that our QuIDD technique asymptotically outperforms other known simulation techniques.

1 Introduction

Richard Feynman observed in the early 1980s that simulating quantum processes on classical hardware seems to require super-polynomial (in the number of qubits) memory and time. Traditional array-based representations are often insensitive to the actual values stored, and even sparse matrix storage offers little improvement for quantum operators with no zero matrix elements (e.g., Hadamard operators). Gottesman[6] identified a number of special-case quantum circuits for which tailor-made simulation techniques require only polynomial memory and runtime. However, he noted that these "restricted types of quantum circuits fall short of the full power of quantum computation." Thus, in cases of major interest, such as Shor's and Grover's algorithms, quantum simulation is still performed with straightforward linear-algebraic tools and requires astronomic resources.

A number of "programming environments" for quantum computing were proposed recently that are mostly front-ends to quantum circuit simulators. Their back-ends typically use linear algebra methods to multiply matrices and require super-polynomial computational resources in the number of qubits. The potential benefits of efficient linear-algebraic operations on compressed arguments are immense.

Our approach uses graph-based techniques to improve asymptotic time and memory complexity of quantum simulations by exploiting the structure of quantum operators. Although abstract worst-case complexity is still exponential, our approach achieves very substantial performance gains in many important cases.

Other advanced simulation techniques, e.g., MATLAB's "packed" representation, include data compression, but often must decompress the operands of matrix-vector multiplication. A notable exception is Greve's simulation[5] of Shor's algorithm that uses *Binary Decision Diagrams* (BDDs).[2] Probability amplitudes of individual qubits are modeled by single decision nodes. This only captures superpositions in which every participating qubit is rotated by ± 45 degrees from $|0\rangle$ towards $|1\rangle$. Though Greve's BDD representation cannot simulate arbitrary quantum circuits, the idea of modeling quantum states with a BDD-*like* structure is appealing and motivates our approach.

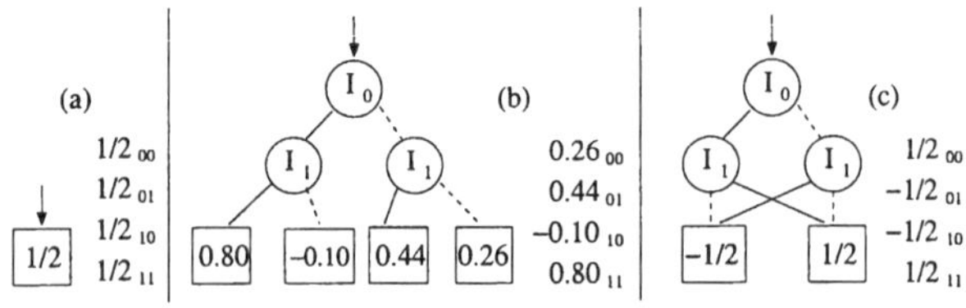

Figure 1. QuIDD examples of (a) best, (b) worst, and (c) mid-range complexity.

2 QuIDD Theory

The *Quantum Information Decision Diagram* (QuIDD) was born out of the observation that vectors and matrices that arise in quantum computing exhibit a lot of structure. More complex operators obtained from the tensor product of simpler matrices continue to exhibit these common substructures, which BDDs can capture. BDDs and operations for manipulating them were originally developed by Lee[1] and extended to Reduced Ordered BDDs (ROBDDs) by Bryant[2] to handle large Boolean functions efficiently. An ROBDD is a *directed acyclic graph* (DAG) with up to two outgoing edges per node, labeled *then* and *else*. Algorithms that perform operations on ROBDDs are typically recursive traversals. While not improving worst-case asymptotics, in practice ROBDDs achieve exponential space compression and runtime improvements by exploiting various types of structure in applications.

Beyond the domain of digital logic design, ROBDD variants have been adopted in many contexts. Multi-Terminal Binary Decision Diagrams (MTBDDs)[3] and Algebraic Decision Diagrams (ADDs)[4] with their integrated linear-algebraic operations are particularly relevant to the task of simulating quantum systems. We have developed a further refinement, the QuIDD, to compress complex-valued matrices and vectors and operate on them in compressed form. Our C++ implementation of QuIDDs, called QuIDDPro, uses ADDs, but can, in principle, use MTBDDs as well. Space and time complexities of our simulations of n-qubit systems range from $O(1)$ to $O(2^n)$, but the worst case is not typical.

Vectors and Matrices. Figure 1 shows the QuIDD structure for three 2-qubit states. We consider the indices of the four vector elements in binary, and define their bits as decision variables of QuIDDs. A similar definition is used in ADDs.[4] For example, traversing the *then* edge (solid line) of node I_0 in Fig. 1(c) is equivalent to assigning the value 1 to the first binary digit of the vector index. Traversing the *else* edge (dotted line) of node I_1 in the same figure is equivalent to assigning the value 0 to the second binary digit of the index. These traversals bring us to the terminal node $-\frac{1}{2}$, which is precisely the value at index 10 in the vector representation.

QuIDD representations of matrices extend those of vectors by adding a second type of variable node and enjoy the same reduction rules and compression benefits. Consider the 2-qubit Hadamard matrix annotated with binary row and column indices shown in Fig. 2(a). In this case there are two sets of indices: The first (vertical) set corresponds to the rows, and the second (horizontal) set corresponds to the columns. We assign the variable name R_i and C_i to the row and column index variables respectively. This distinction between the two sets of variables was

$$R_0R_1 \begin{array}{c} 00 \\ 01 \\ 10 \\ 11 \end{array} \begin{bmatrix} \frac{1}{2} & \frac{1}{2} & \frac{1}{2} & \frac{1}{2} \\ \frac{1}{2} & -\frac{1}{2} & \frac{1}{2} & -\frac{1}{2} \\ \frac{1}{2} & \frac{1}{2} & -\frac{1}{2} & -\frac{1}{2} \\ \frac{1}{2} & -\frac{1}{2} & -\frac{1}{2} & \frac{1}{2} \end{bmatrix}$$

$$\begin{array}{cccc} 00 & 01 & 10 & 11 \end{array}$$
$$C_0C_1$$

(a)

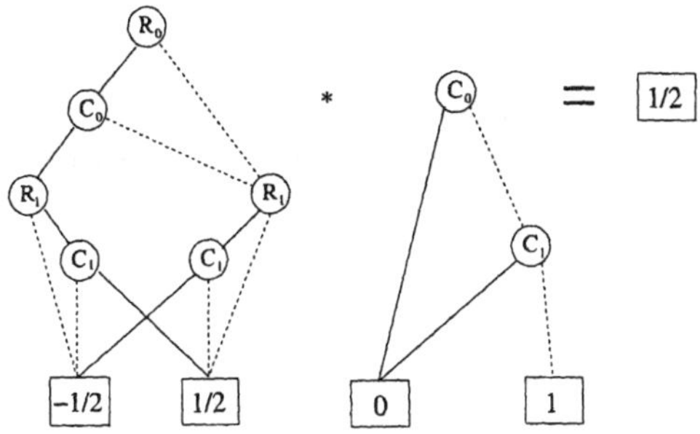

(b)

Figure 2. (a) 2-qubit Hadamard, and (b) its QuIDD representation multiplied by $|00\rangle = (1,0,0,0)$.

originally noted in several works including that of Bahar et al.[4] Figure 2(b) shows the QuIDD form of this sample matrix where it is used to modify the state vector $|00\rangle = (1,0,0,0)$ via matrix-vector multiplication.

QuIDD Operations. Most operations defined for ADDs also work on QuIDDs with only slight modification. A key example is matrix multiplication, which is an extension of the dot-product operation and implemented as a recursive procedure adapted from the well-known *BDD-Apply* function.[2] For more details, see our technical report.[7] Tensor products can be implemented as follows. By definition, $A \otimes B$ multiplies each element of A by the entire matrix (or vector) B producing a new matrix (or vector). Multiplication of the terminal values is done by first shifting the variable numbers in B after those in A followed by a call to the recursive *Apply* function with an argument that directs *Apply* to multiply when it reaches the terminals of both operands.[7] Since QuIDD operations are variants of *Apply*, they have complexity $O(|A| \cdot |B|)$, which is polynomial in the number of qubits if both $|A|$ and $|B|$ are.

3 Simulating Grover's Algorithm with QuIDDs

We simulated quantum circuits for Grover's algorithm[8] in the state-vector representation by performing matrix-vector multiplications and tensor products using QuIDDs. Ideal numbers of iterations for Grover's algorithm are computed following Boyer et al.[9] Oracle circuits are implemented using k-CNOT gates. To evaluate QuIDD representations of all relevant quantum gates, we measured their size at n-qubits, where $n = 20, \ldots, 100$ and observed that memory usage grew linearly.[7] Thus, using QuIDDs, simulation of Grover's algorithm is not memory limited even at 100 qubits. Results in Table 1 deal with an oracle searching for one element out of 2^n. As shown, QuIDDPro achieves asymptotic memory savings compared to known interpreted and compiled numerical analysis packages. The overall runtimes are still exponential in n because Grover's algorithm requires an exponential number of iterations, even on an actual quantum computer. We also studied a "mod-1024" oracle[7] searching for elements whose ten least significant bits are 1. We observed that memory usage for the mod-1024 oracle for up to $n = 25$ qubits grew as $(7.592 + 0.041n)$. For additional details on numerical precision, round-off errors, etc., see our technical report.[7]

Table 1. Simulating Grover's algorithm with n qubits using Octave (Oct), MATLAB (MAT), Blitz++ (B++) and our simulator QuIDDPro (QP). Results were produced on a 1.2 GHz AMD Athlon with 1 GB RAM running Linux. Memory usage for MAT and Oct is lower bounded by the size of the state vector and conditional phase shift operator; B++ and QP memory usage is measured as the size of the entire program. Runtimes for MAT and Oct are not shown past 15 qubits as simulation time was limited to 20 hours.

Runtime (s)				
n	Oct	MAT	B++	QP
10	89.4	14.0	0.22	0.20
11	2.94e2	45.9	0.72	0.39
12	9.26e2	1.53e2	2.22	0.88
13	3.09e3	5.80e2	6.92	1.94
14	1.36e4	5.90e3	23.09	4.79
15	7.10e4	5.92e4	70.4	9.32
16	TIME-OUT	TIME-OUT	2.13e2	22.2
17	TIME-OUT	TIME-OUT	6.34e2	50.7
18	TIME-OUT	TIME-OUT	1.92e3	1.13e2
19	TIME-OUT	TIME-OUT	5.74e3	2.00e2
20	TIME-OUT	TIME-OUT	1.74e4	3.25e2

Memory Usage (MB)				
n	Oct	MAT	B++	QP
10	3.60e-2	2.00e-2	1.95e-2	0.211
11	6.80e-2	4.40e-2	7.03e-2	0.207
12	0.132	9.20e-2	7.42e-2	0.281
13	0.260	0.188	0.129	0.426
14	0.268	0.264	0.250	0.444
15	0.524	0.520	0.500	0.605
16	1.04	1.03	1.00	0.840
17	2.06	2.06	2.00	0.965
18	4.11	4.10	4.00	1.59
19	8.20	8.20	8.00	1.77
20	16.4	16.4	16.0	2.04

4 Conclusions and Future Work

In this work, we proposed and tested a new technique for simulating quantum circuits using a data structure called a QuIDD. We have shown that QuIDDs enable practical, generic and reasonably efficient simulation of quantum computation. Their key advantages are faster execution and lower memory usage. In our experiments, QuIDDPro achieves exponential memory savings compared to other known techniques. Our ongoing work focuses on the growth of required precision and on simulating other quantum algorithms, such as Shor's, where we plan to simulate the effects of errors and decoherence. We are also attempting to describe quantum gates that have polynomial QuIDD representations and thus facilitate fast classical simulation.

Acknowledgments This work was partially supported by the DARPA QuIST program. The views and conclusions contained herein are those of the authors and should not be interpreted as necessarily representing official policies or endorsements of the Defense Advanced Research Projects Agency, or the U.S. Government.

References

1. C. Y. Lee, *Bell System Technical Jour.*, **38**, 985–999 (1959).
2. R. Bryant, IEEE Trans. on Computers **C35**, 677–691 (1986).
3. E. Clarke et al., "Multi-Terminal Binary Decision Diagrams and Hybrid Decision Diagrams," In T. Sasao and M. Fujita, eds, *Representations of Discrete Functions*, pp. 93-108, Kluwer, 1996.
4. R. I. Bahar et al., "Algebraic Decision Diagrams and their Applications", *In Proc. IEEE/ACM ICCAD 1993*, 188-191, 1993.
5. D. Greve, "QDD: A Quantum Computer Emulation Library", 1999 (http://home.plutonium.net/~dagreve/qdd.html)
6. D. Gottesman, quant-ph/9807006.
7. G. Viamontes, M. Rajagopalan, I. Markov, J. Hayes, quant-ph/0208003
8. L. Grover, Phys. Rev. Lett. **79**, 325–328, (1997).
9. M. Boyer, G. Brassard, P. Hoyer and A. Tapp, "Tight Bounds on Quantum Searching", *4th Workshop on Physics and Computation*, Nov. 1996.

QUANTUM LEARNING AND UNIVERSAL QUANTUM MATCHING

M. SASAKI

Communications Research Laboratory, Koganei, Tokyo 184, Japan
CREST, Japan Science and Technology Agency

A. CARLINI

Imai Quantum Computing and Information Proj., Bunkyo-ku, Tokyo 113, Japan
ERATO, Japan Science and Technology Agency

Three quantum systems are given in some unknown states $|f\rangle^{\otimes N}$, $|g_1\rangle^{\otimes K}$, and $|g_2\rangle^{\otimes K}$, and we want to decide which *template* state $|g_1\rangle$ or $|g_2\rangle$, each representing a pattern class C_1 or C_2, respectively, is closest to the input *feature* state $|f\rangle$. We derive two matching strategies. The first consists of a two-stage semiclassical procedure. The second is a fully quantum strategy, without intermediate measurements, that we call the *universal quantum matching machine.* We present Bayes optimal solutions for both strategies in the case of $K = 1$, showing that the fully quantum matching procedure is strictly superior to the semiclassical one.

1 Introduction

Distinguishing quantum systems is one of the central tasks in quantum information theory.[1] In a recent paper,[2] we considered the problem of quantum pattern matching, in which we assumed that the input states $|f\rangle$ are given as quantum information (i.e., unknown quantum states) whereas the template states $|g_i\rangle$'s with known identities are given as classical information. Our goal was to obtain the best template as classical information (i.e., knowledge of the identity of the best $|g_i\rangle$) via a suitable matching strategy represented by a probability operator measure (POM). Here we generalize this model by assuming that we are given only some finite number (K) copies of each template (so our original formulation is equivalent to $K = \infty$). In particular, suppose that we *a priori* know that

$$|f\rangle \equiv \frac{1}{\sqrt{2}}\left(|\uparrow\rangle + e^{if}|\downarrow\rangle\right) \ , \ |g_i\rangle \equiv \frac{1}{\sqrt{2}}\left(|\uparrow\rangle + e^{ig_i}|\downarrow\rangle\right) \ , \ i = 1, 2, \tag{1}$$

where the parameters f, g_1, and g_2 are completely unknown.

2 Semiclassical Matching

For simplicity we set $M = 2$, i.e., we study the problem of binary classification. Thus we start with a system described by the state

$$|\Psi\rangle \equiv |f\rangle^{\otimes N} \otimes |g_1\rangle^{\otimes K} \otimes |g_2\rangle^{\otimes K} . \tag{2}$$

The semiclassical strategy is represented by two kinds of POMs. The first, $\{\hat{\mu}(g_1', g_2')\}$, is for estimating the identities of the templates from the samples

$\hat{g}_1^{\otimes K} \otimes \hat{g}_2^{\otimes K}$. The other, $\{\hat{\Omega}_1(g_1', g_2'), \hat{\Omega}_2(g_1', g_2')\}$, is for classifying the input feature state $\hat{f}^{\otimes N}$ and is the optimal matching strategy for the *estimated* templates $\{\hat{g}_1', \hat{g}_2'\}$.[2] In other words, $\{\hat{\mu}(g_i')\}$ corresponds to the *learning* process to train the classifier $\{\hat{\Omega}_j(g_i)\}$ with given training samples $\{\hat{g}_i^{\otimes K}\}$. In a Bayesian formulation, the optimal estimation strategy $\{\hat{\mu}(g_i')\}$ should then maximize the following average score:

$$\bar{S}^{\mathrm{SC}} = \sum_{g_1', g_2'} \mathrm{Tr}\left[\hat{\mu}(g_1', g_2')\hat{G}(g_1', g_2')\right], \tag{3}$$

where we have introduced $\hat{W}(g_j) \equiv \int \frac{df}{2\pi}\, \hat{f}^{\otimes N} |\langle f|g_j\rangle|^2$ and the *learning score operator* $\hat{G}(g_1', g_2') \equiv \int \frac{dg_1}{2\pi} \int \frac{dg_2}{2\pi}\, \hat{g}_1^{\otimes K} \otimes \hat{g}_2^{\otimes K} \cdot \sum_{j=1,2} \mathrm{Tr}\left[\hat{\Omega}_j(g_1', g_2')\hat{W}(g_j)\right]$, Thus the problem reduces to estimation of the classifier parameters g_1' and g_2' through the learning score operator $\hat{G}(g_i')$. By definition, the POM $\{\hat{\Omega}_j(g_i')\}$ should maximize the average score for $\hat{W}(g_j')$, i.e., $\bar{S}' = \frac{1}{2} + \mathrm{Tr}\left[\Delta\hat{W}(g_1', g_2')\hat{\Omega}_1(g_1', g_2')\right]$, where $\Delta\hat{W}(g_i') \equiv \hat{W}(g_1') - \hat{W}(g_2')$. The score operator $\hat{\Omega}_1(g_i')$ is the projection onto the subspace of the positive eigenvalues λ_m for the operator $\Delta\hat{W}(g_i')$ (see Ref. 4 for details). The optimal strategy maximizing $\bar{S}'$ is given by the POM $\hat{\Omega}_1(\Theta) = \hat{V}(\Theta + \frac{\pi}{2})\hat{\Lambda}_1\hat{V}^\dagger(\Theta + \frac{\pi}{2})$, where $\hat{V}(\Theta) \equiv \sum_{m=0}^{N} \mathrm{e}^{im\Theta} |m\rangle\langle m|$, $\hat{\Lambda}_1 \equiv \sum_{\lambda_m \geq 0} |\lambda_m\rangle\langle\lambda_m|$ and the angle $\Theta \equiv \frac{g_1' + g_2'}{2}$.

2.1 *Optimal learning strategy for $K = 1$*

In the case $K = 1$, the score $\hat{G}(\Theta)$ has the spectral decomposition $8\hat{G}(\Theta) \equiv \tilde{G}(\Theta) \oplus |T\rangle\langle T|$. Then, the learning POM can be written as $\hat{\mu}(\Theta) = \tilde{\mu}(\Theta) \oplus |T\rangle\langle T|$, and the average score is given by $\bar{S}^{\mathrm{SC}} = \frac{1}{8}[1 + \mathrm{Tr}(\tilde{\Gamma})]$, with $\tilde{\Gamma} \equiv \int \frac{d\Theta}{2\pi}\, \tilde{\mu}(\Theta)\tilde{G}(\Theta)$. One example of POM maximizing $\mathrm{Tr}(\tilde{\Gamma})$ is the group covariant, continuous, square-root measurement $\tilde{\mu}(\Theta) \equiv |\tilde{\mu}(\Theta)\rangle\langle\tilde{\mu}(\Theta)|$ based on the maximum eigenvalue state $|a_+(\Theta)\rangle$ of $\tilde{G}(\Theta)$, i.e., $|\tilde{\mu}(\Theta)\rangle \equiv \hat{a}^{-\frac{1}{2}}|a_+(\Theta)\rangle = \hat{V}(\Theta)|\tilde{\mu}(0)\rangle$, where $\hat{a} \equiv \int \frac{d\Theta}{2\pi} |a_+(\Theta)\rangle\langle a_+(\Theta)|$. In fact, it is straightforward to prove that this POM is also optimal,[1,3] and the maximum average score is $\bar{S}_{\max}^{\mathrm{SC}} = \frac{1}{2} + \frac{R_N}{\sqrt{2}}$. where (in the occupation number basis representation of $\downarrow$ for $|f\rangle^{\otimes N}$) $R_N \equiv \frac{1}{2^{N+1}} \sum_{m=0}^{N-1} \sqrt{C_m^N C_{m+1}^N} \langle m|\hat{\Lambda}_1|m+1\rangle$, with $C_m^N \equiv \binom{N}{m}$. Furthermore, there are many equivalent discrete POMs attaining the same average score $\bar{S}_{\max}^{\mathrm{SC}}$. The strategy requiring the minimum number of outputs is given by $\{\tilde{\mu}(0), \tilde{\mu}(\frac{2\pi}{3}), \tilde{\mu}(\frac{4\pi}{3})\}$. There is also an optimal, separable but non-covariant strategy that uses Von Neumann measurements and which achieves the same $\bar{S}_{\max}^{\mathrm{SC}}$.[4]

2.2 *Separable learning strategy for general K*

For general K there is a simple strategy composed of the optimal separate estimation of each template state,[5] which is represented by the discrete and rank one POMs $\{|A_{j_1}\rangle\langle A_{j_1}|\}$ and $\{|B_{j_2}\rangle\langle B_{j_2}|\}$ (with $j_1, j_2 = 0, 1, .., J-1$)

$$|A_{j_1}\rangle \equiv \frac{1}{\sqrt{J}}\sum_{k=0}^{K} \mathrm{e}^{i\frac{2\pi j_1}{J}k}|k\rangle \ ; \ |B_{j_2}\rangle \equiv \frac{1}{\sqrt{J}}\sum_{l=0}^{K} \mathrm{e}^{i(\frac{2\pi j_2}{J}+\phi)l}|l\rangle . \tag{4}$$

The relative angle ϕ between the set $|A_{j_1}\rangle$ and $|B_{j_2}\rangle$ is determined so as to maximize the matching score. The learning strategy can be represented as

$$\hat{\mu}(\Theta_{j_1 j_2}) = |A_{j_1}\rangle\langle A_{j_1}| \otimes |B_{j_2}\rangle\langle B_{j_2}| . \tag{5}$$

The optimal average score is found for $\phi = \pi/J$ and $J = K+1$, and is

$$\bar{S}^{\mathrm{SC}} = \sum_{j_1,j_2=0}^{J-1} \mathrm{Tr}\left[\hat{\mu}(\Theta_{j_1 j_2})\hat{G}(\Theta_{j_1 j_2})\right] = \frac{1}{2} + \frac{2R_N Q_K}{(K+1)\sin[\pi/2(K+1)]}, \tag{6}$$

where $Q_K \equiv \frac{1}{2^K}\sum_{k=0}^{K-1}\sqrt{C_k^K C_{k+1}^K}$. By numerical test, we can show that this separable learning strategy does not satisfy the Bayes optimality condition except for the case $K=1$, for which it reduces to an orthogonal measurement.

3 Universal Quantum Matching

There is a more fully quantum procedure which extracts only the required information, i.e., the classical information on which $|g_i\rangle$ best matches $|f\rangle$, without attempting to obtain any further information about the identities of the template states themselves. For binary classification, the total system at our disposal is still represented by the state from Eq. (2). The optimal strategy can then be defined by a straightforward extension of the Bayesian formulation given in our previous work,[2] with the score operators

$$\hat{W}_i \equiv \int \frac{dg_1}{2\pi}\int \frac{dg_2}{2\pi}\int \frac{df}{2\pi} |\Psi\rangle\langle\Psi| \, |\langle f|g_i\rangle|^2 . \tag{7}$$

The fully quantum optimal strategy is obtained as a POM $\{\hat{\Pi}_i\}$ that maximizes the following average score $\bar{S}^{\mathrm{QM}} = \frac{1}{2} + \mathrm{Tr}\left[(\hat{W}_1 - \hat{W}_2)\hat{\Pi}_1\right]$. As already explained in Sec. 2 below Eq. (3), the problem reduces to finding the subspace of the positive eigenvalues for the operator $\hat{W}_1 - \hat{W}_2$ (see Ref. 4 for details). In the case of $K=1$ the optimal attainable average score is given by

$$\bar{S}^{\mathrm{QM}} = \frac{1}{2} + \frac{\sqrt{2}}{2^{N+4}}\left[2\sqrt{N} + \sum_{k=1}^{N-1}\sqrt{C_k^N (C_{k+1}^N + C_{k-1}^N)}\right]. \tag{8}$$

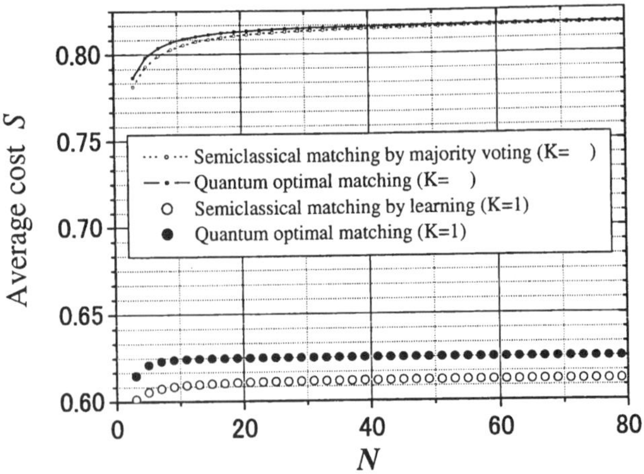

Figure 1. Average score as a function of the number of input feature systems. The big dots and circles represent the attainable scores of the universal quantum-matching machine and the optimal semiclassical matching strategy based on the learning process, respectively, in the case $K = 1$. The solid and dashed lines are the scores in the case of $K = \infty$ derived in our previous paper.

4 Discussion

We explicitly derived the Bayes optimal learning strategy for semiclassical matching and optimal universal quantum matching in the case of one copy, $K = 1$, for the template states, and an arbitrary number N copies of the input state. Our previous results[2] correspond to the case of $K = \infty$. An important aspect of the quantum pattern-matching problem is already seen in this toy model. Namely, there certainly exists a full quantum matching procedure, which tries to extract meaningful information about the best template class excluding any intermediate measurement process, and which is strictly superior to the straightforward extension of semiclassical matching strategies.

References

1. C. W. Helstrom, *Quantum Detection and Estimation Theory* (Academic Press, New York, 1976); A. S. Holevo, *Probabilistic and Statistical Aspects of Quantum Theory* (North-Holland, Amsterdam, 1982).
2. M. Sasaki, A. Carlini, and R. Jozsa, Phys. Rev. A **64**, 022317 (2001).
3. A. S. Holevo, J. Multivar. Anal. **3**, 337 (1973); H. P. Yuen, R. S. Kennedy, and M. Lax, IEEE Trans. **IT-21**, 125 (1975).
4. M. Sasaki and A. Carlini, Phys. Rev. A **66**, 022303 (2002).
5. R. Derka, V. Buzek, and A. K. Ekert, Phys. Rev. Lett. **80**, 1571 (1998).

Part VII

Quantum Control and Measurement

QUANTUM TRAJECTORIES AND QUANTUM CONTROL: THEORY AND CAVITY-QED EXPERIMENT

H. M. WISEMAN, P. WARSZAWSKI
Centre for Quantum Dynamics, School of Science, Griffith University, Nathan, Brisbane, Queensland 4111 Australia
E-mail: H.Wiseman@gu.edu.au

J. REINER, W. P. SMITH, L. OROZCO, S. KUHR
Department of Physics and Astronomy, State University of New York, Stony Brook, New York, USA

Quantum trajectories describe the stochastic evolution of an open quantum system conditioned on continuous monitoring of its output, such as by an ideal photodetector. They are useful for answering questions of principle, for conditional state preparation, and (probably most importantly) for quantum feedback control systems. For the latter two applications, it is necessary to use quantum trajectories for *realistic* detectors, and we outline a theory to do this. Finally, we present the first experimental results for quantum feedback in the "deep quantum" regime where quantum trajectories must be used for designing and modeling the feedback. In a cavity QED system we show that a state conditioned on the detection of a single photon can be frozen (its dynamics stopped) and then released after an arbitrary lapse of time.

Stochastic Schrödinger equations were introduced in quantum optics ten years ago .[1,2,3] By far their widest application has been for numerical simulations of quantum master equations of large systems. However they are also of interest from a more fundamental viewpoint, as describing the conditional evolution of a radiatively damped quantum system, conditioned on the continuous monitoring of its radiated field by photodetection. That is to say, it describes *the dynamics of the knowledge* that an observer (armed with perfect detectors) has about an open quantum system. This interpretation is known as quantum trajectory theory.[4,5] Quantum trajectories describe both quantum jumps for direct detection, and quantum diffusion for homodyne and heterodyne detection etc.

Quantum trajectories are useful for at least three good reasons. The first is that they can answer questions of principle, such as the following: An ideal laser with a mean boson number μ has the stationary state

$$\rho_{\rm ss} = \sum_n e^{-\mu}\frac{\mu^n}{n!}|n\rangle\langle n| = \int \frac{d\phi}{2\pi}|\sqrt{\mu}e^{i\phi}\rangle\langle\sqrt{\mu}e^{i\phi}|.$$

Is it valid to think of the laser as "really" being in an unknown number state $|n\rangle$? What about a coherent state $|\sqrt{\mu}e^{i\phi}\rangle$ of unknown phase ϕ?. In Ref. 6, Wiseman and Vaccaro argued that this question can be rigorously formulated as "is there a way to monitor the system such that it evolves stochastically between states in the ensemble, so that the ensemble average is realized as a time-average." This question is non-trivial, but can be answered for the above case.[6]

Secondly, many conditional (non-deterministic) state preparation schemes have now been proposed for quantum information processing. If the conditioning is done using a continuous measurement scheme then quantum trajectories will be needed to describe the conditioning accurately.

Thirdly, the stage beyond conditioning is quantum feedback, i.e., using the current resulting from monitoring a quantum system to control it. The analytical and numerical advantages of feedback using quantum trajectories were pointed out in Ref. 7. More fundamentally, one's state of knowledge of a system (generated by a QT) is the optimal basis for controlling it, *by definition*.[8,9,10,11]

For the first application above, it is sufficient to consider perfect detectors. But for the latter two, where quantum trajectories are the quantum analog of classical filters (such as the Kalman filter), detector imperfections must be taken into account. It is straightforward[5] to generalize quantum trajectory theories to treat inefficient photodetection. However, a quantum trajectory theory incorporating other realistic imperfections, in particular a finite bandwidth, has only recently been developed.[12,13] It can model both photon counters and photoreceivers (for homodyne detection), and include the effects of efficiency, bandwidth, electronic noise, dead time, and dark noise. The proper treatment of bandwidth limitations and electronic noise are of particular significance as these imperfections are inevitable and predominant concerns in many quantum control protocols.

Until now, experiments in quantum feedback have been in a regime of small quantum noise, where linearized semiclassical treatments are sufficient. That is, quantum noise must be taken into account, but can be treated as classical noise with a size determined by $\hbar$. Very recently, experimental results for quantum feedback in the "deep quantum regime" have been obtained in the Stony-Brook cavity QED experiment.[14] In this regime, linearization is impossible and quantum trajectories must be used as the basis to design the feedback.

The specific experimental scheme is as follows. The cavity QED system consists of a single mode of the electromagnetic field of a cavity interacting with a beam of two-level atoms initially in their ground state, as shown in Fig. 1. The cavity is driven very weakly, so that photodetections of the light transmitted by the cavity are very infrequent and the state before a detection can be taken to be $|\psi_{ss}\rangle$, which is very close to the true steady state.

Following a photodetection, the conditioned quantum state of the system is $|\psi_c(0)\rangle \propto \hat{a}|\psi_{ss}\rangle$, which evolves into $|\psi_c(\tau)\rangle$. Given our knowledge of this evolution, we can, for particular times τ, change the system dynamics (by modulating the driving amplitude) so as to capture the system in that conditioned state. When the parameters are later restored to their usual values, the released system state resumes its interrupted evolution. This feedback-

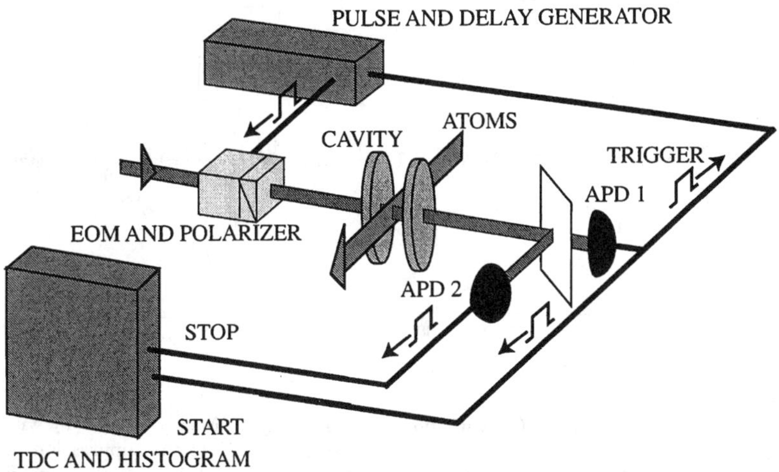

Figure 1. Simplified diagram of the experimental setup. The detection of a photon at the "start" avalanche photodiode (APD) triggers a change in the driving intensity via an electro-optical modulator EOM in front of a polarizer. The $g^{(2)}(\tau)$ correlation function is determined from the distribution of times between "start" and "stop".

modified conditioned state we can denote $|\psi_c'(\tau)\rangle$.

These dynamics can be seen in the $g^{(2)}$ correlation function

$$g^{(2)}(\tau) = \frac{\langle I(t+\tau)I(t)\rangle_{ss}}{\langle I(t)\rangle_{ss}^2} = \frac{\langle I(t+\tau)\rangle_c}{\langle I(t)\rangle_{ss}}, \qquad (1)$$

where $I(t)$ is the photocurrent from the system, and here the subscript c means conditioned on a photodetection at time t in the steady state. In terms of the feedback-modified conditioned state,

$$g^{(2)}(\tau) = \frac{\langle \psi_c'(\tau)|\hat{a}^\dagger \hat{a}|\psi_c'(\tau)\rangle}{\langle \psi_{ss}|\hat{a}^\dagger \hat{a}|\psi_{ss}\rangle} \qquad (2)$$

The experimental results for the measurement of this function are shown in Fig. 2. This experiment directly demonstrates both the reality of the conditioned state and its usefulness for quantum feedback.

Acknowledgments

This work has been supported by the NSF, NIST, DAAD, and the Australian Research Council. HMW thanks John Vaccaro and Hideo Mabuchi for their collaborations on some of the work reported briefly here.

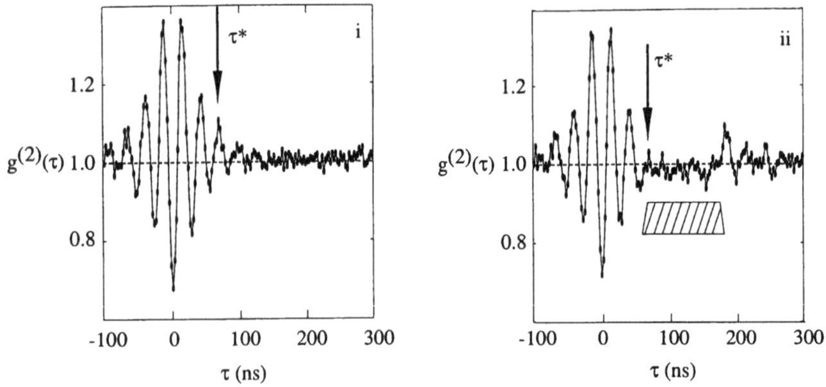

Figure 2. **Left**: Measured $g^{(2)}(\tau)$ with no feedback. **Right**: Measured $g^{(2)}(\tau)$ with an appropriate feedback step applied during the shaded region. Note the suppression of the oscillation at time τ^* by the feedback, and the reappearance of this oscillation when the feedback is turned off (at the end of the shaded region).

References

1. J. Dalibard, Y. Castin and K. Mølmer, Phys. Rev. Lett. **68**, 580 (1992).
2. C. W. Gardiner, A. S. Parkins, and P. Zoller, Phys. Rev. A **46**, 4363 (1992).
3. N. Gisin and I. Percival, J. Phys. A **25**, 5677 (1992).
4. H. J. Carmichael, *An Open Systems Approach to Quantum Optics* (Springer, Berlin, 1993).
5. H. M. Wiseman and G. J. Milburn, Phys. Rev. A **47**, 642 (1993).
6. H. M. Wiseman and J. A. Vaccaro, Phys. Rev. Lett. **87**, 240402 (2001).
7. H. M. Wiseman and G. J. Milburn, Phys. Rev. Lett. **70**, 548 (1993).
8. V. P. Belavkin, "Non-demolition measurement and control in quantum dynamical systems", in *Information, complexity, and control in quantum physics*, edited by A. Blaquière, S. Dinar, and G. Lochak (Springer, New-York, 1987).
9. A. C. Doherty and K. Jacobs, Phys. Rev. A **60**, 2700 (1999).
10. A. C. Doherty, S. Habib, K. Jacobs, H. Mabuchi and S. M. Tan, Phys. Rev. A **62**, 012105 (2000).
11. H. M. Wiseman, S. Mancini, and J. Wang, Phys. Rev. A **66**, 013807 (2002).
12. P. Warszawski, H. M. Wiseman, and H. Mabuchi, Phys. Rev. A. **65**, 023802 (2002).
13. P. Warszawski, H. M. Wiseman, quant-ph/0206125, quant-ph/0206126.
14. W. P. Smith, J. E. Reiner, L. A. Orozco, S. Kuhr, and H. M. Wiseman, Phys. Rev. Lett. **89**, 133601 (2002).

MEASURING THE INDIVIDUAL ELEMENTS OF THE OPTICAL DENSITY MATRIX

K. L. PREGNELL AND D. T. PEGG
School of Science, Griffith University, Nathan, Brisbane 4111, Australia
E-mail: K.Pregnell@mailbox.gu.edu.au
E-mail: D.Pegg@sct.gu.edu.au

We show how any selected element of the optical density matrix can be simply measured by use of two beam splitters, three photodetectors, a phase shifter and a reference field that can be derived easily from a coherent-state field.

1 Introduction

It is now well established that the quantum state of light can be measured. The most common methods involve reconstruction of the Wigner function,[1] from which the density operator can be recovered. Often, however, complete knowledge of the density matrix is not required. For such applications in which only specific off-diagonal information is required a more useful measurement procedure would be to selectively measure the individual density matrix elements of interest. Such a selective measurement scheme has been proposed by Steuernagel and Vaccaro.[2] The major disadvantage of this scheme, however, is that the determination of each matrix element $\rho_{N,M}$ requires the preparation of a two-state superposition of $|N\rangle$ and $|M\rangle$ for use as a probe field. Unfortunately, such probe fields have never been generated in the laboratory.

Measuring the diagonal elements $\rho_{N,N}$ of the density matrix can be done by photon counting. In this paper we extend this technique to measure selected off-diagonal elements $\rho_{N,N+\lambda}$ and $\rho_{N+\lambda,N}$ by use of two beam splitters and a reference field that, remarkably, can be derived from an easily-prepared coherent state.

2 Operator synthesis

The density matrix element $\rho_{N,N+\lambda}$ in the number state representation of a density operator $\hat{\rho}$ is given by

$$\rho_{N,N+\lambda} = \mathrm{Tr}(\hat{\rho}|N+\lambda\rangle\langle N|). \tag{1}$$

This can be compared with the probability for an outcome event e of a measurement on a system in state $\hat{\rho}$, which is given from general quantum measurement theory[3] by

$$P(e) = \mathrm{Tr}[\hat{\rho}\widehat{\Pi}(e)], \tag{2}$$

where $\widehat{\Pi}(e)$ is the element of a probability operator measure (POM) associated with the event e. If we can synthesize the operator $|N+\lambda\rangle\langle N|$ by a linear

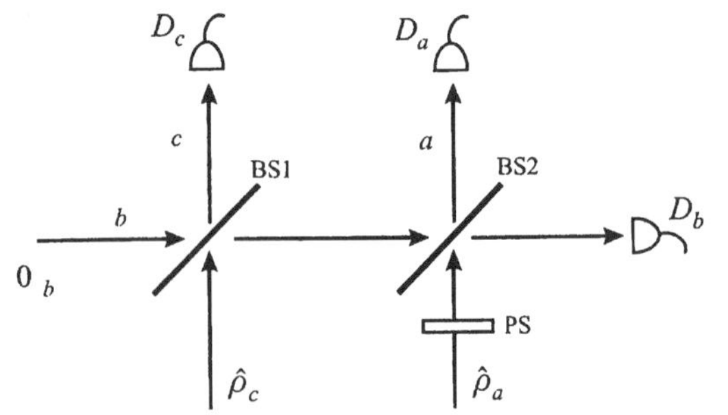

Figure 1. Apparatus for measuring the optical density matrix elements.

combination of different POM elements then we can find the matrix element from the same linear combination of the associated measurable probabilities.

We adopt this operator synthesis approach in this work to discuss an experimentally viable procedure that provides a nonrecursive method for measuring individual density matrix elements of a light field, without having to acquire sufficient information to reconstruct the entire state.

3 Measurement Technique

The proposed measurement technique uses the arrangement shown in Fig. 1. It consists of two symmetric 50/50 beam splitters labelled BS1 with input modes b and c and BS2 with input modes a and b. In the output modes are photodetectors D_a, D_b and D_c. We assign to the input reference fields in modes a and b the density matrices $\hat{\rho}_a$ and $\hat{\rho}_b$. The operator $\hat{\rho}_b$ represents the vacuum field. The state $\hat{\rho}_a$ depends on the value of λ selected for the measurement and has some zero matrix elements:

$$\hat{\rho}_a = \sum_{n=0}^{\lambda} \rho_{n,n}|n\rangle_{aa}\langle n| + (\rho_{0,\lambda}|0\rangle_{aa}\langle\lambda| + \text{H.c.}) + \sum_{m>\lambda}\sum_{n>\lambda} \rho_{m,n}|m\rangle_{aa}\langle n|. \quad (3)$$

We show how to generate the state $\hat{\rho}_a$ later. The field to be measured, in state $\hat{\rho}_c$, is in the input mode c of BS1. In the entry port of BS2 is a phase shifter PS capable of altering the phase of $\hat{\rho}_a$.

We let the distance between the beam splitters be an integer number of wavelengths, which allows us to ignore the phase shift of the light between the beam splitters. Let $e = (n_a, n_b, N)$ represent the event that photodetectors D_a, D_b and D_c register n_a, n_b and N photocounts respectively. The joint probability for this detection event is[4]

$$P(e) = \text{Tr}_c\left[\hat{\rho}_c\hat{\Pi}_c(e)\right], \quad (4)$$

where

$$\hat{\Pi}_c(e) = \mathrm{Tr}_b\left[\hat{\rho}_b\hat{R}_1^\dagger\hat{\Lambda}_b(n_a, n_b)\otimes|N\rangle_{cc}\langle N|\hat{R}_1\right], \tag{5}$$

with

$$\hat{\Lambda}_b(n_a, n_b) = \mathrm{Tr}_a\left[\hat{\rho}_a\hat{R}_2^\dagger|n_a\rangle_{aa}\langle n_a|\otimes|n_b\rangle_{bb}\langle n_b|\hat{R}_2\right], \tag{6}$$

and where $\widehat{R}_1$ and $\widehat{R}_2$ are the unitary operators for the action of beam splitters BS1 and BS2 respectively.[4]

We see from (4) that $\hat{\Pi}_c(e)$ is an element of a POM that represents the set of all detection events $\{e\}$ of the enlarged measuring device comprising all the elements in Fig. 1 except the state to be measured. We now choose events e such that $\lambda = n_a + n_b$. Then using the form of $\hat{\rho}_a$ in (3) we find eventually that

$$\hat{\Lambda}_b(n_a, n_b) = \sum_{n=0}^{\lambda}\sigma_{nn}\rho_{n,n}|\lambda - n\rangle_{bb}\langle\lambda - n| + (\sigma_{0\lambda}\rho_{0,\lambda}|0\rangle_{bb}\langle\lambda| + \mathrm{H.c.}), \tag{7}$$

where

$$\sigma_{0\lambda} = (-1)^{n_a}(2i)^{-\lambda}\binom{\lambda}{n_a}. \tag{8}$$

The specific form of σ_{nn} is not required. Using $\hat{\rho}_b = |0\rangle_{bb}\langle 0|$, we find

$$\hat{\Pi}_c(e) = \sum_{n=0}^{\lambda}\tilde{\sigma}_{nn}\rho_{n,n}|N+\lambda-n\rangle_{cc}\langle N+\lambda-n| + (\tilde{\sigma}_{0\lambda}\rho_{0,\lambda}|N\rangle_{cc}\langle N+\lambda| + \mathrm{H.c.}), \tag{9}$$

where

$$\tilde{\sigma}_{0\lambda} = \sigma_{0\lambda}i^{\lambda}2^{-N-\lambda/2}\binom{N+\lambda}{N}^{1/2}. \tag{10}$$

The effect of the phase shifter PS is to alter the phase of the density matrix elements of $\hat{\rho}_a$ by an amount proportional to the phase shift ϕ, that is

$$\rho_{n,m} \rightarrow \rho_{n,m}\exp[i(n-m)\phi]. \tag{11}$$

For $\phi = \pi\beta/\lambda$, $\rho_{0,\lambda}$ in the POM element (9) is changed to $\rho_{0,\lambda}\exp[-i\pi\beta]$. We denote this new POM element and associated probability by a superscript β and write $\hat{\Pi}_c^\beta(e)$ and $P^\beta(e)$. By repeating the experimental procedure only four times, each with a different phase shifter setting $\beta = 0, 1/2, 1, 3/2$, we gain enough information to synthesize the operator

$$|N\rangle_{cc}\langle N+\lambda| = \frac{\hat{\Pi}_c^0(e) - \hat{\Pi}_c^1(e) + i\left[\hat{\Pi}_c^{1/2}(e) - \hat{\Pi}_c^{3/2}(e)\right]}{4\tilde{\sigma}_{0\lambda}\rho_{0,\lambda}} \tag{12}$$

from a linear combination of physically measurable POM elements. Thus our required matrix elements are given in terms of the measurable probabilities $P^\beta(e)$, corrected for photodetector imperfections,[4] simply by

$$ {}_c\langle N+\lambda|\hat{\rho}_c|N\rangle_c = \frac{P^0(e) - P^1(e) + i\left[P^{1/2}(e) - P^{3/2}(e)\right]}{4\tilde{\sigma}_{0\lambda}\rho_{0,\lambda}}, \tag{13} $$

with ${}_c\langle N|\hat{\rho}_c|N+\lambda\rangle_c$ given by the complex conjugate of this expression.

Interestingly, the reference state $\hat{\rho}_a$ in (3) does not depend on N, the number of photons detected at D_c. As a result $\hat{\rho}_a$ does not need to be changed to measure matrix elements with different values of N. So the probabilities needed to derive *all* matrix elements with a common λ value can be obtained from a single set of measurements.

The required reference state $\hat{\rho}_a$ can be generated as a mixture of coherent states $|\alpha\rangle$ with $\alpha = |\alpha|\exp(i\phi)$ as follows. For a chosen λ and initial phase shifter setting $\phi = \pi\beta/\lambda$, we perform the experiment an equal number of times with phase shifter settings of $\pi\beta/\lambda + 2\pi j/\lambda$ where $j = 0, 1, \ldots \lambda - 1$. This makes the reference state a uniform effective mixture of coherent states, with phases such that the matrix elements $\rho_{n,m}$ with $0 < |m-n| < \lambda$ average to zero as required. This mixed state is a specific realization of $\hat{\rho}_a$.

4 Conclusion

By photocounting we can measure the diagonal elements of the optical density matrix. We have shown here how to extend this procedure to measure any selected matrix element by use of two beam splitters and three photodetectors. For this we require a reference field in a specific mixed state. This reference field can be prepared easily from a field in a coherent state. All that is required for this preparation is a simple phase shifter.

Acknowledgments

D. T. Pegg thanks the Australian Research Council for funding

References

1. U. Leonhardt, *Measuring the Quantum State of Light* (Cambridge University Press, Cambridge, 1997).
2. O. Steuernagel and J. A. Vaccaro, Phys. Rev. Lett. **75**, 3201 (1995).
3. C. W. Helstrom, *Quantum Detection and Estimation Theory* (Academic Press, New York, 1976).
4. K. L. Pregnell and D. T. Pegg, Phys. Rev. A **66**, 013810 (2002)

AN OPTIMALITY PROPERTY OF THE SQUARE-ROOT MEASUREMENT FOR MIXED STATES

JULIO I. CONCHA AND H. VINCENT POOR
Department of Electrical Engineering, Princeton University
Princeton, NJ 08540, USA
E-mail: {jiconcha,poor}@ee.princeton.edu

The square-root measurement (SRM) is a popular quantum detection strategy that has been used, for example, in the proof of the quantum channel capacity theorem, both for pure and mixed states.[1,2,3] The pure-state version has been shown to satisfy a least-squares property.[4] In this article, we extend the SRM to infinite dimensions and show that a similar property holds in that case.

1 Introduction

Consider the quantum detection problem

$$H_i : |\psi\rangle = |\psi_i\rangle \qquad i = 1, \ldots, M \tag{1}$$

where the states are $|\psi_i\rangle$ are linearly independent and have equal prior probabilities. Then the error probability P_e of a POVM $\Pi_i = |w_i\rangle\langle w_i|$ satisfies[5]

$$P_e \leq \frac{1}{M} \sum_{i=1}^{M} \| \, |w_i\rangle - |\psi_i\rangle \, \|^2. \tag{2}$$

Instead of directly minimizing P_e, as in Bayesian detection,[6] one can minimize the right-hand side (RHS) of (2). The solution can be found in closed form:

$$|w_i\rangle \triangleq (\Psi\Psi^\dagger)^{-1/2} |\psi_i\rangle \tag{3}$$

where Ψ is the matrix whose columns are the $|\psi_i\rangle$'s.

The quantum detector defined by (3) has been called 'pretty-good measurement'[7] and 'square-root measurement'[4] in the literature. It has the distinct advantage that it can be computed directly from the given quantum states. Holevo[5,8] showed that the SRM is asymptotically optimal in the Bayes sense, as the quantum states become nearly orthogonal. The SRM was later used to prove the quantum channel capacity theorem for pure states.[1] It has also been shown that the SRM coincides with the minimum probability of error detector for certain state collections having a symmetry property.[4,9] Furthermore, the SRM minimizes the RHS of (2) among all measurements of the form $\Pi_i = |w_i\rangle\langle w_i|$, even if the $|\psi_i\rangle$'s are linearly dependent.[4]

A mixed-state version of the square-root measurement (MSRM) was used to prove the quantum channel capacity theorem for mixed states.[2,3] Our goal is to show that this MSRM minimizes a quadratic cost function analogous to (2). We also generalize the MSRM to infinite-dimensional spaces, and show that there too an optimality property holds.

2 The SRM for finite-dimensional mixed states

Consider now a hypothesis testing problem with mixed states ρ_i. If the ρ_i are infinite-dimensional, we consider a subspace $\mathcal{T}$ of $\mathcal{H}$ of finite dimension, and construct a POVM on $\mathcal{T}$. Let P be the projection onto $\mathcal{T}$, and let the spectral decomposition of ρ_i be

$$\rho_i = \sum_{k=1}^{\infty} \lambda_{ik} \left|\psi_{ik}\right\rangle \left\langle\psi_{ik}\right| . \tag{4}$$

A *typical subspace* for ρ_i is defined as the span of the eigenvectors $|\psi_{ik}\rangle$ of ρ_i whose eigenvalues lie on a certain interval, $L < \lambda_{ik} < U$. Let P_i be the projection onto the typical eigenvectors of ρ_i. The MSRM is defined by[2,3]

$$\Pi_i = Y^+ P P_i P Y^+, \tag{5}$$

$$\text{where} \quad Y = \left(\sum_{i=1}^{M} P P_i P \right)^{1/2} \tag{6}$$

and $(\cdot)^+$ denotes the Moore-Penrose pseudoinverse. The operator $\Pi \triangleq \sum_i \Pi_i$ is the projection onto the range of $P \sum_i P_i P$. By defining an "error operator" $\Pi_e = I - \Pi$, a POVM is obtained. By an appropriate choice of $\mathcal{T}$, one can ensure that the probability of declaring an error is negligible.

Theorem 1 *Let Ψ_i be any operator such that $\Psi_i \Psi_i^\dagger = P P_i P$ (such as $P P_i$). The MSRM (5)-(6) satisfies $\Pi_i = \Upsilon_i \Upsilon_i^\dagger$, where the collection of operators Υ_i minimizes the quadratic cost function*

$$J = \sum_{i=1}^{M} \|\Upsilon_i - \Psi_i\|_2^2 \tag{7}$$

subject to the constraint $\sum_{i=1}^{M} \Upsilon_i \Upsilon_i^\dagger = \Pi$.

Here $\|\cdot\|_2$ is the Hilbert-Schmidt norm. This theorem can be derived from the pure-state result by solving the hypothesis testing problem of determining the indices (i, k) of the most likely eigenvector.

It is interesting to ask whether one can define a SRM without projecting the whole problem to a finite-dimensional subspace. This can be done by considering the weighted version of the SRM.[4,7] Instead of trying to make the columns of Υ_i close to the eigenvectors $|\psi_{ik}\rangle$ of ρ_i, we try to approximate $w_{ik} |\psi_{ik}\rangle$, for some set of weights w_{ik}. The eigenvalues in the expansion (4) can be interpreted as a conditional probability distribution, with each λ_{ik} being the probability of the corresponding eigenvector $|\psi_{ik}\rangle$, given i. If p_i is the prior probability of the mixed state ρ_i, then $p_{ik} = p_i \lambda_{ik}$ is a probability mass function. Of course, this is only a fiction, because there is no observable quantity having such distribution (unless the ρ_i commute). But it does give an idea of how much weight the eigenvector $|\psi_{ik}\rangle$ should be assigned: a low

p_{ik_0} implies a combination of a low prior probability p_i and a low conditional probability of getting the result k_0 if we were to apply the POVM $\Pi_k = |\psi_{ik}\rangle\langle\psi_{ik}|$. Following Ref. 4, we assign the weights $w_{ik} = \sqrt{p_{ik}}$, and redefine the operator Ψ_i to have columns $\sqrt{p_{ik}}\,|\psi_{ik}\rangle$, $k = 1, 2, \ldots$, so that $\Psi_i\Psi_i^\dagger = p_i\rho_i$.

First, we establish a "weighted" version of the finite-dimensional MSRM. Consider the space $\mathcal{K} = \mathcal{H} \otimes \mathbb{C}^M$. We define the operator $\Psi : \mathcal{H} \to \mathcal{K}$ by $\Psi|\psi\rangle = \sum_{i=1}^M \sqrt{p_i\rho_i}\,|\psi\rangle \otimes e_i$, for $|\psi\rangle \in \mathcal{H}$. Here $\{e_i\}$, $i = 1, \ldots, M$ is an orthonormal basis of $\mathbb{C}^M$. The operator Ψ is compact, so that it has a singular value decomposition of the form $\Psi = \sum_{k\in S} \sigma_k |f_k\rangle\langle g_k|$, where $|f_k\rangle \in \mathcal{K}$ and $|g_k\rangle \in \mathcal{H}$ are orthonormal and $\sigma_k > 0$. The set S is either finite or countable. It is easy to see that S is finite if and only if all ρ_i's are of finite rank. If S is countable, then $\sigma_k \to 0$ and the series converges in operator norm. Clearly

$$\Psi^\dagger\Psi = \sum_{i=1}^M p_i\rho_i = \sum_{k\in S} \sigma_k^2 |g_k\rangle\langle g_k|\,.$$

Let $\Pi \triangleq \sum_{k\in S} |g_k\rangle\langle g_k|$ be the projection onto the range of $\sum_i p_i\rho_i$. Let

$$P_K = \sum_{k=1}^K |g_k\rangle\langle g_k| \quad \text{and} \quad Y_K = \left(P_K \sum_{i=1}^M p_i\rho_i P_K\right)^{1/2}.$$

With this setup, we can pose a sequence (in K) of finite-dimensional problems. The proof of the following theorem is similar to that of Theorem 1.

Theorem 2 *The weighted mixed state SRM defined by*

$$\Pi_i^K = Y_K^+ p_i\rho_i Y_K^+ \quad i = 1, \ldots, M \tag{8}$$

(plus an error operator $\Pi_e^K = I - P_K$) satisfies $\Pi_i^K = \hat{\Upsilon}_i(K)\hat{\Upsilon}_i^\dagger(K)$, where $\hat{\Upsilon}_i(K)$ is a solution of

$$\min \sum_{i=1}^M \|\Upsilon_i - P_K\sqrt{p_i\rho_i}\|_2^2 \tag{9}$$

$$\textit{subject to} \sum_{i=1}^M \Upsilon_i\Upsilon_i^\dagger = P_K. \tag{10}$$

3 The infinite-dimensional SRM

Now we are ready to define an infinite-dimensional version of the SRM. Define for $\Upsilon_i : \mathcal{H} \to \mathcal{H}$ an operator $\Upsilon : \mathcal{H} \to \mathcal{K}$ by $\Upsilon|\psi\rangle = \sum_{i=1}^M \Upsilon_i^\dagger |\psi\rangle \otimes e_i$.

Theorem 3 *The sequence of solutions $\hat{\Upsilon}_i(K)$ converges strongly to*

$$\hat{\Upsilon}_i = \sum_{k\in S} \frac{1}{\sigma_k} |g_k\rangle\langle g_k| \sqrt{p_i\rho_i}, \tag{11}$$

which solves the minimum norm problem

$$\min J_1 = \|\Upsilon - \Psi\| \tag{12}$$

$$\text{subject to} \quad \sum_{i=1}^{M} \Upsilon_i \Upsilon_i^\dagger = \Pi. \tag{13}$$

The operators $\Pi_i = \hat{\Upsilon}_i \hat{\Upsilon}_i^\dagger$ *define a POVM, and* $\Pi_i^K \to \Pi_i$ *strongly.*
Note that in (12) we are no longer using the Hilbert-Schmidt norm, which need not be defined for Υ, but the operator norm induced by the norm in $\mathcal{H}$.

The POVM defined in Theorem 3 can be considered the infinite-dimensional extension of the MSRM. Defining

$$Y = \left(\sum_{i=1}^{M} p_i \rho_i\right)^{1/2} = \sum_{k \in S} \sigma_k \left|g_k\right\rangle \left\langle g_k\right|,$$

it follows from (11) that we can formally write $\Pi_i = Y^+ p_i \rho_i Y^+$, just as in the finite-dimensional MSRM. This formula allows one to define an SRM directly in terms of the given quantum states, and does not involve projections onto subspaces. However, care must be exercised when dealing with Y^+, since it is unbounded whenever S is infinite. For a proof of Theorem 3, see Ref. 10.

Acknowledgments

This research was supported by the NSF under Grant No. 99-80590.

References

1. P. Hausladen, R. Jozsa, B. Schumacher, M. Westmoreland, and W. K. Wootters. *Phys. Rev. A* **54**, 1869 (1996).
2. A. S. Holevo. *IEEE Trans. Inform. Theory* **IT-44**, 269 (1998).
3. B. Schumacher and M. D. Westmoreland. *Phys. Rev. A* **56**, 131 (1997).
4. Y. C. Eldar and G. D. Forney, Jr. *IEEE Trans. Inform. Theory* **IT-47**, 858 (2001).
5. A. S. Kholevo. *Problemy Peredachi Informatsii* **15**(4), 3 (1979). English version: *Problems of Information Transmission* **15**(4), 247 (1979).
6. C. W. Helstrom. *Quantum detection and estimation theory.* Academic Press, New York, 1976.
7. P. Hausladen and W. K. Wootters. *J. Mod. Opt.* **41**, 2385 (1994).
8. A. S. Kholevo. *Teoriia Veroiatnostei I Ee Primeneniia* **23**(2), 429 (1978). English version: *Theory of Probability and its Applications* **23**(2), 411 (1978).
9. M. Ban, K. Kurokawa, R. Momose, and O. Hirota. *Int. J. Theor. Phys.* **36**, 1269 (1997).
10. J. I. Concha. *Signal detection in multiaccess quantum channels.* Ph.D. thesis, Princeton University, 2002.

QUANTUM METROLOGY: DETECTION OF WEAK FORCES USING SCHRÖDINGER CAT RESOURCES

K. NEMOTO,[†] W. J. MUNRO,[‡] G. J. MILBURN,[*] AND S. L. BRAUNSTEIN[†]

[†] *School of Informatics, Dean Street, University of Wales, Bangor LL57 1UT, UK*
[‡] *Hewlett-Packard Laboratories, Filton Road, Stoke Gifford, Bristol BS34 8QZ, UK*
[*] *Centre for Quantum Computer Technology, University of Queensland, Brisbane, QLD, Australia*

We investigate the utility of nonclassical states of simple harmonic oscillators (a superposition of coherent states) for sensitive force detection. We find that, like squeezed states, a superposition of coherent states allows the detection of displacement measurements at the Heisenberg limit. Entangling many superpositions of coherent states offers a significant advantage over single-mode superposition states with the same mean photon number.

1 Introduction

Nonclassical states of light have received considerable attention in the field of quantum and atom optics. Many nonclassical states of light have been experimentally produced and characterized. These states include photon number states, squeezed states and certain entangled states. There are a number of suggested, and actual, applications for these states in quantum information processing including quantum computation, communication and cryptography to name but a few. They have also been proposed for high -precision measurements, such as improving the sensitivity of Ramsey fringe interferometry[1] and the detection of weak tidal forces due to gravitational radiation. In this article we consider how nonclassical states of simple harmonic oscillators may be used to improve the detection sensitivity of weak classical forces.

Let us begin by establishing the classical limit for force detection. When a classical force, $F(t)$, acts for a fixed time on a simple harmonic oscillator, it displaces the complex amplitude of the oscillator in phase space with the amplitude and phase of the displacement determined by the time dependence of the force.[2] The action of the force in the interaction picture is simply represented by the unitary displacement operator

$$D(\alpha) = \exp(\alpha a^\dagger - \alpha^* a), \tag{1}$$

where $a, a^\dagger$ are the annihilation and creation operators for the single mode of the electromagnetic field satisfying $[a, a^\dagger] = 1$, and α is a complex amplitude which determines the average field amplitude, $\langle a \rangle = \alpha$. For simplicity we will assume that the force displaces the oscillator in a phase-space direction that is orthogonal to the coherent amplitude of the initial state. To detect the force we would need to measure the signal of the quadrature $\hat{Y} = -i(a - a^\dagger)$. If the oscillator begins in a coherent state $|\alpha_0\rangle$, (α_0 is real) the displacement $D(i\epsilon)$ causes the coherent state to evolve to $e^{i\epsilon\alpha_0}|\alpha_0 + i\epsilon\rangle$. The signal-to-noise ratio is then SNR $= S/\sqrt{V} = 2\epsilon$ which must be greater than unity to be resolved. This establishes the standard quantum limit (SQL)[3] of $\epsilon_{SQL} \geq 1/2$.

It is well known[4] that this limit may be overcome if the oscillator is first prepared in a squeezed state (a uniquely quantum-mechanical state) for which the uncertainty in the momentum quadrature is reduced below the coherent-state level. For a momentum-squeezed state (with mean photon number n_{tot}) it is straightforward to show the minimum detectable displacement is $\epsilon_{min} \geq 1/\sqrt{4n_{tot}}$. This scales as the inverse square root of the mean photon number and means the only way to improve the sensitivity is to increase n_{tot}. Can we do better using different non-classical resources?

2 Weak force detection utilizing Schrödinger cat states.

We now consider another class of nonclassical states, based on a coherent superposition of coherent states, which can be entangled over N modes. The N-mode entangled cat state has the form

$$|\psi\rangle = \frac{1}{\sqrt{2}}(|\alpha, \alpha, \ldots, \alpha\rangle + |-\alpha, -\alpha, \ldots, -\alpha\rangle) \tag{2}$$

where n_{tot} is the total photon number of the entire state. Parkins and Larsabal[5] recently suggested how this highly-entangled state might be formed in the context of cavity QED and quantized motion of a trapped atom or ion. The weak force $D(i\epsilon)$ (for $\epsilon \ll 1$) acts simultaneously on all modes of this N-party entangled state. The resulting state is

$$|\psi(\theta)\rangle = \frac{e^{iN\theta}}{\sqrt{2}}|\alpha + i\epsilon, \ldots, \alpha + i\epsilon\rangle + \frac{e^{-iN\theta}}{\sqrt{2}}|-\alpha + i\epsilon, \ldots, -\alpha + i\epsilon\rangle,$$

where $\theta = \epsilon\alpha$. The theory of optimal parameter estimation indicates that the limit on the precision with which the displacement parameter be estimated is bounded by

$$\epsilon_{min} = \frac{1}{\sqrt{N\left[1 + 4N\alpha^2/(1 + e^{-2N\alpha^2})\right]}} \quad \text{where } n_{tot} = N\alpha^2 \frac{\left[1 - e^{-2N\alpha^2}\right]}{\left[1 + e^{-2N\alpha^2}\right]} \tag{3}$$

and realizes the Heisenberg Limit. For $n_{tot} \gg 1$, Eq. (3) simplifies to

$$\epsilon_{min} = \frac{1}{\sqrt{N\left[1 + 4n_{tot}\right]}} \sim \frac{1}{\sqrt{4Nn_{tot}}}.$$

Let us now compare this to the case in which one has N copies of the single-mode cat state $|\alpha\rangle + |-\alpha\rangle$. In this case (for $\alpha^2 \gg 1$) the minimum detectable displacement is $\epsilon_{min} = 1/\sqrt{[N + 4n_{tot}]}$ whereas a single-mode cat state with mean photon number n_{tot} achieves $\epsilon_{min} = 1/\sqrt{[1 + 4n_{tot}]}$. We show these results graphically in Fig. 1 for $N = 10$.

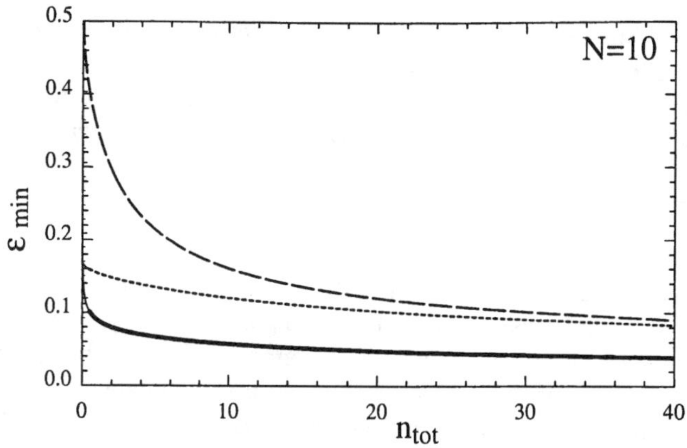

Figure 1. Plot of the minimum detectable displacement e_{min} versus n_{tot} for $N = 10$. The solid curve is for the entangled cat state (2) and the dotted line is for N separable copies of a single-mode cat state $|\alpha\rangle + |-\alpha\rangle$. The final curve (the dashed line) represents a single-mode cat state with mean photon number n_{tot}.

How do we interpret these results? For large n_{tot} (a regime we need to be in to achieve a good sensitivity) we find that the N-mode entangled cat state has an extra critically important $\sqrt{N}$ improvement over N individual copies of a single-mode cat state (both states have the same mean photon number). This is due to the entangled cat state and the collective (Bell-like) measurement. These results indicate that it would seem to be most efficient for a large fixed n_{tot} to have as many modes in the entangled state as possible.

3 Comparison and Discussion

It is enlightening to compare our results to the study of Ramsey-fringe interferometry introduced by Bollinger et al.[6] and discussed by Huelga et al.[1]. In Ramsey-fringe interferometry the objective is to detect the relative phase difference between two superposed states, $\{|0\rangle, |1\rangle\}$. The theory of quantum parameter estimation[7] indicates in this case that we should choose the input state to be $|\psi\rangle_i = (|0\rangle + |1\rangle)/\sqrt{2}$ and the optimal measurement is a projective measurement in the basis $|\pm\rangle = |0\rangle \pm |1\rangle$. The probability for obtaining the result $+$ is $P(+|\theta) = \cos^2\theta$. In N repetitions of the measurement the uncertainty in the inferred parameter is $\delta\theta = 1/\sqrt{N}$, which achieves the classical lower bound for quantum phase parameter estimation. However it was first noted by Bollinger et al.[6] that a more effective way to use the N-level systems is to first prepare them in the maximally-entangled state,

$$|\psi\rangle = \frac{1}{\sqrt{2}}(|0\rangle_1|0\rangle_2 \ldots |0\rangle_N + |1\rangle_1|1\rangle_2 \ldots |1\rangle_N). \tag{4}$$

In this case, parameter estimation gives the Heisenberg lower bound of $\delta\theta = 1/N$. The Hilbert space of N two-level systems is the tensor product space of dimension 2^N. The entangled state in Eq. (4) however resides in a lower-dimensional subspace of permutation symmetric states.[8] It can be written in the form

$$|\psi\rangle = \frac{1}{\sqrt{2}}(|-N/2\rangle_{N/2} + |N/2\rangle_{N/2}), \tag{5}$$

and so we can regard the state as an SU(2) 'cat state' for N two-level atoms. Hence it is straightforward to see that a single N-level atom can achieve the same frequency sensitivity. Their equivalence can be also be understood by noting that the sensitivity of such frequency measurement is proportional to the energy difference of the states involved. What entanglement allows is for one to create an effective state without the need of resorting to a superposition between a certain ground state and a highly excited one.

To conclude, we have in this article shown how superpositions of coherent states can be used to achieve extremely sensitive force detection. For a single mode state $|\alpha\rangle + |-\alpha\rangle$ we have found that the minimum detectable displacement for weak force measurements scales as $1/\sqrt{n_{tot}}$. More importantly, by using an N-mode entangled cat state (and a collective measurement) a sensitivity scaling as $\epsilon_{min} = 1/\sqrt{4Nn_{tot}}$ is achievable. This sensitivity is at the Heisenberg limit and indicates that even with finite mean photon number n_{tot} (or fixed mean energy) it is possible to achieve extremely sensitive displacement detection by letting N become large.

Acknowledgements

WJM, KN and SLB acknowledges funding by the European projects EQUIP, QUICOV and QUIPROCONE. GJM acknowledges support from the Australian Centre for Quantum Computer Technology.

References

1. S. F. Huelga, C. Macchiavello, T. Pellizzari, A. K. Ekert, M. B. Plenio and J. I. Cirac, Phys. Rev. Lett. **79**, 3865 (1997).
2. V. Braginsky and F. Ya. Khalili, *Quantum measurement*, (Cambridge University press, Cambridge, 1992).
3. D. F. Walls and G. J. Milburn, *Quantum Optics*, (Springer, Berlin, 1994).
4. C. M. Caves, K. S. Thorne, R. W. P. Drever, V. D. Sandberg and M. Zimmermann, Rev. Mod. Phys. **52**, 341 (1980).
5. A. S. Parkins, E. Larsabal, Phys. Rev. A **63**, 012304 (2001).
6. J. J . Bollinger, W. M. Itano, D. J. Wineland and D. J. Heinzen, Phys. Rev. A **54**, R4649, (1996).
7. S. L. Braunstein , C. M. Caves and G. J. Milburn, Annals of Physics **247**, 135, (1996).
8. R. H. Dicke, Phys. Rev. **93**, 99 (1954).

BINARY COMMUNICATION IN ENTANGLED CHANNELS

MATTEO G. A. PARIS
Quantum Optics & Information Group, INFM Unità di Pavia, Italy
E-mail: paris@unipv.it, URL: www.qubit.it/~paris

We analyze optical binary communication assisted by entanglement and show that: i) ideal entangled channels have smaller error probabilities than ideal single-mode coherent channels if the photon number of the channel is larger than one; ii) realistic entangled channels with heterodyne receivers have smaller error probabilities than ideal single-mode coherent channels if the photon number of the channel is larger than a threshold of about five photons.

1 Introduction

In order to convey classical information to a receiver using quantum channels a transmitter prepares a quantum state drawn from a collection of known states. The receiver detects the information by measuring the channel, so as to determine the state prepared. Since the given states are generally not orthogonal, then no measurement will allow the receiver to distinguish perfectly between them. The problem is therefore to construct a measurement optimized for distinguishing between nonorthogonal quantum states, and to find realistic signals that minimize the error probability at fixed energy of the channel.

In optical binary communication, say amplitude modulation keyed (AMK),[a] information is conveyed by two quantum states $\varrho_j = |\psi_j\rangle\langle\psi_j|$, $j = 1,2$ with $|\psi_1\rangle = |\psi_0\rangle$ and $|\psi_2\rangle = D(\alpha)|\psi_0\rangle$ where $|\psi_0\rangle$ is a given reference state, usually taken to be the vacuum. Without loss of generality, the amplitude a may assumed to be real, and $D(\alpha) = \exp(\alpha a^\dagger - \bar{\alpha} a)$ is the displacement operator. If we consider equal *a priori* probabilities for the two signals, the optimal quantum measurement to discriminate the $|\psi\rangle$'s with minimum error probability[1] is the POVM $\{M_j\}_{j=1,2}$, $M_1 + M_2 = I$ corresponding to the so-called square-root measurement.[2] We have $M_j = |\mu_j\rangle\langle\mu_j|$, with $|\mu_j\rangle = \sum_k \mu_{kj}|k\rangle$, $\mu_{kj} = [\Psi(\Psi^\dagger\Psi)^{-1/2}]_{kj}$; $[\Psi]_{ij} = \psi_{kj}$ is the matrix of the coefficients of the two signals $|\psi_j\rangle = \sum_k \psi_{kj}|k\rangle$ in a given basis $\{|k\rangle\}$. The error probability is given by

$$P_e = \frac{1}{2}\mathrm{Tr}[M_1\varrho_2 + M_2\varrho_1] = \frac{1}{2}\left[1 - \sqrt{1 - |\langle\psi_1|\psi_2\rangle|^2}\right] .$$

For AMK binary communication we have $|\langle\psi_1|\psi_2\rangle|^2 = \exp(-2N)$, where N is the average number of photons in the channel *per use*, $N = \frac{1}{2}\mathrm{Tr}[a^\dagger a(\varrho_1+\varrho_2)] = \frac{1}{2}|\alpha|^2$. In the following we will refer to this quantity as *the photon number of the channel.*

[a] An equivalent analysis may be performed for phase-shift keyed signals.

In this paper we describe how binary communication can be improved by using realistic sources of entanglement with either ideal or heterodyne receivers for state discrimination. The corresponding error probabilities are denoted by Q_e and R_e respectively. We find that entanglement is of value unless the photon number of the channel is very small.

2 Binary communication in entangled channels

Binary optical communication assisted by entanglement may be implemented using as a reference state the so-called twin-beam (TWB) state of two modes of radiation $|\psi_0\rangle = |\lambda\rangle\rangle = \sqrt{1-\lambda^2}\sum \lambda^p\,|p\rangle|p\rangle$, $|\lambda| < 1$. TWBs are produced by spontaneous downconversion in a nondegenerate optical parametric amplifier. The TWB parameter is given by $\lambda = \tanh G$, G being the effective gain of the amplifier. The two states to be discriminated are now given by $|\psi_1\rangle\rangle = |\lambda\rangle\rangle$ and $|\psi_2\rangle\rangle = D(\alpha)|\lambda\rangle\rangle$, where we consider the displacement performed on the beam a. Since the average number of photons of TWB is given by $N_\lambda = 2\lambda^2/(1-\lambda^2)$, the photon number of TWB channels is given by $N = N_\lambda + \frac{1}{2}|\alpha|^2$. The error probability for the ideal discrimination of the states $|\psi_1\rangle\rangle$ and $|\psi_2\rangle\rangle$ reads as follows $Q_e = \frac{1}{2}\left[1-\sqrt{1-\exp[-2N(1-\beta)(1+\beta N)]}\right]$, where $\beta = N_\lambda/N$ is the fraction of the photon number of the channel used to establish entanglement between the two modes. We have that $Q_e < P_e$ for $N > (1-\beta)^{-1}$, i.e., entanglement is always of value if the photon number of the channel is larger than one. The optimal entanglement fraction is given by $\beta_{opt} = (N-1)/(2N)$, corresponding to an error probability given by $Q_e = P_e$ if $N < 1$ and

$$Q_e = \frac{1}{2}\left[1-\sqrt{1-\exp[-\frac{1}{2}(1+N)^2]}\right], \qquad N \geq 1\,.$$

In assessing the usefulness of entanglement in binary communication it should be noted that for single-mode coherent channels the performance of the ideal detector can be achieved, in principle, by means of the Dolinar's receiver.[3] On the other hand, no suggestion yet exists for realizing ideal performance for TWB entangled channels. Therefore, a question arises whether or not entanglement could be practically used to improve binary communication.

In order to answer to this question, we consider a receiver that measures the real and the imaginary part of the complex operator $Z = a + b^\dagger$, a and b being the two modes of the TWB. The measurement of Re[Z] and Im[Z] can be experimentally implemented, and corresponds to multiport homodyne detection if the two involved modes have the same frequencies,[4] or to heterodyne detection otherwise.[5] The outcome of each Z measurement is a complex number z, and the POVM of the measurement is given by $\Pi_z = |z\rangle\rangle\langle\langle z|$, with $|z\rangle\rangle = D_j(z)\sum_n |n\rangle|n\rangle$ and either $j = a$ or $j =$

b. As an inference rule we adopt the condition "Re$[z] > \Lambda \to |\psi_2\rangle\rangle$", where Λ is a threshold value, chosen to minimize the probability of error R_e. Since the heterodyne distribution, conditioned on a displacement α, is given by $p(z|\alpha) = |\langle\langle z|D(\alpha)|\lambda\rangle\rangle|^2 = \exp\{-|\alpha - z|^2/\Delta_\lambda^2\}/(\pi\Delta_\lambda^2)$ with $\Delta_\lambda^2 = (1-\lambda)/(1+\lambda) = (\sqrt{N_\lambda + 2} - \sqrt{N_\lambda})/(\sqrt{N_\lambda+2} + \sqrt{N_\lambda})$, we have $R_{12} = \int_0^{\mathrm{Re}[z]>\Lambda} d^2z\, p(z|\alpha)$ and $R_{21} = \int_{\mathrm{Re}[z]>\Lambda}^{\infty} d^2z\, p(z|0)$ such that

$$R_e = \frac{1}{2}(R_{12} + R_{21}) = 1 - \frac{1}{2}\left\{\mathrm{Erf}\left[\frac{\Lambda}{\Delta_\lambda}\right] + \mathrm{Erf}\left[\frac{\alpha - \Lambda}{\Delta_\lambda}\right]\right\},$$

where $\mathrm{Erf}[x] = \frac{2}{\sqrt{\pi}}\int_0^x dt e^{-t^2}$ denotes the error function. R_e is minimized by the choice $\Lambda = \alpha/2$, and therefore the minimum probability of error in a realistic entangled channel with heterodyne reception is given by $R_e = \frac{1}{2}[1 - \mathrm{Erf}(\frac{1}{2}\alpha/\Delta_\lambda)]$. The error probability R_e can be further minimized by tuning the entanglement fraction β. Substituting in R_e the expression $\alpha = \sqrt{2N(1-\beta)}$ and Δ_λ we obtain

$$R_e = \frac{1}{2}\left\{1 - \mathrm{Erf}\left[\frac{1}{2}\sqrt{\frac{2N(1-\beta)(\sqrt{\beta N + 2} - \sqrt{\beta N})}{(\sqrt{\beta N + 2} + \sqrt{\beta N})}}\right]\right\}.$$

The optimal entanglement fraction is given by $\beta_{opt} = \frac{1}{2}N/(1+N)$ which maximizes the argument of Erf, and thus minimizes R_e. We do not report the resulting error probability, whose expression is rather cumbersome. Rather, in Fig. 1 we have plotted the error probabilities as a function of the photon number of the channel. We have that $R_e < P_e$ for N larger than the threshold value $N \simeq 5.2$. Although TWB entangled channels with heterodyne reception do not approach ideal performance, it is apparent from Fig. 1 that they can have smaller error probabilities than single-mode coherent channels

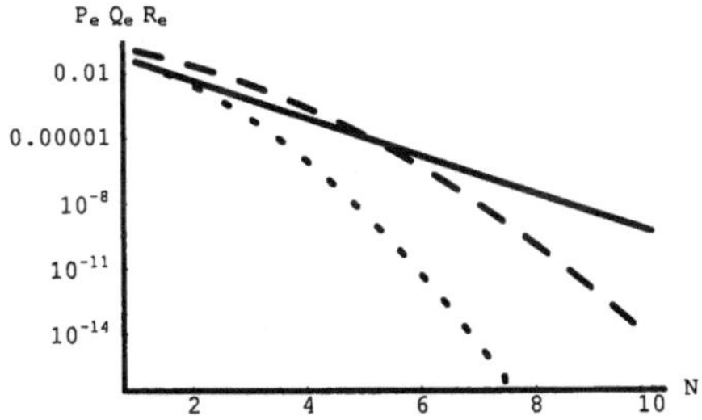

Figure 1. Logarithmic plot of the error probabilities versus the photon number of the channel. The solid line is the error probability P_e for a single-mode coherent channel, the dotted line is Q_e for ideal entangled channels, and the dashed line is R_e for heterodyne-reception entangled channels. Note that $R_e < P_e$ for N larger than the threshold $N \simeq 5.2$.

For large photon number of the channel, we have that asymptotic results $P_e \simeq \frac{1}{4}e^{-2N}$, $Q_e \simeq \frac{1}{4}e^{-\frac{1}{2}(1+N)^2}$ and $R_e \simeq (\sqrt{2\pi}N)^{-1}e^{-\frac{1}{8}N^2}$.

3 Conclusions

We have analyzed binary communication in TWB-based entangled channels, and compared their performances with ideal single-mode coherent channels. We have found that ideal entangled channels show smaller error probability than single-mode ones if the photon number of the channel is larger than one, whereas realistic entangled channels, i.e., channels equipped with heterodyne receivers, show smaller error probabilities than single-mode ones if the photon number of the channel is larger than a threshold of about five photons. We conclude that TWB binary communication represents a realistic alternative to single-mode coherent channels.

Acknowledgments

This work has been sponsored by the INFM through the project PRA-2002-CLON and by EEC through the project IST-2000-29681 (ATESIT).

References

1. C. W. Helstrom, *Quantum Detection and Estimation Theory* (Academic Press, New York, 1976).
2. Y. Eldar, and G. D. Forney, *IEEE Trans. Inform. Theory* **IT-47**, 858 (2001).
3. S. Dolinar, *MIT Res. Lab. Electron. Rep. Prog.* **111** 115, (1973).
4. M. G. A. Paris, A. Chizhov, O. Steuernagel, *Opt. Comm.* **134**, 117 (1997).
5. H. P. Yuen, and J. H. Shapiro, *IEEE Trans. Inform. Theory* **IT-26**, 78 (1980).

OPTIMAL MEASUREMENT STRATEGIES FOR MIRROR-SYMMETRIC STATES

KIERAN HUNTER,[1] ERIKA ANDERSSON,[1] CLAIRE R. GILSON,[2] AND STEPHEN M. BARNETT[1]

[1] *Department of Physics, University of Strathclyde, Glasgow G4 0NG, Scotland*

[2] *Department of Mathematics, University of Glasgow, Glasgow G12 8QW, Scotland*

We find the maximum-fidelity measurement and retransmission strategy for a set of three mirror-symmetric qubit states. We show this to be distinct from the minimum error discrimination measurement.

The problem of finding the optimal measurement to perform on a quantum system has been extensively studied, and is one with obvious implications for quantum communication and computation. Despite this there are relatively few cases in which the optimal measurement is known.

Our problem is this: given the possible states $|\psi_j\rangle$ of the system under consideration and the probabilities p_j of these states occurring, what is the best measurement to perform on the system? The solution will depend on what we want to achieve, that is what kind of information we wish to obtain. We must define a figure of merit, a function which provides a measure of the appropriateness of our strategy. A common example of this is the probability of incorrectly identifying the state p_e,[1,2,3,4] from which we obtain the minimum-error measurement strategy. The error probability p_e is a measure of the recovery of one kind of classical information about the preparation, the number (j) of the selected state.

In this paper we shall be primarily concerned with the fidelity of a measurement and retransmission process. Here we make a measurement on a quantum signal to obtain some classical information and then use this information to generate a new signal which matches the old as closely as possible. The fidelity F of this process is the probability that a subsequent measurement made on the new signal (made by someone who knows which of the $|\psi_j\rangle$ was actually transmitted) finds it to be the same as the original. Thus the fidelity is a measure of how difficult it is to detect that a measurement was made on the signal, as well as a measure of how much of the quantum information in the signal state can be transmitted through a classical channel. This measurement and retransmission process is also equivalent to a $1 \to \infty$ cloner for the specified set of states.

The minimum-error strategy is known for a small number of cases, each of which possesses some simplifying property. The fidelity-maximizing measurement and retransmission strategy has recently been found for two of these cases, when the signal states are symmetric[5] and when there are two signal states.[6] In both of these cases the minimum-error measurement is optimal for the measurement step, although it is not a unique solution for the symmetric states. This might lead us to conjecture that the minimum-error measurement strategy *always* maximizes the fidelity. We shall demonstrate that this conjecture is false by finding the maximum-fidelity strategy for a set of mirror-symmetric states.

We have recently described the minimum-error strategy for a qubit which is known to be one of a set of three mirror-symmetric qubit states.[7] Here mirror symmetric means that the set of states is invariant under the transformation

$$|+\rangle \longrightarrow +|+\rangle, \ |-\rangle \longrightarrow -|-\rangle, \tag{1}$$

with the prior probabilities associated with any mirror-symmetric pair of states being equal. The set of three mirror-symmetric qubit states can be written as

$$\begin{aligned}
|\psi_1\rangle &= \cos\theta|+\rangle + \sin\theta|-\rangle, \ p_1 = p, \\
|\psi_2\rangle &= \cos\theta|+\rangle - \sin\theta|-\rangle, \ p_2 = p, \\
|\psi_3\rangle &= |+\rangle, \ p_3 = 1 - 2p.
\end{aligned} \tag{2}$$

The minimum-error measurement strategy possesses the same mirror symmetry as the states and consists of three elements, except for large values of p for which the best strategy is to optimally distinguish $|\psi_1\rangle$ and $|\psi_2\rangle$, never detecting $|\psi_3\rangle$.

To find the fidelity-maximizing strategy, we express F as a function of the states $|\psi_j\rangle$ and probabilities p_j. We denote the states to be transmitted as $|\phi_k\rangle$ and describe the measurement by its probability operators $\hat{\Pi}_k$. The expectation values $\langle\psi_j|\hat{\Pi}_k|\psi_j\rangle$ of these operators give the probabilities of the measurement outcome k for the state $|\psi_j\rangle$. The $\hat{\Pi}_k$ must be Hermitian, non-negative and sum to the identity in order that they represent probabilities. This set of probability operators $\{\hat{\Pi}_k\}$ is called a *probability operator measure* (POM). This gives F as

$$F = \sum_{j,k} \langle\phi_k|\psi_j\rangle\langle\psi_j|\hat{\Pi}_k|\psi_j\rangle\langle\psi_j|\phi_k\rangle p_j, \tag{3}$$

which is maximized with respect to $|\phi_k\rangle$ by selecting $|\phi_k\rangle$ to be the eigenvector of

$$\hat{O}_k = \sum_j |\psi_j\rangle\langle\psi_j|\hat{\Pi}_k|\psi_j\rangle\langle\psi_j| p_j. \tag{4}$$

corresponding to the largest eigenvalue. F is then just the sum of the largest eigenvalues of these operators.

To evaluate the fidelity we parameterize the operators $\hat{\Pi}_k$ and express F in terms of these parameters and those of the states $|\psi_j\rangle$. An examination the eigenvalues of (4) shows that there must be an optimal measurement which is mirror symmetric and confined to the plane of the Bloch sphere containing the states $|\psi_j\rangle$. We then conduct a variation of the fidelity F subject to the conditions on the parameters of $\hat{\Pi}_k$ by Lagrange's method of unknown multipliers.

The maximization of F gives the solution:[8]

(i) when $p < -\frac{\cos 2\theta}{1-\cos 2\theta}$, $p \neq 0$, $\cos 2\theta \neq 1$, the unique optimal measurement strategy consists of the two elements

$$|+\rangle\langle+|, |-\rangle\langle-|; \tag{5}$$

(ii) when $p > -\frac{\cos 2\theta}{1-\cos 2\theta}$, $p \neq 0$, $\cos 2\theta \neq 1$, then the unique optimal measurement strategy consists of the two elements

$$\frac{1}{2}(|+\rangle + |-\rangle)(\langle+| + \langle-|) = |r\rangle\langle r|, \frac{1}{2}(|+\rangle - |-\rangle)(\langle+| - \langle-|) = |l\rangle\langle l|; \tag{6}$$

(iii) and when $p = 0$ or $p = -\frac{\cos 2\theta}{1-\cos 2\theta}$ or $\cos 2\theta = 1$ then any measurement whose elements are confined to the plane of the states (2) will be optimal.

Conclusions

The maximum-fidelity measurement strategy is always mirror symmetric and consists of two elements. Only two such strategies exist, with one giving the maximum fidelity, and the other the least fidelity, of all strategies composed of elements confined to the plane of the signal states. Which of the two gives the maximum fidelity and which the minimum depends on the parameters of the original signal states (2). If both of these strategies give the same fidelity, then any strategy composed of elements in the plane of the states will also be optimal.

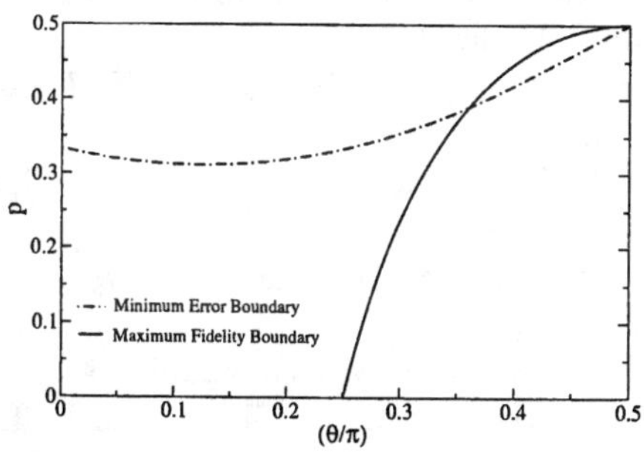

Figure 1. A comparison of the domains in which the $\{|l\rangle\langle l|, |r\rangle\langle r|\}$ strategy is optimal for minimum error, [above the dash-dot line] and for maximum fidelity [to the left of the solid line], in terms of the state parameters p and θ.

The fidelity is always maximized by a two-element strategy, whereas the error is generally minimized by a three-element strategy, so it is clear that the minimum-error strategy does not generally maximize the fidelity. It does so only when there is no unique solution for a fidelity-maximizing measurement and for large values of p (the probability of either of the states $|\psi_1\rangle$ or $|\psi_2\rangle$ being the signal state). The boundary of the domains wherein $\{|l\rangle\langle l|, |r\rangle\langle r|\}$ minimizes the error and where it maximizes the fidelity (Figure 1) seem to be unrelated except for their large-p behavior. This does not rule out a more complicated connection between minimizing error and maximizing fidelity, but they are clearly not equivalent.

The only property of the states (2) which we used to derive the maximum-fidelity measurement was their symmetry and position on a plane of the Bloch sphere. This implies — by the properties of the eigenvalues of (4) — that the measurement also possesses mirror symmetry and is confined to the plane of the states. For *any* set of qubit states possessing this symmetry or allowing the same simplification of the eigenvalues of (4), the optimal measurement must still be one of the two mirror-symmetric two-element strategies.

Acknowledgments

This work was supported by the UK Engineering and Physical Sciences Research Council, the Marie Curie Fellowship Scheme of the European Commission, the Royal Society of Edinburgh and the Scottish Executive Education and Lifelong Learning Department.

References

1. C. W. Helstrom, *Quantum Detection and Estimation Theory* (New York: Academic, 1976).
2. A. S. Holevo, *Probabilistic and Statistical Aspects of Quantum Theory* (Amsterdam: North-Holland, 1982).
3. H. P. Yuen, R. S. Kennedy, and M. Lax, *IEEE Trans. Inform. Theory* **IT-21**, 125 (1975).
4. R. B. M. Clarke, V. M. Kendon, A. Chefles, S. M. Barnett, E. Riis, and M. Sasaki, *Phys. Rev. A.* **64**, 012303 (2001).
5. S. M. Barnett, C. R. Gilson, M. Sasaki, *J. Phys. A: Math. Gen.* **34**, 6755 (2001).
6. C. A. Fuchs and M. Sasaki, private communication.
7. E. Andersson, S. M. Barnett, C. R. Gilson, and K. Hunter, *Phys. Rev. A.* **65**, 052308 (2002).
8. K. Hunter, E. Andersson, C. R. Gilson, and S. M. Barnett, submitted to J. Phys. A: Math. Gen.; quant-ph/0209138.

RESULTS ON CONTINUOUS QUANTUM ERROR CORRECTION VIA QUANTUM FEEDBACK CONTROL

CHARLENE AHN
ANDREW C. DOHERTY
Institute for Quantum Information, Caltech, Pasadena, CA 91106, USA
E-mail: cahn@theory.caltech.edu

ANDREW J. LANDAHL
Center for Bits and Atoms, MIT, Cambridge, MA 02139, USA
Hewlett-Packard Laboratories, Palo Alto, CA 94394, USA
Institute for Quantum Information, Caltech, Pasadena, CA 91106, USA

We review a protocol for continuously protecting unknown quantum states from decoherence that incorporates design principles from both quantum error correction and quantum feedback control. This protocol uses weaker control tools than are typically assumed for quantum error correction. We study its performance numerically, under the non-ideal conditions of bandwidth-limited control and imperfect detection rate.

1 Introduction

Two important, well-studied methods to combat decoherence in quantum systems are quantum error correction and quantum feedback control. Quantum error correction is a powerful tool that can be used to protect unknown quantum states. This discretized method of controlling quantum states postulates the resources of projective measurements and instantaneous unitary gates. Quantum feedback control, on the other hand, usually assumes weaker resources: the information about the quantum state fed into the controller typically comes from continuous measurements and the operations the controller applies in response are typically bounded-strength Hamiltonians.

In a previous paper,[1] we combined the formalism of stabilizer quantum error-correcting codes and the techniques of state-estimation feedback to obtain a protocol for protecting unknown quantum states using continuous measurements and bounded-strength Hamiltonians. Here we will review the main points of that protocol, as well as present some further extensions of that work. In particular, we will discuss some modifications to make our scheme more realistic: bandwidth-limited control and imperfect detection.

2 Continuous quantum error correction protocol

In this section we construct a state-estimation feedback based on the bit-flip code, which corrects for an error model represented by bit flips occurring independently on each qubit at some rate γ. For this code, the stabilizer generators are ZZI and IZZ, and the correction operators are bit-flips on individual qubits. Our protocol involves measuring the stabilizer generators (along with the remaining non-identity stabilizer ZIZ) via a diffusive Wiener process. In addition, we use the Hamiltonian feedback $F = \lambda_1 XII + \lambda_2 IXI + \lambda_3 IIX$, with control parameters λ_k, to correspond to the unitary bit-flip corrections. Parameterizing the measurement strength by κ and the detector efficiency by η yields the following stochastic master equation, which describes the state conditioned upon the measurement results:

$$\begin{aligned} d\rho_c = \; & \gamma(\mathcal{D}[XII] + \mathcal{D}[IXI] + \mathcal{D}[IIX])\rho_c dt \\ & + \kappa(\mathcal{D}[ZZI] + \mathcal{D}[IZZ] + \mathcal{D}[ZIZ])\rho_c dt \\ & + \sqrt{\kappa\eta}(\mathcal{H}[ZZI]dW_1 + \mathcal{H}[IZZ]dW_2 + \mathcal{H}[ZIZ]dW_3)\rho_c \\ & - i[F, \rho_c]dt \end{aligned} \tag{1}$$

$$dQ_1 = 2\kappa\eta\langle ZZI\rangle dt + \sqrt{\kappa\eta}dW_1 \tag{2}$$

$$dQ_2 = 2\kappa\eta\langle IZZ\rangle dt + \sqrt{\kappa\eta}dW_2 \tag{3}$$

$$dQ_3 = 2\kappa\eta\langle ZIZ\rangle dt + \sqrt{\kappa\eta}dW_3, \tag{4}$$

where ρ_c denotes that the state is conditioned upon the measurement results (2)–(4). The γ terms denote the independent decoherence; the $\kappa\mathcal{D}$ terms denote measurement decoherence; the $\sqrt{\kappa\eta}\mathcal{H}$ terms denote measurement localization; and $-i[F, \rho]$ is, of course, Hamiltonian evolution.

In order to choose the control parameters λ_k, it is useful to introduce a cost function. One might envision using a measure of the distance between the evolved state to the target codeword, but as we desire to protect an *unknown* quantum state we choose instead a measure of the distance from the evolved state to the *codespace*: $C = 1 - f$, where $f(\rho) = \mathrm{tr}(\rho\Pi_C)$ and Π_C is just the projector onto the bit-flip code codespace, $\Pi_C = \frac{1}{4}(III + ZZI + ZIZ + IZZ)$. Minimizing the cost at each time step gives the following feedback coefficients:

$$\begin{aligned} \lambda_1 &= \lambda\,\mathrm{sgn}\langle YZI + YIZ\rangle \\ \lambda_2 &= \lambda\,\mathrm{sgn}\langle ZYI + IYZ\rangle \\ \lambda_3 &= \lambda\,\mathrm{sgn}\langle ZIY + IZY\rangle, \end{aligned} \tag{5}$$

where λ is the maximum feedback strength that can be applied. Note that these expectation values are computed by estimating the state based on the entire measurement record.

3 Bandwidth-limited control

The feedback given in (5) is a bang-bang control; that is, the optimal solution occurs when the control parameters λ_k are always at the maximum or minimum value allowable (λ or $-\lambda$, respectively). Indeed, (5) assumes that we are able to change the direction of our feedback infinitely quickly.

Of course, in practice this is not the case, and one might envision replacing the sgn function in the feedback (5) with a sigmoid such as a tanh

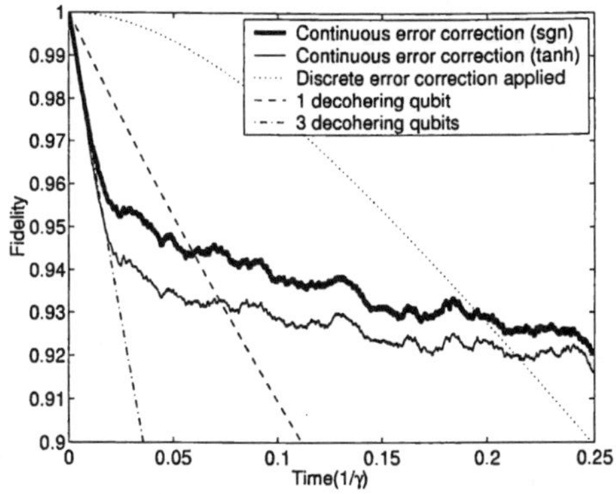

Figure 1. Behavior of our protocol with sgn and tanh feedback for parameters $\kappa/\gamma = 64$, $\lambda/\gamma = 128$, averaged over 10^4 quantum trajectories. The analytical curves shown are as follows: the dashed line is the fidelity of one decohering qubit, the dashed-dotted line is the fidelity of three decohering qubits, and the dotted line is the fidelity of an encoded qubit after one round of discrete error correction at time t. Our simulation results are given by the solid lines: the thick solid line is the codeword fidelity given the sgn feedback in (5), and the thin solid line is the codeword fidelity where $\mathrm{sgn}(x)$ in the feedback has been replaced by $\tanh(50x)$.

function. Fig. 1 shows numerical results for sgn feedback and tanh feedback. The figure of merit here is the codeword fidelity $F_{\mathrm{cw}}(t) = \mathrm{tr}\,(\rho_c(0)\rho_c(t))$, the overlap of the state with the target codeword. This graph is a typical average over 10^4 quantum trajectories for the (scaled) measurement and feedback strengths $\kappa/\gamma = 64$, $\lambda/\gamma = 128$, assuming perfect detector efficiency $\eta = 1$. We can see that the curves describing $F_{\mathrm{cw}}(t)$ for both sgn and tanh feedback are qualitatively similar: they both improve and surpass the fidelity of a single unprotected qubit as well as eventually surpass the fidelity achievable by a round of discrete quantum error correction applied at time t.[a] Further numerical study suggests that, unsurprisingly, the closer the sigmoid gets to a step function, the better the feedback protects the state.

4 Imperfect detection

Another natural question to ask is the following: how do our results change if the detectors are not perfect? For efficiency $0 \leq \eta \leq 1$ we numerically test our protocol (1)–(4) as before. Figure 2 graphs the codeword fidelity at a particular time as a function of η; the time $\gamma t = 0.2$ was chosen as indicative of the general behavior of F_{cw} as a function of η.

[a] In our previous paper we also consider the case in which the resource of discrete error correction is available, and continuous error correction can be performed in between discrete correction cycles. Here, for the sake of brevity, we assume that this resource is not available.

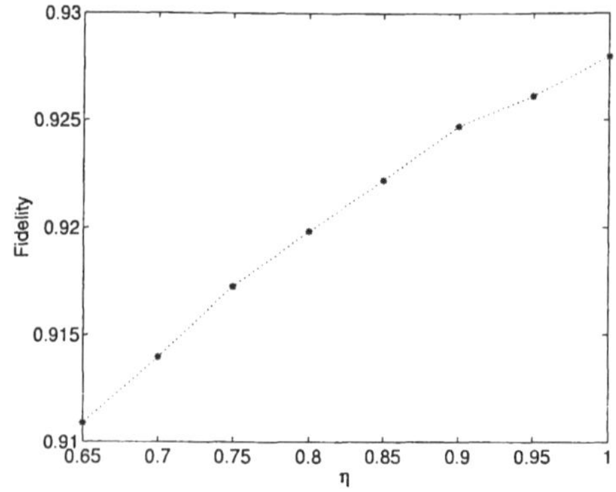

Figure 2. The codeword fidelity at time $\gamma t = 0.2$ as a function of detector efficiency η.

This figure shows that for efficiencies close to 1, the protocol still performs very well. This feedback does not propagate errors badly because it is a function of the entire measurement record, not just instantaneous measurement results, which lends the protocol a limited inherent fault-tolerance.

5 Conclusion

Bandwidth-limited control and imperfect efficiency must be considered if our protocol for protecting unknown quantum states is to be of practical importance. We have shown that these limitations, as long as they are not too severe, do not greatly hinder our ability to protect an unknown quantum state.

Acknowledgments

We would like to thank the organizers of QCMC 2002. This work was supported in part by the National Science Foundation under grant number EIA-0086038 and by the Department of Energy under grant number DE-FG03-92-ER40701. A. L. acknowledges support from an IBM faculty partnership award and C. A. acknowledges support from an NSF fellowship.

References

1. C. Ahn, A. C. Doherty and A. J. Landahl, Phys. Rev. A **65**, 042301 (2002); quant-ph/0110111.

Part VIII
Quantum Cryptography and Bit Commitment

REVERSE RECONCILIATION PROTOCOLS FOR QUANTUM CRYPTOGRAPHY WITH CONTINUOUS VARIABLES

FRÉDÉRIC GROSSHANS AND PHILIPPE GRANGIER
Laboratoire Charles Fabry de l'Institut d'Optique (CNRS UMR 8501)
F-91403 Orsay, France

We introduce new quantum key distribution protocols using quantum continuous variables, that are secure against individual attacks for any transmission of the optical line between Alice and Bob. In particular, it is not required that this transmission be greater than 50%. Though squeezing or entanglement may be helpful, they are not required, and there is no need for quantum memories or entanglement purification. These protocols can thus be implemented using coherent states and homodyne detection, and they may be more efficient than usual protocols using quantum discrete variables.

1 Introduction

1.1 Coherent QKD protocols

In a recent article,[1] we have shown that quantum continuous variables (QCV) may provide a valid alternative to the usual "single photon" quantum key distribution (QKD) schemes, simply by generating and transmitting random distributions of coherent states. More precisely,[1] a whole family of secure protocols can be obtained by using either coherent states, squeezed states, or entangled EPR beams, provided that the transmission of the line is greater than 50% (i.e., the losses are less than 3 dB). The security of these protocols is related to the no-cloning theorem,[2,3] and non-classical features like squeezing or EPR correlations have no influence on the achievable secret key rate. The 3 dB loss limit of these cryptography protocols makes their security demonstration quite intuitive, but there exist in principle multiple ways for Alice and Bob to go beyond this limit, using, e.g., entanglement purification.[4]

In this paper we discuss new protocols that are secure for any value of the line transmission. The basic idea is to use *reverse* reconciliation protocols, that is, Alice will try to guess what was received by Bob, rather than Bob trying to guess what was sent by Alice. In that case, Alice gets an advantage, because she can always guess better than the eavesdropper Eve.

1.2 Direct and reverse reconciliation protocols

In the first step of a generic QKD protocol, Alice prepares a quantum state and sends it to Bob, who makes a measurement on this state. Alternatively, Alice and Bob may share two EPR-correlated systems, and they both make measurements on their parts. In order to warrant security, Alice and Bob must randomly choose to use different measurement basis, and the transmitted data will be significant only when their basis are compatible. After the quantum exchange, Alice and Bob must agree on a common measurement basis, and discard the wrong measurements. At the end of this step, Alice and Bob (and the potential eavesdropper Eve) share a set of correlated Gaussian data.

As a second step, Alice reveals some randomly chosen samples of the data that she sent, and Bob reveals his corresponding measurements. These samples allow them to measure some relevant parameters of the quantum channel, e.g., the error rate and the transmission, that is called "channel gain" for QCV protocols. Knowing the correlations between their key elements, Alice and Bob can evaluate the amount of information they share (I_{AB}), and the information that the eavesdropper Eve can have about their values (I_{AE} and I_{BE}). Therefore they can evaluate the size of the secret key they will generate at the end of the protocol. If Eve knows too much, the size of this secret key will be 0, and Alice and Bob will abort the protocol at this step.

Then Alice and Bob need to use classical communications to extract a common key from their correlated key elements, revealing as little information as possible to Eve. This step also includes error correction, that is done using parity-based algorithms like Cascade. Here we will consider protocols in which Bob sends correction information and Alice corrects her key elements to have the same values as Bob. Since Bob gives the correction information (also to Eve), this type of reconciliation keeps $I_{AB} - I_{BE}$ constant, and will provide a useable key[5] if $I_{AB} - I_{BE} > 0$. We call it "reverse reconciliation" (RR) because Alice adapts herself to what was received by Bob, whereas the opposite is done in more usual "direct reconciliation" (DR) protocols.

Finally, the last step of a practical QKD protocol is that Alice and Bob perform privacy amplification to filter out Eve's information. Since this step is based on an evaluation of the amount of information collected by Eve on the reconciled key, a crucial requirement is to get a bound on I_{AE} for DR, and on I_{BE} for RR. For a coherent-state protocol, the DR bound based on I_{AE} was given in Ref. 1, and security requires a line transmission above 50% as stated above. We will now establish the RR bound, and we will show that it is not associated with a minimum value of the line transmission.

2 Entangling cloner

To eavesdrop a reverse reconciliation scheme, Eve needs to guess the results of Bob's measurement. We will call *entangling cloner* a system allowing her to do so, because this kind of system can be described as a cloner creating two quantum-correlated outputs: Eve keeps one of them and sends the other to Bob. Let (x_{in}, p_{in}) be the input quadratures of the entangling cloner and (x_B, p_B), (x_E, p_E) the quadratures of its two outputs. A good entangling cloner should minimize the conditional variances [6] $V_{x_B|x_E}$ and $V_{p_B|p_E}$. Alice and Bob should assume Eve uses the best possible entangling cloner, knowing the Alice-Bob channel quality. This channel can be described by

$$x_B = g_x(x_{in} + B_x) \qquad p_B = g_p(p_{in} + B_p), \tag{1}$$

with $\langle x_{in} B_x \rangle = \langle p_{in} B_p \rangle = 0$, $\langle x_{in}^2 \rangle = \langle p_{in}^2 \rangle \equiv V N_0 \geq N_0$, and $\langle B_{x,p}^2 \rangle \equiv \chi_{x,p} N_0$, where N_0 is the shot-noise variance.

For reverse reconciliation protocols, Alice needs to evaluate x_B. Her estimator can be denoted αx_A, with $\alpha \in \mathbf{R}$. Eve's estimator for p_B will be εp_E. Their error will be $x_{B|A,\alpha} \equiv x_B - \alpha x_A$ and $p_{B|E,\varepsilon} \equiv p_B - \varepsilon p_E$. It is straightforward to show that $[x_{B|A,\alpha}, p_{B|E,\varepsilon}] = [x_B, p_B]$ and therefore

$$\left\langle x_{B|A,\alpha}^2 \right\rangle \left\langle p_{B|E,\varepsilon}^2 \right\rangle \geq N_0^2. \tag{2}$$

The conditional variances obey by definition the following relations:

$$V_{x_B|x_A} = \min_\alpha \left\{ \left\langle x_{B|A,\alpha}^2 \right\rangle \right\} \qquad V_{p_B|p_E} = \min_\varepsilon \left\{ \left\langle p_{B|E,\varepsilon}^2 \right\rangle \right\}. \tag{3}$$

From Eq. (2) one has $V_{x_B|x_A} V_{p_B|p_E} \geq N_0^2$ and thus

$$V_{p_B|p_E} \geq N_0^2 / V_{x_B|x_A}. \tag{4}$$

By exchanging the roles of x and p one obtains $V_{p_B|p_A} V_{x_B|x_E} \geq N_0^2$ and

$$V_{x_B|x_E} \geq N_0^2 / V_{p_B|p_A}. \tag{5}$$

These inequalities imply that Alice and Eve cannot jointly know more about Bob's field than allowed by the Heisenberg principle.

Now, if Alice creates the field (x_{in}, p_{in}), we can write

$$x_{in} = x_A + A_x \qquad p_{in} = p_A + A_p, \tag{6}$$

where x_A (p_A) is Alice's best estimate of x_{in} (p_{in}) and $\langle A_x^2 \rangle = \langle A_p^2 \rangle \equiv s N_0$ where s is the amount of squeezing used by Alice to generate this field, and must fulfill the condition $s \geq 1/V$. The correlation coefficients are equal to $\langle p_A^2 \rangle = (V - s) N_0$, $\langle p_B^2 \rangle = G_p (V + \chi_p) N_0$, and $\langle p_A p_B \rangle = g_p \langle p_A^2 \rangle$. This allows us to calculate Alice's conditional variance on Bob's measurement:

$$V_{p_B|p_A} = \langle p_B^2 \rangle - \langle p_A p_B \rangle^2 / \langle p_A^2 \rangle = G_p (\chi_p + s) N_0. \tag{7}$$

A similar calculation leads to the symmetric relation

$$V_{x_B|x_A} = G_x (\chi_x + s) N_0. \tag{8}$$

These equations and the constraint $s \geq 1/V$ on the squeezing give finally

$$V_{p_B|p_A} \geq V_{p_B|p_A,\min} = G_p (\chi_p + 1/V) N_0 \tag{9}$$
$$V_{x_B|x_A} \geq V_{x_B|x_A,\min} = G_x (\chi_x + 1/V) N_0. \tag{10}$$

The output-output correlations of an entangling cloner, described, e.g., by $V_{p_B|p_E}$, should only depend on the density matrix of the field (x_{in}, p_{in}) at its input, and not on the way this field was built. The inequality (4) has thus to be fulfilled for every physically allowed value of $V_{x_B|x_A}$, given the density matrix of the field (x_{in}, p_{in}). If we look for a boundary to Eve's knowledge by using Eq. (4), we have thus to use the tightest limit on $V_{x_B|x_A}$, that is given by $V_{x_B|x_A,\min}$ according to (10). Obviously the same reasoning holds for $V_{p_B|p_A}$, with the corresponding tightest limit $V_{p_B|p_A,\min}$. We have then

$$V_{x_B|x_E} \geq V_{x_B|x_E,\min} = N_0/\{G_p(\chi_p + 1/V)\} \tag{11}$$

and, similarly

$$V_{p_B|p_E} \geq V_{p_B|p_E,\min} = N_0/\{G_x(\chi_x + 1/V)\} \tag{12}$$

In a practical QKD scheme Alice and Bob will give the same roles to x and p. Assuming therefore that $G_x = G_p = G$ and $\chi_x = \chi_p = \chi$, the two bounds (11), (12) reduce to a single one, and it is possible to explicitly describe an entangling cloner achieving this limit. We will consider here only the case of $G < 1$, but the limit is tight for any G. The entangling cloner can then be sketched as follows: Eve uses a beam splitter with a transmission G to split up part of the Alice-Bob transmitted signal, and she injects into the other input port a field $E1$, with the right variance to induce a noise of variance $G\chi N_0$ at Bob's end. One has therefore:

$$\langle x_{E1}^2 \rangle = \langle p_{E1}^2 \rangle = G\chi N_0/(1-G). \tag{13}$$

Eve should know the maximum about this injected field $E1$, and will therefore use a half-pair of EPR-correlated beams, so that she does perform an "entangling" attack. We can then write $x_{E1} = x_{\text{known}} + x_{\text{unknown}}$ where x_{known} stands for Eve's best estimate of x_{E1}, given by the measure of its brother-beam, and x_{unknown} stands for the noise she cannot know. We have

$$\langle x_{\text{unknown}}^2 \rangle = N_0^2 / \langle x_{E1}^2 \rangle = (1-G)N_0/(G\chi) \tag{14}$$

$$\langle x_{\text{known}}^2 \rangle = \langle x_{E1}^2 \rangle - \langle x_{\text{unknown}}^2 \rangle. \tag{15}$$

Eve also use an output port of the beam splitter to measure the field $E2$, which gives her information about the input field:

$$x_{E2} = g x_{E1} - \sqrt{1-G}\, x_{in}. \tag{16}$$

She can cancel a part of the noise induced by $E1$ by subtracting the part proportional to x_{known}. Thus she knows

$$x'_{E2} = g x_{\text{unknown}} - \sqrt{1-G}\, x_{in}. \tag{17}$$

We also have $x_B = g x_{in} + \sqrt{1-G}\, x_{E1}$ where Eve already knows the part proportional to x_{known}, injected with x_{E1} and she only needs to guess

$$x'_B = g x_{in} + \sqrt{1-G}\, x_{\text{unknown}}. \tag{18}$$

from x'_{E2}. We have therefore $V_{x_B|x_{E1},x_{E2}} = V_{x'_B|x'_{E2}}$, and the calculation of the quantities $\langle x'^2_B \rangle$, $\langle x'^2_{E2} \rangle$, $\langle x'_{E2} x'_B \rangle$ lead straightforwardly to the conditional variance:

$$V_{x'_B|x'_{E2}} = N_0/\{G\chi + G/V\} = V_{x_B|x_E,\min}, \tag{19}$$

showing that the entangling cloner does reach the lower limit of (11), (12).

3 Reverse quantum cryptography

In a reverse quantum cryptography protocol, Eve's power is limited by the values of $V_{x_B|x_E,\min}$ and $V_{p_B|p_E,\min}$ given by (11) and (12). In the following, we will assume that a "perfect" Eve is able to reach that limit:

$$V_{x_B|x_E} = V_{x_B|x_E,\min} = \frac{N_0}{G_p(\chi_p + 1/V)} \tag{20}$$

$$V_{p_B|p_E} = V_{p_B|p_E,\min} = \frac{N_0}{G_x(\chi_x + 1/V)}. \tag{21}$$

Reverse cryptography is possible when

$$V_{x_B|x_E} > V_{x_B|x_A} \quad or \quad V_{p_B|p_E} > V_{p_B|p_A}. \tag{22}$$

Combining Eqs. (7), (8) and (21), the above conditions become

$$(G_x\chi_x + G_x s)(G_p\chi_p + G_p/V) < 1 \tag{23}$$

$$(G_p\chi_p + G_p s)(G_x\chi_x + G_x/V) < 1. \tag{24}$$

These inequalities give the general conditions for the security of a reverse reconciliation protocol. For simplicity reasons, we will assume in the following that everything is symmetric in (x,p), i.e., $G_x = G_p = G$ and $\chi_x = \chi_p = \chi$, so that these conditions simplify to:

$$(G\chi + Gs)(G\chi + G/V) < 1. \tag{25}$$

Any experimental implementation of this protocol should however estimate these parameters from statistical tests, which are likely not to be exactly symmetric.

The conditions (25) can directly be translated into an information rate by using Shannon's formula:

$$I_{BA} = \frac{1}{2}\log_2 \frac{\langle x_B^2 \rangle}{V_{B|A}} \qquad I_{BE} = \frac{1}{2}\log_2 \frac{\langle x_B^2 \rangle}{V_{B|E}}. \tag{26}$$

The secret information rate for a reverse reconciliation protocol is therefore

$$\Delta I = I_{BA} - I_{BE} = \frac{1}{2}\log_2 \frac{V_{B|E}}{V_{B|A}} \tag{27}$$

$$\Delta I = \frac{1}{2}\log_2 \frac{1}{(G\chi + G/V)(G\chi + Gs)}. \tag{28}$$

It is straightforward to check that ΔI may be positive for arbitrarily high losses ($G \to 0$), even for coherent states ($s = 1$). Therefore, reverse reconciliation provides a simple way to extend the coherent-state protocols of Ref. 1 into the high-loss regime.

4 Implementations using EPR or coherent beam transmission

Here we consider protocols with the same quantum communication part as in Ref. 1, but we assume that reverse reconciliation is used, so that the 3 dB loss limit for security goes away, as explained above. We give below more quantitative estimates of the security thresholds.

If Alice uses EPR beams (or modulates a maximally-squeezed beam), $s = 1/V$, but Alice and Bob have information only every second transmission, since they don't always choose the same measurement basis then,

$$\Delta I_{EPR} = \frac{1}{4}\log_2 \frac{1}{(G\chi + G/V)^2} = \frac{1}{2}\log_2 \frac{1}{G\chi + G/V}. \tag{29}$$

For coherent beams, no squeezing is used, therefore $s = 1$ and the mutual informations are not dependent of the basis choice. We thus have

$$\Delta I_{coh} = \frac{1}{2}\log_2 \frac{1}{(G\chi + G/V)\,(G\chi + G)} \tag{30}$$

$$\Delta I_{coh} = \Delta I_{EPR} - \frac{1}{2}\log_2 G(1+\chi). \tag{31}$$

Since $G\chi \geq (1-G)$, with the equality iff the noise is minimal and $G \leq 1$, we obtain $\Delta I_{coh} \leq \Delta I_{EPR}$, and and $\Delta I_{coh} = \Delta I_{EPR}$ if and only if the noise comes only from losses. Defining the excess noise as $\epsilon = \chi - (1-G)/G$, it is simple to show that the reverse protocols are secure so long as as $\epsilon < (V-1)/(2V) \sim 1/2$ for coherent states, and $\epsilon < (V-1)/V \sim 1$ for EPR beams. This shows again that coherent states are indeed secure, although EPR beams are more robust against excess noise.

5 Conclusion

We have shown that reverse reconciliation protocols can be used to extract a secret key from the exchange of coherent or EPR beams between Alice and Bob. The key is secure against individual attacks for any transmission of the optical line between Alice and Bob, provided that the excess noise (noise beyond the loss-induced vacuum noise) is not too large.

References

1. F. Grosshans and P. Grangier, Phys. Rev. Lett. **88**, 057902 (2002).
2. N. J. Cerf et al., Phys. Rev. Lett. **85**, 1754 (2000); N. J. Cerf and S. Iblisdir, Phys. Rev. A **62**, 040301(R) (2000).
3. F. Grosshans and P. Grangier, Phys. Rev. A **64**, 010301 (R) (2001).
4. L.-M. Duan et al., Phys. Rev. Lett. **84**, 4002 (2000).
5. U. Maurer, IEEE Trans. Inf. Theory **39**, 733 (1993).
6. J.-P. Poizat et al., Ann. Phys. (Paris), **19**, 265 (1994); P. Grangier et al., Nature **396**, 537 (1998).

SECURE COMMUNICATION USING COHERENT STATES

GERALDO A. BARBOSA, ERIC CORNDORF, PREM KUMAR, AND HORACE P. YUEN

Center for Photonic Communication and Computing, ECE Department, Northwestern University, Evanston, IL 60208-3118
E-mail: barbosa@ece.northwestern.edu

G. MAURO D'ARIANO, MATTEO G. A. PARIS, AND PAOLO PERINOTTI

Quantum Optics & Information Group, INFM, Università di Pavia, via Bassi 6, I-27100 Pavia, Italy

We demonstrate that secure communication using coherent states is possible. The optimal eavesdropping strategy for an M-ary ciphering scheme shows that the minimum probability of error in a measurement for bit determination can be made arbitrarily close to the pure guessing value $P_e = 1/2$. This ciphering scheme can be optically amplified without degrading the security level. New avenues are open to secure communications at high speeds in fiber-optic or free-space channels.

Secure communication protocols protected by physical laws instead of mathematical complexities, such as the BB84 quantum protocol for key distribution,[1] seem to have encountered a bottleneck that hampers their utilization in real networks. The same no-cloning theorem that guarantees security forbids the signal amplification that is necessary in long-haul communication links. No alternate quantum scheme using quantum repeaters or entangled states, having practical applicability within a reasonable time span, has been envisaged. The question "is it possible to create a system with available technology that could provide unconditional security in long-distance communication?" has a positive answer. It relies on the use of quantum noise inherent in the coherent states of light, as demonstrated in this paper.

In the presence of noise, it has been shown information theoretically[2] that new shared secret keys can be created between two users. A specific protocol has been proposed by Yuen,[3,4] which has been called the YK protocol. A particular implementation of this YK protocol has been demonstrated,[5] in which detector noise is utilized and hence it is not unconditionally secure. However, the YK protocol can be made unconditionally secure by utilizing the fundamental, unavoidable quantum noise in a quantum signaling scheme.[6] The other known secure scheme is, of course, the BB84,[1] or its variant that involves features of B92,[7] in which coherent states instead of Fock states are employed. The implementations of the YK protocol,[5] and BB84, both suffer from the intrinsic limitation that very weak signals with no more than one photon per mode have to be used, making them severely rate-limited in a lossy channel. This problem can be alleviated in a new protocol, in which mesoscopic coherent states are employed to overcome loss and to allow ordinary amplification, switching and routing. In addition to the use of the fundamentally-unavoidable quantum noise in coherent states, a crucial new ingredient in this protocol is the explicit use of a shared secret key for the cryptographic objective of key expansion. A shared secret key is also needed in the BB84 and the YK protocols for the purpose of user and message authentication amidst the protocol execution.

In the ciphering scheme for this new protocol the sender (Alice) uses an explicit secret key (a short key $\mathbf{K}$, appropriately expanded into a longer key $\mathbf{K}'$ by use of another encryption mechanism such as a stream cipher) to modulate the parameters of, in general, a multimode coherent state. Coherent states span an infinite-dimensional Hilbert space which we refer to as a *qumode.* A qumode can be associated with any physical property of light such as polarization, phase, frequency or time. For the free-space implementation to be presented, the qumodes are the two orthogonal modes of polarization. In this case, Alice uses the running key $\mathbf{K}'$ to specify a polarization basis from a set of M uniformly spaced two-mode bases spanning a great circle on the Poincaré sphere. Each basis consists of a polarization state and its antipodal state at an angle π from it, representing the 0 and 1 bit value for that basis. The message $\mathbf{X}$ is encoded as $\mathbf{Y}_{K'}(\mathbf{X})$. This mapping of the stream of bits onto points of the Poincaré sphere is the *key* to be shared by Alice and the receiver (Bob). Because of his knowledge of $\mathbf{K}'$, Bob is able to make a precise demodulation operation producing the plaintext $\mathbf{X}$. Bob applies $\mathbf{K}'$ to the received sequence of arbitrary polarization states to return them to the linear orthogonally-polarized condition, representing the two original bits of the message $\mathbf{X}$.

We present analysis that covers both polarization as well as phase modulation of optical signals. In the case of *polarization* states, information is encrypted and encoded on two orthogonal polarization modes of radiation with annihilation operators a_1 and a_2. A coherent state $|\psi_0\rangle$ with amplitude α in mode a_2 ($|\psi_0\rangle = |0\rangle \otimes |\alpha\rangle$) is "rotated" by a unitary transformation U_{φ_b} ($\varphi_b = 0$ or π) to create the bit of a message. This rotation is performed by, e.g., $U_{\varphi_b} = \exp[(\varphi_b/2)(a_1^\dagger a_2 - a_1 a_2^\dagger)]$, giving

$$|\psi_b\rangle = U_{\varphi_b}|0\rangle \otimes |\alpha\rangle = |\alpha \sin\frac{\varphi_b}{2}\rangle \otimes |\alpha \cos\frac{\varphi_b}{2}\rangle. \tag{1}$$

For *phase* encoding within a given polarization state, one could start by splitting a coherent state $|\alpha\rangle$ into a two-mode coherent state $|\Psi_0\rangle = |\alpha/\sqrt{2}\rangle_1 \otimes |\alpha/\sqrt{2}\rangle_2$. Bit encoding can be represented by the operation

$$|\Psi_b\rangle = e^{-iJ_z\varphi_b}|\Psi_0\rangle = |e^{-i\varphi_b/2}\alpha/\sqrt{2}\rangle_1 \otimes |e^{i\varphi_b/2}\alpha/\sqrt{2}\rangle_2, \tag{2}$$

where $J_z = (a_1^\dagger a_1 - a_2^\dagger a_2)/2$. Demonstration of the security of the ciphering scheme in both kinds of physical encoding, polarization or phase, can be treated with the same formalism and leads to the same result.

Let us analyze the phase ciphering, applied by the same modulator generating the bit sequence. The ciphering angle ϕ_ν could have ν as a discrete

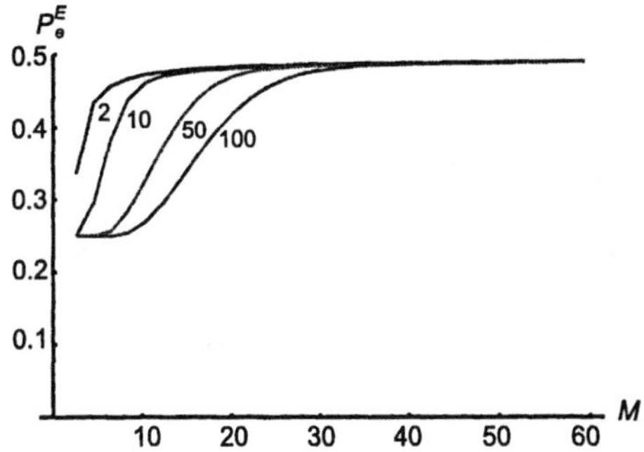

Figure 1. P_e^E as a function of M for $|\alpha|^2 = 2$, 10, 50, 100.

or a continuous variable determined by some general distribution. A ciphered two-mode state is $|\Psi_{b\nu}\rangle = e^{-iJ_z(\varphi_b+\phi_\nu)}|\Psi_0\rangle$ and the corresponding density operator for all possible choices of ν is ρ_b. The problem is to find the minimum probability of error P_e^E that an eavesdropper (Eve) can achieve in bit determination, given that ciphered states are used.

No restriction is imposed on the physical devices available to Eve, including perfect detectors and unlimited computational power. A close-to-source attack is considered, in which no losses have yet occurred that normally would during propagation of the signal. These are the ideal conditions for an eavesdropper.

The optimal POVM for discriminating between ρ_0 and ρ_1 is given by Helstrom's binary discrimination procedure[9] applied to $\Delta\rho = \rho_1 - \rho_0$. Calling Π_1 and Π_0 ($\Pi_1 + \Pi_0 = \mathrm{I}$) the projectors over eigenstates with the positive and negative eigenvalues of $\Delta\rho$, the probability of error P_e^E is

$$P_e^E = \mathrm{Tr}\left[p_1 \Pi_0 \rho_1 + p_0 \Pi_1 \rho_0\right], \tag{3}$$

where p_1 and p_0 are *a-priori* probabilities to find a state in ρ_1 or ρ_0, respectively. In one of Yuen's scheme,[8] closest values of a given k are associated with distinct bits from the bit at position k. For example, $\phi_k = \pi\left[k/M + (1/2)\left(1 - (-1)^k\right)\right]$, $k = 0, 1, ..., M-1$. In this encoding protocol, two closest neighboring states represent distinct bits. Figure 1 shows the minimum probability of error as a function of the number of ciphering levels M. P_e^E goes very fast to the asymptotic pure-guessing limit of $1/2$ as M increases. The quantum noise present in the coherent state of light is what makes these states indistinguishable to an eavesdropper.

Bob, on the other hand, by knowing the key has much more complete information on the state of light that has been sent and can extract the information with great precision. His probability of error is

$$P_e^B = \frac{1}{2}\left(1 - \sqrt{1 - e^{-2|\alpha|^2}}\right). \tag{4}$$

For sufficiently large values of α, the minimum probability of error P_e^B is negligible, leading to an excellent signal recovery by Bob.

Note that the present analysis does not include Eve's attacks using trial keys, which would be exponentially complex. Also, the stream cipher output in the system is not open to observation, thus its seed key is not open to the usual known-plaintext attacks. The complete security analysis for the most general attacks will be presented elsewhere.

This scheme opens up the path for long-distance secure communication based on protection by physical laws instead of mathematical complexities.

Acknowledgments

This work was supported by DARPA/AFRL under Grant No. F30602-01-2-0528.

References

1. C. H. Bennett and G. Brassard, "Quantum cryptography: public-key distribution and coin tossing," in *Proceedings of the IEEE International Conference on Computers, Systems, and Signal Processing*, Bangalore, India, 1984, pp. 175–179.
2. A. D. Wyner, *Bell Syst. Tech. J.* **54**, 1355 (1975); I. Csiszar and J. Korner, *IEEE Trans. Inform. Theory* **24**, 339 (1978); U. M. Maurer, *IEEE Trans. Inform. Theory* **39**, 733 (1993).
3. H. P. Yuen and A. Kim, *Phys. Lett. A* **241**, 135 (1998); *Phys. Lett. A* **246**, 560 (1998).
4. H. P. Yuen, "Quantum versus classical noise cryptography," in *Quantum Communication, Computing, and Measurement 2*, P. Kumar et al., eds., (Plenum, New York, 2000), pp. 399–404.
5. A. Tomita and O. Hirota, *J. Opt. B: Quant. and Semiclass. Opt.* **2**, 705 (2000).
6. H. P. Yuen, "Communication and measurement with squeezed states," in *Quantum Squeezing*, eds. P. D. Drummond and Z. Ficek, (Springer-Verlag, Berlin, to be published).
7. C. H. Bennett, *Phys. Rev. Lett.* **68**, 3121 (1992).
8. H. P. Yuen, "Anonymous key quantum cryptography," (Northwestern University, Evanston, 2000), unpublished; H. P. Yuen, A. Kim, *Phys. Lett. A* **241**, 135 (1998).
9. C. W. Helstrom, *Quantum Detection and Estimation Theory*, Vol. 123, Series: *Mathematics in Science and Engineering*, (Academic Press, New York, 1976).

QUANTUM KEY DISTRIBUTION OVER 67 KM WITH A PLUG & PLAY SYSTEM

HUGO ZBINDEN, NICOLAS GISIN, DAMIEN STUCKI
Group of Applied Physics, 1211 Geneva, Switzerland
E-mail: hugo.zbinden@physics.unige.ch

OLIVIER GUINNARD, GRÉGOIRE RIBORDY
id Quantique S.A., Geneva

Quantum key distribution (QKD) is stepping out of the laboratory. We present a commercial fiber-optic QKD-prototype based on faint laser pulses and the results of field tests.

1 Introduction

Quantum cryptography or, more exactly, quantum key distribution (QKD) is the most advanced subject in the field of quantum information technologies. Since the introduction of the BB84 protocol by Bennett and Brassard[1] many experiments have been performed by numerous groups.[2] However, to our knowledge, all experiments to date were performed in laboratories or used laboratory equipment (e.g., liquid nitrogen cooled the detectors) or needed frequent alignments (e.g., control of polarization or phase). In this paper, we present a commercial turn-key, fiber-optic QKD-prototype.[3,4] We tested the stability of the auto-compensating plug & play system[5] over installed terrestrial and aerial cables. Keys were exchanged over a distance of 67 km.

2 Plug & Play System

The QKD system consists of two 19" casings, one for Alice and one for Bob (see Fig. 1). The two devices are connected to computers by the USB port and linked together through an optical fiber. The two computers communicate via an ethernet/Internet link. The system features the following characteristics:

- Faint laser plug & play setup. The plug & play setup is an autoaligned phase-coding setup with pulses travelling forth and back between Bob and Alice.[5]
- BB84 protocol.
- 5 MHz pulse rate.
- Thermoelectrically cooled, gated InGaAs APD photon counters, with quantum efficiency η_{det} of 10% and dark-count probability of about 10^{-5} per gate.[6,3]

Figure 1. Commercial QKD-system based on the plug & play setup

- Automatic setup, all functions are computer controlled.

3 FIELD TESTS

3.1 Robustness of the plug & play setup

A commercial QKD system must work under all real conditions. In particular, it is important to check that the auto-alignment works with slowly-varying fiber cables. We measured the interference visibilities by sending relatively strong pulses (several photons per pulse) always with the same, compatible phase values and looking at the counts on the two detectors, R_{right} and R_{wrong} (substracting the counts due to detector noise). We then obtained the fringe visibility according to the standard definition:

$$V = \frac{R_{\text{right}} - R_{\text{wrong}}}{R_{\text{right}} + R_{\text{wrong}}} \tag{1}$$

We tested different fibers under different conditions:

A. Installed fibers (underground) of up to 67 km length.

B. Two passages through an aerial cable of 2.5 km length in combination with installed fibers and fibers on a spool.

C. A polarization scrambler in combination with 25 km of fiber on a spool.

In cases A and B the visibilities were always better than 99.6%. In case C, we measured the visibility as function of the scrambling frequency. This frequency is defined as the number of complete circles that the polarization vector would describe per second on the Poincaré sphere, if the birefringence changed uniformly. The visibility drops from 99.7% to 99.5% and to 98% at frequencies of 40 Hz and 100 Hz respectively. This shows that the visibilities decrease under very rapid perturbations, which are unlikely to be found in

Table 1. Data for key exchange over installed fibers.

Fiber	Length [km]	R_{raw} [kHz]	QBER [%]	R_{net} [kHz]
Geneva-Nyon (under lake)	22.0	2.06	2.0 ± 0.1	1.51
Nyon-Lausanne (terrestrial)	37.8	0.50	3.9 ± 0.2	0.26
Geneva-Lausanne (under lake) B	67.1	0.16	5.6 ± 0.3	0.05
Ste Croix (aerial)	22.7	2.32	3.0 ± 0.1	1.57

installed fibers. Hence, $QBER_{opt} = (1 - V)/2$, the quantum bit-error rate due to imperfect interference can almost be neglected.

3.2 Key exchange

We performed key exchange over different installed cables, the longest connecting the cities of Lausanne and Geneva. We measured the raw bit rate R_{raw} and the quantum bit error rate (QBER). Table 1 gives the obtained values for various fibers at an average photon number per pulse of $\mu = 0.2$.

R_{net} is the bit rate after error correction and privacy amplification. On the one hand, errors are essentially due to the detector noise, and the QBER increases with increasing fiber length (loss) and lower μ. On the other hand, we have to take into account that in QKD setups using faint laser pulses, an eavesdropper can take advantage of multi-photon pulses and his information increases with higher μ.[7] Therefore, there is an optimal μ, which maximizes R_{net}. In our case with $\mu = 0.2$, R_{net} is essentially limited by the detector noise and not by the information that the eavesdropper can derive from multi-photon pulses. The trade-off between detector noise and multi-photon pulses depending on the assumptions about the eavesdropper is discussed in Ref. 8.

4 Conclusions

We have tested a commercial QKD-system based on the plug & play setup. It proves to be perfectly stable in different environments, including aerial cables. Purists would prefer a system based on real single photons. However, at the time, the maximum transmission distance is limited by the detector noise rather than by the Eve's information gained from multi-photon pulses. Available technology for single-photon sources or entangled-photon sources is not yet ripe to be integrated into a commercial system. In the near future, better photon counters at telecom wavelengths could significantly improve the performance of fiber-based QKD systems.

Acknowledgments

We would like to thank Swisscom for giving us access to their fiber links. This work was supported by the Esprit project 28139 (EQCSPOT) through Swiss OFES and the NCCR "Quantum Photonics".

References

1. C. H. Bennett, and G. Brassard, "Quantum cryptography: public key distribution and coin tossing", Int. Conf. Computers, Systems & Signal Processing, Bangalore, India, December 10-12, 175 (1984).
2. for a review see, e.g., N. Gisin, G. Ribordy, W. Tittel, and H. Zbinden, Rev. Mod. Phys. **74**, 145 (2002).
3. id Quantique SA, www.idquantique.com.
4. D. Stucki, N. Gisin, O. Guinnard, G. Ribordy, and H. Zbinden, New J. of Phys. **4**, 41 (2002).
5. A. Muller, T. Herzog, B. Huttner, W. Tittel, H. Zbinden and N. Gisin, Applied Phys. Lett. **70**, 793 (1997).
6. D. Stucki, G. Ribordy, A. Stefanov, H. Zbinden, J. G. Rarity, and T. Wall, J. Mod. Opt. **48**, 1967 (2001).
7. G. Brassard, N. Lütkenhaus, T. Mor, and B. C. Sanders, Phys. Rev. Lett. **85**, 1330 (2000).
8. S. Felix, N. Gisin, A. Stefanov, and H. Zbinden. J. of Mod. Optics **48**, 2009 (2001).

QUANTUM BIT COMMITMENT: A COMPLETE CLASSIFICATION OF PROTOCOLS

GIACOMO MAURO D'ARIANO

Quantum Optics & Information Group *of the INFM*
Dipartimento di Fisica "A. Volta", via Bassi 6, I-27100 Pavia, Italy

Department of Electrical and Computer Engineering,
Northwestern University, Evanston, IL 60208

This paper addresses the controversy between Mayers, Lo and Chau[1] on one side, and Yuen[2] on the opposite side, as to whether or not unconditionally secure protocols exist. For such purpose, a complete classification of all possible bit-commitment protocols is given, including all possible cheating attacks. For the simplest class of protocols (non-aborting and with complete and perfect verification), it is shown how a game-theoretical situation naturally arises. For these protocols, bounds for the cheating probabilities are derived, which turn out to be different from those given in the impossibility proof.[1] The whole classification and analysis has been carried out using a *finite open-system* approach. The discrepancy with the impossibility proof is explained on the basis of the implicit adoption of a *closed-system approach*—equivalent to modeling the commitment as being performed by two fixed machines interacting unitarily in an overall *closed system*. However, it is shown that the closed-system approach for the classification of commitment protocols unavoidably leads to infinite dimensions, which then invalidates the continuity argument at the heart of the impossibility proof.

1 Introduction

It is of practical relevance to establish if there exist secure quantum bit commitment protocols, since quantum bit commitment is a crucial element for building up more sophisticated protocols, such as remote quantum gambling, coin tossing, and unconditionally secure two-party quantum computation.

In bit commitment Alice provides Bob with a piece of evidence that she has chosen a bit $b = 0, 1$ which she commits to him. Later, Alice will open the commitment, revealing the bit b to Bob, and proving that it is indeed the committed bit with the evidence in Bob's possession. Therefore, Alice and Bob should agree on a protocol which satisfies simultaneously the following three requirements: (1) it must be *concealing*, namely Bob should not be able to retrieve b before the opening; (2) it must be *binding*, namely Alice should not be able to change b after the commitment; (3) it must be *verifiable*, namely Bob must be able to check b against the evidence in his possession, according to the rules of the protocol. In an in-principle proof of security of the commitment it is supposed that both parties possess unlimited technology, e.g., computational power, space, time, etc., and the protocol is said to be *unconditionally secure* if neither Alice nor Bob can cheat with significant probability of success as a consequence of physical laws.

In 1993, a quantum-mechanical protocol was proposed,[3] and the unconditional security of this protocol was generally accepted for long time. The insecurity of this protocol was shown by Mayers, Lo and Chau[1] in 1997, by recognizing the possibility for Alice to cheat by entangling the committed evidence with a quantum system in her possession, and it was argued that no unconditionally secure protocol is possible. Finally, after 2000, Yuen[2] presented some protocols which challenged the previous impossibility proof, mostly on the basis of the possibility of encoding the bit on an *anonymous state* given to Alice by Bob and known only to him, and suggesting the use of *decoy systems* that make the protocol concealing in the limit of infinitely-many systems, with the possibility for Bob to perform his quantum measurement before Alice opening, whence disputing the general availability of EPR cheating for Alice.

In this paper, in order to clarify the controversy, we will present a classification of all possible bit-commitment protocols based on a single commitment step, analyzing the main cheating strategies for both parties (a full derivation of the classification, the reduction of multi-step commitments to a single step, and a more exhaustive analysis of cheating attacks can be found in Ref. 4, of which the present paper is a much shorter version). For the simplest class of protocols (non-aborting, with complete and perfect verification) we will show how a game-theoretical situation naturally arises. Bounds for the cheating probabilities of these protocols are presented, which are different from those given in the impossibility proof.[1] In the final discussion we will see how the discrepancy between the two opposite analysis arises, due to the implicit adoption in the impossibility proof of a *closed-system approach*, equivalent to modeling the commitment as being performed by two fixed machines interacting unitarily in an overall *closed system*. However, it is shown that such modeling, along with the requirement of unlimited technology, necessarily leads to infinite dimensions, which invalidates the continuity argument at the heart of the impossibility proof.

2 The classification of protocols

The most general bit-commitment scheme with a single step is of the form: (1) Bob prepares the Hilbert space H with the *anonymous state* $|\varphi\rangle \in \mathsf{H}$, and sends H to Alice; (2) Alice *modulates* the value $b = 0, 1$ of the committed bit on the anonymous state $|\varphi\rangle$ and sends the output back to Bob. The *bit modulation* is a quantum operation (QO) $\mathrm{M}^{(b)}$ parametrized by b. Such scheme contains all possibilities, including Yuen's protocols,[2] and the protocols considered by Mayers, Lo and Chau,[1] which correspond to *openly known* $|\varphi\rangle$. In general, the output Hilbert space K of the QO will be different from H, since Alice can send back to Bob a quantum system different from what he sent to her.

In Ref. 4 a complete classification of all possible protocols is derived, on the basis of the fact that since Alice has unlimited technology, she can always achieve the encoding QO's $\mathrm{M}^{(b)}$ of the committed bit value b via a *perfect pure measurement.* For *non-aborting protocols*, this corresponds to the following QO's

$$\mathrm{M}^{(b)}(|\varphi\rangle\langle\varphi|) = \mathrm{Tr}_{\mathsf{F}\otimes\mathsf{P}}[U^{(b)}(|\varphi\rangle\langle\varphi| \otimes |\omega\rangle\langle\omega|_{\mathsf{A}} \otimes \rho_{\mathsf{P}})U^{(b)\dagger}], \qquad (2.1)$$

where A is the preparation ancilla/decoy Hilbert space prepared in the state $|\omega\rangle$; F is the measurement ancilla Hilbert space on which Alice performs a complete von Neumann measurement, and we have that $\mathsf{K} \otimes \mathsf{F} \simeq \mathsf{H} \otimes \mathsf{A}$; P is the space of the *secret parameter*, say j, which is needed in order to make the protocol *concealing* and at the same time *verifiable* (so that the modulation is actually a choice between two *ensembles* of QO's $\{\mathrm{M}_j^{(b)}\}$ for $b = 0, 1$). Therefore, the best option for Alice is to achieve the encoding QO by preparing the ancilla/decoy state $|\omega\rangle_{\mathsf{A}} \in \mathsf{A}$, performing the unitary transformation $U^{(b)}$ on $\mathsf{H}\otimes\mathsf{A}$, making a complete von Neumann measurement on F, with outcome say i, and finally send K to Bob. The partial trace on $\mathsf{F}\otimes\mathsf{P}$ on the basis $\{|i\rangle \otimes |j\rangle\}$, which describes Alice's measurement, corresponds to the Kraus decompositions $\mathrm{M}^{(b)} = \sum_{ji} p_j E_{ji}^{(b)} \cdot E_{ji}^{(b)\dagger}$, where j is the *secret parameter* and i is the *secret outcome*, and the probabilities $p_j = \langle j|\rho_{\mathsf{P}}|j\rangle$ for j will depend on the preparation ρ_{P}. In a protocol which is completely and perfectly verifiable Alice tells b, j and i to Bob, who verifies the state $E_{ji}^{(b)}|\varphi\rangle$. Since the local QO's on K and $\mathsf{F} \otimes \mathsf{P}$ commute, Alice has the possibility of: (1) first sending K to Bob; (2) then performing the measurement on $\mathsf{F} \otimes \mathsf{P}$ at the very last moment of the opening. As we will see, this is the basis for Alice's EPR cheating attacks. Notice that strictly trace-decreasing QO's, i.e., aborting protocols, pose limitations to Alice's EPR cheating. In fact, Alice cannot delay the abortion of the protocol at the opening, and must declare it at the commitment. Since both secret parameters j and i can be conveniently measured by Alice, they can be treated on equal footings as a single parameter $J \equiv (j, i)$. With the notation $E_J^{(b)} \doteq \sqrt{p_j} E_{ji}^{(b)} \in \mathsf{B}(\mathsf{H}, \mathsf{K})$, the maps write

$$\mathrm{M}^{(b)}(|\varphi\rangle\langle\varphi|) = \sum_j p_j \mathrm{M}_j^{(b)}(|\varphi\rangle\langle\varphi|) = \sum_J E_J^{(b)}|\varphi\rangle\langle\varphi|E_J^{(b)\dagger}. \qquad (2.2)$$

3 Cheating

For a discussion of all possibilities for cheating see Ref. 4. Here we analyze the only the attacks that are useful for both Alice and Bob.

Alice cheating. After the commitment and before the opening Alice can try to cheat by performing a unitary transformation V on $\mathsf{F} \otimes \mathsf{P}$: this is the so-called EPR attack. Without changing the QO's $\mathrm{M}^{(b)}$, the maneuver will change their Kraus decompositions—which are relevant at the opening—as $\{E_J^{(b)}\} \to \{E_J^{(b)}(V)\}$, keeping the cardinality, in the following way

$$E_J^{(b)}(V) = \sum_L E_L^{(b)} V_{JL}, \qquad V_{JL} = \langle J|V|L\rangle. \qquad (3.3)$$

The probability that Alice can cheat successfully in pretending to have committed, say, $b = 1$, whereas she committed $b = 0$ instead, is given by

$$P_c^A(V, \varphi) = \sum_J \frac{|\langle\varphi|E_J^{(0)\dagger}(V)E_J^{(1)}|\varphi\rangle|^2}{\|E_J^{(1)}\varphi\|^2}, \tag{3.4}$$

which depends on the anonymous state $|\varphi\rangle$ and on the cheating transformation V. Without any knowledge of $|\varphi\rangle$, the best that Alice can do is to adopt a conservative strategy, by maximizing her probability of cheating in the worst case, corresponding to the *minimax* choice of V

$$(P_c^A)_\mu \doteq \max_V \min_\varphi P_c^A(V, \varphi). \tag{3.5}$$

It is evident that in this way a game-theoretical situation arises, in which Bob chooses $|\varphi\rangle$ and Alice chooses V, with the probability $P(V, \varphi)$ playing the role of a *payoff matrix.* The actual game situation is more complicated—due for example to Bob cheating—and will be analyzed elsewhere.

Bob cheating. Bob can try to cheat by making the *best discrimination* between the two maps $\mathrm{M}^{(b)} = \sum_j p_j \mathrm{M}_j^{(b)}$. However, since he doesn't know the probabilities p_j actually used by Alice, his strategy will be suboptimal, and his actual cheating probability P_c^B will be lower than the probability $(P_c^B)_{\rm opt}$ corresponding to the optimal strategy with the right probabilities p_j. Since map-discrimination is generally more reliable with the map acting locally on an entangled state,[5] instead of preparing $|\varphi\rangle \in \mathsf{H}$ Bob prepares an entangled state on $\mathsf{H} \otimes \mathsf{R}$ and sends only H to Alice. Therefore, for equally probable bit values $b = 0, 1$, Bob's optimal probability of cheating is bounded as follows[4]

$$P_c^B \le (P_c^B)_{\rm opt} = \frac{1}{2} + \frac{1}{4}\left\|\mathrm{M}^{(1)} - \mathrm{M}^{(0)}\right\|_{cb}, \tag{3.6}$$

where $\|\cdot\|_{cb}$ denotes the completely-bounded (CB) norm.

Bounds for cheating probabilities. If the protocol is perfectly concealing the CB-norm in Eq. (3.6) is zero, and the two maps are the same, whence the their Kraus decompositions are connected via a unitary transformation V on $\mathsf{F} \otimes \mathsf{P}$, and Alice can cheat with probability one. Let's consider now the case in which Bob's optimal probability of cheating $(P_c^B)_{\rm opt}$ is infinitesimally close to $\frac{1}{2}$, namely $\|\mathrm{M}^{(1)} - \mathrm{M}^{(0)}\|_{cb} = \varepsilon$. Notice that generally ε is vanishing for increasing dimension of K (such as when the approximately concealing condition is achieved for an increasingly large number of decoy systems[2]), and no obvious continuity argument can be invoked to assert that Alice's cheating probability will approach unity for vanishing ε. More precisely, in the present context the continuity argument of Ref. 1 would imply that

$$1 - (P_c^A)_\mu = \omega\left(\left\|\mathrm{M}^{(1)} - \mathrm{M}^{(0)}\right\|_{cb}\right), \quad \lim_{\varepsilon\to 0}\omega(\varepsilon) = 0, \tag{3.7}$$

with the function $\omega(\varepsilon)$ independent of the dimension of K. However, using anonymous states such assertion may turn out to be false. In fact, it is obvious that if there is an alternative Kraus decomposition $\{E_J^{(0)}(V)\}$ for the map $\mathrm{M}^{(0)}$ such that the two Kraus decompositions $\{E_J^{(0)}(V)\}$ and $\{E_J^{(1)}\}$ are close, then the protocol is approximately concealing and not binding, since[4]

$$(P_c^B)_{opt} - \frac{1}{2} = \frac{1}{4}\left\|\mathrm{M}^{(1)} - \mathrm{M}^{(0)}\right\|_{cb} \leq \frac{1}{2}\sqrt{\left\|\sum_J \left|E_J^{(0)}(V) - E_J^{(1)}\right|^2\right\|}, \quad (3.8)$$

$$P_c^A(V,\varphi) \geq \left[1 - \frac{1}{2}\left\|\sum_J \left|E_J^{(0)}(V) - E_J^{(1)}\right|^2\right\|\right]^2, \quad (3.9)$$

where for any operator A we use the customary abbreviation $|A|^2 \doteq A^\dagger A$. However, the impossibility proof would be true if a bound of the form (3.8) were satisfied in the reverse direction, in which case one would have

$$1 - (P_c^A)_{\mu,av} \leq \min_V \left\|\sum_J \left|E_J^{(0)}(V) - E_J^{(1)}\right|^2\right\| \leq \omega\left(\left\|\mathrm{M}^{(1)} - \mathrm{M}^{(0)}\right\|_{cb}\right), \quad (3.10)$$

which would correspond to the following *continuity argument*: if two CP maps are close in CB-norm, then for a given fixed Kraus decomposition for one of the two maps, there is always an alternative Kraus decomposition for the other map such that the two are close. Since, as regards the cheating probabilities, we have considered only the case of non-aborting protocols with perfect-verification, proving the continuity argument (3.10) or directly the bound (3.7) would mean that a secure protocol could be sought outside such class of protocols. On the other hand, finding a counterexample to Eq. (3.7) would provide a perfectly verifiable and unconditionally secure protocol.

4 Discussion

The discrepancy between the previous analysis and the analysis beneath the impossibility proof[1] is essentially due to the fact that the latter is based on the assumption that the starting state of the commitment protocol is openly known, in the sense that the probability distribution of the state is given, and then the corresponding mixed state can be purified. The general underlying idea is that the protocol should be processed by *machines*, and therefore all probability distributions are defined, and purified inside the machines. However, such an assumption is certainly not realistic for a cryptographic protocol, in which each party has the freedom of changing or tuning the machine, namely choosing any desired probability distribution. One can continue to argue on this line, asserting that changing the machine is equivalent to use of a larger machine. However, this will be equivalent to considering *infinite machines*, corresponding to uniform probabilities on infinite sets, and this would invalidate an impossibility proof based on an unproven continuity argument.

The above ill-posed mathematical framework arises from the Bayesian approach to secret parameters, dictated from *closed-system* modeling with fixed machines and purification of probabilities. As an alternative to this closed-system approach, we have the realistic *finite open-system* approach, in which unknown parameters are treated as such, without the need of any a priori probability distribution, and in which we can address the problem for finite dimension with the parameter ε depending on it. Then, if one proceeds by treating unknown parameters as such, no openly -known state can be assumed, and the anonymous state encoding of Yuen[2] leads to the present classification of protocols. Notice that if the initial state $|\varphi\rangle$ is openly known, then for that given fixed state all QO's can be regarded as random unitary transformations (since all states are connected by unitary transformations), and this leads to the simple form of Alice's cheating probability in terms of fidelities,[1] whereas in the present context the probability of cheating has the more involved form (3.4), due to the fact that the state $|\varphi\rangle$ is unknown, and that there are QO's that don't admit random unitary Kraus decompositions.

Finally, regarding the possibility of aborting protocols, one could always reasonably adopt equivalent protocols which don't abort, since the repeated commitment will eventually be successful. However, such kind of protocols will necessarily be infinite convex-combinations of protocols on infinite-dimensional anonymous spaces H, and again the *closed-system* approach would necessarily lead to infinite dimensions.

Acknowledgments. This work has been jointly founded by the EC under the program ATESIT (Contract No. IST-2000-29681) and by the USA Army Research Office under MURI Grant No. DAAD19-00-1-0177. Extensive discussions with H. P. Yuen, who motivated this work, are acknowledged.

References

1. D. Mayers, Phys. Rev. Lett. **78**, 3414 (1997); H. K. Lo and H. F. Chau, Phys. Rev. Lett. **78**, 3410 (1997); H. K. Lo, Phys. Rev. A **56**, 1154 (1997).
2. H. P. Yuen, in *Quantum Communications and Measurements II*, P. Kumar, G. D'Ariano and O. Hirota, eds., Kluwer Academic/Plenum (New York 2000) p. 399; quant-ph/0006109, 0009113, 0106001, 0109055, 0207089. See also the paper in these proceedings.
3. G. Brassard, C. Crèpeau, R. Jozsa, and D. Langlois, in *Proceedings of the 34th Annual IEEE Symposium on Foundations of Computer Science*, 1993 (IEEE, Los Alamitos, 1993), p. 362.
4. G. M. D'Ariano, quant-ph/0209149.
5. G. M. D'Ariano and P. Lo Presti and M. G. A. Paris, Phys. Rev. Lett. **87**, 270404 (2001).

WHY THERE IS NO IMPOSSIBILITY THEOREM ON SECURE QUANTUM BIT COMMITMENT

HORACE P. YUEN

Department of Electrical and Computer Engineering, Department of Physics and Astronomy, Northwestern University, Evanston, IL 60208-3118, USA

E-mail: yuen@ece.northwestern.edu

The impossibility proof on unconditionally secure quantum bit commitment is critically reviewed. Different ways of obtaining secure protocols are indicated.

1 Introduction

There is a nearly universal acceptance of the general impossibility[1-4] of secure quantum bit commitment (QBC), taken to be a consequence of the Einstein-Podolsky-Rosen (EPR) type entanglement cheating which rules out QBC and other quantum protocols that have been proposed for various cryptographic objectives. Since there is no characterization of all possible QBC protocols, logically there can be no general impossibility proof as maintained to this date. In this article, which is based on Ref. 5, we explain the nature of various gaps and incompleteness in the impossibility proof, in addition to this a priori logical point. They should make clear the fact that there is no impossibility theorem even in the absence of a specific protocol that has been proved unconditionally secure. But we also describe an unconditionally secure protocol **QBC1** and other possible approaches for obtaining secure protocols.

2 The impossibility proof

The essential ideas that constitute the impossibility proof are generally agreed upon.[1-4] Adam and Babe have available to them two-way quantum communications that terminate in a finite number of exchanges, during which either party can perform any operation allowed by the laws of quantum physics. During these exchanges, Adam would have committed a bit with associated evidence to Babe. It is argued that, at the end of the commitment phase, there is an entangled pure state $|\Phi_{\mathsf{b}}\rangle$, $\mathsf{b} \in \{0,1\}$, shared between Adam who possesses state space $\mathcal{H}^A$, and Babe who possesses $\mathcal{H}^B$. For example, if Adam sends Babe one of M possible states $\{|\phi_{\mathsf{b}i}\rangle\}$ for bit b with probability $p_{\mathsf{b}i}$, then $|\Phi_{\mathsf{b}}\rangle = \sum_i \sqrt{p_{\mathsf{b}i}}|e_i\rangle|\phi_{\mathsf{b}i}\rangle$ with orthonormal $|e_i\rangle \in \mathcal{H}^A$ and given $|\phi_{\mathsf{b}i}\rangle \in \mathcal{H}^B$. Adam would open by making a measurement on $\mathcal{H}^A$, say $\{|e_i\rangle\}$, communicating to Babe his result i_0 and b; then Babe would verify by measuring $|\phi_{\mathsf{b}i_0}\rangle\langle\phi_{\mathsf{b}i_0}|$ on $\mathcal{H}^B$, accepting as correct only the result 1.

Generally, Babe can try to identify the bit from ρ^B_{b}, the marginal state of $|\Phi_{\mathsf{b}}\rangle$ on $\mathcal{H}^B$, by performing an optimal quantum measurement that yields the optimal cheating probability $\bar{P}^B_c$ for her. Adam cheats by committing $|\Phi_0\rangle$

and making a measurement on $\mathcal{H}^A$ to open i_0 and $\mathsf{b} = 1$. His probability of successful cheating is computed through $|\Phi_\mathsf{b}\rangle$, his particular measurement, and Babe's verifying measurement; the one optimized over all of his possible actions will be denoted $\bar{P}_c^A$. For a fixed measurement basis, Adam's cheating can be described by a unitary operator U^A on $\mathcal{H}^A$. When $\rho_0^B = \rho_1^B$, i.e., $\bar{P}_c^B = 1/2$, U^A is obtained via the Schmidt decomposition of $|\Phi_\mathsf{b}\rangle$. For unconditional, rather than perfect, security, one demands that both cheating probabilities $\bar{P}_c^B - 1/2$ and $\bar{P}_c^A$ can be made arbitrarily small when a security parameter n is increased.[2] Thus, *unconditional security* is quantitatively expressed as

$$\text{(US)} \qquad \lim_n \bar{P}_c^B = \frac{1}{2}, \quad \lim_n \bar{P}_c^A = 0. \tag{1}$$

This condition (1) says that, for any $\epsilon > 0$, there exists an n_0 such that for all $n > n_0$, $\bar{P}_c^B - 1/2 \leq \epsilon$ and $\bar{P}_c^A \leq \epsilon$, to which we refer as ϵ-*concealing* and ϵ-*binding*, respectively. These cheating probabilities are to be computed purely on the basis of physical laws, and thus would survive any change in technology, including any increase in computational power. One can write down explicitly $\bar{P}_c^B = \frac{1}{4}\left(2 + \|\rho_0^B - \rho_1^B\|_1\right)$. The corresponding $\bar{P}_c^A$ satisfies:[5,6]

$$4(1 - \bar{P}_c^B)^2 \leq \bar{P}_c^A \leq 2\sqrt{\bar{P}_c^B(1 - \bar{P}_c^B)}. \tag{2}$$

The lower bound in (2) yields the impossibility proof [1,7]

$$\text{(IP)} \qquad \lim_n \bar{P}_c^B = \frac{1}{2} \Rightarrow \lim_n \bar{P}_c^A = 1. \tag{3}$$

When random numbers known only to one party are used in the commitment, they are to be replaced by corresponding entanglement purification. For a random k, it is argued from the doctrine of the "Church of the Larger Hilbert Space"[4] that it is to be replaced by the purification $|\Psi\rangle$ in $\mathcal{H}^{B_1} \otimes \mathcal{H}^{B_2}$,

$$|\Psi\rangle = \sum_k \sqrt{\lambda_k}|\psi_k\rangle|f_k\rangle, \tag{4}$$

where the $|f_k\rangle$'s are complete orthonormal in $\mathcal{H}^{B_2}$ kept by Babe while $\mathcal{H}^{B_1}$ would be sent to Adam. Similar purification is to be used for performing any operation during commitment that might otherwise require an actual measurement. As a consequence, it is claimed that a shared state $|\Phi_\mathsf{b}\rangle$ at the end of commitment is known to both parties.

It appears that there is considerable incompleteness in the impossibility proof. For example, one may observe that the cheating probability $\bar{P}_c^A$ depends on Babe's verifying measurement. For an arbitrary protocol, the impossibility proof formulation does not, and in fact cannot, specify what the possible verifying measurements could be. There is *no* proof given that there cannot be more than one verifying measurement for which different cheating transformations are needed. When such a situation occurs, Adam may not know which one to use for a successful cheating. Even though this gap can be closed, in a proof that is not totally obvious, it is indicative of the incompleteness of the impossibility proof. The following situations show that the impossibility proof formulation is actually widely incomplete. A protocol may involve cheating detection during commitment with corresponding possibility of aborting the protocol, a situation different from cheat-sensitive protocols.[8] It has to be decided what would happen when cheating is detected, say in a game-theoretic formulation. It makes no sense to keep trying until one party's cheating is not detected; some limit on the number of detected cheats must be imposed. Assuming both parties are honest not trying to cheat, which is what the impossibility proof formulation does except for Adam to form entanglement instead of sending one $|\phi_{bi}\rangle$, also makes no sense because there would then be no need for a protocol. (Actually, the $|\phi_{bi}\rangle$ entanglement step is often mistakenly described as an honest one.) These possibilities have not been accounted for. In the discussions of a proper framework for QBC protocols in Ref. 5, we have codified some intuitively valid rules for protocol formation under the names *Intent Principle* and *Libertarian Principle.* In the following, we will discuss several of the many gaps in the impossibility proof.

3 No impossibility theorem without QBC definition

A plausible first reaction to the impossibility proof is: why are all possible QBC protocols covered by its formulation? More precisely, how may one define the necessary feature of an unconditionally secure QBC protocol that is required for any proof of a mathematical theorem that says such protocol is impossible? *No* such definition is available. The situation is similar to the lack of a definition of an "effectively computable" function in the context of the Church-Turing thesis. Nobody calls the Church-Turing thesis the Church-Turing theorem. This is because there is no mathematical definition of an effectively computable function. The logical possibility is open that someday a procedure may be found that is intuitively or even physically effective, but which can compute a nonrecursive arithmetical function.

Thus in the absence of a precise definition of a QBC protocol, one would have at best an "impossibility thesis", not an impossibility *theorem.* (This view was emphasized to the author by Masanao Ozawa.) Just as there appear to be many different forms of effective procedures, there are many different QBC protocol types[5] that appear not to be captured by the impossibility proof formulation. To uphold just an "impossibility thesis", one would need to prove that unconditionally secure QBC is impossible in each of these types.

4 Unknown versus random parameter

The impossibility proof regards any unknown number to one party as a random variable with a known probability distribution, from which the purification (4) may be formed. However, as it is well-known in classical statistics, not every unknown parameter is a random variable. In the present situation, there is an infinite number of open possibilities, such as the number of states and operations available, that admits no uniform probability distribution or actual entanglement for the purpose of EPR cheats. Furthermore, there is simply no ensemble here for the unknown parameter to be averaged over. In an analogous situation in the quantum information literature, this error has been recently called the "Partition Ensemble Fallacy Fallacy".[9] More significantly, there is no need for Adam to know the probability $\{\lambda_k\}$ under concealing for every $\{\lambda_k\}$. The proper approach is to regard the state $|\Psi\rangle$ of (4) as an unknown "parameter" in an infinite space. The other party does not need to know it, or to know its probability distribution *even* if it has one, because of the following *Secrecy Principle* which is a corollary of the Intent Principle and Libertarian Principle.

> *Secrecy Principle*: A party does not need to reveal a secret parameter chosen by her in whatever manner if it does not affect the security of the other party, who cannot reject the protocol on such a basis.

Thus, generation of the secret parameter can be automatized by one party, and it can be kept secret just as Adam can keep his bit b secret or a secret key can be kept secret in standard cryptography.

Indeed, with the use of (4) by Babe, it is not sufficient for concealing to assume that one fixed $|\Psi\rangle$ is used by her as done in the impossibility proof. Two examples are given in Ref. 6, which show that Babe can cheat by using another $\{\lambda_k\}$ or $|\Psi\rangle$ than the one prescribed, and nothing in the impossibility proof formulation prevents her from doing that. If one imposes the condition that the protocol is ϵ-concealing for every possible choice of $|\Psi\rangle$, then there is *no* impossibility proof until one shows that there is a cheating transformation for Adam which will work for every possible $|\Psi\rangle$. In the case of perfect concealing, this has been proved[6] for a single use of (4) by Babe. The corresponding ϵ-concealing case is yet to be resolved. See the article by G. M. D'Ariano in this volume for a quantitative discussion.

Note that the Secrecy Principle directly contradicts the claim that a pure $|\Phi_\mathsf{b}\rangle$ is openly known at the end of commitment. One consequence is that because Babe does not know $\{p_{\mathsf{b}i}\}$, the usual specification of the concealing condition is a sufficient but not necessary one needed for a general impossibility proof. Furthermore, one has to show that whatever information Adam lacks on $|\Phi_\mathsf{b}\rangle$, such as the $|f_k\rangle$ of (4), is *not* needed for his cheating. Observe also that (4) is not equivalent to the mere generation of $|\psi_k\rangle$ with probability λ_k, due to the presence of off-diagonal terms $|f_k\rangle\langle f_{k'}|$. Such purification has to be considered because of possible entanglement cheating, not because of the Church of the Larger Hilbert Space. Indeed, entanglement may help determine the bit through such terms, as the example in the next section shows. Even with the Church, the two cases are not equivalent.

5 Shifting of the evidence state space

Even when a pure $|\Phi_\mathsf{b}\rangle$ is openly known, the impossibility proof does not cover the situations in which opening and verification are more elaborate, involving component parts of $\mathcal{H}^A$ and $\mathcal{H}^B$. In particular, consider a protocol in which Babe forms (4) and sends Adam $\mathcal{H}^{B_1}$, with $|\psi_k\rangle = |\psi_{k1}\rangle|\psi_{k2}\rangle$ in $\mathcal{H}^{B_1} = \mathcal{H}^{B_{11}} \otimes \mathcal{H}^{B_{12}}$. Adam randomly switches the state in $\mathcal{H}^{B_{11}}$ to be that of $|\psi_{k1}\rangle$ or $|\psi_{k2}\rangle$ by the unitary permutation P_m, $m \in \{1, 2\}$, modulates the resulting state in $\mathcal{H}^{B_{11}}$ by a single U_b for each b, and sends it to Babe. He opens by revealing b, his random permutation P_m, and *returning* $\mathcal{H}^{B_{12}}$. Babe verifies by testing the appropriate states in $\mathcal{H}^{B_{11}}$ for checking b, and $\mathcal{H}^{B_{12}}$ for checking that there is no change. It is possible that the protocol is both concealing and binding for the following reason. For the final committed state $|\Phi_\mathsf{b}\rangle$ with Adam entangling the P_m with $|e_i\rangle \in \mathcal{H}^{A_1}$, we have $\mathcal{H}^A = \mathcal{H}^{A_1} \otimes \mathcal{H}^{B_{12}}$ and $\mathcal{H}^B = \mathcal{H}^{B_{11}} \otimes \mathcal{H}^{B_2}$. Thus, ρ_0^B can be close to ρ_1^B because $\mathcal{H}^{B_{12}}$ is not available to Babe for her cheating. However, only $\mathcal{H}^{A_1}$, and not $\mathcal{H}^A$, is available to Adam's cheating, so he cannot apply the required cheating U^A without being found cheating with a nonvanishing probability. Using the upper bound in (2) the security condition can be expressed as $\rho_0^B(\mathcal{H}^{B_{12}} \otimes \mathcal{H}^{B_2}) \sim \rho_1^B(\mathcal{H}^{B_{12}} \otimes \mathcal{H}^{B_2})$ and $\rho_0^B(\mathcal{H}^{B_1} \otimes \mathcal{H}^{B_2}) \not\sim \rho_1^B(\mathcal{H}^{B_1} \otimes \mathcal{H}^{B_2})$. To preserve the impossibility proof one would need to show that, in addition to (3), $\lim_n \bar{P}_c^B(\mathcal{H}^{B_{12}} \otimes \mathcal{H}^{B_2}) = \frac{1}{2} \Rightarrow \lim_n \bar{P}_c^B(\mathcal{H}^{B_1} \otimes \mathcal{H}^{B_2}) = \frac{1}{2}$. Clearly, this has *not* been proved.

As an example, consider the case $\mathcal{H}^{B_1} = \mathcal{H}^{B_{11}} \otimes \mathcal{H}^{B_{12}} \otimes \mathcal{H}^{B_{13}} \otimes \mathcal{H}^{B_{14}}$ of four qubits, with $\{|\psi_k\rangle\} = \{|1\rangle|2\rangle|3\rangle|4\rangle, |4\rangle|1\rangle|2\rangle|3\rangle, |3\rangle|4\rangle|1\rangle|2\rangle, |2\rangle|3\rangle|4\rangle|1\rangle\}$, where $\{|1\rangle, |2\rangle, |3\rangle, |4\rangle\}$ are, e.g., a fixed set S_0 of four possible BB84 states on a given great circle of a qubit. Adam permutes each $|\psi_k\rangle$ by one of four possible P_m, and returns the first qubit to Babe unchanged for $\mathsf{b} = 0$, while shifted by π in the great circle for $\mathsf{b} = 1$. Assume first that Babe either did not entangle, or cannot use her entanglement in $\mathcal{H}^{B_2}$. Then $\rho_0^{B_{11}}(\psi_k) = \rho_1^{B_{11}}(\psi_k)$ for all k, and no entanglement of permutations would produce a rotation on the first qubit while not disturbing the others. Thus, Adam cannot cheat perfectly and has a fixed $\bar{P}_c^A$ for this protocol which is not arbitrarily close to one, even though it is perfectly concealing. If one can find a case in which the protocol remains perfectly concealing with entanglement by Babe, which is not the case in this example, (IP) of (3) would be contradicted, and the case can be extended to become an unconditionally secure protocol by repeating it in a sequence. Such a case can indeed be found in this class of protocols which we call Type 2.

6 Protocol QBC1

If carried out honestly, this protocol is conceptually simple and works as follows.[5] Adam sends Babe n qubits with states selected randomly and independently from S_0. Babe then picks randomly one of these qubits and sends it back to Adam, who would leave it unchanged or shift it by π, depending on whether $\mathsf{b} = 0$ or 1, and commit it as evidence. He opens by revealing b and all the qubit states, and Babe verifies by corresponding measurements.

We assume that no cheating by either party, other than entanglement, occurs during commitment as in the impossibility proof formulation, say, under heavy penalty in a game-theoretic formulation in which state checking is done by both parties. Thus the protocol is perfectly concealing. There are many ways for Babe to randomly pick one of the n qubits, say by permutation into a fixed qubit among the n ones, or into a separate fixed qubit, each with its own purification. If Adam knows which particular way Babe chooses, it can be shown that he can cheat successfully. However, his success depends crucially on this knowledge, and no further entanglement purification by Babe is possible over these different ways that would allow her to send back a single qubit to Adam for bit modulation. While the situation here has some similarity to our Type 3 protocols,[5] it is one that cannot be completely purified even with a known probability distribution, and the impossibility proof does not apply. Thus, the protocol becomes ϵ-binding for large n. A full security proof of this protocol and detailed treatment of Type 2 protocols will be presented elsewhere.

Acknowledgements

I would like to thank G. M. D'Ariano, M. Ozawa, and I. L. Chuang for useful discussions. This work was supported by the Defense Advanced Research Projects Agency and the Army Research Office.

References

1. D. Mayers, quant-ph/9603015.
2. D. Mayers, Phys. Rev. Lett. **78**, 3414 (1997).
3. H. K. Lo and H. F. Chau, Phys. Rev. Lett. **78**, 3410 (1997); Fortschr. Phys. **46**, 907 (1998); Physica D **120**, 177 (1998); H. K. Lo, Phys. Rev. A **56**, 1154 (1997); G. Brassard, C. Crépeau, D. Mayers, and L. Salvail, quant-ph/9712023; quant-ph/9806031; J. Mueller-Quade and H. Imai, quant-ph/0010112.
4. D. Gottesman and H. K. Lo, Physics Today, Nov. 2000, p. 22.
5. H. P. Yuen, quant-ph/0207089.
6. H. P. Yuen, quant-ph/0109055.
7. H. P. Yuen, quant-ph/0006109.
8. L. Hardy and A. Kent, quant-ph/9911043.
9. K. Nemoto and S. L. Braunstein, quant-ph/0207135.

LARGE N QUANTUM CRYPTOGRAPHY

ADRIAN KENT
DAMTP, University of Cambridge, Centre for Mathematical Sciences, Wilberforce Road, Cambridge CB3 0WA, U.K.
Email: a.p.a.kent@damtp.cam.ac.uk

In quantum cryptography, the level of security attainable by a protocol which implements a particular task N times bears no simple relation to the level of security attainable by a protocol implementing the task once. Useful partial security, and even near-perfect security in an appropriate sense, can be obtained for N copies of a task which itself cannot be securely implemented. We illustrate this with protocols for quantum bit string commitment and quantum random number generation between mistrustful parties.

1 Introduction

It is now well known that quantum information can guarantee classically unattainable security in a variety of important cryptographic tasks. We know too from no-go results that quantum cryptography cannot guarantee perfect security for every task. We cannot presently characterize precisely the tasks for which perfectly secure quantum protocols exist, or even the range of cryptographic tasks for which perfectly secure quantum protocols *might possibly* exist, because quantum cryptography involves more than devising quantum protocols for tasks known to be useful in classical cryptography. The properties of quantum information allow new and cryptographically useful tasks, which have no classical counterpart. Also, reductions and relations between classical cryptographic tasks need not necessarily apply to their quantum equivalents. This means that there is a wider range of tasks to consider, and that no-go theorems may not necessarily be quite as powerful as classical reasoning would suggest.

These remarks apply in particular to bit commitment and coin tossing, important cryptographic protocols whose potential for physically secure implementation has been extensively investigated. It is known that unconditionally secure quantum bit commitment is impossible for non-relativistic protocols:[1,2,3,4,5] that is, protocols in which the two parties are restricted to single pointlike sites, or more generally, in which the signalling constraints of special relativity are ignored. No unconditionally secure non-relativistic coin tossing protocol has been found; no proof that no such protocols exist has yet been published either.

Unconditionally secure bit commitment is conjectured to be possible between parties controlling appropriately separated pairs of sites, when the impossibility of superluminal signalling is taken into account.[6,7] Unconditionally secure coin tossing is simple to implement under these conditions. However, we restrict attention to non-relativistic protocols in the rest of this paper, taking this as understood rather than inserting "non-relativistic" throughout.

Some variants of bit commitment, for which non-relativistic protocols are not known to be impossible, have previously been studied.[8,9] We consider here a different generalization, bit string commitment, in which one party commits many bits to another in a single protocol. Two non-relativistic bit string commitment protocols, which offer classically unattainable levels of security against cheating, are described.

2 Bit string commitment

Consider the following classical cryptographic problem. Two mistrustful parties, A and B, need a protocol which will (i) allow A to commit a string $a_1 a_2 \ldots a_n$ of bits to B, and then, (ii) at any later time of her choice, reveal the committed bits. The protocol should prevent A from cheating, in the sense that she should have little or no chance of unveiling bits a'_i different from the a_i without B being able to detect the attempted detection. In other words, A should be genuinely committed after the first stage. The protocol should also prevent B from being able to completely determine the bit string. More precisely, it must guarantee that, before revelation, B has little or no chance of obtaining more than m bits of information about the committed string, for some fixed integer $m < n$.

This (m, n) *bit string commitment* problem is a generalization of the standard bit commitment problem, in which $n = 1$ and $m = 0$. Clearly, a protocol for bit commitment would solve this generalized problem, since the protocol could be repeated n times to commit each of the a_i, and B would be able to obtain no information about the committed string. Conversely, classical reasoning implies that a protocol for the generalized problem, for any integers m and n with $m < n$, could be used as a protocol for standard bit commitment. For A and B can use any coding of a single bit a by the n bit string such that none of the m bits available to B give information about a, and then use the protocol to commit A to a.

Classically, then, (m, n) bit string commitment is essentially equivalent to bit commitment. However, there is no obvious equivalence between quantum (m, n) bit string commitment and quantum bit commitment. The impossibility of unconditionally secure quantum bit commitment does not necessarily imply that, with an analogous definition of security, unconditionally secure quantum bit string commitment is impossible. In fact, the next sections show it can be achieved.

3 Protocol 1

Define qubit states $\psi_0 = |0\rangle$ and $\psi_1 = \sin(\theta)|0\rangle + \cos(\theta)|1\rangle$, where $\sin^2(\theta) = \delta$. We take $\theta > 0$ and $r = n - m$ to be security parameters for the protocol.

Commitment: To commit a string $a_1 \dots a_n$ of bits to B, A sends the qubits $\psi_{a_1}, \dots, \psi_{a_n}$, sequentially.

Unveiling: To unveil, A simply declares the values of the string bits, and hence the qubits sent. Assuming that B has not disturbed the qubits, he can test the bit values a'_i claimed by A at unveiling by measuring the projection onto $\psi_{a'_i}$ on qubit i, for each i. If he obtains eigenvalue 1 in each case, he accepts the unveiling as an honest revelation of a genuine commitment. If he obtains eigenvalue 0 in any case, he concludes (assuming that noise is negligible) that A has cheated.

Security against A: Whatever strategy A follows, once she transmits the qubits to B, their respective density matrices ρ_i are fixed. Let $p_i^j = \langle \psi_j | \rho_i | \psi_j \rangle$ be the probability of B accepting a revelation of j for the i-th bit. We have

$$p_i^0 + p_i^1 \leq \cos^2[(\pi/4) - (\theta/2)] + \sin[(\pi/4) + (\theta/2)]\,, \tag{1}$$

which is $\leq 1+\theta$ for small θ. This is the standard definition of security against A for an individual bit commitment, with security parameter θ. In other words, A's scope for cheating on any bit of the string is limited to slightly increasing the probability of revealing a 0 or 1, by an amount $\leq \theta$, which can be made arbitrarily small by choosing the security parameters appropriately.

Security against B: We assume that, prior to the commitment, B has no information about the bit string and regards every possible value as equiprobable. From B's perspective, then, he has to obtain information about a density matrix of the form

$$\rho = (1/2^n) \sum_{a_1 \dots a_n} |\psi_{a_1} \dots \psi_{a_n}\rangle\langle\psi_{a_1} \dots \psi_{a_n}|\,. \tag{2}$$

Holevo's theorem[10] tells us that the accessible information available to B by any measurement on ρ is bounded by the entropy

$$\begin{aligned} S(\rho) = \{&[(1+\sin\theta)/2]\log_2[(1+\sin\theta)/2] + \\ &[(1-\sin\theta)/2]\log_2[(1-\sin\theta)/2]\}^n\,. \end{aligned} \tag{3}$$

Now, for any fixed $\theta > 0$, we have $S(\rho) < n$. For any fixed r, by taking n sufficiently large, we can ensure $n - S(\rho) > r$. In other words we can ensure that, however B proceeds, an average of at least r bits of information about the string will remain inaccessible to him. By choosing n suitably large, we can also ensure that the probability of his obtaining more than $n - r$ bits of information about the string is smaller than ϵ, for any given $\epsilon > 0$.

A more efficient version of this protocol can be devised using qutrit states[11] — an observation I owe to Rob Spekkens.

4 Protocol 2

Protocol 1 ensures bit-wise security against A, but uses a rather inefficient bit string coding which allows B to obtain almost all of the bit string before revelation. For large n, more efficient codings allow the security against B to be greatly enhanced, though with a weakened notion of security against A.

We again take $\theta > 0$ to be a security parameter and write $\epsilon = \sin(\theta)$. Now, for any $\theta > 0$ and large n, explicit constructions are known for sets $v_1, \ldots, v_{f(n)}$ of vectors in H^n such that $|\langle v_i \,|\, v_j \rangle| < \sin(\theta)$ for all $i \neq j$, with the property that $f(n) = O(e^{Cn})$, where C is a positive constant that depends on θ.[12,13] (The use of these constructions for efficient quantum coding of classical information has previously been noted by Buhrman et al.,[14] who describe efficient quantum fingerprinting schemes which reduce communication complexity in the simultaneous message passing model.) A string of $O(Cn)$ bits can thus be encoded by vectors in H^n, such that the overlap between the code vectors for two distinct strings is always less than $\sin(\theta)$, suggesting the following bit string commitment protocol.

Commitment: Let N be the number of bits that can be encoded in H^n by the above construction. To commit a string $a_1 \ldots a_N$ of bits to B, A sends the state $v_{a_1 \ldots a_N}$, treating the index as a binary number.

Unveiling: To unveil, A simply declares the values of the string bits, and hence the state sent. Assuming that B has not disturbed the qubits, he can test A's claim at unveiling by measuring the projection onto $v_{a_1 \ldots a_N}$. If he obtains eigenvalue 1, he accepts the unveiling as an honest revelation of a genuine commitment. If he obtains eigenvalue 0, he concludes that A has cheated.

Security against A: As before, once A transmits a quantum state to B, its density matrix ρ is fixed. Consider some set $i_1, \ldots, i_r$ of bit strings which A might wish to maintain the option of revealing after commitment. Let P_i be the projection onto v_i, let $p_i = \mathrm{Tr}(\rho P_i)$ be the probability of A successfully revealing string i, and write

$$Q = P_{i_1} + \ldots + P_{i_r} \,. \tag{4}$$

It is not too hard to verify that

$$\mathrm{Tr}(\rho Q) \leq 1 + (r-1)\epsilon. \tag{5}$$

In other words,

$$p_{i_1} + \ldots + p_{i_r} \leq 1 + f(\epsilon, r)\,, \tag{6}$$

where, for any fixed r, f can be made as small as desired by choosing θ suitably small.

So, given that A is determined to reveal a bit string from some finite set of size r, her scope for cheating is limited to increasing the probability of revealing any given element of the set by a fixed amount. For any fixed r, that amount can be made arbitrarily small by choosing the security parameters appropriately. If B's concern is to prevent cheating of this type, for some predetermined r, the protocol can guarantee him security.

Security against B: Holevo's theorem implies that the information about the $N \approx Cn$ bit string accessible to B is at most $\log(n)$ bits.

5 Asymptotically secure coin tossing

Consider the following non-relativistic protocol for generating a string of N random bits between mistrustful parties. We assume that N is large, and take M also to be large, with $\log(M) \ll N$. A prepares M batches of N Bell singlet states, and sends one particle from each of the MN singlets to B. B chooses $(M-1)$ of the batches, and asks A to send the second particle from each of the $(M-1)N$ singlets in these batches. B tests that these $(M-1)N$ pairs of particles are indeed singlets. If not, he concludes that A is cheating, and the protocol ends. If so, he accepts that A is honest. A and B then use the last batch of singlets to generate N random bits, by carrying out correlated measurements (say of σ_z) and converting the results to a bit string using a previously agreed protocol.

Security against A: A can only cheat by preparing non-singlet states which bias the outcomes towards those she would prefer. Her scope for cheating is limited by the cut-and-choose step of the protocol, which ensures that, if any batch has low fidelity to N singlet states, her cheating will almost surely be detected.

Security against B: B can cheat by carrying out measurements on every particle from every batch sent to him, deciding which batch gives the bit string most favorable for his purposes, and choosing the other $(M-1)$ for the test. However, this will allow him to fix only $\approx \log(M)$ bits of information about the N bit string. With suitable M, N this is an insignificant fraction.

Acknowledgments

Much of this work was carried out while a visiting academic researcher in the QIP Group at Hewlett-Packard Labs, Bristol. I thank Serge Massar, Bill Munro, Tim Spiller, Rob Spekkens, Terry Rudolph and Alain Tapp for helpful discussions. This work was partially supported by the European collaboration EQUIP.

References

1. H.-K. Lo and H. Chau, Phys. Rev. Lett. **78**, 3410 (1997).
2. D. Mayers, Phys. Rev. Lett. **78**, 3414 (1997).

3. D. Mayers, quant-ph/9603015.
4. H.-K. Lo and H. Chau, Physica D **120**, 177 (1998).
5. D. Mayers, in *Proceedings of the Fourth Workshop on Physics and Computation* (New England Complex System Inst., Boston, 1996), p. 226.
6. A. Kent, Phys. Rev. Lett. **83**, 1447 (1999).
7. A. Kent, quant-ph/9906103, submitted to J. Cryptology.
8. L. Hardy and A. Kent, quant-ph/9911043.
9. D. Aharonov, A. Ta-Shma, U. Vazirani and A. Yao, "Quantum Bit Escrow", in *Proceedings of the 32nd Annual ACM Symposium on the Theory Of Computing* (2000).
10. A. Holevo, "Statistical problems in quantum physics", in *Proceedings of the Second Japan-USSR Symposium on Probability Theory*, ed. by G. Maruyama and J. Prokhorov (Springer-Verlag, Berlin, 1973).
11. R. Spekkens and T. Rudolph, Phys Rev A **65**, 012310 (2002).
12. J. Conway and N. Sloane, *Sphere Packings, Lattices and Groups*, 2nd edition, (Springer-Verlag, New York, 1993)
13. J. Justesen, IEEE Trans. Info. Theory **18**, 652 (1972).
14. H. Buhrman, R. Cleve, J. Watrous and R. de Wolf, quant-ph/0102001.

SECRECY CAPACITY IN THE BB84 PROTOCOL OF QUANTUM CRYPTOGRAPHY

HOWARD E. BRANDT
U.S. Army Research Laboratory
2800 Powder Mill Rd., Adelphi, MD 20783
E-mail: hbrandt@arl.army.mil

I calculate the secrecy capacity of the BB84 protocol in the presence of an individual attack in which the eavesdropping probe is entangled with the signal states, and states of the probe become correlated with the states measured by the legitimate receiver. Emphasis is placed on information leakage to the eavesdropping probe. The calculation generalizes earlier work to include an arbitrary angle between the signal bases.

1 Introduction

The average secrecy capacity C_s' of a quantum key distribution system in quantum cryptography is the number of secret bits produced per bit from the transmitter, and is given by[1]

$$C_s' = \operatorname*{Lim}_{m \to 0} \left\langle \frac{n - e_T - s}{m} \right\rangle . \tag{1}$$

Here the limit of a very long transmission is understood in which m, the number of bits of raw data, is very large. The numerator of Eq. (1), $(n - e_T - s)$, is the size of the final key, where n is the number of bits of sifted data with the inconclusive bits removed, e_T is the number of bits of erroneous discarded data due to error correction, and s is the privacy amplification compression level. The privacy amplification compression level s is given by[1]

$$s = t(n, e_T) + q + \nu + g, \tag{2}$$

where q is the estimated information leakage during error correction, ν is the estimated leakage from any multi-photon bits, g is an extra safety margin, and $t(n, e_T)$ is the defense function. The defense function, in general, depends on the size n of the sifted data, and on the number e_T of errors, and is chosen appropriately by the legitimate users, in order to effectively defend against an eavesdropping attack. The defense function $t(n, e_T)$ is the estimated upper bound on possible information leakage through eavesdropping on the quantum channel. Quantitatively it is determined by the maximum total Renyi information gain I_T^R by the eavesdropping probe. The compression level s must be chosen so that the probability is small that $I_T^R > t(n, e_T)$. An attack is successful if it introduces e_T errors on the n bits of sifted data, and yields a Renyi information $I_T^R > t(n, e_T)$ on the $(n - e_T)$ bits of corrected data. The probability of a successful attack must be negligible. In the presence of noise and channel losses, it is not sufficient, for the security of a quantum key distribution system to detect eavesdropping. It must be insured that the shared data is sufficiently secure.

2 Calculating Secrecy Capacity

The average secrecy capacity, Eq. (1), converges in distribution to[1]

$$C_s' = \left\langle \frac{n}{m} \right\rangle \left(1 - \left\langle \frac{e_T}{n} \right\rangle - \frac{t_F}{n} \Big|_{\frac{e_T}{n} = \left\langle \frac{e_T}{n} \right\rangle} - \lim_{m \to \infty} \left\langle \frac{q}{n} \right\rangle \right) . \tag{3}$$

The factor $\left\langle \frac{n}{m} \right\rangle$ in Eq. (3) is the conclusive rate. Since the inconclusive rate $R_?$ is 1/2 for the BB84 protocol,[1] and remains unchanged in the presence of the individual attack, the conclusive rate must also be 1/2, namely,

$$\left\langle \frac{n}{m} \right\rangle = (1 - R_?) = \left(1 - \frac{1}{2} \right) = \frac{1}{2}. \tag{4}$$

Also in Eq. (3), $\left\langle \frac{e_T}{n} \right\rangle$ is the average intrinsic error rate, and $\left\langle \frac{q}{n} \right\rangle$ is the average information leakage during error correction. Since the present work focuses on the information leakage through eavesdropping [represented by the third term in Eq. (2)], possible additional terms, $\left(-\left\langle \frac{\nu}{n} \right\rangle\right)$ and $\left(-\left\langle \frac{g}{n} \right\rangle\right)$, are dropped in Eq. (3) [see Eq. (2)]. In the third term of Eq. (3), $\frac{t_F}{n}\big|_{\frac{e_T}{n} = \left\langle \frac{e_T}{n} \right\rangle}$ is the average defense frontier t_F evaluated at the average intrinsic error rate. The defense frontier t_F is, for all possible eavesdropping strategies, the upper bound on the information leakage through eavesdropping, based on an optimal eavesdropper in the limit of a long transmission. The defense frontier t_F is chosen to minimize the chance of any successful eavesdropping strategy, and, for the individual attack, it is given by[1]

$$t_F(n, e_T) = \max_{e \le e_T} \left\{ n \left(1 - \frac{e}{n} \right) I_{opt}^R \left(\frac{e}{n} + \xi \right) + \xi \left[n^2 \left(1 - \frac{e}{n} \right) \right]^{1/2} \right\} , \tag{5}$$

where $I_{opt}^R(E)$ is the maximum Renyi information gain on corrected data by the eavesdropping probe conditioned on a fixed error rate $E = (e/n)$, and ξ is defined by

$$\xi = \frac{1}{(2n)^{1/2}} \operatorname{erf}^{-1}(1 - p) , \tag{6}$$

where erf^{-1} denotes the inverse standard error function. The standard error function $\operatorname{erf}(z)$ is defined by

$$\operatorname{erf}(z) = \frac{2}{\sqrt{\pi}} \int_0^z e^{-y^2} dy . \tag{7}$$

Also in Eq. (6), p is the probability for successful eavesdropping $[I_R^T > t(n, e_T)]$ on $(n - e_T)$ bits of corrected data and producing e_T errors; and p can be made arbitrarily small. The defense frontier, Eq. (5), was determined by Slutsky, Rao, Sun, Tancevski, and Fainman[1] by clever use of the central limit theorem of probability theory, and is constructed to minimize the chance of successful eavesdropping. Using Eqs. (3)–(5), the asymptotic secrecy capacity, in the limit of long transmission with $m \to \infty$, $n \to \infty$, and $\xi \to 0$, and for $q = 0$, becomes[1]

$$C'_s\,|_{q=0,n\to\infty,\xi\to 0} \;=\; \frac{1}{2}\left(1 \;-\; E \;-\; \max_{E'\le E}\;(1 \;-\; E')\,I^R_{opt}\,(E')\right), \qquad (8)$$

where E is the error rate, and $\max_{x'\le x} f(x')$ denotes the maximum value of a function $f(x')$ for $x' \le x$. Also in Eq. (8), $I^R_{opt}(E')$ is the maximum Renyi information gain on corrected data by the eavesdropping probe, conditional on fixed error rate E'. In the present work, an individual attack is addressed in which the probe is taken to be a Fuchs-Peres probe[2,3,4,5] which becomes entangled with the signal state, and the state of the probe becomes correlated with the state received by the legitimate receiver.

For the four-state protocol, the maximum Renyi information gain I^R_{opt} on corrected data by a Fuchs-Peres probe, conditional on fixed error rate E, for the individual attack, is given by[2,4,5]

$$I^R_{opt} = \log_2(2 - Q^2). \qquad (9)$$

Here Q is the minimum overlap of the probe states correlated with the signal states, and, for an arbitrary angle between the signal bases, it is given by[4,5]

$$Q = \begin{cases} \frac{1+\left[1-2\csc^2(2\alpha)\right]E}{1-E}, & \alpha \le \pi/8 \\ \frac{1+\left[1-2\sec^2(2\alpha)\right]E}{1-E}, & \alpha \ge \pi/8 \end{cases}, \qquad (10)$$

with

$$\alpha = \frac{1}{2}\left(\frac{\pi}{2} - \bar{\theta}\right), \qquad (11)$$

where $\bar{\theta}$ is the angle between the nonorthogonal linear polarization states of the signal. For $\alpha = \pi/8$, corresponding to the standard BB84 protocol with $\bar{\theta} = \pi/4$, Eqs. (9) and (10) agree with Ref. 2. Substituting Eqs. (9) and (10) in Eq. (8), one obtains for the asymptotic secrecy capacity:

$$C'_s\,|_{q=0,n\to\infty,\xi\to 0} \;=\; \begin{cases} \frac{1}{2}\left(1 - E - \max_{E'\le E}(1-E')\log_2\left[2 - \left(\frac{1+\left[1-2\csc^2(2\alpha)\right]E'}{1-E'}\right)^2\right]\right), & \alpha \le \pi/8 \\ \frac{1}{2}\left(1 - E - \max_{E'\le E}(1-E')\log_2\left[2 - \left(\frac{1+\left[1-2\sec^2(2\alpha)\right]E'}{1-E'}\right)^2\right]\right), & \alpha \ge \pi/8 \end{cases} \qquad (12)$$

For $\alpha = \pi/8$, Eq. (12) also agrees with Ref. 1. It is evident from Eqs. (9)–(12) that as a function of α, for fixed error rate, the overlap of correlated probe states is greatest, the Renyi information gain by the probe is least, and the secrecy capacity is greatest for $\alpha = \pi/8$, which corresponds to the standard BB84 protocol with $\overline{\theta} = \pi/4$.

Acknowledgments

This work was supported by the U.S. Army Research Laboratory and the Defense Advanced Research Projects Agency.

References

1. B. Slutsky, R. Rao, P. C. Sun, L. Tancevski, and S. Fainman, Appl. Opt. **37**, 2869–2878 (1998).
2. B. A. Slutsky, R. Rao, P. C. Sun, and Y. Fainman, Phys. Rev. A **57**, 2383-2398 (1998).
3. C. A. Fuchs and A. Peres, Phys. Rev. A **53**, 2038–2045 (1996).
4. H. E. Brandt, "Probe optimization in four-state protocol of quantum cryptography," Institute of Theoretical Physics, University of California, Santa Barbara, Preprint # NSF-ITP-01-176 (2001), to appear in Phys. Rev. A (2002).
5. H. E. Brandt, "Secrecy capacity in the four-state protocol of quantum key distribution," to appear in J. Math. Phys. (2002).

SHOR-PRESKILL TYPE SECURITY-PROOF FOR QUANTUM KEY DISTRIBUTION WITHOUT PUBLIC ANNOUNCEMENT OF BASES

W.-Y. HWANG[1] , X.-B. WANG[1], K. MATSUMOTO[1] J. KIM[2], AND H.-W. LEE[2]

[1]*IMAI Quantum Computation and Information Project, ERATO, Japan Science and Technology Corporation, Daini Hongo White Bldg. 201, 5-28-3, Hongo, Bunkyo, Tokyo 133-0033, Japan*

[2]*Department of Physics, Korea Advanced Institute of Science and Technology, Taejon 305-701, Korea*

We give a Shor-Preskill type security-proof for quantum key distribution without public announcement of bases [W.Y. Hwang *et al.*, Phys. Lett. A **244**, 489 (1998)]. First, we modify the Lo-Chau protocol once more so that it finally reduces to quantum key distribution without public announcement of bases. Then we show how we can estimate the error rate in the code bits based on that in the checked bits in the proposed protocol, that is the central point of the proof. We discuss the issue of when the bases sequence must be discarded.

In the standard Bennett-Brassard 1984 (BB84) quantum key distribution (QKD) protocol,[1,2] at most half of the data obtained by using expensive quantum communication can be utilized. One method for the full efficiency QKD is to delay the measurements in the BB84 scheme using quantum memories. This is indeed the original proposal by Bennett and Brassard.[1] However, quantum memories would be quite costly with near-future technology. Another method is to assign significantly different probabilities to the different bases.[3] Although unconditional security of the scheme is known,[3] it has a disadvantage that a larger key must be generated at once than in the BB84 scheme in order to get the same level of security. However, in a recently proposed QKD without public announcement of basis (PAB),[4] we can obtain the full efficiency with such problem relaxed.

QKD without PAB is a simple variation of BB84 scheme. In the BB84 scheme, Alice and Bob use different random bases and then discard the cases in which the bases are not matched. In QKD without PAB, Alice and Bob use bases determined by a prior random key, the basis sequence b. When the basis sequence b is used only once, it is clear that the scheme is as secure as the BB84 scheme. However, in this case it is clearly meaningless because they have to consume secret key that is as long as the generated key. Thus, the problem is whether the basis sequence b can be used repeatedly without loss of security. It was shown that it is the case against the individual attacks,[4] and it was suggested that it can be true for coherent attacks.[5]

In this paper, we use mostly the notations of Refs. 6,8, except for that we use $|\bar{0}\rangle$ and $|\bar{1}\rangle$ instead of $|+\rangle$ and $|-\rangle$, respectively, and $|\Phi^+\rangle = (1/\sqrt{2})(|00\rangle + |11\rangle)$.

Here we modify once again the modified Lo-Chau protocol[6] to get the modified Lo-Chau protocol II. The only difference is the following. In the former, Alice and Bob each use independent random bases and then use only the matched cases. In the latter, a prior random key (the basis sequence b) is used to determine the bases of Alice and Bob. The modified Lo-Chau protocol II finally reduces to the QKD without PAB, as in the Ref. 6.

QKD without public announcement of basis

(1) Alice creates $2n$ random bits. Alice and Bob are sharing a prior random $(2n/r)$-bit string, the basis sequence b. (2) Alice encodes each random bit to qubits using the basis sequence b. That is, when the random bit is 0 (1) and the corresponding component of the basis sequence b is zero, she creates a qubit in the $|0\rangle$ ($|1\rangle$) state. When the random bit is 0 (1) and the corresponding component of the basis sequence b is one, she creates a qubit in the $|\bar{0}\rangle$ ($|\bar{1}\rangle$) state. (3) Alice repeats step (2) r times with the same basis sequence b. (4) Alice sends the resulting qubits to Bob. (5) Bob receives the $2n$ qubits and performs measurement S_z or S_x if the corresponding component of the sequence b is zero or one, respectively. Here S_z (S_x) is the orthogonal measurement whose eigenvectors are $|0\rangle$ and $|1\rangle$ ($|\bar{0}\rangle$ and $|\bar{1}\rangle$). (6) Bob repeats step (5) r times with the same basis sequence b. (7) Alice decides randomly on a set of n bits to use for the protocol, and chooses at random n of these to be check-bits. (8) Alice and Bob announce the values of the their check-bits. If too few of these values agree, they abort the protocol. (9) Alice announces $u+v$, where v is a string consisting of randomly chosen code-bits (non-check bits), and u is a random code word in C_1. Alice announces the positions of the randomly chosen code-bits. (10) Bob subtracts each $u+v$ from his each code-bits, $v+\epsilon$, and corrects the result, $u+\epsilon$, to a codeword in C_1. (11) Alice and Bob use the coset of each $u+C_2$ as the key. In this way, they obtain m-bit string.

Since the modified Lo-Chau protocol II reduces to QKD without PAB, it is sufficient for us to show the security of the former protocol. We begin with a reminder about the classicalization of statistics that is stressed by Lo and Chau.[7,8] Then we will see that remaining arguments are similar to what we used for individual attacks.[4] First, let us review the classicalization of statistics in the Shor and Preskill proof.[6] What we consider is the interaction of qubits $|\psi\rangle$ of Alice and Bob and quantum probes $|e\rangle$ of Eve. In general, the state after any interaction by a unitary operator U can be decomposed[9,10] as follows:

$$U|\psi\rangle|e\rangle = \sum_{\{k\}} C_{\{k\}}\sigma_{k_1(1)}\sigma_{k_2(2)}\cdots\sigma_{k_n(n)}|\psi\rangle|e_{\{k\}}\rangle. \tag{1}$$

Here $\{k\}$ is the abbreviation for the $k_1, k_2, ..., k_n$, with $k_i = 0,1,2,3$ ($i = 1,2,...,n$), and $\sigma_0 = I$, $\sigma_1 = \sigma_x$, $\sigma_2 = \sigma_y$, $\sigma_3 = \sigma_z$. The $C_{\{k\}}$'s are coefficients. The vectors $|e_{\{k\}}\rangle$ are normalized but not mutually orthogonal in general. Since Eq. (1) is just the general decomposition of a vector by complete bases, it is clear that the interaction described by Eq. (1) includes coherent attacks as well as individual attacks. What Eve can do is only to control the coefficients $C_{\{k\}}$'s as she likes.

By the classicalization of the statistics,[7,8] as long as the checking measurements are concerned, the mixed state,

$$\rho = \sum_{\{k\}} |C_{\{k\}}|^2 \sigma_{k_1(1)}\sigma_{k_2(2)}\cdots\sigma_{k_n(n)}|\psi\rangle\langle\psi|\sigma_{k_1(1)}\sigma_{k_2(2)}\cdots\sigma_{k_n(n)}, \qquad (2)$$

gives rise to the same results as the pure state in Eq. (1). This is the basis for the classicalization of statistics,[7,8] as a result of which it is sufficient for us to consider classical distributions given by probabilities $P_{\{k\}} = |C_{\{k\}}|^2$.

Once the classicalization of statistics has been performed, it is not difficult to see that the modified Lo-Chau protocol II is secure. In the case of the BB84 protocol, they estimate the error rate or the ratio of σ's that are not the identity operator I among the $\sigma_{k_1(1)}\sigma_{k_2(2)}\cdots\sigma_{k_n(n)}$'s, by doing the checking measurement on some randomly chosen subsets of the qubits. If Eve's operation on a checked qubit is the identity I, the probability of giving rise to an error is zero. If Eve's operation on a checked qubit is not the identity I, it will give rise to errors probabilistically: if the basis matches it will induce no errors, but if the bases do not match it will. (More precisely, the probabilities for giving rise to errors is 1/2, 1/2, and 1, respectively, for σ_z, σ_x, σ_y operations.) What Eve wants to do is to minimize the number of errors in the check bits for a given number of non-identity operations. However, since the checked bits and the bases are randomly chosen by Alice and Bob, Eve knows nothing about them while she has access to the qubits of Alice and Bob. Thus we can assume that the error rate of the checked bits represents that of the code bits, that is a crucial point in the security proof.

Let us now consider the modified Lo-Chau protocol II. This protocol to the first round is obviously stronger than the modified Lo-Chau protocol. Thus it is clear that to the first round the modified Lo-Chau protocol II is as secure as the modified Lo-Chau protocol. Then let us consider the second round. Here one may worry that Eve can extract some information about the basis sequence b after the first round. It is obvious that if Eve knows the basis sequence b she can successfully cheat; this is because in that case she can control the probabilities $P_{\{k\}}$'s so that more bases are matched or that the probability of being detected decreases. However, no matter how many rounds are performed, Eve can extract no information on the basis sequence b by any quantum operations in the ideal case:[4] all elements in the ensemble of qubits with different bases give rise to the same density operator. (For other discussion, including that for non-ideal case, see Ref. 11. Also note that all public discussions between Alice and Bob are performed after all qubits have arrived at Bob in the proposed protocol.) So we need not worry about that point. Now what Eve knows is that the same basis sequence b is used repeatedly. That is, she knows which qubits are in the same basis although she does not know the identity of the basis. *Now the problem is whether Eve can induce statistically smaller number of errors in the checked bits for a given number of non-identity operators in the second round than in the first round. However, we can see that she cannot do so because she does not know which basis it is and thus the probability that the bases are not matched is still 1/2.* For example, let us consider the first two qubits in the first and second rounds. If Eve's basis and the checked bit's basis is matched (not matched) then the probability that it is to be detected is zero (non-zero). Even if Eve knows that the two qubits are in the same basis, that information is not helpful in decreasing the expected error rate since the probability that the bases are not matched is still 1/2. Eve's best strategy here is to choose the same operations for the two qubits. Then, although the average error rate is not changed, the deviation of the probabilistic distribution will be increased. We can easily see that the same thing can be said for the remaining qubits and for all in the later j-th rounds ($j = 3, 4, 5, ..., r$). Therefore we can safely estimate the error rate in the code bits based on that in the checked bits, as we did in the modified Lo-Chau protocol.[6]

However, it should also be underlined[4] that the basis sequence has to be discarded after the final key is used for encrypting a message, because a cryptogram gives partial information about the key by which it is encrypted. The information about the key can then used to extract information about the basis sequence b.

References

1. C. H. Bennett and G. Brassard, in *Proc. IEEE Int. Conf. on Computers, Systems, and Signal Processing, Bangalore* (IEEE, New York, 1984) p.175.
2. N. Gisin, G. Ribordy, W. Tittel, and H. Zbinden, Rev. Mod. Phys. **74**, 145 (2002), and references therein.
3. H.-K. Lo, H. F. Chau, and M. Ardehali, quant-ph/0011056.
4. W. Y. Hwang, I. G. Koh, and Y. D. Han, Phys. Lett. A **244**, 489 (1998).
5. W. Y. Hwang, D. Ahn, and S. W. Hwang, Phys. Lett. A **279**, 133 (2001).
6. P. W. Shor and J. Preskill, Phys. Rev. Lett. **85**, 441 (2000).
7. H.-K. Lo and H. F. Chau, Science **283**, 2050 (1999).
8. H.-K. Lo, Quan. Inf. Com. **1**, 81 (2001).
9. P. W. Shor, Phys. Rev. A **52**, 2493 (1995).
10. J. Preskill, Proc. Roy. Soc. Lond. A **454**, 385 (1998).
11. W.-Y. Hwang, X.B. Wang, K. Matsumoto, J. Kim, and H.-W. Lee, quant-ph/0201053.

QKD PROTOCOLS IN THE DARPA QUANTUM NETWORK

DAVID PEARSON
CHIP ELLIOTT
BBN Technologies, 10 Moulton Street, Cambridge, MA 02138, USA
E-mail: {dpearson, celliott}@bbn.com

Under DARPA sponsorship, a team from BBN Technologies, Boston University, and Harvard University has started a five-year research program to design and build the world's first full-fledged Quantum Network. The first version of this network is operational. We briefly describe the system architecture of the Quantum Network, then focus on its QKD protocols and algorithms. Each of the protocols is described in high-level form, and we show how these components are assembled to form an entire QKD protocol stack. We discuss the major design drivers for the protocol stack, including the notions of round-trips and pipelining.

1 The DARPA Quantum Network

After nearly two decades as a laboratory curiosity, quantum key distribution (QKD) techniques are just now emerging as useful building blocks in highly secure networks. Under DARPA sponsorship, a team from BBN Technologies, Boston University and Harvard University has recently begun a five-year research program to design and build the world's first such highly secure quantum network, one that delivers end-to-end network security via high-speed QKD, and to test that network against sophisticated eavesdropping attacks.

The quantum network has been described elsewhere.[3] The network, shown in Fig. 1, is intended to distribute keys for a virtual private network (VPN) running on top of the public internet. Key distribution may be routed through trusted QKD nodes, or QKD links may be optically switched. The VPN gateway also runs the QKD protocols described here.

2 The QKD Protocol Suite

The QKD protocols were designed to fit into a reliable and secure network environment. Consequently we want the protocols to be robust and reliable, to be efficient in use of network bandwidth, to support a full security system, and to support multiple QKD links. We also want the software to support multiple operating system platforms, to accommodate different QKD hardware, and to be flexible and extensible enough that we can add updated QKD protocols and new functions such as routing and optical switching.

Designing the entire suite together allowed us to meet these goals much more easily, since many of the most difficult protocol issues—reliability, crash/restart, flow control, pipelining, e.g.—can be handled by a common framework, so the individual protocol modules can be much simpler; see Fig. 2.

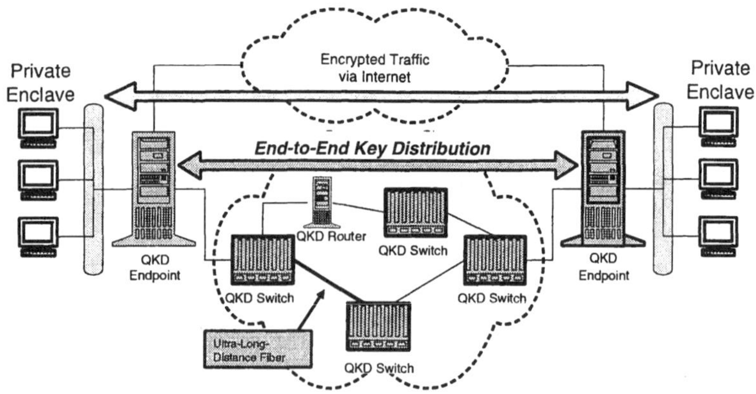

Figure 1. Diagram of the quantum network.

This also allows us to apply security policy uniformly to the entire protocol suite, e.g., adding classical encryption to the public channel.

Aside from public exchanges with peer protocol suites at other network nodes, the QPD protocol driver has two major external interfaces: one with the optical control software through which it obtains raw QKD bits, and one with the consumer (in our case, a modified implementation of the internet security suite, IPsec). Both of these interfaces are designed to be very simple and modular, allowing us (for example) to easily interface another optical implementation of QKD using quite different control software.

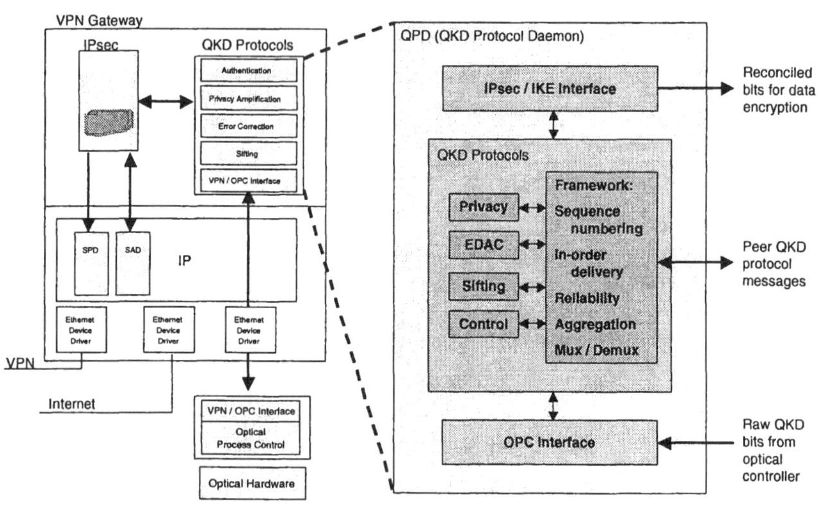

Figure 2. Architecture of the QKD protocol suite.

3 Sifting

In the sifting process Alice (the transmitter) and Bob (the receiver) agree to discard any bits for which their bases disagree and any bits for which Bob did not have a valid detection (in the case of BB84 this could mean neither detector registered or both did, though the former is far more common). In the sifting protocol, Bob sends Alice a list of bits where valid detections occurred, and for each of these detections a single bit encoding the basis used (the bases are omitted in B92). Alice sends back a list of bits indicating which subset of those bits to keep. The only optimization we use is a run-length encoding of the list of valid detections, since with current detector efficiencies and fiber attenuation, the valid detections will be very sparse.

4 Error detection and correction

The error detection and correction (EDAC) protocol starts with the sifted frame. There are likely to be some errors in this result due to various kinds of noise. There may be additional errors due to the presence of an eavesdropper. The protocol's job is to determine the number of errors and correct them, keeping track of both the number of bits in error and the number of bits of information disclosed publicly about the key.

We use a protocol based loosely on the Cascade protocol of Brassard & Salvail.[2] A few differences were introduced for economy of time, key bits, and bandwidth on the public channel. Our EDAC protocol does not disclose a portion of the key string at the beginning to form an initial estimate of the error rate, instead we use an upper bound of the error rate to choose the number of subset parities to try, which results in fewer bits sacrificed. To cut down on the number of round-trips, the two sides take turns in the binary search procedure, and multiple binary searches can take place in parallel when there are known disjoint ranges containing errors. Finally, we use more compact representations of the subsets, which aids pipelining the error correction of multiple frames at the same time.

5 Entropy estimation

After error correction is finished, we must make a conservative estimate of the amount of information an eavesdropper (Eve) may have gained about the QKD bits. We allow two measures currently, one used by Bennett, *et al.*:[1]

$$t = \frac{4e}{\sqrt{2}}, \quad s = \sqrt{(4+2\sqrt{2})e}.$$

The other measure is from Slutsky, *et al.*:[4]

$$t = (b-e)[1+\log_2(1-\frac{1}{2}(\frac{\max(1-3e',0)}{1-e'})^2)], \quad s = \sqrt{b} \text{ where } e' = \frac{e}{b} + \frac{c}{\sqrt{b}}.$$

In either case, we add on terms for other sources of leaked information, including bits revealed during EDAC, beam splitting attacks, and POVM attacks.

6 Privacy amplification

Once we know how much "good" information t is in a frame, privacy amplification is the process of distilling a shorter string that's all good information (i.e., Eve knows less than 1 bit about it, with high probability). To do this, we use a universal family of hash functions, in this case linear functions over $GF[2^b]$. The privacy amplification protocol communicates a b-bit multiplier, an irreducible modulus of degree b, and a number of bits to truncate.

7 Conclusion

The QKD protocol suite is currently running on a network of 3 computers with a mix of real and simulated links. It has proven practical, reliable, and extensible. The modularity of the design allows it to gracefully accommodate heterogeneous realizations of QKD, and we look forward to adding new sources and detectors in the second year of the project.

Acknowledgments

This work was supported under the DARPA QuIST program, and we are deeply indebted to our program manager, Dr. Mike Foster of DARPA ITO, and our agent, Dr. Don Nicholson of the Air Force Research Laboratory, for their support. We are also grateful to our collaborators on the project: John Myers at Harvard, Alexander Sergienko and Gregg Jaeger at Boston University, and Greg Troxel, Alex Colvin, and John Schlafer at BBN.

References

1. C. H. Bennett, F. Bessette, G. Brassard, L. Salvail, and J. Smolin, *J. Cryptology* **5**, 3–28 (1992).
2. G. Brassard and L. Salvail. "Secret-key reconciliation by public discussion," in *Advances in Cryptology — EUROCRYPT* '93 (T. Helleseth, ed.). *Lecture Notes in Computer Science* **765**, 410–423 (1994).
3. C. Elliott, *New J. of Phys.* **4**, 46.1 (2002).
4. B. Slutsky, R. Rao, P. C. Sun, L. Tancevski, and S. Fainman, *Appl. Opt.* **37**, 2869–2878 (1998).

DEMONSTRATION OF ENTANGLED-PHOTON LINK FOR QUANTUM CRYPTOGRAPHY

FABIO ANTONIO BOVINO, PIETRO VARISCO, ANNA MARIA COLLA, GIUSEPPE CASTAGNOLI, ANNA MARTINOLI, PAOLO DE NICOLO, AND SANDRA BRUZZO

Elsag spa, Via Puccini 2, 16154 Genova, Italy
E-mail: Fabio.Bovino@elsag.it

GIOVANNI DI GIUSEPPE* AND ALEXANDER V. SERGIENKO

Departments of ECE and Physics, Boston University, Boston, MA 02215, USA

We present results of experimental demonstration of a quantum key distribution link based on the use of two-photon entangled states produced in the nonlinear process of spontaneous parametric downconversion. The quality of high-rate entangled-state distribution is verified by observing high-visibility ($98 \pm 2\%$) quantum interference and by violating Bell's inequalities at the end-user stations.

1 Introduction

We report some experimental results of production, distribution, and detection of entangled-photon quantum states for secure quantum key distribution (QKD) in a fiber-based communication link between two users that has been designed and built at Elsag spa. Elsag spa, an Italian ITC company based in Genova, designs and implements solutions and services based on innovative technologies in several areas, like Industry & Defense, Banking & Insurance, Public Administration and Services, Healthcare, Transport, Utilities and Postal Services. Elsag, which for many years has been actively researching Quantum Physics applications to information technology, established an in-house Quantum Optics Laboratory in the Fall 2001 to investigate, in particular, methods and devices for secure communication in several applications.

The goal of our research is to implement a prototype of a system of real practical use, by employing entangled-photon pairs generated in the nonlinear process of spontaneous parametric downconversion (SPDC), which have been proven to be a highly desirable carrier[1] for quantum cryptography applications.[2] Cryptographic keys are generated by using as a physical support entangled photon pairs, transmitted over a "quantum channel" (single-mode fiber). Information is encoded in the photon polarization. The photon sequences detected by either user are exploited to generate a totally secure shared key by applying the BB84 protocol. The shared key can then be used to encode messages running over the "public channel".

The prototype requires development and test of the system structural

*Also with Istituto Elettrotecnico Nazionale Galileo Ferraris, Strada delle Cacce 91, 10153 Torino, Italy.

components (entangled photon source, coupling into fibers, user units); of server/user and user/user protocols, of the "public" and "quantum" communication channels, and of the complete key generation software. The full procedure is sketched in Sect. 2. A target key production rate of practical industrial interest must be above 1 kbit per second.

The software architecture of the system builds on the one developed for a previous system[3] for cryptographic key exchange between two users based on single photon techniques, developed within European project *European Quantum Cryptography and Single Photon Optical Technology (EQCSPOT).*

The problems of practical utilization of entangled-photon pairs technology are usually associated with relatively low photon collection efficiency due to spatial distribution of SPDC radiation and with the quality of polarization state control in a fiber environment due to a broad spectral width of entangled-photon wave packets. We were able to partially overcome those problems and to reach a significant increase in the rate of entangled-photon pairs available. The quality of the transmitted Bell-state has been verified by observing the quantum interference visibility at the user units, as described in Sect. 3. Ongoing and future work is reported in Sect. 4.

2 Key generation

The key generation procedure consists of the following steps.

1. Creation of entangled photon pairs by a central SPDC source.
2. Raw quantum transmission of entangled photon pairs over the quantum channels to users A and B.
3. Random basis selection and photon detection — for each pair of incoming photons, A and B randomly and independently choose a base to measure the photon polarization.
4. Public discussion — A and B publicly announce which polarization bases they chose, and discard all the data obtained with mis-matched bases.
5. QBER estimation — A and B verify that data are actually correlated.
6. Error correction and privacy amplification. A and B perform error correction by publicly checking parities of bit blocks. The disclosed information about the key can be reduced by privacy amplification techniques.[4]
7. Authentication based on a modified Wegman-Carter protocol.[5]

3 Experimental demonstration

The experimental setup is shown in Fig. 1. The entangled-photon source consists of a mode-locked Ti:Sapphire laser (Coherent Mira-Verdi system; 76 MHz repetition rate, Δt=150 fsec, 830 nm), frequency doubled by a Second Harmonic Generator (415 nm, 200 mW average power) and focused to a waist of 100 μm by a lens (f = 50) on a 1 mm BBO crystal. The BBO crystal was tilted for non-collinear degenerate (830 nm) type-II phase matching with output semi-angles of about 3.5°, for which the cones superposition is symmetrical. The intersections of the ordinary and extraordinary cones[6] were imaged with $f = 15.4$ mm coupling lenses placed at 75 cm from the output face of the nonlinear crystal, into a single-mode fiber with a Mode Field Distribution (MFD) of 4.2 μm. We used two 40 nm interference filters to cut off noise before the coupling system. The photon pairs were detected by SPAD detectors (Perkin-Elmer SPCM-AQR14).

To perform the Bell inequality test, one of the analyzers was set at 45° and we recorded the coincidences and single counts for different values of the other analyzer angle. For this purpose we used an in-house developed 2-fold coincidence unit, based on PLD technology, with a 3 ns coincidence window. The choice of 45° is necessary to avoid the natural basis dictated by the optical axes of the nonlinear crystal. We obtained a visibility of 97.6% (see Fig. 2). The best coincidence count was about 25,000 pairs per second with about 80,000 single photons detected per channel. This number increases to about 85,000 coincidences with higher pump power and a 3 mm crystal, but efficiency is lower.

4 Future developments

We are now actively investigating the optimization of the photon fiber coupling efficiency. Current results are a coupling efficiency $\eta_c \sim 18\%$ with a 3 mm crystal length and $\eta_c \sim 29\%$ with a 1 mm crystal. Taking into account factors of 50% for detector efficiency and 85% for the filters placed before the coupling lenses, the effective coupling into fibers is 42% and 68%, respectively.

Another important direction is the completion of the software development and the integration of the prototype. Moreover, prospective scalability of the two-user link towards user networks and integration into advanced cryptographic systems will be analyzed.

Acknowledgments

This work was developed within a Project funded by the Italian Ministry of Education, University and Research (MIUR), Grant N. 67679/ L.488/92.

References

1. A. V. Sergienko *et al.*, *Phys. Rev. A* **60**, R2622 (1999); T. Jennewein *et al.*, *Phys. Rev. Lett.* **84**, 4729 (2000); D. S. Naik *et al.*, *Phys. Rev. Lett.* **84**, 4733 (2000); W. Tittel *et al.*, *Phys. Rev. Lett.* **84**, 4737 (2000).
2. Z. Walton *et al.*, *J. Mod. Opt.* **48**, 2055 (2001); N. Gisin *et al.*, *Rev. Mod. Phys.* **74**, 145 (2002).

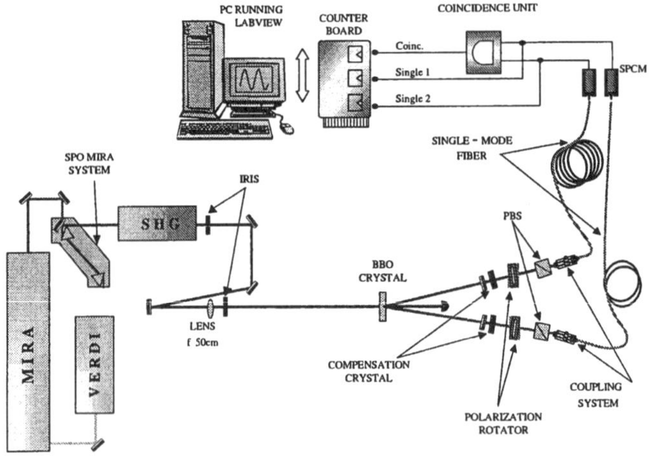

Figure 1. Experimental set up.

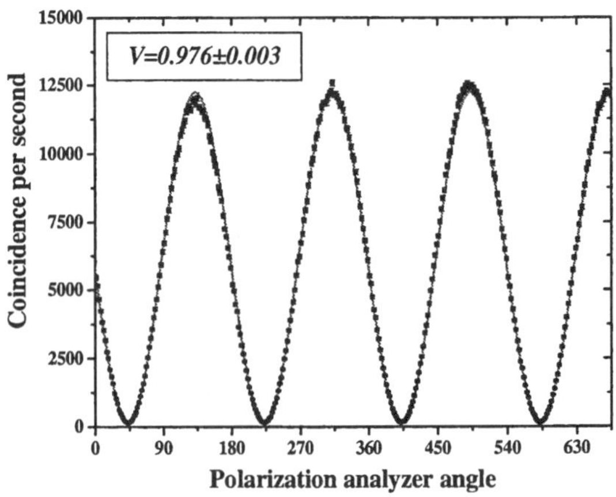

Figure 2. Correlation curve at 45°.

3. A. M. D'Angelo, R. Dell'Eva, H. Inamori, A. Martinoli, *J. Modern Opt.* **48**(13), 1943 (2001).
4. C. H. Bennett, G. Brassard, C. Crepeau, U. Maurer, *1994 IEEE International Symposium on Information Theory*, Trondheim, Norway (1994).
5. M. N. Wegman and J. L. Carter, *Journal of Computer and System Sciences* **22**, 265-279 (1981).
6. P. G. Kwiat *et al.*, *Phys. Rev. Lett.* **75**, 4337 (1995).

CONTINUOUS VARIABLE QUANTUM KEY DISTRIBUTION: BEATING THE 3 DB LOSS LIMIT

N. LÜTKENHAUS, CH. SILBERHORN, G. LEUCHS,
Zentrum für Moderne Optik, Universität Erlangen-Nürnberg, 91058 Erlangen, Germany

T. C. RALPH
Centre for Quantum Computer Technology, University of Queensland, QLD 4072, Australia

We demonstrate that quantum key distribution systems based on continuous variable implementations can operate beyond the apparent 3 dB loss limit that is implied by the beam splitting attack. Here we discuss the information-theoretical background and explain the difference between our approach and that by Grosshans and Grangier.

The distribution of random keys for cryptographic purposes can be made secure by using the fundamental properties of quantum systems. Any intervention of a potential eavesdropper can be detected. Within certain limits, a detected intervention can be neutralized with tools developed in classical information theory, such as error correction and privacy amplification. Quantum key distribution was first discussed for discrete systems, and experimental demonstrations have been carried out using optical sources, which produce low photon number states. More recently, schemes based on continuous quantum variables have been proposed. The expectation of a better performance of such systems is based on an anticipated higher clock rate of realizations, and the availability of a wider variety of correlation data that allow checking for eavesdropping activity. Here we review the background of the problem how to use continuous variable systems on lines with high losses. Then we outline the main idea behind two recent proposals[1,2] to overcome the apparent 3 dB loss limit in a protocol using coherent states.[3]

Let us begin with the information-theoretical background that allows one to establish a secret key from partly compromised data. For that we describe the problem by classical three-party correlations between sender Alice, receiver Bob and eavesdropper Eve. (See Fig. 1.) Given the correlations as joint probability distribution for data of the three parties, Csiszar and Körner[4] showed that it is in principle possible to obtain a secure key via a one-way communication protocol at a rate C bounded by

$$C \geq C_{\min} := \min\{I_{AB} - I_{AE}, I_{AB} - I_{BE}\} \tag{1}$$

where I_{AB}, I_{AE}, I_{BE} denote the Shannon mutual information between the respective parties.[a] If $I_{AE} \geq I_{BE}$, the one-way communication flow goes

[a]Maurer[5] found an upper bound for C in form of the *intrinsic information* $I_{AB\downarrow E}$ that

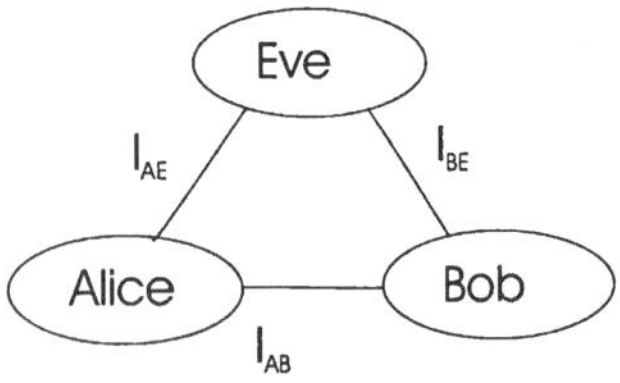

Figure 1. The three-party correlations between Alice, Bob, and Eve lead to Shannon information measures between any two parties.

from Bob to Alice, otherwise it goes in the opposite direction. Note that originally this bound has been established in a non-constructive way.

To obtain a secret key from the given correlations one can proceed in two steps. In the first step, Alice and Bob perform an error correction protocol via a public channel to reconcile their respective data representing the key. As a result of error correction, we are left with only one new relevant mutual information, $I_{(AB)E}$, characterizing Eve's knowledge of the new, corrected key shared by Alice and Bob. In the second step, they shorten this key via mappings described by the generalized privacy amplification procedures[6] in order to end up with a secret key. Here we are interested in the circumstances under which this second step is successful. In the general case, general privacy amplification requires that Alice and Bob can bound Eve's information on their shared key as measured by the *collision probability.* However, when the joint probability distribution between the three parties results from independent events (no correlations between subsequent signals) it is sufficient to derive an upper bound on the mutual information $I_{(AB)E}$ as measured by the mutual information per signal. In that case the reconciled key needs to be shortened precisely by the fraction $I_{(AB)E}$.

There are two main methods of error correction: one-way or two-way error correction. In one-way error correction one party, for example Alice, sends additional information about her version of the key to Bob such that Bob can correct the errors in his key and adapt it to Alice's key. Following Shannon's theory of information, Alice needs to send in the ideal case $1 - I_{AB}$ bits of this redundant information. Then $I_{(AB)E}$ denotes Eve's information on Alice's key after error correction. Note that this quantity in general is not equal to I_{AE} as long as *side information*, such as error correction information, becomes publicly available. However, if we encrypt this side information via a one-time pad, which is information-theoretically proven to be secure, then we have $I_{(AB)E} = I_{AE}$. If we take this approach, Alice and Bob need to share some initial secret[b] and we have to re-define the success of the protocol: we

is defined as the smallest possible value of the mutual information between Alice and Bob given all possible hypothetical announcements Eve could make based on her data.

[b]Alice and Bob need to share a secret anyway to authenticate their public communication.

require the bit rate obtained after privacy amplification, R_{PA}, to be bigger than the rate $R_S = 1 - I_{AB}$ of secret bits used up in the encryption of the side information. The difference is the net rate of generated secure bits

$$C_{A\to B} = 1 - I_{AE} - (1 - I_{AB}) = I_{AB} - I_{AE} \,. \tag{2}$$

Similarly, if Bob sends the error correction information via one-way communication, we find

$$C_{B\to A} = I_{AB} - I_{BE} \,. \tag{3}$$

The situation is different for some widely used two-way communication error correction methods, such as the one proposed by Brassard and Salvail.[7] In these protocols error correction information is effectively sent from Alice to Bob, while Bob sends to Alice information about the positions of errors, which he subsequently corrects. Although the first part can be encrypted again via a one-time pad, the second part of information causes Eve's information about Alice's and Bob's key to become identical. That means that in general $I_{(AB)E} \geq \max\{I_{AE}, I_{BE}\}$. However, in specific cases (e.g., independent noise) one can make the stronger statement $I_{(AB)E} = \max\{I_{AE}, I_{BE}\}$. This is the case in our analysis.[2] Then we find for the generated net rate of secret key

$$C_{A\leftrightarrow B} = I_{AB} - \max\{I_{AE}, I_{BE}\} \,. \tag{4}$$

One can imagine protocols that interpolate between the one-way and the two-way error correction protocols, leaking only partial information about the error positions.[c]

With this information-theoretical background we are ready to explain how one can obtain a positive net rate of secure key from a continuous variable protocol in the presence of high loss. There are two independent approaches, one by Grosshans and Grangier,[1] and one by the present authors.[2] Both are not full security proofs, and model instead the eavesdropper by a specific attack. In the *beam-splitter attack*, Eve replaces the lossy channel by a perfect one. Then she taps this perfect channel with a beam splitter. This strategy is indistinguishable from the lossy channel and makes part of the signal available to Eve. It appears that the wide class of observable correlations in continuous variable protocols will suffice, typically, to narrow down Eve's action to this beam splitting attack. Both articles note that for losses higher than 3 dB we have

$$I_{AE} > I_{AB} > I_{BE} \,. \tag{5}$$

Grosshans and Grangier[1] use this relation to argue that a secure key can be obtained via the one-way communication at the rate $C_{B\to A}$ as discussed above. Our approach, on the other hand, aims at a secure key rate using the two-way communication scenario. This increases the potential for realistic

[c]This point has been raised in a discussion with P. Grangier.

practical implementation since one-way error correction codes usually operate farther from the ideal Shannon limit $1-I_{AB}$ than the two way error correction scheme,[7] which is known to be efficient even for high error rates up to 15%. We introduce a postselection procedure into the coherent state protocol[3] that changes the ordering of the two-party information quantities to

$$I_{AB}^{\text{post}} > I_{AE}^{\text{post}} > I_{BE}^{\text{post}} . \tag{6}$$

Such a postselection procedure has been already proposed and successfully implemented for four-state protocols by Hirano et al.,[8] but is now adapted to our situation. It is based on Bob's measurement, which is one of two conjugate quadrature measurements. Bob's aim is to decide from which half-plane of the phase space, with respect to the quadrature measurement, Alice has chosen the amplitude of the signal state. Clearly, measurement results close to zero have a higher error rate than measurement results farther from the origin. Therefore one can choose cut-off values so that signals are accepted only if they do not fall into the region around the zero-value. Note that this does not change the value of I_{AE} on the post-selected signals, thereby justifying the stronger form for $C_{A\leftrightarrow B}$, since Eve's and Bob's quantum state after the beam splitter is a product state. On the other hand, this procedure decreases the error rate between Alice and Bob, therefore increasing I_{AB} arbitrarily close to one. For more details, please refer to the full publication.[2]

Acknowledgments

This work was supported by the Deutsche Forschungsgemeinschaft and by the EU project IST-1999-13071 (QUICOV); T.C.R. acknowledges the support of the Australian Research Council. The authors would also like to thank N. Korolkova for fruitful discussions.

References

1. F. Grosshans and P. Grangier, quant-ph/0204127.
2. Ch. Silberhorn, T. C. Ralph, N. Lütkenhaus, and G. Leuchs, *Phys. Rev. Lett.* **89**, 167901 (2002).
3. F. Grosshans and P. Grangier, *Phys. Rev. Lett.* **88**, 057902 (2002).
4. I. Csiszar and I. Körner, IEEE Trans. Inf. Theory **IT-24**, 339 (1978).
5. U. M. Maurer, IEEE Trans. Inf. Theory **39**, 1733 (1993).
6. C. H. Bennett, G. Brassard, C. Crepeau, and U. M. Maurer, IEEE Trans. Inf. Theory **41**, 1915 (1995).
7. G. Brassard and L. Salvail in *Advances in Cryptology - EUROCRYPT'93*, Lecture Notes in Computer Science Vol. 765 (Springer, New York, 1994).
8. T. Hirano, T. Konishi, and R. Namiki, quant-ph/0008037; R. Namiki and T. Hirano, quant-ph/0205191.

GAMBLING ON THE QUANTUM INTERNET

R. W. SPEKKENS
University of Toronto, 60 St. George St., Toronto M5S 1A7, Canada.

TERRY RUDOLPH
Bell Labs, 600-700 Mountain Ave., Murray Hill, NJ 07974, U.S.A.

We present a quantum protocol for the task of weak coin flipping. We find that for one choice of parameters in the protocol, the maximum probability of a dishonest party winning the coin flip if the other party is honest is $1/\sqrt{2}$. We also examine the cheat-sensitivity of the protocol. In particular, we calculate the maximum probability of winning that a dishonest party can achieve without running any risk of being caught cheating.

Consider the following simple cryptographic problem, originally introduced by Blum. Alice and Bob are going through a divorce, and are trying to determine who will get to keep the car. They would like to decide the issue by flipping a coin, however they live in different cities and can only communicate by telephone. Of course, it does no good to have one of them flip a coin and announce the result, since they do not trust one another. What they require is a protocol that simulates a coin flip while guaranteeing to each party that if he or she follows the honest strategy, then the other party's ability to bias the coin toss is limited. We call any such protocol a *weak coin flipping* (WCF) protocol. The security of a WCF protocol can be quantified by Alice's maximum probability of winning the coin flip given an honest Bob, $P_A^{\max}$, and by Bob's maximum probability of winning the coin flip given an honest Alice, $P_B^{\max}$.

Such a protocol is termed "weak" because one can demand a stronger form of security, specifically, that Alice and Bob be guaranteed that the other party cannot reliably bias the outcome of the coin flip in *either* direction. Recently,[1] it has been shown that there exist quantum protocols for this "strong" coin flipping wherein the maximum probability of either party biasing the outcome in either direction is 3/4. One would expect that if a party is only trying to bias the outcome in one direction, then his or her opponent is better able to guard against such biasing. Thus, one would expect there to exist a quantum protocol for WCF with $P_A^{\max} = P_B^{\max} < 3/4$.

One can show that, consistent with this expectation, there exists a three-round quantum WCF protocol with $P_A^{\max} = P_B^{\max} = 1/\sqrt{2}$. It proceeds as follows. Alice prepares a pair of systems in a (typically entangled) state $|\psi\rangle \in \mathcal{H}^A \otimes \mathcal{H}^B$, and sends system B to Bob. Bob measures a positive operator valued measure (POVM) $\{E_0, E_1\}$ on system B, and sends a classical bit b indicating the result to Alice. In the honest protocol, Bob wins if $b = 0$ and Alice wins if $b = 1$. We require that $\langle\psi| I \otimes E_b |\psi\rangle = 1/2$ to ensure that these outcomes occur with equal probability.

Of course, a dishonest Bob can always simply announce himself to be the winner, so Alice would like evidence that he actually did the measurement and obtained the outcome $b = 0$. Meanwhile, Bob knows that a dishonest Alice could submit a state different from $|\psi\rangle$, for which the probability of Bob's measurement having the outcome $b = 1$ is increased, and so Bob would like evidence that she actually submitted $|\psi\rangle$. Such evidence is provided to the parties as follows. If Bob announces $b = 0$, then he must resubmit system B to Alice, who then tests whether the state of AB has collapsed to $|\psi_0\rangle = I \otimes \sqrt{E_0}\,|\psi\rangle\,/\sqrt{\langle\psi|\,I \otimes E_0\,|\psi\rangle}$ as one would expect from the collapse rule for POVMs if Bob in fact measured $\{E_0, E_1\}$ and obtained the outcome 0. On the other hand, if Bob announces $b = 1$, then Alice must submit system A to Bob, who then tests whether the final state of AB is $|\psi_1\rangle = I \otimes \sqrt{E_1}\,|\psi\rangle\,/\sqrt{\langle\psi|\,I \otimes E_1\,|\psi\rangle}$, as one would expect if Alice actually submitted $|\psi\rangle$.

By optimizing over all cheating strategies that are consistent with the laws of quantum mechanics, it can be shown that the security achieved by this protocol is $P_A^{\max} = 2\mathrm{Tr}\left(\rho E_0^2\right)$ and $P_B^{\max} = 2\left[\mathrm{Tr}(\sqrt{\rho E_0 \rho})\right]^2$, where $\rho = \mathrm{Tr}_A\left(|\psi\rangle\langle\psi|\right)$. An interesting family of instances of this protocol is defined by $\rho = x\,|0\rangle\langle 0| + (1-x)\,|1\rangle\langle 1|$, and $E_0 = \frac{1}{2x}\,|0\rangle\langle 0|$ with $1/2 < x \leq 1$. As x is varied, there is a trade-off between the magnitude of $P_A^{\max}$ and $P_B^{\max}$ of the form $P_A^{\max} P_B^{\max} = 1/2$. For $x = 1/\sqrt{2}$, one obtains $P_A^{\max} = P_B^{\max} = 1/\sqrt{2}$. It is unknown whether this is the optimal security that can be achieved in a WCF protocol.

The WCF protocol proposed above can offer additional security in the form of *cheat sensitivity:* whenever a party cheats above a threshold amount, he or she runs a risk of being caught. If the cost of being caught cheating is much higher than the cost of simply losing, this can provide a strong disincentive to would-be cheaters. We define the threshold for cheat sensitivity for a party to be the maximum probability of winning that the party can achieve, given that their probability of being caught cheating is strictly zero. By optimizing over all strategies, we find that the thresholds for Alice and Bob are, respectively, $P_A^{\mathrm{thresh}} = 1/\left[2\mathrm{Tr}(\rho\Pi_{(I-E_0)})\right]$ and $P_B^{\mathrm{thresh}} = 1/\left[2\lambda^{\max}(E_0\Pi_\rho)\right]$, where Π_X denotes the projector onto the support of X, and $\lambda^{\max}(X)$ denotes the largest eigenvalue of X. For the family of instances of the protocol defined above, we have $P_A^{\mathrm{thresh}} = 1/2$, $P_B^{\mathrm{thresh}} = P_B^{\max}$. This means that Alice runs a risk of being caught whenever she cheats, whereas Bob can cheat right up to the maximum amount possible without running any risk of being caught. In different instances of the protocol, one can have simultaneously $P_A^{\mathrm{thresh}} < P_A^{\max}$ and $P_B^{\mathrm{thresh}} < P_B^{\max}$. This demonstrates that cheat sensitivity is a useful form of security in its own right.

References

1. A. Ambainis, in *Proceedings of the 33rd Annual Symposium on Theory of Computing 2001* (ACM, New York, 2001), p. 134.

UNCLONEABLE ENCRYPTION

DANIEL GOTTESMAN

Perimeter Institute, 35 King Street N, Waterloo, Ontario N2J 2W9 Canada

Quantum states cannot be cloned. I show how to extend this property to classical messages encoded using quantum states, a task I call "uncloneable encryption." An uncloneable encryption scheme has the property that an eavesdropper Eve not only cannot read the encrypted message, but she cannot copy it for later decoding. Any authentication scheme for quantum states acts as a secure uncloneable encryption scheme. Uncloneable encryption is also closely related to quantum key distribution (QKD), demonstrating a close connection between cryptographic tasks for quantum states and for classical messages. The main results apply to a one-time key with unconditional security, but uncloneable encryption remains secure with a pseudorandom key. To defeat the scheme, Eve must break the computational assumption behind the pseudorandom sequence before Bob receives the message, or lose her opportunity. This means uncloneable encryption can be used in a non-interactive setting, where QKD is not available, allowing Alice and Bob to convert a temporary computational assumption into a permanently secure message.

The primary application of cryptography is to send secret messages. Typically, there is a sender Alice who wishes to communicate with a receiver Bob, but an eavesdropper Eve is listening to their messages. To stop her, Alice encrypts her transmissions; Bob decrypts using a secret key unknown to Eve. While Bob can easily read the secret message, it will be difficult or impossible for Eve to do so, as she lacks the key. Another task is authentication: Alice and Bob do not care if Eve reads the message, but want to make sure she does not change it. Naturally, a message can be both encrypted and authenticated.

Many cryptographic systems are based on computational assumptions: Eve's attempt to learn the contents of a message is equivalent to solving some hard problem. The one-time pad provides unconditional security, whatever Eve's computational power. Alice and Bob share a secret key that is as long as the message, and the encrypted message consists of the bits of the original XORed with the corresponding bits of the key, which is only used once.

However, a "cloning" attack will break even the one-time pad. Suppose Alice and Bob share a secret key k, and Alice encrypts a classical message m using an encryption scheme with key k. Eve intercepts the message, copies it, and passes it on to Bob, who checks if it has been tampered with. If the ciphertext is classical, Eve can copy the message without altering it, so Bob will not detect her interference. At this point, Eve cannot read the encrypted message, but if she later acquires k, she can easily decipher it.

For the one-time pad, perhaps the cloning attack is not a severe worry, since the key is usually destroyed after being used. It is a much more serious problem for computationally secure schemes. In such schemes, the same key is used repeatedly, giving Eve more opportunity to steal it, enabling her to read not only future messages, but past ones as well. Eve may not even need to steal the key: she can simply copy down the message and begin a time-consuming brute-force attack. Alternately, she could wait in the hopes that future improvements in computer hardware or algorithms make it easier to break the encryption scheme. Furthermore, having the ciphertext of many encrypted messages to examine is very helpful when performing cryptanalysis.

Quantum states have the property that they cannot be copied.[1,2] On the surface, this only applies to superpositions of states. If a classical message is sent as a standard set of basis states, it can be copied without being disturbed. In general, an unencrypted classical message can always be copied: reading it constitutes making a copy. However, if we instead encrypt the classical message using quantum states, we can produce *uncloneable encryption* schemes, which are secure even against the cloning attack. In particular, for any attack by Eve, either she gets caught with high probability (e.g., if she steals the message), or she learns almost nothing about the message. In this paper, I give an outline of various results on uncloneable encryption, omitting some of the proofs and discussion of finer points due to space limitations. A more complete discussion is available on the quant-ph e-print archive.

Quantum mechanics has other cryptographic applications, such as quantum key distribution (QKD),[3] which enables Alice and Bob to create a secure classical key despite the potential presence of an eavesdropper. QKD uses only an insecure quantum channel and authenticated (but unencrypted) classical channels, but requires multiple rounds of communication between Alice and Bob. QKD can create a secret key which is then used with the one-time pad to send unconditionally secure messages. In contrast, uncloneable encryption is a noninteractive protocol which can be used to enhance the security of the one-time pad or computationally secure encryption schemes. Alternatively, it can perform QKD with relatively little interaction and other small improvements. Noninteractivity is essential for data storage, and important when there is a substantial transmission lag (for instance, when communicating with a distant space probe). It is convenient for more mundane communication contexts where there is a modest but nonzero time cost for transmissions. Uncloneable encryption is closely related to some forms of QKD, but it can be best viewed as a strong encryption protocol that shares the intrusion-detection ability of quantum key distribution. Another related concept is that of "secure direct communication,"[4] which is, however, also explicitly interactive.

Another side of the subject of quantum cryptography is to create cryptographic protocols to protect quantum states. For instance, it is possible to authenticate quantum states.[5] It turns out that quantum authentication protocols have precisely the properties needed to create uncloneable encryption schemes. To see this, we must first define "uncloneable encryption."

Alice sends Bob a classical message m as $\sigma_k(m)$, with $k \in \mathcal{K}$ a shared key. To encrypt, $\sum_k \sigma_k(m)/|\mathcal{K}|$ must be independent of the message. Eve's attack on the transmission is a superoperator $\mathcal{A}$ acting on $\sigma_k(m)$; $\mathcal{A}$ cannot depend on k. $\mathcal{A}$'s output is split between Bob (who gets $\sigma_{B,k}(m)$) and Eve.

Bob has some efficient checking procedure $(\sigma_{B,k}(m), k) \mapsto \{\text{ACC}, \text{REJ}\}$

which allows him to detect Eve's tampering. He accepts the message when he gets ACC; when he gets REJ he concludes Eve may have stolen the encrypted message. Let $\rho_k(m)$ be Eve's residual density matrix conditioned on Bob accepting the message m, and let $P_k(m)$ be the probability that Bob accepts m. In general, $\rho_k(m)$ and $P_k(m)$ can depend on the attack $\mathcal{A}$.

Definition 1 *An encryption scheme $\sigma_k(m)$ with error ϵ is an uncloneable encryption scheme with error ϵ if, for any two messages $m \neq m'$ and all attacks $\mathcal{A}$ by Eve, for a fraction of at least $1-\epsilon$ of the possible values of the key k, the trace distance $D\big(P_k(m)\rho_k(m), P_k(m')\rho_k(m')\big) \leq \epsilon$.*

In other words, unless Eve has a large chance of being caught, she has little information about the message, even after learning the key. In particular, Eve cannot tell whether the message was m or m'. Note that an uncloneable encryption scheme by definition also encrypts, even if Eve is caught.

A quantum authentication scheme is an encoding on unknown quantum states: $(|\psi\rangle, k) \mapsto \sigma_k(|\psi\rangle)$, where $|\psi\rangle$ is from some Hilbert space $\mathcal{H}$. Eve performs an attack $\mathcal{A}$, producing Bob's state $\sigma_{B,k}(|\psi\rangle)$. Bob's decoding operation $\mathcal{D}(\sigma_{B,k}(|\psi\rangle), k)$ has image $\mathcal{H}_2 \otimes \mathcal{H}$, where $\mathcal{H}_2$ is a qubit with basis $|\mathrm{ACC}\rangle$, $|\mathrm{REJ}\rangle$. A secure authentication scheme should, for any attack $\mathcal{A}$, produce either $|\mathrm{REJ}\rangle$ or the original state $|\psi\rangle$. The following theorem applies:[5]

Theorem 2 *A quantum authentication scheme with error ϵ is an encryption scheme with error at most $4\epsilon^{1/6}$.*

By theorem 2, if we send a classical message as a basis state for a quantum authentication scheme, it is necessarily encrypted. In fact, we can go even further: it satisfies definition 1 for security against cloning attacks.

Theorem 3 *A quantum authentication scheme with error ϵ is an uncloneable encryption scheme with error at most $(15/2)\epsilon^{1/6}$ (for small ϵ).*

Proof:

We can assume Alice's encoding of a pure state $|\psi\rangle$ is again a pure state for a given value k of the classical key. When we send two possible classical messages m and m' with this authentication scheme, we get

$$m \mapsto |\mathrm{ACC}\rangle|m\rangle|\phi_k(m)\rangle + |\mathrm{REJ}\rangle|\xi_k(m)\rangle + |\mathrm{ACC}\rangle|\eta_k(m)\rangle, \tag{1}$$

$$m' \mapsto |\mathrm{ACC}\rangle|m'\rangle|\phi_k(m')\rangle + |\mathrm{REJ}\rangle|\xi_k(m')\rangle + |\mathrm{ACC}\rangle|\eta_k(m')\rangle, \tag{2}$$

where the $|\xi_k\rangle$s and $|\eta_k\rangle$s are split between Bob and Eve, with $|\eta_k\rangle$ orthogonal to the transmitted message. The $|\phi_k\rangle$s are held by Eve. Since this is a secure authentication scheme, $(\sum_k \||\eta_k\rangle\|^2)/|\mathcal{K}| \leq \epsilon$. Since it is a *quantum* authentication scheme, Alice could also have sent $|m\rangle + |m'\rangle$:

$$|m\rangle + |m'\rangle \mapsto |\mathrm{ACC}\rangle\Big(|m\rangle + |m'\rangle\Big)|\phi_k\rangle + |\mathrm{REJ}\rangle|\xi_k\rangle + |\mathrm{ACC}\rangle|\eta_k\rangle. \tag{3}$$

But by linearity,

$$\begin{aligned} |m\rangle + |m'\rangle \mapsto\ & |\mathrm{ACC}\rangle\Big(|m\rangle|\phi_k(m)\rangle + |m'\rangle|\phi_k(m')\rangle\Big) \qquad (4)\\ & + |\mathrm{REJ}\rangle\Big(|\xi_k(m)\rangle + |\xi_k(m')\rangle\Big) + |\mathrm{ACC}\rangle\Big(|\eta_k(m)\rangle + |\eta_k(m')\rangle\Big). \end{aligned}$$

The first term is the most interesting: if Eve's residual states $|\phi_k(m)\rangle$ and $|\phi_k(m')\rangle$ are different, they become entangled with the message. We find

$$|\eta_k\rangle = |\eta_k(m)\rangle + |\eta_k(m')\rangle + \Big(|m\rangle - |m'\rangle\Big) \otimes \Big(|\phi_k(m)\rangle - |\phi_k(m')\rangle\Big)/2. \quad (5)$$

Since $|\eta_k\rangle$, $|\eta_k(m)\rangle$, and $|\eta_k(m')\rangle$ must all have small norm for most k, so must the difference $|\phi_k(m)\rangle - |\phi_k(m')\rangle$. We are now effectively done, since we have shown that Eve's residual states are very similar for the two messages. The remaining details appear in the full version of the paper. QED

Uncloneable encryption is also closely related to QKD: in fact, any uncloneable encryption scheme can be used to perform secure key distribution. In QKD, Alice and Bob create a shared secret key using authenticated classical channels and an insecure quantum channel. Alice and Bob do not generally use any pre-existing secret key beyond that needed for classical authentication.

Given the same resources and uncloneable encryption scheme $\mathcal{S}$, Alice and Bob can perform QKD. First, Alice generates random strings k and x. She sends the message x to Bob using $\mathcal{S}_k$. When Bob receives the message, Alice announces k (classically). Bob checks if the message is valid; if it is, Alice and Bob use x as their new secret key. The uncloneability property guarantees that this is a secure QKD scheme: Eve gets the quantum state and then later learns the key, but her residual density matrices when Bob accepts the transmission are very similar. In particular, she has little information about the established key x. In fact, this is an even stronger security condition than what is usually proved about QKD: most proofs assume Eve retains *classical* information after QKD terminates, whereas here we let Eve retain *quantum* information (although certain proofs[6] contain a very similar statement).

In order to realize uncloneable encryption with near-future technology, it is necessary to have a protocol which does not require coherent storage or complicated quantum manipulations. QKD is a good source of models; for instance, both BB84 and B92 are "prepare-and-measure" (PAM) protocols in which Alice sends unentangled qubits to Bob and Bob measures them immediately upon receiving them, without having to store them at all. We now wish to find an uncloneable encryption protocol with this same structure.

One straightforward solution is simply to take BB84 and add a layer of encryption. That is, Alice encodes her message with an error-correcting code, and further as a set of parity checks (privacy amplification), encrypting the result with a one-time pad. Then she sends each bit of the resulting expanded message in one of two bases, with check bits interspersed at random. The state of the check bits, as well as the bases used and the key for the one-time pad, comprise the key for the uncloneable encryption scheme, and Bob accepts the message only if the error rate on the check bits is within acceptable limits.

In the full version of this paper, I present a PAM protocol motivated by quantum authentication. That protocol is substantially more efficient at checking for errors, requiring fewer qubits and key bits. In the low-error limit, the use of key bits is just over twice the length of the original classical message.

A PAM uncloneable encryption scheme might be suited to experimental realization in the near future. However, it is more challenging than BB84. In particular, in BB84, it is harmless to discard any qubits which are not received by Bob, whereas for uncloneable encryption, discarding bits will eventually destroy the message. Uncloneable encryption thus requires high efficiency single-photon sources and detectors, which are useful for QKD but not required. This need can be seen as a cost of going to a non-interactive uncloneable encryption protocol rather than an interactive QKD protocol. One possible solution is to use squeezed states,[7] which largely avoid this problem.

Experimental constraints are not the only limitation on practical uncloneable encryption schemes. The key requirements of unconditionally secure uncloneable encryption are not immense, but are still more than is desirable in a truly non-interactive setting (where QKD is not available to produce more key). In classical cryptography, we frequently use a computational assumption to encrypt long messages with a short key. Does uncloneable encryption still work if the key is not truly random, but is instead a *pseudorandom* sequence generated from a much shorter secret key shared by Alice and Bob?

Similarly, in BB84, Alice and Bob discard half of all bits received because they have not previously agreed on a basis. If Alice and Bob take their bases from a pseudorandom sequence generated by a short shared key, they could double the key generation rate. But is a key generated this way secure?

In both cases, Eve still cannot learn the secret message without a quantum algorithm to break the pseudorandom sequence. Furthermore, even if she *eventually* overcomes the computational constraint, it does her no good: to defeat Alice and Bob, Eve must break the pseudorandom sequence before Bob receives the quantum transmission. Intuitively, this is sensible: unless she can defeat the scheme during transmission, the uncloneability property holds, preventing her from copying the message. This is easy to show in the case of an uncloneable encryption scheme $\mathcal{S}$ derived from quantum authentication schemes under theorem 3; see the full version of this paper for the proof.

Theorem 4 *If Eve can efficiently defeat uncloneability for scheme $\mathcal{S}$ (derived from an authentication scheme) with pseudorandom key $\mathcal{K}$, then she has an efficient quantum algorithm to distinguish $\mathcal{K}$ from a truly random sequence.*

Many open questions about uncloneable encryption remain. Theorem 3 provides a good way of constructing uncloneable encryption schemes — from authentication schemes. Is this the *only* way to produce uncloneable encryption protocols? There might be uncloneable encryption schemes which do not also authenticate the classical message being sent. Similarly, do QKD protocols always come from uncloneable encryption schemes? There is an uncloneable encryption scheme that corresponds to BB84, but B92[8] does not appear to derive from any uncloneable encryption scheme.

That is, quantum authentication could be slightly stronger than uncloneable encryption, which in turn could be slightly stronger than quantum key distribution. Nevertheless, the differences are quite small; quantum authentication and QKD are closely related. This is surprising, as the tasks of authenticating quantum states and encrypting classical data at first sight appear completely unrelated. There may well be a rich structure of further interconnections between quantum and classical protocols waiting to be uncovered.

Moving to computational security, we have theorem 4, which unfortunately only proves security when the pseudorandom sequence is secure against *quantum* attacks. If we use a PAM protocol and Eve can make only attacks against single photons, the whole scenario can be simulated classically. Intuitively, therefore, Eve has only classical capabilities and should be unable to copy the state, even if the pseudorandom sequence is only *classically* secure. It would be useful to prove that uncloneability still holds in this case. For instance, we could then perform PAM uncloneable encryption for message m today based on an RSA-protected key, and still have information-theoretic security for m in the distant future once quantum computers become available.

We might also wish to give the uncloneability property to other types of classical protocols. One difficulty is that it is unclear to what extent the name "uncloneable encryption" is really deserved. I have not shown that a message protected by uncloneable encryption cannot be copied — only that Eve cannot copy it without being detected. Is it possible for Eve to create two states, neither of which will pass Bob's test, but which can each be used (with the key) to extract much of the message? Or can one instead prove bounds, for instance, on the total information content of the various purported copies?

Finally, uncloneable encryption is not really conceivable in a purely classical context. Are there other novel tasks which simply make no sense for a classical protocol yet are achievable with the aid of quantum information?

Acknowledgements

I would like to thank Claude Crépeau, Hoi-Kwong Lo, Dominic Mayers, and Adam Smith for helpful discussions. This work was performed in part while the author was a Clay Long-Term CMI Prize Fellow.

References

1. W. K. Wootters and W. H. Zurek, Nature **299**, 802 (1982).
2. D. Dieks, Phys. Lett. A **92**, 271 (1982).
3. C. H. Bennett and G. Brassard, in *Proc. of IEEE International Conf. on Computers, Systems, and Signal Processing*, p. 175 (IEEE press, 1984).
4. A. Beige, B.-G. Englert, C. Kurtsiefer, and H. Weinfurter, Acta Phys. Pol. A **101**, 357 (2002).
5. H. Barnum, C. Crépeau, D. Gottesman, A. Smith, and A. Tapp, quant-ph/0205128, to appear in Proc. FOCS '02.
6. D. Mayers, Journal of ACM **48**, 351 (2001).
7. D. Gottesman and J. Preskill, Phys. Rev. A **63**, 022309, 18 pages (2001).
8. C.H. Bennett, Phys. Rev. Lett. **68**, 3121 (1992).
9. P. W. Shor and J. Preskill, Phys. Rev. Lett. **85**, 441 (2000).

PRACTICAL PROTOCOLS FOR SECURE QUANTUM KEY DISTRIBUTION AT HIGH BIT-ERROR RATES

HOI-KWONG LO

MagiQ Technologies, Inc., 275 Seventh Avenue, 26th Floor, New York, NY 10001-6708, USA

Quantum Key distribution (QKD) is the best-known application of quantum cryptography. Classical data—the raw key—resulting from QKD require classical post-processing protocols to remove errors and to ensure that the eavesdropper indeed has a negligible amount of information about the final key. It is, thus, an important question to work out a secure and yet practical protocol for classical post-processing. Entanglement purification has recently become a powerful approach in the design of such protocols. Here, I survey the basic concepts and some recent results of this approach. For instance, generalizing Shor-Preskill's proof, Gottesman and I have shown that using *two*-way classical communications, the standard BB84 protocol can be made secure even at a quantum bit error rate of about 18.8%, which is substantially higher than the figure of about 11% set by the Shor-Preskill proof. Such a protocol may extend the distance of secure QKD and/or increase the key generation rate. Moreover, I have proven the security of a modified version of the Cascade error-correction protocol, which is a practical protocol proposed by Brassard and Salvail

1 Introduction

1.1 Overall strategy

Quantum key distribution (QKD)[1] and entanglement purification protocols (EPPs)[2] are two important ideas in quantum information. The goal of quantum key distribution is to allow two distant parties, Alice and Bob, to share a secure random string of numbers, known as a key, in the presence of an eavesdropper, through noisy quantum communications. The goal of an entanglement purification protocol is to distill perfect Einstein-Podolsky-Rosen (EPR) pairs, i.e., singlets, in the presence of environmental noise (i.e., decoherence). In this paper, I note the connection between these two important ideas by regarding Eve as the source of the environmental noise.

The main goal of this paper is to study the security of BB84—the best-known protocol proposed by Bennett and Brassard in 1984[1] for QKD. BB84 is a simple prepare-and-measure protocol that is close to current experimental implementations. In BB84, Alice picks a time sequence of photons with each placed randomly into one of four polarizations—vertical, horizontal, 45-degrees and 135-degrees and sends them to Bob. For each photon, Bob picks randomly one of the two bases—rectilinear or diagonal—to determine its polarization. Alice and Bob then publicly announce their bases. They keep only the photons that are transmitted and received in the same bases. Those photons should give the same polarization for Alice and Bob, in the absence of noise and eavesdroppers. The power of QKD lies in the fact that any eavesdropping attack will necessarily disturb the photon polarizations and, therefore, will almost surely be caught.

In this paper, one uses EPPs to prove the security of BB84. More specifically, the overall strategy is as follows: A) one constructs an EPP-based QKD scheme and proves its security and B) one shows that the security of the EPP-based QKD scheme implies the security of BB84. As a result, one obtains a simple proof of unconditional security of BB84. [The first but rather complex proof of the unconditional security of BB84 was by Mayers.[3]] I should emphasize that unconditional security means Eve is allowed to use *any* eavesdropping attack within the security model. In particular, Eve is allowed to regard all the photons transmitted by Alice as a single entity, couple a single probe to them, unitarily evolve the combined system, keep part of the system herself and send the rest to Bob. Unconditional security is widely regarded as the Holy Grail of quantum cryptography.

1.2 Classical post-processing

After quantum transmission, each of Alice and Bob have some polarization data—known as the raw key. They then perform classical post-processing on those data. First, they perform a verification test. For instance, they pick a random subset of the polarization data and publicly announce those data. From there, they can compute the bit error rate of the quantum communication. If the error rate is too high, they abort. Otherwise, they go to the next step in which they perform error detection/correction to remove errors from the signals. In the final step, Alice and Bob perform "privacy amplification," whose goal is to reduce eavesdropper's residual information to an arbitrarily small amount (in some security parameters chosen by Alice and Bob).

The current paper mainly concerns the last two steps—error detection/correction and privacy amplification—of the classical post-processing of data generated from QKD.

1.3 Connecting EPPs with QKD

The idea of entanglement purification was introduced in Ref. 2. Suppose two distant observers, Alice and Bob, share N imperfect EPR pairs. They can apply local operations and classical communications (LOCCs) to attempt to distill out a smaller number, say k, EPR pairs of higher fidelity. Entanglement purification protocols (EPPs) that involve only one-way classical communications have been shown to be mathematically equivalent to standard quantum error-correcting codes. They are useful for both storage and communications of quantum information. On the other hand, EPPs that involve two-way classical communications are known to be more powerful than those involving only one-way communications in the sense that they can tolerate higher channel error rates. Such two-way EPPs are, however, useful only for the communication of quantum information, but not for storage.

The connection between EPP and QKD was first suggested by Deutsch *et al.*[4] This idea was substantially developed by Lo and Chau,[5] who proved rigorously that, given quantum computers, QKD can be made unconditionally secure using EPPs. Indeed, an EPP can be turned into a QKD scheme. Alice and Bob can estimate the property of their channel by randomly sampling and measuring a subset of their shared noisy EPR pairs along either the X or Z basis. They broadcast their measurement outcomes of the tested sample and compute the error rates of the two bases. Now, because the tested sample is randomly chosen, the error rate of the tested sample, with high confidence, provides an estimate of the error rate of the untested pairs. Alice and Bob abort if the error rate of the tested sample is too high. Otherwise, they proceed with an EPP to correct the errors of the untested pairs. Assuming that the EPP is successful, they should now share a smaller number, say k, of almost perfect EPR pairs. They can then generate a shared secure k-bit key by, for example, measuring those EPR pairs along the Z-axis. Eve cannot learn anything about the value of the key because k perfect EPR pairs are in a pure state, which is unentangled with Eve's ancilla.

A key insight of the Lo-Chau proof is a quantum-to-classical reduction argument, which shows that it is, indeed, all right to apply *classical* statistical theory to estimate the error rate of the untested pairs by using the error rate of the tested sample. More concretely, it is consistent to assign classical probabilities to eigenvectors in the N-Bell basis. Each basis vector of the N-Bell basis is a tensor product of Bell states, $|\Psi^{\pm}\rangle$ and $|\Phi^{\pm}\rangle$, for a pair of qubits, where $|\Psi^{\pm}\rangle = \frac{1}{\sqrt{2}}(|\uparrow\downarrow\rangle \pm |\downarrow\uparrow\rangle)$, and $|\Phi^{\pm}\rangle = \frac{1}{\sqrt{2}}(|\uparrow\uparrow\rangle \pm |\downarrow\downarrow\rangle)$.

As noted in the Einstein-Podolsky-Rosen paradox, it is generally inconsistent to assign classical probability theory to a quantum problem. The key reason why classical probability theory does apply here is the "commuting observables" idea. Provided that all the relevant observables of interest commute with each other, it is consistent to assign classical probability theory to a quantum problem. The hard part of the Lo-Chau proof is to construct such commuting observables. The observables that they consider are *symmetric*: Each is of the form $M_A \otimes M_B$ where M_A (which acts on Alice's Hilbert space) is the same as M_B (which acts on Bob's Hilbert space). Moreover, each of M_A is a Pauli operator. [A Pauli operator acting on n qubits is a tensor product of individual qubit operators that are of the form I (the identity), $X = \begin{pmatrix} 0 & 1 \\ 1 & 0 \end{pmatrix}$, $Y = \begin{pmatrix} 0 & -i \\ i & 0 \end{pmatrix}$, and $Z = \begin{pmatrix} 1 & 0 \\ 0 & -1 \end{pmatrix}$.] For this reason, all the relevant observables are diagonal with respect to the N-Bell basis and as such they commute with each other.

2 The Shor-Preskill proof

The Lo-Chau proof has the advantage of being conceptually simple, but requires a quantum computer to implement. Therefore, it is a proof of concept, rather than a practical result. Recently, Shor and Preskill[6] have provided a simple security proof of standard BB84 using the entanglement purification approach, thus removing the requirement of quantum computers. The Shor-Preskill proof relies on a class of EPPs with only one-way classical communications. The subclass of EPPs that they consider is based on the so-called Calderbank-Shor-Steane (CSS) codes. EPPs based on CSS codes have the additional feature that each M_A is either i) of X-type (i.e., a tensor product of individual qubit X's and I's only) or ii) of Z-type (i.e., a tensor product of individual qubit Z's and I's only). The eigenvalues of the X-type operators tell Alice and Bob what phase errors have occurred whereas those of the Z-type operators tell Alice and Bob what bit-flip errors have occurred. Consequently, in CSS codes, the bit-flip and phase error correction procedure are decoupled from each other.

Here comes the key point of using CSS codes. Because the final key is generated by measurement along the Z-axis, its value is not affected by phase errors at all. Therefore, it is unnecessary to actually perform the phase-error correction. What is important is to show that phase-error correction would have been successful, if Alice and Bob had performed it. By dropping the phase-error correction procedure, the EPP-based QKD protocol is equivalent to BB84. For this reason, Alice and Bob can perform secure QKD without quantum computers. The Shor-Preskill proof is important because it shows that the systematic machinery of entanglement purification can be applied to prove the security of a near-practical protocol like BB84.

3 EPPs with two-way classical communications

Shor and Preskill showed that the security of those CSS-based EPPs implies the security of BB84 up to a bit error rate of about 11%. Recall that the Shor-Preskill proof employs EPPs with only one-way classical communications. Given that EPPs with two-way classical communications are more powerful than those with only one-way classical communications, it is natural to ask whether one can prove the security of BB84 using EPPs with two-way classical communications. Another motivation for studying EPPs with two-way classical communications is to establish the security of standard protocols such as "Cascade" for the classical post-processing of quantum signals. I remark that, until recently, Cascade has only been proven to be secure against a restricted class of attacks—so-called individual attacks.

Recently, Gottesman and I[7] have proven that EPPs with two-way classical communications can indeed be used to establish the security of BB84. As a consequence, we proved that BB84 can be made secure up to error rates of 18.9%, which is substantially higher than the record set by the Shor-Preskill proof (11%). [We remark that it is known that BB84 is insecure at a bit error rate of 25%. This is due to the intercept-and-resend strategy wherein Eve simply measures a signal from Alice in either of the two bases (rectillinear or diagonal) and resends the result of her measurement to Bob.]

Naively, following the Shor-Preskill idea of employing CSS codes, one might consider two-way CSS-like protocols for EPPs, which involve operators of X-type and Z-type only (i.e., phase and bit-flip types). One basic primitive of such EPPs involves Alice and Bob each measuring $X \otimes X$ on two EPR pairs and broadcasting their outcomes. If their outcomes disagree, they discard both EPR pairs. If their outcomes agree, they keep one of the two EPR pairs. Unfortunately, such a primitive step *cannot* be reduced to BB84. This is because it involves the post-selection of EPR pairs based on measurement outcomes of X-type operators. Without quantum computers, Alice and Bob cannot really know the outcome of the X-type measurements (phase-error syndromes) and, therefore, cannot possibly perform post-selection based on those outcomes.

Having known the above problem, it is natural to allow post-selection based on outcomes of the Z-type operators only, but not X-type operators. After adding one more technical assumption, we have the following Main Theorem:

Main Theorem: Suppose a symmetric EPP, which consists of measurements $M_A \otimes M_B$'s followed by a decoding step, a bit-flip error correction step and finally a phase-error correction step, satisfies the following conditions. Then, it can be reduced to BB84 or the six-state scheme.

(1) It consists of measurements of X-type and Z-type operators only.

(2) It does not contain post-selection based on outcomes of X-type operators.

(3) The decoding step does not depend on the outcomes of X-type operators. The phase-error correction step can depend on the outcome of the X-type operator, but only by factors of Z.

Remark: The condition that the phase error correction step may depend on the outcome of the X-type operator by only factors of Z ensures that phase errors will not change the value of the final key.

The details of the proof of the Main Theorem can be found in Ref. 7. A particular class of EPPs that can tolerate a high bit-error rate is of the form of several iterations of Step B, followed by several iterations of Step P and then by *asymmetric* CSS codes. Here, Step B involves Alice and Bob each measuring $Z \otimes Z$ on two EPR pairs and broadcasting their outcomes. They discard both pairs if their outcomes disagree. On the other hand, if their outcomes agree, they keep one of the two EPR pairs for subsequent steps. Step P is the three-qubit (majority vote) phase code. By asymmetric CSS codes, I mean a quantum error-correcting code that consists of X-type and Z-type operators only that can correct a fraction f_1 of bit-flip errors and a different fraction f_2 of phase errors. Such a class of EPPs can tolerate a bit error rate of up to 18.9%.

Similarly, the entanglement purification approach can be used to prove that the six-state scheme can tolerate a bit error rate of up to 26.4%.[7] Since

BB84 is known to be insecure at bit error rates higher than 25%, this result shows that the six-state scheme can intrinsically tolerate a higher bit-error rate than BB84.

Other recent work on the entanglement purification approach to QKD can be found in Ref. 8. In summary, entanglement purification has become a powerful tool for security analysis of standard BB84 and the six-state scheme. It allows one to show that those standard schemes can tolerate much higher bit-error rates than previously known.

Acknowledgments

This paper describes joint work with Daniel Gottesman in Ref. 7. Discussions with numerous other colleagues are also gratefully acknowledged.

References

1. C. H. Bennett and G. Brassard, in *Proceedings of IEEE International Conference on Computers, Systems, and Signal Processing*, IEEE press, 1984, p. 175.
2. C. H. Bennett, D. P. DiVincenzo, J. A. Smolin, and W. K. Wootters, Phys. Rev. A **54**, 3824 (1996).
3. D. Mayers, Journal of ACM, **48**, 351–406, available at quant-ph/9802025; preliminary version is D. Mayers, *Advances in Cryptology—Proceedings of Crypto' 96* (Springer-Verlag, New York, 1996), p. 343.
4. D. Deutsch, A. Ekert, R. Jozsa, C. Macchiavello, S. Popescu, and A. Sanpera, Phys. Rev. Lett. **77**, 2818 (1996); available at quant-ph/9604039; Erratum Phys. Rev. Lett. **80**, 2022 (1998).
5. H.-K. Lo and H. F. Chau, Science **283**, 2050–2056 (1999); available at quant-ph/9803006.
6. P. W. Shor and J. Preskill, Phys. Rev. Lett. **85**, 441 (2000); available at quant-ph/0003004.
7. D. Gottesman and H.-K. Lo, quant-ph/0105121.
8. D. Gottesman and J. Preskill, quant-ph/0008046 ; H.-K. Lo, Quantum Information and Computation **1**, 81–94 (2001); H.-K. Lo, H. F. Chau and M. Ardehali, quant-ph/0011056; H. F. Chau, quant-ph/0205060.

Part IX
Quantum Computation and Decoherence

PHYSICS, PHILOSOPHY AND QUANTUM TECHNOLOGY

DAVID DEUTSCH
Oxford University, Oxford, United Kingdom
E-mail: david.deutsch@qubit.org

Quantum theory and the classical theory of computation were perfected in the 1930s, and fifty years later they were unified to form the quantum theory of computation. Here I want to tell you about a speculation — I can't call it more than a "speculation" even though I know it's true — about the kind of theory that might, in another fifty years' time, supersede or transcend the quantum theory of computation.

There are branches of science — in fact most of them are branches of physics — that we expect, by their nature, to have philosophical implications. An obvious example is cosmology. There are other sciences, such as, say, aerodynamics, in which, no matter how startling or important our discoveries may become, we do not expect fundamental philosophical implications. So, various sciences fall at different places on a scale (Fig. 1) ranging from the most fundamental on the left to the least fundamental, the most derivative, on the right.

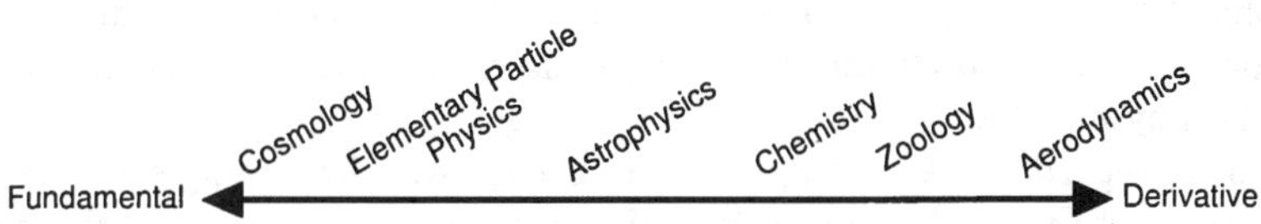

Figure 1. Placing sciences on a scale from fundamental to derivative.

The same holds for mathematics. There are branches of mathematics, such as logic, that we expect by their nature to be relevant to philosophical issues. Then there are other branches, for instance Fourier analysis, which, although they might be very useful both in mathematics itself and in practical applications, are not expected to be philosophically interesting. The vertical axis of Fig. 2(a) measures how mathematical a field is. Halfway up is the line of demarcation between science (which has empirical content) and mathematics (which is purely abstract).

Now, where does the theory of computation lie on that diagram? Traditionally the answer would have been that it is a branch of mathematics, but not a fundamental one: Kronecker said that God made the integers and all the rest is the work of man; more modern formulations give set theory pride of place. So the theory of computation might have been placed at about position 1 on Fig. 2(b). But in the twentieth century, Gödel and Turing argued that the theory of computation ought to be isomorphic to proof theory,

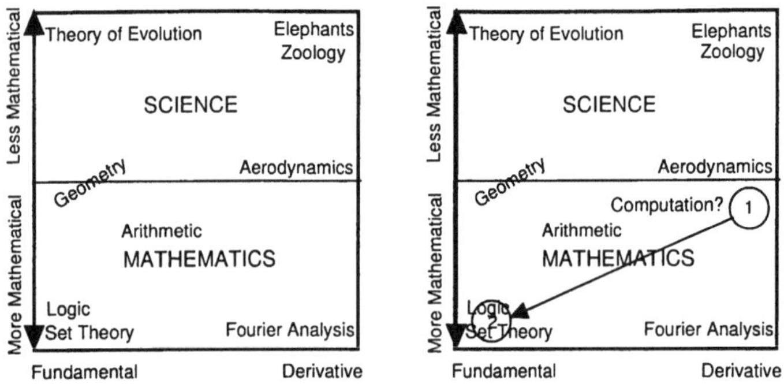

Figure 2. Left panel: (a) assessing the branches of mathematics. Right panel: (b) placing computation in the diagram.

which (it was usually assumed) is at the foundations of mathematics. Such assessments would put it far away at position 2.

What about the theories of information and communication? They were studied under the heading of physics, and would also have been placed well to the right, on the derivative side of the diagram, for all our results in these fields are obtained by taking fundamental theories like the superposition principle and quantum electrodynamics, and deriving conclusions from them. We do not add any new laws.

So we regard our knowledge of the physical world as being structured in the manner of Fig. 3(a): we have laws that apply to absolutely everything, and we apply them to special cases. There's cosmology, and one branch of cosmology would be the physics of galaxies. Within that, there's the physics of solar systems, and within solar systems, planets. On planets, we have quantum computers, elephants, and so on. Alternatively, we can think of elementary particle physics which describes the behavior of all particles in full generality; solid state physics is a special case, and so on up to elephants, humans and quantum computers. Either way, the theory of computers, even quantum computers, would seem to be a highly specialized subfield of a subfield of fundamental physics. After all, it's quite hard to make quantum computers. As far as we know, there are nowhere near as many of them in the universe as there are stars or even elephants. As far as we know there aren't any at all, yet. And in any case, it seems that when we're studying quantum computers we're studying how matter and energy behave under extremely unusual and contrived circumstances — something that may possibly be important to us for practical reasons, but of no fundamental significance. Yet we know that that is the wrong conclusion. We know it because of the existence of computational universality: the laws of physics allow for a machine — a universal quantum computer — with the property that its possible motions correspond

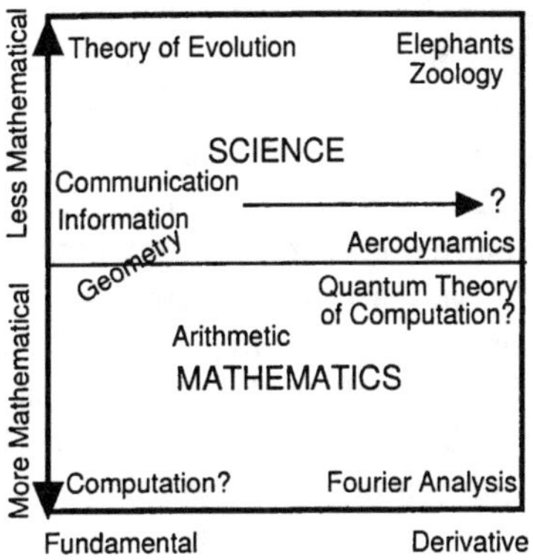

Figure 3. Left panel: (a) placing information and communication in the diagram. Right panel: (b) the encompassing role of quantum computation: does it include all of physics?

in a suitable sense to all possible motions of all possible physical objects. Therefore the whole of physics and more — the study of all possible physical objects — is just isomorphic to the study of all programs that could run on a universal quantum computer.

So the world view portrayed in Fig. 3(a) is wrong, and we're led to a different picture of the relationship between the various sciences, namely Fig. 3(b), in which physics is the quantum theory of computation, and the study of particular physical systems is the study of particular classes of computations. So again galaxies stars and elephants will appear somewhere in this diagram as special cases, but the study of quantum computers is represented by the whole diagram. [As Charles Bennett has pointed out — when I presented this paper at the conference — the quantum theory of computation still does appear as a small region of the diagram as well, but that region has the same structure as the diagram as a whole.]

Yet, even though Fig. 3(b) is our best way of conceiving of the character of physical law, most of our world-views still incorporate something more like the obsolete Fig. 3(a), in which a universal computer is just another physical system. The reason is partly inertia. It is also partly the way in which quantum physics is taught: a course that started with qubits and quantum computational networks instead of the Schrödinger equation and the square well would not only be far closer to the physical foundations of the theory but also inherently simpler. This would have the further merit of allowing quantum theory to be taught earlier in a physics curriculum. But I digress. There is also a good reason for not accepting Fig. 3(b), the computational view of nature, our best available view, as the whole story either.

Admittedly it is very natural, when one has understood the centrality of computation in physics, to make certain speculations about what may be:

maybe the universe that we see — or presumably the multiverse — is really a computer program running on a giant computer. That's an intriguing idea and a rich source of science-fiction plots, but as physics, it is a fundamentally flawed idea. It is a retrograde step in understanding what quantum computation and universality are telling us, and that is for two main reasons. The first is that any cosmology of that type entails giving up on explanations. For if what we see as the laws of physics are actually just attributes of some software, then by the very definition of computational universality, we then have no means of understanding the hardware on which that software is running. So we have no way of understanding the real physics of reality. Thus for this reason, because the properties of this supposed outer-level hardware would never figure in any of our explanations of anything, we have no more reason for postulating that it's there than we have for postulating that there are fairies at the bottom of the garden.

That's a philosophical, or methodological reason. The second reason why I think this idea would be a non-starter is a more technical one, but it too is a killer. We see around us a computable universe; that is to say, of all possible mathematical objects and relationships, only an infinitesimal proportion are ever instantiated in the relationships of physical objects and physical processes. (These are essentially the computable functions.) Now it might seem that one approach to explaining that amazing fact, is to say "the reason why physical processes conform to this very small part of mathematics, 'computable mathematics,' is that physical processes really are computations running on a computer external to what we think of as physical reality." But that relies on the assumption that the set of computable functions — the Turing computable functions, or the set of quantum computable operations — is somehow inherently privileged within mathematics. So that even a computer implemented in unknown physics (the supposed computer that we're all simulations on) would be expected to conform to those same notions of computability, to use those same functions that mathematics designates as computable. But in fact, the only thing that privileges the set of all computational operations that we see in nature, is that they are instantiated by the laws of physics. It is only through our knowledge of the physical world that we know of the difference between computable and not computable. So it's only through our laws of physics that the nature of computation can be understood. It can never be vice versa.

Another of these very natural speculations is that maybe there isn't just one giant computer but an infinite number of them, all running different programs. Or else, forget the computers (the argument I've just given tells us that we have to). We could speculate that there are just many universes all running different laws of physics, as, for instance, in the evolutionary universe idea of Lee Smolin, or the ideas of Seth Lloyd or Max Tegmark. Now I have no objection to the idea that multiple laws of physics in different universes will be implicated in future explanations of the physical world, but it cannot

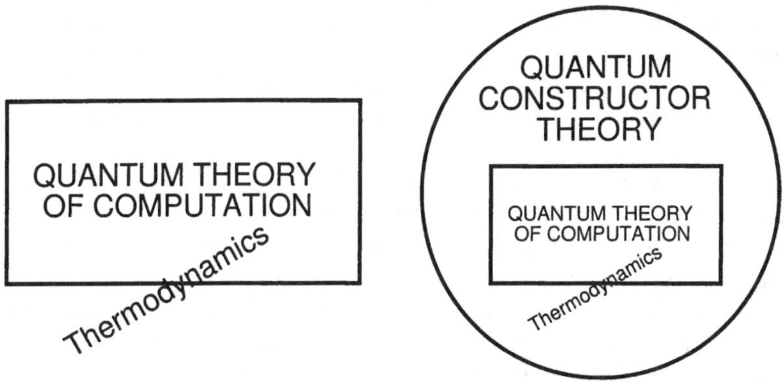

Figure 4. Left panel: (a) thermodynamics is not fully included within the quantum theory of computation. Right panel: (b) quantum constructor theory.

be the whole explanation. It cannot even be the gist of the explanation — for essentially the same reason as the universe-is-a-simulation idea: there is no notion of computation prior to the laws of physics, indeed, there's no notion of laws at all prior to a definition of what is or isn't computable.

Thus, the very power of the principle of the universality of computation, which gives us such a unified view of what physics is, also limits the extent to which physical reality can be regarded as consisting of computations. Because of universality, the nature of computation and the laws governing it are independent of the underlying hardware. Therefore those laws, and that theory, can't explain hardware. Explaining hardware, however, is obviously part of science. Hence there must be something to physics beyond the quantum theory of computation. I think we have to conceive of the quantum theory of computation as a special case of a bigger theory: quantum constructor theory, which is the theory of what physical objects can be constructed, using what resources. Here I don't mean abstract resources, like the number of computational steps or the amount of memory, but physical resources like atoms and energy and entropy and so on.

We do already have some hints about constructor theory: it's not quite true that all of existing physics can be understood as being various aspects of the quantum theory of computation. For instance, we know that it is not possible to build a perpetual motion machine of the second kind. We have a law of physics that tells us so. Yet as far as the quantum theory of computation goes, the time reverse of any physical state is just another physical state. Universality says that the evolution of that state can be simulated by the universal computer with arbitrary accuracy. So the quantum theory of computation does not have the wherewithal to accommodate the whole of, say, quantum statistical mechanics within it [Fig. 4(a)].

Another hint of quantum constructor theory is in the quantum theory of communication. What makes communication different from computation? As in thermodynamics, it is the fact that we have to take into account constraints on computation that are imposed by the actual nature of the physical world. For instance, we may consider two spatially-separated computers, and we have to model what it means for them to 'communicate.' We have to say that certain physical operations, which are perfectly good *computations*, are not allowed because no hardware that is available in nature can implement them because, for instance, that would involve moving information faster than the speed of light. The quantum theory of computation knows nothing of distance; one day, perhaps, distance will be defined in quantum constructor theory, as a certain category of constraints on communication, just as atoms or elementary particles may be defined as certain constraints on the construction of smooth objects. So we have some hints of bits of a future theory that will, in a unified way, address real resources such as energy and volume and time, rather than formal resources such as memory and computational steps and number of computational gates.

The full quantum constructor theory will incorporate the particle physicists' 'theory of everything,' including quantum gravity, as well as the quantum theory of computation and thermodynamics. We may hope that it would be able to answer exotic questions like: can we build a black hole and spin it up until it becomes a time machine? Can we collapse a black hole and have it form new universes which we can design, and if so what are the constraints on that? Before that, we might expect it to resolve more down-to-earth controversies like: can we ever build a controlled fusion reactor? Note that as far as the quantum-theory-of-computation conception of physics goes, the answer would be yes. Building such a device is simply a matter of preparing a certain observable in a fairly sharp state, and in quantum computation that is never a fundamental problem. But that's because the quantum theory of computation doesn't quite capture the whole of physics.

Another such question is of course: can we build a quantum computer? That's a topical issue here, and at the present state of science, still a controversial one. Yet we have to admit that at present, the controversy is not really part of science. It's a bit like glove puppets arguing 'oh yes we can,' 'oh no you can't,' for neither side can appeal to laws of physics. At best they are expressing their intuitions, which may or may not contain wisdom but at the moment are outside physics and outside science. One day the issue will be brought within science, by quantum constructor theory — although I suspect that by then it will have been resolved empirically, by the building of quantum computers.

There will presumably be a constructor generalization of the universal quantum computer, namely the universal quantum constructor, a machine that can be programmed to construct any quantum object that can be constructed, or any quantum object with any achievable properties.

Quantum constructor theory will give us a veritable meta-physics — not metaphysics, the branch of philosophy, but a subject that stands in the same relation to physics as metamathematics does to mathematics. It will be the theory of what can be done, and what can be made, in physical reality. There are some awesome questions waiting for us there in that direction. One of them is: is the human race a universal constructor? — a question with tremendous reverberations for things like epistemology and cosmology, and actual metaphysics.

Our state of knowledge of this field is still very primitive. We are nowhere near answering any such question yet, or even many elementary questions of constructor theory. The subject is still so much in its infancy that even within the quantum theory of computation proper, we don't really have a good idea of what quantum information is, or how entanglement should be quantified and so on. A few years ago the journalist John Horgan wrote a book *The End of Science*, in which he said that all fundamental theories are already known and that from now on fundamental science will all be just dotting the i's and crossing the t's. Horgan concedes that in the year 1900 people were saying much the same things: that physics in the future would be about evaluating the sixth decimal place and so on, and they were proved wrong within a single generation by a series of scientific revolutions. Horgan rightly points out that the fact that those pundits were embarrassingly wrong does not prove that he isn't right. But I think that in 1900 there was a lot more excuse for thinking that physics was almost at an end than there is now. For today's best theories contain within themselves the implication that they can't be complete. There is the well known conflict between the general theory of relativity and quantum theory. There's also the fact I'm stressing, that the principle of universality tells us that there must be a larger unifying theory outside the quantum theory of computation.

So we know, in our field at least, that Horgan is wrong. We know that there are huge gaps in our understanding, and fundamental mismatches between our best theories and the reality they are supposed to explain. We know that if we are at the end of some era then it's only because we are at the beginning of a new one which offers the prospect not only of some quite fundamental discovery but of new kinds of fundamental discovery.

HIGHLIGHTS OF QUANTUM SEARCH BY MEASUREMENT

ANDREW M. CHILDS, ENRICO DEOTTO
EDWARD FARHI, JEFFREY GOLDSTONE
Center for Theoretical Physics, MIT, Cambridge, MA 02139, USA

SAM GUTMANN
Department of Mathematics, Northeastern University, Boston, MA 02115, USA

ANDREW J. LANDAHL
Center for Bits and Atoms, MIT, Cambridge, MA 02139, USA
Institute for Quantum Information, Caltech, Pasadena, CA 91125, USA
E-mail: alandahl@mit.edu

We describe a quantum algorithm for solving combinatorial search problems that uses only a sequence of measurements. The algorithm is similar in spirit to quantum computation by adiabatic evolution, in that the goal is to remain in the ground state of a time-varying Hamiltonian. Indeed, we show that the running times of the two algorithms are closely related. We also show how to achieve the quadratic speedup for Grover's unstructured search problem with only two measurements.

A promising way to develop new quantum algorithmic ideas is to explore alternative formulations of quantum computation. In a previous paper,[1] we explored measurement back-action as a way to simulate adiabatic evolution. In so doing, we developed a generic quantum measurement algorithm for solving combinatorial optimization problems as well as a specific algorithm for solving Grover's search problem[2] with quadratic speedup using only two measurements. In this article, we review these algorithms and highlight some key points of their analysis.

An adiabatic algorithm finds the minimum of a function by applying a slowly changing Hamiltonian to the ground state of the initial Hamiltonian H_B. The final Hamiltonian H_P is chosen so that its ground state encodes the minimum of the function. The adiabatic theorem states that if the evolution is smooth, without level crossings, and applied over a total time $T \gg \Gamma/g^2$, the final state will be the ground state of H_P with high probability, where

$$\Gamma^2 \equiv \max_s \left[\langle E_0(s)|(\tfrac{\mathrm{d}H}{\mathrm{d}s})^2|E_0(s)\rangle - \langle E_0(s)|\tfrac{\mathrm{d}H}{\mathrm{d}s}|E_0(s)\rangle^2\right] \tag{1}$$

$$g \equiv \min_s |E_1(s) - E_0(s)|, \tag{2}$$

and where $E_i(s)$ represents the ith largest energy eigenstate of the interpolating Hamiltonian $H(s)$, with $0 \leq s \leq 1$.

We define the corresponding M-measurement algorithm to be the sequence of M measurements of the interpolating Hamiltonian's value at equally spaced times. No Hamiltonian acts during the measurement algorithm; evolution is generated solely by back-action. For projective measurements, the

Zeno effect predicts that the system will remain in the (changing) ground state with high probability when M is large, resulting in a final ground state population of $\exp(-\Gamma^2/Mg^2)+\mathcal{O}(M^{-2})$, and therefore a successful algorithm when $M \gg \Gamma^2/g^2$.

The running time of the M-measurement algorithm is the product of M and the time τ it takes to perform each measurement of $H(s)$. We calculate this time using von Neumann's measurement model: a Hamiltonian interaction $H(s) \otimes p$ with a pointer followed by a measurement of the pointer's momentum p. To implement this process as a quantum circuit, we digitize the pointer to r qubits, identifying its momentum eigenbasis with the computational basis. We further normalize p as $p\,|z\rangle = 2^{-r}z\,|z\rangle$ so as not to artificially hide algorithmic strength in a growing system-pointer interaction. Finally, we use standard techniques to simulate the interaction Hamiltonian $H(s) \otimes p$ by a quantum circuit.[3,4] In our more detailed paper,[1] we show that this model is equivalent to the quantum phase-estimation algorithm.

This quantum circuit approximates a projective measurement, generating a state whose matrix elements are $|\langle E_a|\,\rho\,|E_b\rangle|^2 \cdot |\kappa(x)|^2$, where $x \equiv (E_b - E_a)\tau/2$ and

$$|\kappa(x)|^2 = \frac{\sin^2(x)}{4^r \sin^2(x/2^r)}\,. \tag{3}$$

Figure 1 depicts this function for $x = 4$. It has a sharp peak of unit height and width of order 1 at the origin, and identical peaks at integer multiples of $2^r\pi$. For this approximation to be sufficiently good, $|\kappa(x)|^2$ must be bounded below 1 by a constant for all relevant energy separations x, and in particular for $x = g\tau/2$. Because the width of the central peak is of order 1, this condition is satisfied when $\tau \geq \mathcal{O}(1)/g$, and therefore the M-measurement algorithm succeeds with high probability whenever its running time $T = M\tau \gg \Gamma^2/g^3$. Finally, this approximation is space-efficient—we show in our more detailed paper[1] that r need be no larger than $\mathcal{O}(\log n)$.

One can use a variant of the M-measurement algorithm to solve Grover's unstructured search problem faster than the best possible classical algorithm. The Grover problem[2] is to find a particular unknown n-bit string w using only queries of the form "Is z the same as w?". This is equivalent to the problem of minimizing the oracle function

$$h_w(z) = \begin{cases} 0 & z = w \\ 1 & z \neq w \end{cases}\,. \tag{4}$$

The best possible classical algorithm for solving this problem requires $\Theta(2^n)$ queries to h_w, whereas the best possible quantum algorithm requires only $\Theta(2^{n/2})$ queries for both the unitary ($U_w|z\rangle = (-1)^{h_w(z)}|z\rangle$) and Hamiltonian ($H_w = 1 - |w\rangle\langle w|$) formulations of the oracle.[5,6,7,8] We propose an analogous *measurement oracle* for this problem: the interaction Hamiltonian $H_w \otimes p$. This proposal is motivated by the fact that repeated alter-

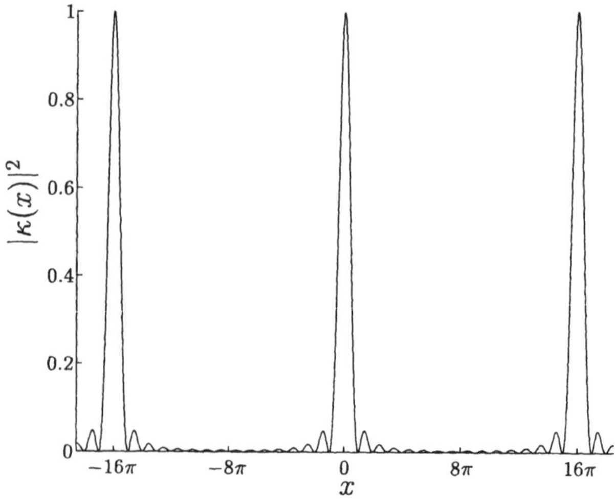

Figure 1. The function $|\kappa(x)|^2$ for $r = 4$.

nation of $H_w \otimes p$ and $H_B \otimes p$ can generate any Hamiltonian of the form $[sH_B + (1-s)H_w] \otimes p$, which is our model for approximating projective measurement of $H(s)$.

For $H_B = \sum_j (1 - \sigma_x^{(j)})/2$, and linear interpolation to H_w, the minimum gap $g \sim 2^{1-n/2}$ and the $s = s^*$ at which it occurs are known and are independent of w.[9] Furthermore, up to terms of order $1/n$, the $H(s^*)$ eigenstates are equal superpositions of the beginning and final ground states, $|\psi_\pm\rangle \simeq [|E_0(0)\rangle \pm |E_0(1)\rangle]/\sqrt{2}$. Hence, a two-measurement algorithm will solve this problem: prepare the system in the state $|E_0(0)\rangle$, measure $H(s^*)$, then measure $H(1)$. This algorithm finds w with probability $\frac{1}{2}$, which can be boosted as close to unity as desired by repetition. This is not a constant-time algorithm, however. Because the $H(1)$ measurement takes constant time and the $H(s^*)$ measurement takes time $\tau = \mathcal{O}(1)/g$, its complexity is $\Theta(2^{n/2})$, the most efficient possible quantum mechanically.[5]

We have shown that an adiabatic algorithm requiring time $T \gg \Gamma/g^2$ can be simulated by a corresponding measurement algorithm requiring time $T \gg \Gamma^2/g^3$. Thus, the measurement algorithm is efficient whenever the adiabatic algorithm is efficient. Moreover, we have presented a measurement algorithm that can achieve quadratic speedup for the Grover problem by using knowledge of the place where the gap g is smallest. Finally, we have argued that it is important to use an explicit dynamical process to model the measurement of complicated observables when they are called for in quantum algorithms. Without a measurement model, the analysis of such algorithms can give misleading results.

Acknowledgments

This work was supported in part by the Department of Energy under cooperative research agreement DE-FC02-94ER40818, by the National Science Foundation under grant EIA-0086038, and by the National Security Agency and Advanced Research and Development Activity under Army Research Office contract DAAD19-01-1-0656. AMC received support from the Fannie and John Hertz Foundation, and ED received support from the Istituto Nazionale di Fisica Nucleare (Italy).

References

1. A. M. Childs, E. Farhi, E. Deotto, J. Goldstone, S. Gutmann, and A. Landahl. *Phys. Rev. A* **66**, 032314 (2002), quant-ph/0204013.
2. L. K. Grover. *Phys. Rev. Lett.* **79**, 325 (1997).
3. S. Wiesner. "Simulations of many-body quantum systems by a quantum computer," quant-ph/9603028.
4. C. Zalka. *Proc. Roy. Soc. London A* **454**, 313 (1998).
5. C. H. Bennett, E. Bernstein, G. Brassard, and U. Vazirani. *SIAM J. Comput.* **26**, 1510 (1997).
6. E. Farhi and S. Gutmann. *Phys. Rev. A* **57**, 2403 (1998).
7. J. Roland and N. Cerf. "Quantum search by local adiabatic evolution," quant-ph/0107015.
8. W. van Dam, M. Mosca, and U. Vazirani. "How powerful is adiabatic quantum computation?," in B. Werner, ed., *Proceedings, 42th Annual Symposium on Foundations of Computer Science*, pp. 279–287, Los Alamitos, CA, 2001. IEEE Press, quant-ph/0206003.
9. E. Farhi, J. Goldstone, S. Gutmann, and M. Sipser. "Quantum computation by adiabatic evolution," quant-ph/0001106.

EFFICIENT CLASSICAL SIMULATION OF MEASUREMENTS IN OPTICAL QUANTUM INFORMATION

STEPHEN D. BARTLETT AND BARRY C. SANDERS
Department of Physics and Centre for Advanced Computing – Algorithms and Cryptography, Macquarie University, Sydney, NSW 2109, Australia
E-mail: stephen.bartlett@mq.edu.au

We present conditions for the efficient simulation of a broad class of optical quantum circuits on a classical machine: this class includes unitary transformations, amplification, noise, and measurements. Various proposed schemes for universal quantum computation using optics are assessed against these conditions, and we consider the minimum resource requirements needed in any optical scheme to generate optical nonlinear processes and perform universal quantum computation.

Information processing using the rules of quantum mechanics may allow tasks that cannot be performed using classical laws.[1] Of the many possible realizations of quantum information processes, optical realizations have the advantage of negligible decoherence. Both qubit[2,3,4] and continuous-variable[5] schemes offer significant potential for optical quantum information processing, especially if efficient processes can be performed that are not efficient on any classical device.

Advanced techniques in linear optics and squeezing are known to be insufficient to perform universal quantum computation[1,5,6]; in particular, optical nonlinear processes (such as a Kerr nonlinearity[7]) have been identified as a necessary requirement. (Schemes that employ only linear optics[8] are not scalable, in that they require resources that grow exponentially in the number of qubits.) However, Kerr nonlinearities suffer either from weak strengths or high losses, and the lack of appropriate nonlinear materials greatly restricts the type of processes that can be performed in practice.

Recently, nonunitary processes such as measurement have been identified as a means to implement nonlinear operations. Proposals for optical quantum computation by Knill, Laflamme and Milburn[3] (KLM) and Gottesman, Kitaev and Preskill[4] (GKP) employ photon counting to induce nonlinear transformations in optical systems. Photon counting is an important example of a process that can be used to achieve nonlinear transformations via feedforward of measurement results. Such a nonunitary transformation appears to enable impressive capabilities equivalent to nonlinear transformations.

It is imperative to determine what type of processes (unitary transformations, projective measurements, interaction with a reservoir, etc.) can be used to implement nonlinear transformations and thus perform universal quantum computation. One approach is to identify classes of processes that can be efficiently simulated on a classical computer. Under the assumption that universal quantum computation is *not* efficiently simulatable classically, such processes are also insufficient to implement optical nonlinear transformations. The Gottesman-Knill (GK) theorem[1] for qubits, the continuous-variable classical simulatability theorem of Bartlett *et al.*[6] (BSBN), and the general optical classical simulatability theorem of Bartlett and Sanders[9] (BS) allow us to investigate the classical complexity of a quantum process using particular classes of initial states, unitary operations and measurements.

Here, we consider the implications of the BS optical classical simulatability theorem on various proposals for quantum computation using optics. This theorem employs the powerful formalism of Gaussian completely positive (CP) maps[10] to describe efficiently simulatable operations on Gaussian states.

Theorem for efficient classical simulatability (BS): *Any quantum information process that initiates in a Gaussian state and that performs only Gaussian CP maps can be* efficiently *simulated using a classical computer.* These maps include (i) the unitary transformations corresponding to linear optics and squeezing, (ii) linear amplification (including phase-insensitive and phase-sensitive amplification and optimal cloning), linear loss mechanisms or additive noise, (iii) measurements that are Gaussian CP maps including, but not limited to, projective measurements in the position/momentum eigenstate basis or coherent/squeezed state basis, with finite losses, and (iv) any of the above Gaussian CP maps conditioned on classical numbers or the outcomes of prior Gaussian CP measurements (classical feedforward).

Our theorem for efficient classical simulation provides a powerful tool in assessing whether a given optical process can enhance linear optics to perform nonlinear transformations or allow quantum processes that are exponentially faster than classical ones. Algorithms or circuits employing Gaussian CP maps can be efficiently simulated on a classical computer, and thus do not provide any sort of quantum exponential speedup.

We now consider some of the key new results of this theorem in terms of known processes.

Corollary 1: Linear optics or squeezing transformations conditioned on the measurement outcome of homodyne detection with finite losses using Gaussian states cannot induce a nonlinearity.

Thus, initiating with Gaussian states, it is not possible to use homodyne measurements and feedforward of measurement results to induce a (possibly nondeterministic) optical nonlinearity in the way that photon counting allows in the KLM scheme. In terms of optical implementations of quantum computing, this theorem reveals why all previous schemes either propose some form of optical nonlinearity,[2,5] use other forms of measurement such as photon counting[3,4] or are not efficiently scalable.[8]

This theorem also places severe constraints on the use of photodetection to perform nonlinear transformations in realizations of optical quantum

Table 1. Efficient classical simulatability for schemes employing various initial states, unitary gates, and measurements.

Initial States	Unitary Gates	Measurements	Efficiently simulatable?
Vacua	Linear optics, squeezing	Gaussian CP (i.e., homodyne)	Yes[6,9]
Vacua	Linear optics, squeezing, Kerr nonlinearity	Homodyne	No (Lloyd & Braunstein[5])
Single photons	Linear optics only	Photon counting	No (KLM[3])
Vacua	Linear optics, squeezing	Photon counting & homodyne	No (GKP[4])
Single photons	Linear optics, squeezing	Homodyne	???

computing. For a threshold photodetector[3,11,12] with perfect efficiency, the POVM is given by two elements, corresponding to "absorption" and "no-absorption" of light. Photon counters are effectively constructed as arrays of such detectors.[12] The vacuum projection describes the non-absorption measurement, and the corresponding map describing this measurement result is Gaussian CP. However, the absorption outcome is not.

Corollary 2: Gaussian CP maps conditioned on the no-absorption outcome of a photodetection measurement are also Gaussian CP, whereas transformations conditioned on the absorption outcome are not.

Note that the same result holds for finite-efficiency photodetectors: such detectors can be modelled as unit efficiency photodetectors with a linear loss mechanism describable using Gaussian CP maps. Thus, the absorption outcome of photodetection and the feedforward of this measurement result is a key resource for optical quantum information processing. This corollary also proves that any nonlinear gate employing linear optics and photon counting *must* be nondeterministic; a photon counting measurement of a Gaussian state could possibly result in an outcome of zero photons, and such a result corresponds to an efficiently classically simulatable process. (Note that nonlinear optics, in contrast, can be deterministic.)

Our classical simulatability theorem may be useful in assessing the "minimum" requirements for universal quantum computation with optics. Table 1 presents various classes of initial states, unitary gates, and measurements (that can be used for classical feedforward) and their classical simulatability according to our theorem. Employing only Gaussian states and Gaussian CP maps results in an efficiently simulatable circuit; one can now consider supplementing this set with various "resources" that may allow for universal quantum computation. As shown by Lloyd and Braunstein,[5] the addition of a Kerr nonlinearity or any higher-order transformation on a single mode results in universal quantum computation. The schemes of KLM and GKP reveal that photon counting is also a resource that allows for universal quantum computation. The KLM scheme also requires single photon Fock states "on demand" as ancilla inputs to their nondeterministic nonlinear gates; such states lie outside the domain of our theorem (they are not Gaussian) and may serve as a resource for performing nonlinear operations.

It is interesting to consider, then, if single photons on demand are by themselves sufficient to bestow Gaussian CP maps with the power to perform nonlinear operations and thus universal quantum computation. Considering the recent progress in creating single photon turnstile devices[13] (with low probability of producing zero or two photons by accident), a scheme that requires single photons but otherwise employs only linear optics, squeezing, and high-efficiency homodyne detection would obviate the need for ultra-high efficiency photon counters.[14]

Acknowledgments

SDB acknowledges helpful discussions with M. A. Nielsen. This project has been supported by an ARC Large Grant and a Macquarie University New Staff Grant.

References

1. M. A. Nielsen and I. L. Chuang, *Quantum Computation and Quantum Information* (Cambridge University Press, Cambridge, 2000).
2. I. L. Chuang and Y. Yamamoto, *Phys. Rev.* A **52**, 3489 (1995).
3. E. Knill *et al*, *Nature (London)* **409**, 46 (2001).
4. D. Gottesman *et al*, *Phys. Rev.* A **64**, 012310 (2001).
5. S. Lloyd and S. L. Braunstein, *Phys. Rev. Lett.* **82**, 1784 (1999).
6. S. D. Bartlett *et al*, *Phys. Rev. Lett.* **88**, 097904 (2002).
7. D. F. Walls and G. J. Milburn, *Quantum Optics* (Springer, Berlin, 1994).
8. N. J. Cerf *et al*, *Phys. Rev.* A **57**, 1477 (1998).
9. S. D. Bartlett and B. C. Sanders, *Phys. Rev. Lett.*, in press, (2002); quant-ph/0204065.
10. G. Lindblad, *J. Phys. A: Math. Gen.* **33**, 5059 (2000).
11. P. Kok and S. L. Braunstein, *Phys. Rev.* A **63**, 033812 (2001).
12. S. D. Bartlett and B. C. Sanders, *Phys. Rev.* A **65**, 042302 (2002).
13. C. Santori *et al*, *Phys. Rev. Lett.* **86**, 1502 (2001).
14. S. D. Bartlett *et al*, in *Proceedings of Free-Space Laser Communication and Laser Imaging II*, Vol. **4821**, ed. J. C. Ricklin and D. G. Voelz (SPIE, Bellingham, WA, 2002); quant-ph/0204073.

NUCLEAR MAGNETIC RESONANCE IMPLEMENTATION OF QUANTUM CHAOTIC MAPS

YAAKOV S. WEINSTEIN

Dept. of Nuclear Engineering, Massachusetts Institute of Technology
Cambridge, MA 02139, USA
E-mail: yaakov@mit.edu

SETH LLOYD

d'Arbeloff Laboratory for Information Systems and Technology
Department of Mechanical Engineering, Massachusetts Institute of Technology
Cambridge, MA 02139, USA

JOSEPH V. EMERSON, DAVID G. CORY

Dept. of Nuclear Engineering, Massachusetts Institute of Technology
Cambridge, MA 02139, USA

We explore the capacity of current nuclear magnetic resonance (NMR) quantum information processors to simulate aspects of quantum chaos. We first review the implementation of the quantum baker's map on a three qubit NMR quantum information processor and show how applied perturbations can be useful in the study of quantum chaos. We also introduce a set of quantum random maps that have no classical analog but exhibit features of quantum chaos. These maps are implementable on NMR quantum information processors.

Quantum information processors, systems with a small number of two-level quantum bits or qubits, are useful test beds for a range of quantum simulations. For example, NMR quantum information processors have been used to simulate properties of entanglement[1] and the dynamics of the quantum harmonic oscillator.[2] Below, we discuss NMR quantum information processor simulations of quantum chaotic maps. We first review our recent implementation the quantum baker's map[3] and then discuss quantum chaotic random maps.

Classically chaotic systems are extremely sensitive to initial conditions.[4] Arbitrarily close points in phase space diverge at an exponential rate given by the system's Lyapunov exponent. However, quantum systems, due to unitary evolution, cannot exhibit this behavior. Nevertheless, sensitivity to small perturbations in the time evolution of a system can be used as a signature of quantum chaotic systems.[5,6,7] Another signature is the equivalence of certain statistical properties for quantum chaotic evolution operators and random matrices.[8] Specifically, quantum chaotic Hamiltonians are known to show level repulsion, the spacings between nearest neighbor eigenvalues follow the Wigner-Dyson distribution.[9] In addition, the magnitude of the elements of the eigenvectors of quantum chaotic operators follow χ^2_ν distributions[10] from the appropriate random matrix ensemble.

To study quantum chaos, Balazs and Voros[11] quantized the baker's map, one of the most basic maps used in the study of classical chaotic phenomenon, in hopes that the resulting operator would show quantum chaotic phenomenon. Their 'quantum baker's map' (QB), is simply a quantum Fourier transform (QFT) on half of Hilbert space followed by an inverse QFT on all of Hilbert space. The QFT is a discrete Fourier transform acting on Hilbert space: $\mathrm{QFT}_q|x\rangle = \frac{1}{\sqrt{q}}\sum_{x'=0}^{q-1} e^{2\pi i x x'/q}|x'\rangle$. The QFT, and, hence, the QB, can be expressed as a sequence of two elementary gates,[12] the one-qubit Hadamard gate, H_j, which rotates a qubit from $|0\rangle \to \frac{1}{\sqrt{2}}(|0\rangle + |1\rangle)$ and $|1\rangle \to \frac{1}{\sqrt{2}}(|0\rangle - |1\rangle)$, and the two-qubit conditional phase gate, $B_{jk}(\theta)$, which applies a phase of θ to qubit k if qubit j is $|1\rangle$. For three qubits, the gate sequence of the quantum baker's map is $\mathrm{QB} = \mathrm{Swap}_{13}H_3B_{23}^{\dagger}\left(\frac{\pi}{2}\right)B_{13}^{\dagger}\left(\frac{\pi}{4}\right)H_2B_{12}^{\dagger}\left(\frac{\pi}{2}\right)H_1\mathrm{Swap}_{23}H_3B_{23}\left(\frac{\pi}{2}\right)H_2$ where Swap_{jk} is a swap gate between bits j and k.[13] The necessary NMR operations to implement these gates, radio frequency pulses for rotations and periods $\sigma_z^j\sigma_z^k$ coupling, are given elsewhere.[14] Swap gates are done by relabeling bits.

The most efficient and least biased way to study quantum chaos is through simulations on a quantum information processor. Though for small Hilbert spaces the same simulations could be done on a classical computer, an actual quantum simulation is necessary to understand the complexity and challenges of future, more elaborate, quantum simulations. In the first experiment, we implemented the QB followed its inverse, to benchmark implementation accuracy. Subsequent experiments involved the implementation of perturbations both unitary, least-bit rotations, and non-unitary, application of a magnetic field gradient, between iterations of the QB. The experiments show that the baker's map is not sensitive to the least-bit rotation perturbation, though it is sensitive to other perturbations. The results of the nonunitary perturbation experiment are in line with the conjecture of Zurek and Paz[7] that, when decohered, quantum chaotic systems produce entropy at a rate given by the classical map's Lyapunov exponent.

In addition to the quantum baker's map, which is an example of a quantized version of a classical map, we would like to study quantum chaos on a purely quantum level without having to rely on classical correspondence. To this aim, we used maps with circular unitary ensemble (CUE) random matrix statistics, that are easy to implement and, by construction, exhibit the full complexity and fulfill the statistical properties of a random unitary operator. These maps serve as paradigmatic systems with which to study aspects of quantum chaos.

A subset of these maps may be chosen for being implementable on today's NMR-based quantum information processors. These maps consist of only a few gates and, though they operate on a low-dimensional Hilbert space, the statistics of a group of these maps can be concatenated and tested against the expected statistics for random matrices.

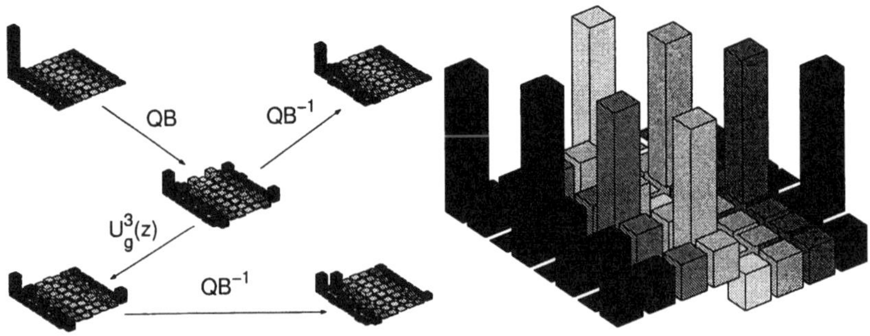

Figure 1. The left figure shows the real part of the experimental density matrices that show the effects of perturbations on a baker's map. The density matrices are in the computational basis. The first row (column) is $|000\rangle$ the next $|001\rangle$ until $|111\rangle$. We start with an initial $|000\rangle$ pseudo-pure state (top left) and implement the baker's map (center). This is followed by an inverse iteration of the map (top right). To test the effect of perturbations we apply a spatially dependent magnetic field gradient along the z-direction $U_g^3(z) = \exp(\frac{ikz}{2}\sigma_z^3)$, where z is the spatial coordinate and k is a wave-number. This introduces a spatially dependent phase that mimics decoherence. The effect of the gradient on the third qubit after one iteration of the baker's map is shown (bottom left). This is followed by an inverse iteration of the map (bottom right). The effect of this perturbation is to produce one bit of information, consistent with the hypothesis of Ref. 7 (see text). The right figure is the real part of the baker's map operator.

Easily implementable operations for NMR quantum information are rotations and nearest neighbor couplings. Therefore, to produce random maps that can be implemented on simple NMR quantum information processors, random rotations and couplings between nearest neighbor qubits are strung together. Figure 3 shows the statistics of a group of 10 three qubit random maps, each map consisting of 8 random rotations and 7 coupling periods.

In conclusion, we have taken a first step toward simulation of quantum chaos on quantum information processors. The quantum baker's map has already been implemented and basic schemes to observe phenomena related to quantum chaos have been tested in rudimentary form. Experiments such as these establish a foundation for further experimental investigations of quantum chaotic dynamics and the exploration of theoretical approaches to quantum chaos. We also introduce random maps that allow the study of quantum chaos without the need to invoke classical mechanics and allow for simulations of quantum chaos on NMR quantum information processors.

The authors thank M. A. Pravia and E. M. Fortunato for help with experiments and J. P. Paz for helpful discussions. This work was supported by DARPA/MTO through ARO grant DAAG55-97-1-0342 and by the Cambridge-MIT Institute.

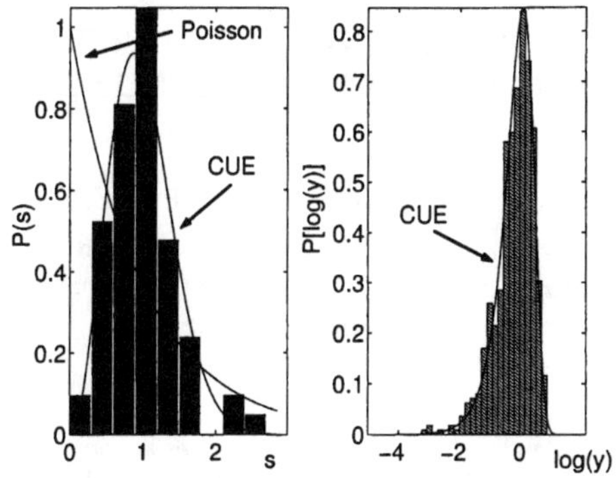

Figure 2. Statistics for a group of 10 'NMR friendly' random maps. Nearest neighbor energy eigenvalue statistics (left) compared to the expected CUE and Poisonnian (for regular maps) curves, s is the nearest neighbor spacing. The eigenvector statistics (right) compared to the expected CUE, y is the magnitude of an element of an eigenvector.

References

1. R. J. Nelson, D. G. Cory, and S. Lloyd, Phys. Rev. A **61**, 022106 (2000).
2. S. Somaroo, C. H. Tseng, T. F. Havel, R. Laflamme, and D. G. Cory, Phys. Rev. Lett. **82**, 5381 (1999).
3. Y. S. Weinstein, S. Lloyd, J. V. Emerson, and D. G. Cory, to appear in Phys. Rev. Lett.
4. A. J. Lichtenberg and M. A. Lieberman *Regular and Chaotic Dynamics* (Springer Verlag, 1992).
5. A. Peres, in *Quantum Chaos, Quantum Measurement* edited by H. A. Cerdeira, R. Ramaswamy, M. C. Gutzwiller, and G. Casati (World Scientific, Singapore, 1991); A. Peres, *Quantum Theory: Concepts and Methods* (Kluwer, Dordecht, 1993).
6. R. Schack and C. M. Caves, Phys. Rev. Lett. **71** 525 (1993); R. Schack, G. M. D'Ariano, and C. M. Caves, Phys. Rev. E **50**, 972 (1994).
7. W. H. Zurek and J. P. Paz, Physica D **83**, 300 (1995).
8. F. Haake, *Quantum Signatures of Chaos* (Springer, New York, 1991).
9. O. Bohigas, M. J. Giannoni, and C. Schmit, Phys. Rev. Lett. **52**, 1 (1984).
10. F. Haake and K. Zyczkowski, Phys. Rev. A **42**, 1013 (1990).
11. N. L. Balazs and A. Voros, Ann. Phys. **190**, (1989); M. Saraceno, Ann. Phys. **199**, 37 (1990).
12. D. Coppersmith, IBM Research Report RC19642 (1994).
13. R. Schack, Phys. Rev. A **57**, 1634 (1998).
14. Y. S. Weinstein, M. A. Pravia, E. M. Fortunato, S. Lloyd, and D. G. Cory, Phys. Rev. Lett. **86**, 1889 (2001).

NEW SUMMING ALGORITHM USING ENSEMBLE COMPUTING

C. D'HELON AND V. PROTOPOPESCU
Center for Engineering Science Advanced Research,
Computer Science and Mathematics Division,
Oak Ridge National Laboratory,
Oak Ridge, TN 37831-6355 USA

We propose an ensemble algorithm that provides a new approach for summing up a set of function samples. The query complexity of the algorithm depends only on the scaling of the measurement sensitivity with the number of distinct spin sub-ensembles. From a practical point of view, the proposed algorithm may result in an exponential speedup, compared to known quantum and classical summing algorithms.

In this paper, we propose an ensemble algorithm for evaluating and summing an arbitrary function, as an alternative to the quantum algorithms that are currently believed to be the most efficient algorithms available in terms of query complexity.

To date, a handful of quantum algorithms have been proposed to solve specific mathematical problems much faster than the best available classical algorithms. Among them, Shor's prime factoring algorithm[1] and Grover's unsorted search algorithm[2] are the best known, as they address problems of direct practical relevance.

The possibility of speeding up the evaluation and summing of a large number of function samples was first noted by Abrams and Williams,[3] who suggested calculating numerical integrals and stochastic processes using quantum algorithms. Quantum algorithms exploit the inherent parallelism offered by entangled quantum states, to perform certain computational tasks much more efficiently than classical devices, using either *pure* or *pseudopure* quantum states[4,5] that are tensor products of multiple qubits. The numerical value of an integral is evaluated by employing either the mean estimation algorithm devised by Grover[6] to calculate the mean of a discrete set of numbers, or by using the quantum counting algorithm proposed by Brassard, Hoyer, and Tapp[7] to determine the number of elements that fulfill a specified condition. Both of these approaches rely on a generalization of Grover's search algorithm, resulting in a quadratic speedup in comparison with classical randomized (Monte Carlo) algorithms, and an exponential speedup in comparison with classical deterministic algorithms for a single processor.

An alternative paradigm for computing has been suggested by Bruschweiler *et al.*,[8] which operates on ensembles i.e., mixed states of identical spin systems. This exploits the parallelism available by acting simultaneously on linear combinations of many different input states in an ensemble of spins.

This type of parallelism is classical in nature, though the evolution of the spin systems is governed by quantum dynamics. In contrast, quantum computing with pure states relies on the parallelism of entangled states, to perform operations in a Hilbert space that is the tensor product of multiple qubits.

Although requiring an exponentially larger set of memory resources to encode the same number of distinct input states, ensemble computing can accommodate decoherence times that are exponentially shorter than that for an equivalent computation involving entangled states. Ensemble algorithms can also be exponentially faster, for adequate measurement sensitivities e.g., Bruschweiler[9] has proposed a new strategy for searching an unsorted database, using the ensemble computing paradigm in the context of NMR technology. The ensemble search algorithm employs binary partition of the N elements in the database, to find the desired element after $O(log(N))$ oracle queries.

We present a new approach to summing up function samples, using an ensemble algorithm, and discuss its query complexity. The algorithm has three main steps. The first step consists of preparing an ensemble mixture of N input states representing the sampling domain. In the second step a function f is applied to the input states, using a single transformation U_f to perform the function evaluation for every input state at once. This parallel application results in an ensemble mixture, which contains all of the function values in the output register. Finally, measurement of the output register automatically averages the contributions from the entire ensemble, giving a signal proportional to the sum of the function samples S_f.

Up to this point, the query complexity of the proposed algorithm is one i.e., only one function evaluation is required. If the measurement sensitivity of the experiment is adequate to distinguish between distinct normalized output signals with a precision equal to or better than $1/N$, then only one run of the algorithm is required to determine the sum S_f. In this case, the ensemble summing algorithm may give an exponential speedup over all known quantum and classical summing algorithms. For a signal-to-noise ratio SNR $\approx 10^4$ in an NMR implementation, the measurement sensitivity is adequate to allow a single application of the ensemble summing algorithm for up to ≈ 100 function samples.

However as the number of sample points N increases, the measurement sensitivity eventually becomes inadequate. Thus significant differences between normalized output signals, differences as small as $1/N$, will not be detectable in a single experimental trial. To enhance the sensitivity, the algorithm is repeated a number of times. For example, in an NMR implementation the proposed algorithm will have to be repeated N^2 times, taking into account the square-root scaling of the signal-to-noise ratio with the number of experimental trials.

The ensemble summing algorithm has an exponential advantage in terms of query complexity, relative to the implementation of the quantum summing algorithm using Grover's search algorithm with pseudopure states in

NMR, as the two algorithms have the same scaling for the measurement sensitivity. Similarly, the query complexity of the ensemble search algorithm is exponentially smaller than that required for Grover's search algorithm using pseudopure states in NMR.

However a comparison with the (theoretical) implementation of Grover's search algorithm using pure states shows that the ensemble summing algorithm will be more efficient only for a total number of samples below a threshold value determined by the measurement sensitivity. The threshold value for the number of function samples, N_t, is given by $N_t \approx (\text{SNR})^{4/3}$.

Finally we note, that the ensemble summing algorithm presented here is applicable to estimating the mean of a continuous function, or the definite integral of a continuous multi-dimensional function.

Acknowledgments

This research was partly supported by the U.S. Department of Energy, Office of Basic Energy Sciences. The Oak Ridge National Laboratory is managed for the U.S. DOE by UT-Battelle, LLC, under contract No. DE-AC05-00OR22725.

References

1. P. Shor, *Proceedings of the 35th Annual Symposium on Foundations of Computer Science*, ed. S. Goldwasser (IEEE Computer Society, Los Alamitos, CA, 1994).
2. L. K. Grover, Phys. Rev. Lett. **79**, 325 (1997).
3. D. S. Abrams and C. P. Williams, quant-ph/9908083.
4. D. P. DiVincenzo, quant-ph/0002077.
5. L. M. K. Vandersypen, M. Steffen, G. Breyta, C. S. Yannoni, M. H. Sherwood and I. L. Chuang, Nature **414**, 883 (2001).
6. L. K. Grover, quant-ph/9711043.
7. G. Brassard, P. Hoyer and A. Tapp, Lect. Notes in Comp. Science **1443**, 820 (1998).
8. Z. L. Madi, R. Bruschweiler and R. R. Ernst, J. Chem. Phys. **109**, 10603 (1998).
9. R. Bruschweiler, Phys. Rev. Lett. **85**, 4815 (2000).

SHORTENING GROVER'S SEARCH ALGORITHM FOR AN EXPECTATION-VALUE QUANTUM COMPUTER

DAVID COLLINS

Department of Physics, Carnegie Mellon University, Pittsburgh PA 15213
Email: collins5@andrew.cmu.edu

Quantum algorithms are conventionally formulated for implementation on a single system of qubits amenable to projective measurements. However, in expectation-value quantum computation, such as nuclear magnetic resonance realizations, the computer consists of an ensemble of identical qubit-systems amenable only to expectation value measurements. The prevalent strategy in such expectation value implementations of quantum algorithms has been to retain the conventional formulation's unitary operations but modify its initialization and measurement steps appropriately. This naive approach is not optimal for Grover's algorithm and a shortened version for expectation-value quantum computers is presented.

Quantum algorithms[1] are usually formulated with the idea that each will be implemented on single quantum system amenable to projective measurements. In contrast, most experimental implementations have used room-temperature, solution-state NMR, which involves an ensemble of non-interacting identical quantum computers and for which the only measurement outcomes available are expectation values of observables.[2,3,4] Consequently, quantum algorithms have been adapted for such expectation-value quantum computers by modifying the preparation and measurement stages.[2,5] However, these adaptations have been constructed so that the expectation-value quantum computer mimics its single quantum system relative as closely as possible. As such, they do not use the multiple identical quantum computers in the ensemble advantageously. In this article we show how the ensemble can be used to shorten Grover's search algorithm for expectation-value quantum computers (a more detailed description appears elsewhere[6]).

We consider an expectation-value quantum computer, consisting of an ensemble of identical, non-interacting quantum computers that (i) can be prepared in any pure or pseudopure initial state,[2,5] (ii) to which any unitary transformation can be applied, and (iii) for which the expectation value (EV) of $\sigma_z(k)$ can be measured for each qubit (labeled by k). This is the case with current NMR realizations.

The standard translation of a quantum algorithm to a form suitable for an expectation value quantum computer can be illustrated via Grover's algorithm for searching a database containing a single marked item in one of N possible locations (for convenience assume that $N = 2^L$ for some integer L; this is not a severe restriction). The database will be represented as $X = \{0, 1, \ldots, N-1\}$ and the search proceeds with the aid of the following oracle, invoked at unit cost: $f(x) = 0$ if $x \neq s$ and $f(x) = 1$ if $x = s$ where s denotes the marked item's location. A classical sequential search requires

$N/2$ oracle queries on average to locate the marked item correctly. A quantum algorithm[1,7] uses an L-qubit data register and an oracle unitary operation, defined on the computational basis states as $\hat{U}_f |x\rangle := (-1)^{f(x)} |x\rangle$ and extended linearly to superpositions of these. The data register is initialized to $|\psi_i\rangle := (1/\sqrt{2^L}) \sum_{x=0}^{2^L-1} |x\rangle$, followed by repeated applications of the Grover iterate $\hat{G} := \hat{D}\hat{U}_f$. Here $\hat{D}\left(\sum_{x=0}^{N-1} c_x |x\rangle\right) := \sum_{x=0}^{N-1} (-c_x + 2\langle c\rangle) |x\rangle$, where $\langle c\rangle = \sum_{x=0}^{N-1} c_x/N$. After m applications of $\hat{G}$, the data register's state is[8]

$$|\psi\rangle = \sin\left[(2m+1)\theta/2\right] |s\rangle + \frac{\cos\left[(2m+1)\theta/2\right]}{\sqrt{N-1}} \sum_{x \neq s} |x\rangle, \tag{1}$$

where $\cos(\theta) = 1 - 2/N$. After $\lfloor \pi/2\theta \rfloor$ applications of $\hat{G}$ the system's state is approximately $|\psi\rangle = |s\rangle$; a projective measurement (PM) in the computational basis would yield s with probability of error, which we henceforth ignore, at most $1/N$. For $N \gg 1$, $\theta \approx 2\sqrt{1/N}$ and the algorithm requires about $\lfloor \sqrt{N}\ \pi/4 \rfloor$ oracle invocations to locate the marked item with near certainty, giving a quadratic speedup over the classical sequential search. To convert between PM and EV outcomes note that, when $|\psi\rangle = |s\rangle$, $\langle \sigma_z(k)\rangle := \langle\psi| \sigma_z(k) |\psi\rangle = (-1)^{s_k}$, where $s = s_L \ldots s_1$ is the binary representation of s. This reveals the marked item if it is possible to distinguish between $\langle \sigma_z(k)\rangle = +1$ and $\langle \sigma_z(k)\rangle = -1$ for each qubit. This *standard EV version* of Grover's algorithm has been used in all NMR realizations to date.

What is crucial for the success of the above translation is that the sign of $\langle \sigma_z(k)\rangle$ for each qubit can be determined. This depends only on which PM outcome would be more likely: positive or negative for PM outcomes 0 or 1 respectively. Therefore, for expectation-value quantum computers, it is not essential that the state prior to measurement be $|s\rangle$, but rather one for which the most likely PM outcome is s. This can be attained with $m < \lfloor \sqrt{N}\ \pi/4 \rfloor$ applications of $\hat{G}$, in which case Eq. (1) yields

$$\langle \sigma_z(k)\rangle = (-1)^{s_k} A_m, \tag{2}$$

where the *EV attenuation*

$$A_m := \frac{\sin^2\left[(2m+1)\theta/2\right] N - 1}{N-1} \tag{3}$$

determines the magnitude of the EV. The EV attenuation increases monotonically with respect to m from 0, prior to any applications of $\hat{G}$, to approximately 1 in the case of the standard EV version. This leads to a *truncated EV version* of Grover's algorithm, which is identical to the standard EV version *except that it terminates after the minimum number of applications of* $\hat{G}$ *such that it is still possible to distinguish reliably between* $\langle \sigma_z(k)\rangle > 0$ *and* $\langle \sigma_z(k)\rangle < 0$ *for all data-register qubits.* In an ideal case (i.e., an infinitely large ensemble and infinitely precise measurements) the truncated EV version succeeds after one application of $\hat{G}$. In practice, noise and statistical limitations effectively establish a threshold EV attenuation, A_{th}, below which the sign of the EV cannot be discerned reliably; the algorithm then succeeds when $A_m > A_{\text{th}}$. The threshold will depend on experimental details, but for many practical expectation-value quantum computers it will be possible to truncate the algorithm compared to the standard EV version.

Searching a database containing more than one marked item is complicated by the fact that the standard version of Grover's algorithm is not deterministic. Here, after about $\lfloor\sqrt{N/M}\,\pi/4\rfloor$ applications of $\hat{G}$, the data register is approximately in the state $|\psi_f\rangle = 1/\sqrt{M}\sum_{x\in S}|x\rangle$, where M is the number of marked items and S denotes the set of their locations.[1] A PM will yield the location of one of the marked items with certainty. However, the bitwise EV technique described earlier may fail in some cases, because averaging over more than one possible database location can produce devastating cancellations.[6] One way to avoid this and still incorporate the truncation described above is to use a *filtered EV* technique, based on iterated runs of the algorithm. The iteration step produces the $k+1$ bit of a marked item's location, if the first k bits have been determined to be $s_k, s_{k-1}, \ldots, s_1$, by combining the EVs of two runs of the algorithm. In the first, the algorithm is run without modification, whereas in the second a *correlation operation* $\hat{C}_{k+1}(s_k,\ldots,s_1)$ is inserted between the last application of $\hat{G}$ and the EV measurements, where

$$\hat{C}_{k+1}(s_k,\ldots,s_1)\,|x_L\ldots x_1\rangle := (\sigma_x(k+1))^{g(x_k\ldots x_1)}\,|x_L\ldots x_1\rangle\,, \tag{4}$$

with

$$g(x_k\ldots x_1) := (x_k\oplus s_k\oplus 1)(x_{k-1}\oplus s_{k-1}\oplus 1)\ldots(x_1\oplus s_2\oplus 1)\oplus 1. \tag{5}$$

Averaging the EVs obtained from the two runs gives[6]

$$\langle\sigma_z(k+1)\rangle_{\text{ave}} = \frac{1}{M}\sum_{x\in S'}(-1)^{x_{k+1}}, \tag{6}$$

identical to an EV performed on $(1/\sqrt{M})\sum_{x\in S'}|x\rangle$ where $S' := \{x\in S : x_k = s_k,\ldots,x_1 = s_1\}$, and whose sign gives s_{k+1} for some marked item whose first k bits are $s_k, s_{k-1},\ldots,s_1$. The process is initiated by inspecting the sign of $\langle\sigma_z(1)\rangle$, giving s_1 for a marked item. The entire filtering procedure requires $\log_2(N)$ runs of the algorithm and $O([\log_2(N)]^2)$ operations to compute g for all stages. Note that the amplitude of the EV scales as $1/M$ and thus for a given experimental realization there will be a threshold (in M) beyond which this scheme fails. We only consider cases in which M lies beneath this threshold.

The truncated EV version of Grover's algorithm for one marked item is extended to multiple marked items if the filtering scheme described above is used. After m applications of $\hat{G}$,

$$\langle\sigma_z(k)\rangle_{\text{ave}} = \frac{A_m}{M} \sum_{x \in S'} (-1)^{x_k}, \tag{7}$$

where S' includes filtering conditions, the EV attenuation is

$$A_m = \frac{\sin^2\left[(2m+1)\theta/2\right] N - M}{N - M}, \tag{8}$$

and the algorithm can be terminated whenever $A_m > A_{\text{th}}$. The reduction in the number of applications of $\hat{G}$ depends on the actual threshold EV attenuation, A_{th}, and the maximum tolerable threshold EV attenuation, $A_{\text{stand}} = 1/M$, for the standard EV version[6]. The minimum number of applications in a truncated EV version is

$$m_{\text{trunc}} \approx m_{\text{stand}} \frac{2}{\pi} \arcsin\left[\sqrt{A_{\text{th}}/A_{\text{stand}} + (1 - A_{\text{th}}/A_{\text{stand}})M/N}\right], \tag{9}$$

where m_{stand} is the number of applications of $\hat{G}$ required for the standard EV version.[6]

Whenever a quantum computing device only offers expectation value outcomes, then the truncated version of Grover's algorithm is superior to the standard version. Here the ensemble's ability to produce decisive expectation values may be used advantageously and a naive translation from the single quantum system version of an algorithm is not always optimal. The extent to which this is applicable to other algorithms is not clear, and would be a worthwhile issue to investigate.

The author would like to thank Bob Griffiths for many useful discussions. This work was supported by NSF grants 9900755 and 0139974.

References

1. M. A. Nielsen and I. L. Chuang, *Quantum Computation and Quantum Information* (Cambridge University Press, Cambridge, 2000).
2. I. L. Chuang, N. Gershenfeld, M. G. Kubinec, and D. W. Leung, Proc. R. Soc. Lond. A **454**, 447 (1998).
3. L. M. K. Vandersypen, M. Steffen, M. H. Sherwood,C. S. Yannoni, G. Breyta, and I. L. Chuang, App. Phys. Lett. **76**, 646 (2000).
4. L. M. K. Vandersypen, M. Steffen, G. Breyta, C. S. Yannoni, M. H. Sherwood, and I. L. Chuang, Nature **414**, 883 (2001).
5. D. G. Cory, M. D. Price, and T. F. Havel, Physica D **120**, 82 (1998).
6. D. Collins, Phys. Rev. A **65**, 052321 (2002).
7. L. K. Grover, Phys. Rev. Lett. **79**, 325 (1997).
8. M. Boyer, G. Brassard, P. Høyer, and A. Tapp, Fortschr. Phys. **46**, 493 (1998).

ENTROPY-ENERGY BALANCE IN NOISY QUANTUM COMPUTERS

MAXIM RAGINSKY

Center for Photonic Communication and Computing, ECE Department
Northwestern University, 2145 N. Sheridan Rd., Evanston, IL 60208-3118, USA
E-mail: maxim@ece.northwestern.edu

We use entropy-energy arguments to assess the limitations on the running time and on the system size, as measured in qubits, of noisy macroscopic circuit-based quantum computers.

Quantum information is essentially a nonequilibrium theory in the sense that its basic primitives are decomposed into temporal sequences of local operations that are performed on physical systems driven far from equilibrium. The requirement of locality becomes all the more important when we consider quantum information processing in macroscopic systems (multi-qubit quantum computers), because local operations will be used to model both the computation proper and the errors affecting it.

An important issue to address is the stability of a macroscopic quantum computer (MQC) in the presence of noise. There are two notions of stability for quantum-mechanical states,[1] namely *global* and *local thermodynamic stability.* For a microscopic system (i.e., one with finitely many degrees of freedom) these are equivalent and amount to the following. Let H be the system Hamiltonian, β the inverse temperature. Then a state (density operator) ρ is thermodynamically stable (both globally and locally) if it minimizes the free energy functional $F_\beta(\rho) = \mathrm{tr}\,(\rho H) - (1/\beta)S(\rho)$, where $S(\rho) = -\,\mathrm{tr}\,(\rho \ln \rho)$ is the von Neumann entropy. However, the two stability notions are rather different for systems with infinitely many degrees of freedom. A state ρ is globally thermodynamically stable (GTS) if it minimizes the specific free energy (i.e., free energy "per particle"), and locally thermodynamically stable (LTS) if no *local* modification of it yields a state with lower specific free energy. It can be shown that any GTS state is also LTS, but the converse is generally false.

States that are LTS but not GTS are referred to as *metastable states.*[1] An apt example comes from laser physics. Imagine an active medium consisting of a large number of three-level atoms with the states $|0\rangle, |1\rangle, |2\rangle$, each atom initially in the ground state $|0\rangle$. The atoms are pumped to the level $|2\rangle$, and then decay nonradiatively to $|1\rangle$. This results in a relatively long-lived metastable state of population inversion. As far as MQC's are concerned, we are interested mainly in their metastable states, and the goal of error correction (and of judicious MQC design in general) is to preserve metastability for the duration of the computation. Specifically, we can isolate two separate aspects of (meta)stability for MQC's — temporal and spatial. The former refers to the maximum number of operations that can be carried out on a noisy MQC using given energy resources, whereas the latter is related to the maximum number of qubits that can be processed reliably on a noisy MQC. We will address these two issues using entropy-energy arguments,[2] a standard technique in statistical physics. Due to lack of space, our presentation will be rather sketchy; we will supply the details in a separate paper.[3] We note that even though we consider *macroscopic systems*, there is no need to pass to the thermodynamic limit because we are concerned with *local* thermodynamic stability.

First of all, let us fix a model of an N-qubit quantum computer. We may imagine its operation as a sequence of alternating computation and noise steps. For a circuit-based QC, a computation step is an application of a tensor product of one- and two-qubit universal quantum gates, and a noise step is described by a general trace-preserving completely-positive linear map T on density matrices. We will henceforth refer to such maps as channels (note that any unitary transformation is an instance of a channel). Specifically, if $\mathcal{H} \simeq \mathbb{C}^2$ is a single-qubit Hilbert space, then the state of the N-qubit computer is a density operator ρ on $\mathcal{H}^{\otimes N}$. The composition of a computation step and a noise step is a mapping $\rho \mapsto T(U\rho U^*)$, where U is unitary. We adopt the model of local stochastic noise,[4] so that T can be written in the form $(1-\epsilon)\,\mathrm{id} + \epsilon R^{\otimes N}$, where id is the identity channel, R is a channel on 2×2 density matrices, and ϵ is a small positive number that quantifies the noise strength.

We make two simplifying assumptions. The first one is needed for the analysis of the temporal stability and concerns the noisy channel R. Namely, we will take R to be bistochastic, i.e., $R(\mathbf{1}) = \mathbf{1}$, and strictly contractive,[5] which means that there exists a constant $C \in [0,1)$ (called the *contraction rate*) such that, for any two density operators ρ, σ, $\|R(\rho) - R(\sigma)\|_1 \leq C\,\|\rho - \sigma\|_1$, where $\|X\|_1 = \mathrm{tr}\,|X|$ is the trace norm. For instance, the much studied depolarizing channel, $R(\rho) = (1-\lambda)\rho + \lambda \mathbf{1}/2$ for some $\lambda \in [0,1)$, fits this description. Our second assumption, necessary only for the analysis of the spatial stability, states that the number of gates applied during any computation step is bounded by a positive number K that depends only on the particular algorithm, but not on the number of qubits n. This means that our analysis will be inapplicable to highly parallelized computation.[6]

We will rely upon the following two theorems, the proofs of which are given elsewhere.[3,7]

Theorem 1. Consider the channel $R_N = R^{\otimes N}$, where R is a bistochastic strictly contractive channel on 2×2 density matrices with contraction rate C. Then, for any $2^N \times 2^N$ density matrix ρ and any positive integer m, we have $S[R_N^m(\rho)] - S(\rho) \geq \frac{1-C^{2m}}{2}\,\|\rho - 2^{-N}\mathbf{1}\|_2^2$, where $S(\rho) = -\,\mathrm{tr}\,(\rho \ln \rho)$ is the von Neumann entropy and $\|X\|_2 = \sqrt{\mathrm{tr}(X^*X)}$ is the Hilbert-Schmidt norm of the operator X.

Theorem 2. Let ρ_i, $i = 1, \dots, n$, be n mutually commuting density operators. Suppose that there exists a constant $\kappa \geq 0$ such that, for any i, $\sum_{j \neq i} \mathrm{tr}\,(\rho_j \rho_i) \leq \kappa$. Let $\rho = n^{-1} \sum_{i=1}^{n} \rho_i$. Then $S(\rho) \geq n^{-1} \sum_{i=1}^{n} S(\rho_i) + \ln(n) - 2\sqrt{\kappa}$.

Let us first consider temporal stability. Suppose that our computer operates on N qubits, and that we are given "energy resources" E (this parameter could be determined, e.g., from the so-called "control Hamiltonian" representation of quantum computation[8]). We are interested in the entropy increase after m steps of noisy computation. Since entropy can only be produced by the channel T and not by the unitarily implemented gates, the entropy gain is given by $\Delta S(\rho, m) \equiv S[T^m(\rho)] - S(\rho)$, where ρ is the initial state of the computer. Now $T^m = \sum_{j=0}^{m} \binom{m}{j} (1-\epsilon)^{m-j} \epsilon^j R_N^j$, where $R_N = R^{\otimes N}$, so that by concavity of the von Neumann entropy we have $\Delta S(\rho, m) \geq \sum_{j=0}^{m} \binom{m}{j} (1-\epsilon)^{m-j} \epsilon^j \left\{ S[R_N^j(\rho)] - S(\rho) \right\}$. Using Theorem 1 we can write

$$\Delta S(\rho, m) \geq \zeta_{\rho,N} \sum_{j=0}^{m} \binom{m}{j} (1-\epsilon)^{m-j} \epsilon^j (1 - C^{2j}), \tag{1}$$

where $\zeta_{\rho,N} \in [0, (2^N - 1)/2^{N+1}]$ depends only on ρ and N. Carrying out the summation in (1) we obtain

$$\Delta S(\rho, m) \geq \zeta_{\rho,N} \left\{ 1 - [1 - \epsilon(1 - C^2)]^m \right\} = \zeta_{\rho,N} m \epsilon (1 - C^2) + o(\epsilon), \tag{2}$$

where $o(\epsilon)$ stands for terms that go to zero faster than ϵ as $\epsilon \to 0$ and therefore can be neglected when ϵ is sufficiently small. The corresponding free-energy shift is $\Delta F_\beta(\rho, m) \equiv E - (1/\beta) \Delta S(\rho, m)$, where β is the inverse temperature. It is now easy to see from the estimate (2) that $\Delta F_\beta(\rho, m)$ will be negative for all $m \geq \bar{\zeta}_{\rho,N,T} \beta E$, where $\bar{\zeta}_{\rho,N,T}$ is a constant that depends on ρ, N, and T. In other words, the state of the MQC will not be metastable for large enough m, or, to put it bluntly, the MQC will "crash" after $O(\beta E)$ operations. However, because the produced entropy may be at least partially drained off by error correction, this estimate merely tells us how often it should be carried out.

We pass now to spatial stability. We note that in a circuit-based computer each computational step is an application of a bounded number of universal quantum gates, and the initial state of the computer may be taken separable without loss of generality. Therefore at every instant of the computation the set $\{1, \dots, N\}$ can be partitioned into L disjoint clusters $C_1, \dots, C_L$, so that the state of the computer has the form $\rho = \bigotimes_{l=1}^{L} \rho^{(l)}$, where $\rho^{(l)}$ is the state of the qubits in the lth cluster.[4] Let us suppose for simplicity that the clusters all have the same size d, so that the computer operates on $N = Ld$ qubits. Let us partition the set $\{C_1, \dots, C_L\}$ into n disjoint blocks $S_1, \dots, S_n$, each of which contains k clusters; thus $N = nkd$. Now, for each $i = 1, \ldots, n$, define T_i to be the channel that acts as a depolarizing channel $\sigma \mapsto (1-\lambda)\sigma + \lambda \mathbf{I}/2^d$ on the state of each of the clusters in S_i and leaves the remaining clusters intact. Then $\rho_i \equiv T_i(\rho)$ are n mutually commuting density operators for which we have the elementary estimate

$$\mathrm{tr}\left(\sum_{j \neq i} \rho_j \rho_i\right) \leq (n-1)\left(1 - \lambda + \frac{\lambda}{2^d}\right)^{2k}. \tag{3}$$

Note that for fixed n, λ, and d we can always choose k so large that the right-hand side of (3) is bounded above by unity. Thus the conditions of Theorem 2 are satisfied with $\kappa = 1$, and the entropy gain due to the channel $T \equiv n^{-1} \sum_{i=1}^{n} T_i$ is $O(\ln n)$. Because the energy shift due to T depends only on the number K of gates applied during each computational step, the free-energy shift will be negative for large enough n. We may thus conclude that the number of qubits that can be processed reliably (that is, kept in a metastable state) in a MQC is bounded from above as $O(e^{\beta E})$, where β is the inverse temperature, and E depends on K.

To summarize, we have shown that there exist upper bounds on the running time and on the size (in qubits) of circuit-based noisy MQC's. However, these constraints become significant only when βE is small (as in, e.g., ensemble quantum computation using NMR). Furthermore, our analysis applies only to circuit-based computers without parallelization; massively parallel non-circuit models, such as the "one-way quantum computer" of Briegel and Raussendorf,[9] are likely to be intrinsically thermodynamically stable.

Acknowledgments

This work was supported by the U.S. Army Research Office and by the Defense Advanced Research Projects Agency.

References

1. G. L. Sewell, *Quantum Theory of Collective Phenomena* (Clarendon Press, Oxford, 1986).
2. B. Simon and D. A. Sokal, *J. Stat. Phys.* **25**, 679 (1981).
3. M. Raginsky, in preparation.
4. D. Aharonov, *Phys. Rev. A* **62**, 062311 (2000).
5. M. Raginsky, *Phys. Rev. A* **65**, 032306 (2002).
6. C. Moore and M. Nilsson, *SIAM J. Comput.* **31**, 799 (2001).
7. M. Raginsky, *J. Phys. A: Math. Gen.* **35**, L585-L590 (2002).
8. G. Ortiz, J. E. Gubernatis, E. Knill, and R. Laflamme, *Phys. Rev. A* **64**, 022319 (2001).
9. H. J. Briegel and R. Raussendorf, *Phys. Rev. Lett.* **86**, 5188 (2001).

RAPID DATA SEARCH USING ADIABATIC QUANTUM COMPUTATION

DARIA AHRENSMEIER,[♯] SAURYA DAS,[♭] * RANDY KOBES,[♯]
GABOR KUNSTATTER,[♯] AND HAITHAM ZARAKET[♯]

[♯] *Dept. of Physics and The Winnipeg Institute for Theoretical Physics*
The University of Winnipeg,
515 Portage Avenue, Winnipeg, MB - R3B 2E9, CANADA
E-mail: dahrens,randy,gabor,zaraket@theory.uwinnipeg.ca

[♭] *Dept. of Mathematics and Statistics,*
University of New Brunswick, Fredericton, NB - E3B 5A3, CANADA
E-mail: saurya@math.unb.ca

We show that, by a suitable choice of time-dependent Hamiltonian, the search for a marked item in an unstructured database can be achieved in unit time, using adiabatic quantum computation. This is a considerable improvement over the $\mathcal{O}(\sqrt{N})$ time required in previous algorithms. The trade-off is that in the intermediate stages of the computation process, the ground state energy of the computer increases to a maximum of $\mathcal{O}(\sqrt{N})$, before returning to zero at the end of the process.

1 Adiabatic Quantum Computation

Adiabatic quantum computation (AQC) is a new paradigm in quantum computation, in which an initial state $|\Psi_0\rangle$ is *adiabatically* transformed into a final state $|\Psi_1\rangle$ by means of a time-dependent Hamiltonian:[1]

$$H(s) = f(s)H_0 + g(s)H_1 \tag{1}$$
$$\text{where} \quad H_0 = I - |\Psi_0\rangle\langle\Psi_0| \tag{2}$$
$$H_1 = I - |\Psi_1\rangle\langle\Psi_1| \tag{3}$$

($s(t)$ is a time-like parameter, which monotonically increases with time t, such that $s(0) = 0$ and $s(T) = 1$, where T is the required running time of the AQC). The boundary conditions on $f(s)$ and $g(s)$ are as follows:

$$f(0) = g(1) = 1 \quad , \quad f(1) = g(0) = 0 \ . \tag{4}$$

Note that $|\Psi_0\rangle$ and $|\Psi_1\rangle$ are ground states of H_0 and H_1, respectively. The *adiabaticity condition*, which must be preserved at all times, is given by:

$$\frac{|\langle -|(dH/dt)|+\rangle|}{(E_+ - E_-)^2} \leq \epsilon \ , \tag{5}$$

$$\text{where} \quad |\pm\rangle = \text{ground state and first excited state}: \quad H|\pm\rangle = E_\pm|\pm\rangle \ .$$

*PRIMARY AUTHOR

The problem is to estimate the running time T for a given computational problem implemented via AQC.

2 Data Search Problem

For a completely unstructured database of N items, one would like to find a marked item (say "m") in the shortest possible time. Schematically:

$$\underbrace{|\cdot|\cdot|\cdot|\cdots \quad \overbrace{|m|}^{\text{Marked item}} \quad \cdots|\cdot|\cdot|\cdot|}_{\text{unstructured database of } N \text{ items}} \rightarrow \text{Find } m \text{ in shortest possible time}$$

Now, it is well-known that classical algorithms require $\mathcal{O}(N)$ steps on average to find m. On the other hand, it was shown by Grover that quantum mechanics can be used to quadratically speed-up the process.[2] That is, by associating each item in the database with an eigenvector in a N-dimensional Hilbert space (such that m corresponds to the ket $|m\rangle$), then starting with the symmetric superposition of all states, and applying a series of unitary operations, one can evolve to the marked state in $\mathcal{O}(\sqrt{N})$ steps.

3 Data Search Using AQC

In this case, the adiabatic Hamiltonian (1) replaces the set of unitary transformations mentioned in the previous section. The final state $|\Psi_1\rangle$ is again the marked state $|m\rangle$. Now, it can be proved, by closely following the arguments of Refs. 3,4, that the following inequality holds (see Appendix):

$$\int_0^T g(s(t)) \geq \frac{k\sqrt{N}}{4} \quad , \tag{6}$$

where k is a constant of order unity. Note that previously[4] it had been assumed that $g(s(t)) = 1 - s = 1 - f(s(t)) \leq 1 \quad \forall s$, for which the above theorem implies that the running time $T \geq k\sqrt{N}/4$ which is at par with Grover's algorithm. Result (6) can be thought of as the AQC generalization of the lower bound on the number of steps of any previously-proven search algorithm.[5]

The 'gap' between the ground state and first excited state of the Hamiltonian is given by:[6]

$$\Delta(s) = \sqrt{(f-g)^2 + \frac{4}{N} fg}. \tag{7}$$

For the choice $g = 1-f = 1-s$, this implies $\text{Min}(\Delta) = \Delta(1/2) = 1/\sqrt{N}$, which is in conformity with the general idea that the running time and minimum gap are inverses of each other. However, (6) and (7) suggest that by suitably changing $g(s(t))$, so as to increase the gap considerably, the running time can

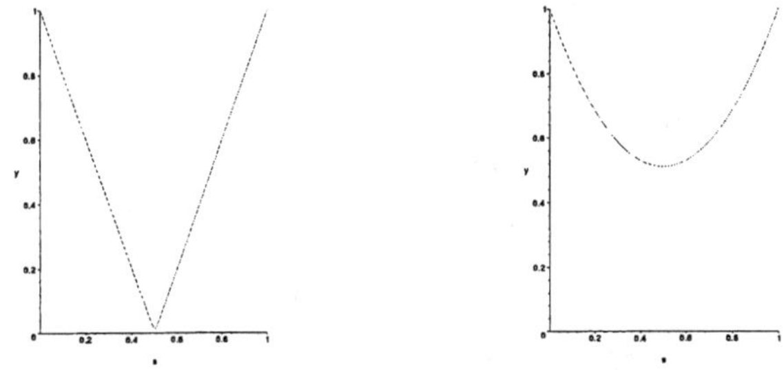

Figure 1. Original gap and modified gap Δ plotted as functions of $s : 0 \rightarrow 1$ for $N = 10,0000$

be significantly reduced. We make such a choice, which satisfies the boundary conditions (4):

$$f = 1 - s + \sqrt{N}s(1-s) \quad , \quad g = s + \sqrt{N}s(1-s) \ . \tag{8}$$

It is easy to see that for the above choice, we achieve $\mathrm{Min}(\Delta) = \mathcal{O}(1)$ and the running time is[6]

$$T = \frac{1}{\epsilon}\left(1 + \frac{\pi}{2}\right),$$

which is a constant. The original gap and the modified gap are plotted in Fig. 1 for $N = 10,000$.

4 Discussion

(1) Note that although the ground state energy rises to $\mathcal{O}(\sqrt{N})$ for intermediate times, no energy is actually being used in the process. Thus, energy need not be regarded as a resource in this context. Furthermore, by subtracting E_- from Hamiltonian (1) at all times, the resultant ground state energy can be made to vanish, without modifying the gap or the running time.
(2) Error correcting processes would presumably entail heat losses, commensurate with the second law of thermodynamics.
(3) A larger gap in our case may signal greater fault-tolerance than previously considered Hamiltonians.[7]
(4) Work is in progress towards similar considerations for structured data searches, to see whether similar speed-ups are possible.[6]

Acknowledgments

The authors would like to thank E. Farhi and S. Gutmann for useful discussions. S.D. thanks V. Husain for useful comments. This work was supported by the Natural Sciences and Engineering Research Council of Canada.

Appendix

To prove (6), first write (1) as:[3,4]

$$H(s) = H_1(s) + H_{2m}(s) \ , \tag{9}$$

where

$$H_1(s) = (f(s) + g(s)) - f(s)|\psi_0\rangle\langle\psi_0| \tag{10}$$

$$H_{2m}(s) = -g(s)|m\rangle\langle m| \ . \tag{11}$$

Consider two computers, $|\psi_m, t\rangle$ and $|\psi_{m'}, t\rangle$, respectively, at any instant t, evolving to states $|m\rangle$ and $|m'\rangle$. The Schrödinger equations are:

$$i\frac{\partial}{\partial t}|\psi_{m,m'}, t\rangle = (H_1 + H_{2m,2m'})\,|\psi_{m,m'}, t\rangle \tag{12}$$

subject to the boundary conditions:

$$|\psi_m, 0\rangle = |\psi_{m'}, 0\rangle = |\psi_0\rangle \ ; \quad |\psi_m, T\rangle = |m\rangle \ , \ |\psi_{m'}, T\rangle = |m'\rangle \quad . \tag{13}$$

From (12), it follows that:

$$\frac{\partial}{\partial t}\sum_{m,m'}\left[1 - |\langle\psi_m, t|\psi_{m'}, t\rangle^2\right] \leq 4N^{3/2}g(s) \ . \tag{14}$$

Integrating (14) from $t = 0$ to $t = T$, and using the boundary conditions (13), we get:

$$\sum_{m,m'}\left[1 - |\langle\psi_m, T|\psi_{m'}, T\rangle|^2\right] \leq 4N^{3/2}\int_0^T g(s(t))dt \ . \tag{15}$$

Finally, using the fact:

$$1 - |\langle\psi_m, T|\psi_{m'}, T\rangle|^2 \geq k \quad , \forall m \neq m', \tag{16}$$

which simply means that different computers evolve the same initial state to sufficiently different final states, we obtain (6), for $N \gg 1$.

References

1. E. Farhi, J. Goldstone, S. Gutmann, M. Sipser, quant-ph/0001106.
2. L. K. Grover, Phys. Rev. Lett. **79**, 325 (1997).
3. E. Farhi and S. Gutmann, quant-ph/9612026.
4. J. Roland and N. J. Cerf, quant-ph/0107015.
5. C. H. Bennett, E. Bernstein, G. Brassard, and U. Vazirani, quant-ph/9701001; L. K. Grover, quant-ph/9809029, quant-ph/0201052, quant-ph/0202033; A. Zalka, Phys. Rev. **A60**, 2746 (1999).
6. S. Das, R. Kobes, G. Kunstatter, quant-ph/0204044;
   D. Ahrensmeier, S. Das, R. Kobes, G. Kunstatter, and H. Zaraket, in preparation.
7. A. M. Childs, E. Farhi, and J. Preskill, quant-ph/0108048.

DYNAMICS OF QUANTUM ADIABATIC COMPUTATION

V. N. SMELYANSKIY AND D. A. TIMUÇIN

NASA Ames Research Center, Mail Stop 269-3, Moffett Field, CA 94035-1000

E-mail: {vadim,timucin}@email.arc.nasa.gov

We present an analysis of the performance of quantum adiabatic evolution algorithms (QAAs) for random combinatorial optimization problems (COPs) using a simple model of a COP that is directly related to the NP-complete Number Partitioning Problem. A key element of our approach is the problem *landscape correlation*; that is, the conditional distribution of the set of strings obtained from a given string by a fixed number of bit flips. We use this entity to describe QAA as a quantum local search and show that in our example of COP, the dynamics of the algorithm can be described as a 1D quantum diffusion process. The ground state remains extended in the energy space, thus leading to an exponential complexity for the algorithm. We discuss the possible generalizations of the presented analysis and the limitations of QAA.

1 Introduction

During last decade, there has been a rapidly growing interest in the development of quantum algorithms capable of solving classically-intractable computational problems. Perhaps the most notable examples are the combinatorial optimization problems (COPs). In the simplest case, the task in a COP is to minimize the cost function (or "energy") $E_{\mathbf{z}}$ defined on a set of 2^n binary strings $\mathbf{z} = \{z_1, \ldots, z_n\}$ $z_j = 0, 1$, each containing n bits. In quantum computation, this cost function can be represented by a Hamiltonian $H_P = \sum_{\mathbf{z}} E_{\mathbf{z}} |\mathbf{z}\rangle\langle\mathbf{z}|$, where the summation is over the 2^n states $|\mathbf{z}\rangle$ forming the computational basis of an n-qubit quantum register. By design, the ground state of H_P encodes the solution to the COP. It has been recognized[1] that many of the spin glass models in physics are in almost one-to-one correspondence with a number of computationally intractable COPs from theoretical computer science that form the NP-complete class. It is an open question whether polynomial-time quantum algorithms exist for the problems in this class.

Farhi and co-workers recently suggested a new quantum algorithm for solving COPs based on the properties of quantum adiabatic evolution.[2] In the quantum adiabatic-evolution algorithm (QAA)[2] one specifies a Hamiltonian $\mathcal{H}(t)$ that depends on time through a "control" parameter $s \equiv s(t)$:

$$\mathcal{H}(t) = H(s) \equiv (1 - s)H_D(s) + s\,H_P, \qquad s(0) = 0, \;\; s(T) = 1, \;\; H_D(T) = 0. \tag{1}$$

Here, $H_D(s)$ is a (generally time-dependent) "driver" Hamiltonian that is designed to cause transitions between the eigenstates of the "problem" Hamiltonian H_P, so that $[H_D(s), H_P] \neq 0$. The Hamiltonian $\mathcal{H}(t)$ guides the quantum evolution of the state vector $|\psi(t)\rangle$ according to the Schrödinger equation

$i\,\partial|\psi(t)\rangle\partial t = H(t)|\psi(t)\rangle$ (we let $\hbar = 1$) from $t = 0$ to $t = T$, the *run time* of the algorithm. In QAA, one prepares the initial state of the system $|\psi(0)\rangle$ to be the ground state of the driver $H_D(0)$. In the simplest case one has

$$H_D(0) = -\sum_{j=1}^{n} \sigma_x^j, \qquad |\psi(0)\rangle = 2^{-n/2} \sum_{\mathbf{z}\in\{0,1\}^n} |\mathbf{z}\rangle, \tag{2}$$

If $\mathcal{H}(t)$ is varying sufficiently slowly in time, then the wave function $|\psi(t)\rangle$ will stay close to the instantaneous (adiabatic) ground state of $\mathcal{H}(t)$ (up to a phase factor). Because $\mathcal{H}(T) = H_P$, one can retrieve the solution to the COP by making a measurement at the final moment, $t = T$. A sufficient condition for the (quasi)adiabatic evolution can be expressed in terms of the instantaneous eigenstates $|\phi_k(s)\rangle$ and eigenvalues $\lambda_k(s)$ of $H(s)$. In particular, for many practical COPs (e.g., Satisfiability), H_P typically has a number (polynomial in n) of distinct energy levels with unit inter-level separations. In those problems, a lower bound for the run-time T is determined by the minimum of the excitation energy gap during the QAA:

$$T = \mathcal{O}\left(C g_{\min}^{-2}\right), \qquad g_{\min} = \min_{0\leq s\leq 1} |\lambda_1(s) - \lambda_0(s)|, \tag{3}$$

where the problem-specific constant C scales polynomially in n. If $g(s)$ is known explicitly, then by adjusting the rate ds/dt so that it is synchronized with the time variation of $g(s)$,[4] one can relax the above condition to $T = \mathcal{O}\left(C' g_{\min}^{-1}\right)$.

The performance of this QAA has been simulated on a classical computer for several NP-complete problems using randomly generated problem instances that are believed to be computationally hard for classical algorithms.[3] Results of these simulations suggest a quadratic scaling law of the run-time of QAA with n. It was also shown[4] that the previously obtained query-complexity argument that leads to the exponential lower bound for unstructured search[5] cannot be used to rule out the polynomial-time solution of the NP-complete Satisfiability problem by QAA. However, so far there have been no studies of the effects of frustration and disorder in random COPs on the performance of QAA.

2 Classical local search and conditional cost distribution.

A key quantity that determines the dynamics of many classical local search algorithms is the following conditional distribution function (or a landscape correlation[6]):

$$\hat{P}_r(\Omega|\mathbf{z}) = \frac{1}{C_n^r} \sum_{\mathbf{z}} \delta(\Omega_{\mathbf{z}'} - \Omega)\, \delta(r - D(\mathbf{z},\mathbf{z}')), \quad C_n^r = \frac{n!}{r!(n-r)!}. \tag{4}$$

Here $D(\mathbf{z},\mathbf{z}') = \sum_{j=1}^{n} z_j(1-z_j') + (1-z_j)z_j'$ is the Hamming distance between the strings (i.e., the number of distinct bit values in) $\mathbf{z}$ and $\mathbf{z}'$. $\Omega_{\mathbf{z}}$ is a certain function of the binary string $\mathbf{z}$ that is related to the cost function, $E_{\mathbf{z}} = c(\Omega_{\mathbf{z}})$, and is an intrinsic characteristic of a given COP. In a typical variant of local search, one randomly flips r bits of the current string $\mathbf{z}$ and thus makes a transition to a new string $\mathbf{z}'$ with some probability, depending on the value of $\Omega_{\mathbf{z}'}$ that favors an overall decrease in $E_{\mathbf{z}}$.

In the simplest case, $\hat{P}_r(\Omega|\mathbf{z})$ depends on $\mathbf{z}$ only via the value of $\Omega_{\mathbf{z}}$: $\hat{P}_r(\Omega|\mathbf{z}) = P_r(\Omega|\Omega_{\mathbf{z}})$. This approximation is used in many studies of random COPs. In particular, for the Number Partitioning problem, $\Omega_{\mathbf{z}}$ is the so-called signed partition residue of a given string $\mathbf{z}$, and one can show[7] that the conditional distribution $\hat{P}_r(\Omega|\mathbf{z})$ has a Gaussian form for $n \gg 1$:

$$P_r(\Omega|\mathbf{z}) \approx P_r(\Omega|\Omega_{\mathbf{z}}) = \frac{1}{\sqrt{2\pi n\sigma^2(q)}} \exp\left[-\frac{(\Omega - q\,\Omega_{\mathbf{z}})^2}{2n\sigma^2(q)}\right], \qquad (5)$$

where $\sigma(q) = \sigma(0)\,(1-q^2)^{1/2}$ and $q \equiv 1-2r/n$. From the above, one can obtain the single-point (unconditional) distribution function $\hat{P}(\Omega) = 2^{-n}\sum_{\mathbf{z}} \delta(\Omega_{\mathbf{z}} - \Omega)$, which is also Gaussian in Ω for $n \gg 1$, with mean zero and standard deviation $n^{1/2}\sigma(0)$. In this case, the dynamics of local search are similar to a classical 1D "diffusion" and "drift" along the Ω-axis. The general limitation of local search is the existence of local minima, separated by large Hamming distances $r = \mathcal{O}(n)$ from the true global minimum. On a classical computer, one would need to do, on average, $\mathcal{O}(C_n^r)$ iterations of local search to cover this distance. On the other hand, in a quantum algorithm, one can make use of simultaneous transitions with all possible values of r.

3 One-dimensional quantum diffusion and the minimum gap

We write a stationary Schrödinger equation for the instantaneous eigenvalues $\lambda_k(s)$ and eigenstates $|\phi_k\rangle$ of $H(s)$ in the form $|\phi\rangle = s\,\hat{\mathcal{G}}(\lambda, s)\,H_P\,|\phi\rangle$, where $\hat{\mathcal{G}}(\lambda, s) = [\lambda - (1-s)H_D]^{-1}$ is the Green function corresponding to the driver Hamiltonian. (In the sequel, we drop the subscript k that indicates the position of an eigenvalue in the sorted array.) One can show that the matrix elements $\langle \mathbf{z}'|\hat{\mathcal{G}}|\mathbf{z}\rangle = G_r$ depend only on the Hamming distance $r = D(\mathbf{z}, \mathbf{z}')$ between the states $\mathbf{z}$ and $\mathbf{z}'$. Then the stationary Schrödinger equation takes the form

$$[1 - s\,G_0(\lambda, s)E(\Omega_{\mathbf{z}})]\,\phi_{\mathbf{z}} = \frac{s\Phi\,2^{-n}}{\lambda + (1-s)n} + s\sum_{\mathbf{z}'\neq\mathbf{z}} G_{h(\mathbf{z},\mathbf{z}')}\,\phi_{\mathbf{z}'}\,E(\Omega_{\mathbf{z}'}), \qquad (6)$$

where $\Phi = \sum_z E_{\mathbf{z}}\phi_{\mathbf{z}}$. In what follows, we will solve the above equation using the model of COP defined in Sec. 2 via Eqs. (4)–(5), and assuming that the energy $E_{\mathbf{z}} = c(\Omega_{\mathbf{z}})$ takes discrete values $\varepsilon_0, \varepsilon_1, \ldots, \varepsilon_{M-1}$ ($M = \mathcal{O}(n)$), corresponding to contiguous intervals (or "bins") of $|\Omega|$.[7]

One can show, based on Eq. (6), that the eigenfunctions $|\phi_k\rangle$ of $H(s)$ with $k = \mathcal{O}(1)$ are given by a sum of two components, $\phi_{\mathbf{z}} = v(\Omega_{\mathbf{z}}) + u_{\mathbf{z}}$.[7]

For example, at the ground state one has $\phi_{\mathbf{z}} \approx v(\Omega_{\mathbf{z}})$ from the initial instant of time, $s = 0$, up until the small vicinity of the avoided crossing at $s = s^*$, between the ground state and the first excited state. This component obeys an equation that corresponds to a 1D quantum diffusion over Ω:

$$[1 - s\, G_0(\lambda, s) E(\Omega)]\, v(\Omega) = \frac{s\Phi\, 2^{-n}}{\lambda + (1-s)n} + s \int_{-\infty}^{\infty} d\Omega'\ \chi(\Omega, \Omega')\, E(\Omega') v(\Omega'), \tag{7}$$

where $\chi(\Omega, \Omega') = \int_0^n dr\, C_n^r\, G_r(\lambda, s)\, P_r(\Omega'|\Omega)$. For $s > s^*$, $\phi_{\mathbf{z}} \approx u_{\mathbf{z}}$, where $u(\Omega_{\mathbf{z}})$ decays rapidly with the Hamming distance $D(\mathbf{z}, \mathbf{w})$ from the ground state $|\mathbf{w}\rangle$ with minimum energy ($c(\Omega_{\mathbf{w}}) \leq E_{\mathbf{z}}$ for all $\mathbf{z}$). At the avoided crossing, the minimum gap $g_{\min}$ is determined by the overlap factor between the extended and the localized states: $g_{\min} \sim |v(\Omega_{\mathbf{w}})|$. Using the explicit form of $G_r(\lambda, s)$, one can show[7] that $g_{\min} = \mathcal{O}(n 2^{-n/2})$. This results in an exponentially large complexity of QAA.

4 Discussion

Using the conditional distribution function (5) and the form of H_D in (2) that results in $G_r \propto 1/C_n^r$, one can show that the function $\chi(\Omega'|\Omega)$ in (7) varies only slightly on the scale of $\Omega, \Omega' \ll n^{1/2}$. It is this fact that leads to the weak compression of $v(\Omega)$ near $\Omega = 0$. QAA with H_D (2) exploits the structure of a COP *only* via the landscape correlation function (5), and the algorithm fails because the correlation is weak for small $\Omega \leq 1$. It is of interest to apply this method to different COPs, and use different forms of $H_D(s)$ (cf. Refs. 8,9), that may result in more complex correlation structure for the QAA to exploit.

Acknowledgments

This research was supported by NASA IS/RCA program (project No: 749-40).

References

1. M. Mezard, G. Parisi, and M. Virasoro, *Spin Glass Theory and Beyond* (World Scientific, Singapore, 1987).
2. E. Farhi *et al.*, quant-ph/0001106.
3. E. Farhi *et al.*, *Science* **292**, 472 (2001).
4. W. Van Dam, M. Mosca, and U. Vazirani, quant-ph/0206003.
5. C. H. Bennett *et al.*, *SIAM Journal of Computing*, **26**, 510-1523 (1997).
6. E. Angel and V. Zissimopoulos, *Discr. Appl. Math.*, **99**, p.261 (2000); http://citeseer.nj.nec.com/198010.html.
7. V.N. Smelyanskiy, U.V. Toussaint, and D.A. Timuçin, quant-ph/0202155.
8. E. Farhi, J. Goldstone, and S. Gutmann, quant-ph/0208135.
9. A. Boulatov and V. N. Smelyanskiy, quant-ph/0208189.

OPERATION TIME OF QUANTUM GATES

LEV B. LEVITIN, TOMMASO TOFFOLI, AND ZACHARY WALTON
Boston University. ECE Dept., 8 Mary's St., Boston MA 02215
E-mails: levitin@bu.edu, tt@bu.edu, walton@bu.edu

We consider a quantum gate that complements the state of a qubit and then adds to it an arbitrary phase shift. It is shown that the minimum operation time of the gate is $\tau = \frac{h}{4E}(1+2\frac{\theta}{\pi})$, where h is Planck's constant, E is the quantum-mechanical average energy, and θ is the phase shift modulo π.

It had been shown in Ref. 1 that there exists a fundamental limit to the speed of dynamical evolution of a quantum system. Namely, the minimum time required for a system to go from a given state to one orthogonal to it is

$$\tau = \frac{h}{4E}, \tag{1}$$

where h is Planck's constant and E is the quantum-mechanical average energy of the system. Expression (1) applies to the *autonomous* time evolution of a system, and it is not immediately applicable to changes in the system state caused by the interaction with another (external) system.

This paper considers the question of what is the minimum time of operation of quantum gates that operate on qubits (i.e., quantum systems with two-dimensional Hilbert space).

Let

$$\psi_1(0) = \begin{bmatrix} 0 \\ 1 \end{bmatrix} \quad \text{and} \quad \psi_2(0) = \begin{bmatrix} 1 \\ 0 \end{bmatrix} \tag{2}$$

be the two initial orthogonal stationary states of a qubit. Consider a "gate" that complements the state of the qubit (a quantum inverter or a controlled-NOT gate with the controlling qubit in logical state 1) and then adds to it an arbitrary phase shift θ. This is a device that applies an external interaction to the system for a certain time τ such that at the end of this time interval

$$\psi_1(\tau) = \psi_2(0)e^{-i\theta} \quad \text{and} \quad \psi_2(\tau) = \psi_1(0)e^{-i\theta} \tag{3}$$

i.e., the two orthogonal states are swapped and a given phase shift θ is added to the resulting state. During this time the evolution of the system is governed by a unitary operator $\mathbf{U}(t)$, so that

$$\psi_i(t) = \mathbf{U}(t)\psi_i(0) = e^{-\frac{i\mathbf{H}}{\hbar}t}\psi_i(0), \quad (i = 1, 2), \tag{4}$$

where $\mathbf{H}$ is the total Hamiltonian of the system (including the interaction Hamiltonian) and $\hbar = h/2\pi$. Note that, owing to linearity, (3) is a necessary and sufficient condition for any *unknown* quantum state of a qubit to be converted into the orthogonal state with a phase shift θ.

Recall that any unitary time evolution operator has a diagonal form,

$$\mathbf{U}_{\text{diag}}(t) = \begin{bmatrix} e^{-i\frac{E_1}{\hbar}t} & 0 \\ 0 & e^{-i\frac{E_2}{\hbar}t} \end{bmatrix}, \tag{5}$$

where E_1, E_2 are the eigenvalues of $\mathbf{H}$. The most general form of a unitary operator with the diagonal form (5) can be written as follows:

$$\mathbf{U}(t) = e^{-i\frac{E_1+E_2}{2\hbar}t} \times \begin{bmatrix} \cos^2\phi_1\, e^{i\frac{E_2-E_1}{2\hbar}t} + \sin^2\phi_1\, e^{-i\frac{E_2-E_1}{2\hbar}t} & ie^{i\phi_2} \sin 2\phi_1 \sin \frac{E_2-E_1}{2\hbar}t \\ ie^{-i\phi_2} \sin 2\phi_1 \sin \frac{E_2-E_1}{2\hbar}t & \cos^2\phi_1\, e^{-i\frac{E_2-E_1}{2\hbar}t} + \sin^2\phi_1\, e^{i\frac{E_2-E_1}{2\hbar}t} \end{bmatrix} \tag{6}$$

where ϕ_1 and ϕ_2 are arbitrary phase parameters. (Note that, in fact, $\mathbf{U}(t)$ has three independent parameters—not four.)

It is readily shown that, to satisfy (3) and to provide for the minimum time τ, one should choose $\phi_1 = \pi/4$ and $\phi_2 = 0$. Hence the operator $\mathbf{U}(t)$ has—in the original basis of the system [the one with basis vectors $\psi_1(0)$ and $\psi_2(0)$]—the following unique form

$$\mathbf{U}(t) = e^{-i\frac{E_1+E_2}{2\hbar}t} \begin{bmatrix} \cos \frac{E_2-E_1}{2\hbar}t & i \sin \frac{E_2-E_1}{2\hbar}t \\ i \sin \frac{E_2-E_1}{2\hbar}t & \cos \frac{E_2-E_1}{2\hbar}t \end{bmatrix}. \tag{7}$$

The corresponding Hamiltonian is

$$\mathbf{H} = \begin{bmatrix} \frac{E_1+E_2}{2} & \frac{E_1-E_2}{2} \\ \frac{E_1-E_2}{2} & \frac{E_1+E_2}{2} \end{bmatrix} = \frac{E_1+E_2}{2}\mathbf{I} + \frac{E_1-E_2}{2}\boldsymbol{\sigma}_x, \tag{8}$$

where $\mathbf{I}$ is the identity operator and $\boldsymbol{\sigma}_x$ one of the Pauli matrices. It follows from (4) and (7) that, for a proper choice of E_1 and E_2,

$$\begin{aligned} \psi_1(\tau) &= \mathbf{U}(\tau)\psi_1(0) = \psi_2(0)e^{-i\theta}, \\ \psi_2(\tau) &= \mathbf{U}(\tau)\psi_2(0) = \psi_1(0)e^{-i\theta}. \end{aligned} \tag{9}$$

Equation (9) holds if E_1 and E_2 are chosen so that

$$\begin{aligned} E_1 &= \frac{\theta}{\theta+\pi}E_2 \quad \text{for} \quad 0 \le \theta < \pi, \quad \text{and} \\ E_2 &= \frac{\theta-\pi}{\theta}E_1 \quad \text{for} \quad \pi \le \theta < 2\pi. \end{aligned} \tag{10}$$

Then the minimum time τ of operation of the quantum gate is given by

$$\tau = \frac{h}{2|E_2 - E_1|}. \tag{11}$$

The average energy of the system is

$$E = \langle\psi_i|\mathbf{H}|\psi_i\rangle = \frac{E_1+E_2}{2}, \quad (i = 1, 2). \tag{12}$$

From (10), (11), and (12) it follows that

$$\tau = \tau(\theta) = \frac{h}{4E}\left(1 + 2\frac{\theta \bmod \pi}{\pi}\right). \tag{13}$$

It may seem that τ could be made arbitrarily small by increasing the energy difference $|E_2 - E_1|$. However, this is not possible in a real physical situation, which is not completely described by the qubit model. For example, if $\psi_1(0)$ and $\psi_2(0)$ are two stationary states of an electron in an atom or ion, with energies E_1' and E_2' respectively, then it is advantageous to let $E_2 - E_1$ be equal to the resonant frequency,

$$E_2 - E_1 = E_2' - E_1'$$

(cf. Ref. 2). As a numerical example, consider experiments[3] made with Ca^+ ions in an ion trap. The characteristic wavelength of the transition between the two relevant Ca^+ energy levels is $\lambda = 397\,\text{nm}$, which yields $\tau = \lambda/2c \sim 6.62 \times 10^{-16}\,\text{s}$.

Consider now a one-qubit quantum gate that makes an arbitrary unitary transformation of a *known* state such that the absolute value of the inner product

$$\left|\langle\psi(\tau_\alpha)|\psi(0)\rangle\right| = \cos\alpha.$$

A similar analysis shows that, for any α $(0 \le \alpha \le \pi/2)$, the minimum time required for this operation is

$$\tau_\alpha = \frac{\alpha h}{2\pi E} = \frac{2\alpha}{\pi}\tau(0). \tag{14}$$

References

1. N. Margolus and L. Levitin, *Physica D* **120**, 188–195 (1998).
2. L. Landau and E. Lifshitz, *Quantum Mechanics, 3rd ed.*, (Butterworth–Heinemann, 1997).
3. A. Steane, *Appl. Phys.* **B64**, 623–642 (1997).

ROBUST CONTROL OF DECOHERENCE IN REALISTIC ONE-QUBIT QUANTUM GATES

V. PROTOPOPESCU, R. B. PEREZ, C. D'HELON, AND J. SCHMULEN

Center for Engineering Science Advanced Research,
Computer Science and Mathematics Division,
Oak Ridge National Laboratory,
Oak Ridge, TN 37831-6355 USA

We present an open loop (bang-bang) scheme to control decoherence in a generic one-qubit quantum gate and implement it in a realistic simulation. The system is consistently described within the spin-boson model, with interactions accounting for both adiabatic and thermal decoherence. The external control is included from the beginning in the Hamiltonian as an independent interaction term. After tracing out the environment modes, reduced equations are obtained for the two-level system in which the effects of both decoherence and external control appear explicitly. The controls are determined exactly from the condition to eliminate decoherence, i.e., to restore unitarity. Numerical simulations show excellent performance and robustness of the proposed control scheme.

The realization of any quantum computer relies on maintaining quantum coherence in the system, for a period of time spanning at least the duration of the desired computation. Unfortunately, due to coupling to the environment, the evolution within the quantum computer loses its unitary character; in other words, the system decoheres.[1] Several approaches have been proposed to eliminate or mitigate the undesirable effects of decoherence in open quantum systems, including open loop (quantum bang-bang) control,[2] decoherence free subspaces (DFS),[3] and quantum feedback.[4]

We focus on open-loop control for a two-level system. Our implementation follows Lloyd and Viola's results [2], but has several new aspects: (i) it is more realistic — the control and decoherence act simultaneously, and the model is able to deal with adiabatic as well as thermal decoherence; (ii) it is relatively simple to calculate, (iii) efficient to implement, and (iv) robust to noise both in the decoherence functions as well as in the control pulses.

The two-level system is described using the spin-boson model,[5] with the external control included from the beginning in the Hamiltonian as an independent interaction term. Adiabatic and thermal decoherence arise from the coupling of the system to the outside world through the matrices σ_z and σ_x, respectively. After tracing out the environment modes, reduced equations are obtained for the two-level system in which the effects of both decoherence and external control appear explicitly.

By equating the elements of the reduced density matrix in the presence of decoherence and (unknown) control with the elements of the density matrix undergoing a unitary evolution, we determine the control that cancels out the effect of the decoherence and momentarily restores unitarity. The control

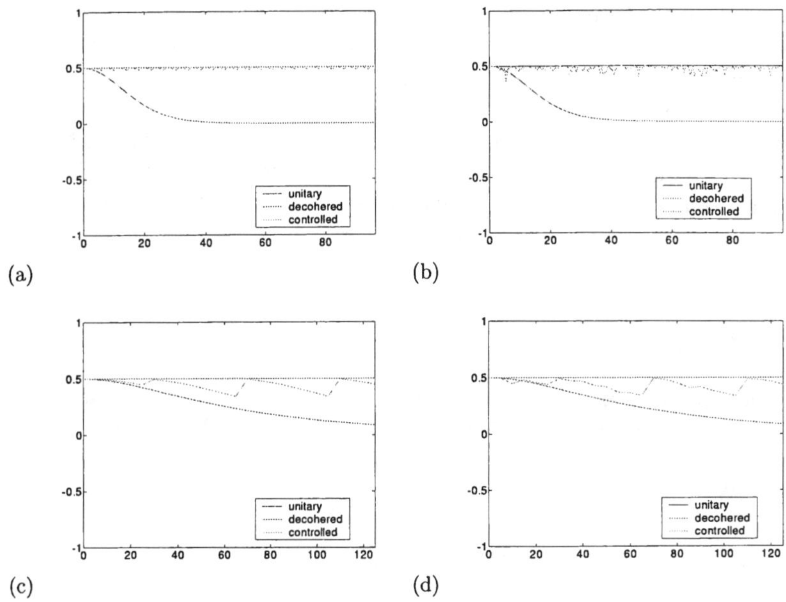

Figure 1. The unitary, adiabatically decohered, and controlled evolution of the $\mathrm{Im}\{\rho_{12}\}$ element of the density matrix for the initial state $i/\sqrt{2}|0\rangle + 1/\sqrt{2}|1\rangle$. The parameters characterizing these plots are: the time between control pulses, T (scaled in terms of the Rabi frequency), the decoherence rate, γ (dimensionless), and the standard deviation, ΔI, of the control pulses after adding normally-distributed noise. (a) $T = 0.5$, $\gamma = 1$, $\Delta I = 0$; (b) $T = 0.5$, $\gamma = 1$, $\Delta I = 0.1$; (c) $T = 5$, $\gamma = 0.1$, $\Delta I = 0$; (d) $T = 5$, $\gamma = 0.1$, $\Delta I = 0.1$.

scheme advances through a cycle of eight time steps, to handle in turn the real and imaginary parts of the matrix elements of the two-level system. In general, resetting any one of the matrix elements to its corresponding unitary value implies that the cumulative effect of the control pulses applied since the last correction cancels out the effect of decoherence.

We note two important things for the applicability of the scheme. First, the knowledge of the decoherence function is needed only for a finite period of time. Second, after initial transients, controls will stabilize and the whole cycle will repeat. This behavior has indeed been observed: the values of the control pulses were stabilized rapidly after the first cycle of eight time steps, as shown in Fig. 1, in the case of adiabatic decoherence.

The relative size of the time step between control pulses determines the deviation of the matrix elements from their unitary values. Also, the size and frequency of the control needed to restore the ideal situation depends on the strength of the decoherence. For $\gamma = 1$ (extremely strong decoherence), the frequency of the control can be decreased to only ≈ 2 times the Rabi frequency. If we keep decreasing the frequency, we cannot restore exact unitarity, at least not by using this scheme. For $\gamma = 0.1$ (strong to medium decoherence), we can decrease the frequency to ≈ 0.2 of the Rabi frequency. Of course, higher frequency results in better restorations of unitarity.

For thermal decoherence, similar results are obtained. However, because this type of decoherence affects all elements of the density matrix, the amount of control needed to restore unitarity is higher than in the adiabatic case. Finally, if the control pulses are perturbed by noise, the control is still very effective.

Acknowledgments

This research was partly supported by the U.S. Department of Energy, Office of Basic Energy Sciences. The Oak Ridge National Laboratory is managed for the U.S. DOE by UT-Battelle, LLC, under contract No. DE-AC05-00OR22725.

References

1. A. O. Pittenger, *An Introduction to Quantum Computing Algorithms* (Birkhauser, Boston 2000); M. A. Nielsen and I. L. Chuang, *Quantum Computation and Quantum Information* (Cambridge University, Cambridge 2000); C. W. Gardiner, *Quantum Noise* (Springer, Berlin 1991); D. Giulini, E. Joos, C. Kiefer, J. Kupsch, I.-O. Stamatescu, and H. D. Zeh, *Decoherence and the Appearance of a Classical World in Quantum Theory* (Springer, Berlin 1996); D. Bouwmeester, A. Ekert, and A. Zeilinger, *Physics of Quantum Information* (Springer, Berlin 2000).
2. L. Viola and S. Lloyd, Phys. Rev. A **58**, 2733 (1998); L. Viola, E. Knill and S. Lloyd, Phys. Rev. Lett. **82**, 2417 (1999); L. Viola, S. Lloyd, and E. Knill, Phys. Rev. Lett. **83**, 4888 (1999).
3. D.A. Lidar, I. L. Chuang, and K. B. Whaley, Phys. Rev. Lett. **81**, 2594 (1999).
4. J. Wang, H. Wiseman and G. J. Milburn, J. Chem Phys **268**, 221 (2001).
5. A. J. Leggett, S. Chakravarty, A. T. Dorsey, M. P. A. Fisher, A. Garg, and W. Zwerger, Rev. Mod. Phys. **59**, 1 (1987); N. G. van Kampen, J. Stat. Phys. **78**, 299 (1995); G. M. Palma, K.-A Suominen, and A. K. Ekert, Proc. R. Soc. London A **452**, 567 (1996); D. Mozyrsky and V. Privman, J. Stat. Phys. **91**, 787 (1998).

DECOHERENCE IN A QUANTUM WALK ON THE LINE

VIV KENDON AND BEN TREGENNA
Optics Section, Blackett Laboratory, Imperial College, London, SW7 2BW, UK
E-mail: Viv.Kendon@ic.ac.uk

We have studied how decoherence affects a quantum walk on the line. As expected, it is highly sensitive, consisting as it does of an extremely delocalized particle. We obtain an expression for the rate at which the standard deviation falls from the quantum value as decoherence increases and show that it is proportional to the number of decoherence "events" occurring during the walk.

Quantum walks on discrete lattices are of interest to the quantum information community because classical random walks underpin important classical algorithms. The aim is to find more powerful quantum counterparts. First it is useful to understand the basic properties of quantum walks on simple lattices. Two versions have been studied, continuous time[1] and discrete-time coined[2] quantum walks. Here we consider only the coined version. Coined quantum walks on a line, cycle, and the hypercube have been solved exactly,[3,4,5] and numerical studies used to explore quantum walks on two-dimensional lattices.[6,7] The quantum walks show a speed up over the equivalent classical random walk, a quadratic increase in standard deviation for a walk on a line, a quadratically-faster mixing time of a walk on a cycle, and an exponential increase in the hitting time to the opposite corner for a walk on a hypercube.[8]

A quantum coin is a d-dimensional quantum system which is "flipped" by applying a unitary operator $\mathbf{C}$. For a quantum walk on a line, $d = 2$ ("left" and "right") and without loss of generality $\mathbf{C}$ can be taken to be a Hadamard ($\pi/2$) rotation. The particle then moves in a superposition of the two possible directions indicated by the coin, $\mathbf{S}|x,a\rangle = |x+a,a\rangle$, where x is the particle position and $a \in \{-1,+1\}$ is the state of the coin. The unitary operator for each step of the walk is thus $\mathbf{U} = \mathbf{S}\cdot(\mathbf{C}\otimes\mathbb{I})$. The moments have been calculated,[3] for asymptotically large times T for a walk starting at the origin,

$$\langle x^2\rangle = (1-1/\sqrt{2})T^2 = \sigma^2(T), \tag{1}$$

independent of initial coin state, and

$$\langle x\rangle_a = a(1-1/\sqrt{2})T, \tag{2}$$

where $a \in \{1,-1\}$ is the initial coin state. The standard deviation (from the origin) $\sigma(T)$ is thus linear in T, in contrast to $\sqrt{T}$ for the classical walk.

To model decoherence in this system we use a discrete master equation

$$\rho(t+1) = (1-p)U\rho(t)U^\dagger + p\sum_i \mathbb{P}_i U\rho(t)U^\dagger \mathbb{P}_i, \tag{3}$$

where the summation runs over the dimensions of the Hilbert space on which the decoherence occurs, either the coin, the particle, or both. The projectors

$\mathbb{P}_i$ act in the computational basis, and p is the probability of a decoherence event happening per time step. This equation was evolved numerically[9] for various choices of $\mathbb{P}$. All choices produced the same general form for the decay of $\sigma(T,p)$ from the quantum ($p=0$) to the classical ($p=1$) value, with small differences in the rates. The slope of $\sigma(T,p)$ is finite as $p \to 0$ and zero at $p=1$. Here we calculate $\sigma(T,p)$ analytically for $pT \ll 1$ and $T \gg 1$ for the case in which $\mathbb{P}$ is the projector onto the preferred basis $\{|a,x\rangle\}$, i.e., decoherence affecting both particle and coin.

The probability distribution for finding the particle in the state $|a,x\rangle$ in the presence of decoherence can be written as,

$$P(x,a,T,p) = (1-p)^T P(x,a,T) + p(1-p)^{T-1} P^{(1)}(x,a,T) + \dots, \tag{4}$$

where $P(x,a,T)$ is the distribution obtained for a perfect walk and $P^{(i)}(x,a,T)$ is the sum of all the ways to have exactly i noise events, e.g.,

$$P^{(1)}(x,a,T) = \sum_{t=1}^{T}\sum_{y}\sum_{b} P(y,b,t) P_{yb}(x,a,T-t), \tag{5}$$

where $P_{yb}(x,a,T-t)$ is the distribution obtained by a perfect (no noise) walk starting in state $|y,b\rangle$ for $T-t$ steps. For the ideal walk, $\sigma^2(T) \equiv \sum_x \sum_a x^2 P(x,a,T)$, and for the walk with decoherence,

$$\sigma^2(T,p) \equiv \sum_x \sum_a x^2 P(x,a,T,p). \tag{6}$$

Taking Eq. (4) to first order in p, and substituting along with Eq. (5) into Eq. (6) gives

$$\sigma^2(T,p) \simeq \sum_{x,a} x^2 \left\{ (1-pT) P(x,a,T) + p \sum_{t=1}^{T} \sum_{y,b} P(y,b,t) P_{yb}(x,a,T-t) \right\}. \tag{7}$$

The first term on the right-hand side is (by definition) $(1-pT)\sigma^2(T)$. Noting that $P_{yb}(x,a,T-t)$ is a translation of a walk starting at the origin, $P_{yb}(x,a,T-t) = P_{0b}(x-y,a,T-t)$, relabeling the summed variable x to $(x+y)$ then enables the sums over x and a to be performed in the second term,

$$\begin{aligned} & p\sum_{t=1}^{T}\sum_{y}\sum_{b} P(y,b,t) \sum_{x}\sum_{a} (x+y)^2 P_{0b}(x,a,T-t) \\ &= p\sum_{t=1}^{T}\sum_{y}\sum_{b} P(y,b,t) \left\{ \sigma_{0b}^2(T-t) + 2y\langle x\rangle_{0b}^{(T-t)} + y^2 \right\}. \end{aligned} \tag{8}$$

From Eq. (1), $\sigma_{0b}^2(T-t)$ does not depend on b, so the summation over y and b may be performed trivially. The summation applied to y^2 gives $\sigma_0^2(t)$ by definition. This leaves only the evaluation of

$$2p\sum_{t=1}^{T}\sum_{y,b} P(y,b,t)y\langle x\rangle_{0b}^{(T-t)} = 2p(1-1/\sqrt{2})\sum_{t=1}^{T}(T-t)\sum_{y,b} yb\ P(y,b,t), \tag{9}$$

where we have used Eq. (2). We note that this term does not depend on whether the initial coin state is plus or minus one, and so we may include both these possibilities equally. Also, by the symmetry of the walk, it is possible to rewrite a probability function for travelling from state $|0,c\rangle$ to $|y,b\rangle$ in the reverse order, i.e., as a probability for moving from $|y,b\rangle$ to $|0,c\rangle$. Care must be taken to ensure that the signs of each term due to the coefficient yb in the summation are maintained. We obtain

$$\begin{aligned}2p\sum_{t,y,b} P(y,b,t)y\langle x\rangle_{0b}^{(T-t)} &= p(1-1/\sqrt{2})\sum_{t=1}^{T}(T-t)\sum_{y,b,c}(1-2\delta_{b,c})yb\ P_{yb}(0,c,t)\\ &= p(1-1/\sqrt{2})\sum_{t=1}^{T}(T-t)\left[\sum_{y,b,c} yb\ P_{y,b}(0,c,t) - 2\sum_{y,b} yb\ P_{yb}(0,b,t)]\right],\end{aligned} \tag{10}$$

treating the two parts with and without a delta function independently. Expanding the summations over b and translating the particle basis by $-y$ gives

$$\begin{aligned}&2p\sum_{t=1}^{T}\sum_{y,b} P(y,b,t)y\langle x\rangle_{0b}^{(T-t)}\\ &= p(1-1/\sqrt{2})\sum_{t=1}^{T}(T-t)\left[\sum_{y,c} yP_{0,-1}(y,c,t) - 4\sum_{y} y\ P_{y,+1}(y,+1,t)\right].\end{aligned} \tag{11}$$

The final summation over y may be bounded above by noting that

$$\begin{aligned}P_{0-1}(y,-1,t) &= |\langle y,-1|U^t|0,-1\rangle|^2\\ &= \frac{1}{2}|\langle y+1,1|U^{t-1}|0,-1\rangle - \langle y+1,-1|U^{t-1}|0,-1\rangle|^2\\ &\le \frac{1}{2}\sum_{c} P_{0,-1}(y+1,c,t-1).\end{aligned} \tag{12}$$

Using this in Eq. (11) gives,

$$\begin{aligned}2p\sum_{t,y,b} P(y,b,t)y\langle x\rangle_{0b}^{(T-t)} &\le p(1-1/\sqrt{2})\sum_{t=1}^{T}(T-t)\left[\langle y\rangle_{0,-1}^{t} - 2\langle y\rangle_{0,-1}^{(t-1)} + 2\right]\\ &\le p(1-1/\sqrt{2})\sum_{t=1}^{T}(T-t)\left[(1-1/\sqrt{2})t + \sqrt{2}\right].\end{aligned} \tag{13}$$

Combining these results in the full expression for $\sigma^2(T,p)$, Eqs. (7) and (8), and performing the simple summations over t gives

$$\sigma^2(T,p) \leq \sigma_0^2(T)\left[1 - \frac{\sqrt{2}}{6}pT + p(\sqrt{2}-1) + \dots\right]. \tag{14}$$

Taking the square root gives as an upper bound on the standard deviation,

$$\sigma(T,p) \leq \sigma(T)\left[1 - \frac{pT}{6\sqrt{2}} + \frac{p}{\sqrt{2}}(1 - 1/\sqrt{2}) + O(p^2, 1/T)\right]. \tag{15}$$

This compares well with simulation data, once a second-order correction for $\sigma(T) = (1 - 1/\sqrt{2})^{1/2}(T - 1/T)$ is taken into account. The $1/T$ form of this correction was found in Ambainis et al.,[3] however, we determined the coefficient $(1 - 1/\sqrt{2})^{1/2}$ numerically for a wide range of evolution times T. The bounding procedure applied here is reasonably accurate; numerical studies give the coefficient of p in the above expansion as 0.09566, compared with the bound of 0.20711. The first-order dependence is thus proportional to pT, the number of decoherence events during the whole quantum walk. Related results for decoherence on the coin only can be found in Brun et al.[10]

We thank Peter Knight, Will Flanagan, Rik Maile, Julia Kempe, Jens Eisert, Todd Brun, and Hilary Carteret for useful discussions. Funded by the UK Engineering and Physical Sciences Research Council.

References

1. E. Farhi and S. Gutmann, Phys. Rev. A **58**, 915–928 (1998), quant-ph/9706062.
2. Y. Aharonov, L. Davidovich, and N. Zagury, Phys. Rev. A **48**(2), 1687 (1992).
3. A. Ambainis, E. Bach, A. Nayak, A. Vishwanath, and J. Watrous, Proc. 33rd STOC pp. 60–69 (2001).
4. D. Aharanov, A. Ambainis, J. Kempe, and U. Vazirani, Proc. 33rd STOC pp. 50–59 (2001), quant-ph/0012090.
5. C. Moore and A. Russell, quant-ph/0104137.
6. T. D. Mackay, S. D. Bartlett, L. T. Stephenson, and B. C. Sanders, quant-ph/0108004.
7. B. Tregenna, W. Flanagan, R. Maile, and V. Kendon, *Tuning quantum walks: coins and initial states* (2002), in preparation.
8. J. Kempe, quant-ph/0205083.
9. V. Kendon, and B. Tregenna, *Decoherence is useful in quantum walks* (2002), submitted, quant-ph/0209005.
10. T. A. Brun, H. A. Carteret, and A. Ambainis, quant-ph/0208195.

Part X
Quantum Communication and Coding

ENTANGLEMENT AND CHANNEL CAPACITY

SETH LLOYD

Massachusetts Institute of Technology, Department of Mechanical Engineering, Cambridge, MA 02139, USA

This paper investigates the capacity of quantum channels, and shows that enhancements in channel capacity can be obtained by coupling together the information degrees of freedom in quantum channels. By coupling together modes in a multimode optical fiber, one can in principle obtain a significant enhancement of the capacity of the fiber for fixed power over the same fiber with uncoupled modes.

Communication channels, like all physical systems, are at bottom quantum mechanical, and their physical limits are calculated using the laws of quantum mechanics.[1–22] A variety of results suggest that enhancements in channel capacity can be obtained by exploiting techniques of quantum information processing.[23–26] For example, quantum systems can be correlated with each other in ways that classical systems cannot, a feature known as entanglement. It has been speculated that entanglement might be used enhance the capacity of quantum communication channels.[24–28] In general, the amount by which entanglement can enhance communication is not known.

A recent paper by the author[29] investigates the question of whether it is possible to enhance the capacity of communication channels by coupling together their information-bearing degrees of freedom in a way that induces entanglement. That paper showed that for fixed power, M coupled, entangled spin chains or modes of the electromagnetic field can in principle transmit information at a rate at least $\sqrt{M}$ times greater than M uncoupled, unentangled chains or modes. Presented herein is a summary of those results.

To understand how quantum mechanics allows enhancements of communication capacity, first review the case of unentangled parallel quantum channels. In particular, it is well established[1–22] that the broadband bosonic channel (a single transverse mode of the electromagnetic field) with power P can transmit $C_{1q} = \alpha\sqrt{P/\hbar}$ bits per second, where $\alpha = \sqrt{\pi/3}(1/\ln 2)$. A similar result holds for propagation of information down spin chains. (The power P is equal to the energy E used to transmit the information, divided by the total time t over which the transmission takes place; as noted in Refs. 8,17, this energy need not be dissipated in the course of transmission.) As a consequence,[1] if the power is spread amongst M unentangled broadband bosonic channels, each with power P/M, the rate of communication is $C_{Mc} = \sqrt{M}C_{1q}$. This is the best known rate for power-limited communication using M unentangled channels, though it is not proven to be the limiting rate. For noiseless channels, however, Refs. 26,27 imply that this rate cannot be surpassed merely by entangling the states of the channels while leaving their dynamics unchanged. By contrast, in Ref. 29 the author showed that if one couples together M spin chains or transverse modes of the electromagnetic field to induce entanglement between the modes in the course of propagation, then using power P one can send information from A to B at a rate $C_{Mq} = \sqrt{2/\pi(1-2^{-M})}M\sqrt{P/\hbar} \approx MC_1 = \sqrt{M}C_{Mc}$. That is, for a fixed power, dynamics that entangle chains or modes can in principle outperform by a factor of $\sqrt{M}$ dynamics that leave the chains or modes unentangled.

To analyze the effect of an entangling dynamics on information propagation, consider a qubit channel that transmits a quantum bit from A to B. Initially, A and B each possess a two-state quantum system, or 'qubit.' A's qubit holds the quantum state $|\psi\rangle$ which is to be transmitted to B, whose qubit is initially in the state $|0\rangle$. The two states $|0\rangle$ and $|1\rangle$ of the qubits are assumed to be degenerate, so that no energy is required to store the qubit. The qubit channel can be used either to transmit classical information — $|\psi\rangle = |0\rangle$ or $|1\rangle$ — or to transmit quantum information — $|\psi\rangle = \alpha|0\rangle + \beta|1\rangle$. The dynamics of the channel transfers the information from A's qubit to B's qubit. After the transfer has taken place, B's qubit is in the state $|\psi\rangle$ and A's qubit is in a standard state such as $|0\rangle$. The sole restriction placed on dynamics of the channel is that it obeys the rules of quantum mechanics: the time evolution of A's qubit and B's qubit, together with their environment and whatever interaction they use to transfer the information, is a unitary, Hamiltonian dynamics. (An arbitrary strictly positive time evolution can be embedded in such dynamics.[30]) This requirement bounds the rate of reliable information transmission down the qubit channel for any possible dynamics given limited power.

Quantum dynamics obey the Margolus-Levitin theorem, which implies that when B's qubit is rotated by π, the average energy of the complete system above its ground state is $E \geq \pi\hbar/2\Delta t$, where Δt is the time over which the transfer takes place.[31] In Ref. 29, the Margolus-Levitin theorem was used to show that the maximum rate at which information can be sent down the qubit channel is $C_{1q} = 1/\Delta t = (2/\sqrt{\pi})\sqrt{P/\hbar}$. This result holds for any dynamics that reliably transfers the qubit from A to B. In other words, the power-limited capacity of the qubit channel differs from that of the broadband bosonic channel by a constant of order unity.

Note, as above, that the energy applied during transmission need not be dissipated: it is merely the energy invested in the propagation of information and can in principle be recovered after transmission. In fact, existing quantum logic devices can swap information from one place to another at rates approaching C_{1q}, with minimal dissipation during the transfer process.

A simple example of an interaction that attains the qubit capacity limit C_{1q} is the application of a 'swap' operation: $S|\psi\rangle_A|\phi\rangle_B = |\phi\rangle_A|\psi\rangle_B$ for all $|\psi\rangle, |\phi\rangle$. Clearly, the swap operator performs the desired transfer, and as shown in Ref. 29, attains the power/capacity limit of the qubit channel. It does so coherently and without dissipation in principle. As noted above, existing quantum logic devices can swap information from one place to another at rates very close to this limit.[35–38]

The proof that swap attains the desired limit C_{1q} relies on the properties of the swap operator:[29] S is unitary, $S^2 = 1$, consequently S is also Hermitian, $S = S^\dagger$. It is straightforward to show that $e^{i\pi S/2} = iS$. The proof that swap attains the desired power-limited information transfer rate for the qubit channel uses S as a Hamiltonian, and applies this Hamiltonian for a time necessary to effect the information transfer.

The 'swap' picture of quantum information transmission assumes a direct transfer of A's qubit to B over a time $\Delta t \geq d(AB)/c$, where $d(AB)$ is the distance between A and B. To look at propagation effects, consider the case in which A's and B's qubits are coupled by an intervening chain of qubits $A_1B_1A_2B_2 \ldots A_nB_n$, where A has access to A_1 and B has access to B_n. Here, it can be shown[29] that the transmission of information from A to B by repeated swapping down the chain of qubits comes within $\sqrt{2}$ of the power/capacity limit C_{1q}.

Now turn to the case of multiple qubit channels that can be coupled to each other during the course of propagation. It is here that entanglement leads to a significant enhancement in power-limited transmission rate. Clearly, M uncoupled qubit channels can transmit information at a rate $\sqrt{M}$ greater than a single quantum channel using the same power P merely by dividing the power equally amongst the channels.[1] Each channel now transmits at a rate $(2/\sqrt{\pi})\sqrt{P/M\hbar}$ giving an overall rate of transmission $C_{Mc} = (2M/\sqrt{\pi})\sqrt{P/Mh} = (2/\sqrt{\pi})\sqrt{MP/h} = \sqrt{M}C_{1q}$. This rate enhancement is the best known enhancement for parallel unentangled channels and holds for both the bosonic channel and for the qubit channel. Because of the square root dependence of transmission rate on power, both the qubit and broadband bosonic channel are more efficient at a lower power. As a result, one improves performance by dividing up information and power among the different channels.

Now we show that one can improve on the unentangled transmission rate C_{Mc} by engineering interactions that entangle the qubit channels in the process of transmission. The goal of the M-channel transfer is to enact the $2M$-qubit analog of the swap above: $S_{1\ldots M} = S_1S_2 \ldots S_M$, where S_1 is the swap operator on the first of A and B's qubit channels, S_2 is the swap operator on the second, etc. The $2M$ qubit swap $S_{1\ldots M}$ swaps A's M qubits with B's M qubits and has the same properties as the 2-qubit swap above (Hermitian, squares to one, etc.). An obvious way to perform the $2M$-qubit swap is just to apply M two-qubit swaps, i.e., one applies the Hamiltonian $S_1 + S_2 + \ldots + S_M$ for an amount of time required to perform the transfer in each of the channels. Since $e^{i\pi(S_1+S_2+\ldots+S_M)/2} = i^M S_1S_2 \ldots S_M$, this method clearly effects the transfer. It is straightforward to verify that this method attains the unentangled transfer limit C_{Mq} above.

But the unentangled limit can be surpassed by the following method. $S_{1\ldots M}$ is Hermitian and can be applied as a Hamiltonian. It is easy to verify that $e^{i\pi S_{1\ldots M}/2} = iS_{1\ldots M}$: accordingly, applying the $2M$-qubit swap operator as a Hamiltonian also swaps the qubits. In addition, it does so more efficiently than swapping the qubits one by one. In fact, in Ref. 29 it is shown that the transmission rate for applying the $2M$-qubit swap Hamiltonian is $C_{Mq} = 1/\Delta t = \sqrt{2(1-2^{-M})P/\pi\hbar}$. Comparing C_{Mq} with C_{Mc} we see that using the $2M$-qubit swap operator as a Hamiltonian gives an enhancement in transmission rate of $\sqrt{M}$ over swapping the qubits one by one.

In addition, applying the Hamiltonian $S_{1\ldots M}$ necessarily entangles the M qubit channels (except in some very simple cases as when the message being transmitted is $00\ldots0$). For example, if A's input state is $|b_M\rangle = |b_1\ldots b_M\rangle$, then at time $\Delta t/2$ (halfway through the controlled flipping operation) A and B's qubits are in the state $(e^{-i\pi/4}/\sqrt{2})\big(|b_1\ldots b_M\rangle_A|00\ldots0\rangle_B + i|00\ldots0\rangle_A|b_1\ldots b_M\rangle_B\big)$. Transferring M bits down M uncoupled, unentangled quantum channels using the same power as a single qubit channel takes $\sqrt{M}$ times longer than transferring the information down coupled, entangled channels. Unentangled transfer corresponds to the application of M two-qubit swap operations with Hamiltonian $S_1 + \ldots S_M$ as opposed to the $2M$-qubit swap Hamiltonian $S_{1\ldots M} = S_1S_2\ldots S_M$, and takes $\sqrt{M}$ times the energy of the entangled swap. As a result, the coupled, entangled channels have a capacity of at least $\sqrt{M}$ times the capacity of the uncoupled, unentangled channels.

The use of entanglement allows the transfer of M bits in the same time and using the same power that it takes to transfer a single bit. In some sense, that it is just as easy in terms of power and energy to rotate $2M$ bits from one state to another as it is to rotate 2 bits from one state to another should not be surprising: no two states in Hilbert space are more than π radians apart in angle. Accordingly, if one can effect arbitrary evolutions on the M-qubit channel Hilbert space, M bits can be transferred using the same power and time as one bit. Effectively, the coupling between the channels allows them to transmit information in the form a 'super-boson' with 2^M internal states. The $\sqrt{M}$ enhancement afforded by exploiting entanglement is typical of quantum information processing and arises from essentially the same source as the $\sqrt{M}$ enhancements in quantum search[32] and quantum positioning.[33]

Of course, enacting the necessary Hamiltonian $\tilde{S}_{1\ldots M}$ is likely to prove experimentally difficult. To attain the $\sqrt{M}$ enhancement of channel capacity allowed by entanglement, an M-qubit entangling operation must be used. The single qubit channel swap operator between A and B can be written $S = \sigma_x^A\sigma_x^B + \sigma_y^A\sigma_y^B + \sigma_z^A\sigma_z^B$, and the corresponding operator for swapping particles such as photons between A and B is $a_Aa_B^\dagger + a_A^\dagger a_B$. The M-channel swap operator $S_{1\ldots M}$ is the product $S_1S_2\ldots S_M$ of the individual swap operators, and corresponds to interaction operators of the form $\sigma_x^1\sigma_x^2\ldots\sigma_x^M$ for spin qubits and $a_{A1}a_{B1}^\dagger\ldots a_{AM}a_{BM}^\dagger + H.C.$ for particle modes. That is, Mth-order nonlinear interactions are required to attain the entanglement-enhanced channel capacity presented here.

The results presented here represent an extension of concepts of quantum information processing to enhancing the power-limited capacity of communication channels using entanglement. The use of entanglement and squeezing to improve the efficiency of power-limited systems appears to be a generic feature of quantum mechanics. Database search, interferometry, quantum clocks, the accuracy of positioning and lithography, and now the capacity of quantum channels, all receive a benefit of $\sqrt{M}$ by using squeezing and entanglement. It is interesting to speculate what other quantum technologies might so benefit. The strength of quantum materials? The power of quantum heat engines? Time will tell.

Acknowledgments

This work was funded by ARDA, NRO, and ARO under a MURI program.

References

1. C. M. Caves and P. D. Drummond, *Rev. Mod. Phys.* **66**, 481-537 (1994).
2. J. P. Gordon, in *Advances in Quantum Electronics*, J. R. Singer ed., (Columbia, New York, 1961), p. 509.
3. D. S. Lebedev and L. B. Levitin, *Dok. Akad. Nauk SSSR* **149**, 1299; *Sov. Phys. Dokl.* **8**, 377 (1963).
4. D. S. Lebedev and L. B. Levitin, *Inf. Control* **9**, 1 (1966).
5. H. Marko, *Kybernetik* **2**, 274 (1965).
6. H. Takahasi, in *Advances in Communication Systems, Vol. 1*, A. V. Balakrishnan, ed., (Academic, New York 1965), p. 227.
7. J. I. Bowen, *IEEE Trans. Inf. Theory* **IT-13**, 230 (1967).
8. R. Landauer and J. W. F. Woo, in *Synergetics*, H. Haken, ed., (Tuebner, Stuttgart 1973), p. 97.
9. C. W. Helstrom, *Proc. IEEE* (Lett.) **62**, 139 (1974).
10. H. P. Yuen and J. H. Shapiro, *IEEE Trans. Inf. Theory* **IT-24**, 657 (1978).
11. J. H. Shapiro, H. P. Yuen, and J. A. Machado Mata, *IEEE Trans. Inf. Theory* **IT-25**, 179 (1979).
12. H. P. Yuen and J. H. Shapiro, *IEEE Trans. Inf. Theory* **IT-26**, 78 (1980).
13. L. B. Levitin, *Int. J. Th. Phys.* **21**, 299 (1982).
14. J. B. Pendry, *J. Phys. A* **16**, 2161 (1983).
15. Y. Yamamoto and H. A. Haus, *Rev. Mod. Phys.* **58**, 1001 (1986).
16. B. E. A. Saleh and M. C. Teich *Phys. Rev. Lett.* **58** 2656 (1987).
17. R. Landauer, *Nature* **335**, 779 (1988).
18. J. D. Bekenstein, *Phys. Rev. A* **37**, 3437 (1988).
19. J. D. Bekenstein and M. Schiffer, *Int. J. Mod. Phys. C* **1**, 355 (1990).

20. M. Schiffer, *Phys. Rev. A* **43**, 5337 (1991).
21. H. P. Yuen and M. Ozawa, *Phys. Rev. Lett.* **70**. 363 (1992).
22. B. E. A. Saleh and M. C. Teich, *Proc. IEEE* **80**, 451 (1992).
23. A. S. Kholevo, *Probl. Peredachi Inf.* **9**, 3 (1973) [*Probl. Inf. Transm. (USSR)* **9**, 177 (1973)].
24. E. H. Lieb and M. B. Ruskai, *J. Math. Phys.* **14**, 1938 (1973).
25. C. H. Bennett and S. J. Wiesner, *Phys. Rev. Lett.* **69**, 2881 (1992).
26. B. Schumacher and M. D. Westmoreland, *Phys. Rev. A* **56**, 131 (1997).
27. A. S. Holevo, *IEEE Trans. Inf. Theory* **44**, 269 (1998).
28. C. H. Bennett, P. W. Shor, J. A. Smolin, and A. V. Thapliy, 'Entanglement-Assisted Capacity of a Quantum Channel and the Reverse Shannon Theorem,' quant-ph/0106052.
29. S. Lloyd, *The power of entangled quantum channels,* submitted to Nature, quant-ph/0112034.
30. A. Peres, *Quantum Theory: Concepts and Methods*, (Kluwer, Hingham) 1995.
31. N. Margolus and L B. Levitin, in *PhysComp96*, T. Toffoli, M. Biafore, J. Leao, eds. (NECSI, Boston) 1996; *Physica D* **120**, 188-195 (1998).
32. L. K. Grover, in *Proceedings of the 28th Annual ACM Symposium on the Theory of Computing*, ACM Press, New York, 1996, pp. 212-218.
33. V. Giovannetti, S. Lloyd, and L. Maccone, *Nature* (2001).
34. Q. A. Turchette, C. J. Hood, W. Lange, H. Mabuchi, and H. J. Kimble, *Phys. Rev. Lett.* **75**, 4710-4713 (1995).
35. C. Monroe, D. M. Meekhof, B. E. King, W. M. Itano, and D. J. Wineland, *Phys. Rev. Lett.* **75**, 4714-4717 (1995).
36. D. G. Cory, A. F. Fahmy, and T. F. Havel, in *PhysComp96, Proceedings of the Fourth Workshop on Physics and Computation*, T. Toffoli, M. Biafore, J. Leão, eds., (New England Complex Systems Institute, Boston) 1996.
37. N. A. Gershenfeld and I. L. Chuang, *Science* **275**, pp. 350-356 (1997).

THE QUANTUMNESS OF A SET OF QUANTUM STATES

CHRISTOPHER A. FUCHS
Bell Labs, Lucent Technologies, Murray Hill, New Jersey 07974, USA
Ctr. for Quantum Communication, Tamagawa University, Tokyo 194-8610, Japan

MASAHIDE SASAKI
Communications Research Laboratory, Koganei, Tokyo 184-8795, Japan
CREST, Japan Science & Technology Corp., Shibuya, Tokyo 150-0002, Japan

We propose to quantify how "quantum" a set of quantum states is. The quantumness of a set is the worst-case difficulty of transmitting the states through a classical communication channel. Potential applications of this measure arise in quantum cryptography, where one might like to use an alphabet of states most sensitive to quantum eavesdropping, and in laboratory demonstrations of quantum teleportation, where it is necessary to check that entanglement has indeed been used.

1 Introduction

How quantum can a single quantum state be? Does this question make sense? One gets the impression it does with even a small perusal of the quantum-optics literature, where coherent states are often called "classical" states of light. Despite the nomenclature, we suggest there is no robust notion of the classicality of a *single* quantum state. Consider any two coherent states $|\alpha\rangle$ and $|\beta\rangle$. The inner product of these states is nonzero. Thus, if a single mode is prepared secretly in one of these states, there is no automatic device that can amplify the signal reliably into a two-mode state $|\gamma\rangle|\gamma\rangle$, where $\gamma = \alpha, \beta$ depending upon the input. Nonorthogonal states cannot be cloned,[1] and this holds whether such states are called "classical" or not.

A notion of the *quantumness of states* can thus only be attached to a *set* of states. The members of a set of states can be more or less quantum with respect to each other, but there is no good sense in which each one alone is intrinsically quantum or not. A set of two nonorthogonal states $|\psi_0\rangle$ and $|\psi_1\rangle$, with $x = |\langle\psi_0|\psi_1\rangle|$, provides a good example.[2] To set the stage, let us work within the metaphor of no-cloning. There, we might take the degree of "clonability"[3] as measure of quantumness of the two states.

A cloning attempt is a unitary operation U that gives $|\psi_i\rangle|0\rangle \longrightarrow |\Psi_i\rangle$, $i = 0, 1$, where $|\Psi_i\rangle$ is a state whose partial trace over either subsystem gives identical density operators. An optimal cloning attempt is one that maximizes the fidelity between the output and the wished-for target state $|\psi_i, \psi_i\rangle \equiv |\psi_i\rangle|\psi_i\rangle$, i.e., maximizes $F_{\rm try} = \frac{1}{2}|\langle\Psi_0|\psi_0,\psi_0\rangle|^2 + \frac{1}{2}|\langle\Psi_1|\psi_1,\psi_1\rangle|^2$. It can be shown that[4]

$$F_{\rm clone} = \max_U F_{\rm try} = \frac{1}{2}\left(1 + x^3 + (1 - x^2)\sqrt{1 + x^2}\right) . \qquad (1)$$

Viewing Eq. (1) as a measure of the quantumness of two states—i.e., the smaller F_{clone}, the more quantum the set of states—one finds that two states are the *most* quantum with respect to each other when $x = 1/\sqrt{3}$.

Equation (1), though we will not ultimately adopt it, exhibits some of the main features a measure of quantumness ought to have. In particular, two states are the most classical with respect to each other when they are either orthogonal or identical. Moreover, the set is most quantum when the states are somewhere in between, in this case when they are 54.7° apart. This point draws the most important contrast between the notions of quantumness and distinguishability.[5,6] As an example, in communication theory it is important to understand the best probability with which a signal can be guessed correctly after a quantum measurement has been performed on its carrier. For the case at hand, the measure of optimal distinguishability is then given by $P_s = \frac{1}{2}\left(1 + \sqrt{1 - x^2}\right)$.[5] This quantity is monotone in the parameter x. No measure of quantumness should have this character. Instead, quantumness should capture how difficult it is to make a copy of the quantum state after some of the information about its identity has been deposited in another system.

The optimal cloning fidelity in Eq. (1) is not completely satisfactory for our purposes, though. One reason is that the idea of cloning does not lead uniquely to Eq. (1). Under minor modifications of the clonability criterion, the particular x for which two states are the most quantum with respect to each other changes drastically. For instance, by another measure in Ref. 4, two states are the most quantum with respect to each other when they are 60° apart. Furthermore, by neither of these measures do we see a potentially desirable connection between quantumness and *angle* in Hilbert space. If there is a connection, one might expect the two states to be the most quantum with respect to each other when they are 45° apart—giving rise to the pleasing slogan: "Two states are the most classical when they are 0° and 90° apart. They are most quantum when they are halfway in between."

For these reasons, we adopt a metaphor more akin to eavesdropping in quantum cryptography. For any set of pure states $\mathcal{S} = \{\Pi_i = |\psi_i\rangle\langle\psi_i|\}$, let us act as if there is a source emitting systems with states drawn according to a probability distribution π_i. (This distribution is an artifice; ultimately it will be discarded after an optimization.) The systems are then passed to an eavesdropper who is required to measure them one by one and thereafter fully discard the originals. To make sure the latter process is enforced, we might imagine that the eavesdropper really takes the form of two people, perhaps Eve and Yves, separated by a classical channel. Eve may perform any quantum measurement imaginable, but then Yves will have access to nothing beyond the classical information obtained to attempt to reproduce the original state.

The question is, how intact can the states remain in this process? To gauge the intactness, we take the average fidelity between the initial and final states. Operationally this corresponds to Yves handing his newly prepared quantum system back to the source. The preparer checks to see whether the system has kept its identity; the probability it passes the test is the fidelity.

Considering the best measurement and resynthesis strategies Eve and Yves can perform gets us most of the way toward a notion of quantumness. The final ingredient is to imagine that the source makes this task as hard as possible. Conceptually, we do this by adjusting the probabilities π_i so that the maximum average fidelity is as small as it can be. The resulting fidelity is what we take to be the quantumness of $\mathcal{S}$. The intuition behind this definition is simple. It captures in a clear-cut way how difficult the eavesdropper's task can be made for reconstructing the set of states. And it does this disregarding the more subtle task of quantifying how much information Eve learns about the state's identity in the process. In a way, it captures the raw sensitivity to eavesdropping that can be imparted to the states in $\mathcal{S}$.

The problem promoted here has its roots in the "state estimation" scenario studied in great detail in the recent literature.[7] The main differences are that we have relaxed the condition that the states in $\mathcal{S}$ be associated with a uniform distribution on Hilbert space, and we have added an extra optimization over the probability distribution π_i. Moreover, the traditional use of "state estimation" has been for purposes of defining a notion of distinguishability for quantum states.[5,8] As explained above, this is exactly what we are *not* trying to get at with a notion of quantumness.[9]

2 Building an Expression for Quantumness

Imagine $\mathcal{S}$ equipped with a probability distribution π_i. Such a set of states along with a set of assigned probabilities, we call an *ensemble* $\mathcal{P}$. (There are no restrictions on the number of elements in $\mathcal{S}$, nor on d, the dimension of Hilbert space for which $|\psi_i\rangle \in \mathcal{H}_d$.) Eve performs a single quantum measurement, i.e., some POVM $\mathcal{E} = \{E_b\}$, on the signal.

Yves makes use of the information Eve obtains—some explicit index b—by preparing his system in a quantum state σ_b. Since the preparation is based solely on classical information, there need be no restrictions on the mapping $\mathcal{M} : b \to \sigma_b$. For instance, it need not be completely positive, etc. Moreover, the σ_b may be mixed states. This corresponds to the possibility of a randomized output strategy on the part of Yves. The conjunction of $\mathcal{E}$ and $\mathcal{M}$ constitutes a protocol for the eavesdropping pair.

Supposing the source emits the state Π_i, and Eve obtains the outcome b for her measurement, then the fidelity Yves achieves is $F_{b,i} = \langle\psi_i|\sigma_b|\psi_i\rangle$. However there is no predictability of Eve's measurement outcome beyond what quantum mechanics allows. Similarly, the most we can say about the actual state the source produces is through the probability distribution π_i. Therefore, the average fidelity for the protocol is

$$F_{\mathcal{P}}(\mathcal{E}, \mathcal{M}) = \sum_{b,i} \pi_i \text{tr}(\Pi_i E_b)\text{tr}(\Pi_i \sigma_b). \tag{2}$$

A convenient intermediate quantity comes from optimizing Yves' strategy alone. For a given $\mathcal{E}$, we define the *achievable fidelity* with respect to the measurement to be $F_{\mathcal{P}}(\mathcal{E}) = \max_{\mathcal{M}} F_{\mathcal{P}}(\mathcal{E}, \mathcal{M})$. In analogy to the quantity known as accessible information[6] in the theory of quantum channel capacities, let us define the *accessible fidelity* of the ensemble $\mathcal{P}$ to be

$$F_{\mathcal{P}} = \max_{\mathcal{E}} F_{\mathcal{P}}(\mathcal{E}) \,. \tag{3}$$

Finally the *quantumness* of the set $\mathcal{S}$ is defined by

$$Q(\mathcal{S}) = \min_{\{\pi_i\}} F_{\mathcal{P}} \,. \tag{4}$$

3 The Accessible Fidelity

It is easy to derive an exact expression for the achievable fidelity $F_{\mathcal{P}}(\mathcal{E})$ for any given $\mathcal{E}$. First note that $F_{\mathcal{P}}(\mathcal{E}, \mathcal{M})$ is linear in the σ_b. Thus, in any decomposition of σ_b into a mixture of pure states, we might as well delete σ_b and replace it with the most advantageous element in the decomposition. Therefore, it never hurts to take the σ_b to be pure states, $\sigma_b = |\phi_b\rangle\langle\phi_b|$.

Rewriting $F_{\mathcal{P}}(\mathcal{E}, \mathcal{M})$ under this assumption, we obtain

$$F_{\mathcal{P}}(\mathcal{E}, \mathcal{M}) = \sum_b \langle\phi_b|M_b|\phi_b\rangle \,, \tag{5}$$

where $M_b = \sum_i \pi_i \Pi_i E_b \Pi_i = \sum_i \pi_i \mathrm{tr}(\Pi_i E_b)\Pi_i$. Now the pure states $|\phi_b\rangle$ are arbitrary. Thus we can optimize each term in Eq. (5) separately. This is done by remembering that the largest eigenvalue $\lambda_1(A)$ of any Hermitian operator A can be characterized by $\lambda_1(A) = \max \langle\alpha|A|\alpha\rangle$. Therefore,

$$F_{\mathcal{P}}(\mathcal{E}) = \sum_b \lambda_1\Big(\sum_i \pi_i \mathrm{tr}(\Pi_i E_b)\Pi_i\Big) \,. \tag{6}$$

Unfortunately, this is where the easy part of the development ends. No explicit expression for the accessible fidelity exists in general. The most one can hope is to understand some of its general properties, a few explicit examples, and perhaps some useful bounds.

In this regard, the first question to ask is how much can said about the measurements achieving equality in Eq. (3). Are we even sure that optimal measurements exist? The answer is yes, and the reason is essentially the same as for the existence of an optimal measurement for the accessible information.[10] Because $\lambda_1(A+B) \le \lambda_1(A) + \lambda_1(B)$, $F(\mathcal{E})$ is a convex function over the the set of POVMs. Since the set of POVMs is a compact set[10] and $\lambda_1(A)$ is a continuous function, it follows that $F_{\mathcal{P}}(\mathcal{E})$ achieves its supremum on an extreme point of the set. Furthermore, by the reasoning of Refs. 11,12, we know that for any extreme point $\mathcal{E}$, all the nonvanishing operators E_b within it must be linearly independent. Thus, we can restrict the maximization in

Eq. (3) to POVMs with no more than d^2 outcomes. Finally, because of the subadditivity of $\lambda_1(A)$, these d^2 operators can be chosen to be rank-one.

One might wish for a further refinement in what can be said of optimal measurements for accessible information. For instance, that the number of measurement outcomes not exceed the number of inputs in analogy to the case of quantum hypothesis testing.[5] This intuition is captured by asking rhetorically, what can Eve possibly do better than make her best guess and pass that information on to Yves? If such is the case, though, a proof remains to be seen. Indeed, because of the nonlinearity in Eq. (3), there may be counterevidence from the case of accessible information.[13]

This brings up the question of how to draw a comparison between the success probability in hypothesis testing and the achievable fidelity for any given measurement. The usual way of posing the hypothesis testing problem is to assume a one-to-one correspondence between inputs Π_i and POVM elements E_i, each element signifying the guess one should make. In that way of writing the problem, the average success probability P_s takes the form $P_s = \sum_i \pi_i \mathrm{tr}(\Pi_i E_i)$. Here, however, we cannot make such a restriction on the number of outcomes. So, we must pose the hypothesis testing problem in a more general way.

Suppose Eve performs a measurement $\mathcal{E}$ and observes outcome b to occur. This information will cause her to update here probabilities for the various inputs according to Bayes' rule:

$$p(i|b) = \frac{p(b,i)}{p(b)} = \frac{\pi_i \mathrm{tr}(\Pi_i E_b)}{\mathrm{tr}(\rho E_b)} , \tag{7}$$

where $p(b) = \mathrm{tr}(\rho E_b)$ and $\rho = \sum_i \pi_i \Pi_i$. Maximum likelihood dictates that Eve's success probability will be optimal if she chooses the value i for which $p(i|b)$ is maximum. Thus her average success probability will be

$$P_s(\mathcal{E}) = \sum_b p(b) \max_i \{p(i|b)\} = \sum_b \max_i \{\pi_i \mathrm{tr}(\Pi_i E_b)\} . \tag{8}$$

Equation (8) compares to $F_{\mathcal{P}}(\mathcal{E})$ through a simple inequality. To see this, note that $F_{\mathcal{P}}(\mathcal{E}) = \sum_b p(b)\lambda_1(\rho_b)$, where $\rho_b = \sum_i p(i|b)\Pi_i$. Suppose $i{=}j$ maximizes $p(i|b)$. Then $\lambda_1(\rho_b) = \max\langle\phi|\rho_b|\phi\rangle \geq \langle\psi_j|\rho_b|\psi_j\rangle = \sum_i p(i|b)|\langle\psi_j|\psi_i\rangle|^2 \geq p(j|b) + \sum_{i\neq j} p(i|b)|\langle\psi_j|\psi_i\rangle|^2 \geq \max_i\{p(i|b)\}$. Therefore, $P_s(\mathcal{E}) \leq F_{\mathcal{P}}(\mathcal{E})$. This inequality is not tight, however. For instance, for $\mathcal{P}$ describing a uniform distribution of states on a qubit, $P_s \to 0$, while $F_{\mathcal{P}} = 2/3$.[8]

Tighter bounds, both upper and lower, on Eq. (3) would be useful. An obvious lower bound comes directly from the convexity of the $\lambda_1(A)$ function. Note in particular that $\rho = \sum_b p(b)\rho_b$. Therefore $F_{\mathcal{P}}(\mathcal{E}) \geq \lambda_1(\rho)$. This inequality is generally tighter than the previous one in that it never falls below $1/d$; moreover, there is a measurement $\mathcal{E}$ that achieves it.

A more interesting lower bound comes about by considering the behavior of $F_{\mathcal{P}}(\mathcal{E})$ with respect to the "square-root measurement."[14] This POVM is constructed from the ensemble decomposition of ρ by multiplying it from the left and right by $\rho^{-1/2}$. Inserting this measurement into $F_{\mathcal{P}}(\mathcal{E})$, we obtain

$$F_{\mathcal{P}} \geq F_{\mathrm{PGM}} = \sum_i \lambda_1\Big(\sum_j \pi_i\pi_j \Pi_j \rho^{-1/2}\Pi_i\rho^{-1/2}\Pi_j\Big). \tag{9}$$

4 Conclusion

Much more can be said about accessible fidelity and quantumness,[15] but lack of space prevents us from saying it here. We end instead with a question. One can define the *quantumness of a Hilbert space* by

$$Q_d = \inf_{\mathcal{S}} Q(\mathcal{S}) , \tag{10}$$

where the infimum is taken over *all* sets of states living on $\mathcal{H}_d$. One has to wonder whether this quantity might not indicate a deep defining property for the quantum system itself—its ultimate "sensitivity to the touch."[16]

Acknowledgments

Much of this work was carried out at Caltech in Spring 1999 and at Tamagawa University in Springs 2000/2001. CAF acknowledges support of a DuBridge Fellowship and the hospitality of Tamagawa University during those periods. MS thanks S. M. Barnett and C. Gilson for valuable discussions.

References

1. H. P. Yuen, Phys. Lett. A **113**, 405 (1986).
2. C. A. Fuchs, `quant-ph/9810032`.
3. V. Bužek and M. Hillery, Phys. Rev. A **54**, 1844 (1996).
4. D. Bruß, *et al.*, Phys. Rev. A **57**, 2368 (1998).
5. C. W. Helstrom, *Quantum Detection and Estimation Theory*, (Academic Press, NY, 1976).
6. C. A. Fuchs, `quant-ph/9601020`.
7. S. Massar and S. Popescu, Phys. Rev. Lett. **74** 1259 (1995).
8. A. Chefles, Contemp. Phys. **41**, 401–424 (2000).
9. S. M. Barnett, C. R. Gilson and M. Sasaki, J. Phys. A **34**, 6755 (2001).
10. A. S. Holevo, J. Mult. Anal. **3**, 337 (1973).
11. A. Fujiwara and H. Nagaoka, IEEE Trans. Inf. Theory **44**, 1071 (1998).
12. E. B. Davies, IEEE Trans. Inf. Theory **IT-24**, 596–599.
13. P. W. Shor, `quant-ph/0009077`.
14. A. S. Holevo, Theor. Prob. Appl. **23**, 429 (1978).
15. C. A. Fuchs and M. Sasaki, "Squeezing Quantum Information through a Classical Channel," in preparation.
16. C. A. Fuchs, `quant-ph/0205039`.

ENCODING AND DECODING QUANTUM INFORMATION VIA ENTANGLEMENT

MIO MURAO
Department of Physics, Graduate School of Science, The University of Tokyo, 7-3-1 Hongo, Bunkyo-ku, Tokyo 113-0033, Japan
E-mail: murao@phys.s.u-tokyo.ac.jp

VLATKO VEDRAL
Blackett Laboratory, Imperial College, Prince Consort Road, London SW7 2BZ, United Kingdom
v.vedral@ic.ac.uk

In order to the characterize encoding and decoding of quantum information represented by an unknown state, we investigate entanglement required to perform remote quantum information distribution (telecloning) and concentration (reverse-telecloning) protocols. These protocols perform encoding and decoding via a generalization of teleportation, using only initially-shared entanglement and local operations and classical communications (LOCC) among spatially separated parties. The asymmetry of encoding and decoding from the viewpoint of required entanglement resource has been analyzed. In an extreme case, the encoding requires entanglement and global operations but decoding can be performed using only LOCC without any entanglement. This strong asymmetry may suggest the possibility of a quantum "one-way" function.

1 Introduction

Encoding and decoding of quantum information represented by an unknown single qubit state $|\phi\rangle = \alpha|0\rangle + \beta|1\rangle$ are fundamental operations for quantum information processing, e.g., quantum error correction and quantum communications. Encoding is a mapping from a single-qubit state $|\phi\rangle$ to a multi-qubit state $|\psi\rangle = \alpha|\psi_0\rangle + \beta|\psi_1\rangle$ where $|\psi_0\rangle$ and $|\psi_1\rangle$ are orthonormal multi-qubit states. Decoding is $|\phi\rangle$ to $|\psi\rangle$. The choice of the orthonormal multi-qubit states for the mappings determines the "performance" of encoding and decoding. Therefore it is important to understand the mapping to characterize encoding and decoding.

With the addition of an ancilla qubit state $|0...0\rangle$, the encoding process can be described by a unitary operation U_e as $|\psi\rangle = U_e|\phi\rangle \otimes |0...0\rangle$. In this case, decoding is described by $U_d = U_e^\dagger$, which is simply the reverse process. However the unitary operations U_e and U_d are over-specific for both encoding and decoding — they include information about the ancilla system.

We consider encoding performed by a generalization of re-exportation, which requires no information regarding the ancilla system. In this generalization, we use a multi-qubit entangled state $|\xi\rangle = (|0\rangle \otimes |\psi_0\rangle + |1\rangle \otimes |\psi_1\rangle)/\sqrt{2}$ instead of the Bell state (the maximally entangled two qubit state). The protocol of the generalization is similar to the standard teleportation protocol,[1] but uses the multi-qubit recovery operations defined by $U_0 \equiv 1$, $U_1|\psi_i\rangle \equiv (-1)^i |\psi_i\rangle$, $U_2|\psi_i\rangle \equiv |\psi_{i\neq j}\rangle$, and $U_3 \equiv U_1 \cdot U_2$ for $i,j = \{0,1\}$ instead of the standard single qubit recovery operations represented by $U_1 = \sigma_z$, $U_2 = \sigma_x$. If the recovery operations are given by products of local unitary operations, the encoding process can be performed by using only the initially shared entangled state and LOCC. In such cases, encoding and decoding can be characterized by the entangled state.

2 Optimal cloning type encoding and decoding

There are a number of different encoding/decoding schemes for different purposes. In this paper, we deal with encoding for quantum optimal universal cloning and its reverse decoding process, and investigate their required entangle states. Quantum optimal universal cloning[2] is the way to obtain the most faithful copies of an unknown state allowed by quantum mechanics, where the perfect duplication of (unknown) quantum information is forbidden by the no-cloning theorem.[3] For the simplest case of two optimal clones, the mappings are $|\phi\rangle = \alpha|0\rangle + \beta|1\rangle \leftrightarrow |\psi_c\rangle = \alpha|\psi_0\rangle + \beta|\psi_1\rangle$, where

$$|\psi_0\rangle = \sqrt{2}\{|0\rangle \otimes |00\rangle + |1\rangle \otimes (|01\rangle + |10\rangle)/2\}/\sqrt{3} \quad (1)$$

$$|\psi_1\rangle = \sqrt{2}\{|1\rangle \otimes |11\rangle + |0\rangle \otimes (|01\rangle + |10\rangle)/2\}/\sqrt{3}. \quad (2)$$

The first qubit is the ancilla. The second and third qubits represent optimal approximate copies. The fidelity of $1 \to 2$ optimal universal cloning is 5/6.

2.1 Encoding (telecloning)

We consider that all the qubits are in the spatially separated locations to make the role of entanglement clear. Then to perform encoding $|\phi\rangle_A \to |\psi_c\rangle_{BCD}$, where the indices A,B,C and D denote the locations of each qubit, we use the following four qubit entangled state (telecloning state):[4]

$$\begin{aligned} |\xi_{tc}\rangle_{ABCD} &= \{|00\rangle \otimes |00\rangle + |11\rangle \otimes |11\rangle \\ &\quad + (|01\rangle + |01\rangle) \otimes (|01\rangle + |01\rangle)/2\}/\sqrt{3}, \end{aligned} \quad (3)$$

where the first qubit functions as the input port, and the last three qubits are the output port. The recovery operations are given by $U_1 = \sigma_z^B \otimes \sigma_z^C \otimes \sigma_z^D$ and $U_2 = \sigma_x^B \otimes \sigma_x^C \otimes \sigma_x^D$.

This telecloning state can be also written as

$$|\xi_{tc}\rangle_{ABCD} = (|0\rangle_A |\psi_0\rangle_{BCD} + |1\rangle_A |\psi_1\rangle_{BCD})/\sqrt{2}, \quad (4)$$

where $|\phi_0\rangle_{AC}$ and $|\phi_1\rangle_{AC}$ are the optimal cloning basis states given by Eq. (1). This duality of representing the telecloning state in the form of Eq. (3) and Eq. (4) is the key for successful encoding. Detailed analysis of entanglement structure for the telecloning state for more general cases is presented in Refs. 4,5.

2.2 Decoding (reverse-telecloning)

For the decoding process $|\psi_c\rangle_{BCD} \rightarrow |\phi\rangle_A$[6] via the generalization of teleportation, we find that several different types of four-qubit entangled states can be used due to the degree of freedom in eliminating ancilla variables. Examples include a 4-qubit GHZ state $(|0000\rangle + |1111\rangle)/\sqrt{2}$, two Bell states $(|00\rangle + |11\rangle)_{BC} \otimes (|00\rangle + |11\rangle)_{Da}/2$, a telecloning state [Eq. (3)] and an unlockable bound entangled state[8]

$$\rho_{ub} = \sum_{i=0}^{3} |\Phi^i\rangle_{AB} \langle\Phi^i| \otimes |\Phi^i\rangle_{CD} \langle\Phi^i| /4, \tag{5}$$

where $|\Phi^i\rangle$ represents the four Bell basis.

The most interesting case is the use of the unlockable bound entangled state. This state is not distillable if we do not allow joint quantum operations (i.e., if all four parties only operate locally), but is not separable either, therefore, it is a bound entangled state.[7] However, if we allow a two qubit joint operation, i.e., Bell joint measurement on any two qubits, we can obtain a maximally entangled state for the other two qubits via LOCC. Thus this state is unlockable. The unlocking mechanism is based on a joint operation for two out of four qubits.

Since we do not allow joint operations on spatially separated qubits, the entanglement we use is indeed bound entangled. It is surprising that a bound entangled state can actually be useful for "transmitting" quantum information in our case. There is no distillable pairwise entanglement in the unlockable bound entangled state, if no joint operations are allowed for qubits in different locations. How can the information be processed and faithfully transmitted using only LOCC?

The answer lies in the optimal cloning state. The three qubits in the optimal cloning state are actually entangled with each other. Each of two clone qubits is entangled (although not maximally entangled) with the ancilla qubits and this entanglement is not bound entanglement. We may conjecture how information processing and transmission have been achieved using only a bound entangled state and LOCC in our scheme as follows: the Bell joint measurement "combines" the optimal cloning state $|\psi_c\rangle_{BCD}$ and the bound entangled state ρ_{BCDA}, which is initially "closed" for transmission. The unbound entanglement of $|\psi_c\rangle_{BCD}$ provides quantum correlation among the qubits of the bound entangled state. The quantum correlation "opens" the channel for transmitting concentrated single qubit information from the three qubits of the input state. Entanglement of the input optimal cloning state and the unlockable bound entangled channel state function in a complementary fashion. This result explains the importance of the ancilla qubit in the optimal cloning state, since the ancilla qubit is necessary for holding entanglement.

3 Asymmetry of encoding and decoding

As we have shown in the previous section, encoding via the generalization of teleportation requires a particular type of entanglement but decoding can be performed equally well using several different types of entanglement. This asymmetry is due to the fact that the encoding process is an entangling process and the decoding process is a disentangling process.

To investigate the asymmetry of encoding and decoding, we consider the most simple two-qubit encoding and decoding $|\phi\rangle_A \leftrightarrow |\psi\rangle_{AB}$. For two-qubit encoding, we found an extreme case that encoding requires entanglement and global operations but decoding can be performed using only local operations and classical communications without any entanglement.

If the two basis states can be written as

$$|\psi_0\rangle = \cos(\theta)|\lambda_0\rangle|\eta_0\rangle + \sin(\theta)|\lambda_1\rangle|\eta_1\rangle \quad (6)$$

$$|\psi_1\rangle = \cos(\theta)|\lambda_0^{\perp}\rangle|\eta_0\rangle + \sin(\theta)|\lambda_1^{\perp}\rangle|\eta_1\rangle, \quad (7)$$

where c_0 and c_0 are real coefficients and $|\lambda_i\rangle$, $|\eta_i\rangle$, and $|\lambda_i^{\perp}\rangle$ form a basis for each qubit satisfying $\langle\lambda_i^{\perp}|\lambda_i\rangle = 0$ and $\langle\eta_i|\eta_j\rangle = \delta_{ij}$ (but not necessary to be $\langle\lambda_0|\lambda_1\rangle = 0$), we can perform $|\psi\rangle_{AB} \rightarrow |\phi\rangle_A$ only by LOCC. No entanglement is required. However to encode $|\phi\rangle_A \rightarrow |\psi\rangle_{AB}$, we require a large amount of entanglement resource, i.e., the initially shared entangled state $|\xi\rangle_{AAB}$ and global recovery operations, as well as classical communications. This strong asymmetry in terms of required resources may suggest the possibility of a quantum "one-way" function.

Acknowledgments

This work was supported partly by the Special Postdoctoral Researchers Program of RIKEN, CREST of JST, the Grant-in-Aid for Encouragement of Young Scientists by JSPS and the Research Foundation for Opto-Science and Technology.

References

1. C. H. Bennett *et al*, Phys. Rev. Lett. **70**, 1895 (1993).
2. V. Bužek and M. Hillery, Phys. Rev. A **54**, 1844 (1996).
3. W. K. Wootters and W. H. Zurek, Nature **299**, 802 (1982).
4. M. Murao et al., Phys. Rev. A **59**, 156 (1999).
5. M. Murao, M. B. Plenio and V. Vedral, Phys. Rev. A **61**, 042311 (2000).
6. M. Murao and V. Vedral, Phys. Rev. Lett. **86**, 352 (2001).
7. M. Horodecki, P. Horodecki, and R. Horodecki, Phys. Rev. Lett. **80**, 5239 (1998).
8. J. A. Smolin, Phys. Rev. A **63**, 032306 (2001).

BOUND ON MEASUREMENT BASED ON NO-SIGNALING

ERIKA ANDERSSON AND STEPHEN M. BARNETT
Department of Physics, University of Strathclyde, Glasgow G4 0NG, Scotland
E-mail: erika@phys.strath.ac.uk
tel. +44 (0)141 548 3376, fax +44 (0)141 552 2891

Quantum mechanics implies the no-signaling condition: No local operation on one quantum system may affect the results of a local measurement on another quantum system, even if the two systems are entangled. This may be used to obtain bounds on quantum operations. As an example, we obtain a tight bound on the measurement which discriminates without error between two non-orthogonal states, without explicit reference to generalized measurements (POM strategies).

Quantum mechanical systems may be entangled with each other, resulting in correlated measurement results for the different systems. This, however, cannot be used to transmit signals between spatially separated quantum systems.[1] We will refer to this statement as the *no-signaling condition.* Quantum mechanics in its standard form implies the no-signaling condition, and is in this sense consistent with special relativity. Turning this around, an operation which does not satisfy the no-signaling condition cannot be allowed within quantum mechanics. Thus, starting from the no-signaling condition, one should be able to obtain explicit bounds on quantum operations. An example is the bound obtained on symmetric cloning.[2] The motivation here is that the no-signaling condition could be used as a more general tool to solve problems in quantum information and quantum measurement theory.

Quantum measurements are usually treated within the POM formalism.[4,5,6] Essentially, POM measurements are equivalent to restricting the transformations of the measured system to be described by completely positive maps. Finding the optimal POM strategy for a measurement situation is often difficult. Here, we will obtain a tight bound on the unambiguous discrimination between two non-orthogonal states, starting from the no-signaling condition, without explicit reference to the measurement transformation. This problem was originally addressed by Ivanovic, Peres and Dieks,[7] who considered the case of two equally probable non-orthogonal states, and subsequently generalized to states with unequal prior probabilities by Jaeger and Shimony.[8] These authors derived their results by considering the unitary interaction between the system of interest and an ancilla, followed by measurement of both systems, a procedure equivalent to a POM strategy. A recent review of unambiguous state discrimination can be found in Ref. 3. The simplicity of the derivation below raises the hope that the no-signaling condition might prove useful, e.g., for obtaining optimal measurement strategies, and demonstrates, in a remarkable way, the power of the no-signaling condition in limiting quantum operations.

Suppose two space-like separated particles are prepared in the entangled quantum state

$$|\psi\rangle = \sqrt{q}|+\rangle_R|a\rangle_L + \sqrt{1-q}|-\rangle_R|b\rangle_L, \tag{1}$$

where

$$\begin{aligned} |a\rangle_L &= \cos(\theta)|+\rangle_L + \sin(\theta)|-\rangle_L \\ |b\rangle_L &= \cos(\theta)|+\rangle_L - \sin(\theta)|-\rangle_L, \end{aligned} \tag{2}$$

and $|+\rangle_{L,R}$ and $|-\rangle_{L,R}$ are orthogonal basis states for the two particles, referred to as "left" and "right", and $0 \leq q \leq 1$. Without loss of generality, we choose $0 \leq \theta \leq \pi/2$. The reduced density matrix of the left system is

$$\rho_L = \mathrm{Tr}_R(|\psi\rangle\langle\psi|) = q|a\rangle_{LL}\langle a| + (1-q)|b\rangle_{LL}\langle b|, \tag{3}$$

corresponding to a statistical mixture of the non-orthogonal states $|a\rangle_L$ and $|b\rangle_L$ with respective prior probabilities q and $1-q$. On this left system, we intend to carry out a measurement to unambiguously distinguish between these two states. The measurement on the left system has three possible outcomes: "a", "b", or "inconclusive", occurring with probabilities P_a, P_b, and $P_? = 1 - P_a - P_b$ respectively. We will obtain a bound on $P_?$, without any further reference to the measurement procedure.

The no-signaling condition requires that no operation performed on the left particle can be detected by observation of the right particle alone[1,6,9]. Hence, measurement of the left particle is not allowed to change the reduced density matrix of the right system,

$$\rho_R = \mathrm{Tr}_L(|\psi\rangle\langle\psi|) = \begin{pmatrix} q & \sqrt{q(1-q)}\cos(2\theta) \\ \sqrt{q(1-q)}\cos(2\theta) & 1-q \end{pmatrix}. \tag{4}$$

Any arbitrarily small, but finite, change in the reduced density matrix of the right system could be detected by preparing a large number of entangled pairs. Measurements on the pair halves located to the right would, with some non-zero probability, reveal a change in their reduced density matrices. This would immediately lead to the possibility of superluminal communication.

If the result of the measurement performed on the left particle is "a" or "b", it is clear from Eq. (1) that the state of the right system after the measurement will be $|+\rangle_R$ or $|-\rangle_R$, respectively. If the result of the measurement is inconclusive, the right system is in an as yet undetermined state with density matrix

$$\rho_? = \begin{pmatrix} \rho_?^{++} & \rho_?^{+-} \\ \rho_?^{-+} & \rho_?^{--} \end{pmatrix}. \tag{5}$$

Putting these together, we find that, after the measurement, the density matrix of the right particle is

$$\rho_R = \begin{pmatrix} P_a & 0 \\ 0 & P_b \end{pmatrix} + P_? \begin{pmatrix} \rho_?^{++} & \rho_?^{+-} \\ \rho_?^{-+} & \rho_?^{--} \end{pmatrix}. \tag{6}$$

By the no-signaling condition, this has to be equal to Eq. (4). After some algebra,[10] this may be shown to result in a general bound

$$P_? \geq 2\sqrt{q(1-q)}\cos(2\theta). \tag{7}$$

Due to the fact that also P_a and P_b have to be positive, it is not always possible to attain this bound. In this case, the minimum value of $P_?$ will lie on the boundary of the parameter space allowed, i.e., either $P_a = 0$ or $P_b = 0$. If $q \leq 1-q$, $P_a = 0$ will be optimal, and the bound is

$$P_? \geq 1-(1-q)\sin^2(2\theta). \tag{8}$$

When $q \geq 1-q$, $P_b = 0$ is optimal, giving

$$P_? \geq 1-q\sin^2(2\theta). \tag{9}$$

Knowing the form (6) of the density matrix ρ_R of the right system, it is possible to reconstruct a measurement on the left system, described by a completely positive map, which produces this particular decomposition of ρ_R.[11] This means that the obtained bound may indeed be attained by a quantum operation on the left system. When P_a, P_b and $P_?$ are all nonzero, the measurement will be described by a generalized measurement strategy, which can be implemented by coupling the system to be measured to an ancilla as considered in Refs. 7,8. Whenever P_a or P_b is equal to zero, a projective von Neumann measurement will be enough: for example, if P_a is equal to zero, the measurement on the left system is a projection in the basis $\{|a\rangle_L, |a^\perp\rangle_L\}$. Obtaining the result "$a^\perp$" will correspond to the result "b", since in this case, the state cannot have been $|a\rangle_L$. The result "a" will be the inconclusive result, since in this case, it is impossible to rule out the possibility that the state was either $|a\rangle_L$ or $|b\rangle_L$, due to their non-orthogonality.

We should also note that unambiguous state discrimination is more than simply a theoretical construction. Unambiguous discrimination between two equiprobable states has indeed been realized in experiments with photon polarization.[12,13]

It has long been appreciated that entangled quantum systems display correlations, but that these do not allow for communication by choice of measurement[1] or other operations[6,9] on one of the systems. Recently, it has been shown that, if one assumes the usual static properties of quantum mechanics, its dynamical properties and the no-signaling condition are connected.[14] On its own, the no-signaling condition does not imply complete positivity, and thus does not imply the framework of standard quantum mechanics.[15] Nevertheless, because quantum mechanics implies no-signaling, in this contribution we have shown that the no-signaling condition may be employed as a physical law and used to obtain bounds on quantum measurement. The example given here is by no means unique. Using a very similar argument, it is possible to use the no-signaling condition to derive a bound on the success of probabilistic cloning. This bound was originally derived by Duan and Guo by assuming that the system to be cloned is subject to a unitary evolution and a subsequent measurement.[16] We have also derived a bound on a minimum-error measurement, and a bound on simultaneous measurement of two spin components of a particle with $S = 1/2$. The obtained bounds all agree with results obtained by considering POM strategies. Because of its simplicity, the no-signaling approach might prove useful for tackling yet unsolved problems in quantum information and quantum measurement theory, for example, problems related to optimal measurement strategies.

Acknowledgments

This work was supported by the Royal Society of Edinburgh, the Scottish Executive Education and Lifelong Learning Department, and by the European Commission through a Marie Curie Fellowship.

References

1. C. G. Ghirardi, A. Rimini, and T. Weber, *Lett. Nuov. Cim.* **27**, 293 (1980); P. J. Bussey, *Phys. Lett.* A **123**, 1 (1987).
2. N. Gisin, *Phys. Lett.* A **242**, 1 (1998).
3. A. Chefles, *Contemp. Phys.* **41**, 401 (2000).
4. C. W. Helstrom, *Quantum Detection and Estimation Theory* (Academic, New York, 1976);
5. A. Peres, *Quantum Theory: Concepts and Methods*, (Kluwer Academic Publishers, Dordrecht 1993);
6. K. Kraus, *States, Effects and Operations: Fundamental Notions of Quantum Theory* (Springer, Berlin, 1983).
7. I. D. Ivanovic, *Phys. Lett.* A **123**, 257 (1987); D. Dieks, *ibid.* **126**, 303 (1988); A. Peres, *ibid.* **128**, 19 (1988).
8. G. Jaeger and A. Shimony, *Phys. Lett.* A **197**, 83 (1995).
9. M. J. Hall, *Phys. Lett.* A **125**, 89 (1987); C. G. Ghirardi, R. Grassi, A. Rimini and T. Weber, *Europhys. Lett.* **6**, 95 (1988); S. M. Barnett and T. Kraemer, *Phys. Lett.* A **293**, 211 (2002).
10. S. M. Barnett and E. Andersson, *Phys. Rev.* A **65**, 044307 (2002).
11. L. P. Hughston, R. Jozsa, and W. K. Wootters, *Phys. Lett.* A **183**, 14 (1993).
12. B. Huttner, A. Müller, J. D. Gautier, H. Zbinden, and N. Gisin, *Phys. Rev.* A **54**, 3783 (1996).
13. R. B. M. Clarke, A. Chefles, S. M. Barnett, and E. Riis, *Phys. Rev.* A **63**, 040305 (2001).
14. C. Simon, V. Buzek, and N. Gisin, *Phys. Rev. Lett.* **87**, 170405 (2001).
15. D. Bruss, G. M. D'Ariano, C. Macchiavello, and M. Sacchi, *Phys. Rev.* A **62**, 062302 (2000).
16. L.-M. Duan and G.-C. Guo, *Phys. Rev. Lett.* **80**, 4999 (1998).

ACTIVE TELEPORTATION OF A VACUUM-ONE PHOTON QUBIT

F. SCIARRINO, S. GIACOMINI, E. LOMBARDI, AND F. DE MARTINI

Istituto Nazionale di Fisica della Materia, Dipartimento di Fisica, Universita' "La Sapienza", Roma, 00185 Italy

We report the experimental realization of "active" quantum teleportation (QST) of a one-particle entangled qubit. This demonstration completes the original QST protocol and renders it available for actual implementation in quantum computation networks. A high value of teleportation "fidelity" was attained, F=90%.

Recently qubit teleportation[1,2] with unprecedented high "fidelity", $F \approx 0.95$, has been experimentally demonstrated by our laboratory. This was done in the context of quantum optics by adopting the concept of "entanglement of one photon with the vacuum", in which each *qubit* was physically implemented by a two-dimensional subspace of Fock states of a mode of the electromagnetic field, specifically the space spanned by the QED "vacuum" and the 1-photon state. Let A and B represent two different modes of the field, with wave vectors k_A and k_B directed, respectively, towards two distant stations (Alice and Bob). These stations may be linked by a nonlocal channel expressed by an entangled state implying the quantum superposition of a *single photon*, e.g., by the *singlet*: $|\Phi\rangle_{\text{singlet}} = 2^{-\frac{1}{2}}(|1\rangle_A |0\rangle_B - |0\rangle_A |1\rangle_B)$ where the mode indexes 0 and 1 denote, respectively, the vacuum and 1-photon Fock-state population of the modes. The relevant conceptual novelty introduced here consists of the fact that the *field's modes* rather than the photons associated with them are taken as the information carriers, i.e., *qubits.*

All previous quantum bit teleportation realizations[2,3] correspond to simplified, incomplete "passive" schemes in which the success of the protocol is demonstrated indirectly by the detection of the nonlocal correlations established a posteriori between the extreme stations, Alice and Bob. These *passive* realizations have the advantage of avoiding the difficult implementation of the final stage of QST: the unitary transformations U restoring the *exact* input qubit at Bob's site under Alice's control through the QST *classical channel.*[1] The main problem faced here is due to the relatively long time T needed to switch, under *single-photon* excitation by the Alice's Bell-measurement apparatus the high-voltage pulses driving the electro-optic Pockels-cells (EOPs) implementing the necessary U-unitaries at Bob's site. Of course, in order to preserve an appreciable QST *fidelity,* we require $T \lll \tau$, where τ is the characteristic time of the decoherence process affecting the *nonlocal channel,* i.e., the one that dephases the corresponding entangled $|\Phi\rangle_{\text{singlet}}$. The present work realizes for the first time the *active* qubit teleportation process by adopting the quoted vacuum-1 photon configuration.[2,4] This scheme provides a discrete-variable optical quantum teleportation that is as complete as

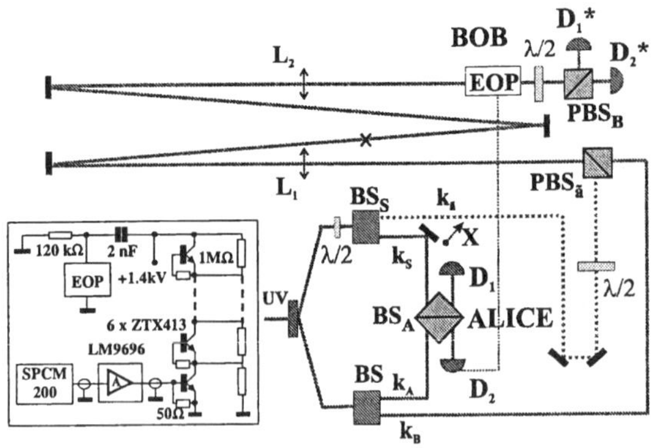

Figure 1. Experimental apparatus realizing active QST. All beams were filtered by interference filters within a bandwidth $\Delta\lambda = 6\,\mathrm{nm}$ and detected by EG&G-SPCM200. INSET: Diagram of the fast electronic switch of the EOP implementing the unitary transformation σ_z. The difficult problem of realizing a fast electronic circuit transforming each small ($\simeq 1\,\mathrm{mV}$) Si-avalanche photodetection signal into a calibrated fast pulse in the kV range was solved by a single linear amplifier chip (LM9696) exciting directly a single chain of six fast avalanche transistors (Zetex ZXT413).

possible using linear optics.

Let us briefly outline the details of the apparatus shown in Fig. 1. A nonlinear $LiIO_3$ crystal slab, cut for type-I phase matching was excited by a cw argon laser. The two photons belonging to each pair emitted by spontaneous parametric downconversion (SPDC) with the same linear vertical (V) polarization had equal wavelengths $\lambda = 727.6\,\mathrm{nm}$. By means of two beam splitters, BS and BS_S, each consisting of a $\lambda/2$ plate plus a calcite crystal (C), inserted in the output modes of the SPDC source, $|\Phi\rangle_{\mathrm{out}}$ was transformed into the product of two entangled states, $|\Phi\rangle_{\mathrm{singlet}} = 2^{-\frac{1}{2}}(|1\rangle_A |0\rangle_B - |0\rangle_A |1\rangle_B)$ and $|\Psi\rangle_{S\tilde{a}} = \alpha |1\rangle_S |0\rangle_{\tilde{a}} + \beta |0\rangle_S |1\rangle_{\tilde{a}}$ with $|\alpha|^2 + |\beta|^2 = 1$, defined over the two pairs of the BS's output modes (k_A, k_B) and $(k_S, k_{\tilde{a}})$, respectively. In our experiment we had four qubits: k_A and k_B in the state $|\Phi\rangle_{\mathrm{singlet}}$, which provided the nonlocal teleportation channel; k_S which represented the qubit to be teleported; and $k_{\tilde{a}}$, the ancilla. The state of the qubit k_S was teleported to Bob into the state of the qubit k_B, thus the overall state $|\Psi\rangle_{S\tilde{a}}$ was transferred into the state of the qubits k_B and $k_{\tilde{a}}$. To verify that the state had been teleported, we transmitted the qubit $k_{\tilde{a}}$ to Bob. The apparatus at the Alice site, consisting of BS_A, D_1, D_2 performed a Bell-state measurement with 50% efficiency by identifying the states $|\Psi^3\rangle_{SA} = |1\rangle_1 |0\rangle_2 = 2^{-\frac{1}{2}}(|0\rangle_S |1\rangle_A - |1\rangle_S |0\rangle_A)$ and $|\Psi^4\rangle_{SA} = |0\rangle_1 |1\rangle_2 = 2^{-\frac{1}{2}}(|0\rangle_S |1\rangle_A + |1\rangle_S |0\rangle_A)$. The other two Bell states involving measurements at Alice's site of either zero or two photons were not

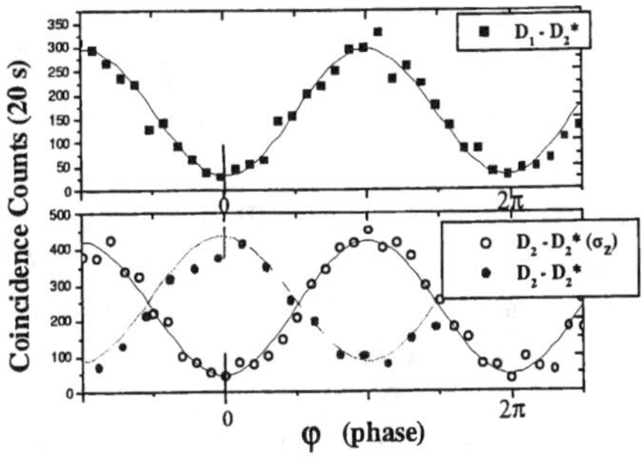

Figure 2. Interferometric fringe patterns due to coincidence experiments involving different pairs of detectors within the *active* QST verification procedure upon variation of the phase φ of the measured fields.

identified by the apparatus, as expected for any linear detection system, and discarded by coincidence electronic circuits. A single photodetection by D_1 implied realization of the state $|\Psi\rangle_{B\tilde{a}} = [\alpha\,|1\rangle_B\,|0\rangle_{\tilde{a}} + \beta\,|0\rangle_B\,|1\rangle_{\tilde{a}}]$, i.e., of the *exact* teleported copy of the input state $|\Psi\rangle_{S\tilde{a}}$. Alternatively, a click at D_2 implied realization at Bob's site of the state $[\alpha\,|1\rangle_B\,|0\rangle_{\tilde{a}} - \beta\,|0\rangle_B\,|1\rangle_{\tilde{a}}]$ The complete QST protocol could be achieved in our experiment by allowing the direct activation by D_2 of an electro-optic (EO) device performing the unitary transformation $U \equiv \sigma_z$ on the mode B. This transformation was implemented in the experiment by a $LiNbO_3$ Pockels Cell (EOP) with <1 nsec risetime. The EOP $\lambda/2$ voltage, leading to a π phase shift of the single-photon state $|1\rangle_B$ with respect to the (phase-insensitive) vacuum state $|0\rangle_B$, was $V = 1.4\,\text{kV}$. The overall risetime achieved by the electronic device was $T_r = 22\,\text{ns}$. This corresponded to the minimum delay we must impart to the teleported single-photon state before entering EOP in order to be transformed into the state $|\Psi\rangle_{B\tilde{a}}$. The optical delay line (DL), 8 m long and corresponding to a delay $\Delta T > T_r$, was realized by multiple reflections using three plane mirrors and two lenses.

An efficient test of the success of the *active* QST operation was carried out by a "passive" interference procedure. The mode $k_{\tilde{a}}$ carrying the ancilla state was injected into the optical delay line by means of a polarizing beam splitter (PBS) and was made to fully spatially overlap the teleportation beam k_B, but with *orthogonal* polarization. The EO crystal of the Pockels cell was oriented in a direction such that the efficiency of the EO phase-shifting operation was maximum for the (V) polarization of mode B and zero for the horizontal (H) polarization of the mode $\tilde{a}$. At the exit of the EOP, the orthogonal linear polarizations of the two (teleported+ancilla) beams were first rotated by the same amount by means of a $\lambda/2$ plate, then linearly mixed by a polarizing beam splitter PBS_B and finally measured by the verification detectors D_1^*, D_2^*. The combination ($\lambda/2$ plate+PBS_B) provided the *variable* beam-splitting action (BS_B) at Bob's site needed to implement the "passive" verification of the QST success through coincidence measurements involving the two detector sets (D_1, D_2) and (D_1^*, D_2^*). Assume that both BS_S and BS_B were set in the *symmetrical* condition: i.e., with equal reflectivity and transmittivity parameters. Micrometric changes of the mutual phase φ of the interfering k_S and k_A modes were obtained by a piezoelectrically driven mirror placed at the exit of BS_S by varying the position X of the mirror at the exit of BS_B. When the EOP was turned off, the phase shift φ was found to affect the coincidence counts rates according to the expressions $(D_1 - D_2^*) = (D_2 - D_1^*) = \frac{1}{2}\cos^2(\frac{\varphi}{2})$ and $(D_1 - D_1^*) = (D_2 - D_2^*) = \frac{1}{2}\sin^2(\frac{\varphi}{2})$ where $(D_i - D_j^*)$, $i, j = 1, 2$, expresses the probability of a coincidence detected by the pair D_i, D_j^*. The upper and lower plots (full circles) shown in Fig. 2 correspond to the actual realization of the states $|\Psi\rangle_{B\widetilde{a}}$ (D_1 click) and $[\alpha|1\rangle_B|0\rangle_{\widetilde{a}} - \beta|0\rangle_B|1\rangle_{\widetilde{a}}]$ (D_2 click) respectively. However the data expressed by open circles (lower plot), taken by EOP activation, correspond to the realization of the EOP-transformed state $\sigma_z\left(\alpha|1\rangle_B|0\rangle_{\widetilde{a}} - \beta|0\rangle_B|1\rangle_{\widetilde{a}}\right) = |\Psi\rangle_{B\widetilde{a}}$, as shown by comparison with the upper plot. In summary, the results show that, allowing the automatic actuation of the EOP-switch by the Alice's detector D_2, the unknown input qubit is teleported *whenever* one of the detectors D_1, D_2 clicks. The QST fidelity is equal to $(90 \pm 2)\,\%$, largely overcoming the limit value implied by quantum teleportation.[3] Because of the key relevance of the quantum teleportation protocol to many important logic networks, the present demonstration represents a substantial step forward towards the implementation of multiple qubit gates in the domain of linear optics quantum computation.[5]

We are greatly indebted with the FET European Network on Quantum Information and Communication (Contract IST-2000-29681:ATESIT), INFM (contract PRA-CLON-2002) and with M.U.R.S.T. for funding.

References

1. C. H. Bennett, et al., Phys. Rev. Lett. **70**, 1895 (1993).
2. E. Lombardi, F. Sciarrino, S. Popescu, and F. De Martini, Phys. Rev. Lett. **88**, 070402-1 (2002).
3. D. Boschi, S. Branca, F. De Martini, L. Hardy and S. Popescu, Phys. Rev. Lett. **80**, 1121 (1998); D. Bouwmeester, et al., Nature (London) **390**, 575 (1997).
4. S. Giacomini, F. Sciarrino, E. Lombardi, and F. De Martini, Phys. Rev. A **66**, 030302(R) (2002).
5. E. Knill, R. Laflamme and G. Milburn, Nature (London) **409,** 46 (2001).

HYBRID DECOHERENCE-FREE ERROR-CORRECTING CODES VIA QUANTUM TRAJECTORIES

K. KHODJASTEH L.

Department of Physics, University of Toronto, 60 St. George st., Toronto, Canada, M5S 1A7

E-mail: kaveh@physics.utoronto.ca,

D. A. LIDAR

Department of Chemistry, University of Toronto, 90 St. George st., Toronto, Canada, M5S 1A9

E-mail: dlidar@chem.utoronto.ca

Generalizing a proposal by Alber et al. (quant-ph/0103042), we develop a hybrid decoherence-free subspace (DFS) quantum error-correcting code (QECC) approach, utilizing the methodology of quantum trajectories. The DFS acts as a first layer of protection against errors due to the conditional evolution, while the QECC acts as a second layer and uses the DFS encoding to offer protection against random quantum jumps. We also study the effect of incorporation of quantum logic gates and hence the possibility of fault tolerant quantum computation. Finally we give an example of the method in cavity QED systems.

In this work we use a hybrid of decoherence free subspaces (DFS) and quantum error correction codes (QECC), along with the concept of quantum trajectories, to devise a coding scheme for qubits that protects them against spontaneous emissions and collective dephasing. This construction also allows for relatively easy means of universal computation with physically available Hamiltonians. It is also shown that this construction is fault tolerant in the sense that, for sufficiently low error rates, the errors do not propagate and quantum computation with this code does not add to the decoherence.

Suppose we have a physical system composed of n qubits (two-level quantum systems, with $|0\rangle$ corresponding to the ground state and $|1\rangle$ corresponding to the excited state). Spontaneous emission, induces a transition from $|1\rangle$ to $|0\rangle$, but leaves $|0\rangle$ unchanged. The operator generating this error on the ith qubit is $F_i = |0\rangle_1\langle i|$. In the quantum trajectories picture, the decoherence cycle has two ingredients: The unitary evolution is replaced by a conditional evolution dictated by a non-Hermitian *conditional Hamiltonian*, which is defined in terms of the system Hamiltonian H_s and the error generators F_i, as:

$$H_c = H_s - \frac{i}{2}\sum_i \lambda_i F_i^\dagger F_i, \tag{1}$$

where λ_i is some measure of the strength of errors acting on the ith qubit.[2] The second ingredient is random occurrence/application of the errors F_i, at random times on random qubits, for our case. In our system we assume all the qubits to be identical with respect to their interaction with the environment, which means, effectively, $\lambda_i = \lambda$.

Consider now the following scalable code structure for logical computational qubit states (as a subclass of a more general formalism introduced in Ref. 2), represented in binary format $|a_1 a_2 \dots a_m\rangle$: For each qubit, we assign 2 qubits in the code and add 2 extra fixed "base" qubits, that gives us $2m+2$ qubits:

$$|a_1 a_2 \dots a_m\rangle \rightarrow \frac{1}{\sqrt{2}}(|b_1 b_2 \dots b_m 01\rangle + |c_1 c_2 \dots c_m 10\rangle), \tag{2}$$

where

$$b_i = \begin{cases} 01 \text{ if } a_i = 0 \\ 10 \text{ if } a_i = 1 \end{cases}, \; c_i = \begin{cases} 10 \text{ if } a_i = 0 \\ 01 \text{ if } a_i = 1 \end{cases}. \tag{3}$$

The above code-words also span the DFS for the conditional Hamiltonian; the DFS condition in our case[4] will be given by,

$$F_i |\psi_j\rangle = |\psi_j\rangle, \tag{4}$$

in which $|\psi_j\rangle$ is a state in the subspace generated by the code words. One can easily check that this translates into using a fixed number of 1's (or 0's) in our code words and is satisfied in our case. This ensures that the code words are protected during the conditional evolution, but they also fulfill the QECC condition,[5] provided that we have the extra information about where (on which qubit) the error has occurred:[2]

$$\left\langle \psi_j \left| \mathbf{F}_i^\dagger \mathbf{F}_i \right| \psi_k \right\rangle = \delta_{jk}. \tag{5}$$

We then show that we can generate all the single qubit operations ($\mathrm{SU}(2)_i$), using single-qubit "logical"[a] Hamiltonians: $X_i^L = X_{2i-1}X_{2i}$ and $Z_i^L = Z_{2i-1}Z_{2m+1}$. This only uses physical[b] Hamiltonians: $H_S = \sum J_{ij}(\sigma_i^x \sigma_j^x + \sigma_i^y \sigma_j^y) + J_{ij}^z \sigma_i^z \sigma_j^z$, with controllable coefficients. One could also think of actual geometries that make the above interactions feasible even with the more common nearest-neighbor interactions.

To perform universal computation, we also need to generate entanglement between two arbitrary logical qubits. We use the fact that, with our construction, the logical Hamiltonian, $Z_i Z_j$, is just another two-body physical Hamiltonian term: $Z_i^L Z_j^L = Z_{2i-1}Z_{2m+1}Z_{2j-1}Z_{2m+1} = Z_{2i-1}Z_{2j-1}$. We further show how to use the $Z_i Z_j$ logical Hamiltonian to generate entanglement. Alternatively, we prove that we can use the nearest neighbor XY interaction, $\sigma_x^i \sigma_x^{i+1} + \sigma_y^i \sigma_y^{i+1}$ and a $\sigma_z^i \sigma_z^{2m+1}$ interaction, to generate the `CPHASE` gate. This is done using a method called *encoded recoupling*.[6]

We note that, in two respects, this construction is fault tolerant. First, the operations we propose never take the states out of the code-space, hence

---

[a] encoded

[b] That means we do not need heterogeneous terms such as $\sigma_x^i \sigma_y^j$.

never make them susceptible to spontaneous emissions. Second, the proposed operations satisfy the fault tolerance property in terms of the stabilizer formalism and its extension to continuous stabilizer. The stabilizer is the set of operators that keep the code words invariant. It is usually a discrete or continuous group generated by the operators $D(\vec{v})$, where $\vec{v}$ is an indexing vector parameter. The fault-tolerance condition is then given by[3]

$$\mathbf{HD}(\vec{v})\mathbf{H} = \mathbf{D}(\vec{v'}), \tag{6}$$

where H is the desired unitary operation and the mapping from $\vec{v}$ to $\vec{v'}$ has to be one to one. It is shown that this condition is satisfied and also provides a method of fault-tolerant syndrome measurement for the QECC part of our code, which uses an ancillary qubit.

We finally provide a method for preparing the states in our code words initially and discuss realization possibilities using the available Hamiltonians in proposals such as quantum dots, or cavity QED with atoms.

Acknowledgments

We thank Dr. L.-A. Wu for helpful discussions and Photonics Research Ontario for financial support (to D.A.L.).

References

1. K. Khodjasteh L. and D. A. Lidar, Phys. Rev. Lett. to appear (2002), quant-ph/02XXXXXX
2. G. Alber, Th. Beth, Ch. Charnes, A. Delgado, M. Grassl, and M. Musinger, Phys. Rev. Lett. **86**, 4402(2001).
3. J. Kempe, D. Bacon, D. A. Lidar, and K. Whaley, Phys. Rev. A **63**, 042307 (2001).
4. D. A. Lidar, I. Chuang, and K. B.Whaley, Phys. Rev. Lett. **81**, 2594 (1998).
5. E. Knill, I. Chuang, and R. Laflamme, Phys. Rev. A **55**, 900 (1997)
6. D. A. Lidar and L.-A. Wu, Phys. Rev. Lett. **88**, 017905 (2002).

PERFORMANCE OF CLASSICAL BINARY CODES FOR QUANTUM CHANNELS: TOWARD HIGHLY RELIABLE QUANTUM COMMUNICATIONS

KENTARO KATO

Core Research for Evaluational Science and Technology (CREST), Japan Science and Technology corporation (JST)
Tamagawa-gakuen 6-1-1, Machida, Tokyo 194-8610, JAPAN
E-mail: kkatop@ieee.org

1 Introduction

Transmission of classical information via a quantum channel is one of the important issues in quantum information theory. Our particular interest lies in the classical coding - quantum decoding[1] case. Fortunately, the channel coding theorem for this case has been already proven by Holevo and Schumacher-Westmoreland,[2,3] and the reliability function has been formulated.[4] Therefore our task is to find good codes predicted from this theorem for realizing highly reliable quantum communication systems. In this paper, the decoding error probabilities for several cases of Bose-Chaudhuri-Hocquenghem (BCH) codes and Reed-Muller (RM) codes are computed. From comparison with the bound on decoding error probability given by the reliability function, the codes examined in this paper are found to be *good* codes.

2 Communication model and the reliability function bound

Our communication model is illustrated in Fig. 1. At the coder, a message m,

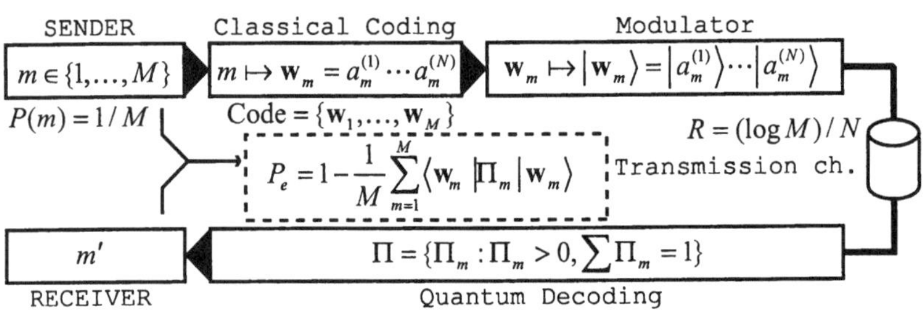

Figure 1. Communication model

chosen from the set of messages $\{1, \ldots, M\}$ with probability $P(m) = 1/M$, is assigned to a codeword $\mathbf{w}_m$ from the code $\mathcal{C} = \{\mathbf{w}_m = a_m^{(1)} \cdots a_m^{(N)} : a_m^{(n)} \in \{0,1\}\}$. From the number M of messages and the length N of a codeword, the information rate is given as $R = \log(M)/N$. At the modulator, the codeword $\mathbf{w}_m$ is transformed into a quantum signal $|\mathbf{w}_m\rangle = |a_m^{(1)}\rangle \otimes \cdots \otimes |a_m^{(N)}\rangle$, called a codeword state, and transmitted to the decoder side. In our case, binary phase-shift keyed coherent states, $\{|0\rangle = |\alpha\rangle, |1\rangle = |-\alpha\rangle\}$ are used in the modulator, and each signal state is called a letter state. Note that these two quantum states are not orthogonal, that is, $0 < \kappa = \langle\alpha|-\alpha\rangle = \exp[-2n_s] < 1$, where $n_s = |\alpha|^2$ is the average number of signal photons per letter. At the decoder, the received quantum signal $|\mathbf{w}_m\rangle$ is decoded into a message $m' \in \{1, \ldots, M\}$, obeying a suitable quantum decoding rule, which is described by a POVM $\Pi = \{\hat{\Pi}_m : \hat{\Pi}_m \geq 0 \ \forall m, \ \sum_m \hat{\Pi}_m = \hat{1}\}$, where $\hat{1}$ is the identity operator on the Hilbert space spanned by the codeword states. From this, the conditional probability decoding into m' when m was sent is given by $P(m'|m) = \langle\mathbf{w}_m|\hat{\Pi}_{m'}|\mathbf{w}_m\rangle$. The performance of this communication system is evaluated by the average probability of decoding error, which is given by $P_e(\mathcal{C};\Pi) = 1 - (1/M)\sum_{m=1}^{M}\langle\mathbf{w}_m|\hat{\Pi}_m|\mathbf{w}_m\rangle$.

According to the quantum channel coding theorem, for this communication system, there exists a code having the average probability of decoding error P_e^* such that[4]

$$P_e^* \leq \exp\left[-N\left\{E_{\mathrm{r}}(R) - \frac{\log 2}{N}\right\}\right], \quad 0 < R < C, \tag{1}$$

where C is the quantum channel capacity calculated[5] as $C = -\lambda_- \log\lambda_- - \lambda_+ \log\lambda_+$, $\lambda_\pm = (1\pm\kappa)/2$, and $E_{\mathrm{r}}(R)$ is the quantum random coding exponent given by $E_{\mathrm{r}}(R) = \max_{0\leq s\leq 1}[E_0(s) - sR]$, $E_0(s) = -\log[\{(1-\kappa)/2\}^{1+s} + \{(1+\kappa)/2\}^{1+s}]$. Hence we call the code satisfying Eq. (1) a *good* code.

3 Numerical simulation for BCH codes and RM codes

In this paper, the following BCH codes[6] and RM codes[6] are employed:

- (7,4,3)-BCH; (15,5,7)-BCH; (15,7,5)-BCH; (31,6,15)-BCH
- (4,3,2)-RM; (8,4,4)-RM; (16,5,8)-RM

For each code, the following decoding schemes are adopted as decoding rules.

- Collective decoding
- Individual decoding with the Helstrom receiver[8]
- Individual decoding with a homodyne receiver

Collective decoding is equivalent to a collective measurement of codeword states. Indeed, the square-root measurement is employed as the collective decoding, which is defined as follows:

$$\hat{\Pi}_m^{\mathrm{SRM}} = |\mu_m\rangle\langle\mu_m|; \quad |\mu_m\rangle = \hat{G}^{-1/2}|\mathbf{w}_m\rangle \ \forall m, \ \hat{G} = \sum_{m=1}^{M} |\mathbf{w}_m\rangle\langle\mathbf{w}_m|. \tag{2}$$

Usuda has proven that the square-root measurement for each code mentioned above is the minimum error decoding rule.[7] On the other hand, the individual decoding scheme is based on individual measurements of letter states and a classical decoding rule, that is, each of letter states of a codeword state is measured individually and the sequence of classical bits obtained by individual measurement is decoded into a message by using a classical decoding rule. In our case, the bounded distance decoding rule[6] is used as the classical decoding rule. Hence the average probabilities of decoding error for both the Helstrom receiver and the homodyne receiver are calculated in a classical manner using bit error probabilities given by $\varepsilon^{\text{Helstrom}} = (1/2)(1 - \sqrt{1 - (\exp[-2n_s])^2})$, $\varepsilon^{\text{homodyne}} = (1/2)(1 - \mathrm{erf}[\sqrt{2n_s}])$, where $\mathrm{erf}[x] = (2/\sqrt{\pi}) \int_0^x \exp[-t^2] dt$. Results of numerical simulation are shown in Fig. 2.

4 Concluding remark

As seen in Fig. 2, the decoding error probabilities of collective decoding for the BCH codes and RM codes do not exceed the quantum reliability function bound, although the individual decoding cases exceed it for some n_s. In other words, the decoding error probabilities of the BCH and RM codes with collective decoding satisfy Eq. (1) for all n_s. Therefore the BCH codes and RM codes considered in this paper are *good* codes, in the sense of the quantum reliability function with the collective measurement.

Acknowledgments

The author would like to thank Prof. Hirota, Dr. Sasaki, and Dr. Usuda for their helpful comments and Dr. Nakamura for his support in CREST.

References

1. C. H. Bennett, P. W. Shor, *IEEE Trans. Inform. Theory* **44**, 2724 (1998).
2. B. Schumacher and M. D. Westmoreland, *Phys. Rev.* A **56**, 131 (1997).
3. A. S. Holevo, *IEEE Trans. Inform. Theory* **44**, 269 (1998).
4. M. V.Burnashev, A. S. Holevo, `quant-ph/9703013 v4`.
5. K. Kato, M. Osaki, O. Hirota, *Phys. Lett.* A **251**, 157 (1999).
6. V. S. Pless, W. C. Huffman, ed., *Handbook of Coding Theory*, (North Holland, 1998).
7. T. S. Usuda, I. Takumi, M. Hata, O. Hirota, *Phys. Lett.* A **256**, 104 (1999).
8. C. W. Helstrom, *Quantum Detection and Estimation theory* (Academic Press, 1976).

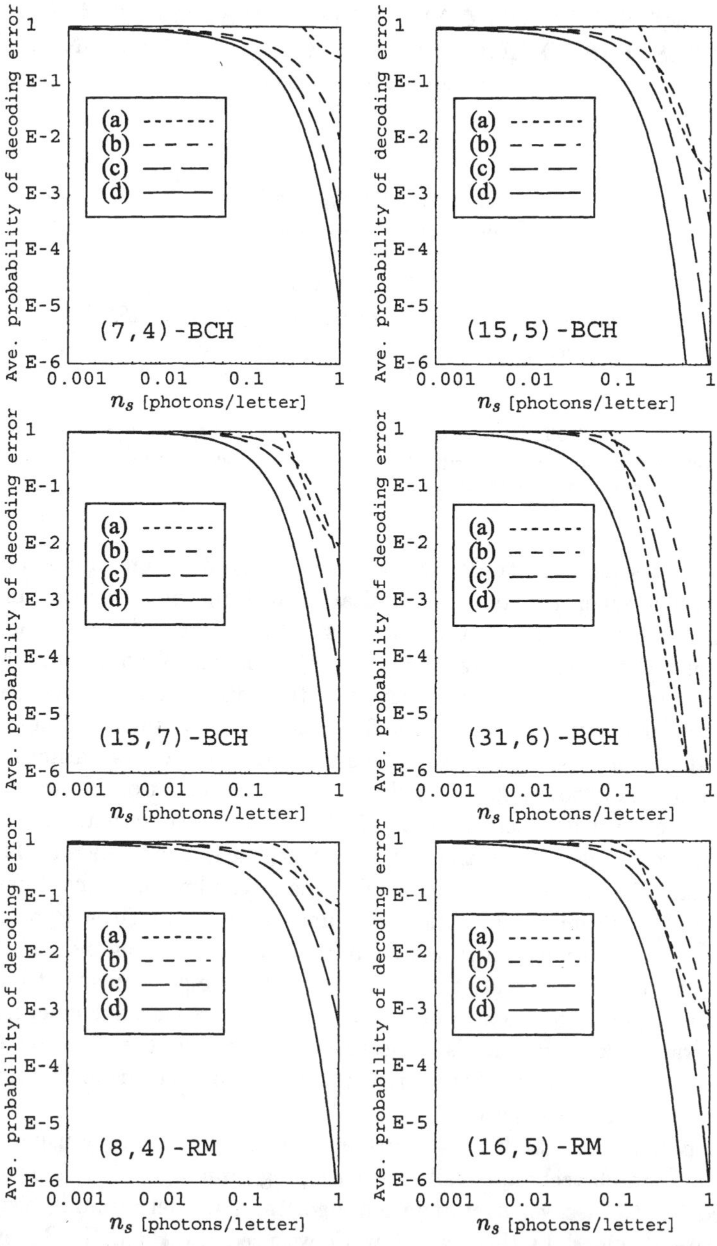

Figure 2. Average probabilities of decoding error for several concrete classical codes — (7,4,3)-BCH, (15,5,7)-BCH, (15,7,5)-BCH, (31,6,15)-BCH, (8,4,4)-RM, and (16,5,8)-RM. (a) quantum reliability function bound of Eq. (1); (b) individual decoding with Homodyne receiver; (c) individual decoding with Helstrom receiver; (d) collective decoding by square-root measurement.

COMMUNICATION CAPACITIES OF SOME QUANTUM GATES, DISCOVERED IN PART THROUGH GENETIC PROGRAMMING

LEE SPECTOR
Cognitive Science, Hampshire College, Amherst, MA 01002, USA
E-mail: lspector@hampshire.edu

HERBERT J. BERNSTEIN
Institute for Science and Interdisciplinary Studies (ISIS) & Natural Science, Hampshire College, Amherst, MA 01002, USA
E-mail: hjbNS@hampshire.edu

We explore tradeoffs between classical communication and entanglement-generating powers of unitary 2-qubit gates. The exploration is aided by a computational search technique called genetic programming.

The question of tradeoffs between classical communication and entanglement-generating powers of unitary transformations in quantum computation has great current interest.[1] If simple general rules of tradeoff are worked out, the power of a transformation U to benefit bi-partite interactions will be characterized by a single number, thus abetting and advancing the "resource" or commodity metaphor for quantum information. Bennett has theorized that a single use of any given two-particle transformation U has a unique maximum power for entanglement or communication (forward, backward or two-way) between Alice and Bob. Which of these various effects U produces would depend on the protocol in which it is embedded. The rule is that only U may connect Alice to Bob, as in the previous investigation of two-qubit Hamiltonian interactions epitomized by the myth of Pyramis and Thisbe.[2] The question is how many c-bits of communication and/or e-bits of entanglement one can create per U. The search for algorithms to deploy this power with or without ancilla, and with or without prior entanglement, begins the general work on Bennett's conjecture. In principle, the power of U may require asymptotic ratios of the number of e- or c-bits generated to instances of U deployed in the algorithm.

We pursue the search for algorithms relevant to this study using a computational search technique called genetic programming (GP). In prior work we used GP to discover new quantum algorithms for determining properties of unitary oracles.[3] In the present work we used the PushGP GP system[4] (http://hampshire.edu/lspector/push.html) in conjunction with the QGAME quantum computer simulator (http://hampshire.edu/lspector/qgame.html).

We first consider the 2-bit Smolin gate suggested by Smolin (personal communication) and shown in Fig. 1 (along with the matrices for most other gates mentioned in this paper). Smolin suggested this gate, which obviously

$$SMOLIN \equiv \begin{bmatrix} \frac{1}{\sqrt{2}} & 0 & 0 & \frac{1}{\sqrt{2}} \\ 0 & 1 & 0 & 0 \\ 0 & 0 & 1 & 0 \\ \frac{1}{\sqrt{2}} & 0 & 0 & -\frac{1}{\sqrt{2}} \end{bmatrix} \quad J(\theta) \equiv \begin{bmatrix} cos(\theta) & 0 & 0 & sin(\theta) \\ 0 & 1 & 0 & 0 \\ 0 & 0 & 1 & 0 \\ sin(\theta) & 0 & 0 & -cos(\theta) \end{bmatrix} \quad SWAP \equiv \begin{bmatrix} 1 & 0 & 0 & 0 \\ 0 & 0 & 1 & 0 \\ 0 & 1 & 0 & 0 \\ 0 & 0 & 0 & 1 \end{bmatrix}$$

$$BS(\theta) \equiv \begin{bmatrix} cos(\theta) & 0 & 0 & sin(\theta) \\ 0 & 0 & 1 & 0 \\ 0 & 1 & 0 & 0 \\ sin(\theta) & 0 & 0 & -cos(\theta) \end{bmatrix} \quad CNOT \equiv \begin{bmatrix} 1 & 0 & 0 & 0 \\ 0 & 1 & 0 & 0 \\ 0 & 0 & 0 & 1 \\ 0 & 0 & 1 & 0 \end{bmatrix} \quad CPHASE \equiv \begin{bmatrix} 1 & 0 & 0 & 0 \\ 0 & 1 & 0 & 0 \\ 0 & 0 & 1 & 0 \\ 0 & 0 & 0 & e^{i\alpha} \end{bmatrix}$$

$$U_\theta \equiv \begin{bmatrix} \cos(\theta) & \sin(\theta) \\ -\sin(\theta) & \cos(\theta) \end{bmatrix} \quad H \equiv \frac{1}{\sqrt{2}} \begin{bmatrix} 1 & 1 \\ 1 & -1 \end{bmatrix} \quad QNOT \equiv \begin{bmatrix} 0 & 1 \\ 1 & 0 \end{bmatrix} \quad SRN \equiv \begin{bmatrix} \frac{1}{\sqrt{2}} & -\frac{1}{\sqrt{2}} \\ \frac{1}{\sqrt{2}} & \frac{1}{\sqrt{2}} \end{bmatrix}$$

Figure 1. Matrices for gates used in this paper.

generates entanglement, as a potential counterexample to Bennett's conjecture, suggesting that this gate could produce one bit of entanglement per use but that it could not communicate. We show here that the Smolin gate *can* communicate one c-bit per use, either forward or backward, with no error and no ancilla. The algorithm evolved by GP is as follows: Initialize both qubits to 0 (qubit 0 is Alice's and qubit 1 is Bob's). Alice leaves her qubit unchanged to send a 0 or flips it to send a 1. Execute: $U_{-\frac{\pi}{4}}$ on qubit 1; $QNOT$ on qubit 0; $U_{\frac{\pi}{8}}$ on qubit 0; square-root-of-not (SRN) on qubit 0; $SMOLIN$ on qubits 1 and 0; $U_{-\frac{\pi}{4}}$ on qubit 1. Bob reads the bit from qubit 1 with no probability of error. By symmetry, Bob and Alice's roles could be reversed for backward classical communication (B to A). Gate array diagrams for the algorithms in this paper can be found at http://hampshire.edu/lspector/qcmc-figures.pdf.

We analyzed the evolved algorithm and, in conjunction with our work on a generalized Smolin gate (below), realized that could be expressed more simply as follows: Initialize both qubits to 0. Alice leaves qubit 0 in the 0 state to send a 0 or flips it to send a 1. Execute: $U_{\frac{\pi}{8}}$ on qubit 0; $QNOT$ on qubit 1; $U_{\frac{3\pi}{4}}$ on qubit 1; $SMOLIN$ on qubits 0 and 1; $U_{\frac{3\pi}{4}}$ on qubit 1. Bob reads from qubit 1 with no probability of error.

We recognized the relation between $\frac{\pi}{8}$ in this algorithm and the $\frac{\pi}{4}$ implicit in the Smolin gate and developed a family of gates generalizing this angle. $J(\theta)$ (see Fig. 1) defines a one-parameter family of gates, all square roots of identity, for which the perfect 1 c-bit communication strategy is an obvious generalization of the strategy we discovered for the Smolin gate. In fact, the entire family of gates, which runs from $CPHASE$ through Smolin (at $\theta = \frac{\pi}{4}$) to a version of $SWAP$ as θ ranges from 0 to $\frac{\pi}{2}$, can be used for perfect communication, forward or back, using our strategy and no prior entanglement or ancilla. The following scheme was discovered by human analysis (GP independently found equivalent results): Initialize both qubits to 0. Alice leaves qubit 0 unchanged to send a 0 or flips it to send a 1. Execute: $U_{\frac{\theta_j}{2}}$ on qubit 0, where θ_j is the value of θ used in J below; $QNOT$ on qubit 1; $U_{\frac{3\pi}{4}}$ on qubit 1; $J(\theta)$ on qubits 0 and 1; $U_{\frac{3\pi}{4}}$ on qubit 1. Bob reads from qubit 1

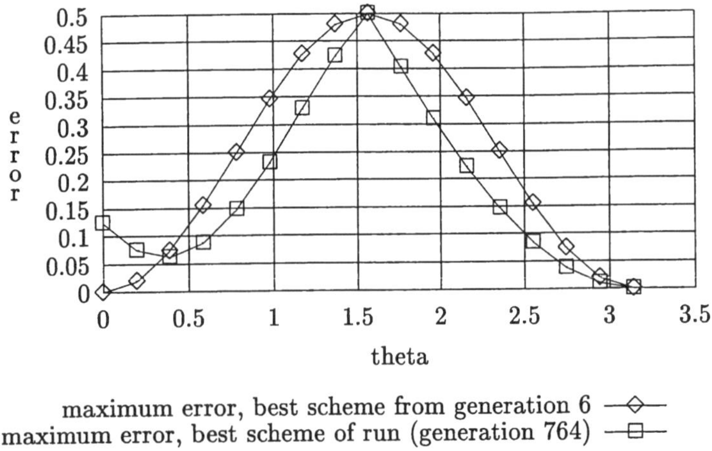

Figure 2. Errors of some evolved strategies for communicating a bit through $BS(\theta)$ with no ancilla and no prior entanglement for various values of θ. The worst case error of a scheme found early in evolution is equivalent to $\frac{sin^2(\theta)}{2}$. A peculiar strategy (using different gates for different θ) found in generation 764 does worse for small θ but better elsewhere.

with no probability of error.

After discovering that the Smolin gate *could* be used for exact communication we developed a new gate that appears to block communication while nonetheless entangling; that is, it seems to fulfill Smolin's initial intent. We define $BS(\theta)$ as in Fig. 1. This ranges from $SWAP \times CPHASE$ through a modified Smolin ($SMOLIN \times SWAP$) to $QNOT \times QNOT$ as θ ranges from 0 to $\frac{\pi}{2}$. Clearly the $\frac{\pi}{2}$ endpoint, as a product of local transformations, can neither communicate nor entangle. For other angles this gate can entangle and has some communication potential. Search by GP has thus far discovered error-free communication strategies through $BS(\theta)$ without ancilla only at θ mod $\pi = 0$; see Fig. 2.

Although we suspect that perfect communication through $BS(\frac{\pi}{4})$ is not possible without prior entanglement, it is indeed possible with one bit of prior entanglement. The following algorithm was found by GP: Initialize both qubits to 0. Then provide entanglement by executing a Hadamard (H) gate on qubit 0 and a controlled-not ($CNOT$) gate with qubit 0 as the control and qubit 1 as the target. Alice then leaves qubit 0 unchanged to send a 0 or flips it to send a 1. Execute: H on qubit 0; H on qubit 1; $BS(\frac{\pi}{4})$ on qubits 0 and 1. Bob reads from qubit 1 with no probability of error. Note that Bob may also use spin-flip choice to simultaneously send 1 bit to Alice.

Knowing that $BS(\pi)$ can communicate one bit with no prior entanglement, we employed GP to find out if a single execution of $BS(\pi)$, in the presence of one bit of prior entanglement, could communicate 2 bits without error. GP found a way, as follows: Initialize four qubits to 0. Then provide prior entanglement by executing H on qubit 1 and $CNOT$ with qubit 1 as the control and qubit 3 as the target. Qubits 0 and 1 are Alice's and qubits 2 and 3 are Bob's. Alice leaves her qubits unchanged to send 0s or flips them to send 1s. Then execute: $CPHASE(\pi)$ on qubit 0 (control) and qubit 1 (target); $BS(\pi)$ on qubits 2 and 1; $CNOT$ on qubits 2 and 3; $U_{\frac{7\pi}{4}}$ on qubit 2. Bob reads the message from qubits 2 and 3 with no probability of error. Qubit 2 will contain the message set by Alice in qubit 0, and qubit 3 will contain the message set by Alice in qubit 1. This is equivalent to dense coding.

Our work on $BS(\theta)$ and $J(\theta)$ led us to an understanding of the importance of the eigenvalue/eigenvector expansion of these gates. In particular there is a close relation between the communication potential of $J(\theta)$ and the presence of an odd number of positive eigenvalues, as opposed to the lack of communication potential of $BS(\theta)$ where there are an even number of positive eigenvalues. Later analytical investigation shows that $BS(\theta)$ for $0 < \theta < \frac{\pi}{4}$ can always entangle a full e-bit of entanglement, too. And of course multiple uses of $BS(\frac{\pi}{4})$—still in the absence of ancilla—can also communicate one bit per gate. This is accomplished in two steps, by alternating a stage of entanglement generation with a stage of the entanglement-consuming 2-way communication mentioned above. But even this strategy fails to close the apparent gap between the entanglement and communication power of $BS(\theta)$ for $0 < \theta < \frac{\pi}{4}$. The two fully entangled states one generates in this case are non-orthogonal. They image distinct non-orthogonal product states whose restoration in stage 2 cannot unerringly signal a c-bit to both Alice and Bob.

Acknowledgments

We thank C. H. Bennett, A. Harrow, D. W. Leung, and J. A. Smolin for discussions. This effort was supported by the Defense Advanced Research Projects Agency (DARPA) and Air Force Research Laboratory, Air Force Materiel Command, USAF, under agreement number F30502-00-2-0611, and by NSF grant PHY-9722614. Support was also provided by Hampshire College for the Institute for Computational Intelligence and for ISIS.

References

1. D. Collins, N. Linden, and S. Popescu. *Phys. Rev. A* **64**, 032302 (2001), quant-ph/0005102 (2000).
2. C. H. Bennett, J. I. Cirac, M. S. Leifer, D. W. Leung, N. Linden, S. Popescu, and G. Vidal. *Phys. Rev. A* **66**, 012305 (2002), quant-ph/0107035 (2001), *cf.* H.J. Bernstein unpubl. talks (Jun 2001).
3. H. Barnum, H. J. Bernstein, and L. Spector. *J. Phys. A: Mathematical and General* **33(45)**, 8047–8057 (2000).
4. L. Spector and A. Robinson. *Genetic Programming and Evolvable Machines* **3**, 7–40 (2002).

PHYSICAL REVERSIBILITY AND ONE-WAY FUNCTION

ELHAM KASHEFI
Department of Computing, Imperial College, London SW7 2BZ, England

VLATKO VEDRAL
Optics Section, The Blackett Laboratory, Imperial College, London SW7 2BZ, England

We discuss the issue of the relationship between computational and physical complexity. We present a simple example of this relationship, exploiting the notion of a one-way function. In physics, one-wayness is traditionally described by the physical entropy, however, this does not tell us anything about the difficulty of performing transformations in general. We argue that we need a more refined definition of physical complexity to explore the interplay between physical and computational one-wayness.

1 Introduction

We want to investigate the relationship between complexity in computing and physics. The computational complexity has a clear definition based on a universal computational model (e.g., the Turing machine, the uniform circuit family).[1] However, in spite of many efforts, a completely satisfactory definition for physical complexity has not been proposed yet.[2,3] In particular, we are interested in the notion of "one-wayness" in physics and computing. The existence of one-way functions is an important open problem in computational complexity and we ask the following question: what are the physical consequences of the existence or (non-existence) of one-way functions?

In thermodynamics, physical states are ordered according to their *entropy*. The entropy measure can be considered as an analog of the computability notation in computing. Entropy, likewise, characterizes whether a process is possible or not. It is not clear, however, that if the entropy of two states a and b is the same, one can still adiabatically design an efficient physical process from a to b and vice versa. Therefore we might need to define a finer ordering of physical states to deal with complexity and efficient processing. In this paper we discuss an example dealing with one-way permutations to establish a simple relationship between physical and computational complexity.

2 One-way Functions

The study of the state and operator complexity is a first step towards exploring the relationship between the physical and computational complexity. The special case of the relationship between the complexity of preparing a state and the complexity of performing the operator of reflection about that state has a close connection with the question of the existence of one-way functions. We introduce a notion of complexity of preparing quantum states and constructing unitary transformations. Define $\mathcal{S}$ to be the set of all sequences $\{|\psi_x\rangle\}_x$ where $|\psi_x\rangle$ is an arbitrary x-qubits state, and $\mathcal{U}$ to be the set of all sequences $\{U_x\}_x$ where U_x is an arbitrary unitary transformation acting on x qubits.

Definition 1 *A family $\{|\psi_x\rangle\}_x \in \mathcal{S}$ of states is polynomial-time computable, if there exists a uniform polynomial-size quantum network family $N = \{N_x\}$ such that on input x, N_x produces output state $|\psi_x\rangle$.*

Definition 2 *A family $\{U_x\}_x \in \mathcal{U}$ of unitary operators is defined to be polynomial-time computable, if there exists a uniform quantum network family $N = \{N_x\}$ such that on input x and $|\psi\rangle$, N_x produces output $U_x(|\psi\rangle)$.*

We consider the relationship between states and reflection operators about those states. The reflection operator, about a given state $|\psi\rangle$, is defined to be

$$2|\psi\rangle\langle\psi| - I\,. \tag{1}$$

For simplicity, we mean by "easy" to be "polynomial computable". It is well-known that if a state ($|\psi\rangle$) is easy, then the reflection about that state ($2|\psi\rangle\langle\psi| - I$) is also easy.[4] We call its inverse, the statement "*if the reflection about a state is easy, the state itself is easy*", the Reflection Assumption. By revisiting Grover's algorithm[5] from this viewpoint we prove the following fact.

Theorem 1 [6] *If there exists a quantum one-way permutation, there exists a counter-example to Reflection Assumption.*

The referred to counter example is based on the strong assumption of the existence of a quantum one-way function, which is equivalent to the open problem of the separation between the complexity classes EQP and UP. It would be interesting to present such a counter example based on a weaker assumption, for example, the open problem of the separation between the complexity classes EQP and PSPACE.

Now we present a theorem on characterization of quantum one-way permutations, the proof of which can be found in Ref. 6. We show that in the quantum setting the problem of inverting a permutation in polynomial time is equivalent to the problem of constructing a polynomial size networks for the reflections about a given quantum states $|\psi\rangle$, i.e., $2|\psi\rangle\langle\psi| - I$.

For any permutation f on n-bit strings, U_f denotes the unitary operator mapping the basis state $|x\rangle|y\rangle$ to $|x\rangle|f(x)\oplus y\rangle$, where $|x\rangle$ and $|y\rangle$ each consist of n qubits. We consider the problem **INVERT**: for any given $x \in \{0,1\}^n$, find $f^{-1}(x)$. When f is given as an oracle, Grover's algorithm can solve **INVERT** with quadratic speed-up over any classical algorithm.[5] Grover's algorithm uses the tagging operator O defined as

$$O|x\rangle|y\rangle = (-1)^{\delta_{x,f(y)}}|x\rangle|y\rangle \tag{2}$$

and the reflection about the uniform superposition defined as

$$|\psi\rangle = \sum_{y\in\{0,1\}^n} |y\rangle, \tag{3}$$

i.e., $2|\psi\rangle\langle\psi| - I$, which is also called the inversion about the average amplitude. It is also possible to efficiently construct the unitary operator $O[k]$ defined by

$$O[k]|x\rangle|y\rangle = (-1)^{\delta_{x_k, f_k(y)} \cdot \delta_{x_{k+1}, f_{k+1}(y)}}|x\rangle|y\rangle, \tag{4}$$

where x_i and $f_i(y)$ for $i = 1, \ldots, n$ represent the i-th bits of x and $f(y)$. This operator $O[k]$ will enable us to mark all the states $|y\rangle$ such that 2 qubits of $|f(y)\rangle$ are equal to the corresponding qubits of $|x\rangle$.

Theorem 2 *A function $f : \{0,1\}^n \rightarrow \{0,1\}^n$ is a quantum one-way permutation (in worst case complexity) if and only if the set $F_n = \{Q_j\}_{j=0,1,\ldots,\frac{n}{2}-1}$ of unitary operators is not easy, where*

$$Q_j = \sum_{x \in \{0,1\}^n} |x\rangle\langle x| \otimes (2|\psi_{j,x}\rangle\langle\psi_{j,x}| - I), \tag{5}$$

and

$$|\psi_{j,x}\rangle = \frac{1}{\sqrt{2^{n-2j}}} \sum_{y: f(y)_{(1,2j)} = x_{(1,2j)}} |y\rangle, \tag{6}$$

This theorem shows that the complexity of efficiently constructing some reflection operator (a physical question) is equivalent to the question of the existence of one-way permutations (a computational question).

3 Discussion

There are two general arguments explaining the origin of irreversibility in physics, which needs to be derived from the fully reversible underlying microscopic laws. One is the loss of information through the interaction of the system with its environment. The second argument is based on the lack of knowledge of the exact state of the system, which then prevents us from reversing the evolution of the system in spite of it being reversible (since we do not have the relevant knowledge).

One can imagine a third approach, however, which is based on the computational one-wayness. Assume that a physical process encodes a reversible one-way function, then it might happen that the final configuration of the system has the same entropy as the initial configuration and still the reverse of the physical process could take an exponential time. Therefore it is reasonable to consider it as an irreversible process even though it is "allowed" by entropy. This was the key of Boltzmann's reply to the objection that entropy of an isolated system can decrease by reversing the evolution thereby contradicting the Second law. Boltzmann maintained that it would be difficult to perform the reversal (although this has never been characterized in terms of computational complexity).

In a very simplified version of Boltzmann's example, we can imagine that the evolution of an isolated gas can be represented as a permutation over the configuration space of the gas (i.e., consisting of all possible positions and momenta in classical physics). It is therefore interesting to see how easy it is to invert such a permutation. Although the answer to this question is not known, we have reduced the problem of the existence of a quantum one-way permutation to the problem of constructing a polynomial size network for performing the specific task of the reflection about a given state. We hope that our work stimulates further discussions and investigations into the important issue of the computational complexity behind the second law of thermodynamics.

Acknowledgments

We are grateful to Harumichi Nishimura for useful discussions. This work was supported by EPSRC, the European grant EQUIP and the QUIPROCONE grant.

References

1. C. H. Papadimitriou, *Computational Complexity*, (Addision-Wesley, 1994).
2. S. Wolfram, *Phys. Rev. Lett.* **54**, 735 (1985).
3. C. H. Bennett in *Complexity, Entropy and the Physics of Information*, ed. W. H. Zurek, (Addison-Wesley, 1990).
4. M. A. Nielsen and I. L. Chuang, *Quantum Computation and Quantum Information*, (Cambridge University Press,2000).
5. L. K. Grover, in *Proceedings of 28th ACM Symposium on the Theory of Computing*, 212 (1996).
6. E. Kashefi, H. Nishimura and V. Vedral, Quantum Inform. Comput. **2**, 379 (2002).

Part XI
Sources of Nonclassical Light

INDISTINGUISHABLE SINGLE PHOTONS FOR QUANTUM INFORMATION SYSTEMS

CHARLES SANTORI,* EDO WAKS,* KYO INOUE,† DAVID FATTAL,* JELENA VUCKOVIC,* GLENN S. SOLOMON,* YOSHIHISA YAMAMOTO*†

**Quantum Entanglement Project, ICORP, JST, Edward L. Ginzton Laboratory, Stanford University, Stanford, CA 94305-4088, USA*

†NTT Basic Research Laboratories, 3-1 Morinosato Wakamiya, Atsugi-shi, Kanagawa 243-0198, Japan

Generation of single photons from a single isolated quantum dot in a post microcavity is reported. Generated single photons are quantum mechanically indistinguishable, so they feature a two-photon interference effect.

1 Introduction

Single-photon sources have recently been demonstrated using a variety of systems, including single molecule,[1,2,3] color center,[4] trapped ion,[5] quantum well,[6] and quantum dot.[7,8,9,10,11] These sources rarely emit two or more photons in the same pulse. Numerous applications for single-photon sources have been proposed in the field of quantum information. However, most, including linear-optical quantum computation,[12] also require quantum indistinguishability. The emitter must produce Fourier-transform-limited single-photon wave packets with negligible jitter. Here, we test the indistinguishability of photons emitted by a semiconductor quantum dot in a microcavity through a Hong-Ou-Mandel-type two-photon interference experiment.[13,14] We find that consecutive photons are largely indistinguishable, with a mean wave-packet overlap as large as 0.81, making this source useful in a variety of experiments in quantum optics and quantum information systems.

2 Indistinguishable Single Photons

When identical single photons enter a 50/50 beam splitter from opposite sides, quantum mechanics predicts that both photons must exit in the same direction, if their wave packets overlap perfectly. This two-photon interference effect originates from the symmetrized wave function of the two identical bosons.[13,14] Most proposed applications for single-photon sources in the field of quantum information (with the notable exception of BB84 quantum cryptography[15]) involve two-photon interference. Such applications include quantum teleportation,[16] post-selective production of polarization-entangled photons,[17] and linear-optics quantum computation.[12]

The experiment used a semiconductor quantum dot as the photon source. Quantum dots are attractive as single-photon sources because they are relatively stable, have narrow spectral linewidths, have rapid radiative decay rates, and can be integrated into larger fabricated structures, such as microcavities, to improve the collection efficiency. A quantum dot excited on resonance by a pulsed source can have an extremely small probability of generating two photons in the same pulse.

Our sample contains self-assembled InAs quantum dots (about 25 μm^{-2}) embedded in GaAs and sandwiched between distributed-Bragg-reflector (DBR) mirrors, grown by molecular-beam epitaxy. Pillars with diameters of $0.3\,\mu m$ and heights of $5\,\mu m$ were fabricated in a random distribution by chemically-assisted ion beam etching (CAIBE), using sapphire dust particles as etch masks. The resulting microcavities, exhibiting three-dimensional photon confinement, have quality factors of approximately 1200 and measured spontaneous-emission rate enhancement (Purcell) factors as high as 5. The sample was cooled to 3–7 K in a cryostat. To generate single photons, we focused 3-ps-duration Ti-Sapphire laser pulses occurring every 13 ns onto these pillars from a steep angle. The laser was tuned to an excited-state absorption resonance of the quantum dot, typically 20–30 nm shorter in wavelength compared to the first-level emission wavelength. The emission was spectrally filtered with a resolution of about 0.1 nm using a diffraction grating, and coupled into a single-mode fiber.

By this method, we obtained bright single-photon sources with excellent two-photon suppression and negligible background emission. We have chosen three quantum dots for this study, denoted as dots 1, 2, and 3, with emission wavelengths of 931 nm, 932 nm, and 937 nm, respectively. A parameter often used to quantify two-photon suppression is $g^{(2)}$, the probability of generating two photons in the same pulse, normalized by the corresponding probability for an equally bright Poisson-distributed source. We estimate $g^{(2)} = 0.053$, 0.067, and 0.071 for dots 1, 2, and 3, respectively. But for the experiment described below, the important parameter is the probability of generating two photons in the same pulse, for either of two consecutive pulses, divided by the probability of generating one photon in each pulse. We estimate this quantity to be $g = 0.039$, 0.027, and 0.025 for quantum dots 1, 2, and 3, respectively. The difference between $g^{(2)}$ and g is due to blinking in our source.

Two other properties of the quantum-dot emission are also important for the two-photon interference experiment described below: the spontaneous emission lifetime and the coherence time. In Fig. 1(a), the average emission intensity of quantum dots 1, 2, and 3 is plotted versus time following an excitation pulse. By fitting decaying exponential functions, we estimate the spontaneous emission lifetimes τ_s of dots 1, 2, and 3 to be 89 ps, 166 ps, and 351 ps, respectively. This variation is due largely to differences in how well each quantum dot couples to its microcavity. In Fig. 1(b), a Michelson interferometer is used to measure the coherence time. The curves show how the interference fringe contrast varies with path-length difference. We estimate the $1/e$ coherence times τ_c for quantum dots 1, 2, and 3 to be 48 ps, 223 ps, and

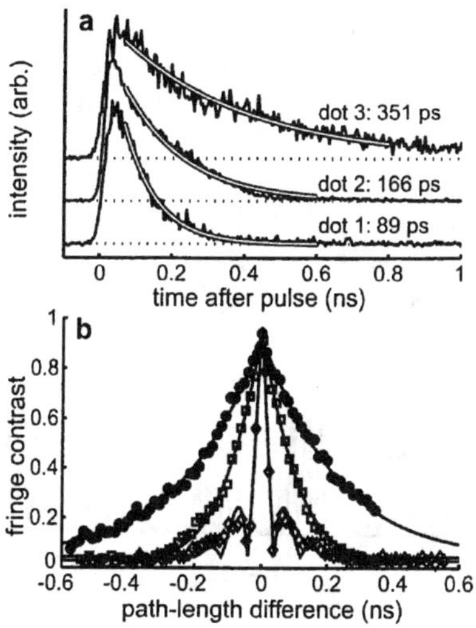

Figure 1. Time-averaged emission properties of quantum dots 1, 2, and 3. (a) Spontaneous emission decay under resonant excitation, measured by a streak camera. The single-photon source. (b) Coherence length, measured using a Michelson interferometer, showing fringe contrast versus path-length difference.

105 ps, respectively. Quantum dot 2 is closest to the Fourier transform limit, with $2\tau_s/\tau_c = 1.5$. When this ratio equals 1, no dephasing can be present, and perfect two-photon interference is expected.

The two-photon interference setup is shown in Fig. 2(a). The quantum dot is excited twice every 13 ns by a pair of equally intense pulses with 2 ns separation. Two pulses emerge from the single-mode fiber. They are split into two arms by a beam splitter, with one arm ($2\,\text{ns} + \Delta t$) longer than the other. The beams then recombine at a different place on the same beam splitter. The two outputs of this interferometer are collected by photon counters, and a photon-correlation histogram is generated of the relative delay time $\tau = t_2 - t_1$ for two-photon coincidence events, where t_1 and t_2 are the times at which photons are detected at detectors 1 and 2, respectively. A histogram obtained in this way for dot 2 with $\Delta t = 0$ is shown in Fig. 2(b).

Five peaks appear within the central cluster, corresponding to three types of coincidence events. For peaks 1 and 5 at $\tau = \mp 4\,\text{ns}$, the first photon follows the short arm of the interferometer, the second photon follows the long arm, and one photon goes to each counter. For peaks 2 and 4 at $\tau = \mp 2\,\text{ns}$, both photons follow the same arm. For peak 3 at $\tau = 0$, the first photon follows the long arm, and the second photon follows the short arm, so that the two photons collide upon their second pass through the beam splitter. Only in this case can two-photon interference occur, and for perfect two-photon

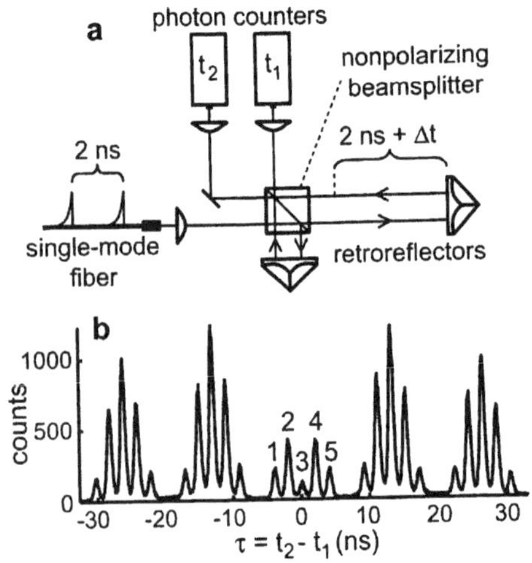

Figure 2. Two-photon interference experiment. (a) Every 13 ns, two pulses, separated by 2 ns and containing 0 or 1 photon, arrive through a single-mode fiber. The pulses are interfered with each other using a Michelson-type interferometer with a (2 ns + Δt) path-length difference. (b) Such a histogram obtained for quantum dot 2, with $\Delta t = 0$. The central peak at $\tau = 0$ (peak 3) corresponds to events in which two photons from opposite arms enter the beam splitter at the same time, and exit in opposite directions.

interference, peak 3 vanishes.

The signature of two-photon interference that we observe is the small size of peak 3 in Fig. 2(b), compared to peaks 2 and 4. We define the quantity $M(\Delta t) = A_3/(A_2 + A_4)$ in terms of the peak areas. This quantity is equal to the conditional probability, given that two photons collide at the beam splitter, that the photons exit in opposite directions, in the limit $g \approx 0$. We measured $M(\Delta t)$ while varying the interferometer path length offset Δt. For all three quantum dots, we observe reductions in the coincidence probability near $\Delta t = 0$, by factors of 0.61, 0.69, and 0.62 for dots 1, 2, and 3, respectively. The remaining coincidences we see are partly due to independently-measured optical imperfections in our setup. Without these imperfections, the coincidence reduction factors would be V(0) = 0.72, 0.81, and 0.74 for quantum dots 1, 2, and 3, respectively.

3 Conclusions

Quantum mechanically indistinguishable single photons are generated from a single isolated quantum dot in a post microcavity.[18] More recently, we have used such single photon sources for various quantum information systems, including quantum key distribution based on BB84 protocol,[19] entanglement formation and violation of Bell's inequality,[20] and entanglement swap gates for linear optics quantum computation.[21]

References

1. F. De Martini, G. Di Giuseppe, and M. Marrocco, *Phys. Rev. Lett.* **76**, 900 (1996).
2. C. Brunel, B. Lounis, P. Tamarat, and M. Orrit, *Phys. Rev. Lett.* **83**, 2722 (1999).
3. B. Lounis and W.E. Moerner, *Nature* **407**, 491 (2000).
4. A. Beveratos *et al*, *Eur. Phys. J. D* **18**, 191 (2002).
5. A. Kuhn, M. Hennrich, and G. Rempe, quant-ph/0204147.
6. J. Kim, O. Benson, H. Kan, and Y. Yamamoto, *Nature* **397**, 500 (1999).
7. P. Michler *et al.*, *Science* **290**, 2282 (2000).
8. C. Santori, M. Pelton, G. Solomon, Y. Dale, and Y. Yamamoto, *Phys. Rev. Lett.* **86**, 1502 (2001).
9. V. Zwiller *et al.*, *Appl. Phys. Lett.* **78**, 2476 (2001).
10. Z. Yuan *et al.*, *Science* **295**, 102 (2002).
11. J.-M. Gérard and B. Gayral, *J. Lightwave Technol.* **17**, 2089 (1999).
12. E. Knill, R. Laflamme, and G. J. Milburn, *Nature* **409**, 46 (2001).
13. H. Fearn and R. Loudon, *J. Opt. Soc. Am. B* **6**, 917 (1989).
14. C. K. Hong, Z.Y. Ou, and L. Mandel, *Phys. Rev. Lett.* **59**, 2044 (1987).
15. C. H. Bennett and G. Brassard in *Proceedings of IEEE International Conference on Computers, Systems and Signal Processing*, Bangalore, India (IEEE, New York, 1984), pp. 175-179.
16. D. Bouwmeester, A. Ekert, and A. Zeilinger in *The Physics of Quantum Information* (Springer-Verlag, Berlin, 2000), pp.49-92.
17. Y.H. Shih and C.O. Alley, *Phys. Rev. Lett.* **61**, 2921 (1988).
18. C. Santori, D. Fattal, J. Vuckovic, G. S. Solomon, and Y. Yamamoto, *Nature* **419**, 594 (2002).
19. E. Waks, K. Inoue, C. Santori, D. Fattal, J. Vuckovic, G. S. Solomon, and Y. Yamamoto, *Nature* **420**, 762 (2002).
20. D. Fattal *et al.*, (to be published).
21. E. Diamanti *et al.*, (to be published).

QUANTUM TECHNOLOGY OF NONCLASSICAL LIGHT: NEW EXPERIMENTS AND PERSPECTIVES

A. I. LVOVSKY

Fachbereich Physik, Universität Konstanz, D-78457 Konstanz, Germany
http://www.uni-konstanz.de/quantum-optics/quantech/

We develop new tools of production, manipulation, and characterization of highly nonclassical states of the light field, with the ultimate goal of making complex photonic building blocks for future quantum optical technology. Based upon our existing experience in synthesis and measurement of the single-photon Fock state, we generate and investigate new, more complex quantum states of light.

1 Introduction

The progress in quantum optical technology relies on our ability to a) create, b) manipulate and c) characterize arbitrary quantum states of the electromagnetic field. Here we summarize a few experiments aimed towards enhancing these abilities. Their common feature is a combination of two experimental techniques that were not used together previously. To *synthesize* the nonclassical states of light we generate entangled pairs of photons by means of parametric downconversion of ultrafast laser pulses. This procedure is commonplace in modern quantum optics and is normally followed by the *characterization* of various properties of the generated ensembles using single-photon detectors. The latter practice, albeit straightforward and intuitive, does not provide full information about the quantum state in question. Therefore we have employed an alternative method, homodyne tomography, which allows us, in principle, to gain complete knowledge about an optical ensemble by means of repeated measurements of its electric field quadratures. Although applying homodyne tomography to highly nonclassical states of light involves a number of challenges, the benefits of this approach are abundant. As we demonstrate below, it opens up the path towards a wide range of new quantum states of light that can be engineered and investigated.

2 Single-photon Fock state

Quantum states containing a definite number of energy quanta (Fock states) play a key role in quantum optics. They constitute the essence of the quantum nature of light and are indispensable in both theoretical description of many optical phenomena, as well as in a wide range of applications, such as quantum cryptography[1] and quantum information processing.[2] In this experiment we have prepared pulsed single photons by conditional measurements on a biphoton state generated via parametric downconversion and characterized them by means of balanced homodyne tomography[3] [Fig. 1(a)].

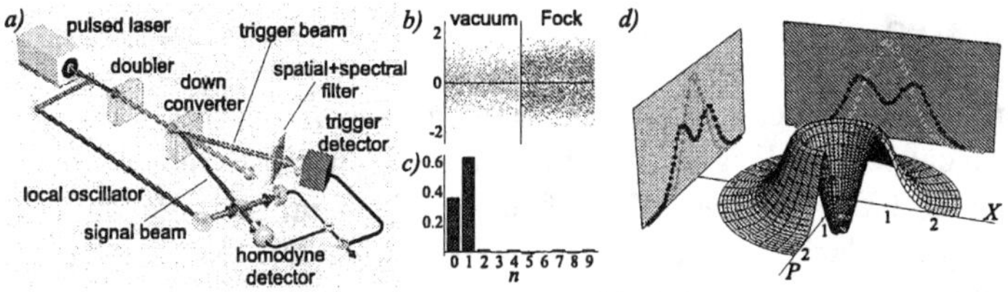

Figure 1. The experiment on quantum tomography of the single-photon Fock state. (a) Simplified scheme; (b) 45000 raw quantum noise data for the vacuum state and the Fock state; (c) the reconstructed density matrix (diagonal elements); (d) phase-randomized marginal distributions for the measured vacuum and Fock states; the reconstructed Wigner function is negative near the origin point. A measurement efficiency of 62% is achieved.

Optical homodyne measurements require that the spatio-temporal mode of the Fock state match that of the local oscillator. Because the Fock state was prepared via a nonlocal measurement and is extremely weak in intensity, this task proved to be a significant challenge.[4]

Another requirement for these experiments is associated with the balanced homodyne detector. Because all measurements are performed in the pulsed regime, our detector has to operate in the time domain and resolve the quantum shot noise of individual laser pulses. It must thus exhibit low electronic noise and a flat amplification profile in a wide radio-frequency range between zero frequency and ~1 MHz.[5]

In an actual experiment, the ensemble measured with the homodyne detector is not an ideal Fock state $|1\rangle$ but rather a statistical mixture whose density matrix can be approximated as $\rho_{\text{meas}} = \eta|1\rangle\langle 1| + (1-\eta)|0\rangle\langle 0|$. The quantity η is the measurement efficiency, which depends on many factors: optical transmission of the signal photon, quantum efficiency of the homodyne detector, trigger dark counts, optical mode matching of the signal photon and the local oscillator, spatio-temporal coherence of the signal photon. The greater η, the deeper the well in the Wigner function; classically impossible negative values are obtained when $\eta > 0.5$.[a] For our setup, the efficiency is $(62 \pm 1)\%$ so the Wigner function does become negative [Fig. 1(b)–(d)].

Quantum state reconstruction of the state $|1\rangle$ has been reported on the vibrational degree of freedom of a trapped beryllium ion[7] as well as in a cavity QED setting.[8] A special feature of this experiment is that the technique of homodyne tomography can be fully understood in the framework of classical physics. In other words, this measurement could have been conducted (and interpreted) by someone who does not believe in quantum mechanics. Yet the result obtained would appear completely absurd, incompatible with the classical picture of the world — thus providing very strong evidence of quantum mechanics.

[a] In fact, even for $\eta \leq 0.5$ ensembles ρ_{meas} are nonclassical according to a weaker criterion[6]

3 Displaced Fock states

The displacement operator $\hat{D}(\alpha) \equiv \exp(\alpha\hat{a}^\dagger - \alpha^*\hat{a})$, acting upon a quantum ensemble, causes its Wigner function to shift in phase space by the vector displacement (X, P), where $X + iP = \alpha$. For example, a coherent state is obtained by displacing a vacuum state: $|\alpha\rangle = \hat{D}(\alpha)|0\rangle$. In this experiment we have studied the displaced single-photon states.

We have implemented the displacement operator by means of a high-reflection beam splitter (in the actual experiment, a dielectric mirror) off which our single photon was reflected [Fig. 2(a)]. A strong coherent laser field entered the beam splitter from the rear, with its tiny fraction being transmitted and displacing the Fock state.

The results of the Displaced Fock state reconstruction are shown in Fig. 2(b),(c).[9] The Wigner function exhibits classically-impossible negative values in the phase space region around the point $X + iP = \alpha$. The photon number distribution shows two peaks, which is also a well-known nonclassical feature of the displaced Fock states.[10]

Displaced Fock states find their application in tomographic reconstruction of random quantum states, yet they themselves have not been synthesized and studied until now. In terms of experimental technology, this work presents the first phase-sensitive tomographic reconstruction of a highly nonclassical optical state.

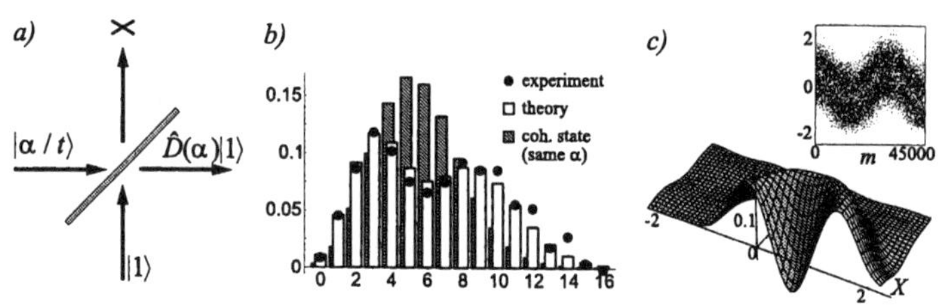

Figure 2. (a) Preparation of the displaced Fock state. The beam splitter transmission t^2 must be low. (b) A reconstructed density matrix for $\alpha = 2.4$ exhibits photon number oscillations. (c) Wigner function ($\alpha = 0.6$).

4 Quantum-optical catalysis

The beam splitter used in the displaced Fock state preparation had two output channels, one of which (reflection of the coherent state) was discarded. In the following experiment this channel was instead subjected to a quantum measurement via a single-photon detector (SPD). In the event of a "click" this detector triggered a homodyne measurement in the other (signal) channel [Fig. 3(a)]. The signal ensemble was thus prepared conditioned on one of the beam splitter output states being the single-photon state, i.e., identical to that in one of the inputs. Contrary to classical intuition we find the signal ensemble to differ from the original ("target") coherent state $|\alpha\rangle$: it is approximated by a coherent superposition $|\psi_s\rangle \propto t|0\rangle + \alpha|1\rangle$, t^2 being the beam splitter transmission. We call the effect of such transformation *quantum-optical catalysis* because of the role of the single photon, which facilitates generation of a nonclassical signal ensemble without being affected by this interaction.[11]

To visualize this phenomenon let us assume $\alpha \sim t \ll 1$ (hence $|\alpha\rangle \approx |0\rangle + \alpha|1\rangle$). Suppose the SPD registers a photon. Where could this photon have originated from? If it comes from the coherent state, the photon $|1\rangle$ from the Fock state input is likely to have been reflected into the signal channel. If, on the other hand, the photon detected by the SPD originates from the Fock state transmitted through a beam splitter, the quantum state in the signal channel is with a high probability vacuum $|0\rangle$.

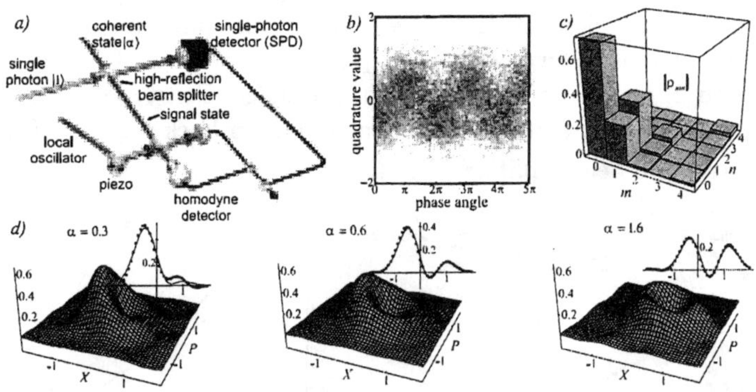

Figure 3. (a) Scheme of the catalysis experiment. Measurements by the balanced homodyne detector are conditioned on the single-photon detector registering a photon; (b) 14153 raw homodyne detector data; (c) absolute values of the density matrix elements in the Fock representation for $\alpha \approx 0.3$. (d): Quantum catalysis ensembles obtained for various values of α. Solid lines show theoretical fits to Wigner functions' cross-section. The beam splitter transmission is $t^2 = 0.075$.

The quantum properties of the beam splitter manifest themselves in the *fundamental indistinguishability* of these two possibilities. If the two initial states are prepared in identical optical modes, there is no opportunity of telling which one of the initial states the photon in the SPD channel is coming from. As a result, the quantum state in the signal channel is not a statistical mixture of the states $|0\rangle$ and $|1\rangle$ but their coherent superposition.

The density matrix of the signal state measured experimentally at $t \approx \alpha \approx 0.3$ is shown in Fig. 3(b). The only non-negligible elements are associated with Fock states $|0\rangle$ and $|1\rangle$; an disproportionately high fraction of the vacuum state is due to experimental inefficiencies in preparing the single-photon state and its measurements.[3]

The reconstructed Wigner functions for the signal state are shown in

Fig. 3(d). At large values of α the photon detector will fire with almost every laser pulse and the signal state approaches a displaced Fock state discussed above. For a constant, small t the increase of α thus implements a gradual transition between highly classical ($|0\rangle$) and highly non-classical ($\hat{D}(t\alpha)|1\rangle$) states of light.

The observed effect of quantum optical catalysis is a direct consequence of beam splitter's capability to generate an entangled two-mode state from a nonclassical but unentangled input. This experiment can be seen as an implementation of the first of two stages of the nonlinear sign shift quantum gate, the basic element of the recently proposed linear-optical quantum computation scheme.[2]

5 Quantum scissors (teleportation via a single photon)

Another important element of this scheme is quantum teleportation (QT) of quantum bits of a form $\alpha_0 |0\rangle + \alpha_1 |1\rangle$. We perform QT by applying the standard Bennett protocol[12] to an entangled Bell-type state $|\Psi^-\rangle = \frac{1}{\sqrt{2}}(|1\rangle |0\rangle - |0\rangle |1\rangle)$ generated when a single-photon Fock state $|1\rangle$ is incident upon a symmetric beam splitter [Fig. 4].

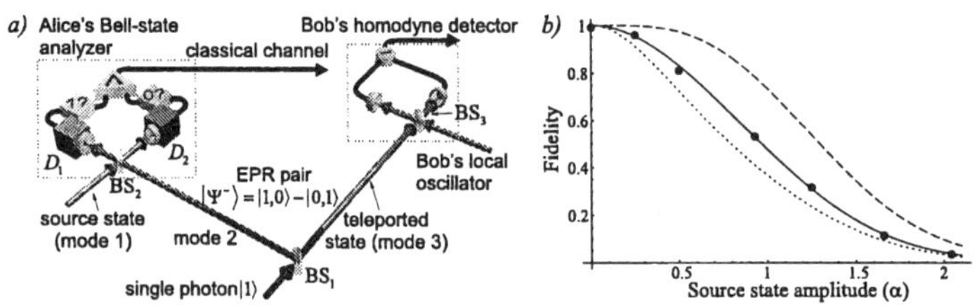

Figure 4. Teleportation by means of a single photon ("quantum scissors"): (a) Scheme; (b) Teleportation fidelity. Shown are the experimental data and the theoretical fit (solid line), the idealized quantum mechanical model with number discriminating detectors (dashed line) and the semiclassical particle model (dotted line).

Alice performs a Bell-state measurement on the source ensemble and her share of $|\Psi^-\rangle$. She overlaps the two modes on another beam splitter and counts photons in the two outputs. If detectors D_1 and D_2 register one and zero photons, respectively, the input state of the Bell-state analyzer is also $|\Psi^-\rangle$ and Bob becomes a copy of the source state. Restricting to these events, we perform homodyne tomography measurements on the teleported state. Note that ideally the above protocol requires number-resolving photon detectors. However, even with commercial detectors the teleportation protocol would exhibit high fidelity for $\alpha_1/\alpha_0 \lesssim 1$.[13] If a weak coherent state $|\alpha\rangle$ is used instead of the superposition $\alpha_0 |0\rangle + \alpha_1 |1\rangle$, QT will cut off the multi-photon terms in the teleported output ("quantum scissors").

To demonstrate the nonclassical nature of teleportation we varied the optical phase of the source state and observed the phase of the teleported state to vary accordingly although nothing was done directly to Bob's share of the original entangled state $|\Psi^-\rangle$. We also characterized the teleported state by means of homodyne tomography for various α's. As expected, the teleportation fidelity approached unity for low α but quickly fell off as this parameter increased [Fig. 4(b)].[14]

6 Perspectives

As shown above, the single-photon state $|1\rangle$ can be used to generate random coherent superpositions of the states $|0\rangle$ and $|1\rangle$. Among our further goals is to extend this technique to produce superpositions of higher number Fock states by means of repeated parametric downconversion in a chain of nonlinear crystals. The nonlocal single-photon state $|\Psi^-\rangle$ is worth further investigation from the point of view of quantum nonlocality.

References

1. For a review, see W. Tittel, G. Ribordy and N. Gisin, Physics World, March 1998, page 41.
2. E. Knill, R. Laflamme and G. Milburn, Nature **409**, 46, (2001); A. P. Lund, T. C. Ralph, quant-ph/0205044.
3. A. I. Lvovsky *et al.*, Phys. Rev. Lett. **87**, 050402 (2001).
4. T. Aichele, A. I. Lvovsky and S. Schiller, Eur. Phys. J. **D 18**, 237 (2002).
5. H. Hansen *et al.*, Opt. Lett. **26**, 1714 (2001).
6. A. I. Lvovsky and J. H. Shapiro, Phys. Rev. **A 65**, 033830 (2002).
7. D. Leibfried *et al.* Phys. Rev. Lett. **77**, 4281 (1996).
8. G. Nogues *et al.*, Phys. Rev. **A 62**, 054101 (2000); see also the paper by S. Haroche in these Proceedings.
9. A. I. Lvovsky and S. A. Babichev, Phys. Rev. **A 66**, 011801 (2002).
10. F.A.M. De Oliveira *et al.*, Phys. Rev. **A 41**, 2645 (1990) and references therein.
11. A. I. Lvovsky and J. Mlynek, Phys. Rev. Lett. **88**, 250401 (2002).
12. C. H. Bennett *et al.*, Phys. Rev. Lett. **70**, 1895 (1993).
13. D. T. Pegg, L. S. Phillips, and S. M. Barnett, Phys. Rev. Lett. **81**, 1604 (1998).
14. S. A. Babichev, J. Ries and A. I. Lvovsky, quant-ph/0208066.

FIBER-OPTIC SOURCES OF QUANTUM ENTANGLEMENT

PREM KUMAR, XIAOYING LI, MARCO FIORENTINO, PAUL L. VOSS, JAY E. SHARPING, AND GERALDO A. BARBOSA

Center for Photonic Communication and Computing, ECE Department
Northwestern University, 2145 N. Sheridan Road, Evanston, IL 60208-3118
E-mail: kumarp@northwestern.edu

We present a fiber-based source of polarization-entangled photon pairs that is well suited for quantum communication applications in the 1.5 μm band of standard telecommunication fiber. Quantum-correlated signal and idler photon pairs are produced when a nonlinear-fiber Sagnac interferometer is pumped in the anomalous-dispersion region of the fiber. Recently, we have demonstrated nonclassical properties of such photon pairs by using Geiger-mode InGaAs/InP avalanche photodiodes. Polarization entanglement in the photon pairs can be created by pumping the Sagnac interferometer with two orthogonally-polarized pulses. In this case the parametrically scattered signal-idler photons yield biphoton interference with $> 90\%$ visibility in coincidence detection, while no interference is observed in direct detection of either the signal or the idler photons.

1 Introduction

Quantum entanglement refers to the nonclassical dependence of physically separable quantum systems. It is an essential resource that must be freely available for implementing many of the novel functions of quantum information processing, such as database searching, clock synchronization, teleportation, computing, and cryptography.[1] Therefore, the efficient generation and transmission of quantum entanglement is of prime importance. With the ubiquitous standard optical fiber serving as the transmission medium and the widespread availability of efficient active and passive fiber devices, technological synergy between the generation and propagation components of the overall quantum network can be achieved by deploying sources of entanglement that rely on the nonlinearity of the fiber itself. In order to develop such sources, we have been conducting experiments with fiber-optic devices that can be used as building blocks for fiber-based sources of either polarization or quadrature entanglement. In the polarization case, our fiber-based setup for single-photon quantum optics has the advantage of modal purity over its crystal counterparts,[2,3] which would be very important for realizing complex networks involving several nonlinear elements.

2 An All-Fiber Source of Quantum-Correlated Photon Pairs

In our effort to develop fiber-based sources of entanglement, we have been investigating nondegenerate four-wave mixing in standard dispersion-shifted fiber (DSF), wherein two pump photons scatter through the Kerr nonlinearity of the fiber to create simultaneous signal and idler photons. Our experiment

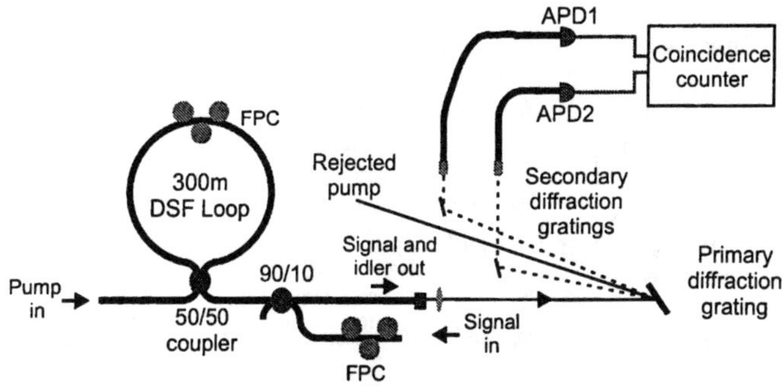

Figure 1. Schematic of the experimental setup. Dispersion-shifted-fiber (DSF) loop and the 50/50 coupler constitute the NFSI. FPC, fiber polarization controller; APD, avalanche photodiode. The signal-in port is blocked during photon-counting measurements.

is conducted near the zero-dispersion wavelength of the DSF, where such scattering is enhanced owing to phase matching of the photon wave functions. It must be pointed out here that in a conventional wavelength-division-multiplexed classical optical communication line, one strives to suppress the four-wave or four-photon mixing process, which otherwise causes cross-talk between the wavelength channels and sets limits on the total data capacity of the communication line.

As shown in Fig. 1, the four-photon mixing takes place in a nonlinear-fiber Sagnac interferometer (NFSI), which we have previously used to generate quantum-correlated twin beams in the fiber.[4] The pump is a mode-locked train of $\simeq$ 3 ps long pulses that arrive at a 75.3 MHz repetition rate. The pulsed operation serves two important purposes: i) the NFSI amplifier can be operated at low average powers and ii) the production of the fluorescence photons is confined to well-defined temporal windows, allowing a gated detection scheme to be used to increase the signal-to-noise ratio. To measure the non-classical (i.e., quantum) correlations between the signal and the idler photons, one must effectively suppress the pump photons from reaching the detectors. Since a typical pump pulse contains $\simeq 10^8$ photons and we are interested in detecting $\simeq 0.01$ signal/idler photon pairs per pulse, a pump-to-signal (idler) rejection ratio in excess of 100 dB is required. We achieve this specification by sending the fluorescence photons through a free-space double-grating spectral filter that separates the signal and idler photons from each other and from the pump photons not rejected by the NFSI (see Fig. 1).

To demonstrate the quantum nature of such four-photon scattering at the "single" photon level, we have assembled a photon-counting apparatus for detecting the signal and idler photons in coincidence. This apparatus is based on commercial InGaAs avalanche photodiodes operating in the gated Geiger mode. Use of this apparatus has allowed us to verify the simultaneous production of the signal and idler photon pairs.[5] In the inset in Fig. 2 we show the number of scattered photons, N_I (N_S), detected in the idler (signal) channel as a function of the number of pump photons, N_P, injected into the

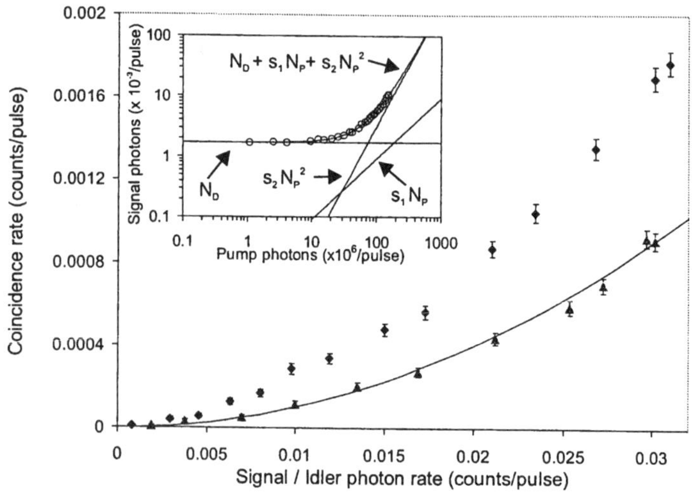

Figure 2. Coincidence rates as a function of the single-photon rates in two different cases: signal-idler fluorescence produced by a pump pulse (diamonds) and signal-idler fluorescence produced by two consecutive pump pulses (triangles). The line represents the calculated "accidental" counts. The inset shows a plot of the detected signal (or idler) photons as a function of the injected pump photons (hollow circles). A second-order polynomial is shown to fit the experimental data. The contributions of the dark counts, linear scattering, and quadratic scattering are plotted separately as well.

NFSI. We fit the experimental data with $N_I = N_D + s_1 N_P + s_2 N_P^2$, where N_D is the number of dark counts during the gate interval, and s_1 and s_2 are the linear and quadratic scattering coefficients, respectively. The fit clearly shows that the quadratic scattering owing to four-photon mixing in the fiber can dominate over the residual linear scattering of the pump due to imperfect filtering. The main body of Fig. 2 shows the coincidence counting results. The diamonds represent the rate of coincidence counts as a function of the geometric mean of the rates of the signal and idler photons generated during the same pump pulse. Dark counts have been subtracted from the plotted count rates. The triangles in Fig. 2 represent the measured coincidence rate as a function of the signal-photon count rate when the signal is delayed with respect to the idler by one pulse period. For two independent photon sources, each with a count rate $R_S \ll 1$, the "accidental" coincidence rate R_C is given by $R_C = R_S^2$, regardless of the photon statistics of the sources. This quadratic relation is plotted as the solid line in Fig. 2, which fits the delayed-coincidence data (triangles) very well. These measurements then show that whereas the fluorescence photons produced by the adjacent pump pulses are independent, those coming from the same pump pulse show a strong correlation, which is a signature of their nonclassical behavior.

With 75 MHz pump-pulse rate, we are now routinely detecting over 1500 photon pairs/s, which we expect to push up by a factor of 20 with further

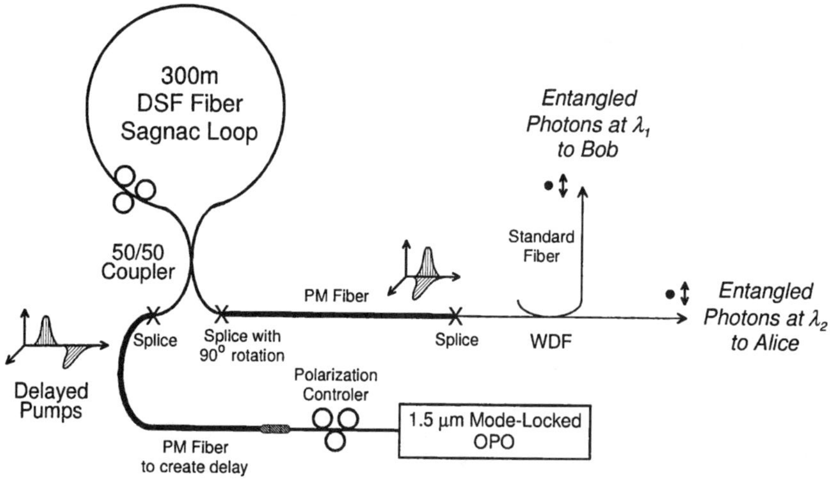

Figure 3. Schematic of an all-fiber experiment to create polarization-entangled photon pairs. In our current implementation, the relatively-delayed, orthogonally-polarized pumps at the input are created with bulk-optic components. The delay at the output, however, is removed by use of a polarization-maintaining (PM) fiber, as shown. Similarly, in our current setup the polarization-entangled photon pairs generated in the Sagnac loop are separated at the output with a bulk-optic wavelength-dependent filter (WDF). An approximately 400-m long all-fiber polarization interferometer is formed between the entrance surface of the input PM fiber and the exit surface (just before the WDF) of the output PM fiber.

refinements in the detection apparatus. Use of higher repetition rate pump pulses (over 10 GHz rate is possible with mode-locked fiber lasers) has the potential of increasing this rate by another two orders of magnitude. As we demonstrate in Sec. 3 below, polarization-entangled photon pairs can then be obtained by polarization multiplexing the signal and idler photons from two orthogonally-polarized pumps.

3 A Fiber-Optic Source of Polarization Entanglement

In this section we present the first, to the best of our knowledge, all-fiber source of polarization-entangled photon pairs. This source has the advantage of modal purity over its crystal counterparts,[2,3] which is very important for realizing complex networks involving many quantum operations.

As demonstrated in Sec. 2 above, the parametric fluorescence accompanying nondegenerate four-wave mixing in standard optical fibers is an excellent source of quantum-correlated photon pairs.[5] The quantum correlations arise because the parametric fluorescence is a result of two pump photons scattering through the Kerr nonlinearity to create simultaneous signal and idler photons. In order to create polarization-entangled photon pairs, we take advantage of

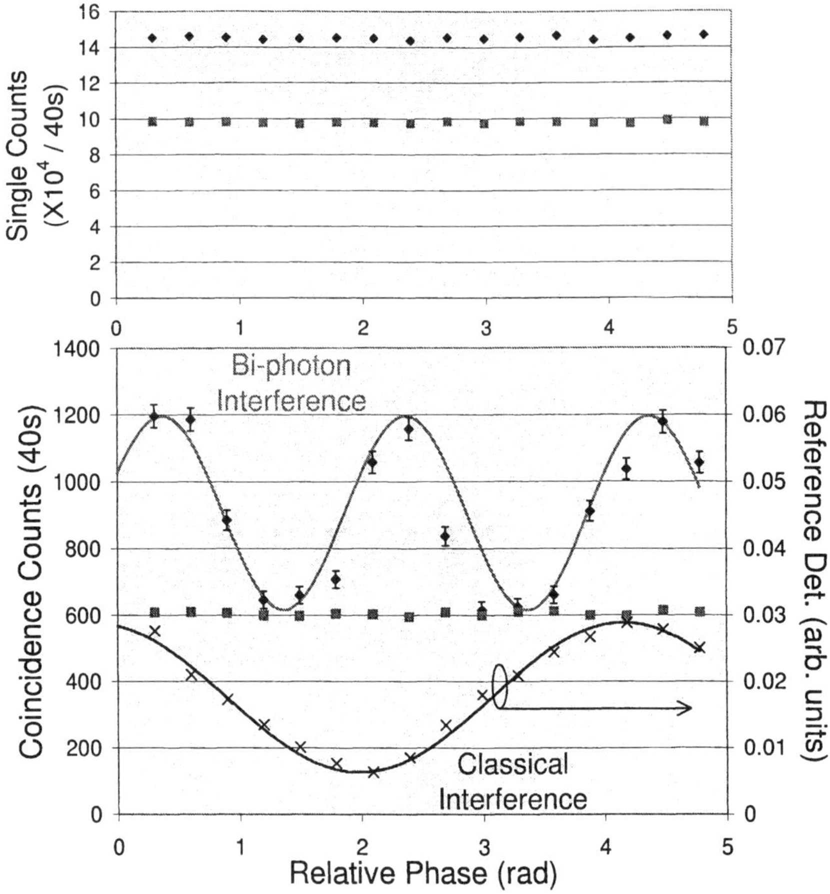

Figure 4. Top Plot: Single-photon counts registered by the signal (diamonds) and the idler (squares) detectors as the phase between the two pump pulses is varied. No phase dependence is observed in either detector's count rate. Bottom Plot: Coincidence-photon counts (diamonds) registered by the signal and idler detectors as the phase between the two pump pulses is varied. The squares represent accidental coincidences that are measured due to less-than-unity detection efficiency and dark counts in the detectors. After subtraction of the accidental counts, the resulting fringe visibility is $> 90\%$. The period of the fringes is half that of the classical interference fringes (crosses, right scale), which were simultaneously monitored by a reference detector during the coincidence measurements. The solid lines are best fits to the expected sinusoidal dependencies.

the fact that the parametric fluorescence in standard fiber is predominantly co-polarized with the pump. When the Sagnac loop is pumped with two delayed orthogonally-polarized pulses, see Fig. 3, the downconverted signal and idler photons originating from the two pulses are co-polarized with the corresponding pumps. However, when the delay distinguishing the downconverted photons is removed and the signal/idler photons are wavelength separated, then a polarized single-photon detection event at the output, in either the signal or the idler arm, cannot determine which pump-pulse produced the photon. This indistinguishability results in polarization entanglement of the signal and idler photons, which we demonstrate by means of interference in coincidence-photon counting of the polarized signal and idler outputs. The coincidence rate should vary sinusoidally as the relative phase between the two pump pulses is scanned.

Similar nonclassical interference has previously been demonstrated by Ou *et al.* with use of two separate $\chi^{(2)}$-crystal based spontaneous parametric down-converters.[6,7] The observed visibility was 40%. The two-interferometer setup in their experiment was of the Mach-Zehnder type, whereas in our experiment the two-interferometer setup is formed by temporally multiplexing an all-fiber polarization interferometer. This interference effect is based on pairs of photons (biphotons) rather than single photons, which led Ou *et al.* to the remark: "Indeed it is possible to modify Dirac's famous statement and argue that pairs of photons are interfering with themselves in these experiments."[7]

A summary of the details of our observations is given in the caption of Fig. 4. We observe a visibility of ¿90% in the interference fringes that occur in coincidence counting. Classically, no interference is expected in such coincidence counts.

Acknowledgments

This work was supported by the Department of Defense Multidisciplinary University Research Initiative (MURI) program administered by the Army Research Office under Grants DAAD19-00-1-0177 and DAAD19-00-1-0469, and by the U. S. Office of Naval Research under Grant N00014-91-J-1268.

References

1. C. H. Bennett and P. W. Shor, *IEEE Trans. Inf. Theory* **44**, 2724 (1998).
2. P. G. Kwiat, E. Waks, A. G. White, I. Appelbaum, and P. H. Eberhard, *Phys. Rev. A* **60**, R773 (1999).
3. S. Tanzilli, H. De Riedmatten, W. Tittel, H. Zbinden, P. Baldi, M. De Micheli, D. B. Ostrowsky and N. Gisin, Electron. Lett. **37** 26 (2001).
4. J. E. Sharping, M. Fiorentino, and P. Kumar, *Opt. Lett.* **26**, 367 (2001).
5. M. Fiorentino, P. L. Voss, J. E. Sharping, and P. Kumar, *Photon. Technol. Lett.* **14**, 983 (2002).
6. Z. Y. Ou, L. J. Wang, and L. Mandel, *Phys. Rev. A* **40**, 1428 (1989).
7. Z. Y. Ou, L. J. Wang, X. Y. Zou, and L. Mandel, *Phys. Rev. A* **41**, 566 (1990).

A SINGLE-PHOTON ON-DEMAND SOURCE WITH DECOUPLED SINGLE AND MULTIPHOTON PROBABILITIES: INITIAL RESULTS

A. MIGDALL, D. BRANNING,* S. CASTELLETTO,† AND M. WARE

Optical Technology Division, National Institute of Standards and Technology, 20899-8441 Gaithersburg, Maryland (USA)

We present an analysis of a multiplexed downconversion system designed to produce a single-photon on-demand source, by a multiple delay line trigger, yielding a single-photon certification of the produced photons. We discuss theoretically a simple implementation of the system together with initial experimental results.

The advent of photon-based quantum cryptography, communication and computation schemes[1,2,3,4] is increasing the need for light sources that produce individual photons; unwanted additional photons can render quantum cryptographic links insecure and degrade quantum-computation efficiencies.[5] More specifically, it would be useful to have these photons created in response to an external trigger, or even to have them arrive repetitively at a fixed, but selectable rate. As currently implemented, single-photon sources cannot be made to produce single photons with high probability, while simultaneously suppressing the probability of yielding two or more photons. Because of this fact, single photon sources cannot really produce single photons on demand. We have previously described a multiplexed parametric downconversion (PDC) system that allows the probabilities of producing one and more photons to be adjusted independently, enabling a better approximation of a source of single photons on demand.[6] Also described was a simplified version of that scheme that retains significant advantages, while greatly easing its implementation (Fig. 1). That implementation allows photons to be produced along with a quantitative "certification" that they are single photons. Some of the single-photon certifications can be significantly better than what is possible with conventional downconversion sources using a unified trigger detector region or with faint laser sources. We present a comparison of the relative merits of these methods along with the first experimental results obtained with a 4-delay-line setup.

Single-photon production schemes, whether based on faint lasers or PDC, suffer from the problem that the rate of producing unwanted multiple photons is tied to the single-photon rate. The two-photon rate grows as the single-photon rate squared. To reduce the multiphoton rate, the single photon rate must be kept small. Moreover it requires operation in a regime where it is mostly likely that no photons are produced at all! Of course, PDC schemes

*CURRENTLY AT UNIVERSITY OF ILLINOIS AT URBANA-CHAMPAIGN

†ALSO AT ISTITUTO ELECTROTECNICO NAZIONALE G. FERRARIS (ITALY)

have an advantage over faint laser sources in that the existence of a twin or "herald" photon allows the discrimination against the case in which no photon is produced.[a]

By adjusting light levels, for a faint laser source (described by Poisson statistics), the maximum fraction of pulses containing just a single photon is 37%. For a conventional PDC source, that is described by thermal statistics (for a single mode of the field), the maximum possible fraction of single-photon pulses is only 25%.[b] Fortunately, the existence of a herald photon in the PDC case provides for the elimination of the cases in which no photon is produced. Eliminating those cases allows the single photon fraction of a PDC source to be improved to 50%.

The multiplexed PDC schemes[6] allow these single-photon fractions to be improved upon by extracting more information out of the herald photon. The simplest of these schemes is shown in Fig. 1. A type-I PDC source is shown producing photon pairs with azimuthal symmetry around the pump beam direction. A series of fibers of increasing lengths is arranged azimuthally, but compactly to collect trigger or "herald" photons, while a single lens collects the photons correlated to those collected by the trigger fibers. Although the deadtime of the detector is such that it prevents more than one photon from being detected from a pump pulse (also the detector has no multiphoton detection capability), the time of detection relative to the pump pulse tells which delay path the photon took to cause the detector firing. This piece of information (along with the detector efficiency) allows us to determine the likelihood or "certification" that the signal channel contains just a single photon. The results of an analysis of this system are as follows .[6] The probability, in the simple scheme, that only one photon was incident into the entire system of delay paths given that the ith delay path caused the firing is

$$P_{\overline{n},\eta,N_{\text{D}}}(i) = \left(\frac{N_{\text{D}}}{\overline{n}+N_{\text{D}}}\right)^{i-1+N_{\text{D}}} \times \left(\frac{N_{\text{D}}+\eta\overline{n}}{\overline{n}+N_{\text{D}}}\right)^{i}, \tag{1}$$

where η is the probability of the detector firing when just one photon is incident, $\overline{n}$ is the mean photon number per pulse, and N_{D} is the number of delay lines. The probability in the simple scheme of producing just a single photon given that the trigger detector did fire is

$$P_{\overline{n}}(1,\eta,N_{\text{D}}|\text{trigger}) = \frac{\overline{n}\eta\left(\frac{N_{\text{D}}}{\overline{n}+N_{\text{D}}}\right)^{1+N_{\text{D}}}}{1-\left(\frac{N_{\text{D}}}{\overline{n}\eta+N_{\text{D}}}\right)^{N_{\text{D}}}}. \tag{2}$$

Figure 2 shows a summary of the overall probabilities of single-photon emission for different sources as a function of detector efficiency. The maximum

[a] For PDC and laser sources the photon production time is restricted to a narrow window.
[b] For both of these cases this maximum is achieved at a mean photon number per pulse of 1.

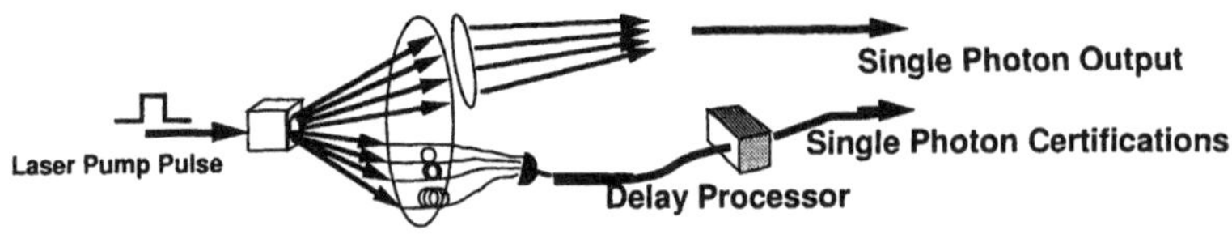

Figure 1. Single crystal and single detector implementation of scheme. Sequential series of delay lines is seen leading to the trigger detector. A lens collects all the modes correlated with those seen by the trigger.

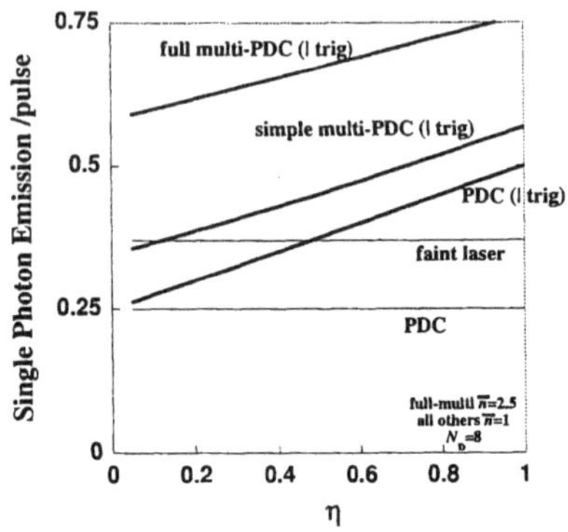

Figure 2. Single photon emission fraction (per pulse). For the full multiplexed PDC $\overline{n} = 2.5$, for all other curves $\overline{n} = 1$. A system of $N_{\text{D}} = 8$ was used for the multiplexed calculation.

single-photon fraction (per pulse) for a faint-laser system and a conventional PDC source is given by the two horizontal lines, as they are independent of η. The maximum fraction of a single-channel PDC source taking advantage of the herald is shown rising to the 50% level at $\eta = 1$. The fraction achievable by the simplified PDC scheme described above is shown surpassing the faint laser fraction at $\eta \approx 0.1$ and rising to 57% at $\eta = 1$. For completeness, we provide the single-photon fraction for the full multiplexed PDC system described in Ref. 6. (This last scheme allows one to take advantage of higher $\overline{n}$'s than is possible with the single-channel systems.)

We implemented the simple multi-PDC scheme of Fig. 2 with 4 fiber-optic delay lines bundled and imaged onto a single-photon counting module detector with a 200-μm-diameter active area. The pump is an 82 MHz mode-locked Argon ion laser operating at 458 nm, with a pulse width of 20 ps. The PDC crystal is KDP cut for an emission angle of approximately 1.5° at the degenerate wavelength. Four lenses couple single modes of downconverted photons to each single-mode fiber.

We have successfully aligned 4 delay lines and observed a well-resolved multicoincidence peak (Fig. 3) with a spacing of 2.42 ns (the difference between delay line lengths). The 4.95 ns gap between the first and second peaks

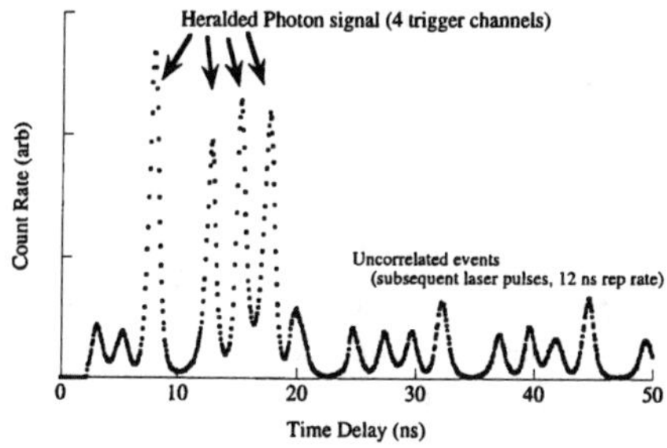

Figure 3. Time correlations between 4-channel trigger and single signal channels.

is because we skipped an intermediate fiber length in our trigger fiber bundle. A raster scan of the signal detector verified that all 4 correlated beams were superimposed at the detector and thus could be collected simultaneously. Careful adjustment of the lens-detector distance is required to make this happen.

We have shown initial results of a single-photon source scheme that has advantages over conventional single-channel single-photon sources. When fully implemented, the system will provide single photons with individualized single certifications. This is the first step in a program to construct a better approximation of a true single-photon on-demand source than is possible using a conventional single PDC setup or a faint-laser source.

References

1. C. H. Bennett and G. Brassard, *Proceedings of the IEEE International Conference on Computers, Systems and Signal Processing*, 175 (1984).
2. A. Ekert, *Phys. Rev. Lett.* **67**, 661 (1991).
3. C. H. Bennett, G. Brassard, and N. D. Mermin, *Phys. Rev. Lett.* **68**, 557 (1992).
4. W. Tittel, J. Brendel, H. Zbinden, and N. Gisin, *Phys. Rev. Lett.* **84**, 4737 (2000).
5. G. Brassard, N. Lutkenhaus, T. Mor, and B. C. Sanders, *Phys. Rev. Lett.* **85**, 1330 (2000).
6. A. Migdall, D. Branning, S. Castelletto, and M. Ware, quant-ph/0209103, in press SPIE Vol 4821., A. Migdall, D. Branning, S. Castelletto, and M. Ware, in press *Phys. Rev. A*.

GENERATION OF SINGLE PHOTONS AND PHOTON PAIRS USING QUANTUM DOTS

R. M. STEVENSON,[1] Z. L. YUAN,[1] M. B. WARD,[1] R. M. THOMPSON,[1,2] P. SEE,[1] B. E. KARDYNAL,[1] A. J. SHIELDS,[1] I. FARRER,[2] C. J. LOBO,[2] K. COOPER,[2] AND D. A. RITCHIE[2]

[1] *Toshiba Research Europe Limited, 260 Cambridge Science Park, Milton Road, Cambridge CB4 0WE, UK*

[2] *Cavendish Laboratory, University of Cambridge, Madingley Road, Cambridge CB3 0HE, UK*

We show that monochromatic emission from a single quantum dot excited electrically as well as optically has at least an order of magnitude less multi-photon pulses than for an attenuated laser with the same intensity. Furthermore, we demonstrate that pairs of photons emitted at different energies due to the radiative decay of the biexciton state are strongly polarization correlated, although the polarization of a pair is random for a given emission period.

Quantum communication by the representation of information using single photons can allow the transmission of encrypted data with security guaranteed by the laws of quantum mechanics. In practice, quantum key distribution systems encode the bit information of the key in the polarization or phase of a photon generated by an attenuated laser beam. However, the proportion of two photon pulses inevitably generated by attenuated lasers can destroy the unconditional security of many systems,[1] highlighting the need for a true source of single photons.

The luminescence spectra of single quantum dots consist of a number of discrete lines, a consequence of the variation of the Coulomb energy for different charge configurations within the quantum dot. It is this property of single quantum dots that dictates that no more than one photon per excitation period will be emitted into a given emission line, provided the excitation time is small in comparison to the radiative lifetime (typically $\sim$1 ns).

We investigate InAs quantum dots formed by deposition of a thin layer of InAs, close to the critical thickness for self-organized island growth, on GaAs. Single quantum dots are isolated by etching $\sim$0.8 μm mesas, or by etching $\sim$ 2 μm apertures in a metallic mask. Optical excitation is provided by a mode locked titanium sapphire laser, typically configured to provide ps pulses with a repetition period of 13.0 ns at an energy above that of the GaAs bandgap. The photoluminescence of a mesa-type quantum dot is shown in Fig. 1(a), for the range of energies that correspond to neutral exciton configurations within the dot. All experiments were carried out at 5 K. The two lines are attributed to exciton (X) and biexciton (X_2) recombination.[2] Emission-time statistics are measured using the Hanbury-Brown and Twiss type system depicted in Fig 1(b). The emission line of interest is selected with a grating spectrometer,

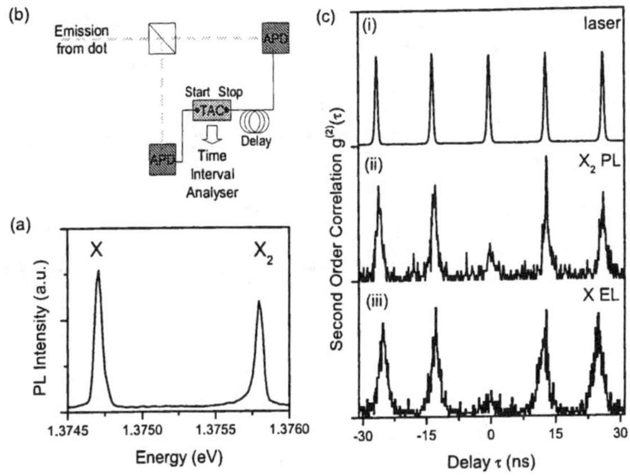

Figure 1. (a) Photoluminescence of an aperture-isolated quantum dot showing emission corresponding to exciton X and biexciton X_2 recombination. (b) Schematic of experiment to measure $g^{(2)}(\tau)$. (c) Second-order correlation for: (i) attenuated laser light; (ii) optically-excited X_2 photon emission; and (iii) electrically-injected X photon emission.

and is incident on a beam splitter. The reflected and transmitted photons trigger a pair of silicon avalanche photodiodes (APDs), and the time intervals between detection events are measured. Figure 1(c) shows histograms of the time intervals, equivalent to the second-order correlation function $g^{(2)}(\tau)$ in the low-intensity regime. Histogram (ii) shows the results for an optically-injected mesa device at the energy of X_2. A suppression by more than an order of magnitude is observed in the probability of coincident detection of two photons, corresponding to the weak peak at $\tau = 0$, in contrast to the corresponding peak in histogram (i), measured for an attenuated laser beam. A device for electrical excitation was fabricated by incorporating the quantum dot layer within a simple p-i-n structure,[3] and isolating the emission from a single dot using an aperture. Similar spectral features were observed as described for optically injected devices. Using square-shaped voltage pulses 0.15 V high and 400 ps wide, on top of a DC offset close to the 'turn-on' voltage of the diode characteristic, $g^{(2)}(\tau)$ was measured at the energy of the X line, as shown in histogram (iii). A similar suppression in multi-photon pulses is observed as for optically injected samples, and the number of remaining multi-photon pulses is consistent with the intensity of stray light originating from other areas of the device.

The biexciton state of the quantum dot decays radiatively to the ground state to emit a pair of photons. We measured the correlation in the linear polarization between biexciton photons and exciton photons using the system depicted in Fig. 2(a). Optically excited emission from an aperture-isolated

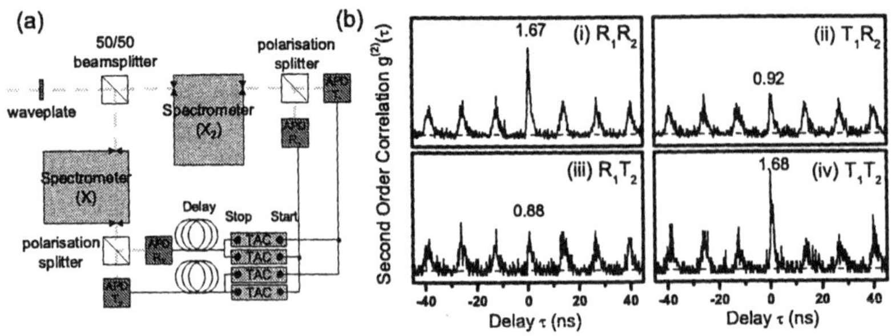

Figure 2. (a) Schematic of polarization-sensitive cross-correlation system. (b) Polarized cross-correlation measured for the four possible combinations of the X-X_2 pair.

quantum dot was divided, using a non-polarizing beam splitter, and passed through two spectrometers to select X_2 and X photons respectively. Polarizing beam splitters then directed the transmitted (T) or reflected (R) photons towards APDs. The second-order correlation was measured for all polarization combinations of X_2 and X. The results of these measurements are shown in Fig. 2(b). All histograms show a series of peaks separated by the laser period of 13 ns. The peaks are asymmetrically shaped due to reduced uncertainty in the biexciton emission time, a consequence of its shorter radiative lifetime.[2] The peak at $\tau = 0$ represents the detection of pairs of photons in the same laser period, and shows a strong correlation for photons of the same linear polarization corresponding to histograms (i) and (iv). The time-averaged emission is unpolarized within experimental error, and the polarization of photons in adjacent periods is random, as can be seen from the equal heights of the peaks at $\tau \neq 0$. We note that the correlation is lost if the polarization measurement axis is rotated away from the [110] and [1$\bar{1}$0] directions of the sample. This means that the photon pairs are not polarization entangled.

To understand the origin of the polarization correlation, polarization-dependent PL spectra were recorded with a resolution better than 30 μeV for a single quantum dot isolated by an aperture in a metal mask, and are shown in Fig. 3. Similar polarization-dependent second-order correlation was observed for this dot as described above. As the polarization is rotated away from the [110] and [1$\bar{1}$0] directions by angle θ, a clear doublet structure is observed in the X and X_2 lines of the PL spectra. The components of the doublets are linearly polarized, and the total energy is conserved for X and X_2 lines of identical linear polarization. This can be understood if we consider a quantum dot with a nondegenerate exciton level, a consequence of the loss of in plane rotational symmetry,[4] as shown in Fig. 3(b). Photon pairs have either vertical (V) or horizontal (H) polarization, which tend to align with

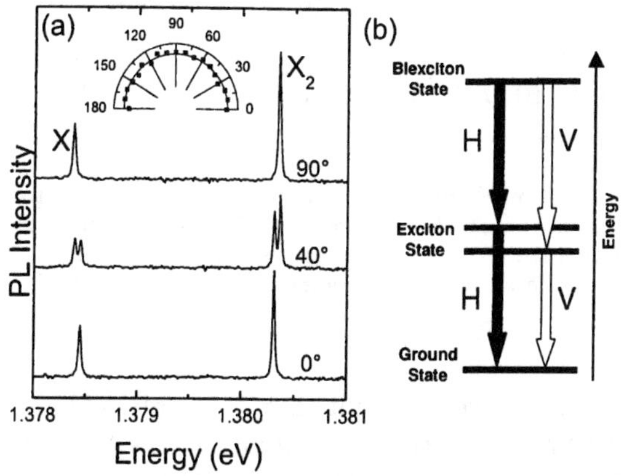

Figure 3. (a) PL spectra of X and X_2 as a function of polarization analyzer angle θ. Inset shows integrated intensity of X as a function of θ. (b) Schematic of exciton level splitting caused by an asymmetry in the shape of the dot.

the [110] and [1$\bar{1}$0] direction of the sample due to the typical elongation of quantum dots along the [1$\bar{1}$0] direction, in agreement with our results. Which-path information is present in such a nondegenerate system, which is why the entanglement predicted for a quantum dot with four-fold rotational symmetry is not observed.[5]

The generation of polarization-correlated photon pairs by quantum dots,[6] recently confirmed by others,[7] opens up the possibility of encoding the state of a transmitted photon using the randomly selected polarization in combination with passive optics. The bit sent is determined by the sender by the measurement of the correlated partner. The broadening of the emission spectra helps remove the spectral information that would reveal the bit sent. Even for our mesa samples, the probability of determining the bit in this way is only 0.515, very close to total randomness.

References

1. G. Brassard *et al.*, Phys. Rev. Lett. **85**, 1330 (2000).
2. R. M. Thompson*et al.*, Phys. Rev. B **64**, 201302(R) (2001).
3. Z. Yuan, *et al.*, Science **295**, 102 (2002).
4. V. D. Kulakovskii *et al.*, Phys. Rev. Lett. **82**, 1780 (1999).
5. O. Benson *et al.*, Phys. Rev. Lett. **84**, 2513 (2000).
6. R. M. Stevenson *et al.*, Phys. Rev. B **66**, 081302(R) (2002).
7. C. Santori *et al.*, Phys. Rev. B **66**, 045308 (2002).

DETERMINISTIC N-PHOTON GENERATION

K. DANI, K. BROWN, D. STAMPER-KURN, K. B. WHALEY

Departments Of Physics and Chemistry, University of California, Berkeley 94720

We present a scheme for N-photon generation with N three-level atoms in a cavity using an external laser pulse as a trigger. We show that during this process, the atom-cavity system lives in an optically dark state, thus minimizing photon losses due to spontaneous decay. We present numerical simulations for $N \leq 5$ to support our analysis.

The fully quantized theory of light affords us states of light that are highly nonclassical in nature. In particular, number states and squeezed states of light exhibit sub-Poissonian photon statistics that are of fundamental interest in the field of quantum optics. From a technological standpoint, deterministic generation of number states would lead to substantial advances in the fields of quantum cryptography and communication. We discuss here a scheme for deterministic N-photon generation, which is an extension of the single-photon generation scheme previously suggested.[1,2]

We first briefly discuss the single-photon generation scheme. Consider a Λ-type atom with states $|0\rangle$, $|1\rangle$ and $|2\rangle$ interacting with a quantized cavity field and an external classical field as shown in Fig. 1[A].

The state $|1\rangle$ is an excited state with a spontaneous emission rate of γ. Initially, we ignore the cavity loss rate κ. The Hamiltonian of the system is,

$$\mathbf{H} = -\Delta\sigma_{11} + r(t)\left(\sigma_{01} + \sigma_{10}\right) + g\left(a\sigma_{12} + a^{\dagger}\sigma_{21}\right) \tag{1}$$

where g denotes the atom-cavity coupling, $r(t)$ denotes the atom-laser coupling and a and $a^{\dagger}$ are the annihilation and creation operators for the quantized cavity field. The atomic operators σ_{ij} are simply $|i\rangle\langle j|$. One can show the existence of a null-valued eigenstate,[2] which excludes any contribution from the excited state $|1\rangle$. Thus the eigenstate is immune to spontaneous decay. It is given by

$$|\Psi\rangle = \frac{1}{\sqrt{r^2 + g^2}}\left[g|0,0\rangle - r|2,1\rangle\right] \tag{2}$$

where the state $|i,l\rangle$ denotes an atom in the state $|i\rangle$ and l photons in the cavity. If we initially start our system in the $|0,0\rangle$ state with the laser pulse off, and we adiabatically turn up the laser field intensity, we follow the above eigenstate. Thus for large values of r, we end up, with a high probability, in the state $|2,1\rangle$, i.e., we produce a cavity photon. Ultimately, this photon would decay into a preferred mode outside the cavity, giving us our single photon source.

Now consider N noninteracting atoms in the cavity. As before, first let us assume no losses from the excited state or from the cavity. We also assume that each atom interacts identically with the laser field and the cavity

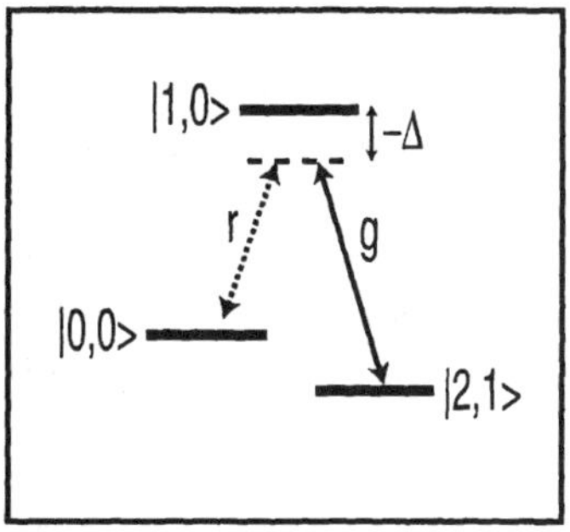

Fig A

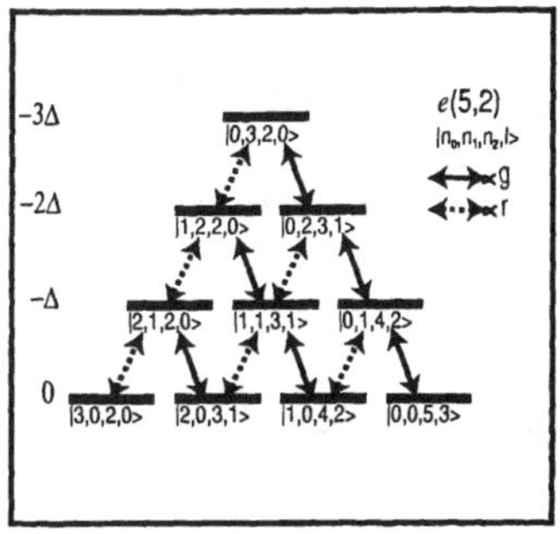

Fig B

Figure 1. [A] $|i, l\rangle$ represents atom in state $|i\rangle$ and l cavity photons. r is coupling due to external laser field, g is coupling due to cavity. [B] Pictorial representation of the Hamiltonian in $e(5,2)$. The dark state is a superposition of states in the bottom-most row such that any contribution from higher rows is effectively cancelled out.

field. Thus the Hamiltonian for the ith atom is also given by Eq. (1). The Hamiltonian for the whole system is simply the sum over all N atoms.

Clearly, such a Hamiltonian is symmetric under the exchange of any two atoms. Thus, if our initial state were symmetric, we would only evolve to states that are symmetric under the exchange of two atoms. As in the single atom case, our initial state is all atoms in the state $|0\rangle$. Hence we may reduce our effective Hilbert space to only the symmetric states. With this aim in mind, we introduce the notation $|n_0, n_1, n_2, l\rangle$ to denote the symmetric state with n_i atoms in state $|i\rangle$ and l photons in the cavity.

This allows us to think of the Hilbert space simply as the tensor product of four different bosonic modes — a mode corresponding to each atomic state and the Fock space of the cavity. Let $b_i^\dagger$ and b_i be the creation and annihilation operators for the atomic modes corresponding to state $|i\rangle$. The Hamiltonian $\mathbf{H}$ can now be rewritten in terms of these operators as

$$\mathbf{H} = -\Delta b_1^\dagger b_1 + r\left(b_1^\dagger b_0 + b_0^\dagger b_1\right) + g\left(b_1^\dagger b_2 a + a^\dagger b_2^\dagger b_1\right). \tag{3}$$

It is clear from the above Hamiltonian that the total number of atoms is conserved. In other words, the operator $\mathbf{T} = b_0 b_0^\dagger + b_1 b_1^\dagger + b_2 b_2^\dagger$ commutes with the Hamiltonian. Its eigenvalues N are natural numbers, denoting the total number of atoms in our system. The corresponding eigenspace is simply $\{|n_0, n_1, n_2, l\rangle : n_0 + n_1 + n_2 = N\}$.

In addition to the conservation of the total number of atoms, we see that a photon is created (destroyed), only when the $|2\rangle$ atomic mode is excited (de-excited). This suggests that a difference operator of the form $\mathbf{D} = b_2^\dagger b_2 - a^\dagger a$ commutes with the Hamiltonian. Moreover, $\mathbf{D}$ also commutes with $\mathbf{T}$. This allows us to look for eigenstates of the Hamiltonian that are simultaneously eigenvalues of **T** and **D**. The eigenvalues of **D** are integers k and the corresponding eigenspace is $\{|n_0, n_1, n_2, l\rangle : n_2 - l = k\}$. Thus for given initial eigenvalues N, k the system is restricted to the subspace $e(N,k) = \{|n_0, n_1, n_2, l\rangle : n_0 + n_1 + n_2 = N, n_2 - l = k\}$. Figure 1[B] shows a pictorial representation of $e(5,2)$. Dotted arrows represent the laser field coupling and solid arrows represent cavity coupling. The bottom-most row contains states without any contribution from the excited states. In analogy to the one-atom case, the correct superposition of states in this row gives us an eigenstate of the Hamiltonian for which any contribution from higher rows cancels due to destructive interference. This is true for every subspace $e(N,k)$. The state is given by

$$|\Psi_k^N\rangle = \frac{1}{Z}\sum_{l=0}^{N-k} \frac{(-x)^l}{\sqrt{(N-k-l)!(l+k)!(l)!}}|N-k-l, 0, l+k, l\rangle, \qquad (4)$$

where Z is the normalization constant and $x = r/g$. It is possible to show that on resonance the null-valued eigenspace of the Hamiltonian is degenerate, but that a nonzero detuning lifts the degeneracy. Hence, if we start out in the state $|N,0,0,0\rangle = |\Psi_k^N\rangle$, and we adiabatically turn on the laser pulse intensity to a large value, $x >> 1$, we can develop a scheme to ultimately end up in the state $|0,0,N,N\rangle$, with a high probability, giving us N photons in the cavity. As before, in order to obtain an N-photon source, the photons must decay into preferred modes outside the cavity. Thus, it is necessary to extend the above closed-system analysis to an open system, in which allowing for cavity decay is required.

The formalism of quantum trajectories[4] lends itself nicely to the study of this open system. In this approach, the system dynamics are characterized by nonunitary evolution, interspersed with random jumps related to photon losses from the cavity and spontaneous scattering from the excited atomic state. The nonunitary evolution is given by the conditional Hamiltonian

$$H(t) = H_0(t) - i\kappa a^\dagger a - i\gamma b_1^\dagger b_1, \qquad (5)$$

where H_0 is the closed-system Hamiltonian given by Eq. (1). The dark states, given by Eq. (4), are no longer eigenstates of the conditional Hamiltonian. In addition, the finite ramp-up time of our laser pulse intensity also causes deviations from the dark states. This gives some probability of being in the excited state and leads to loss of photons through spontaneous decay. Using a perturbative approach, it is possible to analytically characterize this loss of photons.[3] However, that is beyond the scope of this paper. We will instead quantify the spontaneous loss using numerical simulations averaged over a large number of quantum trajectories for $N \leq 5$. We use a driving field that is ramped up linearly with time given by $r(t) = g^2t/100$. The parameters are $(g, \kappa, \gamma)/2\pi = (45, 4.5, 2.25)$ MHz. The ramping-up time for the field is long enough so that the probability of an atom staying in the original state $|0\rangle$ is

Part I
Entanglement

$$\Sigma^2_A = \sum_\lambda q_\lambda \Pi^\dagger_\lambda \Sigma^2_Q \Pi_\lambda \tag{16}$$

where we used the fact that $\Sigma_B\Sigma^\ddagger_Q\Sigma_Q = \Sigma_B$, since for lemma 1 one has $\Sigma^2_Q \geq p\Sigma^2_B$.

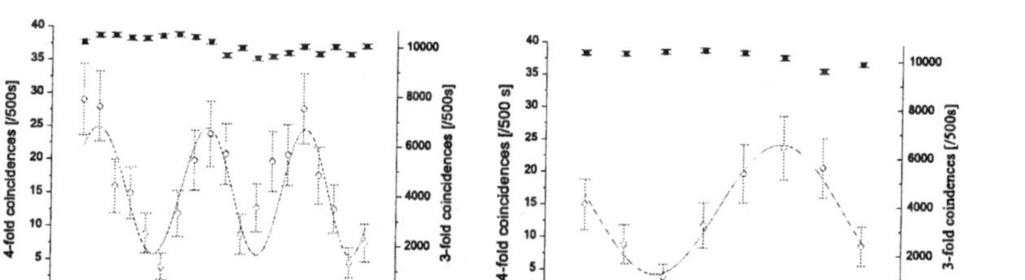

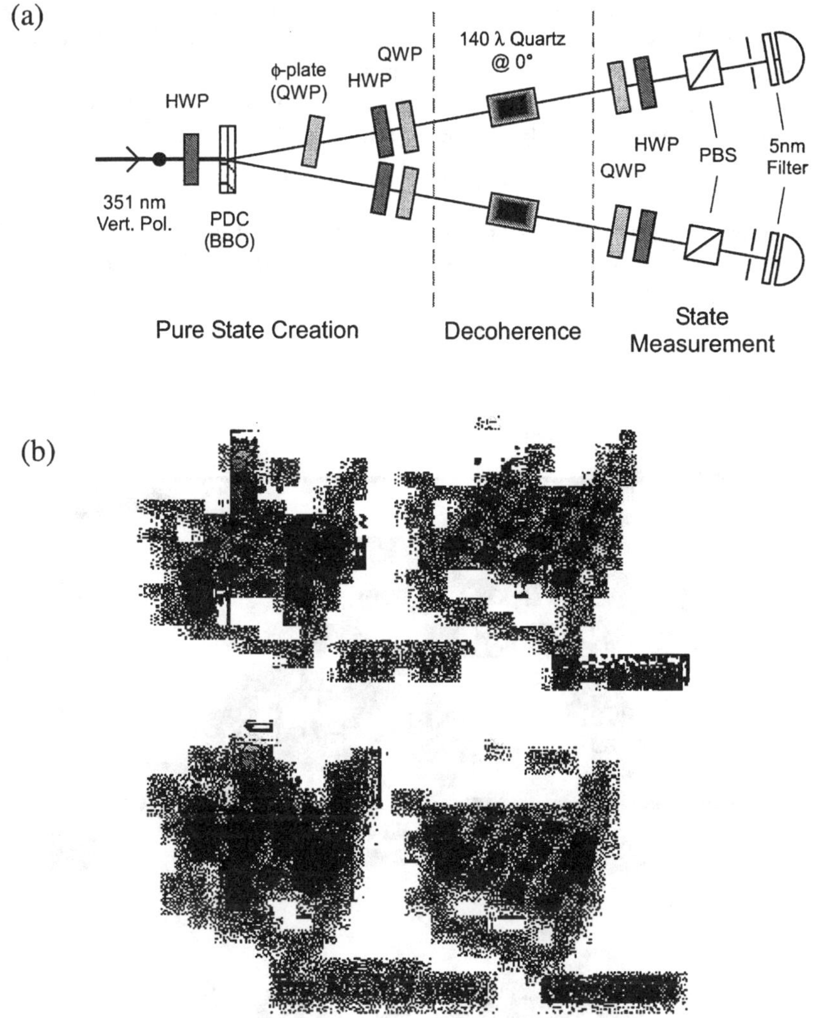

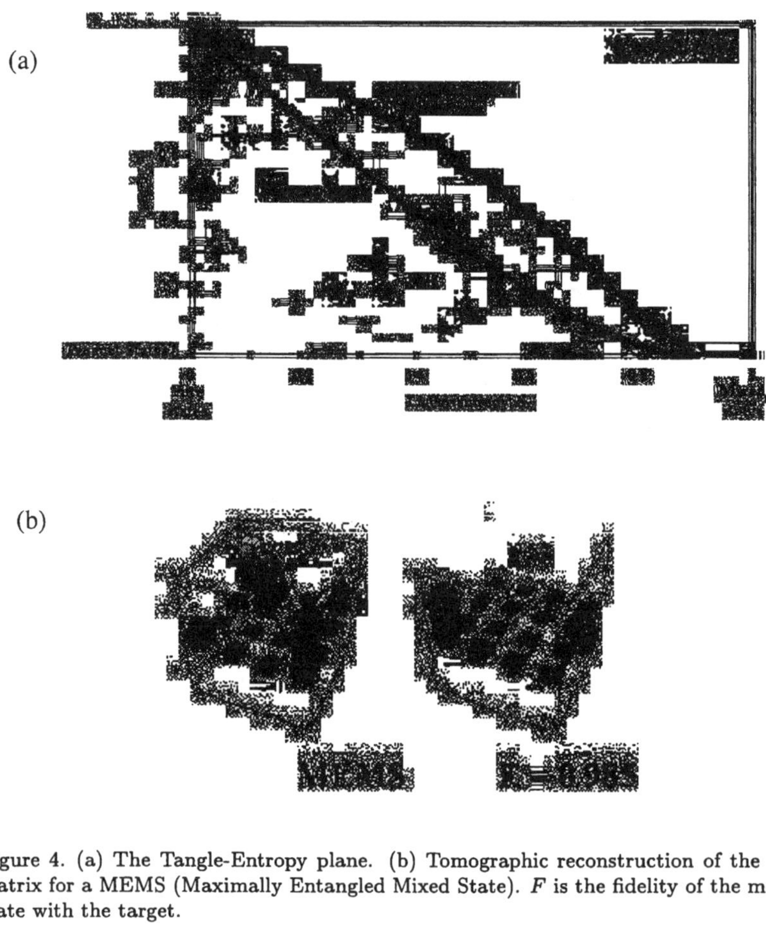

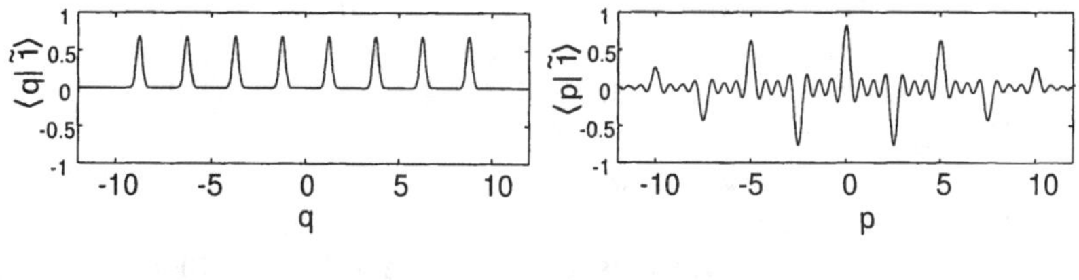

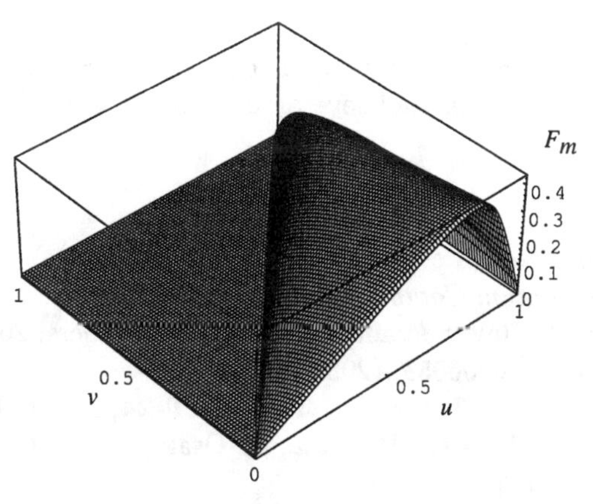

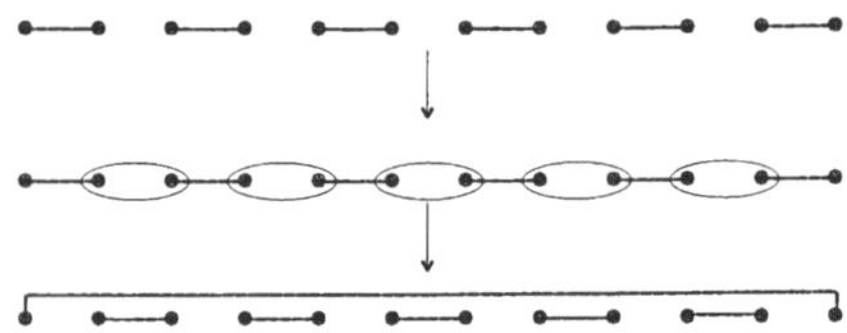

$$\begin{aligned}\lambda(\tilde{\varrho},\delta,n) \equiv \operatorname{tr}\Big\langle &\left[(n+1)(\tilde{\varrho}+\delta)^n + n(\tilde{\varrho}+\delta)^{n-1}\right]\mathcal{L}(\varrho+\delta)\\ &-\left[(n+1)\tilde{\varrho}^n + n\tilde{\varrho}^{n-1}\right]\mathcal{L}(\varrho)\Big\rangle,\end{aligned} \tag{12}$$

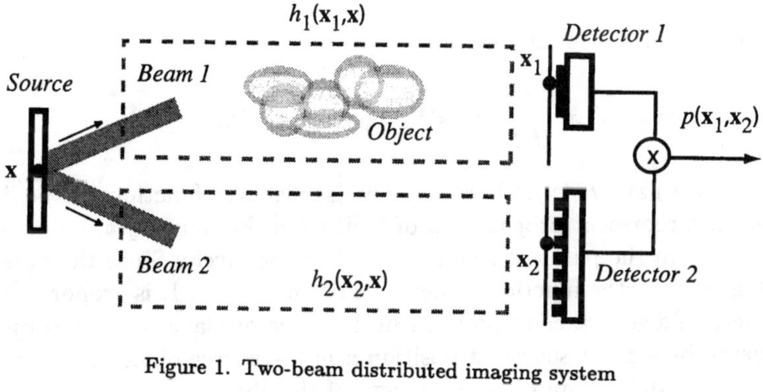

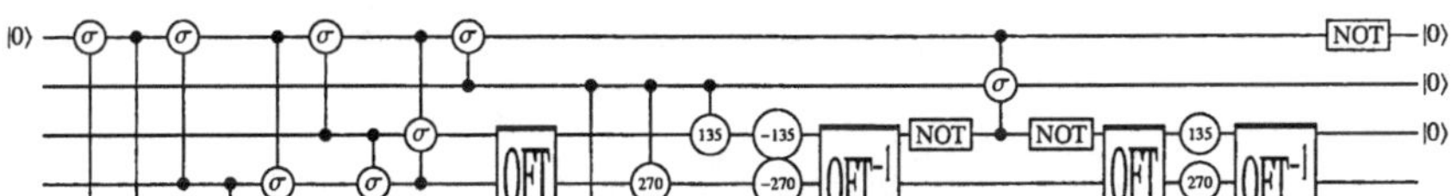

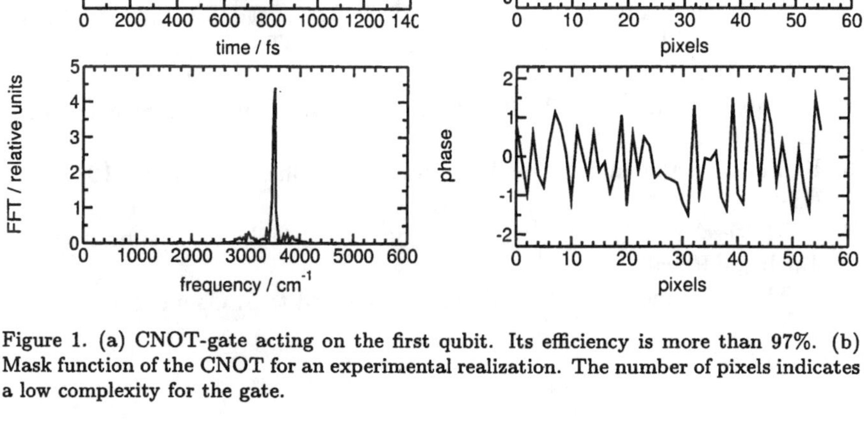

$$\begin{aligned}\hat{\mathbf{H}}_{ij} &= \frac{1}{2}[J^{s}_{ij}(\sigma^{x}_{i}\sigma^{x}_{j} + \sigma^{y}_{i}\sigma^{y}_{j}) + J^{a}_{ij}(\sigma^{x}_{i}\sigma^{x}_{j} - \sigma^{y}_{i}\sigma^{y}_{j})] \\ &+ \frac{1}{2}[K^{s}_{ij}(\sigma^{x}_{i}\sigma^{y}_{j} - \sigma^{y}_{i}\sigma^{x}_{j}) + K^{a}_{ij}(\sigma^{x}_{i}\sigma^{y}_{j} + \sigma^{y}_{i}\sigma^{x}_{j})], \qquad (1)\end{aligned}$$

where $J^{s}_{ij} = \frac{1}{2}(J^{xx}_{ij} + J^{yy}_{ij})$, $J^{a}_{ij} = \frac{1}{2}(J^{xx}_{ij} - J^{yy}_{ij})$, $K^{s}_{ij} = \frac{1}{2}(J^{xy}_{ij} + J^{yx}_{ij})$ and $K^{a}_{ij} = \frac{1}{2}(J^{xy}_{ij} - J^{yx}_{ij})$.

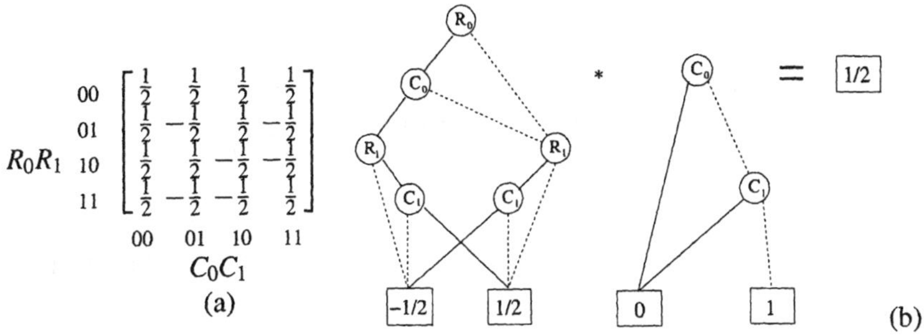

$$\rho_{n,m} \to \rho_{n,m}\exp[i(n-m)\phi]. \tag{11}$$

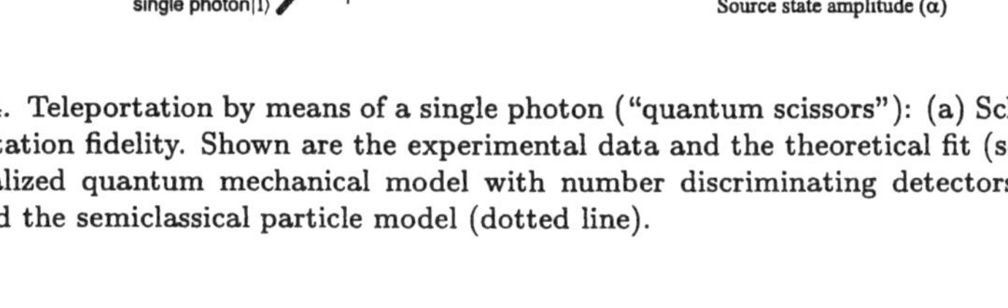

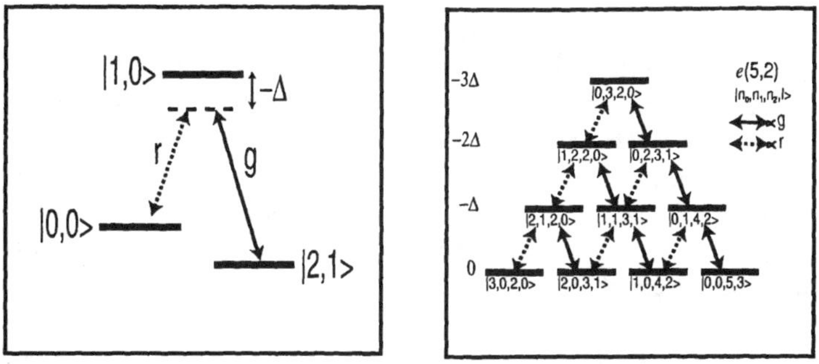

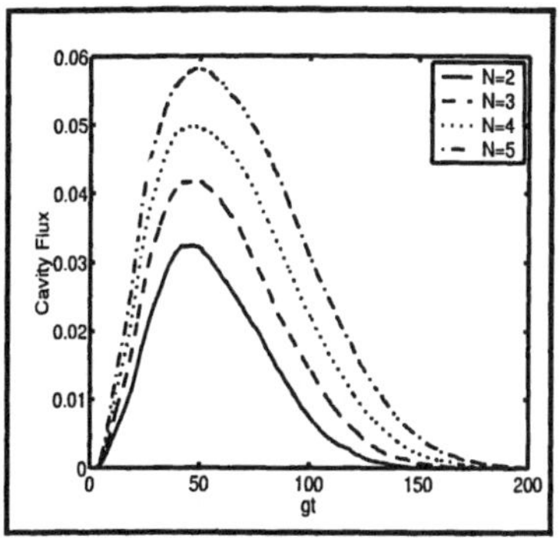

Fig. A

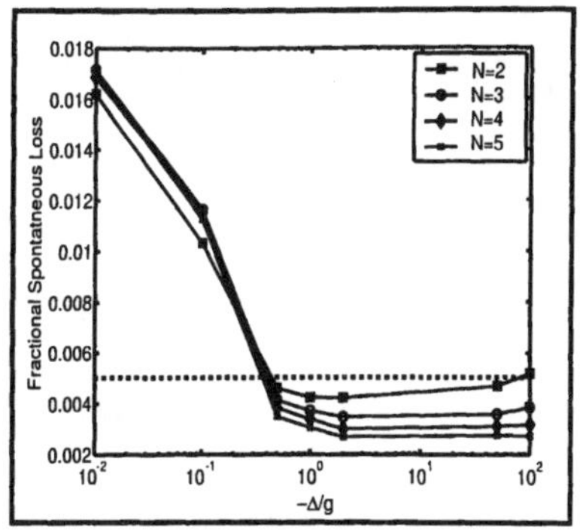

Fig. B

Figure 2. [A] Probabilistic flux of photons exiting the cavity over time for a linear ramping up of laser field with N atoms in the cavity. The area under the curve is the number of photons decaying via the cavity mode. [B] Plot of photons lost due to spontaneous emission as a function of Δ (in units of g) for different values of N.

less than 0.001. Figure 2[A] shows the probabilistic flux of photons decaying from the cavity as a function of gt. The area under the curve denotes the number of photons coming out of the cavity averaged over many trajectories. Figure 2[B] shows the fractional loss of photons to spontaneous decay as a function of Δ in units of g. The simulations suggest that the fractional loss decreases as a function of N for large Δ. Analytical estimates show a constant fractional loss as an upper bound for large detuning.[3]

We conclude that N three level atoms in a cavity can indeed provide a deterministic source of Fock states with a high fidelity. We also note that, by starting out in a superposition over the states $|N-k,0,k,0\rangle$ for different values of k, one can produce other highly non-classical states of light.

References

1. C. Law and H. J. Kimble, *Journal Of Modern Optics* **44**, 2067 (1997)
2. A. Kuhn, et al. *Appl. Phys. B* **69**, 373 (1999).
3. K. Brown, et al. *to be submitted.*
4. H. Carmichael in *An Open System Approach to Quantum Optics* (Springer, Berlin, UK, 2000).